BLACK FLA

BIG BOOK OF FALSE FLAC
AND WORLD CONSPIRACY

Andrè RavenSkül Venås

2021 A Public Domain Reference

KraKRabit Studios Production

ISBN: 9798804236824

This book is a compilation or gathering of *'False Flags'* and *'Conspiracy Theories'* from as far back as I could find. This book does not necessarily reflect the views and beliefs of the Author, all of these theories have been acquired through public files on the internet, and we all know, if it's on the internet, it must be true. This book is strictly for your enjoyment and never forget to *'Read between the Lies'*...

1. *"False Flag and Conspiracy Theory' Defined*

'FALSE FLAG;'

A covert operation designed to deceive, i.e., to create the appearance of a friendly or trustworthy party, group, or nation. Consequently, being responsible for an action that has been designed to create fault on a specific party, group, or nation, resulting in a specifically designed conclusion.

The term 'False Flag' originally referred to pirate ships that flew flags of other countries as a disguise to prevent their victims from fleeing or preparing for battle. Sometimes the flag would continue to fly with the intention of laying blame of the attack on another an enemy or opposing country. The term today extends beyond naval encounters to include countries organizing attacks on themselves making it appear as if enemy nations or terrorists organizations perpetrated the offenses, thus giving said nation a pretext for domestic tyranny and foreign military aggressions. Operations carried out during peacetime by civilian organizations, as well as covert government agencies are also referred to as false flag operations, if the intention is to conceal the factual offending party behind the so called transgression.

'CONSPIRACY THEORY;'

'The theory that an event or phenomenon occurs as a result of a conspiracy between interested parties; spec. a belief that some covert but influential agency (typically political in motivation and oppressive in intent) is responsible for an unexplained event'...

It has been noted that a 1909 article in The American Historical Review as the earliest example, although it also appears in journals as early as April 1870. The word 'Conspiracy' derives from the Latin con- (with, together) and spirare (to breathe). Lance deHaven-Smith has stated that the term entered everyday language in the United States in the year 1964, in which the New York Times ran five stories referencing of the term. Robert Blaskiewicz notes examples as early as the nineteenth century and finds that the term has always been derogatory. A 'Conspiracy Theory' is not simply a conspiracy.

Barkun wrote that conspiracies are 'Actual covert plots planned and/or carried out by two or more persons.' A 'Conspiracy Theory,' on the other hand, is 'An Intellectual Construct,' a 'Template imposed upon the world to give the appearance of order to events.' Positing that 'some small and hidden group' has manipulated events; a 'Conspiracy Theory' can be local or international, focused on single events or covering multiple incidents and entire countries, regions, and periods of history. 'Conspiracy Theorists' see themselves as having privileged access to special knowledge or a special mode of thought that separates them from the masses who believe the official account.

FROM CONSPIRACY TO FRONT PAGE NEWS…

After explosive devices were sent to prominent critics of President Donald Trump, including Barack and Michelle Obama, Bill and Hillary Clinton, and former CIA Director John Brennan many on the far right and even some people with close ties to the White House had a theory of the case.

'The bombing attempts on prominent liberals were ginned up by the left to help them win the midterms.'

On Friday, even President Trump appeared to hint at this argument, saying that in the midst of Republicans 'Doing so well' in early voting, 'Now this 'Bomb' stuff happens, and the momentum greatly slows;' with 'Bomb' in quotes. Alex Jones's 'Conspiracy Theory' site Infowars, made its claim even clearer: The bombing attempts are a 'False Flag;' an attack committed under false pretenses used to drive public perception in a certain direction. Under this scenario, some on the right argue that the goal of the left is to 'Frame' conservatives for the mailings and drive Democrats to the polls in November.

On Friday, authorities announced that a man in Florida had been arrested in connection with the attempted bombings, however truly little information has been released about the bomber or bombers and their motives at this point. Maybe it'll turn out that the motivations were a form of political jujitsu, or a 'False Flag,' or maybe the motives will turn out to be something completely off the wall, not tethered to political polarization at all. We just don't know, but there are those on the right that leapt right at the 'False Flag' narrative without any basis for their claim. And this is not the first time the 'False Flag' narrative has emerged in response to a tragedy or a scare involving mass shootings at elementary schools to the attacks on the Twin Towers on 9/11.

Some people react to events that don't make sense by trying to argue it didn't happen the way we're being told, or maybe it didn't even happen at all. Liberals have baselessly claimed 'False Flags' in these situations as well, the right isn't always culpable. In 2016, for example, a Black Lives Matter activist argued that the shootings of police officers in Dallas that resulted in five deaths could have been a 'False Flag', stating, 'From my experience, whenever public opinion shifts to strongly support the movement, an act of violence against the police happens.' 'Conspiracy Theories' like 'False Flags' appeal to people along the political spectrum. According to a survey conducted in 2014 and reported by the Washington Post, Republicans and Democrats responded equally when asked if they agreed with similar statements such as, 'Much of our lives are being controlled by plots hatched in secret places.'

In the current political environment, it seems that 'Conspiracy Theories' are going mainstream. Ideas that used to remain confined to pamphlets or small networks leapt from the dark corners of the internet into lines contained in speeches, and tweets from internet trollers to the President himself, who is a long time boaster of 'Conspiracy Theories.' 'Social media has given us the power to spread nonsense further and faster than ever before,' said Becket Adams, a commentary writer at the Washington Examiner, who has written extensively on 'Conspiracy Theories' and once stated in an interview, 'A solidly insane Conspiracy Tweetstorm or YouTube video can reach more people now than any newsletter or pamphlet from the 1850s or 1960s ever could.' The result is that a large swath of the public is casting off the working set of facts necessary to truly engage in honest political debates. They prefer, instead, to reject information that might challenge their preexisting ideas, a dangerous position in a moment when many people, our President included, are already committed to 'Alternative facts.'

WHAT IS A 'FALSE FLAG'?

The term 'False Flag' is an old political concept, referring to an operation or attack that is essentially fake, staged by a group that wants a reason to retaliate against the person or people they have accused of the attack. For example, the Nazi invasion of Poland in 1939 began with a 'False Flag' attack on a German radio transmission tower that made it appear as if Polish forces were responsible, thus giving Adolf Hitler carte blanche to launch the invasion. And in the early 1960s, the US government contemplated using a 'False Flag' attack to provoke Americans into supporting a war with communist Cuba.

This plan, known as Operation Northwoods, included the potential destruction of a US ship in Cuban waters and then blaming the Cuban government. One military official wrote, 'Casualty lists in U.S. newspapers would cause a helpful wave of national indignation.' So 'False Flag' attacks have happened, but not often. In the world of 'Conspiracy Theorists,' though, 'False Flags' are seemingly everywhere. They are relied on to explain away events that seem too big or too terrible to be real, and moreover, 'False Flags' help people who can't imagine that someone who shares their political, cultural, or religious worldview would do something so wrong.

In 1944, a member of the antiwar America First movement argued in a pamphlet that the attacks on Pearl Harbor that launched the United States into a war with Japan was a 'False Flag', saying that the United States let the attack happen so that the American people would support a war. 'Conspiracy Theories' involving the government gained wider sway after the Vietnam War. Several American generations experienced firsthand the fact that the federal government is extremely capable of lying and engaging in far-reaching cover-ups. It was the rise of the internet in the 1990s that spread the idea of 'False Flags' from pamphlets and magazines aimed at fringe groups to the broader world, and one 'Conspiracy Theorist' in particular who popularized them all, Alex Jones.

ALEX JONES AND 'FALSE FLAGS'

In the 1990s, as the internet started taking 'Conspiracy Theories' from the gutters of chat rooms to the mainstream media, Alex Jones, the founder of Infowars, was featured on local access TV news in Austin Texas, where he presented anti-government and anti- 'New World Order Conspiracy Theories' to a small audience. The Oklahoma City bombings of 1995, where Timothy McVeigh and Terry Nichols orchestrated a domestic terror attack on a federal building ultimately killing at least 168 people sparked Jones's interest in 'False Flags.' To be clear, McVeigh, who visited Waco, Texas, during the infamous siege at a cult compound in 1993 that resulted in a fire killing more than 80 people, was radicalized by what he viewed as tyrannical government action taken at Waco, writing to the Bureau of Alcohol, Tobacco, and Firearms before the Oklahoma City bombing, 'All you tyrannical people will swing in the wind one day for your treasonous actions.' But Jones was convinced that a cover-up was afoot.

Jones started advocating his belief that the government was involved in the attack, 'I understood there's a kleptocracy working with psychopathic governments, clutches of evil that know the tricks of control.' Then he started spreading that the Oklahoma City bombing was a 'False Flag' that was actually committed by our government to frame the political right and help Bill Clinton win the 1996 Presidential election. 'They set it up to make it look like 'Oh, the feds got hit back' because Waco hurt them so bad it was going to lose them the election,' he stated in April of 2018 to the Austin American-Statesman's Jonathan Tilove. 'It is a 'False Flag,' one hundred percent.' Since 1995, the 'Conspiracy Theorizing' has continued from Jones. He has promulgated the idea that the 9/11 attacks were also a 'False Flag' operation organized by the Bush administration in order to popularize a war in the Middle East, and that the Boston Marathon bombings of 2013 were a 'False Flag' event aimed at expanding government intrusion.

In fact, Infowars sent one of its personalities, Dan Bidondi, to a press briefing with Massachusetts Gov. Deval Patrick held just hours after the Boston bombings to ask if the bombings were a 'Staged attack to take our civil liberties and promote homeland security while sticking their hands down our pants on the streets.' Governor Patrick responded with a resounding 'No.' More recently, Jones has argued repeatedly that mass shooting incidents like the murder of 20 children and six adults at Sandy Hook Elementary School in 2012 or the shootings at Marjory Stoneman Douglas High School earlier this year were also 'False Flag' efforts committed by the US government in order to push gun control measures. In 2015, Jones said, 'Sandy Hook is synthetic, completely fake with actors; in my view, manufactured. I couldn't believe it at first. I knew they had actors there, clearly, but I thought they killed some real kids, and it just shows how bold they are, that they clearly used actors.' This, of course, is not true? And families of the victims of Sandy Hook Elementary have since sued Jones for defamation.

THE PSYCHOLOGY OF 'FALSE FLAGS'

To Alex Jones, and people who think like him, a 'False Flag' is a way to make sense of events that don't make sense, or worse, that might contradict his fervently held political beliefs. To Jones, it's inconceivable that an American veteran like Timothy McVeigh could have been behind the murder of 168 people, so it was obvious that the Oklahoma City bombing was a 'False Flag.' Little children couldn't have been murdered with the same weapons many responsible God loving Americans own and enjoy using every day, so the Sandy Hook shooting was of course a 'False Flag.' And no right-thinking conservative would send Democratic figures bombs in the mail because they were enraged by anti-Trump Democrats, so once again a 'False Flag.' Like 'Conspiracy Theories' themselves, the 'False Flag' idea offers an impenetrable barrier of denial against the reality that sometimes bad people do bad things, and occasionally, those bad people might share your political, social, or cultural viewpoints.

2. *Klik, Klik, Booom This… Vatican City*

Augusto Ferrara's 2010 book '1943; Bombe sul Vaticano', declares that the attack was orchestrated by leading Italian fascist politician and anti-clericalist Roberto Farinacci. The intention was to take out Vatican Radio, which was suspected of sending coded message to the

Allies. The aircraft that delivered the bombs was a SIAI Marchetti S.M.79, a three-engine Italian medium bomber known as the 'Sparviero,' which had taken off from Viterbo, some 80 kilometres north of Rome. One of the pieces of evidence on which Ferrara bases his account of the responsibility of Farinacci was a telephone call from a priest named Giuseppe to the Jesuit Pietro Tacchi Venturi. In fact, a note on page 705 of volume 7 of the Actes et documents du Saint Siège relatifs à la seconde guerre mondiale cites Eitel Friederich Moellhausen as stating that rumors in Rome immediately blamed Farinacci and spoke of Viterbo as the base from which the plane must have flown.

Tardini's note quoted above also says that, from the start, it was the general opinion that Italian Republican Fascists were to blame, a view that Tardini himself discounted on the basis of the information given by Monsignor Carroll. Owen Chadwick also reported that Farinacci was rumored from Rome to have arranged the raid at the Viterbo airfield, something that Farinacci, who was killed together with Mussolini on 28 April 1945, could never himself deny, but Chadwick considered the story 'Very unlikely'. In Ferrara's account, five bombs were dropped, of which one did not explode. According to the Actes et documents du Saint Siège relatifs à la seconde guerre mondiale, the report of an examination carried out by Vatican authorities after the event spoke only of fragments being found making it difficult to determine whether the high-explosive bombs, which had been in the range of 100 to 150 kg each were of British, German, or Italian manufacture.

The 2007 book Venti Angeli Sopra Roma by Cesare De Simone speaks of a supposed admission of responsibility by the RAF in the postwar period. A 2011 article by Raffaele Alessandrini in the January 10 issue of the Vatican newspaper L'Osservatore Romano says that the identity of those responsible has still not been absolutely clarified. However, research published in a 2016 article gives a more definitive identification of the bomber and presents an intriguing account of the motive behind it. Throughout 1943 the Italian Intelligence Service routinely intercepted and recorded telephone conversations to and from the Vatican. On November 8, 1943, Ugo Guspini, one of the intelligence agents involved, recorded the conversation between Fr. Giuseppe and the Jesuit Pietro Tacchi Venturi.

In this verbatim account Fr. Giuseppe informed the Jesuit that he had just returned from the Viterbo Air Force base, north of Rome, where he had been told by an undisclosed informant who was present throughout the entire operation that the bombing was undertaken by Roberto Farinacci and a Roman pilot in an Italian Savoia-Marchetti aircraft with five bombs on board destined to knock out the Vatican Radio because Farinacci believed it was transmitting military information to the Allies. This confirms the account given by Augusto Ferrara above and is further corroborated by Eitel Möllhausen, at the time was Chargé d'affaires at the German Embassy in Rome, who in his post war memoir claimed that Farinacci was responsible having never denied the allegations.

The report by Monsignor Walter S. Carroll, who had just returned from Allied headquarters in Algeria, informed 'Very confidentially' that the bombing was due to an American pilot who had lost his way, and that another American pilot had reported seeing an Allied plane dropping its load on the Vatican, correctly representing opinion at Allied headquarters, Algeria, at the time. On November 8, 1943, Harold Macmillan, the then resident British Minister in Algiers, informed the British Foreign Office in a 'Most Secret' telegram… 'I think we probably did bomb the Vatican.' On the night in question one of seven British Boston bombers, which had been in operation just north of Rome at the time the Vatican was bombed, developed engine trouble and 'Jettisoned it's payload' through clouds over an unknown location in order to lighten its load and return to base.

This was thought to have been the bombs which fell on the Vatican. But at the Foreign Office it was noted that it had been a clear and cloudless night over Rome when the Vatican was bombed. And a subsequent confidential Air Ministry investigation into the incident established that the impaired Boston had actually dropped its bombs over Arce, some fifty miles southeast of Rome, and that neither it nor any other British aircraft in operation that night was responsible. The American pilot who witnessed the bombing probably saw the Savoia-Marchetti aircraft which, from a distance, is not dissimilar to the Merlin Baltimore light bomber frequently used over Italy and mistook it for an Allied aircraft. The weight of evidence, therefore, points to Farinacci, who, as seen, never denied it, because he died with Mussolini.

As to the motive behind it, McGoldrick questions the claim it was intended to silence Vatican Radio. The radio station's transmissions to the enemy and anti-Nazi broadcasts already ceased in May 1941 when Mussolini, under pressure from Hitler, threatened to invade the Vatican and close it down. But from September 8, 1943, when Germany invaded and occupied Rome, both British and American media outlets unleashed a series of totally untrue 'Fake News' reports that the Nazis had invaded the Vatican, imprisoned the Pope, and arrested a number of Cardinals. This inflamed Catholic opinion in Latin America but especially in Argentina, the last South American country to maintain diplomatic relations with Nazi Germany. From September 1943 to the end of October 1943 the German Ambassador in Buenos Aires, Eric Otto Meynen, sent a series of urgent telegrams to Berlin warning that, in the light of these reports, Argentina was about to break off relations with Germany.

It was not enough, Meynen said, to deny the allegations; a concrete counter action was needed. This, together with a carefully choreographed German propaganda operation blamed the British, suggesting that when Farinacci bombed the Vatican with British bombs, he did so under instruction from his German handlers, anxious to discredit the Allies and counter harmful Allied propaganda which threatened their diplomatic relations with Argentina, the last friendly country open to them in Latin America.

The Bombing of March 1, 1944

There is no obscurity about the identity of the British plane that dropped bombs on the edge of Vatican City on 1 March 1944 as this was explicitly acknowledged, at least in private, by the British Air Ministry as an accidental bombing when one of its aircraft on a bombing raid over Rome dropped its bombs too close to the Vatican wall. It caused human casualties, killing a workman who was in the open and injuring a Dutch Augustinian in the College of Saint Monica. The six low-caliber bombs dropped also caused physical damage to the Palace of the Holy Office, to the Oratory of Saint Peter, and to the Pontifical Urbanian College on the nearby Janiculum Hill.

Claims persist, nevertheless, that this was an Italian plane which was seen to strike an obstacle, perhaps a tree on the Janiculum, after which it jettisoned its bombs, but crashed after hitting a house on Via del Gelsomino with its wing. The Italian authorities quickly removed the wreckage and the dead pilot. Monsignor Giulio Barbetta, who recounts his experience of this bombing, says that, while almost all the windows of the Holy Office building were shattered, the glass covering an image of Our Lady between it and the entrance to the Oratory of Saint Peter remained intact and the oratory itself suffered no more than the effects of shrapnel against its wall.

THE NEW WORLD POPE, SATANISM, FREEMASONRY AND OCCULT SIGNS

POPE FRANCIS and the ABSENCE OF CHRIST

Dear brothers and sisters living in this confused world of today: in this segment will be analyzed some of the points made by Francis during his Good Friday homily on April 18, 2014. In total confidence and under the eyes of distracted faithful people, pope Bergoglio turns the Stations of the Cross into social welfare and economics analysis. First, here are the words of Jesus Christ in a message left ten days prior to this event which can be found in The Book of Truth. 'From Holy Week, this year, the cracks will appear, and the meaning of My Crucifixion will be twisted. New interpretations will be presented before the faithful and lies will pour forth from the mouths of my enemies. My Passion will be mocked in subtle ways and will not be immediately apparent. But when the focus moves from my death on the Cross and when strange gestures take place in My Churches, you will know that this is the beginning of the dismantling of My Church on Earth.'…Jesus' message from April 08, 2014

Here is a list of just some of Pope Francis's reflections on some of the Stations of the Cross. His personal approach to the mediation of Christ's Passion is of little mystical depth and of empty spiritual nature; indeed, he diminishes the greatness of Christ's heroism of Self-Sacrifice in favor of 'His' equalization with the average person of today. Francis makes an inappropriate use of the sufferings of today's individuals (illness, poverty, imprisonment, marginalization, immigration, racism, unemployment and more) as if in the attempt to exalt his own goodness over Christ's Redemptive love, which is now obscured. Therefore, such 'Altruistic' words of social justice and care become weapons to be used in the building of what is to come: a religion of social justice and humanitarian works, the conspiracy of the papacy, the church and lucifer.

Some of Francis Reflections on the Stations of the Cross.

FIRST STATION~ Jesus is condemned to death

…For Pilate, the case is closed. Jesus' hasty condemnation thus embraces the easy accusations, the superficial judgements of the crowd, the insinuations and the prejudices which harden hearts and create a culture of racism and exclusion, a throw-away culture of anonymous letters and vicious slanders. Once we are accused, our name is immediately splayed across the front page; once acquitted, it ends up on the last! And what about us? Will we have a clear, upright, and responsible conscience, one which never forsakes the innocent but courageously takes the side of the weak, resisting injustice and defending truth whenever it is violated?

SECOND STATION~ Jesus takes up his cross.

It is also the burden of all those wrongs which created the economic crisis and its grave social consequences: job insecurity, unemployment, dismissals, an economy that rules rather than serves, financial speculation, suicide among business owners, corruption and usury, the loss of local industry. This is the cross which weighs upon the world of labor, the injustice shouldered by workers. Jesus shoulders it himself and teaches us to reject injustice and to learn, with his help, to build bridges of solidarity and of hope, lest we be like sheep who have lost our way amid this crisis.

THIRD STATION~ Jesus falls for the first time.

With the inner strength which comes to him from the Father, Jesus also helps us to accept the failings of others; to show mercy to the fallen and concern for those who are wavering. And he gives us the strength not to shut the door to those who knock and ask us for asylum, dignity, and a homeland. In the awareness of our own weakness, we will embrace the vulnerability of immigrants, and help them to find security and hope.

FIFTH STATION~ Jesus is helped by Simon of Cyrene to carry his cross.

Only by opening my heart to divine love am I drawn to seek the happiness of others through the practice of charity: a night spent in hospital, an interest-free loan, a tear wiped away in the family, heartfelt generosity, farsighted commitment to the common good, a sharing of our bread and labor, the rejection of all jealousy and envy.

SEVENTH STATION~ Jesus falls for the second time.

In him we glimpse the bitter experience of those locked in prisons of every sort, with all their inhumane contradictions. Confined and surrounded, 'pushed hard' and 'falling'. Prisons today continue to be set apart, overlooked, and rejected by society. Marked by bureaucratic nightmares and justice delayed. Punishment is doubled by overcrowding: an aggravated penalty, an unjust affliction, one which consumes flesh and bone. Some – too many! – do not survive… And when one of our brothers and sisters is released, we still see them as 'ex-convicts', and we bar before them the doors of social and economic redemption.

NINTH STATION~ Jesus falls for the third time.

May our contemplation of Jesus, who falls yet rises once more, help us to overcome the kinds of narrowness which fear of the future impresses on our hearts, especially at this time of crisis. Let us leave behind our unhealthy nostalgia for the past, our complacency, and our refusal to change, and the attitude that says: 'but we've always done it this way!' Jesus who stumbles and falls, but then rises, points us to a sure hope which, nourished by intense prayer, is born precisely at the moment of trial, not after or apart from it!

ELEVENTH STATION~ Jesus is crucified.

Today many of our brothers and sisters, like Jesus, are nailed to a bed of pain, at hospital, in homes for the elderly, in our families. It is a time of hardship, with bitter days of solitude and even despair: 'My God, my God, why have you forsaken me?'

TWELFTH STATION~ Jesus dies on the cross.

'Remember me…' (Lk 23:42). The fraternal plea of the thief who became his companion in suffering, pierces Jesus' heart; it is an echo of his own pain. And Jesus grants that request; 'Today you will be with me in paradise' the pain of others always redeems us since it draws us out of ourselves. 'Woman, here is your son! …' (Jn 19:26). But it is his mother, Mary, who stood with John at the foot of the cross, who dispels all fear. She fills that scene with tenderness and hope. Jesus no longer feels alone. So, it is with us, if beside our bed of pain there is someone who loves us! Faithfully. To the end. 'I am thirsty' (Jn 19:28).

Like the child who asks his mother for drink, like the patient burning with fever… Jesus' thirst is the thirst of all those who yearn for life, freedom, and justice. And it is the thirst of the one who is thirstiest of all: God, who, infinitely more than us, thirsts for our salvation. 'It is finished' (Jn 19:30). Everything: every word, every action, every prophecy, every moment of Jesus' life. The tapestry is complete. The thousand colors of love now shine forth in beauty. Nothing is wasted. Nothing thrown away. Everything has become love. Everything completed for me and for you! And so, even dying becomes meaningful!

THIRTEENTH STATION~ the body of Jesus is taken down from the cross.

Leader: We adore you, O Christ, and we praise you.
All: Because by your holy cross you have redeemed the world. Jesus, how brutally you were put to death. How gently you are taken from the cross. Your suffering and pain are ended, and you are put in the lap of your mother. The dirt and blood are wiped away. You are treated with love. As a child, sometimes I treat others better when they're sad or in pain. When somebody dies, I become very gentle and kind. I notice the good and kind things people say about those who have died. As an adult, I seem to be kinder when someone dies. If only I could learn to see the good things about them while they were alive.

If only I would tell those around me how much I love them, while I still have the opportunity to do so. Help me look for the good in those around me, especially those I love the most. Help me live this day as if it were the last. Help me become a gentler and more loving person through my greater appreciation for those around me. O Mary, Mother most sorrowful, the sword of grief pierced thy soul when thou didst see Jesus lying lifeless on thy bosom; obtain for me hatred of sin because sin slew thy Son and wounded thine own heart, and grace to live a Christian life and save my soul.

Our Father.... Hail Mary.... Glory be to the Father....

Leader: Jesus Christ Crucified.

All: Have mercy on us.

Leader: May the souls of the faithful departed, through the mercy of God, Rest in peace.

All: Amen.

ORIGIN AND MEANING OF THE WORD LUCIFER

lucifer (/ˈluːsɪfər/ or /ˈljuːsɪfər/)

Is the King James Version rendering of the Hebrew word הֵילֵל from Isaiah 14:12. This word, transcribed hêlêl or heylel, occurs only once in the Hebrew Bible and according to the KJV-influenced Strong's Concordance means 'Shining one, morning star, light bearer.' The word lucifer as a noun is taken from the Latin Vulgate, which translates הֵילֵל as lucifer from the same Isaiah 14:12 passage, meaning 'The morning star as the planet Venus'. As an adjective, lucifer means 'Light-bringing.' The Septuagint renders הֵילֵל in Greek is ἑωσφόρος (heōsphoros), a designation which literally translates into 'Bringer of dawn' as the morning star. In a subsequent passage, Isaiah relates to a king of Babylon the image of the morning star fallen from the sky, an image he is generally believed to have borrowed from a legend in Canaanite mythology. Isaiah 14:12 (Latin Vulgate) 'Quomodo cecidisti de caelo lucifer qui mane oriebaris corruisti in terram qui vulnerabas gentes.'

The Hebrew word translated as 'lucifer' in Isaiah 14:12 in the KJV is heylel (hay-lale'), and literally means 'Shining one,' 'Morning star,' 'Light bearer.' Isaiah 14:12 is the only place in scripture where this Hebrew word appears. The use of the name 'Lucifer' is ancient in Latin, referring to the planet Venus as the first appearing star in the morning. Although some early Christian Latin writings seem to refer to the devil as 'Lucifer,' it was the Latin Vulgate that was generally responsible for its current widespread use. The Vulgate was produced by Jerome (Cir. 347-420) while translating the available Greek and Hebrew manuscripts into Latin. Starting in approximately 382 A.D. and completing around the year 405 A.D., this version was used as scriptures for almost 1,000 years by the Catholic Church.

In the Vulgate version above, the word lucifer is used with a lower case: 'Quomodo cecidisti de caelo lucifer qui mane oriebaris corruisti in terram qui vulnerabas gentes.' The meaning of the Hebrew word heylel as light bearer was conveyed by Jerome through the parallel and precise concept which, in Latin, was expressed by the word lucifer. Indeed, this word was utilized in reference to the planet Venus, which was considered the light bearer as it was the first visible light after each night. The word lucifer, composed by the Latin lux (light) and the Latin ferre (to bear or to bring), was used from Jerome's time up until the era of the King James Version translation (405 A.D. to 1611). The genitive version of the word Lux is Lucis (possessor of the light). Please take a look at the United Nations based organization Lucis Trust (Lucifer Publishing Company), detailed below.

Since Jerome believed that the Isaiah passage pertained to the evil king of Babylon, he made the connection with Satan by morphing the two together and igniting the evolutionary meaning of the word lucifer from a representation of Venus to today's representation of Satan. Therefore, we could declare that due to a common popular interpretation of the passage, lucifer, additionally to the morning star Venus, began to be perceived as Satan. Early church fathers believed that lucifer was not to indicate the formal name of the devil, but rather the former state from which he fell. Because of all these variations and evolutions, lucifer can be utilized in contrasting fashions and for vastly different purposes such as Jesus, Satan, and Venus, Pagan deities, a light bearer, an enlightened person, an angel, and the morning depending on the perspective. The pseudepigrapha of pre-Christian Enochic Judaism, the form of Judaism witnessed to in 1 Enoch and 2 Enoch, which enjoyed much popularity during the Second Temple period, gave Satan an expanded role, interpreting Isaiah 14:12-15, with its reference to the morning star, as applicable to him, and presenting him as a fallen angel cast out of heaven for refusing, according to Jewish writings, to bow to Adam, of whom Satan was envious and jealous of the power over the earth granted to Adam, motives to which Christians were to add pride, which they mention more frequently than envy or jealousy with regard to humanity.

The word lucifer as an adjective, in meant 'Light-bringing' and was applied to the moon. As a noun, the Latin word lucifer meant 'Morning star.' The word was also used in reference to the Greek mythological goddess 'Eos,' the goddess of dawn giving birth to the morning star Phosphorus. In Roman mythology, its divine personification meant 'The fabled son of Aurora and Cephalus, and father of Ceyx' while in poetry it meant 'Day.' Isaiah 14:12 is not the only place where the Vulgate uses the word lucifer. It uses the same word seven more times, in contexts where it clearly has no reference to a fallen angel:

2 Peter 1:19 – meaning 'Morning star'

Job 11:17 – meaning 'The light of the morning

Job 38:32 – meaning 'The signs of the zodiac'

Psalms 110:3 – meaning 'The dawn'

Sirach 50:6 – referring to the actual 'Morning star'

Revelation 2:28 – of uncertain reference

Revelation 22:16 – referring to 'Jesus'

Indications that in Christian tradition the Latin word lucifer, unlike the English word, did not necessarily call a fallen angel to mind and exist also outside the text of the Vulgate. In the works of Latin grammarians, Lucifer, like Daniel, was discussed as an example of a personal name. Two bishops bore that name, Saint Lucifer of Cagliari, and Lucifer of Siena. In Latin, the word is applied to John the Baptist and is used as a title of Christ himself in several early Christian hymns. The morning hymn Lucis Largitor Spendide of Hilary contains the line, 'Tu verus mundi lucifer.' Some interpreted the mention of the morning star in Ambrose's hymn Aeterne rerum conditor as referring allegorically to Christ and the mention of the cock, the herald of the day or praeco in the same hymn as referring to John the Baptist, likewise, in the medieval hymn 'Christe qui lux es et dies.' Some manuscripts have the line 'Lucifer lucem proferens.' The Latin word lucifer is also used of Christ in the Easter Proclamation prayer to God regarding the paschal candle.

'Flammas eius lucifer matutinus inveniat; Ille, inquam, lucifer, qui nescit occasum. Christus Filius tuus, qui, regressus ab inferis, Humano generi serenus illuxit, et vivit et regnat in saecula saeculorum'.

'May this flame be found still burning by the Morning Star: the one Morning Star who never sets, Christ your Son, who, coming back from death's domain, has shed his peaceful light on humanity, and lives and reigns for ever and ever' In the Litany of Loreto, the Blessed Virgin Mary is invoked as 'Stella matutina', Morning Star, and a popular English hymn addressed to her has the stanza, 'Mary Immaculate, Star of the Morning, Chosen before the creation began, Destined to bring, through the Light of your Dawning, Conquest of Satan, and rescue to Man'.

A CLARIFICATION ON POPE FRANCIS INVOCATION OF LUCIFER

One of the reasons for having such an introduction about the use and meanings of the word 'lucifer' and of the name 'Lucifer' is due to the viral sensationalism caused by a video displaying the Easter Mass celebrated in 2013 soon after Francis' election. Due to the scandal, it caused among many believers of other denominations, it was deemed necessary found to provide an explanation. It is also important to underline that Pope Francis is certainly not the first to celebrate the Easter Mass through the use of the perceived scandalous text, as other Popes have done the same from times long past. Without either defending or attacking such ritual and/or the head of the Catholic Church, further objective explanation is provided below, narrating the meanings of the word 'lucifer' within the different Bible versions and throughout the centuries.

Although the choice of such language can easily be disputed as the use of the adjective 'lucifer' can somewhat be confusing when compared to the use of 'Lucifer' as a noun, it is also necessary to ratify that whenever used in Catholic prayers, the word is always printed with a lowercase 'l,' therefore remaining only an adjective referring to Christ as the 'light bringer.' Aligning perfectly with Scriptures, as we read, 'The people who walked in darkness have seen a great light; those who dwelt in a land of deep darkness, on them has light shined' from Isaiah 9:1, and 'An angel of the Lord appeared to them and the glory of the Lord shone around them' from Luke 2:9. For the sake of considering all possibilities, we can speculate that whether the introduction of such a term was done by some Satanists who infiltrated the Catholic Church centuries ago (with the intent of purposely worshiping the angel Lucifer and to create confusion between his role and Christ's), or whether it was done with the pure intention of using the adjective 'lucifer' to solely honor Jesus Christ (as the Light Bearer) remains unknown. And, as it remains a mystery, here is a quote from a message contained in 'The Warning Second Coming' given to Maria Divine Mercy and which might have something to do with it.

'There is to be a particular insult, which will be inflicted upon My Holy Name, in an effort to desecrate me, during Holy Week. This wicked gesture, during Holy Week, will be seen by those who keep their eyes open, and this will be one of the signs by which you will know that the imposter, who sits on the throne in My Church on earth, does not come from me.

LUCIFER AND FREEMASONRY

Jesuit Léo Taxil (1854–1907) in the 'Taxil Hoax' claimed that Freemasonry was associated with worshiping Lucifer and that leading Freemason Albert Pike had addressed 'The 23 Supreme Confederated Councils of the world', instructing them that Lucifer was God, and was in opposition to the evil god Adonai. In the book 'Morals and Dogma,' Albert Pike spoke of Lucifer in these terms.

'Lucifer, the Light-bearer! Strange and mysterious name to give to the Spirit of Darkness! Lucifer, the Son of the Morning! Is it he who bears the Light, and with its splendors intolerable, blinds feeble, sensual, or selfish souls? Doubt it not!'

Another quote from the same book speaks of Lucifer in the following statement.

'The Apocalypse is, to those who receive the nineteenth Degree, the Apothesis of that Sublime Faith which aspires to God alone and despises all the pomps and works of Lucifer. Lucifer, the Light-bearer! Strange and mysterious name to give to the Spirit of Darkness! Lucifer, the Son of the Morning! Is it he who bears the Light, and with its splendors intolerable blinds feeble, for traditions are full of sensual or selfish Souls? Doubt it not! Divine Revelations and Inspirations: and Inspiration is not of one Age nor of one Creed. Plato and Philo, also, were inspired. The Apocalypse, indeed, is a book as obscure as the Sohar. It is written hieroglyphically with numbers and images; and the Apostle often appeals to the intelligence of the Initiated. "Let him who hath knowledge, understand! Let him who understands, calculate!" he often says, after an allegory or the mention of a number. Saint John, the favorite Apostle, and the Depositary of all the Secrets of the Saviour, therefore, did not write to be understood by the multitude."

Although apologists of Freemasonry contend that Albert Pike and other Masonic scholars referred to the 'Luciferian path' as the 'Morning Star,' and that Freemasonry had been infiltrated and corrupted by 'Subgroups'. These factions, such as the Order of the Illuminati, the P2, or Skull and Bones, are just a few of the many factions of secret societies sprawling throughout the hidden net. Taxil acquired very truthful information from the Order of the Illuminati, which infiltrated the Jesuit order prior to being reabsorbed into the Catholic Church in 1814. Although Taxil's 'Hoax' was publicly known in the 1790's, it was only released from the masonic archives in 1924. And, although he promoted a book written by Diana Vaughan (that he actually wrote himself, as he later confessed publicly) his information seems to be very truthful. In fact, he speaks of a third world war conflict between the Muslims and the Zionists in the Middle East and at a time prior to the unimaginable formation of the state of Israel in 1948.

The information he revealed in his writings, although dismissed by many as he self admittedly denied its veracity in regards to Free Masonry during a press conference on April 19, 1897, is still an important key to understand the relationship between the corrupt parts and persons in the Jesuit Order and the dishonest individuals of the Zionist Order forming the Illuminati. They secretly come together and infiltrate the world's governments and high positions of power in all major industries, above all the banking cartels. The Sigil of Lucifer (Seal of Satan) a magical sigil used occasionally as an emblem by Satanists. In the modern occultism of Dolores North (alias Madeline Montalban), Lucifer's identification as the Morning Star equates him with Lumiel, whom she regarded as the Archangel of Light, and among Satanists he is seen as the 'Torch of Baphomet' and Azazel. In the Satanic Bible of 1969, Lucifer is acknowledged as one of the Four Crown Princes of Hell, particularly that of the East. Lord of the Air, Lucifer has been named 'Bringer of Light, the Morning Star, Intellectualism, and Enlightenment.'

THE FREEMASONS WELCOME POPE FRANCIS

'The crowning of the False Prophet will be celebrated by Masonic groups in all corners who plan the final stages of persecution of all my children.'

'With Pope Francis nothing will ever be the way it was before. The choice of fraternity for a Church of dialogue and not contaminated by the logic and temptations of a temporal power.' Grand Master Gustavo Raffi~

On 14 March 2013, Grand Master Gustavo Raffi of the Grand Orient of Italy, speaks of Pope Francis as if almost prophesying a perfectly accurate profile of the man, as well as the actions and words he will soon display in front of the world. Here is the translation of his entire speech.

'A man of the poor and far from the Curia. Fraternity and dialogue are his first concrete words: maybe in the new Church nothing will ever be like before. It is our auspicious that the Francesco's pontificate, the Pope who
"Comes from the end of the world" may signify the return of the Church-Word versus the Church-institution, promoting an open relationship with the contemporary world, with non-believers and not through the springtime of Vatican II.' 'The Jesuit who is close to the last of history,' continues Raffi 'Has the great opportunity to show the world the face of a Church that must recuperate the annunciation of a new humanity, not the weight of an institution sheltered in defense of its own privileges. Bergoglio knows real life and will remember the lesson of one of his landmark theologists, Romano Guardini, who said truth and love cannot be separated.' 'The simple cross that he wore on his white vest, the Grand Master concludes gives us hope that a Church of the people may find again the ability to dialogue with all men of good will and with Free Masonry which, as the Latin America experience teaches, works for the common good and progress of humanity, following Bolivar, Allende and Jose' Marti' to mention a few. This is the 'White smoke' that we are waiting for from the Church of our time,' Gustavo Raffi ~

Romano Guardini, who was mentioned by Grand Master Gustavo Raffi, is usually acknowledged as a major player in the theological and liturgical movements of the '30s and '40s that led to the reforms of Vatican II. The main lines of his theology opened the way for the adaptation of the Church to the modern world, especially the drastic changes of the Catholic Mass (the role of the priest; the facing toward the people rather than the altar; the diminishing importance of the altar as a sacred place). He also was a continuator of Modernism as well as a progressivist. As early as 1927, Guardini was saying the Mass versus populum and in German in a redesigned chapel at Burg Rothenfels. Discarding the Gothic altars and elaborate décor, he stripped the church, painted the walls white and installed a moveable altar surrounded on three sides by simple stools. Today, Romano Guardini remains Pope Bergoglio's main source of inspiration. It is remarkably interesting how all the hints and messages bring our attention to the intricate and hidden plots that the Free-masonic organizations have been carefully designing for centuries in order to penetrate the Holy Catholic and Apostolic Church and, consequently, destroy the Truth in order to substitute it with a false religion: the One World Religion.

When speaking of Freemasonry, we must never forget that the fruit of their deviated philosophies is a religion of boundless, yet false, tolerance toward what may seem righteous to the modern people of today's sick world, but which are most intrinsically evil insofar as the obliteration of the only Begotten Son of God into total absence by a decreed intolerance towards the mere pronouncing of His Holy Name within the lodge and under a stipulated agreement expected to be fulfilled by the members. What was born out of Albert Pike's Morals and Dogma were, in particular, the promoting of religious and cultural tolerance, theorizing that all religions shared the same roots, the same traits and the same symbols, starting with the Orphic Egg or the Cosmic Egg, and then landing towards Ancient Egyptian, Phoenician, Buddhist and Hindu Texts as well as The Abrahamic Religions. This chaotic paste of Pagan doctrines, hermetic ancient traditions (they being astrology, numerology, alchemy, and theosophy) and Abrahamic religions is the same brainwashing mystery cult of Babylon we are exposed to through today's media. This liberal attitude is what promotes the immoral tendencies that, not too long ago, were considered abhorrent by any standard in society: abortion, divorce, sexual freedom, homosexuality and so forth. Among the warnings that the faithful have received in order to know their hiding enemies consisted of the messages given by the Virgin Mary to a seer in Quito, Ecuador, in 1610. In the following quote we read the prophetic words that Our Lady of Good Success used to paint a most accurate portrait of our time, to say the very least.

'Thus, I make it known to you that from the end of the 19th century and shortly after the middle of the 20th century…the passions will erupt and there will be a total corruption of morals…As for the Sacrament of Matrimony, which symbolizes the union of Christ with His Church, it will be attacked and deeply profaned. Freemasonry, which will then be in power, will enact iniquitous laws with the aim of doing away with this Sacrament, making it easy for everyone to live in sin and encouraging procreation of illegitimate children born without the blessing of the Church… In this supreme moment of need for the Church, the one who should speak will fall silent.' ~ Our Lady of Good Success, Quito, Ecuador, 1610 A.D. ~

The subversive plan to conquer the Bride, the Immaculate Spouse, dates back to the obscure corners of time immemorial, and after the first official take-over back in 1958 as the Church was assaulted by the army of liberals, modernists, human rights, and sexual liberation supporters during the tragic Second Vatican Council, it has almost come to its completion. With the entry of the False Prophet nothing shall ever be the same. One of the most vital resources revealing the Masonic invasion within the Vatican walls is 'The Permanent Instruction of the Alta Vendita,' a Masonic blueprint for the subversion of the Holy Catholic and Apostolic Church. This document, originally published in Italian in the 19th century, was purportedly produced by the highest lodge of the Italian Carbonari and written by Piccolo Tigre, the codename for Giuseppe Mazzini. The document details a Masonic plan to infiltrate the Catholic Church and spread liberal ideas within it. The Carbonari, being part of Freemasonry, render this booklet a must-see Masonic document for whoever desires to know the truth behind the scarlet Vatican curtains. So crucial was the issue of the infiltration of freemasonry in the Mystical Body of Christ that in the 19th century, Pope Pius IX, and Pope Leo XIII both asked for it to be published.

It was first published by Jacques Crétineau-Joly in his book L'Église romaine en face de la Révolution in 1859. It was popularized in the English-speaking world by Monsignor George F. Dillon in 1885 with his book 'The War of Anti-Christ with the Church and Christian Civilization'. The important document is still being consulted by true Catholics as it accurately describes the changes within the Church during the post-Vatican II era. The Strategy outlined in the Permanent Instruction of the Alta Vendita is astonishing in its diabolicalness, cunning and audacity. The document reveals a lengthy process which will involve decades to accomplish in its final goal. Indeed, the authors of the plot were very well aware of the fact that they would not see the day of its fulfillment. Just like black widows spinning their webs of deceit while making sure they will continue to exist as a species through reproduction, these masters of the craft began a task that will be carried on by the succeeding generations of initiated members. This concept is expressed very concisely in a statement contained within The Permanent Instruction saying, 'In our ranks the soldier dies, and the struggle goes on.' The mandate sought for the propagation of liberal ideas and fundamentals throughout every country's society and within the institutions of the Catholic Church so that, over time, prelates, clerics, seminarians, and laity would systematically be ingrained with such innovative principles.

Eventually this progressive outlook would be so ubiquitous that cardinals, bishops, and priests would respectively be ordained, consecrated, and nominated while having adopted the latter-day philosophies entrenched in the French Revolution's Declaration of the Rights of Man and of the Citizen passed in 1789. Let us remember that, among these, are found the separation of church and state, the equality of religions, and the religious pluralism. Ultimately, the depraved members of these altered ranks would elect a Pope from these same hierarchies: a vicar who would lead the Catholic Church on the revolutionary path of enlightenment and renewal from the Chair of Peter. Their initial goal was to ignite the circumstances necessary in order to induce a Pope (and a hierarchy) to embrace and promote the ideas of liberal Catholicism, all the while believing themselves to be faithful Catholics. These Catholic leaders, then, would no longer oppose the modern ideas of the French Revolution the same way it was done by those Popes who were given authority between 1789 and 1958, but would amalgamate them into the church. The end result would be a Catholic Church marching under the banner of the Enlightenment, all the while believing to be instead marching under the banner of the apostolic keys. From what one can see, the plan of the Church's enemies has come to accomplish its wanted objective. The most liberal pope in the history of this Church was elected on March 13, 2013, and as seen earlier, was welcomed with open arms by the Grand Orient of Italy. Some may not be aware of the fact that on March 13, 1826 (187 years earlier to the date), Pope Leo XII issued the Quo Graviora, a document against Freemasonry. This choice comes as both an audacious act of mockery against the Catholic Church and a sign of victory over the same; the 'Architects' are obsessed with dates and numbers and having imposed a Freemason over the

Catholic Church is nothing less than their ultimate triumph. These are excerpts from the same document:

[…when Clement XII, Our Predecessor, saw that the sect de' Liberi Muratori or des Francs-Macons, or otherwise named, was increasing every day and that they were acquiring new strength, which he knew with certainty from many proofs to be not only suspect but even altogether inimical to the Catholic Church, condemned it with his magnificent Constitution, beginning with In eminenti, published on the 28th of April 1738, the text of which is supplied…"To be sure, even as the very voice of the public testifies, it has become known to us that spreading far and wide and each day gaining strength are some societies, assemblies, meetings, gatherings, fellowships, or associations commonly called de` Liberi Muratori or Francs–Macons, or identified by whatever other designation according to the variety of idioms in which men of any religion and sect whatsoever.

Satisfied by a certain feigned appearance of natural honesty, are mutually united by a strict as well as impenetrable covenant according to the laws and statues established by them, and which at the same time they both secretly dedicate themselves to by a strict oath administered on the Sacred Bible, and which under the accumulation of severe penalties they are bound to conceal by an inviolable silence…We have established and Decreed, that from the counsel of several of Our Brother Cardinals of the Holy Roman Church, and especially by Our own motion and from the fullness of Apostolic Power, those same societies, assemblies, meetings, gatherings, fellowships, or associations commonly called de' Liberi Muratori or Francs–Macons, or called by any other name whatever, must be condemned and prohibited, as by Our present Constitution, perpetually valid, We condemn and prohibit them.]

POPE FRANCIS AND THE ROTARY CLUB

Pope Francis, while he was still Archbishop Jorge Mario Bergoglio of Buenos Aires, was named and accepted an honorary membership in the Rotary Club in 1999 and also received the 2005 Silver Laurel Award of the Club as 'Person of the Year'. Both Pope Pius VI and Pope John Paul II gave speeches at The Rotary Club but only Pope Francis can claim actual membership. On January 11, 1951, The Vatican issued a Decree banning members of the clergy from belonging to a Rotary club association. The Wild Voice continues to research this, but to the best of our knowledge this Decree has never been officially rescinded or annulled. Here below is the full text of the Papal Decree issued on January 11, 1951.

Papal Decree – Pope Pius XII

Jan 11, 1951, first published in Osservatore Romano, Vatican City daily
(English translation below by the Archdiocese of Chicago)
The Supreme Sacred Congregation of the Holy Office: a decree. Wednesday, Dec. 20, 1950.
The question has been asked of this Supreme Sacred Congregation whether Catholics may be members of the association commonly called 'The Rotary club.'

After ascertaining the opinion of the Reverend Fathers Consultors, Their Eminences the Cardinals, charged with safeguarding faith and morals, decreed in their plenary meeting of Wednesday, Dec. 20, 1950, as follows. 'Members of the clergy may not belong to a Rotary club association or take part in its meetings;' laymen are to be urged to observe the provisions of Canon 684 of Canon Law. And on the 26th of the same month and year, His Holiness Pope Pius XII approved the resolution and ordered it published, after hearing it in an audience granted to His Excellency the Assessor of the Holy Office. Given in Rome at the offices of the Holy Office on Jan. 11, 1951. Marino Marani, Notary of the Supreme Sacred Congregation of the Holy Office.

THE MYSTERY OF THE HIDDEN HAND

Master of Second Veil: 'Three Most Excellent Masters you must have been, or thus far you could not have come; but farther you cannot go without my words, sign, and word of exhortation. My words are Shem, Japhet, and Adoniram; my sign is this: (thrusting his hand in his bosom). It is in imitation of one given by God to Moses, when He commanded him to thrust his hand into his bosom, and, taking it out, it became as leprous as snow. My word of exhortation is explanatory of this sign, and is found in the writings of Moses, viz., fourth chapter of Exodus:

'And the Lord said unto Moses, Put now thine hand into thy bosom. And he put his hand into his bosom; and when he took it out, behold, his hand was leprous as snow.' The Royal Arch Degree (the 13th degree of the Scottish rite or the 7th degree of the York Rite) is also known as the Mason of the Secret. During this Degree, initiates are said to receive great Masonic truths.

THE CURIOUS HORNS OF THE DEVIL ON POPE FRANCIS: COINCIDENCE?

"My dearly beloved daughter, the times ahead will shake the world from its slumber, irrespective as to what religion, if any, people follow, for the voice of the 'Little Horn' will command attention from all over the world. Seated in the Chair of Peter, this imposter will shout aloud and proudly proclaim his solution to unite all churches as one. Hailed as a modern innovator, he will be applauded by the secular world because he will condone sin." Interestingly, the prophecy given above from Jesus Christ in The Book of Truth speaks of this pope as the 'Little Horn' from the Book of Daniel. In the photograph on Time magazine depicting horns above the Popes head, the 'little horns' might be a signal. Obviously, we do not attest given signs as absolute truth but rather, as curious data. Prophecy? It might, as said above, be the fruit of mere coincidence, but nonetheless: as you scroll down this page, a picture can be put together in a puzzling series of suspicious hints which are hard to believe if compared to the lack of prophecy interest among us, the catholic faithful. We have emphasized in red the words in the photo. They have nothing to do with the content related to the pope and yet: if connected, they read 'Bilingual after the end'. It is curious to analyze the meaning of such phrase as broken down here below.

Bilingual.

It is further to be observed, that the mouth of the serpent was occasionally opened by means of a horsehair skillfully adjusted for the purpose, at the same time that by similar means the animal darted out its biforked (bi-lingual) tongue to the terror of the amazed bystanders. Lingual comes from Old Latin dingua which is a cognate (kindred) with Old English tunge, The change of d (in Old Latin dingua) to l (in Latin lingua) was probably due to dialectal influence (the so-called "Sabine l"). It was facilitated by a folk-etymological association with lingere, 'To lick,' the tongue having been conceived as 'the licking organ.' Bi-lingual represents the double toungue, or forked tongue of a snake. Also, the 'Two red horns' of the devil appearing on top of Francis' head, are a representation of the forked tongue of the serpent. Bilingual after the end might signify the revelation of the serpent after the end, the fall of the Catholic Church. Interestingly, in Revelation 13:11–17, the Beast from the earth, also referred to as the False Prophet has often been equated with an individual Antichrist.

'Then I saw another beast that rose out of the earth; it had two horns like a lamb, and it spoke like a dragon'

To continue on this interesting subject, which many Catholics will find humorous and superstitious, another curious hint comes from the mouth of a nun, who declares Jorge Bergoglio to have been a 'Little devil' at a youthful age. Of course, as we said previously, we take these many coincidences very lightly, if not humorously; yet we find these same coincidences to be intriguingly recurring when it comes to Pope Francis I, knowing that darkness often hides behind jokes and coincidences.

MYSTERY OF THE NUMBER 13 WITH POPE FRANCIS: COINCIDENCE?

The use of the number 13 in Scriptures

This article was written on Friday, June 13, 2014. As this date was not planned, you must take this coincidence as another 'Interesting' occurrence found like a strange rock on a journey's path. Anyone who has closely followed Pope Francis knows that the number 13 has been a constant from the day he became Pope, on March 13 of the thirteenth year of the new millennium. We know that, so far, he's been fulfilling the role of 'Teacher', or 'New Christ', as truly little attention has been paid to Our Lord. All the media talks about is him as the 'Innovator', and the 'New example'. The innovation begins on October 13, 2014, the anniversary day of the last apparition of Our Lady in Fatima. On such day, right in the middle of the 2014 family synod, Jorge Mario Bergoglio decided to announce a change in the Church's view on homosexuality. Interestingly, the first passage found in the Bible was John 13:13, which says:

'You call me 'Teacher' and 'Lord,' and rightly so, for that is what I am'.

It is even more interesting when we know that such passage comes right after the following. When he had finished washing their feet, he put on his clothes and returned to his place. 'Do you understand what I have done for you?' he asked them.

Now, we know how much of a stir Pope Francis has caused by his two consecutive controversial 'Foot washing' rituals. In 2014, he washed the feet of paralyzed people, almost as to signify the immobility of a new Church incapable of evangelizing under his new influence. Let's not forget that it is in John 13 (John 13:18) that we learn about Jesus' betrayal. Not referring to all of you; you know those who have chosen. But this is to fulfill this passage of Scripture: 'He who shared my bread has turned against me'. Not to mention that the name Judas Iscariot contains 13 letters.

- March 13 is also the 72nd day of the year.
- Here are a few interesting aspects of the number seventy-two (72):
- The number of languages spoken at the Tower of Babylon, according to later tradition, were 72.
- The number of names of God, according to Kabbalah, were 72.
- The number of books composing the Holy Bible in the Catholic version, is 72.
- The Book of Revelation is the 72nd (and the last) book in the Bible.
- The current distribution of the Book of Revelation is 22 chapters, adopted since the 13th century, but the oldest known division of the text is that of the sixth century Greek commentator Andrew of Cesary in 72 chapters.
- The number of warriors on the Muslim side at the Battle of Badr, was 72.
- The number of people martyred along with Imam Hussain at the Battle of Karbala was 72.
- The 72 old men of the synagogue, according to the Zohar.
- The number of houri each Muslim martyr (or every Muslim male, according to some ahadith) shall receive as companions in Paradise, s 72.
- The good god Osiris was enclosed in a coffin by 72 evil disciples and accomplices of Set.

- There are 72 demons and other spirits in the Goetia – The Lesser Key of Solomon.

Number 13 as Rebellion in Scriptures

In the Old Testament, the number 13 appears with Nimrod. His name means The Rebel; he, the 13th descendant of Adam, was also known for his rebellion in building the Tower and City of Babel. In 2 Thessalonians 2:8, there is a parallel with the Antichrist figure called The Lawless One (...He will use all sorts of displays of power through signs and wonders that serve the lie). Nimrod was a king (the beginning of his kingdom was Babel) in Genesis 10:10 and, as we can see in Daniel 11:36, the Antichrist is also termed king. Also, Nimrod's headquarters were in Babylon, as he was its King, (Genesis 10:10 and 11:1-9); in the same way, we also notice that the Man of Sin is called the king of Babylon (Isa. 14:4), while in the Apocalypse he is connected with mystery Babylon (Rev. 17:3-5). Later we discover that Nimrod's ambition was to establish a world-empire. Then, always in Genesis – this time in 14:4 – we find: "Twelve years they served Chedorlaomer, and in the thirteenth year they rebelled." Here again, the number 13 represents rebellion, when the king of Sodom and the king of Gomorrah declared war against the four kings. Therefore, powerful kings of impure cities were connected with the number 13 of rebellion. Interestingly, in Revelation 13:13 called 'The Beast Out of the Earth', we read.

'He exercises all the authority of the first beast in his presence. And he makes the earth and those who dwell in it to worship the first beast, whose fatal wound was healed. He performs great signs, so that he even makes fire come down out of heaven to the earth in the presence of men. And he deceives those who dwell on the earth because of the signs which it was given him to perform in the presence of the beast, telling those who dwell on the earth to make an image to the beast who had the wound of the sword and has come to life'.

In Genesis 13:13 we find the following line, which contains 13 words:

'But the men of Sodom were wicked and sinners before the Lord exceedingly.'

Furthermore, in Deuteronomy 13:13: 'Certain men, the children of Belial, are gone out from among you, and have withdrawn the inhabitants of their city, saying, Let us go and serve other gods, which ye have not known.' Here, in this chapter under the title 'Idolatrous Cities to Be Destroyed' are the sons of Belial who rebelled. Beli ya'al means primarily that which is low, hence worthlessness, naughtiness, wickedness. In Deuteronomy 15:9, Belial is rendered in the Authorized Version as an adjective, 'Wicked'. In the New Testament, Mark 7:21-23 says that there are 13 evils in the human heart: 'For from within, out of the heart of men, proceed evil thoughts, adulteries, fornications, murders, Thefts, covetousness, wickedness, deceit, lasciviousness, an evil eye, blasphemy, pride, foolishness: All these evil things come from within, and defile the man.' We see another number 13 In Revelation 13:18, where it is written: 'Let him that hath understanding count the number of the beast: for it is the number of a man; and his number is Six hundred threescore and six. Here is wisdom: The one who has understanding must calculate the number of the beast, because it is the number of a man. His number is 666.' Indeed, everyone knows that the number 6 represents man. The sixth word of the sixth verse of the sixth chapter of the sixth book of the New Testament is the word 'man'. In Romans 6:6 from the King James Bible, we read: 'Knowing this, that our old man is crucified with him, that the body of sin might be destroyed, that henceforth we should not serve sin.' Curiosities: coincidences or not?

More facts about the number 13 in the Bible:

- The number 13 is used 28 times in the Old Testament, and it is never used in the New Testament.
- Numbers 17, 22, and 120,000 are used 13 times in the Bible, and the number 120 is used 13 times in the Old Testament in its cardinal form.
- In the Gospel of Saint John, Jesus uses on the whole 13 titles to designate who He Is.
- 13 were the guests at the Last supper of the Christ.
- The 13th chapter of the Revelation is reserved to the Antichrist and to the Beast.
- In the 13th psalm, it is written: 'The fool has said in his heart, there is no God'.
- The mystery of the Seven Churches of the Revelation presents the winner of 13 rewards on the whole.

- The 13 sons of David were born when he was in Jerusalem.

- It is on the 13th day of the twelfth month, named Adar, that people celebrated the victory of Judas Maccabaeus on the army of Nicanor to Adasa.

- A decree of Jew extermination was decided by Haman during of a convocation addressed to scribes on the 13th day of the first month.

- The words 'Sickness', 'Tear', 'Dragon' and the term 'Son of God' are used 13 times in the New Testament.

- The words 'Carnal' and 'Treason' are used 13 times in the entire Bible.

- In the Bible, 26 numbers, written in their cardinal form, are multiples of 13.

- In the New Testament, 8 chapters possess 13 verses on the whole.

- And always in the New Testament, only 13 different numbers are equal or higher than 2000.

The Occult Numerology of the 03-13-13 Papal Conclave

- Pope Francis elected 13th March 2013.
- 13 days after Benedict Resigns
- Pope Francis age on 03/13/13 was 76 = 13
- White smoke at 7:06 PM = 13
- Exact name announced at 8:13 PM local time
- Italian time and began speaking at 8:23 = 13
- Ordained priest on 13 of December 1969
- First non-European Pope in 1,300 years
- 6 Minutes past 7 = 66 minutes past 6 – 666

Speaking of 666, here are some other strange coincidences:

ASCII is the code read by all computers for simple text. It is the universal language of computers for basic letters, symbols, and functions. Each letter is represented by a number. If you translate the name 'Bergoglio' from letters into ASCII code and add up the numbers, the result is 666. Dave Evans ('The Edge', guitarist from the band U2) played at the Sistine Chapel in May 2016. His daughter, Hollie Evans shared a photo on Instagram upon her arrival at the Vatican for her dad's concert, writing 'Just arrived with my family for a once in a lifetime Papal blessing at the Vatican. And this is the hotel room number I get. Ha!' the number 666. And now back to the number 13, here below are just a few (of many) examples featuring the appearance of the number of rebellion associated to Pope Bergoglio.

In the latest update here below, Pope Francis announces the approaching of a Third World War on September 13, 2014. It seems to be one more too-much-to-be-just-a-coincidence fact that such date was used to announce a war in which will begin from the regions he recently visited during his 'Peace mission'. To the unaware ears of the masses, this public statement came as a surprise, but not for those who follow the prophecies present on the Warning Second Coming website. A message left by the Mother of Salvation given to Maria Divine Mercy on September 6th, 2014, declares what the False Vicar would say seven days later. Here is the message. Mother of Salvation: A new, bitter world war will be declared Friday, September 6th, 2013. My dear child, I must, on the instructions of my Son, Jesus Christ, reveal that the wars, which will unfold now, in the Middle East, will herald the great battle, as a new, bitter world war will be declared. How this breaks the Sacred Heart of my poor suffering Son. The hatred, which infuses the hearts of those leaders, entrusted with the responsibility of running their countries, by ordinary people, will spread. They will betray their own nations. Millions will be killed, and many nations will be involved. You must know that the souls of those who will be murdered and who are innocent of any crime will be saved by my Son. The speed of these wars will escalate, and no sooner will four parts of the world become involved than the Great War will be announced. Sadly, nuclear weapons will be used, and many will suffer. It will be a frightening war, but it will not last long. Pray, pray, pray for all the innocent souls, and continue to recite my Most Holy Rosary, three times a day, in order to ease the suffering, which will result because of World War III. Thank you, my child, for responding to my call. Know that there is great sadness in Heaven at this time and it is with a heavy heart that I bring you this difficult news. You're Mother. Mother of Salvation

Number 13 in Religions: Interesting Facts

We could have not found a better opening image for this chapter than the cover of Black Sabbath's album '13' which came out on June 10, 2013, a few months after the election of Pope Francis and a year to date before the beginning of the Christian persecutions by ISIS on June 10, 2014. The band's name is Black Sabbath, which means 'Black Day of the Lord,' or 'Black Sunday,' or 'Black Holy Day.' Along with the photo, the ensemble It seems to represent a curse on God's people as the violent fire burns onto a dark sky that is to fall upon us soon and which, ironically, has already begun on June 10, 2014. Of course, we are leaning toward some 'Fun' speculation and fantastical satire in this analysis of the band's latest album, which contains 13 songs. But, although all these numbers might only represent a source of amusement for some readers, it is still uncanny that so many details seem to find their perfect placement within a larger and unknown plan: the one of the Antichrist.

Roman Catholicism

- The apparitions of the Virgin of Fátima in 1917 were claimed to occur on the 13th day of 6 consecutive months – from May 13, 1917, to October 13, 1917.
- Pope Pius XII was buried on October 13, 1958, in the Basilica of Saint Peter. He was consecrated a Bishop on May 13 and he fulfilled the second prophecy of Fatima consecrating the world to the Immaculate Heart of Mary. Both May 13 and October 13 were days that the visions of Fatima happened.
- The number 13 has a connection with the Templars who were arrested on October 13, 1307 – the origin of Friday the Thirteenth. De Molay has said to have placed a curse upon the Pope and the King of France at the time of his burning at the stake. The King and Pope later died within a brief time after the Templar Grandmaster's death.
- The apostle James says the Minor directed the Church of Jerusalem during 13 years.
- The 13 ecclesiastical titles of the sacerdotal hierarchy of the Roman Church.
- The father of Job had 13 children, according to the visions of Ann-Catherine Emmerick.
- The celebration of the Epiphany takes place on the 13th day after the nativity of the Lord. The number 13 is called 'theophanicus' for this reason.

We often find the number 13 associated with the Blessed Virgin Mary.

- Her Assumption occurred a Friday 13, in August, at 3 o'clock at night, according to visions of Mary Agreda. However, according to revelations of Mary Jane Even in 1994, the Virgin would have died on August 13 and would have resuscitated two days later, that is to say on August 15 to be then received Body and Soul in the Sky.

- Also, the first and the last appearance of the Virgin Mary in Fatima occurred respectively on May 13 and on October 13, 1917, and it is on July 13, 1917, that the children of Fatima had their vision of Hell, showing thus that 13 is also closely in relation to suffering and to death. Still today, in the end of time, the Virgin appears to some seers and clairvoyant only the 13 of each month. The 13th day of the month in the Christendom would be thus particularly dedicated to the Virgin Mary.

- Moreover, several received particular messages tend to show it as it is the case of following messages. In one of messages given to a privileged soul of Quebec, Our-Lord recommended that the 13 of each month is in the honor of his Mother and established in each family. In another message given by the Virgin Mary to Sister Lucy of Fatima the 1st of May 1987 for the celebration of the 70th anniversary of the day when she appeared her to Fatima on May 13, 1917, she asked her to celebrate the 13 of each month by songs and the praises in spirit of repair and of expiation.

- On May 13, 1981, that occurred the attack of the Pope John-Paul II, in Saint Peter Square. What saved him from the death, it is that he turned the head to look an engraving of Our Lady of Fatima at the same moment where the ball of the gunner passed. France, being devoted to Our Lady since Louis XIII, celebrated her by processions.

- According to visions of Maria Valtorta, during the descent of the Holy Spirit on apostles in prayer in the upper room (Cenacle), the Fire of the Holy Spirit, then in form of sphere very shining above the head of Mary, was shared in 13 very shining melodious flames to go down on the 12 apostles and the Virgin Mary.

- The value of the letter M of Mary, center of the Latin alphabet, is 13.

- Likewise, 13 words compose the invocation to the Virgin on the Miraculous Medal: 'O Mary, conceive without sin, pray for us who have recourse to thee'.

- For believer, Friday 13 (of the month of Nisan) is the day where the Christ is dead on the Cross.
- It is also a Friday 13, day placed under the sign of Venus that Eve, tempted by the demon, made eat an apple to Adam, what entailed their expulsion of the terrestrial Paradise.
- In the visions of Maria Valtorta, Jesus speaks about the 13 veins of humanity by which are distributed the divine graces, first by Himself, and then by His 12 apostles, choose by Him to represent the whole humanity and in which all the humanity is gathered in His 12 apostles.
- The 13th glorious mystery of the Holy Rosary refers directly to Pentecost.
- According to the Rule in the Order of the Saint Saviour, given by the Christ to saint Brigitte of Sweden (1303-1373), 13 priests have to sing the daily mass and the office of the ecclesiastical year.

Judaism

- The number 13 signifies the age at which a boy matures and becomes a Bar Mitzvah.
- 13 is the number of principles of Jewish faith according to Maimonides.
- 13 are the Attributes of Mercy that God has, according to rabbinic commentary on the Torah.
- 13 is the number of circles, or "nodes", that make up Metatron's Cube in Kaballistic teachings.
- Zoroastrianism
- The number 13 had been considered sinister and wicked in ancient Iranian civilization and Zoroastrianism.
- Since beginning of the Nourooz tradition, the 13th day of each new Iranian year is called Sizdah Be-dar, and this tradition is still alive among Iranian people both within modern Iran and abroad.
- Since Sizdah Be-dar is the 13th day of the year, it is considered a day when evil's power might cause difficulties for people.

Islam

- In Shia Islam 13 signifies the 13th day of the month of Rajab (Lunar calendar), which is the birth of Imam Ali.
- 13 also is a total of 1 Prophet and 12 Imams in the Shia school of thought.
- The word star is used 13 times in the Koran.

Number 13 in relation to Fatima and May 13

- May 13, 1917 – Fatima Vision
- May 13, 1941 – Stalin divides Russia into 7 districts in preparation for war
- May 13, 1981 – Pope's attempted assassination

- May 13, 2000 – Third secret partially revealed. Relates to Popes shooting on May 13, 198
- May 13, 2000 – Pope alludes to the Beast rising out of the sea in Revelation. The Beast has 7 heads.
- May 13, 2000 – Putin divides Russia into 7 districts in order to 'facilitate federal administration'

Occult Symbolism of the Number 13

The number 13 is a major symbol in the occult, death, and Satanism. The number 13 is incredibly significant in witchcraft and the occult. 13 is a number which cleans and purifies. The number 13 brings the test, the suffering, and the death. It symbolizes the death to the matter or to oneself and the birth to the spirit: the passage on a higher level of existence. For the Cabalist, the number 13 is the meaning of the Snake, the dragon, Satan, and the murderer. If we take it as prime number, 13 is maleficent. It is especially maleficent when we are at table and when one believes in his power. But, as observed judiciously Grimod, 'the number 13 is to be feared only insofar as there would be to eat only for 12'. The 13th mystery of the Tarot does not have a name. It marks the uncertainty, the hesitation, the fickleness or again a transformation, the end of something (the death) and a renewal, a rupture, which is to say an especially important change. The number 13 has always been associated with magic and the occult as it is believed to possess mysterious and concrete power at the same time. It is an emblem of a secret knowledge, a knowledge which does indeed confer power upon those conversant with it. It is a knowledge that religious orthodoxies have long feared and tried to suppress. Thirteen may be perceived as unlucky to those who fear the secret gnosis it represents, but for adherents of that same gnosis it is truly a sacred number.

Traditionally, there are 13 witches in a coven.

In a pentagram with a circle ratio of 13, each arm of the star equals 12.36, the number of lunar months, days, and hours in a solar year. Add the arms together and you get the number of full moons in five years. It is remarkably interesting to notice the recurring use of the number 13 on the United States'

One Dollar Bill:

- 13 stars above the eagle
- 13 stripes on the middle shield
- 13 arrows on its left side
- 13 leaves and 13 berries on its right side
- 13 layers forming the pyramid
- 13 are the Colonies
- 13 letters are contained in 'New World Order'
- 13 letters are contained in 'E Pluribus Unum' on the ribbon
- 13 feathers in the tail
- 13 letters in 'Annuit Coeptis' (God Has Prospered)

Additionally, 1913 is the year in which the private agency called The Federal Reserve was founded. Since then, the American Dollar has only decreased in value and the entire country's economy has been in the hands of the very few powerful people. The Bilderberg Group has a core of 39 members who are broken into 3 groups of 13 members in each group. The core of 39 answers to the 13 who make up the Policy Committee. The 13 members of the Policy

Committee answer to the Round Table of Nine. The original number of states in the United States of America was 13.

MS 13 Gang: Markings and Signs

Many Mara Salvatrucha members cover themselves in tattoos. The most common markings visible on their skin are 'MS', '13', the 'Devil Horns' and 'Salvatrucha'. Members of this gang – like other gangs – use hand signs to communicate with each other in ways not known to others. One of the most commonly displayed is through the 'devil's head' which forms a 'M' if made upside down. This hand sign is similar (if not identical) to the same symbol commonly made by rock bands, heavy metal bands, pop stars, all their fans, politicians belonging to secret societies, members of families of certain blood lines, Satanists. This gang has grown to become the largest criminal group worldwide: from North America to South America; from Europe to Asia.

The use of the number 13 in movies

- 13th Warrior
- 13 Tzameti
- 13 Frightened Girls
- 13 East Street
- 13 Floors
- 13 West Street
- 13 Fighting Men
- 13 Lead Soldiers
- 13 Men and a Gun
- 13 Assassins
- 13 Beloved
- 13 Rue Madeleine,
- 13 Curses,
- 13 Seconds
- 13 Conversations about One Thing

- 13 Hours in a Warehouse
- 13 Going on 30
- 13th Child: Legend of the Jersey Devil
- 13 Ghosts
- 13 Days
- 13 Women, Thirteen
- District B13
- Las 13 Rosas
- The 13 Ghosts of Scooby-Doo
- 13 ghosts, Friday the 13th
- Ocean's Thirteen
- Apollo 13
- District 13
- Ultimatum, Redboy 13
- Lucky 13
- Dementia 13
- Assault on Precinct 13
- Lastly, an album from the band 'The Doors' was titled '13'

The list is never ending when it come to the numbers 13 and 666, moving on…

BENEDICTS BOOK

As you likely know, there are currently two living Popes. Although this isn't the first time in history that there have been multiple Popes, previous instances were more like power struggles over who the 'Real Pope' was. When Benedict XVI stepped down, he was not declared illegitimate, which has led to a situation where we have two people with an apparent direct line to God. Despite the fact that Benedict has repeatedly stated 'There is only one Pope—Francis,' some of the more traditional factions within the church argue that Francis is illegitimate due to the fact that his predecessor is still alive. With Benedict being considered a conservative Catholic, and Francis a liberal, it was only a matter of time before the two Popes disagreed on an issue of morality, which came in the form of clerical celibacy.

Francis has recently been considering allowing an exemption to clerical celibacy for potential priests living in extremely remote regions, such as the Amazon. These 'Men of virtue' would be allowed to marry, but also act as a priest. In response to this, Benedict co-authored a book with his right-hand man, Cardinal Robert Sarah, in which they implore Francis not to make the change. But when a 92 year old man, who retired 7 years ago due to 'Lack of strength of mind and body' and just so happens to be one of the most influential people on Earth, suddenly drafts a book, suspicions are raised. Cardinal Sarah quickly found himself accused of coercing and manipulating a vulnerable old man. Although Benedict has said that is not the case, and they have removed him as an author, history won't soon forget the time one Pope may have been used as a weapon against another.

FORCED RESIGNATION

Pope Benedict XVI announces his resignation; we've already mentioned that some people believe that Benedict, not Francis, is the one true Pope, and according to this theory, which may include Benedict himself. The official reason given for Benedict's resignation was that he no longer felt capable of executing the duties of the office. But it is worth remembering that his resignation came less than a year after the Vatileaks scandal rocked the Church. The leak contained letters and memos from the Pope himself and painted a picture of a corrupt institution with a weak leader, which theorists claim was used to force his resignation. They point to his continued use of the title 'Pope Emeritus' and white robes as subtle signals that he sees himself as the true leader of the church. But wait, there's more! You may have assumed that Wikileaks was behind the scandal, or at least church insiders, but you'd be wrong. As it turns out, Hillary Clinton, Barack Obama, and George Soros were the ones to end his conservative reign, as part of their plans for a 'Catholic Spring.' While we are now seven years in and spring does not yet appear to have sprung, if we know the Obama-Clinton-Soros machine, they are simply biding their time.

THE ZIONIST POPE

Pope Francis visits major sites in Jerusalem; Theories about election interference or regime change are nothing new, especially not when they involve Clinton, Obama, or Soros.

What makes these theories so believable is that they don't necessarily require conspiracy. You don't have to meet secretly with your preferred candidate, but simply do all their dirty work from the sidelines. They may never have instructed you to do anything, but they never needed to. But while many theorists believe that Benedict was forced to resign over his leadership (too radical, too conservative, or too weak, depending on who you ask), there are some who believe he was ousted to install his hand-picked replacement, Pope Francis. According to this theory, Pope Francis is a puppet Pope, 'Communist wolf,' who lives only to serve the Zionist wishes of George Soros. Although this is definitely a subcategory of the previous theory, and is held by far fewer people, there is a rabbit hole of books, photos, and articles that claim to validate it. But like so many Zionist conspiracy theories, this one is pretty much relegated to the darkest corners of the web.

THE MURDER OF JOHN PAUL I

If there's one thing we know that Catholic Church is good at, it's cover-ups, so it should come as no surprise that one of the most shocking moments in the history of the church is alleged to be one. The death of a Pope is always a moment that sends shockwaves across the globe, but the death of a Pope just 33 days into his Papacy and 53 days after the last Pope died was particularly startling, especially given that John Paul I was just 65 years old. It didn't take long for people to start floating 'Conspiracy Theories,' with the first major example coming in the form of 'In God's Name: An Investigation into the Murder of Pope John Paul I,' a book by a man named David Yallop. Yallop claims that John Paul was murdered by a group of Freemason plants in the Vatican. Yallop claims the Pope was taken out because he was about to expose major scandals involving the Vatican Bank and mafia money-laundering. Yallop 's book is well-respected among conspiracy circles, with numerous authors building on his research since it was published. Other theories include that he was killed because he planned to reintroduce Latin mass, that he was assassinated by the CIA/KGB, or that the KGB was spreading conspiracies about what really was a natural death.

A POLITICAL HITJOB

Another important thing to remember about the Papacy is that it is an elected position. Sure, not many people get to vote in the election, but it is an election, and it is not immune from the kind of political games we see elsewhere. So, when the most recent victor turned out to be someone who is seen as liberal, and who wants to reform the Church, conservative branches of Catholicism started pushing back. One such critic was Carlo Maria Vigano, a former Vatican ambassador to the U.S. While Francis was on an apology tour to Ireland, where he apologized for the abuse carried out by members of the clergy, Vigano released an 11 page letter accusing the Pope of conspiring to cover up the abuse allegations against Archbishop Theodore McCarrick in the US. Vigano is alleged to be part of a larger group hell-bent on taking down Pope Francis, and apparently working with Steve Bannon. Bannon has been a vocal critic of the Pope, going so far as to tell the Italian Prime Minister that the Pope is 'The enemy,' and currently has plans to build 'A gladiator academy for the Judeo-Christian West.' But, despite the devastatingly thorough list of sexual abuse scandals in the Church, the group only managed to draw a very tenuous connection to Francis. They also suffered from some infighting and splits, with clergy opposing Bannon's political aims, while Bannon floated conspiracies about a gay lobby running the Church. While Vigano's letter still may reflect badly on Francis, the Pope's record doesn't appear to come anywhere near the level of cover up or conspiracy that you would expect from the Church, so it is unlikely that this will really pick up speed.

THE KNOW NOTHINGS

'Know Nothings' is the name given to members of what began as a secret society, the Order of the Star Spangled Banner, and eventually became a political party, the American Party. Their nickname comes from the fact that, when asked about the group, members would reply 'I know nothing.' Although briefly lived, the 'Know Nothings' were a powerful nationalist force at a time when immigration was a major issue. Ireland was in the midst of a famine, and the German economy was lagging, both of which led to an explosion of European Catholics moving to the US. In addition to the usual stereotypes you would expect, such as the Irish being nothing more than a bunch of drunkards, or the Germans being little more than a band of boozers, the 'Know Nothings' used conspiracies to stoke up fear around these groups to win power. And an effortless way to do that was to focus on their Catholic faith. In addition to a fraudulent undercover investigation, which apparently uncovered priests forcing themselves on nuns and then strangling the babies, the Know Nothings alleged that the flood of immigrants would drastically affect election results and change the landscape of US politics forever. Americans were already wary of European powers trying to control them, but according to the Know Nothings, it was much worse. The Pope wasn't planning to run America from the Vatican. He was planning to move the Vatican to Mississippi. But almost as quickly as they shot to prominence, the Know Nothings faded into obscurity. The Irish had their potatoes back, the Germans had an industrial revolution, and the nation was much more concerned about the issue of slavery. Fears that the Pope was taking over dissipated, and Mississippi realtors presumably slashed the prices of their Basicallas.

THE ATTEMPTED MURDER OF JOHN PAUL II

Ali Agca, 'When I shot the Pope did not want to kill him, just hurt.' Given how rare it is for a serious attempt to be made on the Pope's life, it is quite surprising that it may have happened twice in a row, to Popes with the same name. When John Paul II succeeded John Paul I, he took the same name as a mark of respect for the papacy cut short. Little did he know that his own papacy would come perilously close to the same fate? On Wednesday, May 13, 1981, Mehmet Ali Agca shot John Paul II in St. Peter's Square. The Pope was hit four times, and required emergency surgery for over 5 hours, but survived. Agca was apprehended at the scene, and police found a suicide note claiming he killed the Pope to expose 'Imperialism.' Agca had previously escaped from jail after assassinating a newspaper editor and had sent a letter to another newspaper claiming the Pope was 'An agent of Russian and U.S. imperialism.' But it doesn't end there. Agca first claimed to be a lone wolf, then the Messiah, then an agent of the Palesinian Liberation Organization, followed by the KGB/Bulgarian intelligence. The press ran with the idea that Agca was part of a larger group, and at one point, even a judge claimed he had help. After being released from jail, Agca brought flowers to John Paul II's grave, and requested a meeting with Pope Francis. The request was denied.

A FALSE PROPHET

While everyone already knows that the Pope is the head of the Catholic Church, it is worth understanding why this is the case, according to Catholic beliefs. Peter was one of the 12

Apostles, and according to Matthew 16, Peter is the 'Rock' upon which Jesus will build the Church, he would receive 'The keys of the kingdom of Heaven', and he would be given the power of 'Binding and loosing', which means the ability to permit or forbid an action without question. This passage is the most cited in terms of legitimizing the Pope as God's representative on Earth. Of course, these days you can't hold any position of power without some people believing you have sinister intentions. But when it comes to the theory that the Pope is the Antichrist, that belief can be traced back hundreds of years. Famed theologian Martin Luther made this accusation in 1537, explicitly stating 'This teaching shows forcefully that the Pope is the very Antichrist', a belief he based on the fact that the Bishop of Rome is elevated to a higher status than all other Bishops. This was followed by Archbishop Cranmer, who claimed the Pope was tricking people into thinking certain sins are okay. Even Isaac Newton jumped on the bandwagon, using some mythical math to connect the Pope with 666. It would be incredibly easy to fill this list with blogs of theorists and clairvoyants who claim the Pope is the Antichrist. What makes this theory particularly interesting is that it stretches back hundreds of years, with every Pope since the 9th Century accused of being a fraud. Unlike most conspiracies, this is one that changed nations, caused wars, and dramatically altered the course of world history.

THE POPE AND THE NAZIS

Given that the Pope is meant to embody God and all that is good, you wouldn't be surprised to hear that the Church were vocal and vociferous opponents of the Nazis. But you might be surprised to learn that that's not true at all. The Vatican, which had become an official independent country in 1929, actually adopted a policy of neutrality during World War 2 and declined to disavow Nazism. Pius XII became Pope 6 months before the war began, and remained in office throughout, meaning he was solely and exclusively responsible for the Church's response to the ongoing atrocities. But while Pius did speak of the tragic loss of Christians, he never addressed the issue of Jewish victims. Despite receiving intelligence from the US, Poland, and the World Jewish Congress, the Pope just never found the time to speak about the ethnic cleansing that was taking place. Perhaps the treaty Pius had negotiated with the Nazis before he became Pope, the one where the Church promised not to be critical in exchange for preferential treatment under the Nazi regime, had something to do with it. Certain historians cushion this fact by stating that the Church only teamed up with the Nazis to defeat the Communists. Others claim the Pope was actually saving Jewish people, but in secret. And then there are those who believe it was just convenient to stay silent. With the archives of Pius set to be made public this year, we may soon know the answer.

SECRET OF FATIMA

Fatima your last chance: The Third Secret Regarding the Church – Fr Gruner. In 1917, three Portuguese children named Lucia Santos, Jacinta Marto, and Francisco Marto claimed to have received 6 visits from the Virgin Mary. The apparition, known as Our Lady of Fatima, is said to have given three secrets to the children: the first was a vision of hell; the second was a prediction that WW1 would end (at some point), along with the suggestion that the Russians convert; but the third secret was a secret. Benedict XV was the Pope at the time of the apparition, and the secret was kept hidden by 5 successive Popes, until John Paul II decided it was time to share the truth with the world. By then, the third secret of Fatima had become a bit of a cultural icon, with the general consensus being that, whether you believe it or not, the secret foretold the end of the world. The Vatican had even stated that it was "most probable the Secret would remain, forever, under absolute seal." Even Lucia, who witnessed the apparition and held the secret, required written permission from the Pope before agreeing to write it down. So, imagine the disappointment when it turned out to be a generic message about penance and salvation, and not a description of the destruction of the Earth. Fortunately, the conspiracy didn't end there. Once the disappointing secret was released, people began to claim it was a fake. To support this, the point to the fact that Lucia said she wrote a letter one a piece of paper. The document revealed was not a letter, and was on four sheets, with many claiming the writing style was totally different. As a result, there are still those who believe that the Vatican is hiding the real secret, which is either how the world will end, or how Satan will infiltrate the Church. You'll just have to wait to find out which one it is.

CAESAR'S MESSIAH

It is being argued that the New Testament Gospels were written by a group of individuals connected to the Flavian family of Roman emperors: Vespasian, Titus, and

Domitian. The authors were mainly Flavius Josephus, Berenice, and Tiberius Julius Alexander, with contributions from Pliny the Elder. Although Vespasian and Titus had defeated Jewish nationalist Zealots in the First Jewish–Roman War of 70 AD, the emperors wanted to control the spread of Judaism and moderate its political virulence and continuing militancy against Rome. Christianity, a pacific and pro-Roman authority religion, was their solution. The Jesus mythicist theory contradicts the mainstream historical view that while the Gospels include many mythical or legendary elements, these are religious elaborations added to the biography of a historical Jesus who did live in 1st-century Roman province of Judea, was baptized by John the Baptist, and was crucified by the order of the Roman Prefect Pontius Pilate.

There is evidence that the Flavian family was involved with early Christianity. It is claimed that the Roman theology of Victory fueled the family's goal to destroy Jerusalem and their imperial ambition. It is not clear who was the first Flavian to convert to Christianity; possible converts include Vespasian's nephew Titus Flavius Clemens and his wife Flavia Domitilla. According to the legendary sixth-century Acts of Saints Nereus and Achilleus, Pope Clement I--whose name clearly references the Flavian family--was the son of Titus Flavius Sabinus. In the First Epistle of Clement, Clement's epistle to the Christians of Corinth, it is argued, Pope Clement describes himself as being like a Roman prefect, giving orders to his soldiers which he expects to be obeyed (1 Clem. 37:2-3). Speculations are that Saint Veronica may be the same person as Berenice, mistress of Emperor Titus. Assuming that at least some of this information linking the Flavian family to early Christianity is correct, Atwill points out that these early connections are exceedingly difficult to explain if Christianity was a struggling grassroots movement originating in Judea. In addition, the sacraments of the early Christian church, its College of Bishops, and the title of its leader (the Pontiff) were all based in Rome, and on Roman, rather than Judaic traditions.

Echoes of Old Testament stories are often found in the New Testament, in a relationship in which the Old Testament model is called the 'Type' and the New Testament reprise is called the 'Antitype.' The study of these types and antitypes is called typology, there are claims that similar typological relationships knit together the Gospels and the works of Flavius Josephus. It is noted that according to the Preterist School of biblical interpretation, the prophecies of Jesus and Daniel were fulfilled by the destruction of Jerusalem in 70 AD, suggesting that this is evidence that the Gospels (including the prophecies of the coming of the Son of man) were actually written after the Jewish War, and that the Gospels are ironically predicting that Titus is the anticipated 'Son of Man'. Jesus's mission in the Gospels foreshadows the military campaign of Titus in Judea, this indicates that the Gospel authors wanted to signal that the character Jesus Christ, as the fulfillment of the messianic prophecies of the Hebrew Scriptures, was a representation of Titus Flavius. Also, that Josephus's narrative in The Jewish War is built around the idea that Daniel's prophecy was fulfilled by Titus's conquest of Jerusalem and the destruction of the Second Temple. Is this as an ironic juxtaposition of events, as Titus Flavius destroyed the Temple and conquered Jerusalem, and turned it over to the Romans?

Scholarly debate over Josephus's knowledge of Christianity has centered on two explicit passages in the Antiquities of the Jews: the Testimonium Flavianum (Ant. 18.3) and a passage that mentions James as the brother of Jesus (Ant. 20.9), that in addition to those brief passages, Josephus wrote several vicious satires of the Gospel narrative and Christian faith, indicating that he was highly familiar with its tenets, but also disdainful. The first occurs at The Jewish War 3.10, where Josephus describes an attack by Titus against Jewish rebels (led by a man named Jesus) at the lake of Gennesareth, in which the rebels are drowned and speared like fish. The Sea of Galilee is the lake where Jesus told his disciples that they would become 'Fishers of men' in Luke 3:21. Josephus enigmatically describes the lake of Gennesereth as 'A vein of the Nile' where 'Coracin fish' grow. 'Chorazain' was a Galilean rebel town, cursed by Jesus at Matthew 11:21.
In Wars 4.7, the rebel leader John is described as suffering a sort of inflammation or distemper. His party meets Vespasian at Gadara, where the rebels are driven into the River Jordan. The passage contains dense verbal parallels to the Gospel description of Jesus meeting the demoniac at the land of Gadarenes, who contains a legion of unclean spirits that enter into herd of swine and then drown themselves in the sea. According to Josephus, the Romans captured a 'Mighty prey' of livestock, but no swine.

The Gospel narratives of Luke 10:38-42 and John 12:2-3 describe a dinner just after Lazarus has been raised from the dead. 'They made him a supper,' John says, and 'Mary has chosen the good portion.' Was this as a macabre cannibalistic double entendre, and a parallel to Wars 6.3, in which Josephus describes a woman named Mary who is pierced by famine. She roasts her baby son as if he were a Passover lamb, eating half of him while saving 'A very fine portion' to be eaten later. 'Come, eat of this food,' she says, in words which are reminiscent of the Catholic Eucharist. Wars 6.5 describes the fate of a certain Jesus, the son of Ananus. This Jesus cries 'A voice from the east, a voice from the west, a voice from the four winds, a voice against Jerusalem and the holy house, a voice against the bridegrooms and the brides, and a voice against this whole people!' No matter how severely whipped, this Jesus simply repeats repeatedly, 'Woe, woe to Jerusalem.' Finally, he says, 'Woe to me also,' and he is killed by a stone from the Roman artillery. In these passages, Atwill sees a parody of Jesus's sayings in Matt. 23:13-33, 24:27-25:1 and Luke 11:43-52. Another sprawling satire in the Gospels and Josephus, called the 'New Root and Branch.' The purpose of this particular satire is to document that the 'root' and 'branch' of the Judaic messianic lineage has been destroyed and that a Roman lineage has been 'Grafted on' in its place.

Arguments that the Testimonium Flavianum (Ant. 18.3) is genuine because it is seen as the introduction to a literary triptych. Immediately following the Testimonium Flavianum is the story of Decius Mundus, who pretends to be the god Anubis, to trick a woman named Paulina into having sex. Atwill sees Decius's name as a pun on Publius Decius Mus, a sacrificial hero of the Roman Republic. As the story continues, Paulina's husband Saturninus agrees that it would be no sin for Paulina to have sex with a god. So, Paulina and Decius Mundus sleep together, but Mundus returns on the third day to boast that he is not a god. The authors of the Gospels were mainly Flavius Josephus, the Herodian princess Berenice, and the military general Tiberius Julius Alexander, with contributions from (the Gentile) Pliny the Elder.

THE UNITED NATIONS IS A LUCIFERIAN CULT CONTROLLED BY THE KNIGHTS OF MALTA, JESUITS, ROTHSCHILDS, AND ROCKEFELLERS

'No one will enter the New World Order unless he or she will make a pledge to worship Lucifer. No one will enter the New Age unless he will take a Luciferian Initiation.' – David Spangler, Director of Planetary Initiative, United Nations, 'Reflections on the Christ,' 2012

The Rockefeller Connection with the United Nations

It is a widely-known fact, that on April 25, 1945, in New York City, the non-governmental organization, known as the United Nations came into being; but did you know that the United Nations was founded, funded, chartered, and established under the auspices of the oil and banking Rockefeller family; the very same (Luciferian) family, that funded American and Nazi eugenics programs, and is now working with the U.N. to build a one world government?

On October 23, 2015, Andrew Glass of Politico Magazine, reported the following facts, regarding the Rockefeller family's connection to the founding of the United Nations. Glass stated, 'On Oct. 24, 1949, four years after the charter went into effect, the cornerstone was laid for the U.N. headquarters building near the East River in mid-Manhattan. Nelson Rockefeller arranged for the purchase, after an initial offer to locate it on the Rockefeller family estate in Westchester County was rejected as being too far from New York City. The $83.4 million purchase, as adjusted to reflect current dollars, was funded by Nelson Rockefeller's father, John D. Rockefeller Jr., who donated the land to the city. Technically, the U.N. headquarters complex in New York remains an extraterritorial site that remains beyond the jurisdictional reach of the surrounding city and state as well as the federal government. However, in exchange for police and fire protection and other essential services, the U.N. has agreed to abide by most local, state, and federal laws. United Nations Day is celebrated on this day each year.

Notice how the United Nations has been designated as an 'Extraterritorial site that remains beyond the jurisdictional reach of the surrounding city and state as well as the federal government.' This is done so that, like the Vatican in Rome, London in England, and D.C. in Washington (all globalist centers of power), the United Nations in New York is legally shielded from any National charges of high treason… Andrew Glass, of Politico, also stated in the 2015 article, that; 'Nelson Rockefeller arranged for the purchase of the U.N. headquarters, after an initial offer to locate it on the Rockefeller family estate in Westchester County was rejected as being too far from New York City.' This brazen display of Rockefeller control over the U.N. (the Family being so arrogant, as to literally attempt to place the headquarters of the United Nations in their own backyard), should make it noticeably clear to any critically-thinking person, who's in control. The United Nations has been, since it's very inception, nothing more than a Jesuit-Rothschild-Rockefeller tool of global control; in short, the United Nations acts as a central banking front-organization, designed, and built with the sole purpose of eliminating National sovereignty, by bringing about 'Global governance' through global dependence.

Considering the evil past of the Rockefeller Foundation, should anyone be surprised? In 1933 (and for 20 years after that), the Rockefeller Foundation spent $1.5 million, funding the CIA's 'Operation Paperclip'; which referred to the task of identifying, finding, hiding, aiding, and assisting 10,000 Nazi scientists and 'Scholars' from Nazi Germany, which were to be safely relocated to U.S. universities, and other U.S. allied locations around the world. Unbelievably, ardent Nazis, such as Dr. Wernher Von Braun, and Dr. Josef Mengele, were given safe haven. The Rockefeller family and Foundation are still engaging in a global war against National sovereignty, and individual rights/freedoms; but why, and for who? If the United Nations was established under the auspices of the Rockefeller family, who's in control of the Rockefellers? To put it simply… the House of Rockefeller works under the House of Rothschild; and the House of Rothschild works under the Jesuits of Rome. Both families have been affiliated with the Jesuits, since the 1700's.

To further understand this fact, one must possess a deeper knowledge of the history of the Rockefeller and Rothschild families. For instance; in 1722, the Jesuits, being expelled from every Catholic country in Europe, found that Russia, Great Britain, and the United States was their only refuge. To carry on their eternal war against the Christian Reformation, thousands of Jesuits entered the United States, under the banner of 'Tolerance and freedom of religion for all.' Among the thousands of Jesuit families that entered the U.S., were the Morgans, Roosevelts, and German Roggenfelders; to make the name sound less German, they changed the Roggenfelder surname to Rockefeller. As for the Rothschild family… many still believe that they control the world, via their central banking system, but that can't be (entirely) true; considering the fact, that the House of Rothschild has always been an agent of the old Holy Roman Empire. If the Rothschilds were in control of the world, why would they waste their time serving Jesuits, and the Vatican? They act as the Pope's official Papal Barons and Bankers. Also, why would they, as a 'Jewish' family, swear allegiance to the 'Holy Father at Rome, the Pope, and the Roman Catholic Church Universal throughout the world,' as the Jesuit Oath demands? Who's really in control? One who swears allegiance, or the one who demands it? Mayer Amschel Rothschild Knight of the Sovereign Military Order of Malta.

So, you see; just as the Morgans, Roosevelts, Rockefellers were Jesuits in 1722, Mayer Amschel Rothschild was of the Sovereign Military Order of Malta (Knights of Malta), and his family considered, Imperial (Holy Roman Empire) Crown Agents, in 1800! In truth, both the Rockefeller and Rothschild families, serve the Pope of Rome as Papal Knights; who, to this very day, continue to serve as the Papal Barons and Bankers of the new Holy Roman Empire. The official title of the House of Rothschild is the 'Guardians of the Vatican's Treasury '! Therefore, the new world order is not new, but a rebirth of the old world order (or old Holy Roman Empire). Just as Sol Invictus (Nimrod/Baal) was the official Sun 'God' (false light/Lucifer) in the later Roman Empire; the Jesuits of Rome, still worships Lucifer! This explains why their Order's emblem is a sun; it represents Sol Invictus (Nimrod/Baal), or Lucifer.

The Canaanite god Baal (who is Nimrod) has always been associated with Beelzebub; and in theological sources (mostly Christian), Beelzebub is just another name for Satan! Clearly, the 'New age' movement is the externalization of the elite's 'Secret doctrine' of Lucifer, onto society and culture; turning the whole of global society into a U.N. Luciferian cult. The United Nations (Jesuit-Rothschild-Rockefeller) new world order agenda is in reality, an anti-Christian war against the Way, the Truth, and Life, Jesus Christ; and real the children of Light (God). The Rothschilds, who have held the title of 'Guardians of the Vatican's Treasury,' since 1776. Even now, the House of Rothschild still works directly under the Jesuit Order, as Papal Knights, Barons, and Bankers (centralizing the world's political, economic, and spiritual power for Rome)! The 'Secret cabal' is the Jesuit Order; and all roads do lead to Rome!

New World Government of the United Nations

Here are three good and obvious reasons, not just and free-thinking Nation should ever willingly cooperate with the United Nations; a highly treasonous, 'Non-governmental' organization. The first reason being, that the main goal of the U.N. is to build a 'One world government,' which would require the speedy elimination 'National autodetermination;' meaning, the elimination of every Nation's sovereignty, along with the elimination of every individual's chartered rights and freedoms. Free-thinking sovereign Nations should not co-operate with the United Nations. It is an act of treason to do so; forcing the free people of free

Nations to follow the 'Recommendations' of an unelected 'Intellectual elite,' working for a non-governmental organization called the United Nations (which was established under the auspices of 'World bankers,' like Rockefeller, etc.), while politicians, bankers, teachers, and police, etc. are ignoring the recommendations (i.e., the free will), of the Nation's people!

'We are grateful to the Washington Post, the New York Times, Time magazine and other great publications whose directors have attended our meetings and respected the promises of discretion for almost forty years. It would have been impossible for us to develop our plan for the world if we had been subject to the bright lights of publicity during those years. But the world is now more sophisticated and prepared to march towards a world-government. The supranational sovereignty of an intellectual elite and world bankers is surely preferable to the National autodetermination practiced in past centuries.' – David Rockefeller in an address to a Trilateral Commission meeting in June of 1991.

New World Economy of the United Nations

'It is well enough that people of the nation do not understand our banking and monetary system, for if they did, I believe there would be a revolution before tomorrow morning.' – Henry Ford. The second reason being, that the United Nations promotes the idea of an inevitable 'Great reset,' which is really the building of a new world economy. A global stock market crash will act as the global catalyst; but, before the needed market crash occurs, the people of the world must be brainwashed with socialism/communism, to the point that they will actually (in the words of Aldous Huxley) 'Come to love their servitude.' The central bankers will buy up their debt, and literally own anyone in debt, or anyone too poor to keep up with the ever-growing costs of inflation... A future of digital assets for the rich, and perpetual debt for the poor. As Klaus Schwab (Executive Chairman of the World Economic Forum) recently proclaimed; 'You will own nothing, and you will be happy.' For the debtor is slave to the lender; and the 'Great reset,' is a euphemism for new world order. On page 405 of David Rockefeller's "Memoirs", he reveals the whole (NWO) truth; that is:

1. My family and I are 'Part of a secret cabal working against the best interests of the United States.'

2. My family and I are 'Internationalists' (globalists).

3. My family and I are 'Conspiring with others around the world.'

4. My family and I are working to build a new 'Global political and economic structure — one world, if you will.'

5. My family and I feel no guilt for our actions; on the contrary, 'I stand guilty, and I am proud of it.'

'Some even believe we are part of a secret cabal working against the best interests of the United States, characterizing my family and me as 'Internationalists' and of conspiring with others around the world to build a more integrated global political and economic structure — one world, if you will. If that is the charge, I stand guilty, and I am proud of it.'

New World Religion of the United Nations

The third and last reason being, that the United Nations promotes religious 'Ecumenism', the World Council of Churches, along with the global Inter-Faith movement; a movement that hides behind the cause of 'World peace'; but in reality, the Inter-Faith movement is nothing more than a global religious deception; mainly involving, the U.N.'s 'Acrane School' of the 'Lucis Trust', and 'The Temple of Understanding', which is the official ecumenical 'Spiritual U.N.' for the six major faiths of the world. The Temple of Understanding was originally supported by globalists, like Defense Secretary and President of the World Bank, Robert S. McNamara, along with Eleanor Roosevelt, and the Bodman foundation, in 1969. Hayden Ludwig, of Capital Research wrote the following, regarding the U.N.'s Temple of Understanding. 'Spearheading the charge was a new coalition formed in 1993: the National Religious Partnership for the Environment (NRPE). The coalition included the U.S. Conference of Catholic Bishops, Jewish Council for Public Affairs, and National Council of Churches of Christ (mostly composed of mainline, liberal denominations).'

The NRPE was always ecumenical, so much so that its initial executive director, Paul Gorman, is a historical ally of atheists. Gorman was a press secretary for arch-liberal Sen. Eugene McCarthy (D-MN) and a radical environmentalist who once called 'The relentless magnitude of environmental degradation' the defining feature of his generation's 'Struggle for social justice.' In the 1980s, Gorman headed the Temple of Understanding in New York City's Episcopal Cathedral of St. John the Divine, then the headquarters of the Gaia Institute, a Pagan organization that worships an earth spirit called 'Gaia' (the personification of the Earth in ancient Greek mythology).

We can only assume that their end-goal is to completely erode Judeo-Christian culture (especially Christianity); then, 'Re-educate' the global population, to accept the 'New world religion' of the 'New Age,' the doctrine of Lucifer, a doctrine of Self-Worship, also known as 'Apotheosis.' In an effort to confuse everyone and draw people further away from the Truth that is Jesus Christ, all the while drawing them ever closer to the father of lies, Lucifer; they've merged the paganism, hermeticism, gnosticism, cabalism, and magick, of the 'Western esoteric tradition,' with the paganism, mysticism, yoga, Zen meditation, and magick of the 'Eastern esoteric tradition.' The very history of 'Elite' foundations proves the existence of a grand conspiracy against Judeo-Christian culture; our God, our beliefs, and us. In short; the U.N. is a satanic cult, warring against the children of the One True Living God.

For instance, do your research, and you will discover that, since its founding in London in 1922, Lucis Trust has been the world's leading satanic cult. It is the controlling force behind The Temple of Understanding. Luciferianism is the false doctrine that will sweep the globe, before God sends a 'Strong delusion' to disbelievers, 'So that they may believe what is false.' Coming soon, is the time of 'Falling away.' Do not be deceived by the United Nations. 'Let no man deceive you by any means: for that day shall not come, except there comes a falling away first, and that man of sin be revealed, the son of perdition...'
– 2 Thessalonians 2:3

'And with all deceivableness of unrighteousness in them that perish; because they received not the love of the truth, that they might be saved. And for this cause God shall send them strong delusion, that they should believe a lie... "
– 2 Thessalonians 2:10-11

Followers of the Luciferian doctrine have flipped the Biblical Garden story on its head; seeing Lucifer as an enlightened liberator, and God as a brutal and unjust tyrant. They believing that God (Jehovah) was keeping Adam and Eve captive (as prisoners), in the Garden of Eden; and that Lucifer did not trick man into a life of sin, but freed him, with the gift of intellect. With intellect; they believe that they will subdue nature with science, conquer physical death and live forever with transhumanism, and by their own will, become Gods with Luciferian gnosis.

The (Luciferian) sponsors of the Lucis Trust include the usual (globalist) suspects; such as.

1. The Rockefeller Foundation
2. Robert McNamara (former Secretary of Defense, one of Henry Ford's "Whiz Kids," former President of Ford Motor Company, and former President of the World Bank)
3. Henry Clausen (the former Supreme Grand Commander of Scottish Rite Freemasons)
4. Thomas Watson, Jr. (of IBM)
5. Rabbi Marc Tannenbaum (of the American Jewish Committee)

Is it just me…? Or are many of these names, the same, that made World War II possible? They are mixing lies (false gods) with the Truth (Jesus Christ), the spirit of the ecumenical movement is entirely anti-Christian. They claim that 'All paths lead to God' (meaning, Hindus, Buddhists, Pagans, and even Satanists, will all go to heaven, because in their twisted view of the reality, all Gods are but an expression of the 'Light,' Lucifer). The Luciferian goal of the United Nations inter-faith movement is to introduce a Lucifer 'New world religion;' ever drawing humanity further away from the Way, the Truth, and the Life, Jesus Christ. However, Christians will not be fooled. We know that the God is the Father, the Son, and Holy Spirit. In the future, the Christian's inability to 'Pledge to worship Lucifer' in a world of spiritual relativism, will lead to a global conflict; then, Christians all over, will be seen as the global 'Enemies of peace and tolerance,' by the lost and fallen Nations of the world, who will chose to follow the U.N.'s gnostic-cabalistic Luciferian Doctrine. Little does the average person know, the U.N.'s ecumenical movement has always drawn its Luciferian inspiration from past occult organizations; such as the Knights of Malta, the Jesuits, Prieure de Sion, Knights Templar, Cathars, Ordre de la Rose-Croix Veritas, Illuminati, Free Masons, Ordre Martiniste, and most recently, the Theosophical Society. The U.N.'s Lucis Trust openly promotes the Theosophical Society's evil doctrine of Lucifer by teaching a blasphemous 'Esoteric gnostic form of

Christianity' called, 'Theosophy.' (Lucifer, was the name of the Theosophical magazine, published by Helena Blavatsky.)

The 'New Atlantis,' the 'New age,' the 'New World Order,' and the 'Great reset' all represent the same Luciferian agenda; to use the U.N., to promote the notion of a global 'Utopian' pseudo-Christian society of ecumenism, ruled by a, relatively unknown, Luciferian 'Priesthood;' a 'Priesthood' dedicated to the doctrine, and steady execution, of the Luciferian agenda, to rule the entire world (and seamlessly legalize evil and lawlessness). To Luciferians; 'Freedom of religion' and 'Tolerance,' means liberty from the holy law of God. Remember, Lucis Trust is not just same crazy fringe group; they are in their own words, the 'Spiritual foundation of the United Nations'… and they don't even bother to hide the fact that they're Luciferians! In fact, if you visit the Lucis Trust website, you will see exactly what the 'Spiritual foundation of the United Nations' is promoting. In a Lucis Trust document entitled, 'Department of Religion' (notice, they are already prepared for a World 'Department of Religion'), you will find proof of the obviously Luciferian (Satanic) belief system held by the United Nations. The document states that in the 'New World Religion,' the whole world will acknowledge/worship Lucifer as the 'Ruler of Self-consciousness.'

Still believe there's no 'New World Order' conspiracy; to build a one world government, one world economy, and one world religion? Keeping your eyes closed, is worse than being blind Lucis Trust has six thousand members worldwide. All members were/are globalist 'Insiders,' like Robert McNamara, Henry Kissinger, David Rockefeller, Paul Volker, George Shultz, etc. The Rockefeller Foundation does not only manage the United Nations, but also the 'Spiritual foundation of the United Nations;' that is, Lucis Trust. The 'Founder' of Lucis Trust, Alice Bailey was a fellow Luciferian, which used the Lucis Press in 1924, to publish 20 or so books, written and distributed by Bailey herself. These books consisted of her own writings, and the writings of a 'Channeled' disembodied Tibetan she called, 'Djwhal Khul.' If that's not crazy enough; or enough to prove the connection between Lucis Trust and Luciferian cults… Upon the death of Helena Petrovna Blavatsky (leader of the Theosophical Society), Bailey assumed the leadership of the Luciferian (Satanic) Theosophical Society (remember… the U.N.s Lucis Trust teachings and curriculum were adopted by this same, Luciferian, Theosophical Society). Now, to prove, beyond a shadow of a doubt, that the U.N., Lucis Trust, and the

Theosophical Society is, are in fact, Satanic. Here's a telling quote from Helena Petrovna Blavatsky herself.

'It is Satan who is the God of our planet and the only God.' – Helena Petrovna Blavatsky

Isn't it strange, that Lucis Trust, an openly Luciferian spin-off organization of the mystical (occult) 'New-age' spiritual movement of Theosophy; was one of the first NGOs to be granted 'Consultative' status with the U.N.? Maybe… Until you understand who's in control. Do you think it was a complete coincidence that the Nazis also believed in occultic powers? It wasn't. In fact, Hitler was not just 'Dabbling' in magick, he was actually a long-time occult student of the German O.T.O. offshoot, the Thule Society, and was an avid follower of Helena Petrovna Blavatsky's teachings. It is a well-known fact that Hitler was so obsessed with Luciferianism that he actually slept with a copy of Helena Petrovna Blavatsky's book, entitled The Secret Doctrine, by his bedside. By the way, the 'Secret doctrine,' is the 'Doctrine of Lucifer,' and that is the doctrine that 'Man is God;' which is also very same doctrine that the United Nation's Lucis Trust is now trying to promoting to the entire world. The United Nations is now selling the same lie that Lucifer sold to Adam and Eve, in the Garden of Eden. It was Blavatsky's 'Secret Doctrine' that laid the occult foundation for Nazi racism, and the outright evil that came with it; the doctrine promotes 'Seven root races,' 'Aryan god-men,' and Lucifer's Garden lie. In Genesis 3, Lucifer seductively suggests to Adam and Eve that God is trying to fool them, by hiding the truth of who they really are… Gods.

'3 now the serpent was more subtle than any beast of the field which the Lord God had made. And he said unto the woman, Yea, hath God said, ye shall not eat of every tree of the garden? 2 And the woman said unto the serpent, we may eat of the fruit of the trees of the garden: 3 But of the fruit of the tree, which is in the midst of the garden, God hath said, ye shall not eat of it, neither shall ye touch it, lest ye die. 4 And the serpent said unto the woman, ye shall not surely die: 5 For God doth know that in the day ye eat thereof, then your eyes shall be opened, and ye shall be as gods, knowing good and evil. 6 And when the woman saw that the tree was good for food, and that it was pleasant to the eyes, and a tree to be desired to make one wise, she took of the fruit thereof, and did eat, and gave also unto her husband with her; and he did eat.' – Genesis 3:1-6

Sin itself, is a sacred act of expression (a sacrament to Lucifer if you will), in their unholy war against the Judeo-Christian God of life and light; believing Lucifer to be the light. In their unholy quest to accomplish the 'Great work' of 'Apotheosis,' Luciferians will engage in cabalistic sex magick with men, women, and children; even demons. They will also contact and commune with unseen spirits (demons). They 'Eat the fruit' of occult knowledge from the cabalistic 'Tree of knowledge of good and evil,' in a grand effort to achieve what Luciferians would call 'Gnosis,' 'Self-realization,' 'Self-empowerment,' or 'Self-enlightenment.' Instead of saying what they really mean, they hide behind new age phrases; like 'Manifest the divinity within,' or 'Awaken the divinity within,' or 'Awaken your higher self' (etc.). But, what they're always saying (in a covert way that is), is… 'Become the God you are.' The message that you don't need God, is one thing, and bad enough; but, getting people to believe that the Christian God is evil, and that Man is God, is Satanic. 'And no marvel, for Satan himself is transformed into an angel of light.' – 2 Corinthians 11:14

Madame Blavatsky, the founder of modern Theosophy, was clearly a worshipper of Satan. You just need to read her quotes regarding Satan, and you'll see, it's very evident. 'And now it stands proven that Satan, or the Red Fiery Dragon, the 'Lord of Phosphorus,' and Lucifer, or 'Light-Bearer,' is in us: it is our Mind.' – Helena Petrovna Blavatsky. 'Curriculum is being drafted to indoctrinate our children in what John D. Rockefeller Jr. called, 'the church of all people.'' – Edith Roosevelt, 1962, 'Universal Theocratic State'.

Waking Up From the U.N. Spell of 'Peace and Safety'

Face it; America, and the world at large, has been misled by a 'Secret cabal' of Luciferian central bankers, elitist intellectuals, corrupt politicians, greedy judges, etc. For one to willingly work with such an openly treasonous organization, such as the United Nations, goes against everything we were taught in the past; that a good citizen loves God, demanding work, and family values. We were taught to fight for these things; to preserve the truth, our freedom, and our County. Where there's Truth, there too is freedom. But now, the world is being tricked by the U.N. into trading individual rights for 'Global peace' and individual freedom for 'Global safety.' If the world trades the Truth for a lie, than world will be doomed! If the world weren't being conditioned to accept lies; long ago, the free people of the free Nations of the world would have laid charges of treason against politicians openly cooperating with the United Nations.

It's sad that the average American is unable to grasp the truth… that the United Nations is a Central Banker's 'Globalist' tool of world domination (it's a non-governmental organization "beyond the jurisdictional reach of the surrounding city and state as well as the federal government"); designed solely for the purpose of creating 'Order', a new world order, out of National instability and dependence (caused by the economic and political chaos) they secretly cause and manage on a global scale, all the while, pretending to be wise men, ushering in a time of 'Global peace and safety'. When in reality, the tyrannical goal of the U.N. is to normalize global inter-dependence (or dependence) of Nations on (in the telling words of David Rockefeller) … 'An intellectual elite and world bankers;' which comprises a 'Secret cabal' that works day and night, 'Against the best interests of the United States.' The United Nations says that they promote 'Global peace and safety' among the free and independent, sovereign Nations of the world; in reality, they're actions promote trauma, confusion, fear, anger, desperation, and dependence, on an internationalist 'Secret cabal' of Luciferians, comprised of the world's most powerful (evil) central banking families.

In short, the secret new world order cabal consists of an 'Intellectual elite' (of Luciferians). They, manage the agenda for 'World bankers' (such as the Rothschild's, and Rockefeller's, etc.); the Houses that fund and control the new world order agenda, from behind the scenes. When a Nation foolishly makes it known to the United Nations that they need something, like money, or military protection; the U.N. doesn't help, instead, they start plotting, behind the scenes, work against the best interests of that Nation (i.e., funding radical communist or fascist 'Social movements' and violent street riots, 'Pandemics', economic crashes, famines, martial law, etc.), making the problems of that Nation even worse off than they already were. Then, when the timing is perfect (in other words, when the Nation is economically and emotionally broken, and on its knees, literally begging for a solution; that's when the United Nations will begin discussions with that particular Nation, offering 'Friendship' and solutions, while playing the role of global heroes. In doing so, that Nation's people become dependent on their apparent heroes, as they now feel a false sense of 'Peace and safety.' This allows for that Nation to be further manipulated and fleeced in the future.

For too long, the Luciferian megalomaniacs in charge of the.U.N., have been playing with entire Nations like pawns on a chessboard. Like witches and warlocks, they've casted their spell of 'Peace and safety' on unsuspecting Nations. The new world order mantra of United Nations, sums up their entire Hegelian dialectic scam with one this phrase; 'Global problems, require global solutions.' The United Nations is dividing and conquering the free Nations of the world; by saying one thing and doing another. For instance, they say they're ambassadors of 'World peace;' but they also admit to acting against the best interests of America, and other free Nations around the world. Who do think is funding the riots; promoting the socialism, causing the social division, poverty, and economic dependence? Never forget; you were born with God-given rights, to life, freedom, liberty, property, and the pursuit of happiness.

3. *Mommy Please, Can We Blow Up the Russians*

The Russian apartment bombings were a series of explosions that hit four apartment blocks in the Russian cities of Buynaksk, Moscow and Volgodonsk between 4 and 16 September 1999, killing 293 people and injuring more than 1,000, spreading a wave of horror across the country. To date, no one has taken credit for these bombings. The Russian government blamed Chechen militants, although they, along with Chechen President Aslan Maskhadov, denied any responsibility. The bombings, together with the Dagestan War, led the country into the Second Chechen War. Then Prime Minister Vladimir Putin's handling of the crisis boosted his popularity and helped him attain the Presidency within a few short months.

Again, on September 22, an explosive device similar to those used in the bombings was found and defused in an apartment block in the Russian city of Ryazan. The next day, Putin praised the vigilance of the inhabitants of Ryazan and ordered the air bombing of Grozny, marking the beginning of the Second Chechen War. Thirty-six hours later, local police arrested the perpetrators, who were discovered to in fact be three FSB agents. The Russian government declared that the incident had simply been a training exercise, and the agents were released on Moscow's orders. Parliament member Yuri Shchekochikhin filed two motions for a parliamentary investigation, but the motions were rejected by the Russian Duma in March of

2000. An independent public commission to investigate the bombings was chaired by Duma deputy Sergei Kovalev, but the commission was rendered ineffective due to the Russian government's refusal to respond to its inquiries.

The official Russian investigation of the bombings was completed in 2002 and concluded that all the bombings were organized and led by Achemez Gochiyayev, who remains at large, and ordered by Islamist warlords Ibn Al-Khattab and Abu Omar al-Saif, who have been killed. Five other suspects have been killed and six have been convicted by Russian courts on terrorism-related charges. A number of historians and observers have stated that the bombings were a 'False flag' attempt, coordinated by Russian state security services to bring Putin into the presidency. Those who hold this view point to a number of pieces of evidence, including the Ryazan incident, the fact that the Volgodonsk bombing was erroneously announced three days before it happened by Russian Duma speaker Gennadiy Seleznyov, and the fact that supposed prime suspect Achemez Gochiyayev told police that he was being set up by the FSB, and notified police about two still-unexploded bombs, which they were able to find and deactivate in time.

Also notable are the untimely deaths of various observers who called the official story into question, Kovalev Commission members Sergei Yushenkov and Yuri Shchekochikhin (both of whom were apparently assassinated in 2003), and former FSB officer Alexander Litvinenko, who blamed the FSB for the bombings in two books he wrote, was allegedly poisoned by FSB agents in London in 2006. Additionally, the Commission's lawyer and investigator, Mikhail Trepashkin, was arrested and served four years in prison for revealing state secrets.

Operation Trust was a counterintelligence operation of the State Political Directorate (GPU) of the Soviet Union. The operation, which ran from 1921 to 1926, set up a fake anti-Bolshevik resistance organization, 'Monarchist Union of Central Russia', or MUCR in order to help the OGPU identify real monarchists and anti-Bolsheviks. The cover story used for discussion was to call the organization the Moscow Municipal Credit Association. The head of the MUCR was Alexander Yakushev, a former bureaucrat of the Ministry of Communications of Imperial Russia, who after the Russian Revolution joined the Narkomat of External Trade, when the Soviets began to allow the former specialists called 'Spetsy,' to resume the positions of their expertise. This position allowed him to travel abroad and contact Russian emigrants. MUCR kept the monarchist general Alexander Kutepov from active actions, as he was convinced to wait for the development of internal anti-Bolshevik forces. Kutepov had previously believed in militant action as a solution to the Soviet occupation, and had formed the 'Combat organization,' a militant splinter from the Russian All-Military Union led by General Baron Pyotr Nikolayevich Wrangel.

Kutepov also created the Inner Line as a counter-intelligence organization to prevent Bolshevik penetrations. It caused the Cheka some problems but was not overly successful. Among the successes of Trust was the luring of Boris Savinkov and Sidney Reilly into the Soviet Union, where they were captured. Some modern researchers say that there are reasons to believe that both persons had doubts in MUCR, and they went into the Soviet Union for their own reasons, using MUCR as a pretext. The Soviets did not organize Trust from scratch. The White Army had left sleeper agents, and there were also Royalist Russians who did not leave after the Civil War. These people cooperated to the point of having a loose organizational structure. When the OGPU discovered them, they did not liquidate them, but expanded the organization for their own use. Still another episode of the operation was an "illegal" trip (in fact, monitored by OGPU) of a notable émigré, Vasily Shulgin, into the Soviet Union. After his return he published a book 'Three Capitals' with his impressions. In the book he wrote, in part, that contrary to his expectations, Russia was reviving, and the Bolsheviks would probably be removed from power.

The one Western historian who had limited access to the Trust files, John Costello, reported that they comprised thirty-seven volumes and were such a bewildering welter of double-agents, changed code names, and interlocking deception operations with 'The complexity of a symphonic score,' that Russian historians from the Intelligence Service had difficulty separating fact from fantasy. Defector Vasili Mitrokhin reported that the Trust files were not housed at the SVR offices in Yasenevo but were kept in the special archival collections (spetsfondi) of the FSB at the Lubyanka. In 1967 a Soviet adventure TV series Operation Trust was created.

The 'Zinoviev letter' was a fraudulent document published by the British Daily Mail newspaper four days before the general election in 1924. It purported to be a directive from

Grigory Zinoviev, the head of the Communist International in Moscow to the Communist Party of Great Britain, ordering it to engage in all sorts of treasonable activities. It said the resumption of diplomatic relations by a Labor government would hasten the radicalization of the British working class. This would have constituted a non-trivial interference in British politics, and as a result it was deeply offensive to British voters, turning them against the Labor Party. The letter seemed authentic at the time, but historians now agree it was a forgery. The letter aided the Conservative Party, by hastening the collapse of the Liberal Party vote that produced a Conservative landslide. A. J. P. Taylor argues that the most important impact was on the psychology of Laborites, who for years afterward blamed their defeat on foul play, thereby misunderstanding the political forces at work and postponing necessary reforms in the Labor Party.

Prime Minister Ramsay MacDonald, head of the short-lived Labor government of 1924 Grigory Zinoviev, head of the Executive Committee of the Comintern A cartoon from Punch, published after the letter was released, depicting a stereotypical Bolshevik wearing a sandwich board with the slogan 'Vote for MacDonald and me.'

Background

In 1924, the socialist Labor Party formed a government for the first time. However, it was a minority government and was liable to fall if the conservatives and liberals combined against it. In foreign policy, the government recognized the Soviet Union in February 1924, and proposed to lend it money. On 8 October 1924, the Labor government of Ramsay MacDonald suffered defeat in the House of Commons on a motion of no confidence; this forced MacDonald to go to King George V to seek a dissolution of Parliament and a new election. The immediate cause of the parliamentary defeat had been the government's decision to drop the prosecution of communist editor John Ross Campbell under the Incitement to Mutiny Act 1797, for publication of an open letter in Workers' Weekly calling on soldiers to 'Let it be known that, neither in the class war nor in a military war, will you turn your guns on your fellow workers.' A general election was scheduled for 29 October.

Letter

Near the end of the short election campaign, there appeared in the press the text of a letter purporting to have originated from Grigory Zinoviev, head of the Executive Committee of the Comintern and Secretary of the Comintern Otto Wille Kuusinen and Arthur MacManus, a British representative at a conference of the Executive Committee and addressed to the Central Committee of the Communist Party of Great Britain (CPGB). One particularly damaging section of this letter read. 'A settlement of relations between the two countries will assist in the revolutionizing of the international and British proletariat not less than a successful rising in any of the working districts of England, as the establishment of close contact between the British and Russian proletariat, the exchange of delegations and workers, etc. will make it possible for us to extend and develop the propaganda of ideas of Leninism in England and the Colonies.'

Publication

The damning document was published in the conservative British Daily Mail newspaper four days before the election. The letter came at a sensitive time in relations between Britain and the Soviet Union, owing to Conservative opposition to the parliamentary ratification of the Anglo-Soviet trade agreement of 8 August. The publication of the letter was severely embarrassing to Prime Minister MacDonald and his Labour Party. Although his party faced the likelihood of losing office, MacDonald had not given up hope in the campaign. Following the letter's publication, any chance of an upset victory was dashed, as the specter of internal revolution and a government oblivious to the peril dominated the public consciousness. MacDonald's attempts to cast doubt as to the authenticity of the letter were in vain, hampered by the document's widespread acceptance among government officials. He told his Cabinet that he "felt like a man sewn in a sack and thrown into the sea.

Election result

The Conservatives decisively won the October 1924 election, ending the country's first Labor government. After the conservatives formed a government with Stanley Baldwin as Prime Minister, a Cabinet committee investigated the letter and concluded that it was genuine. The conservative government did not undertake any further investigation, despite continuing allegations that the letter was forged. On 21 November 1924, the government cancelled the unratified trade agreement with the Soviet Union. However, MI5 decided at the same time that the letter was a forgery. In order to protect its reputation, it did not inform the government, which continued to believe it was genuine.

Denial by Zinoviev

The Comintern and the Soviet government vehemently and consistently denied the authenticity of the document. Grigory Zinoviev issued a denial on 27 October 1924 (two days before the election), which was finally published in the December 1924 issue of The Communist Review, the monthly theoretical magazine of the CPGB, well after the MacDonald government had fallen. Zinoviev declared, 'The letter of 15th September 1924, which has been attributed to me, is from the first to the last word, a forgery. Let us take the heading. The organization of which I am the president never describes itself officially as the 'Executive Committee of the Third Communist International;' the official name is 'Executive Committee of the Communist International.' Equally incorrect is the signature, 'The Chairman of the Presidium.' The forger has shown himself to be very stupid in his choice of the date. On the 15th of September 1924, I was taking a holiday in Kislovodsk, and, therefore, could not have signed any official letter'. It is not difficult to understand why some of the leaders of the Liberal-Conservative bloc had recourse to such methods as the forging of documents. Apparently they seriously thought they would be able, at the last minute before the elections, to create confusion in the ranks of those electors who sincerely sympathize with the Treaty between England and the Soviet Union. It is much more difficult to understand why the English Foreign Office, which is still under the control of the Prime Minister, MacDonald, did not refrain from making use of such a white-guardist forgery.

Impact

Christian Rakovsky dictates the Note to the British government in response to the 'Zinoviev letter.' Historians now agree that the letter had negligible impact on the Labour vote—which held up. It aided the Conservatives by inducing a collapse in the Liberal vote; this led to a Conservative landslide. Robert Rhodes James says the letter provided Labour 'With a magnificent excuse for failure and defeat. The inadequacies that had been exposed in the Government in its brief existence could be ignored.' Indeed, many Laborites for years blamed their defeat on the letter, thereby, as Taylor notes, misunderstanding the political forces at work and postponing necessary reforms in the Labor Party. The result of the election was not disastrous to Labour. The Conservatives were returned decisively, gaining 155 seats, making a total of 413 Members of Parliament. Labor lost 40 seats, retaining 151. The Liberals lost 118 seats, leaving them with only 40, and their vote count fell by over a million. The real significance of the election was that the Liberals—whom Labour had displaced as the second-largest political party in 1922—were now clearly a minor party.

A 1967 British study deemed that the Labor Party was destined for defeat in October 1924 in any event and argues that the primary effect of the purported Comintern communication was upon Anglo-Soviet relations. Under Baldwin, the British Government led the diplomatic retreat from Moscow. Soviet Russia became more isolated, and, of necessity, more isolationist. The Zinoviev letter hardened attitudes and hardened them at a time when the Soviet Union was becoming more amenable to diplomatic contact with the capitalist world. The proponents of world revolution were being superseded by more pliant subscribers to the Stalinist philosophy of 'Building Socialism in One Country.' Thus, after successfully weathering all the early contradictions in Soviet Diplomacy, Britain gave up when the going was about to become much easier. And it gave up largely because the two middle-class parties suddenly perceived that their short-term electoral advantage was best served by a violent anti-Bolshevik campaign.

RUSSIA ACCUSED OF 'FALSE FLAG' ATTACK ON OLYMPIC OPENING

Russia couldn't compete under its own flag at PyeongChang, and US officials suggest, they used a 'False flag' malware attack to disrupt them. Russia couldn't compete under its own flag at PyeongChang, and US officials suggest, they used a 'False flag' malware attack to disrupt them. The cyber-attack that disrupted some networks and servers at the opening of the Winter Olympics in PyeongChang left a number of conflicting forensic clues about its source. The attack used a blend of techniques, tools, and practices that blended the fingerprints of threat groups connected to North Korea, China, and Russia. But according to a report by Ellen Nakashima of the Washington Post, US intelligence officials have determined with some confidence that the attack was in fact a 'False flag' operation staged by individuals working on behalf of a Russian intelligence agency, an attack that went as far as to route traffic through IP addresses associated with North Korea to mask the attack's origin.

In the wake of the February 9 attack, which affected Web servers and network routers connected to the Winter Games organizing committee—including the press center's network, public Wi-Fi networks, and Web servers associated with ticket sales for the Games' events— several security firms rapidly assessed malware connected to the attack. Initial evaluation of the malware showed some commonalities in techniques with NotPetya, the 'Wiper' malware attributed to Russia by UK and US intelligence. Cisco's Talos Labs later revised its report, originally published on February 12, after discovering that the malware samples actually used credential-stealing tools to obtain logins and passwords and then wrote those credentials into the code used to spread the infection across the network. Today, Talos researchers Paul Rascagneres and Martin Lee warned against making an attribution for the attack, as forensics of the malware suggested three different potential attackers. 'The threat actor responsible for the attack has purposefully included evidence to frustrate analysts and lead researchers to false attribution flags,' the pair wrote. 'This false attribution could embolden an adversary to deny an accusation, publicly citing evidence based upon false claims by unwitting third parties.'

The researchers found that in addition to the similarities to NotPetya, the 'Olympic Destroyer' malware (as Talos dubbed it) used a file-naming convention similar to the one used in the SWIFT banking malware used by a branch of the North Korean Lazarus Group. Additionally, small fragments of code within the malware bore hallmarks of the work of three different Chinese threat groups. The use of these telltales is a classic bit of 'Anti-forensics' work by the attackers, making attribution much more difficult based just on the malware itself. But Talos did not make a determination of how the attackers got into the network in the first place. The Post report offers a possible explanation and possibly a better attribution: US intelligence officials told the Post that routers in South Korea had been compromised in advance of the Olympics. Those officials believe the routers were compromised by attackers in the employ of the GRU, Russia's largest foreign intelligence agency. Compromising routers could have allowed the attackers to re-route network traffic, allowing surveillance of the traffic or 'Man in the middle' attacks, including the injection of malware into network traffic.

Router exploitation tools have generally been the domain of state intelligence agencies. Documents leaked by Edward Snowden showed the National Security Agency used these sorts of capabilities as part of Turbine, the automated cyber-attack system component of the NSA's Tailored Access Operations toolkit. In the case of the Olympic attack, officials told the Post that members of the GRU's Main Centre for Special Technology (GTsST) were the most likely culprits. GTsST is also believed to have been responsible for NotPetya, according to the CIA. NSA's automated hacking engine offers hands-free pawning of the world Motive also plays a major part in most attribution calls, and Russia had the most obvious motive amongst the three potential attackers: payback for the International Olympic Committee's banning of many Russian athletes from the Games and its refusal to allow Russian athletes to participate as representatives of Russia. There's also Russia's previous Olympic hacking track record: attacks on the World Anti-Doping Agency (WADA) and Olympic officials at the 2016 Summer Olympic Games in Brazil have been attributed to Russian intelligence.

RUSSIA SENT A MASSIVE NAVAL ARMADA TO SYRIA AND LOOKS TO BE READYING TO FIGHT THE US

Russia has positioned a considerable naval armada in the Mediterranean near Syria after accusing the US of plotting a 'False flag' chemical-weapons attack there. International investigators have found that Syria's government, backed by Moscow, has carried out dozens of deadly chemical attacks on its civilians. But Russia is accusing US-linked forces of secretly conducting these same attacks. But Russia's massive navy buildup in Syria can't actually stop the US from striking Syria in response to the Syrian government's chemical attacks, as it has twice in the past two years. If Russia were to counterattack US Navy ships firing on Syria, the US would most likely crush it in short order. Instead, Russia will probably just keep up its propaganda effort, which includes ship deployments. Russia has positioned a considerable naval armada in the Mediterranean near Syria after accusing the US of plotting a false-flag chemical-weapons attack in rebel-held areas and it looks as if it's preparing for war with the US. A Russian Defense Ministry spokesman, Maj. Gen. Igor Konashenkov, recently said the US had built up its naval forces in the Mediterranean and accused it of 'Once again preparing major provocations in Syria using poisonous substances to severely destabilize the situation and disrupt the steady dynamics of the ongoing peace process.'

But the Pentagon on Tuesday denied any such buildup, calling Russia's claims, 'Nothing more than propaganda' and warning that the US military was not 'Unprepared to respond should the president direct such an action,' CNN's Ryan Browne reported. Business Insider reviewed monitors of Mediterranean maritime traffic and found only one US Navy destroyer reported in the area. The same naval monitors suggest Russia may have up to 13 ships in the region, with submarines on the way. International investigators have linked Syria's government to more than 100 chemical attacks since the beginning of Syria's civil war, and Russia has frequently made debunked claims about the existence or perpetrators of chemical attacks in Syria. Anna Borshchevskaya, an expert on Russian foreign policy at the Washington Institute for Near East Policy, told Business Insider that Moscow was alleging a US false flag possibly to help support a weak Syrian government in cracking down on one of the last rebel strongholds, crackdowns for which chemical attacks have become a weapon of choice.

'Using chemical weapons terrorizes civilians, so raising fear serves one purpose: It is especially demoralizing those who oppose' Syrian President Bashar Assad, Borshchevskaya told Business Insider, adding that Assad may look to chemical weapons because his conventional military has weakened over seven years of conflict. Since President Donald Trump took office, the US has twice struck Syria in response to what it called incontrovertible evidence of chemical attacks on civilians. Trump's White House has warned that any further chemical attacks attributed to the Syrian government would be met with more strikes.

This time, Russia looks as if it's up to more than simply conducting a public-relations battle with the US. Russia's navy buildup around Syria represents the biggest since Moscow kicked off its intervention in Syria with its sole aircraft carrier in 2015. But even with its massive naval presence, Moscow doesn't stand a chance of stopping any US attack in Syria, Omar Lamrani, a military analyst at the geopolitical-consulting firm Stratfor, told Business Insider. 'Physically, the Russians really can't do anything to stop that strike,' Lamrani said. 'If the US comes in and launches cruise missiles' as it has in past strikes 'The Russians have to be ideally positioned to defend against them, still won't shoot down all of them, and will risk being seen as engaging the US,' which might cause US ships to attack them.

Lamrani said that in all previous US strikes in Syria, the US has taken pains to avoid killing Russian forces and escalating a conflict with Syria to a conflict between the world's two greatest nuclear powers 'Not because the US cannot wipe out the flotilla of vessels if they want to,' he said, but because the US wouldn't risk sparking World War III with Russia over the Syrian government's gassing of its civilians. 'To be frank,' Lamrani said, 'The US has absolute dominance' in the Mediterranean, and Russia's ships wouldn't matter. If Russian ships were to engage the US, 'The US would use its overwhelming airpower in the region, and every single Russian vessel on the surface will turn into a hulk in a truly short time,' Lamrani said. So instead of an epic naval and aerial clash, expect Russia to stick to its real weapon for modern war: propaganda. The US would most likely avoid striking Syria's most important targets, as Russian forces integrated there raise the risk of escalation, and Russia would most likely then describe the limited US strike as a failure, as it has before. Russia has made dubious and false claims about its air defenses in Syria, and it could continue down that path as a way of saving face should the US once again strike in Syria as if Russia's forces inspired no fear.

QANON REVEALS EFFORT TO FRAME RUSSIA IN 'FALSE FLAG' NUCLEAR ATTACK ON US, THE FOURTH REICH CONNECTION

QAnon has repeatedly referred to the movie the Sum of All Fears in posts dating back to November 2017 that suggest the Deep State is involved in an effort to foment a nuclear 'False flag' attack on the United States. In the most recent post QAnon explicitly says that a nuclear weapons facility being secretly assembled in Syria would use uranium that could be linked to Russia. QAnon revealed that after a false flag nuclear attack on US territory, the uranium would be traced back to Russia, and the stage would be set for forcing the US military to launch a retaliation that would precipitate World War III. Before examining QAnon's posts, it's worth repeating that the consensus of many analyzing his/her posts is that QAnon represents a group of very senior military intelligence officials working with the Trump Administration. According to Dr. Jerome Corsi, it was a group of three military generals that approached Trump to run for

President in 2015, in order to help the US break free from Deep State control and prevent covert efforts to orchestrate World War III.

QAnon's posts reveal the inner thinking of senior military intelligence officials connected to the Trump White House. The posts provide the general public a unique opportunity to fathom what is really happening in the rarefied world of military intelligence and special operations, despite mainstream media efforts to distract the public through fake news reports. In the movie, The Sum of All Fears, the US and Russia come to the brink of war when a nuclear device is detonated in the city of Baltimore. The nuclear attack is blamed on Russia and the world stands on the brink of World War III until the movie's main protagonist, a CIA analyst (Ben Affleck), shows the uranium used for the device was in fact a stolen US nuclear device.

The term 'Bad actors' is a reference to rogue operators that are linked to the Deep State, who enabled this nuclear facility to be secretly assembled. Presumably, Iran's and Syria's leadership was being tricked, manipulated, or blackmailed, into building this secret nuclear facility that would be controlled by shadowy individuals linked to the Deep State. It's worth pointing out that QAnon has repeatedly said that the Deep State involves a global Satan worshiping group linked to the Rothschild family. This group uses its vast wealth and occult power to compromise politicians and elites around the world, which are subsequently controlled to do the Deep State's bidding. QAnon goes on to say that the nuclear material being used in this satellite Nuclear facility in Syria had been arranged by the Deep State: Here QAnon asserts that the Uranium One (U1) deal reached between the Obama administration and Russia back in 2009, when Hillary Clinton was Secretary of State, was designed to supply Russia with uranium that could be traced back to the US. The Deep State plan was to use the U1 uranium at the secret nuclear facility in Norther Syria, to build a nuclear device that would be detonated in the US.

In the movie the uranium came from a US source. In the secret Iranian nuclear facility in northern Syria, the U1 uranium sold to Russia by the Obama administration, provided a means of incriminating Russia. According to QAnon, this would have led to WAR – a military retaliation by the US covertly planned to escalate to World War III. QAnon's next reference is important for understanding the real target of the US, French and British military strikes into Syria on April 14, QAnon is telling us that the chemical weapons justification used by President

Trump to authorize the strike was a charade, a cover. The US military was really targeting the secret nuclear facilities ostensibly controlled by Iran but were in fact Deep State assets. This would help explain why the Russians stood down in the US coalition attack on its ally, Syria. Russia was briefed in advance, and highly likely approved the plan to take out the secret Iranian nuclear facility which it could not do itself given its alliance with Iran in the Syrian Civil War. Furthermore, in the movie, the actors involved in the 'False flag' attack is connected to a secretive neo-Nazi group. In a March 10 post, QAnon also links the effort to frame Russia in a nuclear attack on the US to a secretive Nazi group. Here QAnon is suggesting that the North Koreans had likewise been helped by a Deep State/Nazi group that had supplied it secret nuclear assistance. After Kim Jong-Un realized that the Deep State had betrayed him by attempting to frame North Korea in a failed nuclear attack on Hawaii, the North Koreans decided to end their cooperation with the Deep State.

The failed 'False flag' attack on Hawaii was therefore the real reason for North Korea's change of heart and decision to cooperate with President Trump. As discussed in a different article, the U.S. military shot down the ballistic missile intended to frame North Korea and stood down its forces rather than retaliate against the North Koreans. This is the meaning of the stage being set for 'Freedom' for North Korea. Apparently, the same thing is happening now in Syria and Iran, by the Deep State's Iranian satellite nuclear facility being destroyed in the US military strike. The picture that is emerging from QAnon's April 30, March 10 and other posts is that the repeated references to The Sum of All Fears movie is revealing a secretive effort by the Deep State to contrive a nuclear war through a 'False flag' attack on the US. QAnon's information here dovetails well with my own research into a breakaway World War II Nazi group linked to occult secret societies that established underground facilities in South America and Antarctica.

This occult led Nazi group established a Fourth Reich possessing highly advanced weapons and aerospace vehicles that is a key pillar of a global control system established by Deep State Satan worshipers. If I am interpreting QAnon's posts correctly, then it is clear that The Sum of All Fears movie was a Deep State initiative to hide the truth in plain sight, which is a well-established occult principle. QAnon is telling us that there is a global network of Deep State actors who are Satan worshipers that work closely with a secretive Nazi group that survived World War II. This Dark Alliance is intent on fomenting a catastrophic World War.

Recent events in Syria and North Korea, firmly point to Presidents Trump and Putin secretly cooperating to put an end to these evil Deep State plans.

DID ANASTASIA ESCAPE THE FIRING SQUAD THAT ANNIHILATED HER ENTIRE FAMILY?

The Romanov family ruled Russia for more than 300 years. The last Russian czar, Nicholas II, had been in power for more than 23 years. However, in 1917, Russia's belief in a ruling czar was well on its way to oblivion. The Russian economy was in shambles, in part due to the country's involvement in World War I, which began in 1914 and had already claimed more than 1 million lives. The Bolshevik revolution, led by Lenin, had created a Red Army that was marching to seize power, while loyalists to the czar, called the White Army, were trying to fend off the coup. Then a curse was put upon the royal family by Grigori Rasputin, the peasant confidant, mystic, and advisor to the czar. Many Russian people blamed Rasputin for their miseries because of his ill advice to the czar, which included getting their country involved in a bloody world conflict. Sensing danger was near, a paranoid Rasputin prophesized to Nicholas II.

'Czar of the land of Russia, if you hear the sound of the bell which will tell you that Grigori has been killed, you must know this: If it was one of your relations who have wrought my death, then no one in the family, which is to say, none of your children or relations, will remain alive for more than two years. They will be killed by the Russian people.' Both of Rasputin's premonitions came true. Two weeks after his warning, Rasputin was murdered by Prince Felix Yusupov, who was married to a niece of the czar, and therefore it was a family relation responsible for his death, as he had alluded to. And 1½ years later, the entire Romanov family was executed after the Bolshevik rebels seized power of the country, which was within the time frame that Rasputin predicted the event would occur. But were they all wiped out?

Did Anastasia Survive the Curse?

The entire royal family, along with their servants, were said to have been murdered and dumped in a mass grave. However, the grave wasn't discovered until some 60 years later. It was always assumed that 11 bodies of the Romanov family and their entourage would be in the same grave. But the remains of only 9 bodies were discovered and Anastasia's body couldn't be confirmed. Whispers that Anastasia had been whisked away with a stash of the royal family's jewels sewn into her clothes, before the Romanov family massacre occurred, ran rampant throughout Russia. Had she been in hiding all these decades, living a secret life?

Let's take a step back and look at the evolution of this mystery. Anastasia Nikolavena Romanov was born on June 18, 1901. Her birth greatly distressed her father because he already had 3 daughters (Olga, Tatiana, and Maria) and was hoping for a son to be heir to his throne. Nicholas II eventually sired a son, but the most famous of all the Romanov children was his youngest daughter, Anastasia. Anastasia was raised in a royal family but didn't always behave as prim and proper as one would assume a child bred into royalty would act. She was a spirited, mischievous child with a sweet sense of humor. Anastasia was engaging and an endlessly entertaining little girl. She would play pranks on her sisters and little brother and on her tutors. She did not enjoy the confines of the classroom; lessons at school bored her. Anastasia was rambunctious and active and preferred the outdoors, where she could frolic about, climb a tree, or play with her dog. She was prone to mischief, sometimes persuading her young brother, Alexei, to join her. But as the son of the court's physician (a man who was executed along with the Romanov family) once remarked, 'She undoubtedly held the record for punishable deeds in her family, for in naughtiness she was a true genius.'

When she grew older, Anastasia took up smoking on the sly. Anastasia had a close relationship with her father's advisor, Rasputin; she considered him a close friend and mentor and grieved mightily after his murder. Anastasia had a good heart. During World War I, a hospital was set up in an area of her palace. Anastasia and her sister Maria would regularly visit the wounded soldiers and try to cheer them up. The girls would play checkers or backgammon with the wounded to help them pass the time. Other times, they would read out loud letters the soldiers received from home, or they'd help soldiers compose letters to be sent to loved ones. But Anastasia's life would soon come crashing down with a thud heard round the world caused by insurgents opposed to the crown. The Lenin-led Bolshevik Revolution was winning the Russian civil war against the old-line forces loyal to the czar. Nicholas II was forced to abdicate. The Romanov family was put under house arrest by their Bolshevik captors. As the rebellion raged in its final stages, the family was moved to several distinct locations, they were told, in order to keep them safe and out of harm's way. Then, on July 17, 1918, the Romanov family was told they were going to be relocated once again. They were moved to a basement room along with their associates. An execution squad entered the room and massacred them all in a torrent of gunfire. The bodies were buried in a mass grave outside the city of Yekaterinburg.

Here's where it gets confusing. Because the Romanovs were of German descent, Germany had gotten indirectly involved in the conflict and demanded that the Bolsheviks ensure 'The safety of the princesses of German blood.' The Bolsheviks indicated that the 2 youngest Romanov children had survived the massacre because they somehow escaped beforehand. Was it true? Or was it said to placate the Germans? Speculation about Anastasia's survival had started to circulate throughout Russia. The exact location of the mass grave where the Romanov family was dumped was never really known, except by the rebels who buried them there. It wasn't until 1991 that the Romanov family grave site was discovered near Yekaterinburg by an amateur Soviet archeologist. It was always assumed that Anastasia was slaughtered with her family and close associates, which would have resulted in 11 bodies, but there were only the remains of 9 bodies found in the gruesome grave. Scientists identified the 2 missing members of the Romanov family as Alexei and either Maria or Anastasia. The fact that Anastasia's body could not be confirmed conclusively only fueled speculation that she did indeed disappear and not die.

Rumors of the missing bodies bolstered the escape theory, which then led to at least 5 imposters crawling out of the woodwork claiming that they were the Grand Duchess Anastasia Nikolaevna Romanov, daughter of the last czar of Russia. Other imposters appeared and claimed to be a sister of Anastasia (Maria, Olga, or Tatiana), but none captured the imagination of the Anastasia imposters. Then, in 2007, a Russian archeologist discovered 2 bodies in another grave in close proximity to the burial site where the slaughtered Romanov family was found. The Russians reported that the human remains were that of a boy who was about 10 to 13 years old and a girl who was about 18 to 23 years old. Anastasia would have been 17 years old at the time of her death. About 6 months later, in 2008, Russian forensic scientists claimed that DNA recovered from the bodies matched that of Anastasia and Alexei. But the validity of their claim is unclear. Perhaps political propaganda played a role. Russia has always strived to be a secretive society. Maybe the Russians wanted to forever put to rest the rumors that Anastasia and Alexei survived. Perhaps the Russians didn't want to have their history tainted; that is to say, maybe they didn't want the world to think that the Bolsheviks, who ultimately became the Communist Party of the Soviet Union, led by the beloved Vladimir Lenin, didn't get the job done completely. We'll never know for sure. The disappearance of Anastasia is one of those mysteries that might remain a mystery until the end of time. The media has been fascinated with the story of Anastasia. Books have been written about her. A Broadway play about her was produced, as well as a musical. And several films have also tackled her tale, with the 1997 animated feature Anastasia, released by Warner Bros, being the most popular.

5 MYTHS AND TRUTHS ABOUT RASPUTIN

The life and death of Grigory Efimovich Rasputin is shrouded in mythology, making him an almost larger than life figure in Russian history. A sexual deviant, mystic healer, political saboteur and renegade monk, the mysterious Rasputin was both reviled and revered during his lifetime and became a scapegoat for various dissident groups of the time period. Here, we take a look at five myths and truths about the legendary Siberian holy man:

Myth 1: He had mystical powers

Born to peasants in a small village in Western Siberia, the young Rasputin turned to religion early in his life. Even as a child, rumors among the local populace were that Rasputin had certain mystical gifts. Despite marrying and fathering several children, Rasputin abandoned family life in search of Orthodox Christian religious devotion and piety. Following years of wandering and religious teaching, Rasputin ended up in St. Petersburg, the seat of royal power. Through various connections, Rasputin became known to Tsar Nicholas and his wife, the Tsarina Alexandra. Michael Cohen, President Trump's Former Lawyer, Pleads Guilty to Lying to Congress. Watch Vladimir Putin and Crown Prince Mohammed bin Salman Embrace at the G20Desperate to find a cure for their ailing son's hemophilia, one night they called upon Rasputin. After his session with the young boy, the bleeding seemed to stop for some time. Some historians, such as Pierre Gilliard, have speculated that the bleeding likely stopped as a result of Rasputin's insistence on disallowing the administration of aspirin (a known blood-thinning agent), and not any 'Mystical' powers he may have had. The Tsarina was amazed, and immediately enlisted the services of Rasputin as a close adviser.

Myth 2: He was a sexual deviant and the Queen's lover

Tales of Rasputin's sexual exploits began to spread early into his time with the royal court, as his eccentric behavior, like drinking heavily and visiting brothels, was seen to clash with his religious piety. According to some historians who believe Rasputin may have been a member of, or at least influenced by the Khlyst religious sect, such sinful behavior brought him closer to God. However, though he did frequently entertain in salons, there is no evidence to suggest Rasputin was a sex-crazed maniac who had a secret affair with Russia's queen. Much like the rest of his life, his behavior in this realm has been exaggerated, and following the February Revolution of 1917 embellished by his enemies in attempts to propagandize his life.

Myth 3: He was Russia's secret ruler

Because of his constant presence in the royal court, whispers grew that Rasputin was acting as a puppet master over the royal couple. Alexandra's growing dependence on Rasputin and his apparent healing abilities with her hemophilic son only exacerbated these rumors. Occasionally, the monk did offer military advice as well as medical help, but his ideas never proved beneficial for the Russian army or Tsar Nicholas personally. In fact, after Tsar Nicholas took personal control over his armies on Aug. 23, 1915, under the advice of Rasputin and the Tsarina Alexandra, the Tsar became the target of blame for Russia's battlefield defeats. Meanwhile, with the Tsar away fighting, a vacuum of leadership was filled by the Tsarina. Here, the myth does approach the truth. Though the Tsarina was in charge, Rasputin did wield great power as her adviser. The mystic healer wasted no time in appointing his own church ministers and other public officials.

Myth 4: He was impossible to kill

Rasputin's behavior and influence came to symbolize everything negative in Russian politics and society at the time. Even prior to his final assassination, other attempts on his life were made. In June of 1914, a beggar woman stabbed the monk in the stomach, claiming he was seducing the innocent. Rasputin made a full recovery, even though he had lost a lot of blood and was close to death after the incident. Two years later, a group of nobles led by a man named Felix Yusupov plotted to get rid of the holy man for the last time. On Dec. 30, 1916, Yusupov invited Rasputin to dine at his home. After a heavy meal, complete with wine and dessert, all supposedly heavily laced with poison, the men looked on, as amazingly, Rasputin showed no symptoms that the poison was having an effect on him. The men proceeded to shoot Rasputin, who, according to legend still drew breath after a barrage of bullets and only died after he was thrown into an ice-cold river to drown. However, while Rasputin's death was in fact plotted by Yusupov and other nobles, autopsy reports show that no poison was found in Rasputin's system and that he seems to have died from a single bullet to the head.

Myth 5: He rose from the dead

Much like the tale of his murder, the aftermath of Rasputin's death has been mythologized over the years. According to legend, after Rasputin's poisoned and shot body was thrown into the ice-cold river, he was fished out by a group of passersby, who found that he was still alive when they dragged his body to the shore of the river. However, the truth is that after Rasputin's already deceased corpse was thrown into the Malaya Nevka River, it took days for the police to find the body because the water had already frozen in the sub-zero Russian winter. On March 15, 1917, Tsar Nicholas II abdicated the Russian throne as a result of the February Revolution. The following year, Bolsheviks eliminated the last vestiges of the Romanov dynasty. But myths about Rasputin endured—and, underneath those myths, there does reside some truth. Several historians have speculated that Rasputin's influence did indeed play a role in the contempt for the royal household and everything it came to represent. The tale of Rasputin indeed shows that mythology can take a life of its own and grow to become more important than the truth.

The Murder of Rasputin, 100 Years Later

`How does the killing of the so-called Mad Monk fit into the larger picture of the Russian Revolution? 'The holy man is he who takes your soul and will and makes them his.

When you choose your holy man, you surrender your will. You give it to him in utter submission, in full renunciation.'

– Feodor Dostoyevsky, the Brothers Karamazov

The murder of Rasputin, Russia's infamous 'Mad Monk,' is the fodder for a great historical tale that blends fact and legend. But the death of the controversial holy man and faith healer had a combustible effect on the tense state of affairs in pre-revolution Russia. Rasputin was killed on December 30, 1916 (December 17 in the Russian calendar in use at the time), in the basement of the Moika Palace, the Saint Petersburg residence of Prince Felix Yussupov, the richest man in Russia and the husband of the Czar's only niece, Irina. His battered body was discovered in the Neva River a few days later. In the decade prior, Rasputin had risen rapidly through Russian society, starting as an obscure Siberian peasant-turned-wandering-holy-man, and then becoming one of the most prominent figures in the Czar's inner circle. Born in 1869 in the village of Pokrovskoye, on the Tura River that flows eastward from the Ural Mountains, where Europe meets Asia in Siberia. He seemed destined for an ordinary life, despite a few conflicts in his youth with local authorities for unruly behavior. He married a local woman, Praskovya Dubrovina, became the father of three surviving children, Maria, Dmitri, and Varvara, and worked on his family's farm.

Rasputin's life changed in 1892, when he spent months at a monastery, putting him on the path to international renown. Despite his later nickname, 'The Mad Monk,' Rasputin never took Holy Orders. Men in Rasputin's position usually gave up their past lives and relationships, but Rasputin continued to see his family, his daughters later lived with him in Saint Petersburg, and he supported his wife financially. His religious fervor, combined with an appealing personal charisma, brought Rasputin to the attention of some Russian Orthodox clergymen and then senior members of the Imperial family, who then introduced him to Nicholas II and his wife, Alexandra. Nicholas wrote to one of his ministers in October 1906, 'A few days ago I received a peasant from the Tobolsk district, Grigori Rasputin, who brought me an icon of St. Simon Verkhoturie. He made a remarkably strong impression both on Her Majesty and on myself, so that instead of five minutes our conversation went on for more than an hour.'

The Imperial couple had consulted unconventional spiritual advisors in the past, but Rasputin filled this role by his ability to read their inner hopes and tell them what they wanted to hear. He encouraged Nicholas to have more confidence in his role as czar, and Alexandra found that his counsel soothed her anxieties. By the First World War, Rasputin was also providing political advice and making recommendations for ministerial appointments, much to the dismay of the Russian elite. Rasputin cemented his relationship with the czar and czarina when he supposedly helped alleviate their only son Alexei's hemophilia. Rasputin's alleged healing powers continue to be debated today. The Czar's sister, Grand Duchess Olga, wrote that she observed Rasputin healing Alexei by kneeling at the foot of his bed and praying; the calming atmosphere that he created in the palace may have assisted with the recovery. Alexandra's lady-in-waiting, Baroness Sophie Buxhoeveden, thought that Rasputin employed peasant folk medicine used in Siberian villages to treat internal bleeding in horses.

Historians continue to debate Rasputin's impact on Alexei's health. In his 2016 book, Rasputin: Faith, Power and the Twilight of the Romanovs, Douglas Smith observes, 'Rasputin's assurances calmed the anxious, fretful mother and filled her with unshakeable confidence, and she, in turn, transferred this confidence to her ailing son, literally willing him back to health.' In addition to increasing confidence in recovery, a key variable may have been Rasputin's insistence that doctors keep away from Alexei. Medical knowledge was still sparse, even though drugs like aspirin were available for treatment. Unfortunately for Alexei, aspirin, considered a cure-all remedy, had the then-unknown side effect of thinning the blood, which would have exacerbated hemophilia symptoms. French historian Hélène Carrère d'Encausse argued that when Rasputin insisted that remedies prescribed by the doctors be thrown in the fire, the discarded medicine likely would have included aspirin. Rasputin's insistence that the doctors leave him alone would have improved his condition and appeared to create a miraculous improvement in his symptoms. Rasputin presented himself in the Imperial Court as holy man, despite no formal affiliation with the Russian Orthodox Church, and spoke as a self-appointed representative of the peasantry, but his behavior away from court offered a different portrait. His drunkenness and affairs with women of all social backgrounds, from street prostitutes to society ladies, scandalized the public. Rasputin appeared to bask in his fame, showing off shirts embroidered for him by the Empress and inviting her friends and servants to his home in

Prokovskoye. (Rasputin's wife appeared untroubled by his infidelities, commenting 'He has enough for all.')

The press, unshackled thanks to rights granted to them by Nicholas II in 1905, spread lurid tales about Rasputin both within Russia and abroad. Rumors about Rasputin's influence over the Czarist regime spread throughout Europe. Petitioners, believing that Rasputin lived with the Imperial family, mailed their requests to 'Rasputin, Czar's palace, Saint Petersburg.' Soldiers on World War I's Eastern front spoke of Rasputin having an intimate affair with Alexandra, passing it off as common knowledge without evidence. As the war progressed, outlandish stories expanded to include Rasputin's supposed treason with the German enemy, including a fantastical tale that he sought to undermine the war effort by starting a cholera epidemic in Saint Petersburg with 'Poisoned apples imported from Canada.' What the public thought they knew about Rasputin had a greater impact than his actual views and activities, fueling demands that he be removed from his position of influence by any means necessary.

Until he murdered Rasputin, Felix Yussupov lived a comparatively aimless life of privilege. One of Nicholas II's daughters, also named Grand Duchess Olga, worked as a nurse during the war and criticized Yussupov's refusal to enlist, writing to her father, 'Felix is a 'downright civilian,' dressed all in brown…virtually doing nothing; an utterly unpleasant impression he makes – a man idling in such times.' Plotting Rasputin's murder gave Yussupov the opportunity to reinvent himself as a patriot and man of action, determined to protect the throne from a malign influence. For Yussupov and his co-conspirators, the removal of Rasputin could give Nicholas II one last chance of restoring the reputation and prestige of the monarchy. With Rasputin gone, the czar would be more open to the advice of his extended family, the nobility, and the Duma and less dependent on Alexandra. There was hope that he would return from military headquarters and once again govern from Saint Petersburg. The most well-known account of Rasputin's murder was the one that Yussupov wrote in his memoirs, published in 1928. Yussupov claimed to have invited Rasputin to his palace to meet his wife Irina (who was in fact away at the time) and then served him a platter of cakes and numerous glasses of wine laced with potassium cyanide. To Yussupov's astonishment, Rasputin appeared to be unaffected by the poison. A desperate Yussupov borrowed the revolver of the Grand Duke Dmitri, the czar's cousin, and shot Rasputin multiple times, but was still unable to kill him.

According to the memoir, 'This devil who was dying of poison, who had a bullet in his heart, must have been raised from the dead by the powers of evil. There was something appalling and monstrous in his diabolical refusal to die.' There was reputedly water in his lungs when his remains were discovered, indicating that he had finally died by drowning. Yussupov's account of Rasputin's murder entered popular culture. The lurid scene was dramatized in numerous films about Rasputin and the Romanovs and even made it into a 1970s disco hit by Boney M., which included the lyrics 'They put some poison into his wine…He drank it all and said, 'I feel fine'. Rasputin's actual murder was probably far less dramatic. His daughter Maria, who fled Russia after the Revolution and became a circus lion tamer billed as 'The daughter of the famous mad monk whose feats in Russia astonished the world,' wrote her own book in 1929 that condemned Yussupov's actions and questioned the veracity of his account. She wrote that her father did not like sweets and never would have eaten a platter of cakes. The autopsy reports do not mention poison or drowning but instead conclude that he was shot in the head at close range.

Yussupov transformed the murder into an epic struggle of good versus evil to sell books and bolster his own reputation. The responses from the public were mixed, reflecting Rasputin's checkered reputation. The elite, from whence Yussupov and his co-conspirators came, rejoiced, and applauded the killers when they appeared in public. The peasantry mourned Rasputin as one of their own, seeing the murder as one more example of the nobility controlling the Czar; when a peasant rose to a position of influence with the Czar, he was murdered by wealthy men. To the dismay of Yussupov and his co-conspirators, Rasputin's murder did not lead to a radical change in Nicholas and Alexandra's polities. To the emergent Bolsheviks, Rasputin symbolized the corruption at the heart of the Imperial court, and his murder was seen, rather accurately, as an attempt by the nobility to hold onto power at the continued expense of the proletariat. To them, Rasputin represented the broader problems with czarism. In the aftermath of the Russian Revolution, Provisional Government leader Alexander Kerensky went so far as to say, 'Without Rasputin there would have been no Lenin.'

Russian National Charged In Election Interference Conspiracy

Alexandria, Va. A 44-year-old Russian national was charged Friday as part of a conspiracy to disrupt the U.S. political system, including the looming midterm elections, federal authorities announced. A criminal complaint was unsealed here naming Elena Alekseevna Khusyaynova of St. Petersburg, Russia, who allegedly served as chief accountant for the disruption campaign funded by businessman Yevgeniy Viktorovich Prigozhin, a close associate of Russian President Vladimir Putin. While the case involves Russian election interference, the charges were not brought by Justice Department special counsel Robert Mueller, who is leading the ongoing inquiry into election meddling by the Kremlin. Nevertheless, Prigozhin was among the 13 Russians indicted earlier this year by Mueller's team, in connection with a wide-ranging political interference effort involving an Internet firm tied to the Kremlin. Prigozhin was not charged in Friday's action, though two of the companies he controlled, Concord Management and Consulting LLC., and Concord Catering were listed as assisting in the case involving Khusyaynova. Both of the companies were also charged, along with Prigozhin, in the earlier Mueller indictment. Khusyaynova, who is not in U.S. custody, is charged with managing the finances of a $35 million campaign, known as Project Lakhta, which targeted the United States and other countries in an influence operation that funded activists, purchased advertising, and promoted postings across social media platforms. During the first six months of this year, the campaign's operating budget totaled more than $10 million, federal authorities said Friday. In Arizona as part of a three-day mid-term campaign swing, President Donald Trump said the added charges have 'Nothing to do with my campaign.' 'All the hackers and everything you see - nothing to do with my campaign,' he said.

The alleged conspiracy, according to court documents, sought to engage in 'Information warfare against the United States,' in part by spreading distrust toward candidates for political office. Prosecutors said the project involved a number of associates who took 'Extraordinary steps to make it appear that they were ordinary American political activists.' 'This included the use of virtual private networks … They used social media platforms to create thousands of social media and email accounts that appeared to be operated by U.S. persons and used them to create and amplify divisive social and political content targeting U.S. audiences,' the government alleged. 'These accounts also were used to advocate for the election or electoral defeat of particular candidates in the 2016 and 2018 U.S. elections. Some social media accounts posted tens of thousands of messages and had tens of thousands of followers.' The Russian campaign allegedly sought to arouse political responses to a range of hot-button issues in the U.S., from immigration and gun rights to race, including National Football League players' protests during the pregame national anthem.

The operation sought to exploit the raw emotion related to the 2015 Charleston, South Carolina, church massacre; last year's mass shooting in Las Vegas; the white nationalists' rally in Charlottesville, Virginia, and various fatal police shootings of African-American men. The conspirators 'alleged activities did not exclusively adopt one ideological view; they wrote on topics from varied and sometimes opposing perspectives,' prosecutors asserted. 'Members of the conspiracy were directed, among other things, to create 'political intensity through supporting radical groups' and to 'aggravate the conflict between minorities and the rest of the population.'' Operatives allegedly developed "playbooks and strategic messaging documents" that guided others on target strategies. The guidance included the proper timing of messaging and how to frame the most controversial communications. Included in that effort, according to court documents, operatives called for assailing the records of Trump opponent Sen. John McCain, R-Ariz., who died in August; and Mueller, claiming that the continuing Russia investigation is 'Damaging to the country.' 'Special prosecutor Mueller is a puppet of the establishment,' campaign operatives advised. 'Emphasize that the work of this (special counsel) is damaging to the country and is aimed to declare the impeachment of Trump.'

Sen. Mark Warner, the ranking Democrat on the Senate Intelligence Committee, said the new charges underscore that the 'Threat is not over.' 'These attacks continue to this day,' Warner said. 'It is critical for Congress to step up and immediately act to employ much-needed guardrails on social media." Sen. Ben Sasse, R-Neb., said the added charges only highlight Putin's 'Shadow war' against the U.S. 'America needs to see what Vladimir Putin is doing,' Sasse said. Election after election, Putin and his cronies are working to undermine our public trust. 'We have to keep exposing his effort for what it is: political warfare. It's good to see DOJ push back on Putin's shadow war by publicly indicting his shadow warriors and bring his war to light.' The charges do not include allegations that Khusyaynova or the broader conspiracy had any effect on the outcome of an election. The complaint also does not allege that any American knowingly participated in the Project Lakhta operation. John Demers, chief of the Justice Department's National Security Division, characterized the alleged Russian campaign as an attack on American democracy. 'Our nation is built upon a hard-fought and unwavering commitment to democracy,' Demers said. 'Americans disagree in good faith on all manner of issues, and we will protect their right to do so. Unlawful foreign interference with these debates debases their democratic integrity, and we will make every effort to disrupt it and hold those involved accountable.' Despite American enforcement efforts, U.S. Attorney Zachary Terwilliger and FBI Director Christopher Wray said foreign interference efforts are continuing. 'The strategic goal of this alleged conspiracy… is to sow discord in the U.S. political system and to undermine faith in our democratic institutions,' Terwilliger said.

Trump, Meeting With His Counterpart or His Handler?

On June 14, 2016, the Washington Post reported that Russian hackers had broken into the Democratic National Committee's files and gained access to its research on Donald Trump. A political world already numbed by Trump's astonishing rise barely took notice. News reports quoted experts who suggested the Russians merely wanted more information about Trump to inform their foreign-policy dealings. By that point, Russia was already broadcasting its strong preference for Trump through the media. Yet when news of the hacking broke, nobody raised the faintest suspicions that Russia wished to alter the outcome of the election, let alone that Trump or anybody connected with him might have been conspiring with a foreign power. It was a third-rate cyber burglary. Nothing to see here. The unfolding of the Russia scandal has been like walking into a dark cavern. Every step reveals that the cave runs deeper than we thought, and after each one, as we wonder how far it goes, our imaginations are circumscribed by the steps we have already taken. The cavern might go just a little farther, we presume, but probably not much farther. And since trying to discern the size and shape of the scandal is an exercise in uncertainty, we focus our attention on the most likely outcome, which is that the story goes a little deeper than what we have already discovered. Say, that Donald Trump Jr., Jared Kushner, and Paul Manafort told their candidate about the meeting they held at Trump Tower with a Russian lawyer after they were promised dirt on Hillary Clinton; and that Trump and Kushner have some shady Russian investments; and that some of Trump's advisers made some promises about lifting sanctions. But what if that's wrong? What if we're still standing closer to the mouth of the cave than the end?

5 of the Most Blatantly Unethical Moves by the Trump Administration

The media has treated the notion that Russia has personally compromised the president of the United States as something close to a kook theory. A minority of analysts, mostly but not exclusively on the right, have promoted aggressively exculpatory interpretations of the known facts, in which every suspicious piece of evidence turns out to have a surprisingly innocent explanation. And it is possible, though unlikely, that every trail between Trump Tower and the Kremlin extends no farther than its point of current visibility. What is missing from our imagination is the unlikely but possible outcome on the other end: that this is all much worse than we suspect. After all, treating a small probability as if it were nonexistent is the very error much of the news media made in covering the presidential horse race. And while the body of publicly available information about the Russia scandal is already extensive, the way it has been delivered, scoop after scoop of discrete nuggets of information has been disorienting and difficult to follow. What would it look like if it were reassembled into a single narrative, one that distinguished between fact and speculation but didn't myopically focus on the most certain conclusions?

A case like this presents an easy temptation for conspiracy theorists, but we can responsibly speculate as to what lies at the end of this scandal without falling prey to their fallacies. Conspiracy theories tend to attract people far from the corridors of power, and they often hypothesize vast connections within or between governments and especially intelligence agencies. One of the oddities of the Russia scandal is that many of the most exotic and sinister theories have come from people within government and especially within the intelligence field. The first intimations that Trump might harbor a dark secret originated among America's European allies, which, being situated closer to Russia, have had more experience fending off its nefarious encroachments. In 2015, Western European intelligence agencies began picking up evidence of communications between the Russian government and people in Donald Trump's orbit.

In April 2016, one of the Baltic States shared with then–CIA director John Brennan an audio recording of Russians discussing funneling money to the Trump campaign. In the summer of 2016, Robert Hannigan, head of the U.K. intelligence agency GCHQ, flew to Washington to brief Brennan on intercepted communications between the Trump campaign and Russia. The contents of these communications have not been disclosed, but what Brennan learned obviously unsettled him profoundly. In congressional testimony on Russian election interference last year, Brennan hinted that some Americans might have betrayed their country. 'Individuals who go along a treasonous path,' he warned, 'do not even realize they're along that path until it gets to be a bit too late.' In an interview this year, he put it more bluntly, 'I think Trump is afraid of the president of Russia. The Russians may have something on him personally that they could always roll out and make his life more difficult.'

While the fact that the former CIA director has espoused this theory hardly proves it, perhaps we should give more credence to the possibility that Brennan is making these extraordinary charges of treason and blackmail at the highest levels of government because he knows something we don't. Suppose we are currently making the same mistake we made at the outset of this drama, suppose the dark crevices of the Russia scandal run not just a little deeper but a lot deeper. If that's true, we are in the midst of a scandal unprecedented in American history, a subversion of the integrity of the presidency. It would mean the Cold War that Americans had long considered won has dissolved into the bizarre spectacle of Reagan's party's abetting the hijacking of American government by a former KGB agent. It would mean that when Special Counsel Robert Mueller closes in on the president and his inner circle, possibly beginning this summer, Trump may not merely rail on Twitter but provoke a constitutional crisis. And it would mean the Russia scandal began far earlier than conventionally understood and ended later, indeed, is still happening. As Trump arranges to meet face-to-face and privately with Vladimir Putin later this month, the collusion between the two men metastasizing from a dark accusation into an open alliance, it would be dangerous not to consider the possibility that the summit is less a negotiation between two heads of state than a meeting between a Russian intelligence asset and his handler. A crazy quilt of connections.

It is often said that Donald Trump has had the same nationalistic, zero-sum worldview forever. But that isn't exactly true. Yes, his racism and mendacity have been evident since his youth, but those who have traced the evolution of his hyper nationalism all settle on one year in particular: 1987. Trump 'Came onto the political stage in 1987 with a full-page ad in the New York Times attacking the Japanese for relying on the United States to defend it militarily,' reported Edward Alden, a senior fellow at the Council on Foreign Relations. 'The president has believed for 30 years that these alliance commitments are a drain on our finite national treasure,' a White House official told the Washington Post columnist Josh Rogin. Tom Wright, another scholar who has delved into Trump's history, reached the same conclusion. '1987 is Trump's breakout year. There are only a couple of examples of him commenting on world politics before then.'

What changed that year? One possible explanation is that Trump published 'The Art of the Deal,' which sped up his transformation from an aggressive, publicity-seeking New York developer to a national symbol of capitalism. But the timing for this account does not line up perfectly, the book came out on November 1, and Trump had begun preaching loudly on trade and international politics two months earlier. The other important event from that year is that Trump visited Moscow. During the Soviet era, Russian intelligence cast a wide net to gain leverage over influential figures abroad. (The practice continues to this day.) The Russians would lure or entrap not only prominent politicians and cultural leaders, but also people whom they saw as having the potential for gaining prominence in the future. In 1986, Soviet ambassador Yuri Dubinin met Trump in New York, flattered him with praise for his building exploits, and invited him to discuss a building in Moscow. Trump visited Moscow in July 1987. He stayed at the National Hotel, in the Lenin Suite, which certainly would have been bugged. There is not much else in the public record to describe his visit, except Trump's own recollection in 'The Art of the Deal' that Soviet officials were eager for him to build a hotel there. (It never happened.)

How do you even think about the small but real chance that the President of the United States has been influenced or compromised by a hostile foreign power for decades? Trump returned from Moscow fired up with political ambition. He began the first of a long series of presidential flirtations, which included a flashy trip to New Hampshire. Two months after his Moscow visit, Trump spent almost $100,000 on a series of full-page newspaper ads that published a political manifesto. 'An open letter from Donald J. Trump on why America should stop paying to defend countries that can afford to defend themselves,' as Trump labeled it, launched angry populist charges against the allies that benefited from the umbrella of American military protection. 'Why are these nations not paying the United States for the human lives and billions of dollars we are losing to protect their interests?' Trump's letter avoided the question of whom the U.S. was protecting those countries from. The primary answer, of course, was the Soviet Union. After World War II, the U.S. had created a liberal international order and underwritten its safety by maintaining the world's strongest military. A central goal of Soviet, and later Russian, foreign policy was to split the U.S. from its allies. The safest assumption is that it's entirely coincidental that Trump launched a national campaign, with himself as spokesman, built around themes that dovetailed closely with Soviet foreign-policy goals shortly after his Moscow stay. Indeed, it seems slightly insane to contemplate the possibility that a secret relationship between Trump and Russia dates back this far. But it can't be dismissed completely. How do you even think about the small but real chance, 10 percent? 20 percent? That the President of the United States has been covertly influenced or personally compromised by a hostile foreign power for decades?

Russian intelligence gains influence in foreign countries by operating subtly and patiently. It exerts different gradations of leverage over distinct kinds of people and uses a basic tool kit of blackmail that involves the exploitation of greed, stupidity, ego, and sexual appetite. All of which are traits Trump has in abundance. Throughout his career, Trump has always felt comfortable operating at or beyond the ethical boundaries that constrain typical businesses. In the 1980s, he worked with La Cosa Nostra, which controlled the New York cement trade, and later employed Michael Cohen and Felix Sater, both of whom have links to the Russian Mafia. Trump habitually refused to pay his counterparties, and if the people he burned (or any journalists) got in his way, he bullied them with threats. Trump also reportedly circulated at parties for wealthy men featuring cocaine and underage girls. One might think this notoriety immunizes Trump from blackmail. Curiously, however, Trump's tolerance for risk has always been matched by careful control over information. He maintains a fanatical secrecy about his finances and has paid out numerous settlements to silence women. The combination of a penchant for compromising behavior, a willingness to work closely with criminals, and a desire to protect aspects of his privacy makes him the ideal blackmail target.

It is not difficult to imagine that Russia quickly had something on Trump, from either exploits during his 1987 visit or any subsequent embarrassing behavior KGB assets might have uncovered. But the other leverage Russia enjoyed over Trump for at least 15 years is indisputable — in fact, his family has admitted to it multiple times. After a series of financial reversals and his brazen abuse of bankruptcy laws, Trump found it impossible to borrow from American banks and grew heavily reliant on unconventional sources of capital. Russian cash proved his salvation. From 2003 to 2017, people from the former USSR made 86 all-cash purchases, a red flag of potential money laundering of Trump properties, totaling $109 million. In 2010, the private-wealth division of Deutsche Bank also loaned him hundreds of millions of dollars during the same period it was laundering billions in Russian money. 'Russians make up a pretty disproportionate cross-section of a lot of our assets,' said Donald Jr. in 2008. 'We don't rely on American banks. We have all the funding we need out of Russia,' boasted Eric Trump in 2014. Since Vladimir Putin, a former KGB agent, rose to power in 1999, money has become a key source of Russian political leverage. The Russian state (and hence Putin) controls the most lucrative sectors of its economy, and Russian investment is not designed solely to maximize return. Shady business transactions offer the perfect cover for covert payments, since just about the entire Russian economy is shady. Trump's adamant refusal to disclose his tax returns has many possible explanations, but none is more obvious than the prospect that he is hiding what are effectively bribes.

During the Obama administration, Russia grew more estranged from the United States as its aggressive behavior toward its neighbors triggered hostile responses from NATO. Putin grew increasingly enamored of reactionary social theories portraying traditional, conservative, Christian Europe as pitted in a civilizational struggle against both decadent liberalism and radical Islam. Also, during this time, Trump carved out a brand as a populist hero of the right by publicly questioning Obama's birthplace and legitimacy. In July 2013, Trump visited Moscow again. If the Russians did not have a back-channel relationship or compromising file on Trump 30 years ago, they highly likely obtained one then. Former FBI director James Comey recounts in his book that Trump was obsessed with reports that he had been recorded in a hotel room watching prostitutes urinate on a bed that Barack Obama had once slept in. Trump, Comey wrote, 'Argued that it could not be true because he had not stayed overnight in Moscow but had only used the hotel room to change his clothes.' The journalists Michael Isikoff and David Corn have reconstructed Trump's trip to Moscow and established that he did in fact stay overnight. This was not the only allegation Trump forcefully and implausibly denied in his early meetings with Comey. He also denied that he had offered a pornographic-film star money to come to his room, grabbed a woman sitting next to him on an airplane, and mocked a disabled reporter at a rally. The other denials have gained no credence in the media. (Indeed, the last incident was broadcast on national television.)

But Trump's dismissal of the Moscow-hotel-room allegation has been given the benefit of the doubt by most reporters, who typically describe the charge as "salacious" and "unverified," which it most certainly is, and treat that to mean "absurd," which it is not. There is growing reason to think the pee tape might indeed exist. There has never been much doubt about Russia's motive to engineer a caper like this. Russian intelligence has a documented and long-standing practice of gathering compromising intelligence on visiting dignitaries. The use of prostitutes and the bugging of hotel rooms are standard. The skepticism has instead focused on both the source of the allegations, former British-intelligence official turned private investigator Christopher Steele, and Trump himself. Steele's dossier burst into public view in January 2017, introducing so many astonishing claims into the public domain that it read like politicized fiction, a modern-day Protocols of the Elders of Zion. 'There has been no public corroboration of the salacious allegations against Mr. Trump, nor of the specific claims about coordination between his associates and the Russians,' the Times stated authoritatively last fall. In fact, some of those claims have been challenged with supporting evidence.

For instance, Mr. Trump's longtime personal lawyer, Michael D. Cohen, produced his passport to rebut the dossier's claim that he had secret meetings in Prague with a Russian official last year. The truth is that much of the reporting of the Russia scandal over the past 18 months has followed the contours of what Steele's sources told him. Steele reported that 'The Kremlin had been feeding Trump and his team valuable intelligence on his opponents, including Democratic presidential candidate Hillary Clinton, in June 2016, days after the Trump Tower meeting occurred but a year before it would be publicly confirmed. Steele obtained early news of the Kremlin's strategy to exploit divides within the Democratic Party through social media; the role of Carter Page, a member of Trump's foreign-policy team whom Russia had been trying to cultivate as a spy since at least 2013; and other now-familiar elements of the story. Even the accusations in the dossier that have purportedly been refuted have gained support from law enforcement. Mueller has reportedly obtained evidence that Cohen actually did visit Prague during the 2016 campaign, contrary to his denials. The FBI has learned that Cohen 'Was in frequent contact with foreign individuals" who "had knowledge of or played a role in 2016 election meddling,' according to BuzzFeed News.

Then there is Trump himself. While the President's character has never been exactly deemed above reproach, some doubts have lingered about whether he would really hire prostitutes to defile a bed merely because Obama had slept there and whether a tape of such a thing would truly shame him. These questions have been answered in the affirmative. Trump's payment of hush money to Stormy Daniels and other women proves that he holds his sexual privacy dear. And the obsessive hatred of Obama that grew out of Trump's humiliation at the 2011 White House Correspondents' Dinner has blossomed into a perverse and often self-destructive mania. People both inside and outside the administration report that Trump will ultimately pick whatever option he believes is the negation of Obama's legacy. 'He will ask, 'Did Obama approve this?' And if the answer is affirmative, he will say: 'We don't,'" a European diplomat told BuzzFeed News. Isikoff and Corn reported that Trump and many of the people who accompanied him on the 2013 trip to Moscow had, earlier that year, visited a club in Las Vegas that regularly performed 'Simulated sex acts of bestiality and grotesque sadomasochism,' including shows in which strippers simulated urinating. Isikoff and Corn do not establish what kind of performance was on display the night Trump visited. It may or may not have involved bodily fluids. But the notion that a display of exotic sex acts lies totally outside the range of behavior Trump would enjoy is quaint and unfounded.

It's not necessary to believe that Putin always knew he might install Trump in the Oval Office to find the following situation highly plausible: Sometime in 2015, the Russian president recognized that he had, in one of his unknown number of intelligence files, an inroad into American presidential politics. The Republican nominees from 2008 and 2012 had both run on a hawkish position against Russia (Mitt Romney had called the country America's 'No. 1 geopolitical foe'). Now, on the fringes of the GOP primaries, there was a candidate opening up what was, from Putin's standpoint, a much-needed flank against not just Obama but his former secretary of State Hillary Clinton and her aggressive position against Russia. Trump praised Putin's toughness and called for a thaw in relations between the two countries. At first, Putin likely considered him simply a way to goad his American foes. Then Trump captured the nomination and his value increased exponentially. At that point, it would have been strange if

Russia didn't help Trump. After all, Russians covertly support allied politicians abroad all the time.

Putin naturally sees intelligence work as central to foreign policy, and his foreign policy is fundamentally threatened by democratic, socially progressive Western Europe. During his tenure, Russia has formed overt or covert ties to right-wing parties in France, Germany, Austria, Hungary, Greece, and Bulgaria. France's right-wing party received an $11 million loan from Russia; its counterparts in Bulgaria and Greece were alleged (but not proved) to have taken funding under the table, too. More often, Russians intermingle financial dealings with political subterfuge in a complex web that appears superficially legitimate. The closest model for how Russia covertly operates may be the Brexit campaign in the U.K., which took place months before the 2016 American election. Driving Britain out of the European Union advanced the decades-long Russian goal of splitting Western nations apart, and Russia found willing allies on the British far right. Not only did Russia use social media to covertly promote Brexit, but Russian officials also met secretly several times with Arron Banks, the millionaire British businessman who supported the Brexit campaign, with the largest political donation in British history. Leaked documents reveal that the Russians discussed letting Banks in on a gold-mining deal that could have produced several billion dollars in easy profit. It might seem preposterous that a national vote that changed the course of British history was determined by a secret Russian operation. British conservatives long dismissed suspicions of covert Russian involvement as a 'Conspiracy Theory.' Yet the conspiracy appears to have been very real.

Another useful model can be found in Ukraine, where a Russian oligarch backed the 2010 political campaign of the pro-Russian apparatchik Viktor Yanukovych. The effort to install Yanukovych prefigured many elements of Trump's campaign. His campaign exploited ethnic divisions and portrayed his opponent, Yulia Tymoshenko, as corrupt and the election as rigged. Yanukovych called for closer ties with Russia while obscuring the depth of his own furtive Russian connections. Most significant, the consultant brought in to manage Yanukovych's campaign was the same one who managed Trump's six years later, Paul Manafort. For all the ambiguous, suspicious facts surrounding Trump's ties to Russia, Manafort's role is the most straightforward. He is an utterly amoral consultant and spent at least a decade directly advancing Russian foreign-policy interests while engaging in systemic corruption. The story begins in

2005, when Manafort proposed to work for billionaire Russian aluminum magnate Oleg Deripaska. Manafort, a Republican operative who had hired himself out to a variety of global villains, promised he would 'Influence politics, business dealings, and news coverage inside the United States, Europe, and former Soviet Republics to benefit President Vladimir Putin's government' in a memo described by the Associated Press.

Russia's oligarchs put their wealth and power at Putin's disposal, or they don't remain oligarchs for long. This requirement is not lost on Deripaska. 'I don't separate myself from the state,' Deripaska told the Financial Times in 2007. 'I have no other interests.' A 2006 U.S. diplomatic cable described him as 'Among the 2-3 oligarchs Putin turns to on a regular basis.' Working for Deripaska meant working for Putin. There's no doubt Manafort's offer was taken up. Deripaska hired Manafort for $10 million a year, and Manafort worked to advance Russian interests in Ukraine, Georgia, and Montenegro. Manafort brought on as his business partner in these endeavors Konstantin Kilimnik, a former member of Russia's foreign military-intelligence agency who according to an indictment by Mueller, still has ties to Russian intelligence. The mystery is exactly when, or whether, Manafort's service to Deripaska, which is to say, to Putin, ended. He has hidden many of his proceeds and indeed now faces charges of money laundering. In 2010, Manafort received a $10 million loan from Deripaska, which he funneled through his shell company.

Manafort had used the same shell company to buy an apartment in Trump Tower, for cash, in 2006. Spending lavishly and deep in debt, Manafort went underground in 2014. Deripaska, seeking to recover funds he believed Manafort owed him, went to court, where one of his lawyers stated, 'It appears that Paul Manafort and Rick Gates,' Manafort's longtime associate 'Have simply disappeared.' Two years later, Manafort resurfaced as Trump's campaign manager, with Gates as his deputy, and set out to use his position to regain favor with his estranged patron. In leaked emails to Kilimnik, Manafort referred to his new standing and asked, 'How do we use to get whole?' Kilimnik assured Manafort, 'We will get back to the original relationship.' That is, Manafort was asking about, and Kilimnik was confirming, the possibility of trading his position as Trump's campaign manager for debt forgiveness from Deripaska. This much was clear in March 2016. The person who managed the campaign of a pro-Russian candidate in Ukraine was now also managing the campaign of a pro-Russian candidate in the United States. And Trump's campaign certainly looked like the same play Putin had run many times before: Trump inflamed internal ethnic division, assailed the corruption of the elite, attacked Western allies while calling for cooperation with Russia, and sowed distrust in the fairness of the vote count. And in addition to deploying social-media bots and trolls, Russia apparently spent directly to help elect Trump.

The FBI is investigating Alexander Torshin, a Russian banker who built ties to Republicans and allegedly funneled campaign funds to the National Rifle Association, which spent three times as much to help Trump as it had on behalf of Romney four years earlier. Trump surrounded himself with several staffers, in addition to Manafort, with unusually close ties to Russia. His national-security adviser, Michael Flynn, had traveled to Moscow in 2015 to fête Putin at a banquet; George Papadopoulos met with Russian officials during the campaign; Russia had marked Carter Page as a possible asset. Michael Cohen and Felix Sater, the two business associates of Trump's with decades-long ties to Russian organized crime, engaged in a mix of diplomatic and commercial negotiations with Russia during the campaign. Several Trump advisers knew Russia was working to help Trump. Papadopoulos let it slip that Russia had dirt on Clinton; Roger Stone, a former longtime business partner of Manafort's who communicated regularly with Trump throughout the campaign, knew what material WikiLeaks had obtained, according to two associates.

Stone also repeatedly boasted of his back-channel contacts to Julian Assange and flaunted advance knowledge of what dirt Assange had. Between a pair of phone conversations Donald Jr. had to set up his Trump Tower meeting, he spoke with someone with a blocked phone number. (His father has a blocked phone number.) John K. Mashburn, a former campaign and current White House staffer, testified in March that he recalled receiving an email in early 2016 that Russia had negative information on Clinton. Russia's hacking appears, in short, to have been common knowledge within the campaign. Despite that, Trump repeatedly denied that Russia had any involvement with the email hacking, suggesting China or a 400-pound man might be the true culprit. Trump and his advisers also made at least 20 false public denials that they had any contact with Russian officials during the campaign.

It is possible that the current list of known campaign contacts accounts for most, or even all, of the direct cooperation. But that is hardly a safe assumption. Very little of the information we have about connections between the Trump campaign and Russia was voluntarily disclosed. The pattern of anyone implicated is to lie about everything, construct the most plausible-sounding cover story for the known facts, and when their lies are exposed, retreat to a new story. The Trump Tower meeting alone required three different cover stories over the course of two days as the truth dribbled out. (There is circumstantial evidence that Putin himself helped shape one of the stories: Trump admitted to speaking with the Russian president about adoption policy at a G20 dinner and, the next morning, dictating his son's misleading explanation that the meeting was about adoptions.) Stone testified to Congress that he had had no illicit contacts with Russians and repeated this defense fervently in public. When the Washington Post reported that he had been offered campaign dirt by a man with a heavy Russian accent, Stone insisted he had forgotten about the episode. How much more evidence of collusion is yet to come out? Maybe a lot more.

One example of the kind Trump's campaign may still be hiding came briefly to light two summers ago. In July 2016, a loose-knit community of computer scientists and cybersecurity experts discovered a strange pattern of online traffic between two computer servers. One of those servers belonged to Alfa Bank in Moscow and the other to the Trump Organization. Alfa Bank's owners had "assumed an unforeseen level of prominence and influence in the economic and political affairs of their nation," as a federal court once put it. The analysts noted that the traffic between the two servers occurred during office hours in New York and Moscow and spiked in correspondence with major campaign events, suggesting it entailed human communication rather than bots. More suspiciously, after New York Times reporter Eric Lichtblau asked Alfa Bank about it but before he brought it up with the Trump campaign, the server in Trump Tower shut down. The timing strongly implied Alfa Bank was communicating with Trump. In October, Slate's Franklin Foer broke the story of the servers and the computer scientists' analysis about what it seemed to mean, which he called 'A suggestive body of evidence that doesn't absolutely preclude alternative explanations.' When Foer's story landed, the political world treated it as insane.

Vox, which had dismissed reports about Trump's secret Russian ties as 'Poorly evidenced 'Conspiracy Theories,'' savaged the server report. The Intercept called it 'Wacky.' Lichtblau reported that the FBI was investigating the server but that it 'Ultimately concluded that there could be an innocuous explanation, like a marketing email or spam, for the computer contacts.' That story became famous primarily for its headline conclusion, 'Investigating Donald Trump, FBI Sees No Clear Link to Russia.' And yet, CNN reported in March 2017 that the FBI's investigation into the server remained open. Meanwhile, the biggest mystery of Foer's story, why did Trump and Russia need a computer server to communicate? Now has a coherent answer. It was already apparent in 2016 that the highest-profile parts of Russia's messaging machine, like RT and Sputnik, were biased toward Trump. But now we know that its social-media activity employed precise demographic and geographic targeting far more precise than a foreign country would be expected to have and notably concentrated on 'Key demographic groups in areas of the states that turned out to be pivotal,' CNN reported. That information is highly valuable.

When a Republican staffer named Aaron Nevins received stolen Democratic Party voter-profile data from Guccifer 2.0, the Russian-backed hacker, that summer, he wrote to the hacker, 'This is probably worth millions of dollars.' The Alfa Bank server connection might not have been put to the exact same kind of collaborative purpose, but Russia's social-media operation needed some fine-grained expertise to direct its targeted messages. It likely got it from somebody connected to Trump and quite possibly used the server to transmit directly with Trump Tower. If that server was transmitting data to and from Moscow, who in Trump Tower was feeding it?

Since the election, Trump and his advisers have continued to act like people who have a great deal to hide. In January 2017, Cohen solicited consulting payments from a firm controlled by a Russian oligarch and, when Flynn became national-security adviser, delivered to him a 'Peace plan' that would have consolidated the gains from Russia's invasion of Ukraine. In December 2016, Jared Kushner and Russia's ambassador discussed setting up a back-channel communications line through the Russian embassy. Erik Prince, the founder of Blackwater and brother of Trump's Education secretary, traveled to the Seychelles and met with a Putin ally in what European and Middle Eastern officials believe was another attempt to establish a back channel. Prince also appears to have lied to Congress about the meeting. Of course, at that point, if Trump had legal diplomatic business to discuss with Russia, the president-elect could have held a normal meeting. It is possible to construct an innocent explanation for all the lying and skullduggery, but it is not the most obvious explanation. More likely, collusion between the Russians and the Trump administration has continued beyond the campaign.

The largest source of suspicion and curiosity is, again, Manafort. He left the campaign in August, when some of his ties to Deripaska were exposed and the campaign was floundering. But contrary to Trump's recent efforts to depict his relationship with Manafort as distant and short-lived, the two continued to speak regularly even after the inauguration. We know this because U.S. investigators had convinced a FISA judge to wiretap Manafort's phone. Mueller has indicted Manafort on a series of white-collar crimes unrelated to the election itself. He has also convinced Rick Gates to cooperate with the investigation and plead guilty to conspiring against the United States. Trump has dangled the prospect of a presidential pardon to dissuade his former campaign manager from spilling his guts, but the pardon alone is not likely to spare Manafort a lengthy prison sentence. (Presidents can pardon only federal crimes, and Manafort is also facing prosecution for state-level crimes committed in Virginia and appears vulnerable to state charges in New York.) Manafort even allegedly took the reckless step of trying to coach a fellow witness to coordinate his story and was thrown in jail for it while he awaits trial. Why would Manafort, who has a law degree from Georgetown and years of experience around white-collar crime, behave like this?

Of all those in Trump's camp, he is the furthest thing from a true believer, and he lacks any long-standing personal ties to the president or his family, so what incentive does he have to spend most or all of his remaining years in prison rather than betray Trump? One way to make sense of his behavior is the possibility that Manafort is keeping his mouth shut because he's afraid of being killed. That speculation might sound hyperbolic, but there is plenty of evidence to support it. In February, a video appeared on YouTube showing Manafort's patron Deripaska on his yacht with a Belarusian escort named Anastasia Vashukevich. In the video, from August 2016, Deripaska could be seen speaking with a high-ranking Kremlin official. The video was such a source of embarrassment to Moscow that it fought to have it removed from YouTube. Vashukevich, who was then in a Thai jail after having been arrested there for prostitution, announced that she had heard Deripaska describe a plot to interfere in the election and that she has 16 hours' worth of audio recordings from the yacht to support her charges. In a letter to America authorities, her associate wrote, 'We risk our lives very much.'

Vashukevich's name has disappeared from the news media. In all probability, either the FBI or Russian intelligence has gotten to her. Whatever has happened to her, her testimony suggests both that Russia is still hiding secrets about its role in Trump's election and that someone who knows Deripaska well believes he would and could kill her for violating his confidence. The latter fear is hardly paranoid. Russia murders people routinely, at home and abroad. In the nine months after Trump's election, nine Russian officials were murdered or died mysteriously. At least one was suspected to have been a likely source for Steele. The attorney for the firm that hired Steele told the Senate last August, 'Somebody's already been killed as a result of the publication of this dossier.'

Here is another unresolved episode that might be weighing on Manafort's decision. In the summer of 2016, veteran Republican activist Peter W. Smith set out to obtain hacked emails from Clinton and contacted Matt Tait, a cybersecurity expert, for help in the project. Smith represented himself as working for the Trump campaign, though he had formed a Delaware-based company, as Smith wrote to Tait, 'To avoid campaign reporting.' Tait later said that he warned Smith that such a search would bring him into likely collusion with Russian hackers but that Smith 'Didn't seem to care.' At minimum, the episode is just another example of a person working for Trump who was eager to collude with Russia. It might indicate something more. In the spring of 2017, Wall Street Journal reporter Shane Harris found Smith and asked about this episode. Smith told Harris he had been acting independently of the Trump campaign. Within ten days of speaking with Harris, the 81-year-old Smith was found dead in a hotel room, with a bag over his head attached with rubber bands and two helium tanks. His suicide note claimed 'No foul play whatsoever' and attributed his decision to a 'Recent bad turn in health since January 2017' and the timing of his 'Life insurance of $5 million expiring.'

Asphyxiation is not unheard of as a method of suicide, and Smith had sold his condominium the previous year under a foreclosure threat, evidence in favor of the hypothesis that Smith did indeed kill himself for financial reasons. Harris noted, however, that when they spoke, 'I had no indication that he was ill or planning to take his own life.' Local police, who initially ruled the death a suicide, stopped taking questions shortly after his role in the campaign became widely known. Smith's family has not publicly affirmed that he committed suicide or that they had an expiring life-insurance policy, nor has the FBI made any statement about his death. Smith may well have killed himself for the reasons cited in the note. Alternatively, he might have killed himself out of fear of being questioned by the FBI, or potentially he was killed by somebody else for that same reason. If he were, or if Manafort merely suspected he was, it would explain his otherwise senseless refusal to cooperate with Mueller's investigation.

In a Republican meeting a month before Trump clinched the 2016 nomination, the recording of which later leaked, House Speaker Paul Ryan mused about how Russia 'Hacked the DNC … and, like, delivered it to who?' House Majority Leader Kevin McCarthy replied, 'There's two people I think Putin pays: Rohrabacher and Trump.' When others laughed, he added, 'Swear to God.' When the Washington Post published this exchange in May 2017, Ryan and McCarthy indignantly insisted they were joking, but if so, it was a 'Joke' akin to a workplace watercooler joke that the angry misfit downstairs might one day shoot up the office. Dana Rohrabacher, a California Republican, has been known for years in Washington as 'Putin's favorite congressman' for his idiosyncratic attention to, and support for, a wide array of pro-Russian positions. (He has worked to weaken sanctions meant to punish Russia for human-rights violations, compared pro-Russian separatists who helped Russia seize Ukrainian territory to the American Founders, and denounced the 'Hypocrisy' of U.S. opposition to the Crimean invasion.) He is widely suspected of having an ulterior motive. That Republican leaders would either gossip or joke about Rohrabacher and Trump in the same breath indicated a deep concern about the man who as none of them expected at the time would go on to win the Presidency. The leaked conversation also revealed something else about the Republican Party, Putin had, by then, made very few American allies. Among elected officials, Trump and Rohrabacher stood alone in their sympathy for Russian positions. Trump had drawn a few anomalously pro-Russian advisers into his inner circle, but by early 2017, Manafort had been disgraced and Flynn forced to resign, and Page had no chance of being confirmed for any Cabinet position.

Trump's foreign-policy advisers mostly had traditionally hawkish views on Russia, with the partial exception of Secretary of State Rex Tillerson, the former Exxon CEO who had won a

Russian Order of Friendship award for his cooperation in the oil business. (Romney had been Trump's initial choice for that position, The New Yorker reported, but Steele, in a separate dossier with a 'Senior Russian official' as its source, said that Russia used "unspecified channels" to influence the decision.) Now that he's in office, Trump's ties to Russia have attracted close scrutiny, and he has found his room to maneuver with Putin sharply constrained by his party. In early 2017, Congress passed sanctions to retaliate against Russia's election attack. Trump lobbied to weaken them, and when they passed by veto proof supermajorities, he was reportedly 'Apoplectic' and took four days to agree to sign the bill even knowing he couldn't block it. After their passage, Trump has failed to enforce the sanctions as directed. Trump also moved to return to Russia a diplomatic compound that had been taken by the Obama administration; announced that he and Putin had 'Discussed forming an impenetrable Cyber Security unit' to jointly guard against 'Election hacking;' and congratulated the Russian strongman for winning reelection, despite being handed a card before the call warning: 'Do not congratulate.'

More recently, as Trump has slipped the fetters that shackled him in his first year in office, his growing confidence and independence have been expressed in a series of notably Russophilic moves. He has defied efforts by the leaders of Germany, France, Britain, and Canada to placate him, opening a deep rift with American allies. He announced that Russia should be allowed back into the G7, from which it had been expelled after invading Ukraine and seizing Crimea. Trump later explained that Russia had been expelled because 'President Obama didn't like Putin' and also because 'President Obama lost Crimea, just so you understand. It's his fault, yeah, it's his fault.' During the conference, Trump told Western leaders that Crimea rightfully belongs to Russia because most of its people speak Russian. In private remarks, he implored French president Emmanuel Macron to leave the European Union, promising a better deal. Trump also told fellow leaders 'NATO is as bad as NAFTA, reserving what for Trump counts as the most severe kind of insult to describe America's closest military alliance.

At a rally in North Dakota last month, he echoed this language, 'Sometimes our worst enemies are our so-called friends or allies, right?' Last summer, Putin suggested to Trump that the U.S. stop having joint military exercises with South Korea. Trump's advisers, worried the concession would upset American allies, talked him out of the idea temporarily, but, without warning his aides, he offered it up in negotiations with Kim Jong-un. Again, confounding his advisers, he has decided to arrange a one-on-one summit with Putin later this month, beginning with a meeting between the two heads of state during which no advisers will be present. 'There's no stopping him,' a senior administration official complained to Susan Glasser at The New Yorker. 'He's going to do it. He wants to have a meeting with Putin, so he's going to have a meeting with Putin.' Even though the 2018 version of Trump is more independent and authentic, he still has advisers pushing for and designing the thrusts of Trumpian populism. Peter Navarro and Wilbur Ross are steering him toward a trade war; Stephen Miller, John Kelly, and Jeff Sessions have encouraged his immigration restrictionism. But who is bending the President's ear to split the Western alliance and placate Russia? If you're Putin, embarking upon a summit with the most Russophilic President since World War II, who is taking a crowbar to the alliance of your enemies, why wouldn't you help him again in 2018 and 2020?

Trump's determination to conciliate Putin can't be dismissed as casual trolling or some idle attraction to a friendly face. It has a serious cost: He is raising suspicions among the public, and among probably some hawkish Republican senators, whose support he very much needs against Mueller. His motive for these foreign-policy moves is obviously strong enough in his mind to be worth prolonging an investigation he is desperate to terminate. There is one other way in which Trump's behavior has changed in recent months. As Mueller has plunged deeper into his murky dealings with Russia, the president has increasingly abandoned the patina of innocence. Trump used to claim he would be vindicated, and his advisers insisted his periodic fits sprang from an irrational resentment that Mueller was tarnishing his election and obscuring his achievements.

Trump barely puts much effort into predicting a clean bill of health anymore. He acts like a man with a great deal to hide declining to testify, dangling pardons to keep witnesses from incriminating him, publicly chastising his attorney general for not quashing the whole investigation and endorsing Russia's preposterous claims that it had nothing to do with the election at all. 'Russia continues to say they had nothing to do with Meddling in our Election!' he tweeted last month, contradicting the conclusion of every U.S. intelligence agency. Trump's behavior toward Russia looks nothing like that of a leader of a country it attacked and exactly like that of an accessory after the fact. 'After' could be optimistic. The logic of Russia's role in helping Trump has not changed since the election. If Trump's campaign hired hackers to penetrate his opponent's communications or voting machines, they would risk arrest. But Putin can hire hackers with impunity. Mueller can indict Russians, and he has, but he can't arrest them unless they decide to leave Russia. Outsourcing Trump's hacking work to Putin made perfect sense for both men in 2016, and still does.

Ever since the fall of 2016, when Republican Senate Majority Leader Mitch McConnell privately turned down an Obama-administration proposal for a bipartisan warning to Russia not to interfere in the election, the underlying dynamic has been set: Most Republicans would rather win an election with Putin's help than lose one without it. The Democrats, brimming with rage, threaten to investigate Russian activity if they win a chamber of Congress this November. For Putin to redouble his attack by hacking into voting machines or some other method would be both strategic and in keeping with his personality. Why stop now? Meanwhile, the White House has eliminated its top cybersecurity position. That might simply reflect a Republican bias against bureaucratic expertise. But it might also be just what it looks like, the cop on the beat is being fired because his boss is in cahoots with the crooks. Shortly before Trump's inauguration, according to Israeli journalist Ronen Bergman, Israeli intelligence officials gathered at CIA headquarters, where they were told something astonishing.

Russia, the agency believed, had 'Leverages of pressure' over the incoming president. Therefore, the agency advised the Israelis to consider the possibility that Trump might pass their secrets on to Russia. The Israelis dismissed the warning as outlandish. Who could believe that the world's most powerful country was about to hand its presidency to a Russian dupe? That the United States government had, essentially, fallen? A few months later, Trump invited Russian diplomats into the Oval Office. He boasted to them that he had fired 'Nut job' James Comey. 'I faced great pressure because of Russia. That's taken off.' At the same meeting, Trump passed on to the Russians an extremely sensitive intelligence secret Israel had captured from a valuable source inside ISIS. It was the precise danger Israel had been cautioned about. Like many of the suspicious facts surrounding Trump's relations with Russia, it was possible to construct a semi-innocent defense. Maybe he just likes to brag about what he knows. Maybe he's just too doddering to remember what a secret is. And as often happens, these unwieldy explanations gained general acceptance. It seemed just too crazy to consider the alternative: It was all exactly what it appeared to be.

IS VLADIMIR PUTIN A TIME TRAVELER OR IMMORTAL VAMPIRE?

Did Vladimir Putin order the death of Alexander Litvinenko? What about Sergei Skripal? Was the Russian government involved in swaying the 2016 American presidential election? Who cares? The real question is whether Vladimir Putin is a time traveler...or an immortal vampire? According to official accounts, Putin was born in Leningrad (now St. Petersburg) in 1952. After studying law, he took a position with the KGB, where he served as a spy in East Germany. Afterward, he became an adviser to the government in St. Petersburg, eventually rising to the position of acting president after Prime Minister Boris Yeltsin resigned. In 2000, Putin was elected president of Russia and has since held onto executive power (even successfully lobbying to change Russia's constitution to allow him additional terms in office). However, according to some photos allegedly taken in 1920 and 1941, Putin has been serving the Russian people for nearly a century as some kind of ageless ubermensch. The photos appear to be military portraits of soldiers who bear a striking resemblance to the man himself, though their authenticity is still in question. If there's one thing we know about Putin, he loves posing for photos from horseback riding in the country to butterfly swimming in rivers to rifle hunting in the wilderness (all while shirtless), Putin could fill galleries with his glamour shots. Though the old photographs brought to light do look like him, they don't quite match up with Putin's own photos of his young self—he appears to have a much broader jaw and a slightly different face. Despite theories that Putin is actually Vlad Dracula or an immortal Russian hero, the best explanation for the photos is that some young Russian guys had a passing resemblance to him— or that these photos have been airbrushed and edited a little to make a good hoax.

4. *From Whom Tommy, Ze Germans*

Operation Himmler (less often known as Operation Konserve or Operation Canned Goods) was a 1939 'False Flag' project planned by Nazi Germany to create the appearance of Polish aggression against Germany, which was subsequently used by the Nazis to justify the invasion of Poland. This included staging false attacks on themselves using innocent people or concentration camp prisoners. Operation Himmler was arguably the first act of the Second World War in Europe.

Planning

For months prior to the 1939 invasion, German newspapers and politicians like Adolf Hitler had carried out a national and international propaganda campaign accusing Polish authorities of organizing or tolerating violent ethnic cleansing of ethnic Germans living in Poland. The plan, named after its originator, Heinrich Himmler, was supervised by Reinhard Heydrich and managed by Heinrich Müller. The goal of this false flag project was to create the appearance of Polish aggression against Germany, which could be used to justify the German invasion of Poland. Hitler also might have hoped to confuse Poland's allies, the United Kingdom and France, into delaying or stopping their declaration of war on Germany.

Implementation

The operations were mostly carried out on 31 August 1939. The operation - as well as the main German offensive - was originally scheduled for 26 August; the shifting diplomatic situation resulted in a delay until 31 August/1 September - but one of the German undercover units was not informed and carried out its attack on a German customs post; several Germans were killed before the incident ended. The operations were carried by agents of the SS and the SD. The German troops, dressed in Polish uniforms, would storm various border buildings, scare the locals with inaccurate shots, and carry out acts of vandalism, and retreat, leaving behind dead bodies in Polish uniforms. The bodies were in fact prisoners from concentration camps; they were dressed in Polish uniforms, killed (by a lethal injection, then shot for appearance) and left behind. They were described in plans as 'Konserve,' i.e., 'canned goods' (which also led to the more informal name of the operation, Operation Konserve). There were several separate operations, including staged attacks on:

- The strategic railway at Jablunka Pass (Jabłonków Incident), located on the border between Poland and Czechoslovakia

- The German radio station Sender Gleiwitz (Gliwice) (this was arguably the most notable of Operation Himmler operations; see Gleiwitz incident)
- The German customs station at Hochlinden (today part of Rybnik-Stodoły)
- The forest service station in Pitschen (Byczyna)
- The communications station at Neubersteich
- ("Nieborowitzer Hammer" before 12 February 1936, now Kuznia Nieborowska)
- The railroad station in Alt-Eiche (Smolniki), Rosenberg in Westpreußen district
- A woman and her companion in Katowice

THE GLEIWITZ INCIDENT

Gliwice Radio Tower today. It is the highest wooden structure in Europe. Further information: Gleiwitz incident. On the night of 31 August 1939, a small group of German operatives, dressed in Polish uniforms and led by Alfred Naujocks, seized the Gleiwitz station and broadcast a short anti-German message in Polish (sources vary on the content of the message). Several prisoners (most likely from the Dachau concentration camp) and a local Polish-Silesian activist (arrested a day before) were left dead on the scene in Polish uniforms.

Aftermath

On 1 September, in a speech in the Reichstag, Adolf Hitler cited the 21 border incidents as justification for Germany's 'Defensive' action against Poland. I can no longer find any willingness on the part of the Polish Government to conduct serious negotiations with us. These proposals for mediation have failed because in the meanwhile there, first of all, came as an answer the sudden Polish general mobilization, followed by more Polish atrocities. These were again repeated last night. Recently in one night there were as many as twenty-one frontier incidents: last night there were fourteen, of which three were quite serious. I have, therefore, resolved to speak to Poland in the same language that Poland for months past has used toward us... This night for the first time Polish regular soldiers fired on our own territory. Since 5:45 a. m. we have been returning the fire... I will continue this struggle, no matter against whom, until the safety of the Reich and its rights are secured. By mid-1939, thousands of Polish Volksdeutsche had been secretly prepared for sabotage and guerrilla warfare by the Breslau

(Wrocław) office of the Abwehr; the purpose of their activities was to provoke anti-German reprisals that could be claimed as provocations by the Germans.

Those German agents indeed cooperated with the German forces during the invasion of Poland, leading to some reprisals, which were highly exaggerated by the German Nazi propaganda. One of the most notable cases of such a scenario was reportedly carried out during Bydgoszcz Bloody Sunday. An instruction issued by the Ministry of Propaganda for the press said, must show news on the barbarism of Poles in Bromberg. The expression 'Bloody Sunday' must enter as a permanent term in the dictionary and circumnavigate the globe. For that reason, this term must be continuously underlined. The operation failed to convince international public opinion of the German claims. The Reichstag fire (German: Reichstagsbrand, was an arson attack on the Reichstag building (home of the German parliament) in Berlin on 27 February 1933, one month after Adolf Hitler was sworn in as Chancellor of Germany. Hitler's government stated that Marinus van der Lubbe, a Dutch council communist, was found near the building and attributed the fire to communist agitators in general though in 1933, a German court decided that van der Lubbe had acted alone, as he claimed. After the fire, the Reichstag Fire Decree was passed.

The Nazi Party used the fire as evidence that communists were plotting against the German government, and the event is considered pivotal in the establishment of Nazi Germany. The term Reichstag fire has come to refer to false flag actions perpetrated or facilitated by an authority to promote their own interests through popular approval of retribution or retraction of civil rights. The fire started in the Reichstag building, the assembly location of the German Parliament. A Berlin fire station received an alarm call that the building was on fire shortly after 21:00. By the time the police and firefighters arrived, the main Chamber of Deputies was engulfed in flames. The police conducted a thorough search inside the building and found van der Lubbe. He was arrested, as were four communist leaders soon after. Hitler urged President Paul von Hindenburg to pass an emergency decree to suspend civil liberties and pursue a 'Ruthless confrontation' with the Communist Party of Germany. After passing the decree, the government instituted mass arrests of communists, including all of the Communist Party parliamentary delegates.

With their bitter rival communists gone and their seats empty, the Nazi Party went from being a plurality party to the majority, thus enabling Hitler to consolidate his power. In February 1933, three men were arrested who were to play pivotal roles during the Leipzig Trial, known also as the "Reichstag Fire Trial": Bulgarians Georgi Dimitrov, Vasil Tanev and Blagoy Popov. The Bulgarians were known to the Prussian police as senior Comintern operatives, but the police had no idea how senior they were: Dimitrov was head of all Comintern operations in Western Europe. The responsibility for the Reichstag fire remains an ongoing topic of debate and research. Historians disagree as to whether van der Lubbe acted alone, as he said, to protest the condition of the German working class. The Nazis accused the Comintern of the act. Some historians endorse the theory, initially proposed by the Communist Party, that the arson was planned and ordered by the Nazis as a false flag operation. The building remained in its fire-damaged state until it was partially repaired from 1961 to 1964, then completely restored from 1995 to 1999.

Prelude

Hitler was sworn in as Chancellor and head of the coalition government on 30 January 1933. As Chancellor, Hitler asked German President Paul von Hindenburg to dissolve the Reichstag and call for a new parliamentary election. The date set for the elections was 5 March 1933. Hitler's aim was first to acquire a National Socialist majority, to secure his position and to remove the communist opposition. If prompted or desired, the President could remove the Chancellor. Hitler hoped to abolish democracy in a more or less legal fashion, by passing the Enabling Act. The Enabling Act was a special law that gave the Chancellor the power to pass laws by decree, without the involvement of the Reichstag. These special powers would remain in effect for four years, after which time they were eligible to be renewed. Under the Weimar Constitution, the President could rule by decree in times of emergency using Article 48.

The unprecedented element of the Enabling Act was that the Chancellor possessed the powers. An Enabling Act was only supposed to be passed in times of extreme emergency and had only been used once, in 1923–24 when the government used an Enabling Act to end hyperinflation (see hyperinflation in the Weimar Republic). To pass an Enabling Act, a party required a vote by a two-thirds majority in the Reichstag. In January 1933, the Nazis had only

32% of the seats. During the election campaign, the Nazis alleged that Germany was on the verge of a Communist revolution and that the only way to stop the Communists was to pass the Enabling Act. The message of the campaign was simple: increase the number of Nazi seats so that the Enabling Act could be passed. To decrease the number of opposition members of parliament who could vote against the Enabling Act, Hitler planned to ban the Kommunistische Partei Deutschlands (the Communist Party of Germany or KPD), which at the time held 17% of the seats, after the elections and before the new Reichstag convened.

Fire

Shortly after 21:00 on 27 February 1933, the Berlin Fire Department received a message that the Reichstag was on fire. Despite the best efforts of the firefighters, most of the building was gutted by the blaze. By 23:30, the fire was put out. The firefighters and police inspected the ruins and found twenty bundles of flammable material (firelighters) unburned lying about. At the time the fire was reported, Adolf Hitler was having dinner with Joseph Goebbels at Goebbels' apartment in Berlin. When Goebbels received an urgent phone call informing him of the fire, he regarded it as a 'Tall tale' at first and hung up. Only after the second call did he report the news to Hitler. Both left Goebbels' apartment and arrived by car at the Reichstag, just as the fire was being put out. They were met at the site by Hermann Göring who told Hitler, 'This is Communist outrage! One of the Communist culprits has been arrested.' Hitler called the fire a 'Sign from God' and claimed it was a Fanal (signal) meant to mark the beginning of a Communist Putsch (revolt). The next day, the Preussische Pressedienst (Prussian Press Service) reported that 'This act of incendiarism is the most monstrous act of terrorism carried out by Bolshevism in Germany.' The Vossische Zeitung newspaper warned its readers that "the government is of the opinion that the situation is such that a danger to the state and nation existed and still exists".

Political consequences

The day after the fire, at Hitler's request, President Hindenburg signed the Reichstag Fire Decree into law by using Article 48 of the Weimar Constitution. The Reichstag Fire Decree suspended most civil liberties in Germany, including habeas corpus, freedom of expression, freedom of the press, the right of free association and public assembly, the secrecy of the post and telephone. These rights were not reinstated during Nazi reign. The decree was used by the Nazis to ban publications not considered 'Friendly' to the Nazi cause. Despite the fact that Marinus van der Lubbe claimed to have acted alone in the Reichstag fire, Hitler, after having obtained his emergency powers, announced that it was the start of a Communist plot to take over Germany. Nazi newspapers blared this 'News.' This sent the Germans into a panic and isolated the Communists further among the civilians; additionally, thousands of Communists were imprisoned in the days following the fire (including leaders of the Communist Party of Germany) on the charge that the Party was preparing to stage a putsch.

Speaking to Rudolph Diels about Communists during the Reichstag fire, Hitler said 'These sub-humans do not understand how the people stand at our side. In their mouse-holes, out of which they now want to come, of course they hear nothing of the cheering of the masses.' With Communist electoral participation also suppressed (the Communists previously polled 17% of the vote), the Nazis were able to increase their share of the vote in the 5 March 1933, Reichstag elections from 33% to 44%. This gave the Nazis and their allies, the German National People's Party (who won 8% of the vote), a majority of 52% in the Reichstag. While the Nazis emerged with a majority, they fell short of their goal, which was to win 50%–55% of the vote that year. The Nazis thought that this would make it difficult to achieve their next goal, which was to pass the Enabling Act, a measure that required a two-thirds majority.

However, there were crucial factors weighing in the Nazis' favor. These were: the continued suppression of the Communist Party and the Nazis' ability to capitalize on national security concerns. Moreover, some deputies of the Social Democratic Party (the only party that would vote against the Enabling Act) were prevented from taking their seats in the Reichstag, due to arrests and intimidation by the Nazi SA. As a result, the Social Democratic Party would be under-represented in the final vote tally. The Enabling Act, which gave Hitler the right to rule by decree, passed easily on 23 March 1933. It garnered the support of the right-wing German National People's Party, the Centre Party, and several fragmented middle-class parties. This measure went into force on 27 March and, in effect, made Hitler dictator of Germany. The Kroll Opera House, sitting across the Königsplatz from the burned-out Reichstag building, functioned as the Reichstag's venue for the remaining twelve years of the Third Reich's existence.

Reichstag fire trial – 'Leipzig Trial' redirects here. For the post-World War I trials, see Leipzig War Crimes Trials. In July 1933, Marinus van der Lubbe, Ernst Torgler, Georgi Dimitrov, Blagoi Popov, and Vasil Tanev were indicted on charges of setting the Reichstag on fire. From 21 September to 23 December 1933, the Leipzig Trial took place and was presided over by judges from the German Supreme Court, the Reichsgericht. This was Germany's highest court. The presiding judge was Judge Dr. Wilhelm Bürger of the Fourth Criminal Court of the Fourth Penal Chamber of the Supreme Court. The accused were charged with arson and with attempting to overthrow the government. The window through which Marinus van der Lubbe supposedly entered the building. The Leipzig Trial was widely publicized and was broadcast on the radio. It was expected that the court would find the Communists guilty on all counts and approve the repression and terror exercised by the Nazis against all opposition forces in the country.

At the end of the trial, however, only Van der Lubbe was convicted, while his fellow defendants were found not guilty. In 1934, Van der Lubbe was beheaded in a German prison yard. In 1967, a court in West Berlin overturned the 1933 verdict, and posthumously changed Van der Lubbe's sentence to 8 years in prison. In 1980, another court overturned the verdict, but was overruled. In 1981, a West German court posthumously overturned Van der Lubbe's 1933 conviction and found him not guilty by reason of insanity. This ruling was subsequently overturned. However, in January 2008, he was pardoned under a 1998 law for the crime on the grounds that anyone convicted under Nazi Germany is officially not guilty. The law allows pardons for people convicted of crimes under the Nazis, based on the idea that the laws of Nazi Germany 'Went against the basic ideas of justice.'

The trial began at 8:45 on the morning of 21 September, with Van der Lubbe testifying. Van der Lubbe's testimony was extremely hard to follow as he spoke of losing his sight in one eye and wandering around Europe as a drifter and that he had been a member of the Dutch Communist Party, which he quit in 1931, but still considered himself a communist. Georgi Dimitrov began his testimony on the third day of the trial. He gave up his right to a court-appointed lawyer and defended himself successfully. When warned by Judge Bürger to behave himself in court, Dimitrov stated: 'Herr President, if you were a man as innocent as myself and you had passed seven months in prison, five of them in chains night and day, you will understand it if one perhaps becomes a little strained.' During the course of his defense, Dimitrov claimed that the organizers of the fire were senior members of the Nazi Party and frequently verbally clashed with Göring at the trial. The highpoint of the trial occurred on 4 November 1933, when Göring took the stand and was cross-examined by Dimitrov. The following exchange took place.

Dimitrov: Herr Prime Minister Göring stated on February 28 that, when arrested, the 'Dutch Communist Van der Lubbe had on his person his passport and a membership card of the Communist Party'. From whom was this information taken?

Göring: The police search all common criminals and report the result to me.

Dimitrov: The three officials who arrested and examined Van der Lubbe all agreed that no membership card of the interrogation of Van der Lubbe had not been concluded. In any case I do not see that anyone has any right to complain because it seems proved in this trial that Van der Lubbe had no such card on him.

Dimitrov: I would like to ask the Minister of the Interior what steps he took to make sure that Van der Lubbe's route to Hennigsdorf, his stay and his meetings with other people there were investigated by the police to assist them in tracking down Van der Lubbe's accomplices?

Göring: As I am not an official myself, but a responsible Minister it was not important that I should trouble myself with such petty, minor matters. It was my task to expose the Party, and the mentality, which was responsible for the crime.

Dimitrov: Is the Reichsminister aware of the fact that those that possess this alleged criminal mentality today control the destiny of a sixth part of the world – the Soviet Union?

Göring: I don't care what happens in Russia! I know that the Russians pay with bills, and I should prefer to know that their bills are paid! I care about the Communist Party here in Germany and about Communist crooks who come here to set the Reichstag on fire!

Dimitrov: This criminal mentality rules the Soviet Union, the greatest and best country in the world. Is Herr Prime Minister aware of that?

Göring: I shall tell you what the German people already know. They know that you are behaving in a disgraceful manner! They know that you are a Communist crook who came to Germany to set the Reichstag on fire! In my eyes you are nothing, but a scoundrel, a crook who belongs on the gallows!" Communist Party was found on him. I should like to know where the report that such a card had been found came from.

Göring: I was told by an official. Things which were reported to me on the night of the fire...could not be tested or proven. The report was made to me by a responsible official, and was accepted as a fact, and as it could not be tested immediately it was announced as a fact. When I issued the first report to the press on the morning after the fire.

In his verdict, Judge Bürger was careful to underline his belief that there had in fact been a Communist conspiracy to burn down the Reichstag, but declared, with the exception of Van der Lubbe, there was insufficient evidence to connect the accused to the fire or the alleged conspiracy. Only Van der Lubbe was found guilty and sentenced to death. The rest were acquitted and were expelled to the Soviet Union, where they received a heroic welcome. The one exception was Torgler, who was taken into "protective custody" by the police until 1935. After being released, he assumed a pseudonym and moved away from Berlin. Hitler was furious with the outcome of this trial. He decreed that henceforth treason among many other offenses would only be tried by a newly established People's Court (Volksgerichtshof). The People's Court later became associated with the number of death sentences it handed down, including those following the 1944 attempt to assassinate Hitler, which were presided over by then Judge-President Roland Freisler.

Execution of Van der Lubbe

At his trial, Van der Lubbe was found guilty and sentenced to death. He was beheaded by guillotine (the customary form of execution in Saxony at the time; it was by axe in the rest of

Germany) on 10 January 1934, three days before his 25th birthday. The Nazis alleged that Van der Lubbe was part of the Communist conspiracy to burn down the Reichstag and seize power, while the Communists alleged that Van der Lubbe was part of the Nazi conspiracy to blame the crime on them. Van der Lubbe, for his part, maintained that he acted alone to protest the condition of the German working class.

Dispute about Van der Lubbe's role in the Reichstag fire.

According to Ian Kershaw, in Hitler 1889–1936: Hubris, written in 1998, the consensus of nearly all historians at the time of writing was that Van der Lubbe did set the Reichstag on fire, and that it was generally believed that he acted alone, and that the Reichstag fire was merely a stroke of good luck for the Nazis. Although Van der Lubbe was certainly an arsonist and clearly played a role, there has been considerable popular and scientific debate over whether he acted alone; the case is still discussed. It is alleged that the idea Van der Lubbe was a 'Half-wit' or "mentally disturbed" was propaganda spread by the Dutch Communist Party, to distance themselves from an insurrectionist anti-fascist, who was once a member of the party and took action where they failed to do so. John Gunther, who covered the trial, described him as 'An obvious victim of manic-depressive psychosis,' and said that the Nazis would not have chosen 'An agent so inept and witless.' Citing a letter allegedly written by Karl Ernst before his death during the Night of Long Knives, he believed that Nazis who heard Van der Lubbe boast of planning to attack the Reichstag started a second simultaneous fire they blamed on him.

Hans Mommsen concluded that the Nazi leadership was in a state of panic on the night of the Reichstag fire, and they seemed to regard the fire as confirmation that a Communist revolution was as imminent as they said it was. British reporter Sefton Delmer witnessed the events of that night, and his account of the fire provides a number of details. Delmer reports Hitler arriving at the Reichstag and appearing uncertain how it began and concerned that a Communist coup was about to be launched. Delmer viewed Van der Lubbe as being solely responsible but that the Nazis sought to make it appear to be a 'Communist gang' who set the fire, whereas the Communists sought to make it appear that Van der Lubbe was working for the Nazis, each side constructing a plot-theory in which the other was the villain. In private, Hitler said of the chairman of the Communist Party, Ernst Torgler, and I'm convinced he was responsible for the burning of the Reichstag, but I can't prove it. In 1960, Fritz Tobias [de], a West German SPD public servant and part-time historian, published a series of articles in Der Spiegel, later turned into a book, in which he argued that Van der Lubbe acted alone. Tobias was widely attacked for his articles, which showed that Van der Lubbe was a pyromaniac, with a long history of burning down buildings or attempting to burn down buildings. Tobias established that Van der Lubbe attempted to burn down several buildings in the days prior to 27 February.

In March 1973, the Swiss historian Walter Hofer organized a conference intended to rebut the claims made by Tobias. At the conference, Hofer claimed to have found evidence that some of the detectives who investigated the fire had been Nazis. Mommsen commented on Hofer's claims by stating, 'Professor Hofer's rather helpless statement that the accomplices of Van der Lubbe 'could only have been Nazis' is tacit admission that the committee did not actually obtain any positive evidence in regard to the alleged accomplices' identity.' Mommsen also had a counter-study supporting Hofer, which was suppressed for political reasons, an act that he admits was a serious breach of ethics. In 1946, Hans Gisevius a member of anti-Hitler resistance within the German government and former member of the Gestapo, Abwehr, and foreign ministry, indicated his supposition that the Nazis were the arsonists. Gisevius posits that Karl Ernst by order of possibly Goebbels, collected a commando of SA men headed by Hans Georg 'Heini' Gewehr, who set the fire.

Among them was a criminal named Rall, who later made a (suppressed) confession before he was murdered by the Gestapo. Almost all participants were murdered in the Night of the Long Knives; Gewehr survived this purge but was later reported, inaccurately, to have died in the war. Gewehr actually lived until 1976 and was involved in much of the post-war controversy about the origins of the fire. New work by Bahar and Kugel, as of 2001, has revived the theory that the Nazis were behind the fire. It uses Gestapo archives held in Moscow and available to researchers only since 1990. They argue that the fire was almost certainly started by the Nazis, based on the wealth of circumstantial evidence provided by the archival material. They say that a commando group of at least three and at most ten SA men, led by Hans Georg Gewehr, set the fire using self-lighting incendiaries, and that Van der Lubbe was brought to the scene later. Der Spiegel published a 10-page response to the book, arguing that the thesis that Van der Lubbe acted alone remains the most likely explanation. Benjamin Carter Hett [de]'s

2014 study rejects the possibility of a single perpetrator, van der Lubbe, as he had neither time nor appropriate resources for a successful arson attack.

Göring's commentary

In The Rise and Fall of the Third Reich, William L. Shirer wrote that at Nuremberg, General Franz Halder stated in an affidavit, that Hermann Göring boasted about setting the fire: On the occasion of a lunch on the Führer's birthday in 1943, the people around the Führer turned the conversation to the Reichstag building and its artistic value. I heard with my own ears how Göring broke into the conversation and shouted, 'The only one who really knows about the Reichstag building is I, for I set fire to it.' And saying this he slapped his thigh. Under cross-examination at the Nuremberg trial in 1945/6, Göring was read Halder's affidavit and denied he had any involvement in the fire, characterizing Halder's statement as 'Utter nonsense'. Göring stated: I had no reason or motive for setting fire to the Reichstag. From the artistic point of view, I did not at all regret that the assembly chamber was burned; I hoped to build a better one. But I did regret very much that I was forced to find a new meeting place for the Reichstag and, not being able to find one, I had to give up my Kroll Opera House ... for that purpose. The opera seemed to me much more important than the Reichstag.

'Counter-trial' organized by the German Communist Party

During the summer of 1933, a mock counter-trial was organized in London by a group of lawyers, democrats, and other anti-Nazis under the aegis of German Communist émigrés. The chairman of the mock trial was Labour barrister (and Stalin apologist) D N Pritt KC, and the chief organizer was the KPD propaganda chief Willi Münzenberg. The other "judges" were Meester Piet Vermeylen of Belgium, George Branting of Sweden, Maître Vincent de Moro-Giafferi and Maître Gaston Bergery of France, Betsy Bakker-Nort of the Netherlands, Vald Hvidt of Denmark, and Arthur Garfield Hays of the United States. The mock trial began on 21 September 1933. It lasted one week and ended with the conclusion that the defendants were innocent, and the true initiators of the fire were to be found amid the leading Nazi Party elite. The counter-trial received much media attention and Sir Stafford Cripps delivered the opening speech. Göring was found guilty at the mock counter-trial. The mock trial served as a workshop, during which all possible scenarios were tested, and all speeches of the defendants were prepared. Most of the 'Judges,' such as Hays and Moro-Giafferi, complained that the atmosphere at the "Counter-trial" was more like a show trial, with Münzenberg constantly applying pressure behind the scenes on the 'Judges,' to deliver the 'Right' verdict without any regard for the truth. One of the 'Witnesses,' a supposed SA man, appeared in court wearing a mask and claimed that it was the SA that really set the fire; in fact, the 'SA man' was Albert Norden, the editor of the German Communist newspaper Rote Fahne.

Another masked witness whom Hays described as 'Not very reliable,' claimed that Van der Lubbe was a drug-addicted homosexual, who was the lover of Ernst Röhm and a Nazi dupe. When the lawyer for Ernst Torgler, asked the mock trial organizers to turn over the 'Evidence' exonerating his client, Münzenberg refused the request because he lacked any 'Evidence' to exonerate or convict anyone of the crime. The counter-trial was an enormously successful publicity stunt for the German Communists. Münzenberg followed this triumph with another by writing under his name, the best-selling The Brown Book of the Reichstag Fire and Hitler Terror, an exposé of what Münzenberg alleged to be the Nazi conspiracy to burn down the Reichstag and blame the act on the Communists. (As with all of Münzenberg's books, the real author was one of his aides; in this case, a Czechoslovak Communist named Otto Katz. The success of The Brown Book was followed by another best-seller published in 1934, again ghost-written by Katz, The Second Brown Book of the Reichstag Fire, and the Hitler Terror.

The Brown Book was divided into three parts. The first part, which traced the rise of the Nazis (or 'German Fascists' as Katz called them, in conformity with Comintern practice, which forbade the use of the term Nazi), portrayed the KPD as the only genuine anti-fascist force in Germany and featured a bitter attack on the SPD. Formed from dissidents within the SPD, the KPD led the communist uprisings in the early Weimar period which the SPD crushed. The Brown Book labelled the SPD 'Social Fascists' and accused the leadership of the SPD of secretly working with the Nazis. The second section deals with the Reichstag fire, which is described as a Nazi plot to frame the Communists, who are represented as the most dedicated opponents of Nazism. The third section deals with the supposed puppet masters behind the Nazis.

NAZIS STAGE FAKE ATTACK AT THE START OF WWII

On Aug. 31, 1939 — 75 years ago this week — Nazi agents staged a fake attack on the German radio transmission tower at Gleiwitz, on the German-Polish border. Adolf Hitler used this 'Attack' as a pretext for the invasion of Poland the next day. By the summer of 1939, relations between Germany and Poland were quickly deteriorating. Hitler had insisted that Poland return the Polish Corridor to Germany, a strip of land that gave Poland access to the sea and the free city of Danzig but cut off Germany proper from its East Prussian territory. The Polish Corridor had been granted to the new state of Poland in the 1919 Treaty of Versailles, a document that Hitler and most Germans had denounced. For the previous few years, Hitler had been bloodlessly acquiring more and more territory in Europe in violation of the treaty. In 1936, Hitler sent his army into the Rhineland, which, though German, had been demilitarized by the treaty. England and France did nothing to stop him. In March 1938, Hitler's army moved into Austria. A few days later, Germany annexed the central European nation, again in violation of the treaty. In September 1938, Hitler demanded the return of the Sudetenland from Czechoslovakia, territory Germany had lost after World War I. Allied with France and friendly toward Britain, Czechoslovakia was the only stable democracy in central Europe. Prague called upon Paris to help defend its borders. Fearing Germany's strength and a repeat of the 1914-1918 war, Britain and France wanted a settlement and signed the Munich Pact with Germany. With its allies refusing to fight, Czechoslovakia gave up the Sudetenland to Hitler.

Hitler had stated throughout this crisis, as he had in his earlier bloodless invasions that he was only working in the interests of protecting ethnic Germans throughout central Europe. Indeed, in Czechoslovakia there were several violent attacks on ethnic Germans by the Czech population, though these instances were relatively few. To strengthen his hand, Hitler had sent special units into the Sudetenland to fake anti-German attacks and increase anti-German propaganda. These false-flag operations gave Hitler the leverage he needed to issue ultimatums during the crisis, which led to his diplomatic victory. In March 1939, Hitler made a mistake by invading and annexing the rump of Czechoslovakia. Not only was this move in violation of the September 1938 agreement at Munich but it also showed Hitler for what he really was a madman with vast territorial ambitions in Europe who could not be trusted. There were virtually no ethnic Germans in the rump of Czechoslovakia. Soon after, when Hitler announced that he wanted the Polish Corridor returned, Britain and France took a firm line and offered Poland a guarantee of its borders.

That summer Hitler repeatedly accused Poles of attacking ethnic Germans in Poland, and again he sent agitators to fake incidents. Finally, Hitler decided to attack Poland. To give Germany its excuse, Hitler wanted a dramatic provocation that he could use to justify his actions. Hitler's most loyal and fanatical followers belonged to the Schutzstaffel, the Protection Squad or SS. Headed by Heinrich Himmler, the SS controlled the machinery of the German police and concentration-camp system, as well having a stake in the Sicherheitsdienst, the Security Service, or the SD, which essentially functioned as Nazi Party intelligence. The head of the SD was Reinhard Heydrich. A man of such ice-cold nerves that Hitler once called him 'The Man with the Iron Heart,' Heydrich was one of those rare individuals who could accomplish anything he set his mind to. A concert-level violinist, an Olympic-level fencer and an ace fighter pilot, Heydrich had created in the SD an efficient organization that could take care of the dirty tricks that Hitler so often employed.

Heydrich's tool within the SD for these missions was something known as the Einsatzgruppen, Special Action Squads, which later would prove to be an integral part of the Holocaust. One of the men Heydrich used for such operations was Alfred Naujocks. Not yet 30 years old, Naujocks had been an early street brawler for the Nazis in the days before the party came to power. In the book 'Who's Who in Nazi Germany,' historian Robert Wistrich wrote, 'A well-known amateur boxer, (Naujocks) was frequently involved in brawls with communists. He joined the SS in 1931 and three years later enrolled in the SD, becoming one of Heydrich's most trusted agents. In 1939 he was made head of the sub-section of Section III of SD Ausland, (foreign section), and put in charge of such special duties as fabricating false papers, passports, identity cards and forged notes for the SD agents operating abroad.' Heydrich had devised a scheme to give Hitler his justification for an attack upon Poland. Several border incidents would be created, under what was called 'Operation Himmler,' after Heydrich's boss. An Einsatzgruppe unit under Naujocks would attack the Gleiwitz radio tower along the border then broadcast Polish propaganda into the Reich.

This attack would be the centerpiece of 'Operation Himmler.' Hitler had ordered his military to invade Poland on Aug. 26. Heydrich and Naujocks had only a few days to get things prepared for the attack on Gleiwitz on Aug. 25. Naujocks and his team traveled to the town and checked into a hotel, claiming to be engineers looking for suitable materials to mine in the area. Under various pressures to avert war and sensing the Poles and their Western allies might back down, Hitler postponed the invasion until Sept. 1. Naujocks and his men spent nearly two weeks in Gleiwitz waiting for the order to proceed. It wasn't nearly enough, however, to broadcast anti-German propaganda. If the incident was to have a look of authenticity to it, it would have to appear as though a small skirmish had indeed taken place near the radio tower. To that end, Heinrich Müller, the head of the Gestapo, had several concentration-camp inmates shot or drugged and their bodies transported to the area. With Polish army uniforms and paybooks supplied by Adm. Wilhelm Canaris, the head of German military intelligence, the former camp prisoners now appeared to be Polish casualties of the battle. This aspect of plan was cynically named 'Operation Canned Goods.' Finally, on Aug. 31, the order arrived at Oberschlesischer Hotel in Gleiwitz, and Naujocks' team went into action and rendezvoused en route to the tower with Müller, who handed over the bodies. In the book "SS Intelligence," historian Edmund L. Blandford wrote:

'Naujocks then took his squad into the radio station, finding the two men on duty ready and compliant. The Polish speaker then yelled a short tirade into the microphone calling for war to begin between Poland and Germany. The squad then ran outside, firing off their pistols as they went. Years later, Naujocks would try to cash in on his claim as the 'man who started the war.' '

The attack, such as it was, was a success. Hitler had his propaganda weapon with which to start the war. In his speech to the Reichstag the following day in which he formally declared war on Poland, Hitler cited the various border incidents and Gleiwitz in particular as 'Frontier violations of a nature no longer tolerable for a great power.' American journalist William L. Shirer, reporting from Berlin when the war broke out, noted in his book 'The Rise and Fall of the Third Reich' that the New York Times and other American newspapers reported on the Gleiwitz incident as one of the events that touched off the war. Additionally, Shirer suggests that many of the SS men who were involved in the operation were 'Put out of the way.'

Whether they were killed or merely assigned to dangerous combat duty in Poland, Shirer doesn't say. In any event, most of the hard facts of what happened at Gleiwitz come from Naujocks himself, who defected to the Americans in November 1944 after falling out of favor with his Nazi superiors. Little is known for certain about the SS men under his command who participated in the attack, though given the almost astronomical casualty rates suffered by Waffen-SS units in the war, it is entirely possible they were indeed all killed. The attack on Gleiwitz was another criminal act and deception in a long line of lies and falsehoods perpetrated by Hitler and his regime. It was certainly not the last. With the invasion of Poland, the Einsatzgruppen sought out Polish professionals, politicians, clergy, and others who the Nazis believed would make trouble for them. Approximately 60,000 of Poland's intelligentsia were summarily shot by these SD thugs at the beginning of the conflict, and as it progressed millions more Poles died in the war or in the death camps.

GERMAN SOLDIER POSING AS A SYRIAN REFUGEE ARRESTED FOR PLANNING 'FALSE FLAG' TERROR ATTACK INVESTIGATORS SAY LIEUTENANT STASHED GUN AT VIENNA AIRPORT TO BE USED IN 'ACT OF STATE-THREATENING VIOLENCE'

A German soldier found posing as a Syrian refugee has been arrested for allegedly planning a 'False flag' shooting attack that would be blamed on asylum seekers. The unidentified soldier was detained when he went to retrieve a loaded pistol he had hidden in a bathroom at Vienna International Airport. The public prosecutor's office in Frankfurt said the 28-year-old is suspected of planning a serious 'State-threatening act of violence', fraud and violating firearms laws. More than 90 German police officers have worked alongside Austrian and French security forces to search 16 locations across three countries on Wednesday, when a suspected accomplice was arrested in Bavaria. Investigations have revealed that the Bundeswehr lieutenant was stationed at Illkirch-Graffenstaden in France before registering as a refugee back in Germany. He gave false information to authorities in Giessen, Hesse, on 30 December 2015 – as Germany was overwhelmed by the arrival of almost a million asylum seekers. Posing as a Syrian refugee but reportedly speaking in French, rather than Arabic, the man submitted an asylum application at Zirndorf in Bavaria in January last year.

'As a result, he was given shelter in a refugee home and has received monthly financial benefits under this false identity,' the Frankfurt prosecutor's office said. 'These findings, as well as other evidence, point towards a xenophobic motive for the soldier's suspected plan to commit an attack using a weapon deposited at Vienna airport.'

If his plan had succeeded, his fingerprints would have registered on the refugee records system and led investigators to his false identity as a Syrian asylum seeker, turning fresh scrutiny on migrants in Germany. Isis has previously used a similar ploy, giving its militants fake Syrian passports that were found at the scene of the Paris attacks. The man's suspected accomplice, a 24-year-old student, was arrested in Hammelburg for alleged involvement in the plot. Police have searched the homes of the two suspects as well as their friends and workplaces, with detectives seizing "extensive material" including mobile phones, laptops, and documents. Prosecutors said the soldier had no permission for the 7.65mm pistol stashed in Vienna, while illegal weapons were also found at his accomplice's house. Both men remain in custody in Frankfurt as the probe continues. The soldier was arrested days after prosecutors revealed that the man who orchestrated the Dortmund bus bombings had attempted to frame Isis to make money on shares.

Police chief says Germany 'On high alert' after attack Sergej W, a dual German-Russian national, detonated three bombs targeting a bus carrying the Borussia Dortmund football team, seriously injuring one player on 11 April. He left misspelled letters at the scene claiming the attack was retaliation for German military intervention against Isis, but investigations found he was not an Islamist but a trader planning to profit from short-selling shares. A series of Isis-inspired terror attacks and plots in Germany have raised tensions leading into September's federal elections, where Angela Merkel is battling to win a fourth term as Chancellor. Right-wing groups have blamed her decision to open borders to refugees in 2015, while extremists have launched hundreds of attacks on asylum seekers' accommodation. At least two neo-Nazi terror plots have been uncovered, while security services have cracked down on the anti-government Reichsbürger movement after one of its members killed a police officer. Division over asylum, immigration and security has driven clashes at protests and political rallies, driving a record year for politically-motivated crime in Germany.

A second soldier has been arrested for allegedly planning a 'False Flag' terror attack to be blamed on refugees in Germany amid fears of a wider neo-Nazi network within the army. The plot was exposed with the arrest of a German lieutenant, Franco A, who was found to be posing as a Syrian refugee in order to carry out a shooting attack targeting left-wing politicians. One of his friends at Illkirch-Graffenstaden barracks in France has now been detained for allegedly covering for the soldier's absences as he periodically returned to Bavaria to continue the ruse. Maximilian T, a 27-year-old German national, was also a member of Jägerbataillon 291 and was arrested on Tuesday after being questioned by military intelligence officers. He had joined his friend on a trip to Vienna in January supposedly for an officers' ball where Franco A. stashed an unregistered gun to be used in the attack at the city's main airport. Maximilian T was also part of an online messaging group where he, Franco A and other members exchanged far-right posts, photos and audio files, Der Spiegel reported. German defense minister Ursula von der Leyen is to visit Illkirch barracks in France during investigation to an alleged far-right terror cell in the German army (EPA). He is assumed to be 'Number three' in the plot, following Franco A and Mathias F, a friend from his hometown who was also arrested in April.

'They were willing, or at least claimed to be, to kill for their cause,' an investigator said. As well as the loaded 7.65mm pistol stashed in a toilet at Vienna International Airport, around 1,000 rounds of ammunition were found at Mathias F's home in Offenbach – mostly stolen from the German army. The federal prosecutor's office said the three suspects were suspected of planning to attack senior politicians and public figures "who are committed to an immigration and refugee policy which has failed in the view of the defendants." The names of the former German President, Joachim Gauck, and left-wing justice minister Heiko Maas (SPD) were on a list of potential targets, said spokesperson Frauke Köhler. She told a press conference Franco A planned to frame Islamist militants for the attack, which would have been linked to his fake identity as a Syrian refugee.

'The three suspects wanted to direct suspicion at asylum seekers living in Germany after the attack,' she added. 'Especially with regard to the ongoing public discussion over immigration and refugee policy, an alleged terrorist attack by a registered asylum seeker would have attracted particular attention and contributed to the sense of threat.'

Numerous asylum seekers have been arrested on terror charges in Germany, including former members of Isis, al-Qaeda, and the Taliban. Franco A had created a fake persona under the name David Benjamin, telling immigration officials he was a Damascus fruit seller from a Christian family with French roots. No doubts appear to have been raised over the credibility of the 28-year-old's background, despite him speaking mainly French with a smattering of Arabic from a language course. The lieutenant registered in Giessen, Hesse, on 30 December 2015, as Germany was overwhelmed by the arrival of almost a million asylum seekers - then submitted an asylum application at Zirndorf in Bavaria in January last year. Despite having to return to Germany to collect monthly welfare payments, Franco A continued his army post in France until the day of his arrest because his friend covered for him, prosecutors said. 'Maximilian T is strongly suspected of planning a serious act of violence against the state out of a right-wing extremist conviction,' a spokesperson added. 'The resulting absences were at least partly covered up by Maximilian T, who had excused Franco A to his superiors.'

Officials said he obtained a Second World War era Unique Model 17 pistol for the attack, which he hid in a disabled toilet in Vienna International Airport while passing through in January. Franco A's double life was only discovered when he was arrested after returning to retrieve the gun in February. A fingerprint check revealed his fake identity as a Syrian refugee, but when 'David Benjamin' failed to answer a court summons in Austria, a wider investigation was triggered, and the plot unraveled. The soldier had not raised alarm over extremism in the army, despite writing a master's thesis on 'Political change and subversion strategy 'at a French university in 2014 that was found to contain far-right thinking.

GERMAN-RUSSIAN MAN 'CARRIED OUT DORTMUND ATTACK TO AFFECT SHARE PRICE'

An assault rifle case carved with a swastika was found in his barracks room, where the letters HH [Heil Hitler] were inscribed on the wall and a Nazi-era pamphlet depicting a Wehrmacht soldier was discovered. The unprecedented plot has shocked Germany, prompting investigations within the army and interior ministry over how Franco A was able to lead a double life for more than a year. The defense minister, Ursula von der Leyen, has come under fire for her handling of the case after attacking 'Weak leadership' following the discovery of 275 suspected right-wing extremists within Germany's military. She has since apologized for her blanket criticism, following scandals including sexual abuse and hazing at another military base. Angela Merkel defended the minister, who has been widely tipped as her successor as Germany heads of federal elections in September. 'It is right that the defense minister did not trivialize what has happened,' the Chancellor said. 'She calls it by its name [right-wing extremism] and is saying that we have to look at whether something like this is happening more often.'

HITLER DEATH CONSPIRACY THEORIES: THE GOOD, THE BAD, AND THE CRAZY

What really happened to the Führer? These Hitler death conspiracy theories, from the plausible to the outlandish, claim to have the answers.

On May 1, 1945, With World War I is About to End, The Soviet Army Was Fighting Its Way into the Central District of Berlin. Meanwhile, American, and British forces were beginning the mammoth task of processing the thousands of German prisoners taken in the fighting in Nuremberg, where an entire SS division had made its last stand, and of cataloging the vast treasures they had captured there. On that day, the Grand Admiral of the German Navy, Karl Dönitz, delivered a radio broadcast to the broken Reich. In it, he announced that Adolf Hitler was dead and that he had died gallantly leading men in battle against Soviet forces. Dönitz claimed that Hitler had named him as his successor in his last testament and that everything was, basically, fine. Business would continue as normal, with the German government 'Temporarily' headquartered in Flensburg. Ten days later, Dönitz was in Allied custody, as were many other leading Nazis. In his effects was found a single telegram from Nazi propaganda minister Joseph Goebbels in Berlin, also now dead, announcing Hitler's death and omitting the bit about the Führer having fallen in combat, which seems to have been Dönitz's own invention, since he had no other evidence of what had actually happened to Hitler in Berlin. Within days, the war was over, and the Third Reich was no more, but the fact that Hitler's body hadn't turned up rankled the Western Allies. Hitler wasn't supposed to mysteriously vanish into history — he was supposed to either stand trial or drop dead and leave a corpse to be verified. Thus, was born a myth of Hitler's survival and a host of Hitler death conspiracy theories, one that still persists and was even reignited by the 2015 release of secret FBI documents containing reports that Hitler had escaped Germany in a U-boat and fled to Argentina. The myth, it seems, lives on.

'The Obstinate Love of Fiction'

Konstantin ZAVRAZHIN/Gamma-Rapho via Getty Images The skull once claimed to be that of Adolf Hitler on display in Moscow on April 26, 2000. Part of the problem with investigating the Führer's demise and easily debunking some of the Hitler death conspiracy theories is that the only people who were in a position to know what happened with any certainty were the Soviets, and they weren't eager to share information or be honest with the Allies who became their Cold War enemies. Between the end of the war in the spring of 1945 and the fall of the USSR in 1991, Soviet authorities put out so many contradictory and self-refuting statements about Hitler's death that some of it must have been conscious disinformation. After initially claiming that Hitler was dead and that they had the remains to prove it, the Soviets then put out word that they didn't have the body and then accused the British of smuggling Hitler and Braun out of Germany. After that, they claimed to have a fragment of Hitler's skull with a conveniently positioned bullet hole in it. Then, decades later, forensic examination revealed that the fragment was that of a woman. Despite such misinformation, Allied investigators tried to get to the bottom of things by interviewing anybody in Germany who might have known what happened inside Hitler's bunker in the last days of the war. One of the people deposed by the British was an SS general named Walter Schellenberg, who was apprehended after the war in Sweden. According to him, Himmler had poisoned Hitler on his advice.

The advantages to telling this story of betraying Hitler were obvious for a former Gestapo general looking to avoid punishment, and since he hadn't actually been present for many of the meetings he claimed to have led, the Allies dismissed his story. Another informant was a woman who claimed she had been at the center of a German intelligence ring from inside the concentration camp at Ravensbrück. This woman, whose name was Carmen Mory, swore she had firsthand knowledge that Hitler, Eva Braun, and others were living in Bavaria under assumed names. She also threatened to kill herself if the British didn't make concessions to her regarding her treatment and let her go. Mory, as it happens, was facing trial for war crimes at the time for having actually been a Gestapo spy inside Ravensbrück, where her information got 60 other women killed. She committed suicide in 1947 after the British sentenced her to hang. Yet another unreliable witness was Luftwaffe pilot Peter Baumgart, who claimed he had personally flown Hitler to Denmark on April 30, 1945. He eventually checked himself into an insane asylum and stopped claiming to have aided Hitler's escape. The British report on these informants, written by historian Hugh Trevor-Roper, concluded that none of the "firsthand accounts" were credible, and neither was that of Dönitz, writing that: 'Reason is powerless against the obstinate love of fiction.'

Escaping Nazis

While the British were leaving esteemed historians (and deep-cover MI-6 spooks, like Trevor-Roper) to despair of ever knowing the truth, the Americans were, ironically, lending credence to Hitler death conspiracy theories stating that he and other prominent Nazis had escaped. The Americans did so by actually helping prominent Nazis escape themselves. Operation Paperclip was a project of the Office of Strategic Services (the U.S. intelligence agency at the time) to identify and extract German scientists and counterintelligence officers in order to keep them out of Soviet hands. These Germans, like Wernher von Braun, went on to lead the American space program and use their experience as Nazi torturers to uncover and frustrate communist subversion of the new West German state. The Soviets were surely aware of all this, which may have motivated some of their refusal to clear up the details surrounding Hitler's death for their Cold War enemies. The subject of Nazis escaping justice came up from time to time in the decades after the war. Some Nazi diehards, such as SS officer Otto Skorzeny, were known to have set up a 'Rat line' to smuggle their former comrades out of occupied Europe and (usually) into South America, where friendly governments would shelter them from prosecution. With such prominent individuals as SS leader Adolf Eichmann and infamous concentration camp doctor Josef Mengele making it out of Germany this way, it didn't seem impossible that their leader had also made it out, thus fueling plenty of Hitler death conspiracy theories.

Sighting Reports

During his life, Adolf Hitler made public appearances and speeches to tens of millions of people. Between 1933 and 1945, his face was printed on hundreds of millions of postage stamps, picture postcards, newspapers, and magazines, as well as other mass-circulation items. His face, in other words, was well-known. If the Hitler death conspiracy theories were true and he had escaped, it wouldn't be easy for him to hide, and it would be easy for passerby to recognize him. So, when informants started cropping up all over the world, such as one Argentine expat in Los Angeles in September 1945, who claimed he had personally seen Hitler and his entourage getting settled into their new homes at the foot of the Andes, the FBI stepped in to investigate. The FBI's investigation pulled from multiple sources all over the world and it was eventually joined by a parallel investigation by the CIA. The CIA effort, which ran into the early 1960s, included a sighting report from an SS veteran named Phillip Citroen, who claimed to have been in regular contact with Hitler in Colombia, and that the former Führer moved to Argentina in January 1955 during a spell of bad health. The CIA report on Citroen's statements even included a microfilmed photograph that purported to show Citroen sitting with Hitler in South America. In the end, after chasing down hundreds of leads on at least three continents, both the FBI and CIA concluded they couldn't prove anything without some hard evidence and closed their cases.

Hitler Death Conspiracy Theories in Popular Culture

The official FBI and CIA search for the fugitive Adolf Hitler may have ended with a whimper, but unofficially, the idea that the most wanted man in history may have faked his death and escaped was too good not to enter the culture in many ways, with Hitler death conspiracy theories popping up again and again. A 2011 book by British authors Simon Dunstan and Gerrard Williams, titled Grey Wolf: The Escape of Adolf Hitler, purported to be a factual examination and biography of the postwar Hitler family: Adolf, Eva, and their daughter Ursula. The book was blasted like a furnace by mainstream historians, who called it trash upon its release. But as the ancient proverb goes: 'If it's trash and it involves Hitler, it'll be on The History Channel during May sweeps.' So it was that, in 2015, The History Channel began running a pseudo-documentary series called Hunting Hitler, which put forward the Hitler death conspiracy theory that he had escaped war-ravaged Europe with his wife aboard a U-boat to

Argentina. The program's writers, evidently not having easy access to a world map, claimed that the U-boat stopped briefly in Madagascar on its way to Buenos Aires.

A Fitting Tribute

In a bizarre way, all the circus-like speculation and Hitler death conspiracy theories would probably have pleased the man himself no end. Based on statements made by people who had actually been present in the bunker at the end, many of them spoken in confidence to WWII researcher and bestselling author David Irving, it is clear that Hitler was serious about disappearing from the world without a trace. Hitler's adjutant, SS officer Otto Günsche, reported being ordered to find several liters of gasoline, suitable for burning remains, a day or two before Hitler's suicide. Furthermore, Hitler seems to have settled on April 30 as his suicide date because it was the latest day when he could be sure there would still be time to burn him properly and disperse the ashes before the Red Army took the Chancellery. His concern seems to have been that no trace of his remains should ever be recovered to serve his enemies as a trophy. Funny enough, such drama was predicted years before it happened by a then-obscure document commissioned by the Office of Strategic Services. In 1943, the OSS asked prominent psychologists to assess what was then known about Hitler from his public and private utterances as well as anecdotal statements from people who had known the man personally. The resulting report goes on for a bit about how Hitler saw himself in relation to his place in history, and then it offers a list of likely outcomes for when the fighting inevitably turned against Germany and Hitler's fall became a certainty. Among the eight possible endings the team saw for Hitler, the outcome they rated as most likely read as follows.

'It is probably true that he has an inordinate fear of death but being a hysteric, he could undoubtedly screw himself up into the super-man character and perform the deed. In all probability, however, it would not be a simple suicide. He has too much of the dramatic for that and since immortality is one of his dominant motives, we can imagine that he would stage the most dramatic and effective death scene he could possibly think of. He knows how to bind the people to him and if he cannot have the bond in life he will certainly do his utmost to achieve it in death.'

Antarctica's Greatest Mysteries, From Lost Civilizations to a Secret Nazi Space Base

Antarctica is effectively a freezing time-capsule that contains clues about life on the planet before humans. IT'S the last great unexplored wilderness on the face of planet Earth and is shrouded in icy mysteries. But what's the truth about the frozen continent of Antarctica? For scientists, it's a freezing cold time-capsule that contains clues about life on the planet before meddling humans came along and ruined everything. But for conspiracy theorists, the icy continent contains much, much more than just a few frozen bacteria and a hidden lake. The wilder minds of the internet have made a series of sensational claims about the South Pole, suggesting its home to alien bases and even a lost human civilization. Few readers are going to have the chance to explore Antarctica any time soon, so we've collected together some of the mysteries which have intrigued scientists — and a few of the wild theories which have lit up the internet.

Blood Falls

A wound-like gash that spurts red liquid out of the Taylor Glacier has puzzled scientists since its discovery in 1911. An Australian geologist stumbled upon the Antarctic waterfall in 1911 and put forward the theory that the "blood" was just water that had been stained by microscopic red algae. The Blood Falls have captivated scientists since their discovery. But researchers from the University of Alaska Fairbanks and Colorado College claimed that Blood Falls is flowing from a large lake which has been trapped under the ice for one million years. This mystery is far from solved, however, because scientists haven't been able to fully explore this lake, which has remained liquid when it probably should have frozen over. It's believed that oxidized iron gives the water its rusty tinge.

The Lost City Of Atlantis

You won't find this theory in any science books, but a quick Google search will throw up screeds of bizarre claims that Atlantis is frozen in Antarctic ice. Conspiracy theorists suggested the object was man-made, hailing it as proof that a city was buried beneath the ice.

But scientists have since said the strange mound was sastrugi — sharp grooves formed on snow by fierce winds.

A Nazi Space Base

Some conspiracy theorists believe the Nazis claimed an area of Antarctica as German territory and sent an expedition there. German scientists then mapped the area to discover a network of rivers and caves, one of which led to a large underground lake. A city-sized base was built near the lake called 'Base 22' or 'New Berlin', which was supposedly was home to not only Nazis, according to Vladimir Terziski, from Bulgaria. But this theory loses credibility quickly because it's claimed the base was used to launch missions to the moon. Colin Summerhayes, a geologist at the University of Cambridge, has previously published an entire paper dedicated to quashing rumors about a secret Nazi space base. However, the Nazis really did have a base in the Arctic, which was abandoned more than 70 years ago when its crew was poisoned by polar bear meat.

A Hidden Mountain Range

With ice and snow everywhere, you'd think the Gamburtsev Mountain Range would be perfect for skiing or sledging. But the whole mountain range is actually frozen under ice near the Southern pole of inaccessibility, the point on the Antarctic continent which is furthest away from the Southern Ocean. The mountains are believed to be roughly the same size as the Alps, standing 2,700 meters high and 1200 kilometres long. They were first discovered in the 1950s but were fully mapped in 2009. It's believed they first formed more than one billion years ago and should have been eroded down to nothing by water and ice but were brought back to life by the collision of two continents.

The Site of an Asteroid 'Mega Impact'

A huge and mysterious 'Anomaly' is thought to be lurking beneath the frozen wastes of an area called Wilkes Land. This 'Wilkes Land gravity anomaly' was first uncovered in 2006, when NASA satellites spotted gravitational changes which indicated the presence of a huge object sitting in the middle of a 480km-wide impact crater. One team of NASA Boffins suggested it is the remains of a truly massive asteroid which was more than twice the size of the Chicxulub space rock which wiped out the dinosaurs. If this explanation is true, it could mean this killer asteroid caused a 'Mega impact' which resulted in the Permian Triassic extinction event that killed 96 per cent of Earth's sea creatures and up to 70 per cent of the vertebrate organisms living on land. However, the wilder minds of the internet have come up with their own theories, with some conspiracy theorists claiming it could be a massive UFO base or a portal to a mysterious underworld called the Hollow Earth. We're going to go with the NASA theories on this one.

Mysterious Life Forms

Researchers have spotted some truly bizarre creatures in Antarctica, although we haven't yet found any aliens. In 2014, it was revealed that tiny life forms are living in a lake locked under half a mile of ice. This lost world has not seen sunlight or fresh air for more than one million years. Yet it supports more than 4,000 species of organisms and suggests life could survive almost anywhere, even on other planets or moons. 'It's the first definitive evidence that there's not only life, but active ecosystems underneath the Antarctic ice sheet, something that we have been guessing about for decades,' said lead researcher Brent Christner, professor of biology at Louisiana State University. 'I think that this does nothing but strengthen the case for life on other icy bodies in solar system and beyond.'

Nazis And Pyramids: What's Really Going On In Antarctica?

Antarctica is one of the last remaining unexplored places on Earth so it's no wonder theories are rife about what's really happening at the bottom of the world. From secret pyramids to hidden Nazis, and speculation about military operations, the inhospitable continent is a favorite topic of discussion for many people across the internet. So, what is going on in Antarctica?

Flat Earth

For a group who call themselves the Flat Earthers, the claim by Pythagoras and Aristotle that our planet is round is absurd and they believe scientists have been deliberately misleading the public ever since. At the core of that deception? They say Antarctica is in fact a large, mostly flat plane surrounding the rest of the world, culminating in a large ice wall guarded by NASA employees. But what about the 24-hour sunlight and darkness that we've been told Antarctica experiences every year? Flat Earthers say it simply isn't true, claiming fake videos are used to manipulate the public. Kiwi documentary maker Anthony Powell has lived in Antarctica for both summer and winter seasons, enduring 24-hour daylight for months on end, and 24 hour darkness for months on end. He's filmed a number of time lapses showing the sun as it dips, but fails to graze the horizon, in summer. He says Flat Earthers often comment on his videos, something he finds very entertaining. He's even issued a challenge to them: He'll reimburse any Flat Earther who travels to Antarctica in summer and can prove his video is fake. 'I even had one person email me to say they were going to take me up on it, and I gave them advice on filming and which cruise ships go to the same location,' he told Newshub. 'We'll see if it actually happens or not.' Antarctica NZ's website also hosts a webcam stream from New Zealand's Scott Base, which refreshes every 15 minutes. At Ross Island, where Scott Base is found, the next sunset won't happen until February.

The pyramids

In 2016, a striking screenshot from Google Earth showed a set of near perfect pyramids, partially covered by snow. Immediately speculation was rife. How were they created? How old were they? Why had they been kept secret until now? At some point someone claimed they were 100 million years old. The quote was assumed to be factual and repeated across the internet unchecked. So, had humans with the technology to build pyramids really been in Antarctica 100 million years ago? Unfortunately, that's not the case. Firstly, humans have only existed in today's form for around 200,000 years. Secondly, the pyramids were revealed to be part of the Ellsworth Mountains, in the Heritage Ranges. 'Pyramid shapes are not impossible - many peaks partially look like pyramids, but they only have one to two faces like that, rarely four,' US researcher Eric Rignot told LiveScience when the images began circulating.

The Nazis

After a secret Nazi mission to Antarctica in 1939, it's been widely speculated the Nazis managed to build a base on the continent - with some even believing Hitler may have escaped there before Germany surrendered in 1945. The evidence for this? It's claimed a German U-boat arrived at an Argentine base in Antarctica two months after the war ended. This boat allegedly carried not just Hitler, but other high-ranking Nazis, securing their safety and taking them to a secret base near the South Pole. However, a study by marine geologist Dr. Colin Summerhayes, from the UK, has already debunked this rumor. Wartime documents proved the Nazis never decided to build a base in Antarctica. They certainly never began constructing one. The initial 1939 mission was scoping out a base so Germany could carve out a slice of the prolific whaling industry. There was no connection to wartime planning.

The military

Travel to Antarctica is strictly controlled under the Antarctic Treaty which aims to protect the continent for peace and scientific research. The 53 countries under the treaty, including New Zealand, apply to conduct operations on the ice. The majority of work is carried out by the military or contractors. McMurdo Station, the US base, has military personnel serving as staff and pilots, while New Zealand's nearby Scott Base works with the Kiwi Defense Force. The majority of air travel into the continent is also military-run, with New Zealand and the US sharing C-17s and Hercules C-130s to transport personnel and cargo, as they have the skills, equipment and experience needed to safely travel to Antarctica. Each plane is huge and has to make its way, in a single trip, across the vast expanse of the ocean and into the freezing landscape. When the weather packs in, it really packs in, making it impossible to land and forcing the flight to turn back. When the ice softens at the peak of summer, only aircraft equipped with skis, like the US Hercules, can land. Antarctica's vast, freezing emptiness has captured the imaginations of people for generations - and with the majority of the continent still untouched, its likely wide-ranging theories will continue to propagate for generations to come.

Us Navy Spies Learned Of Nazi Alliance With Reptilian Extraterrestrials During WWII.

In today's episode of Exonews TV, William Tompkins reveals an astonishing secret acquired by U.S. Navy spies embedded within Nazi Germany's advanced technology projects during the World War II, the Nazi war effort was being assisted by extraterrestrial visitors. The spies had reported to a covert Naval Intelligence operation, located at Naval Air Station San Diego, that Adolf Hitler had signed a secret agreement with representatives of a Reptilian extraterrestrial race. In today's newly released ExoNews TV interview, Tompkins reveals how 'Reptilian consultants' were helping the Nazi SS develop advanced weapons technologies. They had, if you want to call them, 'Consultants,' who are Reptilian consultants assisting on all of these different things that it takes to design and build these spacecraft carriers, and propulsion systems. So, this is an extremely well developed program and documented like crazy. Getting copies of the documents was hard for them, hard for our spies. This was an open program in the upper level of the SS. The spies learned that the goal of the Reptilian plan was not only to assist the Nazis to win the war and achieve planetary conquest, but to build fleets of antigravity spacecraft carriers that could be used for interplanetary conquest in other star systems: Holy cats the thing went way beyond that [world conquest].

Again, what we just said about this was the tip of the iceberg of what they were doing. Already Reptilians were doing it to other stars' planets all over this area of the Galaxy…. These young kids, the operatives, they couldn't believe half of what they brought back, what was going on. But some of them were really good people, and they knew how to get into places and listen to what's going on, and finding what that guy he had talked to, or he heard, and going to so and so, because yes they were doing that over there. Tompkins information is startling, but it is not the first time claims have been made about Nazi Germany receiving extraterrestrial help during the War. The father of German rocket science, Herman Oberth, said the following in response to a question about Nazi Germany's rapid technological development: We cannot take credit for our record advancement in certain scientific fields alone. We have been helped." When asked by whom, he replied, "the peoples of other worlds.

In a 1998 interview with Linda Moulton Howe, a former CIA agent, who from 1957 to 1960 was given access to highly classified briefing files, said that the documents revealed that the Nazis had indeed been helped by an extraterrestrial race in their advanced aeronautical weapons projects: When Vril was building that first craft, the Vril had one or two of the aliens that worked with them in Germany where they fired rockets from Peenemunde. The documents I read in Washington said that's where the first Vril vehicle was made…. The aliens were helpers to Germany. More recently, Secret Space Program whistleblower, Corey Goode says that from 1987 to 2007, he read intelligence briefings on smart-glass pads that detailed what had happed during World War II. He describes how German Secret Societies were helped before and throughout World War II by Draconian extraterrestrials who were assisting the former in the development of advanced antigravity space battle fleets.

At the same time these [German Secret] Societies had made contact with the Draco Federation and another group that avoided the Draco's. The German Occultists were very busy from the early 1900's, especially the time just before, during and after World War One. Their major breakthrough's occurred in the late 1930's. Goode said that the ultimate goal of the Reptilians, in helping German Secret Societies and the Nazi SS, was to create advanced space carrier groups that would be capable of interplanetary conquest. The eventual German/Nazi space battle groups became what Goode described as the "Dark Fleet." It operates outside of our solar system, and is described at length in the book, Insiders Reveal Secret Space Programs and Extraterrestrial Alliances. Consequently, the whistleblower testimonies by the CIA Agent and Corey Goode support Tompkins' claims that intelligence briefing files dating from World War II did indeed refer to Nazi Germany being assisted by extraterrestrials. Significantly, the ultimate goal of the German Reptilian alliance went far beyond planetary conquest, as Tompkins claimed the U.S. Navy had learned from its spies.

In addition to the preceding whistleblower testimony, there are important documents that support Tompkins extraordinary claims. In his autobiography, Selected by Extraterrestrials, Tompkins supplied a number of significant documents. Bill Tompkins - Mission Orders The two most pertinent to his specific claims that Navy spies were reporting on advanced Nazi aerospace projects, are Tompkins' mission orders and two passes he received to enter and leave Naval Air Station with multiple 'Information' packages. His mission orders confirm that he was authorized to work as a 'Disseminator of Aircraft Research and Information.' This is compelling documentary evidence that the packages Tompkins was carrying contained classified Naval intelligence on advanced aircraft designs, which included those developed in Nazi Germany. In last week's ExoNews TV interview, Tompkins revealed how he participated in the debriefings of Navy spies, who returned periodically from Germany to give updates on what they were seeing in advanced technology projects. Tompkins job was to then design briefing packets that he would disseminate to leading U.S. corporations, think tanks and universities that could properly study and evaluate the information.

Over the four years of his covert Naval Intelligence service (1942-1946) Tompkins estimates giving 1200 briefings at various locations, where he revealed Nazi secrets to those U.S. scientists most capable of understanding what the Germans were secretly developing. This week's episode of ExoNews TV is likely to be deeply disturbing to those believing the question of extraterrestrial life is still largely a speculative question, arising from thousands of sightings of UFOs. Tompkins information sheds considerable light on probably the most closely guarded secret in the entire history of the U.S. Intelligence Community. Nazi Germany had been secretly helped by a race of Reptilian extraterrestrials prior to, during and after the Second World War! The U.S. Navy was to subsequently play the lead role in developing a strategic response to this threatening alien alliance, which would continue long after official military hostilities had ceased in Europe.

Secret Nazi Space Program Joined Reptilian Alliance in Interstellar Conquest

The most highly classified space program currently in existence emerged out of a secret alliance between Nazi Germany and Reptilian extraterrestrials, according to whistleblower Corey Goode. In his most recent interview on Cosmic Disclosure, Goode explained the origins of the 'Dark Fleet' as the secret space program established by German Secret Societies and the Nazi SS in Antarctica during the Second World War era. During his interview, Goode described how the Dark Fleet is currently comprised entirely of humans drawn from all over the world who have a totalitarian ideology initially inspired by Nazi ideals: They looked very stern, very arrogant, like they felt very elite. They wore black Stormtrooper kind of clothes, just very stern like. Very totalitarian acting. And a lot of the people that ended up going into this program came from a lot of the German secret society Nazi kind of programs. He says the Dark Fleet works alongside Draconian space battle fleets in interstellar conquest. And all we've really known about them is that they fight . . . They're an offensive force. They are for going and doing offensive type of work alongside the Draco. They go outside the solar system on, I guess, conquests or defending Draco territory, helping the Draco on military expeditions.

Goode says information currently known about the Dark Fleet, comes mainly from defectors who were trapped inside of our solar system after a frequency fence had been created by the Sphere Being Alliance, which left most of the Dark Fleet outside of our solar system, and blocked their re-entry. Goode also discussed a secret base established on the Moon by the Dark Fleet, which has a trapezoid shape, and was previously described by Carolyn Hamlet in an interview where she described physically entering this base. Hamlet recalls being inside a spacecraft approaching the moon base which she witnessed. She says that she next recalled being inside the moon base and witnessed a council type meeting with up to 30 global leaders from around the world led by a prominent female. Another whistleblower, former USAF radar tracking operator, Niara Isley, says that in 1980 she was taken between eight and ten times to a secret moon base, which used human workers and was guarded by Reptilian beings: In interviews, people always want to know what my moon experiences were like, and I can certainly understand such avid curiosity. I can only state that it was terrible on multiple levels. I was terrified for my life the whole time. I was very poorly fed and worked hard during the day cycle, operating some kind of electronic equipment for excavation at times, and doing hard physical manual labor at others, such as lifting and stacking boxes.

Worst of all, I was used for sex during what passed for night there, from man to man. I was allowed extraordinarily little sleep, and I've since learned that this is another facet of mind control abuse. I shut down during all of this to the point that I didn't even feel alive anymore. (Facing the Shadow, Embracing the Light, p.271) This was highly likely the Dark Fleet base that Goode and Hamlet later described. A number of the advanced space vehicles possessed by the Dark Fleet were detailed by Goode including some that appear terribly similar to the imperial star cruisers in the Star Wars series. Other ships were cited as diamond shaped or pumpkin seed shaped. All these craft possess powerful offensive weapons systems, which had been developed by another secret space program called the Interplanetary Corporate Conglomerate, with some enhanced further by the Draconian Reptilians, as Goode explains.

This [Draco] group is working alongside a human group that has all of this technology that has been enhanced by . . . the ICC has helped them build out a lot of this – these vessels and weaponry. And then the Draco group has helped them enhance it even more so for offensive duties outside of the solar system. And they spend almost all of their time completely outside the solar system. Goode says up until recently, the Dark Fleet possessed a decisive technological advantage over all the other space programs, especially the Solar Warden program, which had been established by the U.S. Navy in the 1980's. Over much of the time of his secret space program service, Goode said all five secret space programs, described at length in Insiders Reveal Secret Space Programs, cooperated extensively. This is no longer the case with the Solar Warden program, along with defectors from the Dark Fleet, Interplanetary Corporate Conglomerate, and other smaller groups, which now coordinate with each other as the Secret Space Program Alliance. In previous episodes, Goode has described secret negotiations aimed at bringing about a cessation of military hostilities between the secret spaces programs and introducing 'Full disclosure' to the world.

In the April 12 Cosmic Disclosure interview, Goode discussed his meeting with a White Royal Draco, the Draconian Reptilian leader, which took place in April 2015. This meeting with the 14 foot tall alien was very intimidating, according to Goode. The White Royal Draco possessed highly developed psychic abilities, which Goode found to be very invasive during their telepathic communications: When it was interfacing with me, its eyes were morphing the whole time. It was a very psychically powerful being. And it penetrated the frontal lobe. It was almost like there were microwaves or something shooting into the front of your frontal lobe. It was very invasive. And both Gonzales [pseudonym used by Goode's liaison with the Secret Space Program Alliance] and I, for several days, at least three days, we had headaches. We were nauseated. Goode's information has been corroborated recently by the remarkable testimony of William Tompkins; a serviceman who was assigned to a covert U.S. Navy program that involved spies embedded in Nazi Germany reporting back the developments within the Nazi's top secret aerospace projects. Tompkins has supplied critical documents in his book, Selected by Extraterrestrials, which support his claims.

In recent interviews on ExoNews TV, Tompkins confirmed that an agreement had indeed been reached between Adolph Hitler and Reptilian extraterrestrials. Tompkins was present when the Navy spies described learning about Reptilian consultants that helped German scientists develop sophisticated weapons and antigravity propulsion systems. Hitler, therefore, highly likely participated in a similar meeting with a Royal White Draco as Goode experienced in 2015. In fact, there is evidence that such a meeting did take place. Hermann Rauschning, the Governor of Danzig, revealed that Hitler had met a mysterious leader who was the 'Superman' destined to rule the world. Hitler allegedly said: What will the social order of the future be like? Comrade I will tell you. There will be a class of overlords, after them the rank and file of the party members in hierarchical order, and then the great mass of anonymous followers, servants, and workers in perpetuity, and beneath them again all the conquered foreign races, the modern slaves. And over and above all these, will reign a new and exalted nobility of whom I cannot speak … but of all these plans the militant members will know nothing. The new man is living amongst us now! He is here. Isn't that enough for you? I will tell you a secret. I have seen the new man. He is intrepid and cruel. I was afraid of him.

Hitler's meeting with the 'Superman' or 'Secret world leader,' if true, echoes Goode and Gonzales' encounter with the Royal White Draco whose psychic abilities were very invasive and capable of inducing terror. Significantly, Hitler's description outlines the hierarchical nature of the New World Order he was seeking to create with Germany's secret space programs, which were ultimately under the leadership of this mysterious "superman" who was almost certainly the same Royal White Draco described by Goode. The Reptilians' leader, the Royal White Draco, was therefore at the apex of power, ultimately controlling the Dark Fleet being built by the Nazis, and the fleet's current interstellar imperial operations. Tompkins also reported that the Nazis had established secret bases in Antarctica as a result of their alliance with Reptilian extraterrestrials, confirming Goode again. Out of these Antarctic bases, the Nazi secret space program was launched, and later established a presence elsewhere in our solar system, and beyond. Importantly, Tompkins states that the Nazi bases were built under the protection of, and adjacent to larger caverns of, Reptilians, which all but confirm that a White Royal Draco was in ultimate control of the Nazis secret space program. Tompkins' information is, therefore, consistent with the emergence of the Dark Fleet, as described by Goode.

In conclusion, Goode's revelations about the Dark Fleet in his April 12 Cosmic Disclosure interview are extremely significant. They reveal that elements of humanity have joined in galactic wide wars of conquest, unbeknownst to the rest of the planet's population. For decades, Earth has provided personnel, technology, and resources for unjust wars in space because proponents of a Nazi inspired ideology, in league with an imperial extraterrestrial race, continue to cast a dark shadow over global leaders. This iniquitous situation needs to come to a quick end; Goode and Tompkin's disclosures are an important first step in achieving this vital goal.

5. *How About a Jog in the Park?*

Here is a look at the Boston Marathon terror attack On April 15, 2013, double bombings near the finish line of the Boston Marathon killed three people and injured at least 264.

Facts: The bombs exploded 12 seconds apart near the marathon's finish line on Boylston Street. According to Richard DesLauriers, the special agent in charge of the FBI's Boston office, the bombs contained BB-like pellets and nails. The bombs were contained in pressure cookers, hidden inside backpacks, according to the FBI.

Victims: Martin Richard, 8, a student at Neighborhood House Charter School in Boston. Krystle Campbell, 29, of Medford, Massachusetts. Lingzi Lu, a graduate student at Boston University. She was originally from China.

Timeline: April 15, 2013 - At approximately 2:50 p.m., two bombs explode near the finish line of the Boston Marathon. The bombs explode within 8-12 seconds of each other, about 50-100 yards apart. At 6:10 p.m., President Barack Obama speaks to reporters at the White House, 'We will find out who did this. We'll find out why they did this. Any responsible individuals, any responsible groups, will feel the full weight of justice.'

April 16, 2013 - President Obama, speaking at the White House, describes the bombings as an act of terrorism. Officials confirm that there were only two bombs, despite earlier reports that other unexploded devices had been found. Authorities, including bomb experts, search an apartment in Revere, Massachusetts and remove items. Officials caution that there are no clear suspects, and the motive remains unknown.

April 17, 2013 - A federal law enforcement official tells CNN that the lid to a pressure cooker thought to have been used in the bombings has been found on a rooftop at the scene. Purported miscommunication between government officials lead several news organizations, including CNN, to report prematurely that a suspect has been arrested and is in custody.

April 18, 2013 - Attorney Kenneth Feinberg, an expert on victim compensation, is announced as the administrator of the One Fund Boston, a fund to assist individuals affected by the attacks. At a press conference, the FBI releases pictures of the suspects they are seeking in connection with the bombings. The suspects are later identified as brothers, Tamerlan Tsarnaev, 26, and Dzhokhar Tsarnaev, 19. Late in the evening, Massachusetts Institute of Technology police officer Sean Collier is shot and killed on campus. Soon after, Tsarnaev brothers carjack a driver in Cambridge. The driver is released about 30 minutes later. As the police chase them, Tamerlan Tsarnaev and Dzhokhar Tsarnaev throw explosives out the windows and exchange gunfire with officers. Tamerlan is wounded and later dies at Beth Israel Hospital. He had bullet wounds and injuries from an explosion, according to officials.

April 19, 2013 - Boston police identify the bombers as Tamerlan Tsarnaev and Dzhokhar Tsarnaev, brothers from Cambridge, Massachusetts. They are of Chechen origin and legally immigrated to the United States. Tamerlan is identified as the person killed in the encounter with police while Dzhokhar Tsarnaev, a student at the University of Massachusetts-Dartmouth, remains at large. Throughout the day, hundreds of law enforcement officers go door-to-door on 20 streets in Watertown, looking for Dzhokhar Tsarnaev, who authorities believe is still in Massachusetts. Boston-area residents are asked by authorities to stay inside as the hunt continues for Tsarnaev. Between 6 and 7 p.m., Watertown resident David Henneberry goes out to inspect his boat soon after the lockdown is lifted and sees 'A man covered with blood under a tarp.' 8:15 p.m. - Authorities announce they have a person they believe to be Dzhokhar Tsarnaev cornered. Law enforcement agents later take Tsarnaev into custody. He is hospitalized in serious condition.

April 22, 2013 - Tsarnaev is charged with one count of using and conspiring to use a weapon of mass destruction resulting in death and one count of malicious destruction of property by means of an explosive device resulting in death.

May 1, 2013 - Three 19-year-olds are arrested in connection with the bombings. The three men are accused of helping Dzhokhar Tsarnaev after the bombing. Federal prosecutors say Azamat Tazhayakov, Dias Kadyrbayev, and Robel Phillipos took items from Tsarnaev's dorm room after the bombing to throw investigators off their friend's trail. Tazhayakov and Kadyrbayev are foreign nationals charged with obstruction of justice. They are initially held on unrelated visa issues. Phillipos, an American citizen, is charged with lying to federal agents.

May 9, 2013 - Tamerlan Tsarnaev is buried in a Muslim cemetery in Doswell, Virginia. This is after cemeteries in Massachusetts and elsewhere refuse to allow his burial.

May 22, 2013 - An FBI agent shoots and kills Ibragim Todashev in Orlando, Florida, while questioning him about his relationship with Tamerlan Tsarnaev after cell phone records connect the two. Todashev tells the agent that Tsarnaev participated in a 2011 triple homicide that was drug-related. The confrontation between the FBI agent and Todashev turns violent after Todashev lunges at the agent with a weapon, according to a law enforcement source.

July 10, 2013 - Dzhokhar Tsarnaev pleads not guilty to 30 federal charges.

August 13, 2013 - Dias Kadyrbayev and Azamat Tazhayakov plead not guilty to conspiracy to obstruct justice and obstructing justice with intent to impede authorities.

August 19, 2013 - The testimony of the trauma surgeon who treated Dzhokhar Tsarnaev is unsealed, revealing the extent of his wounds, including multiple gunshot wounds that pierced the base of his skull, mouth, and vertebrae. Unsealed documents also reveal that Tsarnaev was not read his Miranda rights until three days after he was detained.

September 13, 2013 - Robel Phillipos pleads not guilty to making false statements to federal officials, and Dias Kadyrbayev and Azamat Tazhayakov reenter their not guilty pleas. Tamerlan

Tsarnaev's in-laws appear before a federal grand jury in Boston. Details of the four-hour session are not immediately released.

October 21, 2013 - In a court document, prosecutors confirm that Tamerlan Tsarnaev was accused of participating in a 2011 triple homicide outside Boston.

January 30, 2014 - A notice is filed with a federal court after US Attorney General Eric Holder says that federal prosecutors will seek the death penalty against Dzhokhar Tsarnaev.

May 30, 2014 - Authorities arrest a friend of the Tsarnaev brothers, Khairullozhon Matanov and charge him with one count of destroying, altering, and falsifying records, documents, and tangible objects in a federal investigation, specifically information on his computer. He is also charged with three counts of making materially false, fictitious, and fraudulent statements in a federal terrorism investigation. He later pleads guilty to misleading investigators.

August 21, 2014 - Dias Kadyrbayev pleads guilty to obstructing justice. As part of the plea agreement, a sentence of seven years will be recommended by the US attorney, and Kadyrbayev, a Kazakh national, has agreed to be deported after serving his sentence.

October 28, 2014 - Robel Phillipos, a friend of Dzhokhar Tsarnaev, is convicted on two counts of lying to federal agents.

January 5, 2015 - Tsarnaev's trial begins.

March 3, 2015 - Jury selection is completed.

March 4, 2015 - Opening statements begin in Tsarnaev's case. Testimony lasts 15 days. Over the course of the trial, prosecutors call 92 witnesses; the defense calls four.

April 8, 2015 - After deliberating 11 and a half hours, the jury returns a guilty verdict on all 30 charges.

May 15, 2015 - Tsarnaev is sentenced to death.

June 2, 2015 - Dias Kadyrbayev, a friend of Dzhokhar Tsarnaev who pleaded guilty in August 2014, is sentenced to 72 months in prison for obstructing justice.

June 5, 2015 - Azamat Tazhayakov is sentenced to three and a half years in prison for conspiring to obstruct justice and obstructing justice with intent to impede the investigation. Another college friend of Tsarnaev, Robel Phillipos, is sentenced to three years in prison for making false statements to law enforcement in a terrorism investigation.

June 24, 2015 - Tsarnaev is formally sentenced to death. Addressing the court, he apologizes and admits he is guilty.

July 18, 2015 - Tsarnaev is placed in Supermax prison in Florence, Colorado, also home to inmates Ted Kaczynski, the 'Unabomber,' and 9/11 co-conspirator Zacarias Moussaoui.

December 22, 2015 - Stephen Silva, the man who loaned Tsarnaev the gun that was later used to kill an MIT officer, is sentenced to time served and three years' supervised probation. Silva is also ordered to pay $800 in penalties.

January 15, 2016 - Tsarnaev is ordered to pay more than $101 million in restitution to victims and his request for a new trial is denied.

University of Washington researcher Kate Starbird's research into online rumors lead her to an information war being waged through a web of highly politicized conspiracy theories. In 2013, in the time between when two homemade bombs detonated near the Boston marathon finish line and when police cornered and caught bomber Dzhokhar Tsarnaev, a conspiracy theory began to spread online. Internet sleuths, analyzing pictures released by the FBI, said they saw evidence of a false flag attack - proof that the bombing had been staged or carried out by the US government. University of Washington professor Kate Starbird and some of her research team noticed these accusations on Twitter, since they were studying how rumors spread on social media during events like mass shootings and terror attacks. While other online rumors would gain traction and die away as facts became clear, the Boston false flag speculation did not abate, even after Tsarnaev and his brother Tamerlan were identified as the bombers. At the time, Starbird and her team saw the conspiracy theory as something of a curiosity.

'We didn't want to go there,' she says. 'It just seemed messy.' But after taking a closer look at those rumors, she now says her research suggests there is an "emerging alternative media ecosystem" that is growing in reach, and that may have underlying political agendas. Researcher Kate Starbird first began exploring social media rumors during the 2013 Boston Bombing Starting in January 2016, she and her team began mapping sites generating conspiracy theories. They tracked Twitter reaction to shootings along with references to terms like 'False Flag' and 'Hoax' and the websites that used them. Starbird has dubbed what they discovered the 'The information wars.' The work is nominated for best paper at an international web and social media conference in Montreal this week. Highly politicized alternative narratives to events were being spread by a mishmash of websites: anti-mainstream media sites, anti-corporatist 'Alt-Right' and 'Alt-Left' sites, conspiracy-focused White Nationalist and anti-Semitic sites, Muslim Defense sites and Russian propaganda. 'There are different actors,' she says. 'Some are (acting) for financial motives, some are for political motives. Some people are true believers.' Calling her finding an 'Information war' is not a nod towards talk show host Alex Jones' alternative news website Infowars, which focuses on Alt-Right and conspiracy theory themes.

His site rose to mainstream prominence during the 2016 American election. But she has written tongue-in-cheek that 'This work suggests that Alex Jones is indeed a prophet.' Looking back on their older research, they found hints of similar conspiracy activity around the 2010 BP Deepwater Horizon oil spill, which devastated the Gulf Coast of the US. In 2016, the university researchers found sites that helped propagate these conspiracy theory tweets were often so-called 'Alternative media' domains like VeteransToday.com and BeforeItsNews.com. The researchers also found sites like TheRealStrategy.com, which appeared to be generating automated conspiracy theory tweets with "bots" in order to propagate politicized content. Many of the tweets had a political element. For example, a mass shooting might be blamed as a "false flag" by the US government, with speculation that the attack was planned to gain support for gun control. While belief in certain conspiracy theories can be sometimes linked political beliefs, Starbird's research suggested that political content on sites pushing the alternative narratives was less about left-wing versus right-wing - no political leaning was immune - but instead had a broad anti-globalist bent. There was also plenty of anti-vaccine, anti-GMO, and anti-climate science content, as well conspiracies about the world's wealthy and powerful citizens. Starbird's research points to an intentional use of disinformation to muddle thinking and 'Undermine trust in information just generally.'   She says big questions remain, like who might be behind any possible intentional disinformation campaigns and to what extent these messages are coordinated. But she says she is concerned that as these fringe theories gain traction in the public sphere, 'It is not healthy for society when there's no shared reality, there's no set of facts, society at large can become easily manipulated,' she says.

6.   *The Recipe for Meatballs*

The Russo-Swedish War of 1788–90, known as Gustav III's Russian War in Sweden, Gustav III's War in Finland and Catherine II's Swedish War in Russia, was fought between Sweden and Russia from June 1788 to August 1790. The conflict was initiated by King Gustav III of Sweden for domestic political reasons, as he believed that a short war would leave the opposition with no recourse but to support him. Despite establishing himself as an autocrat in a bloodless coup d'état that ended parliamentary rule in 1772, his political powers did not give him the right to start a war. Also, he was becoming increasingly unpopular, an issue which became obvious during the parliament session of 1786. This unpopularity was also encouraged by Russia, which believed an autocratic king to be a threat to its interests. However, Russian support for his opposition did not go unnoticed by Gustav III and was one of the reasons why he thought of the war as inevitable. The Western powers such as Great Britain, the Dutch Republic and the Kingdom of Prussia were alarmed by a string of Russian victories in the Russo-Turkish War (1787–92) and lobbied for the war in the north, which would have diverted the attention of Catherine II of Russia from the Southern theatre. It was at their instigation that Gustav concluded an alliance with the Ottoman Empire in the summer of 1788. However, only the Ottoman Empire was willing to ally with Sweden while Great Britain, the Dutch Republic, and Prussia rejected efforts to form an alliance before the grand opening of the Riksdag in 1789, King Gustav III had the Riksdag Music commissioned. [Clarification needed] The Parliament then decided on the creation of a National Debt Office to raise funds and finance the war, a move that gave rise to a wave of inflation of the Swedish Riksdaler.

Preparations for the war

The Swedes initially planned a naval assault on Saint Petersburg. One Swedish army was to advance through Finland; a second army, accompanied by the Swedish coastal flotilla, was to advance along the Finnish coast into the Gulf of Finland; while a third army sailed with the Swedish battlefleet in order to land at Oranienbaum to advance on Saint Petersburg. The goal was to instigate a coup de état in Russia and depose Empress Catherine II of Russia. Sveaborg was set as the forward base of operations for the campaign. However, the whole concept was based on the assumption that the Swedish open sea fleet would be able to decisively defeat its Russian counterpart. Incidentally, Russian forces were not totally unprepared for the war since the bulk of the Russian Baltic Fleet was planned to be transferred against the Ottoman Empire and had made preparations of its own for war. War was far from popular, even less so in the eastern part of Sweden (modern day Finland). Even senior military leaders voiced their opposition to the plans to go to war. Especially amongst the officers of the army, unrest spread widely. This could partly be explained by the still remaining supporters of Georg Magnus Sprengtporten's plans for Finnish independence. In 1788, a head tailor of the Royal Swedish Opera received an order to sew a number of Russian military uniforms that later were used in an exchange of gunfire at Puumala, a Swedish outpost on the Russo-Swedish border, on 27 June 1788.

The staged attack, which caused outrage in Stockholm, was to convince the Riksdag of the Estates and to provide Gustav with an excuse to declare a 'Defensive' war on Russia. This was important since Gustav III did not have the constitutional right to start an offensive war without the agreement of the estates, who had already made clear that their acceptance would not be forthcoming. The Swedish open sea fleet sailed from Karlskrona on 9 June 1788, with Duke Charles of Södermanland as its commander. On 21 June, the fleet met a Russian squadron off Saaremaa Island and after chasing the Russians down tried to provoke a conflict by demanding Russians render honors to the Swedes from which Russians had been exempted in the previous peace treaties. Vice Admiral Wilhelm von Dessin who commanded the small

Russian squadron agreed to render honors to the Duke Charles but not to the Swedish flag and managed to dissolve the threatening situation and continue towards Copenhagen. Since the Swedish wanted to avoid initiating the conflict they had lost their chance to provoke the Russians into war and were left empty-handed.

On 7 July, the Swedish fleet was notified that a state of war with Russia was in effect, and already on 8 July surprised two unprepared Russian frigates, 32 gun Jaroslavets (Jarislawits) and 24 gun Hektor (Gektor), which were promptly captured together with their crew of 450 men. The Swedish fleet met a Russian fleet sailing under the command of Admiral Samuel Greig and fought an engagement, the Battle of Hogland, in which neither side managed to gain advantage. Upon return to Sveaborg to repair and resupply Duke Charles' fleet, the Swedes found that Sveaborg had been stocked only with coastal fleet in mind, which amongst other things meant that it didn't store ammunition for the heavy cannons of the open sea fleet and lacked suitable stocks of equipment required to repair large sailing ships. The coastal fleet's Stockholm's squadron departed for Finland on 25 June, carrying over 9,000 troops. It reached its destination of Sveaborg on 2 July and started constructing an encampment on the island of Sandhamn, next to Helsingfors. The coastal fleet's Sveaborg squadron under Colonel Mikael Anckarsvärd had been readied for action already by mid-June.

On 26 July, the coastal fleet under Colonel Anckarsvärd departed for Frederikshamn, carrying 6,000 men, while a 4,000-strong unit advanced on land under General Carl Gustaf Armfeldt. The Swedish coastal fleet clashed briefly with a group of Russian galleys outside Frederikshamn on 28 July and forced them to retire within the protection of the fortifications. Initial Swedish landing attempts began on 2 August, but harsh weather prevented the main force from landing and a Russian counter-attack forced the 300-man Swedish landing party to return to their ships. On 3 August, landings were successful, some 10 km south-east of the town, and by the evening Swedish forces were advancing towards Frederikshamn. However, inspired Russian resistance in the early hours of 4 August convinced the Swedish landing force to return to its ships. Attempts to swiftly capture Frederikshamn ended in total failure for several reasons, one of the most glaring being the increasing unrest against the king amongst the officers.

Attempts by Colonel Berndt Johan Hastfer's 1,700-man-strong Savolax brigade to storm Nyslott by surprise on 2 July ended in a siege which, given the besiegers' total lack of siege artillery, caused the Swedish advance to bog down. The siege had to be abandoned on 21 August. General Carl Gustaf Armfeldt's 4,000 men were to support the coastal fleet's capture of Frederikshamn and crossed the border on 18 July, reaching its staging ground just north of Frederikshamn on 20 July. A further 1,100 men were under the command of Colonel Gustaf Mauritz Armfelt. When the failure at Frederikshamn became apparent, the Swedish troops were pulled back to the border. The war being perceived illegal as it didn't have the support of the estates, along with its lack of success, contributed to rising unrest. Already on 9 August, a group of officers had pleaded for peace with Russia, and on 12 August had signed what became known as the Anjala declaration, with the whole matter being later known as the Anjala conspiracy.

King Gustav III's position, surrounded by rebellious officers, was greatly improved when news of a threat of war from Denmark–Norway became known, and he could head back to Sweden on 25 August without being accused of deserting his troops. The Swedish attack on Russia caused Denmark-Norway to declare war on Sweden in August, in accordance with its treaty obligations to Russia. A Norwegian army briefly invaded Sweden and won the Battle of Kvistrum Bridge, before peace was signed on 9 July 1789, following the diplomatic intervention of Great Britain and Prussia. Under their pressure, Denmark-Norway declared itself neutral in the conflict, bringing the Lingonberry War to an end.

The Russian fleet had already in early August, soon after the Battle of Hogland, moved to blockade the Swedish open sea fleet in Sveaborg, as the Swedes were unable to get their fleet ready for battle. A small detachment, under command of James Travene, from the Russian fleet cut the safe coastal sea route past Hangö in late August 1788. This caused severe supply troubles for the Swedish fleets and armies, which were mostly east of the cape. A small coastal fleet detachment under Lieutenant-Colonel Victor von Stedingk sortied to drive off the Russians but lacked the strength to do so. After receiving reinforcements, the Swedes managed on 17 October to engage large Russian units for long enough for the small gunboats to slip past the blockade and protect the transports west of the cape, which probably saved the transports containing army and fleet supplies from capture. A few days later, the Russians abandoned their position, allowing Swedish transports to deliver supplies unhindered. Since Sveaborg could not repair and refit the ships of the open sea fleet, it had to set sail for Karlskrona.

However, preparations and unsuitable weather delayed departure until 20 November, when the sea at Sveaborg was already frozen over and some ships had to be freed by sawing the ice open for them. The fleet, however, reached Karlskrona one week later without any losses, just days before that port also froze over. In an attempt to prevent Russian ships from cutting off coastal sea routes, the Swedes built several fortifications at Hangö and on its surrounding islands during the winter of 1788/1789. Additional fortifications were constructed west of Hangö, near Korpo. However, Porkala cape was left without fortifications. The bulk of the Swedish army in Finland, consisting of 13,000 men under General Johan August Meijerfeldt (the younger), was placed at the Kymmene river, with a further 5,000 men in Savolax. While the troops still lacked supplies, their discipline and morale had been greatly improved from what it had been in 1788.

On the naval front, Sweden had not been so lucky; the crews of the open sea fleet based at Karlskrona suffered heavily from fever, making both fitting and manning the ships very difficult, and it took until 6 July before the fleet was able to set sail, under command of Duke Charles of Södermanland, who had the experienced naval officer Admiral Otto Henrik Nordenskiöld as his flag-captain. Swedish and Russian navies during a battle in July 1789, Öland. In stark contrast to Swedish troubles, the Russian open sea fleet had set sail already in mid-May; by 22 May, a few ships reconnoitered the Swedish defenses at Hangö, but after a short engagement the Russian ships chose to break off. The main body of the Russian fleet under Admiral Vasily Chichagov met the Swedish fleet on 26 July and engaged it in what became known as the Battle of Öland. As in the previous year, the battle was indecisive, with the Swedes heading to Karlskrona and the Russian fleet joining up with a Russian squadron from Danish waters. The raging epidemic then confined the Swedish fleet to Karlskrona for most of the year.

The Swedish coastal fleet had been unable to sail for Sweden for the winter and had to be fitted out in Finland. In addition to the problems, the commander of the coastal fleet Colonel Anckarsvärd was arrested for being involved with the Anjala conspiracy and replaced with Admiral Carl August Ehrensvärd. The Swedish coastal fleet was able to sail from Sveaborg in late May and moved to the vicinity of Frederikshamn. However, after Hangö had been fortified, the Russians had moved in to blockade the coastal sea route at Porkala on 10 June. This effectively split the Swedish coastal fleet, as reinforcements from Sweden were unable to join with the main body, putting the coastal fleet at a severe disadvantage against the Russian coastal fleet. In mid-June 1789, the Russians attacked Savolax from three different directions, with total forces of roughly 10,000 men against 4,000 Swedish defenders. Despite a clear victory at the Battle of Porrassalmi, the Swedish army was forced to withdraw, leaving the important Puumala straits to the Russians. Meanwhile, King Gustav III had assumed control of the main body of the Swedish army and started an offensive towards Villmanstrand on 25 June. The Swedes won a resounding victory at Utti on 28 June, but instead of advancing to Villmanstrand, the king headed for Frederikshamn.

Once again, however, the Swedish offensive was bogged down. It took until 18 July for Russian defenses outside Frederikshamn to be cleared, and during this time the Russian army had kept moving its forces south from Savolax. Small detachments (roughly 2,000 men) sent to stop the Russians were defeated at Kaipiainen and the Swedish army had to withdraw to the border once again. The Russian departure from Savolax enabled Swedish units in the area under the command of Colonel von Stendingk to go onto the offensive. His forces advanced towards Nyslott and won several engagements against the Russians, first at Parkuinmäki Hill and later at Laitaatsilta. When forces moved to their winter encampments, truly little had changed from the spring, with the Savolax brigade having recaptured lost land, and only Puumala had remaining in Russian control. The Russian coastal fleet under Charles Henry of Nassau-Siegen started attacking the Swedish coastal fleet on 15 August, by driving away the Swedish squadron which was scouting the area near Frederikshamn. This was followed by an attack against the main staging ground of the Swedish coastal fleet at Svensksund, leading to the first battle of Svensksund. The Russians tried to take advantage of their victory over the Swedes with a coordinated offensive of both the coastal fleet and the army, which managed to drive the remaining Swedes beyond the Kymmene River. The battered Swedish coastal fleet was soon reinforced with ships from Sveaborg, while its commander Admiral Carl August Ehrensvärd was replaced, first by Colonel Karl Nathanael AF Klercker, who oversaw the repairs, and later by Lieutenant-Colonel Georg Kristian de Frese.

The Russian blockade caused considerable trouble to the Swedes. Starting already in early July, Swedish gunboats engaged the much larger Russians on a daily basis, under the command of Admiral Salomon von Rajalin, who was in overall command of the Swedish coastal fleet in the Porkala region. Since von Rajalin's forces lacked the strength to overpower the Russian blockade, they instead covered the Swedish transports in their passage through Barösund strait. The Swedish forces were repeatedly reinforced during the summer and already in mid-July consisted of 2 frigates, 10 galleys and several gunboats. Several artillery batteries were constructed to protect the area. Fighting at sea near Porkala cape continued until September. The Russian blockade at Porkala was after 24 August 1789 under the command of Captain James Trevene, who started the effort to break the Swedish hold on Barösund. The Russian attack against Barösund started on 18 September. The attacking force consisted of 4 ships of the line, 1 frigate and 6 cutters. Fighting continued for two hours and cost the Swedes a single galley and the Russians one ship of the line (Severny Oryol) and several others damaged, but it gained the Russians the control of the Barösund strait. Sporadic fighting in the archipelago near Porkala continued and on 23 September the Russians captured the island of Älgsjön from the Swedes but lost it on 30 September when Swedish reinforcements under Colonel Gustaf Mauritz Armfelt arrived. The Russian fleet left the area suddenly on 23 October, possibly due to the news that the Swedish open sea fleet had set sail, which it had done on 13 October, only to return to Karlskrona on 22 October. The Russian departure opened the safe coastal sea route to Swedish transports.

In 1790, King Gustav revived the plan for a landing close to Saint Petersburg, this time near Viborg. In addition, a determined effort was made to bolster the strength of the fleets as much as possible so as to be able to get them under sail as soon as possible. The coastal fleet especially was being reinforced with new and stronger ships, some of them donated by the various Swedish towns. The first action took place on 17 March 1790, when two Swedish frigates plundered the Russian-controlled port of Rågersvik (Russian- 'Baltiyskiy Port'). Swedish squadrons from Stockholm started towards Sveaborg on 21 April and also from Pommern on 3 May. Even though the Swedish main effort was on the sea, they attacked also on land, where Swedes led by Colonel Gustaf Mauritz Armfelt defeated Russian defenders on 15 April in southern Savolax, while the army led by King Gustav III and Colonel Gustav Wachtmeister won another victory in the battle of Valkeala. A Russian attack on 5 May close to the Kymmene River gained some success, capturing Anjala, but was thrown back before the end of the month. Fighting on land, however, reached stalemate, and already in June had turned into static warfare.

The Swedish open sea fleet under Duke Charles arrived on 10 May at Hangö and moved on 12 May to the vicinity of Reval. As some ships of the fleet were still separated from the main body, Duke Charles refused to carry out the attack on 12 May, when favorable winds still existed, and instead chose to attack on 13 May, leading to the Swedish failure at the battle of Reval. The Swedish fleet stayed near Reval until late May, when it set sail to protect the flank of the coastal fleet; this led to another naval engagement, at the battle of Kronstadt. Failing to inflict a decisive defeat on the Russians, or to prevent separate Russian squadrons from joining together, the open sea fleet sailed to the Bay of Viborg. The coastal fleet started its offensive on 8 May, under command of King Gustav III with de Frese as his flag-captain, without waiting for the coastal fleet's squadrons from Sweden or Pommern. The Swedish coastal fleet attacked the Russian fleet at Frederikshamn on 15 May, winning a clear victory over the defenders in the battle of Fredrikshamn. However, attempts to capture the town and its fortifications failed. Instead of blockading the town, the Swedes chose to continue further towards Vyborg while raiding Russian supplies along the coast, and reached the Beryozovye Islands on 2 June, from where it attempted to support the open sea fleet in the battle of Kronstadt.

The Russian fleet, under command of Admiral Vasily Chichagov, blockaded the Swedish fleets with their 30,000 men in Viborg Bay. The blockade continued for a month and on 21–23 June, with supplies running out, the Swedes chose to attempt a breakout as soon as favorable winds would allow it. The Swedish coastal squadron under Lieutenant-Colonel Carl Olof Cronstedt arrived at Svensksund on 19 June and supported the ground forces of General Meijerfeldt in driving away Russian forces from its vicinity. However, Cronstedt's squadron could not get past a Russian frigate detachment under Captain Rowan Crown (orig. Robert Cronin) blocking the coastal sea route near modern-day Virolahti and had to return to Svensksund. The Swedish escape from the Viborg Bay started on 3 July and lost several ships when they ran aground due to bad visibility in the treacherous waters.

The Swedish battle fleet retired to Sveaborg for repairs while the Swedish coastal fleet made for a strong defensive position at Svensksund. The Russian coastal fleet, led by Charles Henry of Nassau-Siegen started its attack against the Swedes on 9 July 1790, in what became known as the second battle of Svensksund, which ended in a decisive Swedish victory. Despite recent success, King Gustav III believed that his chances of successfully continuing the war were low. His government was also rapidly suffering from ever-increasing debt caused by the war expenses. On the other hand, Empress Catherine II became convinced that the Swedes would not be easily defeated and was anxious for peace in a war which was not important for her. The Russian Vice-Chancellor Bezborodko immediately agreed to negotiations, and the war was ended by the Treaty of Värälä on 14 August.

Aftermath

The Russo-Swedish War of 1788–1790 was, overall, mostly insignificant for the parties involved. Catherine II regarded the war against her Swedish cousin as a substantial distraction, as her land troops were tied up in the war against Turkey, and she was likewise concerned with revolutionary events unfolding in the Polish–Lithuanian Commonwealth (the 3 May Constitution) and in France (the French Revolution). The Swedish attack foiled the Russian plans of sending its navy into the Mediterranean to support its forces fighting the Ottomans, as it was needed to protect the capital, Saint Petersburg. The war solved Gustav III's domestic problems only briefly, as he was assassinated at the opera in Stockholm, in 1792.

7. *Abracadabra 9-11*

Seventeen years ago, four planes were hijacked by Islamic extremists in the United States. What happened to the passengers of United Airlines flight 93 on 9/11? One aircraft was deliberately crashed into the Pentagon near Washington DC, while two were flown into the World Trade Center in New York City. A fourth plane came down in Pennsylvania after passengers attempted to wrestle back control from the terrorists. The crashes, combined with the subsequent collapse of the two main towers of the World Trade Center, killed 2,996 people, making it the deadliest terrorist attack in recorded history. The blame was laid at the feet of al-

Qaeda and its founder, Osama Bin Laden, kick starting a series of major conflicts in the Middle East and Afghanistan, as well as America's largest and most costly manhunt of all time. However, to some, this is not the full story. Conspiracy theories have been an inevitable consequence of one of the most momentous events of the past century - one that shaped global geopolitics for the next two decades. Here are some of the most commonly repeated conspiracy theories.

It Was an Inside Job

By far the most widespread tale espoused by 9/11 conspiracy theorists - often referred to as 'Truthers' - is that the United States government either helped the attackers succeed or orchestrated the entire thing themselves. "Experts say part of the reason for the persistence of such conspiracy theories is the dissonance that results when people hear that a relatively small group of men using low-tech weapons caused such cataclysmic carnage," says the BBC. Truthers claim the attacks were staged to justify the subsequent wars in Afghanistan and Iraq, a theory peddled by Andreas von Bulow, a former research minister in the German government.

Controlled demolition

The BBC reports that investigations in the wake of the attack 'Made it clear that the tower structures were weakened by the inferno from the planes and felled by the weight of collapsing floors.' However, it adds, 'Even now some people refuse to believe this version of events.' A widely believed theory is that the towers were brought down in a controlled manner using demolition explosives. The Daily Express points out that some Truthers believe 'The towers would not have collapsed in the way they did if they were hit by aircraft.' In footage of the incident, the two main towers can be seen collapsing in on themselves floor by floor in a downward fashion with the debris landing over a relatively small footprint. However, the National Institute of Standards and Technology (NIST) concluded that a 'Very large quantity' of explosives would have been required to bring down the buildings, in an operation that could not have been hidden from the public.

Tower Seven

Also tied into this theory is the fate of Tower Seven of the World Trade Center, which also collapsed despite not being directly hit by any planes. The building, located next to the main towers, was hit by debris from the collapsing buildings and was damaged by fires which burned for seven hours until its collapse later the same evening. Theorists believe that the building may have been demolished as it contained clandestine Secret Service and CIA offices, science, and tech site Popular Mechanics reports. This theory was initially fueled by BBC News's live coverage of the event, during which reporter Jane Standley accidentally announced the collapse of the building 20 minutes before it occurred, blaming the mistake on conflicting reports from other news agencies.

Military stood down

In the 17 years since the attacks, speculation has been rife in regards to the immediate reaction of the US government during the first moments of the attack, once the planes were hijacked and it became clear a terrorist incident was occurring. In a hijacking situation in the US or Canada, standard procedure specifies that the North American Aerospace Defense Command (NORAD) will provide an 'Escort service' when requested by 'The FAA Hijack Coordinator' and will scramble jets to investigate the suspect aircraft. 'America seemingly had the most powerful air force in the world but failed to intercept any of the planes that day, which theorists believe is an indication of a government conspiracy to let the attacks go ahead,' the Daily Star says. However, later investigations specified that not only did the attackers turn off their aircrafts' transponders upon hijacking them, making them far harder to track on radar, but that NORAD was given nowhere near enough time to intercept the planes.

Pentagon missiles

The History Channel states that 'Early video footage and photos taken from the scene of the Pentagon attack did not seem to show much evidence of plane wreckage,' and that 'Theorists maintain this was evidence that the Pentagon was not struck by Flight 77, but by a missile or unmanned drone instead'. However, the US government has hit back at these claims, stating that 'The passenger and crew remains from American Airlines flight 77 were recovered at the

Pentagon crash site,' and that 'Eyewitness reports and photographs show plane debris at the Pentagon crash site'.

It was the work of a different agency

Perhaps a more outlandish theory is that the attack was perpetrated by neither the US government nor solely al-Qaeda, but that it was orchestrated - or at least funded - by a different, foreign government or organization. Fingers have been pointed at everyone from the government of Saudi Arabia to the Pakistani Intelligence Agency (ICI) to the Israeli Secret Service (Mossad). However, the 9/11 Commission Report - the final inquiry report on the incident - states: 'We have seen no evidence that any foreign government or foreign government official supplied any funding.'

'The threat posed by Iraq's weapons of mass destruction will be removed.'
- Secretary of Defense Donald Rumsfeld

In the wake of the 9//11 attacks, President George W. Bush and his administration deliberately led the American public to believe that the U.S. invasion of Iraq was justified because its government, due to the alleged possession of Weapons of Mass destruction, represented an 'Imminent threat' to the United States. The Bush administration later recanted, claiming it never told the public that Iraq was an 'Imminent' threat. (Read more for yourself about how the Bush administration did indeed report that Iraq had Weapons of Mass Destruction. Moreover, there is evidence that the Bush administration had drawn up plans to use military force to overthrow the regime of Saddam Hussein before the 9/11 attacks on the World Trade Center and the Pentagon. This article suggests that 9/11 was 'Seized on as a pretext for stampeding public opinion to accept US military intervention.'

Bush: Saddam Was Not Responsible For 9/11

George Bush last night admitted that Saddam Hussein had no hand in the 9/11 terror attacks, but he asked Americans to support a war in Iraq that he said was the defining struggle of our age. On a day of sorrow and remembrance, beginning with a moment of silence at Ground Zero and ending in a prime time TV address from the Oval Office, Mr. Bush tried to steel Americans for the long war ahead against al-Qaida which he described as an epochal struggle. His speech was also focused on November's congressional elections where the Republicans face a groundswell of discontent about the war in Iraq. The President conceded some crucial ideological ground, formally disavowing the neo-conservative accusation that Saddam had played a role in the attacks on September 11, 2001. But he was unapologetic about the decision to invade Iraq. 'I am often asked why we are in Iraq when Saddam Hussein was not responsible for the 9/11 attacks,' Mr. Bush said. 'The answer is that the regime of Saddam Hussein was a clear threat. My administration, the Congress, and the United Nations saw the threat - and after 9/11, Saddam's regime posed a risk that the world could not afford to take.'

'The world is safer because Saddam Hussein is no longer in power.'

The admission that Saddam had no connection to the attacks on the World Trade Centre and the Pentagon was a departure for a president who is famously averse to any expression of regret. But Mr. Bush, angling to regain the trust of US voters in his leadership of the war on terror, made another display of humility, admitting to other unspecified mistakes in the war on Iraq. However, the president brushed aside any idea of an early exit from Iraq, saying a withdrawal of US forces would hand a victory to al-Qaida. 'Whatever mistakes have been made in Iraq, the worst mistake would be to think that if we pulled out, the terrorists would leave us alone. They will not leave us alone. They will follow us,' Mr. Bush said. 'If we yield Iraq to men like bin Laden, our enemies will be emboldened ... they will gain a new safe haven ... and they will use Iraq's resources to fuel their extremist movement.' Last night's address crowned a series of speeches intended to retune the political agenda to the Republicans' traditionally strong suit: national security. Although the 2,600 US forces killed in Iraq now approaches the toll on September 11 and polls this month showed some 60% of Americans opposed to the administration's handling of the war in Iraq, Mr.

Bush continues to inspire confidence for his leadership on terrorism and in matters of national security. With that in mind, Mr. Bush moved last night to cast himself as a wartime leader in the mould of the two US presidents who presided over the epic battles of the last century. Both were Democrats: Franklin Roosevelt against Germany and Japan in the Second

World War, and Harry Truman in the cold war. Mr. Bush said he was leading a struggle that in these early days may seem just as daunting as the beginning of the Second World War. But he said that the war on terror was as much an existential struggle, and that America could not afford to lose heart now, despite the excessive cost in Iraq. "The war against this enemy is more than a military conflict. It is the decisive ideological struggle of the 21st century, and the calling of our generation," he said. 'If we do not defeat these enemies now, we will leave our children to face a Middle East overrun by terrorist states and radical dictators armed with nuclear weapons.'

9/11 Commission Report

Many respected and distinguished university professors have expressed significant criticism of the 9/11 Commission Report. A number even allege government complicity in the terrorist acts of 9/11. Below are the highly revealing public statements on this vital topic of over 100 university professors with links for verification and further investigation. The collective voices of these respected professors along with over 50 senior government officials, over 250 pilots and aviation professionals, and over 3,000 architects and engineers give credibility to the claim that the 9/11 Commission Report is tragically flawed. These dedicated individuals from across the political spectrum cannot be simply dismissed as irresponsible believers in some 9/11 conspiracy theory. Their sincere concern, backed by impeccable credentials, demonstrates that criticism of the 9/11 Commission Report is not only reasonable, but also in fact a patriotic duty. There are tons of reports and websites dedicated to 9/11 conspiracies, so let's move on.

8. *Who Do That Voodoo, You Do So…?*

Last week, iconic Portland bakery Voodoo Doughnut was the subject of a devastating rumor. Online conspiracy theorists alleged that the bakery is at the center of a child sex-trafficking ring. As internet-fueled rumors increasingly do, it all began with a YouTube video. Before diving in, it's important to note that this is a familiar story. In 2016, the internet watched in first confusion and then horror as a D.C.-area pizza shop became the target of a rumor regarding child abuse. The unraveling of the so-called Pizzagate conspiracy theories led one believer to bring a gun to the pizza shop in December 2016. Now, Voodoo Doughnut finds itself in an eerily similar position. The trendy doughnut shop opened in 2003 as a distinctly different sort of bakery. Instead of cutesy cakes with pink frosting and sprinkles, Voodoo has menu items like the 'Cock 'n balls' and the 'Maple blazer blunt.' Much of Voodoo's branding is dripping in double entendres: Its motto is 'The magic is in the hole;' its boxes bear the quip 'Good things come in pink boxes.' The original shop is located in Portland's gritty Old Town, a bright-pink bastion amid gray buildings and grayer skies. Voodoo went from something of a punk twist on a bakery to a tourist trap. There are now multiple locations, including shops in Denver and L.A., and the store's once grungy look has transformed into a more calculated take on the aesthetic. Lines wrap around its two buildings in Portland, the blaring pink brick becoming something of an Instagram playground for visitors.

Voodoo Doughnut is not without mild political affiliation. During the 2016 election, the shop featured donuts of Hillary Clinton and Bernie Sanders, and Voodoo owner Tres Shannon even delivered a box to Sanders's campaign staff during their stop in Portland. As to why Voodoo didn't make a Donald Trump donut, Shannon said: 'Trump supporters like doughnuts, too. I'd love to do a Donald Trump doughnut with flames and devil eyes, but I don't want to alienate an entire group of people.' He might have anyway. In a video published August 4 (which has since been removed), a man named Michael Whelan explained on the conspiracy YouTube channel Lift the Veil that he recently attended an event at Shannon's home, where he witnessed partygoers abusing children. Whelan even threw in a connection to Comet Ping Pong, the pizza shop at the center of Pizzagate, saying some employees of the pizzeria were at the Voodoo Doughnut party.

Lift the Veil, which has almost 63,000 subscribers, features videos about how the moon landing is rigged, the iPhone 7 can control your mind, and a handful of recent clips linking Macaulay Culkin to Pizzagate and now Donutgate (alternately spelled Doughnutgate). Shortly after the first Whelan interview, the story was picked up by Infowars and QAnon, the latter of which has only recently come into the collective consciousness. The New York Times explained QAnon as 'An interactive conspiracy community' following the reports of Q, who claims to be a government insider whose mission is to spill government secrets. QAnon followers gather IRL and online on YouTube, 4chan, and Reddit, among other sites. It is simultaneously a disparate, tangled franchise and also an incredibly well-connected and mobilized group. On August 10,

Lift the Veil interviewed Whelan again, and both Whelan and host Nathan Stolpman spent some time distancing themselves from any political affiliation in an attempt to prove their credibility. On August 13, Lift the Veil published a call to arms to the Portland police on its Twitch channel, and the rumors began picking up steam on Twitter. The Portland police are not investigating the allegations against Voodoo. Sergeant Peter Simpson told me via email 'that the bureau is aware of the information being shared on social media but at this time has not received any reports substantiating these allegations. Should an actual police report be filed, the Police Bureau would take appropriate investigative measures to follow-up on information regarding criminal activity.'

In the thick of the misinformation age, it is crucial to explore what exactly about both Pizzagate and Donutgate inflamed conspiracy theorists. For starters, Donutgate centers on child sex-trafficking and abuse. A recent Wired story explored this particular type of accusation as a viral hoax-spreading tactic: 'Alleging that your enemy preys upon children is an ancient propaganda tool that's been used by everyone from medieval Catholics to the Soviet Union. It's a powerful indictment because it trades on fundamental human fears. It's designed to otherize the opposition and sabotage any sympathy you might have for them. It's a ubiquitous tactic because it works.' The allegation has been levied against politicians, pizza places, and even Tom Hanks. Both '-gate'-suffixed hoaxes are also a product of current affairs. Conspiracy theories thrive in times of turmoil, argued Professor Jim Kline, who teaches psychology at Northern Marianas College. He authored a paper on this idea, exploring how throughout history, hoaxes have flourished in uncertain and hysteria-ridden periods—including two years ago. 'During the volatile 2016 U.S. presidential campaign, a flurry of conspiracy theories erupted, aimed at demonizing the candidates,' Kline wrote. 'One of the most outrageous conspiracy theories, involving child sex trafficking, ritual murder, and cannibalism, is examined to reveal its archetypal elements and relevancy to hard-wired taboos shared by all of humanity.' He is, of course, talking about Pizzagate. But he could've been talking about the medieval witch hunt or the early days of Christianity, two eras also plagued by what would today be labeled 'Fake news.'

These times can affect the psyche of conspiracy theorists and also encourage those already flirting with the idea of spreading outright lies into doing so with the intention of starting flame wars. 'All of us are susceptible to believing in outrageous plots and perversions. The human brain is an insatiable maker of cause-effect connections. Magical thinking remains prevalent, encouraging individuals to make connections between events that have no cause-effect relationships,' Kline told me via email. He goes on to explain that researchers have found that people who are more susceptible to conspiracy theories are often obsessed with religion or a god or a value system. They're also fearful of and angered by 'The omnipotence of elites,' characterizing them as inhuman (reptilian, even) or capable of inhuman acts (like child abuse). Kline agreed that what's happening with Voodoo seems to closely resemble Pizzagate. 'Conspiracy theorists choose their targets by creating faulty cause-effect relationships with controversial facts,' he said. 'In the case of Pizzagate, the theorists plowed through the emails of John Podesta, released by WikiLeaks, and began making faulty assumptions about what Podesta was actually referring to in some of his emails, specifically about his association with the manager of Comet Ping Pong.'

Conspiracy theorists connected those references to long-standing falsehoods claiming the Clintons are pedophiles, and the new conspiracy was born. 'As for #donutgate, it's the same 'logic," Kline said. 'There are many similarities between the two theories.' Beyond the nature of the allegations, Comet Ping Pong and Voodoo Doughnut share an aesthetic and attitude. Of Comet, the educational journal Committee for Skeptical Inquiry wrote, 'the place is a haven for artists, punks, gays, and other marginal groups: a tangible emblem of inclusivity, tolerance, and other progressive values that are threatening to the conspiracy-prone alt-Right.' Voodoo Doughnut shared these qualities and found itself similarly threatened. 'A legend such as Pizzagate can only spread if the regressive values it reflects nativism, racism, and xenophobia are alive and well and resonate with a sympathetic audience.' Two years post-Pizzagate, this remains true. Donutgate continues to live on Twitter, where some users are mocking it while others remain convinced. As with those of Comet Ping Pong, the Yelp and Facebook pages of Voodoo Doughnut have been flooded with outraged conspiracy believers.

Based on Twitter activity, Donutgate doesn't seem like it's yet reached the hysteria level of Pizzagate—but that doesn't mean it won't. Researchers from the Social Informatics Lab at Wellesley University studied Pizzagate and found that initially the story was a small hoax circulating on Twitter before a Turkish journalist elevated the news with a tweet, and then echo chambers formed to discuss it, causing it to go viral weeks after the initial rumor had first emerged. 'One might wonder whether there was any skepticism during the spreading of the rumor. The answer is no, because the rumor spread in a dense echo chamber, creating a perfect environment for growing the conspiracy theory,' the researchers wrote. Takis Metaxas, a Wellesley computer science professor who worked on the Pizzagate study, pointed out that Donutgate has the potential to grow if it likewise finds international media traction. "What made Pizzagate get bigger over time was that it was promoted by journalists outside the U.S. who wanted to believe it for their own reasons," he said. Metaxas says it helps that so far no 'Trusted agent' has picked up the Donutgate story, and the fact it sounds so much like Pizzagate, something that most people now recognize as a hoax is a factor in limiting its spread. In brief time, the theory could die down just as quickly as it surfaced.

Pizzagate: From Rumor, To Hashtag, To Gunfire in D.C.

December 6, 2016, what was finally real was Edgar Welch, driving from North Carolina to Washington to rescue sexually abused children he believed were hidden in mysterious tunnels beneath a neighborhood pizza joint. What was real was Welch a father, former firefighter and sometime movie actor who was drawn to dark mysteries he found on the Internet terrifying customers and workers with his -assault-style rifle as he searched Comet Ping Pong, police said. He found no hidden children, no secret chambers, and no evidence of a child sex ring run by the failed Democratic candidate for president of the United States, or by her campaign chief, or by the owner of the pizza place. What was false were the rumors he had read, stories that crisscrossed the globe about a charming little pizza place that features ping-pong tables in its back room. The story of Pizzagate is about what is fake and what is real. It's a tale of a scandal that never was, and of a fear that has spread through channels that did not even exist until recently.

Pizzagate — the belief that code words and satanic symbols point to a sordid underground along an ordinary retail strip in the nation's capital is possible only because science has produced the most powerful tools ever invented to find and disseminate information. What brought Welch to the District on a crisp Sunday afternoon in early December was a choking mix of rumor, political nastiness, technological change, and the intoxicating thrill that can come from running down a mystery. His actions Sunday in one of Washington's wealthiest neighborhoods reminded Americans that last month's election did not quite conclude the strangest political season in the nation's history. Welch did not shoot anyone in the disturbance on Connecticut Avenue NW, but he delivered a troubling message about the shattering of trust in a troubled time. On Oct. 28, FBI Director James B. Comey told Congress that he was reopening the investigation of Hillary Clinton's use of a private email server when she was secretary of state. New emails had been found on a computer belonging to disgraced former New York congressman Anthony Weiner, the estranged husband of top Clinton aide Huma Abedin. Two days later, someone tweeting under the ¬handle -@DavidGoldbergNY cited rumors that the new emails 'Point to a pedophilia ring and ¬@HillaryClinton is at the center.' The rumor was retweeted more than 6,000 times. The notion quickly moved to other social-media platforms, including 4chan and Reddit, mostly through anonymous or pseudonymous posts. On the far-right site Infowars, talk-show host Alex Jones repeatedly suggested that Clinton was involved in a child sex ring and that her campaign chairman, John Podesta, indulged in satanic rituals.

'When I think about all the children Hillary Clinton has personally murdered and chopped up and raped, I have zero fear standing up against her,' Jones said in a YouTube video posted on Nov. 4. 'Yeah, you heard me right. Hillary Clinton has personally murdered children. I just can't hold back the truth anymore.' Jones eventually tied his comments about Clinton to U.S. policy in Syria. A man from North Carolina fired shots in D.C. restaurant Comet Ping Pong on Sunday. He told authorities he came to check out a fake news story involving Hillary Clinton. A man from North Carolina fired shots in D.C. restaurant Comet Ping Pong on Sunday. He told authorities he came to check out a fake news story involving Hillary Clinton. The business reopened after Edgar Maddison Welch from North Carolina discharged his assault rifle at the popular Chevy Chase restaurant claiming he was there to investigate a fake news story on the Internet about a child sex ring. Nikki Kahn/the Washington Post. According to YouTube, that video has been viewed more than 427,000 times. Over the next couple of days, the wild accusations against Clinton gradually merged with a new raft of allegations stemming from WikiLeaks' release of Podesta's emails. Those emails showed that Podesta occasionally dined at Comet Ping Pong. On Nov. 7, the hashtag #pizzagate first appeared on Twitter. Over the next several weeks, it would be tweeted and retweeted hundreds or thousands of times each day. An oddly disproportionate share of the tweets about Pizzagate appear to have come from, of all places, the Czech Republic, Cyprus, and Vietnam, said Jonathan Albright, an assistant professor of media analytics at Elon University in North Carolina. In some cases, the most avid retweeters appeared to be bots, programs designed to amplify certain news and information.

'What bots are doing is really getting this thing trending on Twitter,' Albright said. 'These bots are providing the online crowds that are providing legitimacy.' Online, the more something is retweeted or otherwise shared, the more prominently it appears in social media and on sites that track "trending" news. As the bots joined ordinary Twitter users in pushing out Pizzagate-related rumors, the notion spread like wildfire. Who programmed the bots to focus on that topic remains unknown? On the Friday before the election, James Alefantis, who owns two restaurants on the same block in upper Northwest Washington, noticed something odd in his Instagram feed: a stream of comments calling him a pedophile. Upset, Alefantis told some of his young employees at Comet Ping Pong about the hateful comments, and they poked around online. They found rapidly burgeoning discussions on Reddit, 4chan and Instagram about a purported child sex ring operating out of their restaurant.

Alefantis, who grew up in an affluent section of the District, was no stranger to politics. He had held a fundraiser for the Clinton campaign at Comet. He'd had a relationship with David Brock, the erstwhile Clinton nemesis who had a midcareer political conversion and became a pro-Clinton advocate. And Alefantis had lots of customers and friends in liberal Democratic circles. When Alefantis opened Comet a decade ago, he'd had a run-in with an advisory neighborhood commissioner, a local official who did not like it when Comet put ping-pong tables on the sidewalk. That commissioner had warned that having game tables on the sidewalk might bring 'Rapes and murders' to the virtually crime-free neighborhood. Now, a decade later, a Washington Post column about that dispute was trending on Twitter. Somewhere out there, thousands of people were hungrily searching the Internet for anything remotely troubling about Comet Ping Pong. In the final days before the election, other shopkeepers on the block began to receive threatening phone calls and disturbing emails. Strangers from faraway places demanded to know about symbols on their shop windows or photos on their walls. Across from Comet, at the French bistro Terasol, co-owner Sabrina Ousmaal noticed a disturbing Google review of her restaurant that alleged that Terasol, too, was involved in a plot to abuse children. Then, more online comments appeared, focusing on a photo on Terasol's website that showed Ousmaal and her daughter posing with Clinton, who had eaten there several years earlier. The Internet sleuths also fixated on a heart logo that appeared on the restaurant's site as part of a fundraiser for St. Jude Children's Research Hospital, which Ousmaal, a cancer survivor, has supported for years.

'These maniacs thought that was a symbol of child pornography,' said her husband and business partner, Alan Moin. 'It's crazy.' The family removed the symbol from their site, but the online comments adapted to the new reality: Terasol must be hiding something. The anonymous calls increased. 'What can we do?' Ousmaal said. 'There is no basement. There is no tunnel. There is nothing.' Alefantis and other merchants were mystified: Where was this all coming from? Can't anyone make it stop? The merchants approached Facebook and Twitter and asked that disparaging, fictitious comments about them be removed. The shopkeepers said the replies they got advised them to block individual users who were harassing them. The owner of 4chan, Hiroyuki Nishimura, said in an email to The Post that 'Pizzagate reminds me that a country indicated [there were] stockpiles of weapons of mass destruction in Iraq and many people and countries were deceived. It is same old story.' Nishimura, a Japanese Internet entrepreneur, said the rumors about Comet could be false: 'Some people, who believe they do something good, may be deceived by false information.' But, he said, their motive was good; they 'did it for saving children.'

On Connecticut Avenue, the hate calls and death threats kept mounting. Surely, the shopkeepers thought, this will all go away after the election. On Election Day, Brittany Pettibone, a right-wing online activist in California who writes science-fiction novels with her twin sister, tweeted drawings of children under the label 'Sexualized children, child abuse, pools, and bondage.' She wrote that the images were 'A look inside Hillary Clinton's friend Tony Podesta's house.' Tony Podesta, a Washington lobbyist, is John's brother.

Pettibone attached the hashtag #PizzaGate. 'We need to expose this,' she wrote in another tweet. Dozens of commenters responded almost immediately. 'How do we make this VIRAL?' one wrote. Several of the most frequent and prominent purveyors of the Pizzagate rumors said they first learned about the supposed conspiracy from Pettibone's postings. 'I was one of the first,' Pettibone said in a brief conversation Tuesday. She said she would not take part in an interview: 'I'm uninclined to speak to mainstream media because during the election cycle, they made the right look like nut jobs because we suspected Hillary had a health issue, and it turned out she did.' For a few days after Donald Trump's victory, a relative calm returned to Comet. But along the block, merchants were hearing from all manner of strange callers. At Besta Pizza, owner Abdel Hammad got an urgent message from the company that maintains his website. A reviewer alleged that his shop's simple, pizza-shaped logo was a symbol of child pornography. Hammad, an Egyptian immigrant who voted for Trump, was stunned. "It's a slice of pizza,' he said. Hammad removed the image from his site but could not afford more than $2,000 to pay for new signs out front.

'Why did you change the website?' Anonymous callers screamed at him on the phone. 'We're going to put a bullet in your head,' one threatened.

Down the block, at Politics and Prose Bookstore, employees noticed tweets and other online posts that included them on a list of stores linked by underground tunnels that do not exist. The fact that one of the shop's co-owners, Lissa Muscatine, had worked as Clinton's speechwriter and adviser for two decades quickly became one more data point in the Pizzagate activists' conspiracy theory. The shop's phone rang off the hook with profane, abusive calls from across the country. Employees simply hung up, over and over. Frustrated and frightened, merchants along the block talked to the police. They called the FBI, which said the threats were a local matter. On Nov. 16, Jack Posobiec, a former Navy Reserve intelligence officer who had spent much of the previous year as a leader of a pro-Trump grass-roots organization, decided he'd had enough of just reading tweets and blog posts about the pizza place in his city. Posobiec, 31, had never eaten at Comet; he had never even heard of the place until he started reading about it on conservative, antigovernment media sites. 'I didn't pay much attention to it before Election Day because I was focused on the campaign,' he said. 'With that going on, who wants to talk about pizza?'

Now, with Trump elected, he read the posts more closely. Any story that accused Clinton, John Podesta and Brock of nefarious deeds deserved some investigation, he thought. He believed the Clinton campaign was 'Full of secrecy and deception.' It seemed reasonable to Posobiec that Podesta might have organized a sex ring in cahoots with Brock. But the only part of the scenario that was real was that Podesta had been known to eat pizza at Comet. This part is false: pictures purporting to show that symbols, such as butterflies and spirals, in signs at Comet and other shops were statements about pedophilia. Posobiec said he was curious and confused.

He and a friend decided to go have some pizza. They walked into Comet eight days after the election, sat down and ordered. Posobiec got the garlic knots. His friend got a beer. But they were not just hanging out. Posobiec was using his phone to broadcast his evening at Comet on Periscope, an app that allows users to stream video live.

'Part of the experience of living in 2016 is live, on-the-scene broadcasts,' he said. 'People have lost faith with government and the mainstream media being any real authority. After the Iraq War, after Benghazi, people are searching for other sources of information. If I can do something with Periscope and show what I'm seeing with my own two eyes, that's helpful.' Posobiec said he never made any disturbance inside Comet, but the restaurant's managers saw him take his camera into a back room where a child's birthday party was underway. It did not seem appropriate for a child's party to be broadcast on a stranger's Periscope feed. The manager asked two D.C. police officers who happened to be across the street to assist. Posobiec and his friend 'Were gently refused service and asked to leave,' said a person familiar with the restaurant's decision. Posobiec offered to pay for what he had ordered. The manager said it was on the house. Posobiec said he was not there to make a scene. 'I didn't have any preconceived notions,' he said. 'I wasn't sure. I thought I could just show it was a regular pizza place.' That evening, after Posobiec was ushered out of Comet, Pettibone tweeted: 'You're my hero for doing this, Jack. Never let go.'

On Twitter, the hashtag #pizzagate peaked in the hours after Posobiec's video appeared. On Nov. 22, Reddit closed its 'r/pizzagate' subreddit, a site forum focused on a particular topic. The site said it was concerned that Pizzagate posts were revealing private information about people at Comet and nearby stores. 'We don't want witch-hunts on our site,' it said. The decision sparked allegations of censorship from some people who were spreading the Pizzagate rumors. They moved their discussion to a similar site, Voat. On Sunday of Thanksgiving weekend, two men carrying protest signs showed up outside Comet. Alefantis went outside and offered the men coffee. They declined the offer. On the phone and online, threats poured in, with as many as 150 calls a day. The shopkeepers approached D.C. police for help. An officer advised them that the online rumormongering was constitutionally protected speech. Ousmaal replied in an email that she respects freedom of speech but that 'Derogatory libelous and hateful blogs and emails should not and cannot qualify.' The officer, Anthony Baker, responded, 'I don't have any more options to give unfortunately.' A D.C. police statement issued Tuesday said that the department 'Became aware of the fictional allegations contained in the false news story last month; however, despite postings of offensive language, we did not receive reports of any specific threats. Officers advised the staff to immediately report to police any threats made against the establishment or individuals.'

Earlier this fall, in Salisbury, N.C., Edgar Maddison Welch saw some friends doing drugs and he started preaching at them, aggressively. Danielle Tillman, 23, was the best friend of Welch's girlfriend. She said she had just taken acid when Welch got upset, chanting Jesus' name at her. 'He grabbed my hand and got in my face and was like, 'Let the demons out of her,' Tillman recalled. 'It was super weird.' Welch, known to friends as Maddison, had struck friends as a sweet young man who'd had trouble finding his way. He had dabbled in acting; his father ran a small movie studio out of his house and in writing and firefighting. None of it stuck. He liked to hike, long stretches out West, through mountain ranges, over rivers, into national forests. A few years ago, he told his hometown newspaper that through hiking, he had broken his addiction to the Internet. But Welch had another habit. He was arrested several times on drug-possession charges and his name appeared on a forged prescription, according to police records. He was convicted of marijuana possession and public drinking and was sent to a substance-abuse program. Friends say Welch, 28, in recent months grew far more outwardly religious. 'He sees himself as someone who is a protector,' said his friend Charles Dobson, 28. 'He is just a thrill-seeking guy.' On his Facebook page, Welch has posted biblical verses and psalms, some related to the end of days, along with photos of his two children. 'Only by your power can we push back our enemies,' one verse reads. 'Only in your name can we trample our foes.'

A few years ago, Welch told a longtime friend and former roommate, Dane Granberry, about stories he had read online describing miles of secret tunnels under the Denver airport. Welch, who had also been fascinated by conspiracy theories about the Sept. 11, 2001, attacks having been staged by the United States, had become obsessed with the tunnels idea, and spent long hours reading articles, watching videos, and searching for details. 'He's into doing his own research,' Granberry said. 'I don't think he has very much faith in the media, but none of us do.' Granberry said her friend needed to see things for himself. On Friday or Saturday, Welch drove to the District, according to court testimony. He showed up at Comet on Sunday about 3 p.m. Gareth Wade, 47, and Doug Clarke, 50, were sitting down for pizza and beer when a server told them that someone had walked in with a gun. As Welch passed by their table, he told them to vacate the building. They rushed out. Outside, dozens of D.C. police officers swarmed the area, evacuating businesses and blocking off streets. A police helicopter circled overhead. Inside Comet, Welch, armed with a Colt AR-15 assault rifle, a .38-caliber Colt revolver and a folding knife, fired his gun two or three times, police said. Welch, dressed in jeans, a T-shirt, and a hooded sweatshirt, remained inside for about 45 minutes, searching for underground vaults or hidden rooms, police said. At least one gunshot broke off a lock to a door. It led not to hidden sex workers but to a computer room. The bullet damaged a computer tower. At some point, a Comet worker who had been in the back freezer retrieving dough and had missed the earlier commotion heard the shots and emerged into the restaurant. Welch swung the rifle in his direction and the worker fled out onto the avenue, police said.

Finally, Welch responded to police calls for him to leave the building and surrender. He put his AR-15 on top of a beer keg and his revolver on a table. He came out with his hands up, following police commands to walk backward toward them. Welch was handcuffed, and Sgt. Benjamin Firehock asked him why he had done it. Welch said, according to the arrest affidavit, 'That he had read online that the Comet restaurant was harboring child sex slaves and that he wanted to see for himself if they were there. [Welch] stated that he was armed to help rescue them. [Welch] surrendered peacefully when he found no evidence that underage children were being harbored in the restaurant.' Within hours of Welch's arrest, online conspiracy theorists had already decided that he was not one of them. Some suggested he was a 'False Flag,' a government plant an enemy of their cause who had been used in an elaborate plot to conceal the truth. For years, people have made similar claims about everything from the 9/11 attacks (a government conspiracy to justify war, they say) to the Sandy Hook Elementary School shooting (a government conspiracy to justify gun control, they say). Now, in Welch's case, the conspiracy theorists insisted that the real news about his dangerous assault was, in fact, fake news. Comet Ping Pong reopened Tuesday night; the crowd was large and supportive. For some months now, Stefanie MacWilliams, 24, a stay-at-home mother of a 1-year-old boy in Ontario, has written nearly every day, usually about politics, for Planet Free Will, a conservative website based in the United States. Her husband, a mechanic, is the family's main breadwinner, but MacWilliams has been earning some money, too, writing a lot about how good Trump would be for America, and a fair amount about how bad President Obama was.

Starting in early November, MacWilliams noticed that stories based on the Podesta emails were making waves. A friend "who knows I'm interested in politics and shares conspiracy things with me" sent MacWilliams stories about Comet Ping Pong. Then she happened upon Posobiec's live stream from Comet. This, she decided, was a story. She told the Pizzagate tale in a YouTube video, on Twitter and on Planet Free Will. In the third paragraph of her story, MacWilliams wrote that 'We must stress that there is as yet no concrete evidence of any wrongdoing.' She thought she was being quite responsible. She had read Internet chatter about strange happenings and code words, and she thought this needed investigation. She was miffed that Posobiec had been escorted out of Comet when his video tour might have gotten to the bottom of the mystery. MacWilliams's story spread via social media. She became part of what she called a 'Worldwide citizen investigation' of Pizzagate. When she saw Reddit and Twitter react to the conspiracy theory, respectively shutting down a discussion forum and suspending the accounts of some users, she worried that a cover-up was underway.

'As soon as you tell people they can't talk about something, they're going to talk about it a whole lot more,' she said. MacWilliams calls herself a journalist, but she does not try to be '100 percent accurate,' either. She believes the beauty of the Internet is that people can crowdsource the truth. Eventually, what is real will emerge, she said. Pizzagate, she said, is "two worlds clashing. People don't trust the mainstream media anymore, but it's true that people shouldn't take the alternative media as truth, either." The lack of stories about Pizzagate in the mainstream press meant that the back channels of the Internet would step into the breach. But how does this end? What could constitute proof that there is no conspiracy? Some Pizzagate buffs want a video tour showing that there are no secret rooms or tunnels. Others say they would need more. MacWilliams remains caught up in the thrill of the chase. 'There is a camaraderie to it,' she said. 'It is like sitting around with your friends saying, 'What really happened to JFK?' It is like a giant game, especially nowadays when you can crowdsource thousands of emails and figure out what's going on. It's like a real-life Kennedy assassination where all the stuff is at your fingertips, and it's happening today." When the New York Times mentioned her site on Nov. 21 as a source of fake news, MacWilliams got a little angry, but she also had reason to smile: The traffic on Planet Free Will soared as never before. The story is everywhere. Some Americans especially keen on Pizzagate find themselves being accused of being Russian stooges, or of working for hacker's intent on disrupting the American political process.

Did President Trump Endorse Q Info On Secret Indictments Of Pedophile Network?

On November 25, President Donald Trump re-tweeted an alternative news article lauding many of the accomplishments achieved during his administration so far. The site he retweeted, MAGAPILL soon crashed as many of the President's 42 million followers went there to learn more. What is significant about the article and site he retweeted is that it featured a November 19 story about an alleged whistleblower called Q, who has been releasing a lot of information about what is really going on behind the scenes in Washington DC. In retweeting the story and link to the MAGAPILL site, which he lauded as a genuine news site in contrast to 'Fake news' sites, was Trump indirectly endorsing Q's information as genuine? If so, then the ramifications are enormous. First, let's begin with Trump's re-tweet. The article he referred to is titled 'President Donald Trump's Accomplishment List' and an archived copy is available here. It lists his accomplishments across a broad spectrum of political, economic, and national security areas. What is arguably more significant is that at the very top of this article was a large banner linking to a featured story 'Q Clearance Patriot: The Storm and the Awakening: follow the white rabbit.' The Q material discusses an enormous number of topics such as secret indictments of the political elite, current events in Saudi Arabia and Trump's national security briefings by figures such as NSA Director, Admiral Michael Rogers. He preface found on the MAGAPILL site mentions the enormity of the information released in this article and provides some highlights of the released material. Among the more interesting is the view that rather than former FBI Director Robert Mueller conducting a serious investigation into the links between Russia and the Trump Presidential campaign, Mueller is really investigating a corrupt pedophile network that has secretly monopolized power in the US.

The Special Counsel is not corrupt. Let me say that again, the special counsel, headed by Mueller, is not running a corrupt investigation. He's doing the job properly under the guise of investigating the Trump team. This has lowered the guard of the true targets because nobody anticipated it, including the media. There are an unprecedented number of sealed indictments across the nation right now that have not been executed, over 1100 sealed indictments at last glance.

Many high level officials will soon be arrested to actually 'Swamp 'beyond what anyone thought was possible. Once the corruption and the 'type of corruption' is revealed to the American people, it will trigger 'The Awakening.' This event will be something unlike anything you've ever witnessed, Americans will unite behind Trump and his administration for cleaning house. There have been persistent rumors of hundreds of secret Grand Jury indictments that are on the verge of being unleashed. These rumors have been circulating for weeks and a number of alternative media figures have closely analyzed some of the Q material that refers to them. Among these figures is Jordan Sather, whose "Destroying the Illusion" YouTube channel has gained over 65,000 subscribers due to his cogent analyses of the Q material and other topical issues. Sather released a video on November 26 analyzing Trump's retweet of the MAGAPILL article and was the first to raise the possibility that Trump was indirectly endorsing the legitimacy of the Q material.

While the Q material is quite extensive, its core claim that Mueller, as Special Counsel, has really been investigating a corrupt pedophile network, rather than the alleged Russia Trump campaign connection, is very significant. Of special interest is Mueller's background as a former US Marine Corps Captain (1968-1971) who was highly decorated for his bravery during the Vietnam War. It's worth noting that the Secretary of Defense, James Mattis is a retired four star USMC general, as is Trump's Chief of Staff, John Kelly. Given the deep loyalty of former USMC personnel to their military service (semper fidelis – always faithful), it's very possible that Mueller is secretly following an agenda sanctioned by Mattis and Kelly. We also need to keep in mind claims that on November 18, a number of USMC helicopters allegedly buzzed the CIA's Headquarters in Langley, Virginia. While initial reports erroneously referred to the CIA's HQ being stormed by the USMC, a former FBI agent, Hal Turner confirmed through credible sources that the helicopters had only 'Buzzed' the CIA HQ for roughly 30 minutes. Did nearby residents in McLean suddenly notice a large number of loud helicopters overhead, moving toward or from the area of the CIA?

The repeated answer to that question has been 'Yes.' Many (very many) residents of McLean, VA have confirmed they found themselves hearing large numbers of loud aircraft overhead on Saturday, and that the sounds lasted more than 30 minutes! The intent was clear, the USMC was threatening the CIA's clandestine services division to get on board with the Trump administration or else. This is not the first time that the CIA has been intimidated by a US President threatening to unleash the US military against its facilities. In 1958, President Eisenhower threatened the CIA's Area 51 facilities in Nevada with invasion by the US First Army stationed at Colorado if the CIA did not fully disclose all its classified programs there. In a May 2013 video interview, a former CIA operative revealed what he heard Eisenhower tell his boss to relay to the mysterious MJ-12 Committee in charge of the Area 51 facility, for which the CIA provided operational security: 'We called the people in from MJ-12, from Area 51 and S-4, but they told us that the government had no jurisdiction over what they were doing…. I want you and your boss to fly out there. I want you to give them a private message…. I want you to tell them, whoever is in charge, I want you to tell them that they have this coming week to get into Washington and to report to me. And if they don't, I'm going to get the First Army from Colorado. We are going to go over and take the base over. I don't care what kind of classified material you got. We are going to rip this thing apart.'

This takes us finally to the testimony of Michael Gerloff, who has served with the USMC, US Army Rangers and Seattle Police over a period spanning 20 years from 1978 to 2001. Gerloff says that he was part of a secret USMC intelligence group established by President Eisenhower in the early 1950's that continues to the present day. According to Gerloff, the USMC was given special responsibility by Eisenhower to act as an institutional bulwark against systemic corruption that threatened the US Constitution and the Republic. This corruption stemmed from the creation of secret space programs that worked closely with major defense contractors at remote locations such as Area 51. What we are witnessing now with over a thousand secret indictments allegedly generated by Mueller, Trump's USMC/Navy dominated administration, USMC helicopters buzzing CIA HQ and Gerloff's claims, is that we are on the verge of major revelations about deep systemic corruption that has plagued the US. The role of the USMC in taking the lead in cleaning up this systemic corruption is slowly being revealed. Trump's retweet of the MAGAPILL article appears to be an endorsement of the view that secret indictments established by Mueller are on the verge of being disclosed, thereby triggering many further revelations that will awaken the general public. In the meantime, Trump is encouraging those among the American public who are ready, to go down the rabbit hole to learn the truth about systemic corruption, powerful pedophile networks, and secret space programs.

9. *Shoot the Ball Coop*

The Granddaddy of American Conspiracy Theorists

Decades before QAnon, 'False Flags,' 'Crisis actors' and Alex Jones, there was Milton William Cooper. An exclusive excerpt from 'Pale Horse Rider' by Mark Jacobson Even a broken clock is right twice a day; that's what they say about people who are supposed to be crackpots. It's the idea that there is a moment in time when even the most outlandish contention, the most eccentric point of view, the most unlikely person, somehow lines up with shifting reality to produce, however fleetingly, what many perceive to be the truth. But to accept the notion of the "broken clock" is to embrace the established, rationalist parameters of time, 24 hours a day, day after day, years arranged in ascending numerical order, decade after decade, eon upon eon, a forever forward march to an undetermined future, world without end, amen. For some people, people like the late Milton William (Bill) Cooper, collector of clocks, time did not work that way. American shortwave talk-show host, author, and lecturer during the millennial period of the late 1980s onward to the advent of the current century, Bill Cooper chose not to adhere to the mandated linear passage of existence. For Cooper, the entire span of time, the beginning, the middle, and the end was all equally important, but there could be no doubt where the clock had stopped. A minute to midnight that was Bill Cooper's time. This wasn't because Cooper, a voracious reader and self-schooled savant, was anti-science or anti-intellectual. He believed in evolution, and, like his philosophical hero Aristotle, Cooper treasured the supremacy of knowledge and its acquisition. He had a massive collection of jazz records. But somewhere along the way, dating at least back to his service as river-boat captain in a hot zone during the Vietnam War, Cooper came to believe that something wasn't right. What he'd always accepted as truth, what he was willing to give his life to protect, wasn't true at all.

It was part of a vast web of lies that stretched back through the centuries, contrived to rob the common man of his unalienable right to know the reality of his place on the planet. It was a deep-seated conviction that became an obsession and a potent bridge to the current environment, where no one seems to believe anything they're told, where long-respected bastions of truth are thought to be so corrupt as to be what Donald Trump calls 'The enemy of the people.' The idea of 'Fake news,' along with personages like Alex Jones and QAnon (notably influenced by Cooper) are not unprecedented in American life. But none of them would have manifested as they have without Bill Cooper as an immediate predecessor. Cooper sought to dramatize the compounding urgency of the moment on The Hour of the Time, the radio program he broadcast from 1992 until November 2001, his resonant, sometimes folksy, sometimes fulminating voice filling the airwaves via satellite hookups and shortwave frequencies. Nearly every episode of The Hour of the Time began the same way, with the show's singular opening, one of the most arresting sign-ons in radio history. It starts with a blaring air-raid siren, a blast in the night. This is followed by a loud, distorted electronic voice: 'Lights out!' comes the command, as if issued from a penitentiary guard tower. 'Lights out for The Hour of the Time! Lights out for the curfew of your body, soul, and mind.' Dogs bark, people shriek, the bleat of the still half-sleeping multitudes. There is the sound of tramping jackbooted feet, growing louder, closing in. 'It's Past Time': Rep. Barbara Lee on Black Women in Democratic Power what's going on with This Julian Assange Indictment?

Now is the time, a minute to midnight, 60 seconds before enslavement, one last chance. Some citizens will rise, if only from not-quite-yet-atrophied muscle memory. They will shake themselves awake as their forebears once did at Lexington and Concord, heeding Paul Revere's immortal call. They will defend their homes, families, and the last shreds of the tattered Constitution, the most close-to-perfect political document ever produced. The vast majority, however, won't even get out of bed. Some will cower under the covers, but most will simply roll over and go back to sleep. They slept through life, so why not sleep through death? This is how it will be at a minute to midnight, according to Bill Cooper. At the End of Time, a broken clock is always right. Reputed instances of Cooper's prescience are legion.

An early roundup of these forecasts can be found in the August 15th, 1990, edition of the newsletter of the Citizens Agency for Joint Intelligence (CAJI), an organization Cooper created, billing it as 'The largest clandestine intelligence-gathering agency in the world.' Published on a dot-matrix printer, carrying the tagline 'Information, not money, will be the power of the nineties,' Cooper ran an article entitled 'Every Prediction Has Come True.' He listed 16 of his most recent prognostications that had come to pass "or will soon be fulfilled.' These included the disclosure that 'The CIA and the military are bringing drugs into the United States to finance their black projects.' Cooper also predicted that 'The rape of the Savings and Loans by the CIA is only the tip of the iceberg. At least 600 banks will go under in the next two years.' The current monetary structure, Cooper said, 'Will be replaced by a cashless system that will allow the government to monitor our every action by computer. If you attempt to stay out of the system you will not be allowed to buy, sell, work, get medical care, or anything else we all take for granted.'

Cooper continued to make predictions in his watershed book, Behold a Pale Horse. Published in 1991 by Light Technology, a small New Age–oriented house then located in Sedona, Arizona, Behold a Pale Horse is something of a publishing miracle. With an initial press run of 3,500 (500 hardcover, 3,000 paperback), by the end of 2017, the book was closing in on 300,000 copies sold. 'Behold a Pale Horse is the biggest-selling underground book of all time, Cooper often told his audience. Yet sales figures represent only a fraction of the book's true reach. For one thing, as its author often bragged, Behold a Pale Horse routinely topped lists of the most-shoplifted books in the country. To this day, Barnes & Noble stores keep BAPH, as it is sometimes called, behind the cashier's counter to reduce pilferage. This was because, as one clerk at the Barnes & Noble near my house in Brooklyn told me, 'That book has a habit of walking out all by itself.' There is also the captive audience. Since its release, Behold a Pale Horse has been among the most popular 'Prison books' (in that prisoners read them), a distinction it shares with Robert Greene's 'The 48 Laws of Power'.

During the crack epidemic of the 1990s, it was not unusual for a single copy of Behold a Pale Horse to go through enough hands in the cellblocks of places such as Attica to break the book's spine. Some of Cooper's best-known predictions appear in Behold a Pale Horse, which runs a densely typed 500 pages. Eight years before the Trench Coat Mafia murders at Columbine High School, Cooper wrote: "The sharp increase of prescriptions of psychoactive drugs like Prozac and Ritalin to younger and younger children will inevitably lead to a rash of horrific school shootings." These incidents, he said, "will be used by elements of the federal government as an excuse to infringe upon the citizenry's Second Amendment rights." For many, including those who would later claim that the seemingly endless series of school shootings were part of a plot by gun-control advocates to take away America's weapons, Cooper's words took on the air of prophesy.

But Bill Cooper never claimed to be a prophet. He never imagined himself in the line of Ezekiel, Jeremiah, and Daniel, the ancient Hebrew seers carried off by King Nebuchadnezzar II to a 70-year captivity in Babylon. Neither did Cooper compare himself to John, an exile on the island of Patmos, author of the Book of Revelation, which is where the title Behold a Pale Horse comes from. The phrase appears in chapter 6, verse 8, in which John is witness to the opening of the Seven Seals, the preview of God's secret plan to once again destroy the world prior to its rebirth as the Kingdom of Jesus Christ. When the Fourth Seal was revealed, John wrote, 'and I looked, and behold a pale horse: and his name that sat on him was Death, and Hell followed with him.' 'I am no Prophet, I am no Nostradamus, I have no crystal ball,' Cooper proclaimed. He was 'Just an ordinary guy.'

There was nothing supernatural about his predictions. Anyone could do it. It was all in the methodology, summed up in what he called his 'Standard admonition,' the one rule every prospective Hour of the Time listener had to obey, 'No matter what.' 'You must not believe anything you hear on this show,' Cooper declared. Nor was the listener to believe anything they heard from any other shortwave host, or Larry King Live, Dan Rather, George Bush, Bill Clinton, or anyone else in this entire world, whether you hear it on radio, on television, or from the lips of someone standing right in front of you. 'Listen to everyone, read everything, believe nothing until you, yourself, can prove it with your own research,' Cooper told the audience. 'Only free-thinking, intelligent people who are prepared to root through all the crap and get at the truth should be listening to this show. Everyone else should just turn off their radio. We don't even want you to listen. "Listen to everyone. Read everything, believe nothing . . . until you can prove to yourself whether it is true or false or lies between the many shades of gray. If you don't do this, if you cannot do this, or are just plain too lazy to do this, then I can assure you that you will march into the New World Order as a docile slave." Then Cooper made the sound of a sheep. 'Baaa! Baaa! Baaaing all the way.'

Cooper's most famous prediction was made during the June 28th, 2001, broadcast of The Hour of the Time. A little past his 58th birthday and drinking heavily, Cooper was doing his program from a studio he'd built in the den of his house at 96 North Clearview Circle, atop a hill in the small White Mountains town of Eagar, Arizona, 15 miles from the New Mexico line. 'Can you believe what you have been seeing on CNN today, ladies and gentlemen?' Cooper asked the Hour of the Time audience that evening. 'Supposedly, a CNN reporter found Osama bin Laden, took a television camera crew with him, and interviewed him and his top leadership, lieutenants, and his colonels, and generals…in their hideout!.' 'Now don't you think that's kind of strange, folks?' Cooper asked with his signature chuckle. Because the largest intelligence apparatus in the world, with the biggest budget in the history of world, has been looking for Osama bin Laden for years, and years, and years, and can't find him! 'But some doofus jerk-off reporter with his little camera crew waltzes right into his secret hideout and interviews him!'

This meant one of two things, Cooper told the audience. Either 'Everyone in the intelligence community and all the intelligence agencies of the United States government are blithering idiots and incompetent fools, or they're lying to us.' The fact was, Cooper told the audience, no one in the U.S. intelligence services was really looking for Osama bin Laden. They knew where he was. They had since the beginning of the Soviet invasion of Afghanistan. Bin Laden, along with his entire family, was a wholly owned subsidiary of the Central Intelligence Agency. 'They created him. They're the ones funding him. They supported him to make their new utopian worlds…and he has served them well.' There were rumors floating around the mass media that bin Laden was planning attacks on the United States and Israel, but this was just subterfuge, Cooper said. 'If Osama bin Laden is an enemy of Israel, don't you think the Mossad would have taken care of that a long time ago?' Cooper asked. Something else was in the wind. There was no other reason for the government to allow the CNN report but to further stamp bin Laden's bearded, pointy face upon the collective American mind-set. Bogeyman of the moment, the Saudi prince was being readied for his close-up.

'I'm telling you to be prepared for a major attack!' Cooper declared. The target would be a large American city. 'Something terrible is going to happen in this country. And whatever is going to happen they're going to blame on Osama bin Laden. Don't you even believe it?' Two and a half months later, on September 11th, 2001, after two commercial airliners flew into the

Twin Towers of the World Trade Center in a cataclysm that killed 2,996 people, including 343 New York City Fire Department personnel, Cooper's prediction came to pass. By the time Cooper got on the air that morning, the towers had already fallen. Several hours passed before the name Osama bin Laden surfaced on the BBC feed Cooper was monitoring. The British station, which Cooper regarded as marginally more reliable than the American networks, was doing an interview with the former Israeli Prime Minister General Ehud Barak and Richard Perle, chairman of George W. Bush's Defense Policy Board Advisory Committee. Widely known as the Prince of Darkness, in part for his Reagan-era support of Edward Teller's $100 billion Strategic Defense Initiative, known as Star Wars, Perle said the attacks on New York and Washington were 'clearly an act of war.'

'All our Western civilization is under attack,' Barak put in. The interviewer asked Perle if he thought the United States would be justified in firing cruise missiles at Kabul, the capital of Afghanistan. Perle, who along with fellow neocons Dick Cheney, Paul Wolfowitz, and Donald Rumsfeld would soon push hard for the reinvasion of Iraq, answered in the affirmative. The Afghani authorities had 'Allowed Osama bin Laden to operate in their territory,' Perle said. That alone was reason enough for a military strike. Bin Laden was involved, no doubt about it. Yes, Barak agreed, there was 'Every reason to believe' bin Laden was behind the attack. It was then Cooper interrupted the transmission, shouting, 'How do they know who did it? If the United States government had no warning like they say, if they didn't know who was going to mount these attacks, and there are no survivors from the people in these planes, how do they know Osama bin Laden is behind it?'

So, yet again, Cooper was right. Events were transpiring exactly as his research had indicated. Osama bin Laden, the Saudi mama's-boy prince, was about to be officially blamed for the most spectacular foreign attack on America since Pearl Harbor. Not that Cooper was gloating about his latest successful prediction. What had happened in New York City thousands dead, their bodies crushed beneath tons of twisted rubble, a toxic cloud rising over the metropolis was just the beginning of a new torrent of death. On the radio feed, Perle and Barak were discussing logistics; Afghanistan would be a target, possibly, Iraq as well. 'How can they determine that they should bomb Afghanistan?' Cooper shouted with alarm. 'Who are we going to be bombing? The terrorists, or the innocent people of Kabul?' Cooper made another prediction. 'Folks, I can assure you that 72 hours from now we will be at war. We will be bombing two or maybe three countries…. Because that's how it works. When governments are attacked, they lash out. Thousands of people who had nothing whatsoever to do with what is happening at the World Trade Center and the Pentagon are going to die.'

'Nothing will be the same after today,' Cooper said grimly. "Get ready for it, folks, because that's what you're going to be hearing in the next weeks and months on radio and television: Nothing will be the same after today…. Because I'll tell you, ladies, and gentlemen, that's what the people who really did this want you to think, that nothing, nothing, will be the same after today. 'And you know what? They're right. They're telling the truth about that. Within weeks the Congress will pass draconian legislation aimed at restricting the rights of American citizens. You're going to have surveillance cameras on every street corner. You think your phones are being tapped now, just wait. No one is going to gain from this except a very small group of people. Everyone else will lose. No one will lose more than the American people.' This would be the most grievous casualty of the 9/11 attacks, Cooper told the audience, the nation itself, the America that could have been. Freedom, the most elusive of qualities, best distilled in the inspired documents of the Constitution and the Bill of Rights, had been dealt a fatal blow, 'From now on, freedom will be whatever the law allows you to do.' That wasn't going to stop him, Cooper told listeners. He'd stay behind his microphone up in his hilltop studio. He'd keep sending out The Hour of the Time, speaking truth to the ultimate power, if it were the last thing he did. It was soon after that Cooper's final prediction came true. 'They're going to kill me, ladies and gentlemen,' he told the audience. 'They're going to come up here in the middle of the night, and shoot me dead, right on my doorstep.' And, around midnight on November 5th, 2001, less than two months after the 9/11 attacks, that's exactly what happened.

10. Out Of Site Mutha' Fuckin' Out Of Mind

SECRET PRESIDENTIAL MEMORANDUM ISSUED TO DECLASSIFY ANTI-AGING & FREE ENERGY TECHNOLOGIES

According to secret space program whistleblower, Corey Goode, President Donald Trump issued a highly classified Memorandum soon after his January 20th inauguration ordering the release of group of classified patents concerning anti-aging and health, along with free energy technologies. The Top Secret Memorandum was sent to the Department of Defense and the Intelligence Community, and due to its classification status it will not be accessible to major media for reporting. The information received from Goode comes from a senior official in an interagency secret space program comprising the USAF, NRO, NSA, and DIA which he describes as the Military Industrial Complex Secret Space Program (MIC-SSP). The official, whom he calls "Sigmund," is investigating Goode's claims and conducting an "information exchange" with Goode in the process (see Part One). On March 16, Goode briefed me about his ongoing meetings with Sigmund and/or his two subordinates. The information provided by Goode was originally slated for release in an article, "Endgame III," as the sequel to the popular Endgame II article and video. However due to the urgency of releasing this information without delay, it was passed on to me to get it out now.

In one of his 'Meetings' with Sigmund (and/or his subordinates) in late January, Goode was told about Trump issuing a Presidential Memorandum to declassify over 1000 patents from a pool of over 5000. Most of the 1000 patents deal with anti-aging and health technologies, yet some deal with material science and biochemistry and a few involve free energy inventions. These technologies are widely used in a number of secret space programs, and the patents dealing with these have been repressed under national security orders. The USPTO has issued Federal Regulations that govern when patents are classified on the grounds of national security, and subsequently withheld from the general public: Whenever the publication or disclosure of an invention by the publication of an application or by the granting of a patent is, in the opinion of the head of an interested Government agency, determined to be detrimental to national security, the Commissioner for Patents at the United States Patent and Trademark Office (USPTO) must issue a secrecy order and withhold the grant of a patent for such period as the national interest requires. A patent will not be issued on the application as long as the secrecy order is in force. If a secrecy order is applied to an international application, the application will not be forwarded to the International Bureau as long as the secrecy order is in force.

When a Department of Defense entity or a member of the Intelligence Community consider a patent to be a threat to national security, then the Patents Commissioner will issue a secrecy order preventing the patent from being publicly released. The current number of patents that have been classified are approximately 5700 according to the U.S. Patent and Trademark Office (USPTO), which matches the information given to Goode by Sigmund. As the above table shows, the number of secret patents that are declassified each year has averaged roughly 0.5 percent annually. Goode learned that the Pentagon and Intelligence agencies told Trump it would take 10 years to release them, but Trump told them to get it done within two to three years. Evidence for Trump taking the bold step of declassifying secret patents as quickly as possible can be found in his inauguration speech. Towards the end of his speech, Trump uttered one sentence that contained his most developed vision of the future for America and its citizenry, which would result from the kind of declassification Memorandum Goode was told about. Trump said:

We stand at the birth of a new millennium, ready to unlock the mysteries of space, to free the earth from the miseries of disease, and to harness the energies, industries, and technologies of tomorrow. If Trump succeeds in having over 1000 of these declassified over the next two to three years, it will represent 20% of the total. This would be a staggering average yearly increase of up to 2000 percent over previous years. Trump's Secret Memorandum to the Department of Defense and the Intelligence Community is aimed at ultimately having the Patents Commissioner, who is currently Drew Hirshfeld, lift the secrecy orders issued by his predecessors on the 1000 patents marked for declassification. Furthermore, monitoring the USPTO's records of Secrecy Orders Rescinded for 2017, will offer a concrete means of verifying that Trump did indeed issue such a memorandum. According to Goode, most of the secret patents ordered to be declassified deal with anti-aging and health. In particular, he said that telomere technology is very advanced in classified projects and can enable healthy cell reproduction without aging and disease. This is consistent with the claims of retired aerospace engineer, William Tompkins, who says that in early 2016, he was told by Navy officials that anti-aging technologies would be released in a two year period. Tompkins was involved in the original corporate development of anti-aging technologies during his time as a systems engineer at TRW from 1967 to 1971. These technologies were subsequently used in secret space programs, which routinely use personnel for '20 year and back' programs that Goode and other whistleblowers claim they were subjected to.

The patents for these technologies developed at TRW are likely part of the 1000 patents marked for declassification under Trump's Memorandum. Furthermore, Tompkins identified the San Diego headquarters of the Scripps Research Institute as being heavily involved in the study of anti-aging technologies, and it will be a major player in releasing these classified technologies to the public. Support for Goode and Tompkins' testimony regarding classified anti-aging technologies comes from geneticists who have recently publicly identified the genes that control the aging process. In stunning experiments, the results of which have been released in peer reviewed scientific journals, geneticists have demonstrated that they were able to reverse the aging process to varying degrees of success. The lead genetic scientist in publicly announced age reversal studies is Dr. David Sinclair, who discussed in a November 2014 interview the results of his genetic experiments first conducted on mice: We've discovered genes that control how the body fights against ageing and these genes, if you turn them on just the right way, they can have very powerful effects, even reversing ageing – at least in mice so far…

We fed them a molecule that's called NMN, and this reversed ageing completely within just a week of treatment in the muscle, and now we're looking to reverse all aspects of ageing if possible. Declassifying anti-aging patents would revolutionize the medical and health industry, which have already made significant inroads into understanding and reversing the aging process. Another industry that would be revolutionized by Trump's Secret Memorandum is the energy sector. Declassifying free energy inventions would revolutionize the automotive and aviation industries and make it easier for private industries such as SpaceX to develop far more efficient and advanced space propulsion technologies. Most importantly, the release of free energy inventions will effectively end the power and influence of the oil industry. In a surprising case of synchronicity, one of the oil lobby's biggest supporters, David Rockefeller, died on March 20 at the age of 101. Rockefeller was notably known for his staunch support of maintaining the secrecy status quo.

The importance of Trump's Memorandum to the Pentagon and Intelligence Community to declassify secret patents cannot be underestimated due to the revolutionary changes it would usher in. Opposition to such changes helps explain the rumors that Trump would not be allowed to take the office of the President despite the 2016 election result. According to the information received by Goode from Sigmund, Trump was going to be assassinated before or during his Presidential Inauguration. However, the Pentagon in response threatened to launch an open military coup if Trump was assassinated. The CIA, NSA, and Department of Homeland Security (DHS) in particular were warned that they would be surrounded by U.S. military personnel, and that top CIA, NSA, and DHS leaders would end up being arrested for facilitating the assassination.

Goode estimates that approximately 80% of the personnel in these civilian intelligence agencies are Cabal (Deep State) controlled, while approximately 50% of the FBI is under 'White Hat' control. He was told that these agencies refuse to give the same briefings as given to President Reagan (see Part 1) about the MIC SSP, and the handful of alien groups known to them. The impending declassification of over a thousand secret patents will clearly help Trump succeed in revitalizing the U.S. manufacturing industry and providing millions of jobs. It appears that the release of these patents is timed to coincide with impending disclosures regarding discoveries in Antarctica, where advanced technologies have allegedly been discovered, and which will also have a revolutionary impact on a number of major industries.

A Shadowy and Controversial Secret Club Meets in the California Woods Every Year — and At Least 5 Us Presidents Were Members

- Bohemian Grove is the Sonoma County, California campground where the Bohemian Club meets annually.

- The Bohemian Club, a San Francisco-based private club that has counted a number of US presidents among its members, is a controversial group.

- The club's reported rituals and secretive status have spawned sinister internet rumors.

• But experts and insiders conclude Bohemian Grove goings-on are no more or less troubling than a group of extremely wealthy men letting loose in the forest.

Bohemian Grove is a place where strange things happen. In June and July, some of the wealthiest and most powerful men in the country flock to the redwood grove in Sonoma County, California. They're all members of the Bohemian Club, a private, all-male club that's counted US presidents, military officials, artists, and business leaders as members. The Bohemian Grove grounds are dotted with camps bearing strange names, 'Mandalay,' 'Lost Angels,' 'Isle of Aves,' and 'Silverado Squatters.' Guests are welcome, but women and minors must vacate the premises at night. A hollow concrete owl towers over the Grove's artificial lake, where prominent individuals often visit to give lakeside talks on pressing public policy matters. And, during the first weekend of the summer encampment, robed figures sacrifice an effigy as part of a ritual meant to banish all worries from the gathered members. Over the years, a number of those gathered club members have happened to be US presidents. Here's a look at the club's background and at the presidents who Business Insider could confirm were in fact Bohemian Club members:

The Bohemian Club is almost 150 years old

The traditions go back to the earliest days of the private gentleman's club, which sprang up in 1872 in San Francisco. The Bohemian Club began renting the campground for an annual retreat, before purchasing it outright in 1899. 'You come upon it suddenly,' poet and club member Will Irwin wrote of the Grove in 1908. 'One step and its glory is over you.' Originally a cluster of newspaper writers who'd adopted a 'Bohemian lifestyle,' the club expanded overtime to include artists, businessmen, military leaders, and politicians. While the club has diversified in terms of its members' professions, women have been barred from joining since its inception. A 1978 lawsuit did result in the Bohemian Club being required to hire female employees, however. So how do you land a coveted spot in the approximately 2,500-member club?

Vanity Fair reported that you either need to snag invitations from several members or languish for decades on the club's waiting list. You've also got to be prepared to drop $25,000 on your initiation fee. G. William Domhoff, a University of California, Santa Cruz professor emeritus of psychology and sociology, has studied the Bohemian Club extensively. In a post on the site Who Rules America? he described the Grove as '... a place where the powerful relax, enjoy each other's company, and get to know some of the artists, entertainers, and professors who are included to give the occasion a thin veneer of cultural and intellectual pretension.' The motto of the Bohemian Club is 'Weaving spiders, come not here.' It's a line from William Shakespeare's 'A Midsummer Night's Dream,' reflecting the idea is that members are not supposed to worry about work or business deals while at the club. The activities at the Bohemian Grove have become increasingly controversial, especially in the advent of the internet

Because of its secrecy, strange ceremonies, and elite body of members, the Bohemian Club has long been the subject of sinister online rumors. Right-wing conspiracy theorist Alex Jones even attempted to film a cremation ceremony there in 2000. The Bohemian Grove has also attracted a number of protestors who aren't concerned with the allegedly occult aspects of the proceedings. 'The thing we should be concerned about is the lakeside talks,' activist Mary Moore told Vice in 2011. 'They are public policy talks, where these powerful people discuss and choose policy, but they do so in secrecy, with no public scrutiny.' A number of journalists have managed to infiltrate the campground — with mixed success. Alex Shoumatoff investigated reports the Club was illegally logging for Vanity Fair and was caught and detained for trespassing. Philip Weiss snuck into the Bohemian Grove in 1987 and spent a few days mingling with the rich and powerful as they attended speeches, boozed it up from breakfast to nightfall, and urinated on trees. He wrote about the strange experience for Spy magazine. On Gawker, Sophie Weiner also described her own stint working as a dining server at the Grove in 2016. She described the retreat as a place where the elite could 'Engage in behavior that doesn't usually fly for people of their stature in the regular world.' While many politicians have attended Bohemian Grove functions, the number of presidents who were actually club members is seemingly greatly overstated. Calvin Coolidge and Gerald Ford, for example, are often erroneously cited as members. Domhoff concluded that the Bohemian Club reveals that there is a "socially cohesive upper class" in the US, but the Grove activities are 'Harmless.' 'The Grove encampment is a bunch of guys kidding around, drinking with their buddies, and trying to relive their youth, and often acting very silly,' he wrote.

As President, Theodore Roosevelt accepted an honorary club membership

Theodore Roosevelt was granted honorary club membership when he became president. In a brief 1903 letter to Bohemian Club member Edgar D. Peixott, he expressed gratitude for the 'Honor conferred upon me.' He also offered his regrets that he could not make it to a club function.

Herbert Hoover was an active and enthusiastic club member

Hoover joined the Bohemian Club in 1913. By that point, he had amassed a fortune of $4 million in the mining and engineering industry. Hoover and a group of fellow Stanford alumni ultimately founded their own camp in the Bohemian Grove: the Cave Man Camp. An abandoned statue of a caveman that had been previously used in a club production inspired the name, according to the book 'Hoover, the Fishing President: Portrait of the Private Man and His Life Outdoors.' In 'Ike and Dick: Portrait of a Strange Political Marriage,' Jeffrey Frank writes Hoover always "treasured his membership" and was avid about scouting out new club recruits. In 1950, he invited then-congressman Richard Nixon on a trip to the Bohemian Grove.

Nixon was recorded trashing the Bohemian Club on the Watergate tapes

Hoover at the Bohemian Grove in 1950, Nixon happened to bump into his future running mate, according to 'Ike and Dick: Portrait of a Strange Political Marriage.' General Dwight D. Eisenhower was also there, meeting with the Cave Man Camp. Two years later, the pair would make up the Republican presidential ticket in 1952. He would also go on to join the Cave Man Camp after becoming a member in 1953. Domhoff characterized the camp as 'Highly conservative,' even for the Bohemian Club. Nixon would also, reportedly, use his position in the Bohemian Club to launch his ultimately successful run for the White House. According to the book 'Kennedy, Johnson, and the Nonaligned World,' Nixon delivered a Lakeside Speech to his fellow club members in July 1967. He outlined his ideas on American foreign policy, in what he called the 'First milestone on my road to the presidency.' Domhoff wrote that Nixon also got verbal confirmation from club guest Ronald Reagan that he would not challenge him in the Republican primary that year. According to Domhoff, Nixon was 'So full of himself over the

Bohemian Grove' that he wanted to give the lakeside talk in 1971. The idea of a sitting US president giving an off-the-record speech before a cluster of some of the most powerful people in the country sparked controversy in the press. The club leaders asked him to back out, and Nixon acquiesced. But the Watergate tapes indicated that Nixon may have had mixed feelings about the Bohemian Club. He was recorded describing the Bohemian Grove activities using derogatory slurs.

Ronald Reagan avoided the Grove during the 1980 presidential election

Ronald Reagan was officially inducted into the Bohemian Club in 1975, the year before he tossed his hat into the 1976 presidential campaign. He belonged to the Owl's Nest Camp, which he shared with execs from United Airlines and a number of other companies that were powerful in the 1970s. During the 1980 presidential election, Reagan avoided the Bohemian Grove because he thought he 'Might be an embarrassment to our fellow Bohemians because of the round-the-clock surveillance by the press. They camp down at my driveway these days,' according to 'Reagan: A Life in Letters.'   In his Spy magazine expose, Weiss reported that he was able to meet with Reagan in the Owl's Nest Camp. They made some small talk, and Reagan off-handedly confirmed that he had assured Nixon he 'Wouldn't challenge him outright for the Republican nomination in 1968.'   Weiss wrote that Reagan gave the lakeside talk that year and took questions from club members afterwards, during which he called for four year terms for congress members and greater regulation of the press.

George H. W. Bush bunked with executives from influential companies

George H.W. Bush joined the club in 1973, while chairing the Republican National Committee during the Watergate scandal. Domhoff writes that Bush belonged to a camp called Hill Billies, along with top executives from Bank of America, General Motors, and Procter & Gamble. Bush also brought along a future president as a guest on one trip to Bohemian Grove. He introduced his son George W. Bush at a lakeside talk in 1995, saying that he'd make a great president, according to Domhoff.

Creepy Stories and Theories about Bohemian Grove

Every summer, the world's most elite and powerful men meet in the woods north of San Francisco. They don't talk about work. Instead, they perform Druid-like rituals, burning coffin effigies in reverence to the large redwoods that surround their camp. Nixon, Bush, Ford, Reagan, Rumsfeld, Kissinger, Rockefeller—all of these men have been members of the super-secretive Bohemian Club. And this isn't some conspiracy theory: the Bohemian Club is very, very real. And so is their annual retreat at their private camp, Bohemian Grove. Here are some shocking Bohemian Grove stories, some documented, some rumored that might just make you start believing in conspiracies. Some background information - the Bohemian Club was founded in 1872 by reporters who wanted to build a community in which they could appreciate the arts. Artists and musicians were welcome, and, over time, the club relaxed its rules: anyone who appreciated the arts could join, even non-creatives.

This opened the floodgates, because if there's one thing rich people who fancy themselves sophisticates love, its private clubs. Soon, the club was overrun by the wealthy elite, and the artists and journalists were pushed to the margins. As per club rules, at least ten percent of members must be artists, but realistically, only the most famous artists are allowed in. And, oh yeah: no women allowed. One thing is truly clear about Bohemian Grove: they don't like outsiders. In 2008, a Vanity Fair reporter who infiltrated the camp was arrested for trespassing. It took an hour for members and security to suss out the fact that he didn't belong. Impressive, since there were a few hundred men at the camp. You wouldn't think it'd be too hard to blend into a crowd, right? But not this crowd. This crowd can tell who belongs and who doesn't. Despite the closed ranks, a few people have snuck into the club, and their testimonies give Bohemian Grove theories credence. Yet even those who got into the Bohemian Club weren't able to stay long enough to really integrate and figure out exactly what's happening in those woods. Until that happens, we're left to speculate about a Bohemian Grove conspiracy. This list will take you through some theories about this exclusive camp. Get ready to put on your tinfoil hats.

Was a Child Murdered There in 1984?

Mark Evans writes of a man named Paul Bonacci, who claims he saw a snuff film of a child being killed among some large trees. To quote Evans, 'John DeCamp's book, The Franklin Cover-Up, includes Paul Bonacci's testimony about a snuff film of a child being murdered on July 26, 1984, in California in 'An area that had big trees.' At a meeting in Santa Rosa, DeCamp told a group that he had edited out Bonacci's references to an enormous, moss-covered owl and men in hooded red robes because he not know [sic] then about the owl at the Grove and thought it 'too farfetched for people to believe.' In the fall of 1992, Paul Bonacci was shown a black and white photo of the moss-covered owl at the Grove and quickly identified it as the site of the July 1984 snuff film described in DeCamp's book. Although this testimony has been available to law enforcement officials since mid-October 1992, no official investigation has been made." Moloch, indeed.

Human Sacrifice

An article on North Star Zone, a bonkers conspiracy theory website, details allegations of human sacrifice at Bohemian Grove. 'About the mid-1980s there were rumors of murders in remote parts of the property. A local police investigation went nowhere. State investigators on related criminal acts went nowhere. An observer and near victim has described the Bohemian Grove inner hideaways, the closed sanctum, even the decor at secret locations, places where no outsider goes (or servants according to our sources). Apparently there is an Underground lounge (sign spelled U.N. derground) a Dark Room, a Leather Room, and a Necrophilia Room.'

They Perform Druidic Rituals

Filmmaker Alex Jones snuck into Bohemian Grove with a video camera and filmed a very weird ritual: the Cremation of the Care. Members burnt a coffin in front of a 40-foot-tall owl, which they claim is a way of respecting the forest. The ritual involved elaborate costumes and torches, and the footage is undeniably creepy. In an extensive piece on the Bohemian Club, journalist Mark Evans writes, 'Peter Weiss, writing in Spy Magazine, November 1989, states, 'Bohemian Club literature . . . boosts that the Cremation of Care ceremony derives from Druid rites, medieval Christian liturgy, the Book of Common Prayer, Shakespearean drama, and nineteenth-century American lodge rites.' Is this the straight goods, or is it PR sugar coating of a darker sacrificial rite, terrifying even on a symbolic level?' Moloch is an ancient Canaanite god associated with child sacrifice, who appears in the form of a massive bull with a human torso. In his video recording on the Cremation of Care ceremony, Alex Jones often refers to the giant owl as Moloch. But why? In the '90s, Mark Evans wrote an article in which he compared worship of the owl to that of Moloch. Though the ceremony performed at Bohemian Grove and those performed in deference to Moloch differ in key ways, similarities between the two are striking. Both involve massive effigies of animal-gods and a sacrifice by fire. In ancient times, children were sacrificed to Moloch so parents could gain the favor of the god. Some posit Moloch symbolized the terrifying power of nature, and the sacrifice of the child, the ultimate sacrifice, showed the lengths to which power-hungry people will go to rid themselves of powerlessness.

The Fate of the World Is Decided at the Bohemian Grove

A user named Forestlady posting on the Above Top Secret message board claims to have lived only four miles from Bohemian Grove. She says that some of her friends worked at the camp, and the father of one of her friends was a member. She writes, 'Why is the BG so feared? Because policy IS made there. That is where Ronald Reagan and Nixon made the deal that Nixon would run for prez in '72 and Reagan would run in '80, which is what happened. They have Lakeside Talks, given by well-known policymakers, CEO's, and politicians about various policies. I have seen the topics discussed and oddly enough, 10 years later, these 'suggested' policies become actual policies in the real world. (Nuclear rearming is a good example of this, we are now rearming again - that talk was given about 12 years ago or so.) Policy is made behind closed doors, without the input of the public. This is most undemocratic.'

11. The Fallen, Slain, Killed and Tortured…

Telling secrets is a dangerous endeavor, particularly when powerful people don't want those secrets to get out. Here are 10 haunting cases of whistle-blowers who revealed secrets, only to die a short time later under mysterious or even suspicious circumstances.

Russian Treasury Whistle-Blower

Alexander Perepilichny had a sweet life in Russia. He was a rich, successful businessman who traveled the world. But when he refused to keep a secret, he had to give it all up. As an investment banker, Perepilichny began to investigate fraud within the Russian economy and stumbled onto one of the biggest thefts from taxpayers in history. He gave a series of documents to Swiss officials that exposed a massive money laundering scheme in which Russia's mafia and its government conspired to steal $230 million from the Russian treasury. Swiss prosecutors froze a Swiss bank account worth $11 million that belonged to a high-ranking government official who was implicated in the crimes. After exposing the secrets to the public, Perepilichny began to receive death threats, reportedly from 'Powerful enemies in Moscow.' He promptly fled Russia for Britain, where he secretly moved to a private estate. There, he tried to live a quiet life until one fateful morning in November 2012 when he was seen leaving his house to go jogging. A short time later, Perepilichny was found lying dead on the road by a neighbor. He had no injuries on his body and no outstanding medical conditions that would have threatened his life. When an autopsy was performed, a rare poison was found in his stomach from the deadly Gelsemium genus of plants. After his death, an acquaintance revealed to the press that Perepilichny's name had been put on a hit list by the perpetrators of the theft he had exposed. Perepilichny was still providing information to investigators probing the case when he died. According to a judicial inquiry, Russia's domestic intelligence agency FSB may have played a role in Perepilichny's death.

Marc Dutroux Sex Ring Whistle-Blowers

In August 1996, a 14-year-old girl in Belgium suddenly vanished from a public swimming pool. An eyewitness spotted her being taken into a suspicious van owned by Marc Dutroux and his wife. Police searched the couple's home but didn't find the girl. Two days later, Dutroux and his wife astonishingly confessed. They led investigators into their horrifying basement dungeon where the missing girl was still alive almost a week after her kidnapping. Then Dutroux led police to the dead bodies of two more girls who had been held captive in another home. After his arrest, the Belgian public became outraged over the poor police handling of the case. Dutroux wasn't put on trial until 2004. As a result, some Belgians began to allege that there was a cover-up of a larger sex ring which included powerful government officials and police in Belgium. Jean-Marc Connerotte, the first judge overseeing the case, was dismissed for participating in a fundraiser for the parents of one of the murdered girls. In response to his dismissal, around 300,000 people marched through Brussels in protest.

During the trial, Connerotte testified that 'Murder contracts had been taken out against the magistrates' overseeing the investigation to prevent wider inquiries into Dutroux's underage sex ring. In fact, 20 potential witnesses had died before they could give testimony in court, many under mysterious circumstances. One of those witnesses was Bruno Tagliaferro, a scrap metal merchant who told prosecutors he knew Dutroux and had crucial information about the car in which two of the victims had been kidnapped. But soon afterward, Tagliaferro was found dead of an apparent heart attack. Refusing to accept this, his wife claimed that she sent tissue samples of his body to the US, which showed that he was poisoned. A short time later, her teenage son found her dead in her home. Hubert Massa, a top prosecutor investigating the case, also died suddenly in an apparent suicide before the trial began. He didn't leave a suicide note. Massa had been an effective prosecutor who had procured death sentences for killers in past trials. After his trial, Dutroux was given a life sentence for his crimes. But the public was so disgusted that over one-third of Belgians with the surname Dutroux applied to legally have their names changed.

ISIS Whistle-Blower

Serna Shim was a naturalized American citizen who worked as a reporter for an Iranian news organization called Press TV. In October 2014, she was sent to the border between Turkey and Syria to report on the conflict between Iraqi Kurdish forces and ISIS as the Islamist militants attempted to capture a Syrian town. While stationed at the border, Shim reported that ISIS-affiliated Al-Qaeda militants were being smuggled over the Turkish border into Syria by hiding in the back of aid vehicles owned by nongovernmental organizations. Some of these vehicles had emblems of the World Food Organization, part of the United Nation's humanitarian branch. These activities suggested that the government of Turkey was sheltering and supporting ISIS. Turkey had previously refused to assist Kurdish fighters in their war against ISIS. Other reports suggested that Turkey had trained ISIS militants and supplied key intelligence information that gave them an advantage when fighting the Iraqi Kurdish army. After Shim reported on ISIS militants being moved in UN trucks from Turkey into Syria, she was accused by Turkey's intelligence agency of being a foreign spy. This frightened Shim because Turkey had been labeled by Reporters without Borders as 'The world's largest prison for journalists.' Two days later, she was returning to her hotel in Suruc, Turkey, when her rental car suddenly collided head-on with a large cement mixer truck. Shim died in the crash. Press TV called the car accident 'Suspicious' and claimed that the journalist had been 'Assassinated by the government of Turkish president Recep Tayyip Erdogan.' After the crash, the driver of the cement truck that killed Shim was arrested, but he soon disappeared.

Enron Whistle-Blower

John Clifford Baxter was an Enron executive when the company's massive criminal activities were discovered. Earlier, he had reportedly challenged Enron's management team, including CEO Jeff Skilling, about the company's corrupt transactions and then resigned in protest. When Congress initiated hearings to investigate Enron, Baxter was considered to be crucial to the case because his close relationship to Enron's CEO could have provided valuable insights into the company's criminal activities. But two weeks before he was set to testify, Baxter was found dead in his car from a gunshot wound to the head. Police said the death was a suicide, but many details of Baxter's death raised doubts about that conclusion. The pistol that shot and killed Baxter used rat-shot, a fairly unusual form of ammunition that is untraceable by forensics. There were also strange, unexplained wounds on Baxter's hands and unexplained shards of glass on his shirt. The way the police handled the crime scene raised alarms, too. They moved the body and all the evidence, including the gun that killed Baxter before taking photographs of the crime scene. Despite being legally mandated, no autopsy was performed on Baxter's body to determine a cause of death. By the time an autopsy was finally ordered, Baxter's body was already being prepared for burial by a funeral home. When talking with a former business associate two days before his death, Baxter had said that he might need a bodyguard after agreeing to assist in the Enron investigation.

South African Mob Witnesses

When South African crime boss George 'Gewald' Thomas was finally arrested, he faced 52 charges, including seven murders, three attempted murders, weapons charges, racketeering, and breaking and entering. A four-year trial ensued that contained nearly as much bloodshed as the actions with which he was charged. Thomas was (or perhaps still is) the head of the 28s gang, one of the most dangerous gangs in South Africa. At least 12 people linked to the case—including six whom the state intended to call as witnesses at the trial—were murdered. One of those witnesses was Haywin Strydom, who was murdered by a gang-affiliated gunman shortly before he could testify. Despite his untimely death, Strydom's last words may have helped to convict Gewald and his gang. When paramedics arrived, Strydom used his last breaths to identify his killers as 'Gewald's henchmen.' Eventually, Gewald was convicted and given seven life sentences plus an additional 175 years in prison.

Barry Seal

A gifted pilot, Barry Seal used his personal plane to smuggle cocaine for the Medellin drug cartel. Seal claimed that he had earned up to $100 million and smuggled as much as $5 billion worth of cocaine into the US. After he was indicted on conspiracy to smuggle Quaaludes into Florida in 1984, he tried to cut a deal to avoid jail time. When the US attorney heading the case refused to drop all charges in exchange for Seal's work as an informant, Seal hopped in his Learjet and flew to the White House. There, he met with members of the Reagan administration, including Vice President George H.W. Bush's task force on crime. The task force made Seal an undercover DEA operative and supplied him with a military cargo plane to smuggle cocaine from Nicaragua into the US as part of a sting operation. The cocaine in Seal's plane was allegedly provided by the Sandinista government shortly before the Reagan administration became embroiled in the Iran-Contra scandal for illegally supplying arms and assistance to the Sandinistas' enemies, the Contras. Hidden cameras on the plane took photographs of the smuggling operation. The Reagan administration distributed the photos to the press, later using them to try to justify arming the Contras. At this time, Barry Seal also worked for the CIA, which had allegedly been sponsoring Contra groups that smuggled cocaine into the US. The money from drug sales then allegedly funded the Contras. If true, this meant that the CIA was backing a drug smuggling operation into the US. Seal was now a free man, who community service instead of jail timed for the crimes he committed. However, the leak of information showed Seal's face and allowed the cartel to identify him as a traitor. Before Seal could begin his public service work at a Salvation Army in Louisiana, he was found dead in his car with multiple bullet wounds riddling his body. At the time of his death, Seal purportedly had the personal, unlisted phone number of Vice President Bush in his wallet. The killers were believed to be Colombian assassins who were apprehended at Louisiana's border after Seal's murder. They were sentenced to life in prison without parole. Seal's death ended the DEA's investigation into Medellin drug smuggling.

Iranian Secret Police Doctor

Iran's 2009 presidential elections didn't go as planned. After the results were announced and incumbent President Mahmoud Ahmadinejad defeated a strong opposition candidate, protests erupted across the country. Critics claimed that there were irregularities in the voting results and alleged that the election was rigged. Police were called in to suppress the increasingly visible protests, which were dubbed the 'Green Revolution.' Some 4,000 Iranians were arrested as part of police actions against the protests. Iranian police called Dr. Ramin Pourandarjani to administer medical care to the arrested protesters who were being interrogated and tortured by Iranian authorities. Pourandarjani tried to give medical care to protester Mohsen Ruholamini, who died in prison from multiple blows to the head. As a result of Ruholamini's death, Pourandarjani was called to testify before a committee in the Iranian parliament about the incident. His testimony was instrumental in getting Ayatollah Khamenei to close the prison in which the incident had occurred.

However, Pourandarjani was arrested by Iranian authorities after he testified. He was taken to jail, interrogated, and eventually released on bail. However, Iranian authorities threatened to strip him of his medical license or even imprison him indefinitely if he disclosed anything more about what he had seen at the prison when he treated detainees. After he returned to his family and friends, Pourandarjani claimed to be receiving threats against his life. Then he was suddenly found dead. The Iranian authorities kept changing the cause of death from injuries sustained in a car accident to a heart attack to suicide to poisoning. A salad Pourandarjani had eaten before his death was purportedly laced with a lethal dose of a medication used to treat blood pressure. Iranian authorities prevented Pourandarjani's family from investigating his cause of death by performing an autopsy on his body.

Chilean Coup Whistle-Blowers

In 1973, Charles Horman was an American journalist reporting on politics in Chile when Socialist Salvador Allende was president. Horman—who supported Allende—went to the coastal town of Vina del Mar to investigate a violent military coup headed by Augusto Pinochet that had thrown the country into chaos. To his surprise, Horman found US military personnel on the ground and US warships in the waters nearby. Supposedly, he documented some members of the US military taking responsibility for the coup, which pointed to US government involvement. Horman received a ride back to his home in Santiago from Captain Ray Davis, who supposedly worked for the US Embassy. In reality, Davis was commanding the covert US military operation in Chile to back the military coup against Allende. He was also supposedly investigating Americans in Chile who might be radicals or subversives. Believing his knowledge put them in danger, Horman and his wife decided to leave the country. But before they did, Horman was abducted from his home by Chilean soldiers while he was alone. He was taken to a prison camp and disappeared. Horman's friends and family frantically searched for him. A month later, they found his body. He had been executed by the Chilean military.

Frank Teruggi, another American journalist in Chile, was also found dead. For the next 40 years, Horman's family fought to identify Horman's murderers and bring them to justice. Decades after his death, the State Department released a declassified memo on the coup which said, 'US intelligence may have played an unfortunate part in Horman's death. At best, it was limited to providing or confirming information that helped motivate his murder by the government of Chile. At worst, US intelligence was aware the government of Chile saw Horman in a rather serious light and US officials did nothing to discourage the logical outcome of Chilean paranoia. A Chilean spy charged as an accomplice in Horman's death claimed that a CIA agent was present during Horman's kidnapping and interrogation. Supposedly, the CIA agent was also present when Chilean authorities decided to execute Horman. In November 2011, a Chilean court indicted Ray Davis. A year later, their Supreme Court approved a request to extradite Davis to Chile so he could be tried for his role in the deaths of Horman and Teruggi.

AMIA Bombing Investigator

The 1994 AMIA terrorist attack was the most lethal bombing in Argentina's history, killing 85 people and injuring over 300. It occurred in one of the largest Jewish communities outside Israel, prompting the Israeli government to send Mossad agents to Argentina to investigate the attack. The investigation was stalled by alleged incompetence and cover-ups. In September 2004, all suspects tied to Buenos Aires and its police force were found not guilty of any wrongdoing. The judge who made that ruling was impeached the following year because of his grave mishandling of the case. The not guilty verdicts sparked public outrage and resulted in a new investigation into the bombings, headed by lawyer Alberto Nisman. Nisman soon claimed that Iran had orchestrated the terrorist attack and Hezbollah had carried it out. Supposedly, the attack was spurred by Argentina's suspension of a contract to supply nuclear technology to Iran. Nisman also accused Argentine politicians, including President Cristina Kurcher, of deliberately hiding from the public the identity of the Iranians involved in the bombing.

All charges against the president were later dismissed by an appeals court. Nisman published a nearly 300-page report on his investigation. But just a few hours before he was scheduled to testify about his findings in front of Argentina's congress, he was found dead in his home from a gunshot to the head. There were no signs of forced entry into his home, but a hidden entrance was open. An autopsy ruled that Nisman's death was a suicide even though there was no gunpowder residue on his hands. Another autopsy, undertaken at the request of Nisman's wife, found that there was no muscular spasm in his right hand which would have been necessary to fire the gun. His body also appeared to have been moved after his death. Video footage released five months later allegedly showed Argentine police tampering with evidence at the scene of Nisman's death. His computer had also been accessed over 60 times after he died

Iraq War Whistle-Blower

In 2003, David Kelly, a weapons inspector for the British government, was thrust into the public spotlight when BBC journalist Andrew Gilligan published their off-the-record conversation revealing that the British government's investigators had not found any weapons of mass destruction in Iraq, despite the Bush administration's claims otherwise. Unknown to Kelly, the journalist then published the information he had received from Kelly and cited him as the source. The British and American public if not the world altogether was outraged at the revelation, which suggested that the Bush administration and the British government were lying about their reasons for invading Iraq. Kelly was summoned to appear at a committee hearing in British parliament on July 15, 2003. He was rigorously questioned about his conversation with the BBC journalist and why it was revealed to the public.

Around the same time, Kelly met with British ambassador David Broucher. Kelly told Broucher that he had promised Iraqi officials that there would be no war if they cooperated but that he would probably be found dead if Iraq were invaded. Two days after Kelly's testimony to the British parliament, he was found dead outside his home. He had answered some emails that morning and then left for his morning walk. Kelly's body was found in a woodlands area about 1.5 kilometers (1 mi) from his home. He had ingested 29 pain pills, and his left wrist was slashed with a knife he had owned since childhood. An investigation was launched into the suspicious circumstances surrounding his death. The official conclusion was that Kelly had committed suicide. After the announcement, his medical reports were sealed from public view for 70 years. However, a series of doctors published a rebuttal of the cause of death in The Guardian, arguing that the cuts on Kelly's wrist would not have resulted in a fatal amount of blood loss. They also claimed that the amount of painkillers that Kelly had ingested were not enough to kill him. As a result, Dr. Andrew Watt told British authorities that he believed Kelly had been murdered.

Georgi Markov, September 1978

In one of the most chilling episodes of the cold war, the Bulgarian dissident was poisoned by a specially adapted umbrella on Waterloo Bridge. As he waited for a bus, Markov felt a sharp prick in his leg. The opposition activist, who was an irritant to the authoritarian communist government of Bulgaria, died three days later. A deadly 1.7mm-wide pellet containing the poison ricin was found in his skin. His unknown assassin is thought to have been from the secret services in Bulgaria, which was then in the orbit of Soviet Russia.

Alexander Litvinenko, November 2006

The fatal poisoning of the former officer with the Russian spy agency FSB sparked a major international incident. Litvinenko fell ill in November 2006 after drinking a cup of tea laced with radioactive polonium. He met his killers in a ground-floor bar of the Millennium hotel in Mayfair, central London. The pair were Andrei Lugovoi, a former KGB officer turned businessman, who is now a deputy in Russia's state Duma and Dmitry Kovtun, a childhood friend of Lugovoi's from a Soviet military family. Vladimir Putin denied all involvement and refused to extradite either of the killers from Moscow.

Woman in Russian spy mystery is Sergei Skripal's daughter

The exiled Russian banker survived an attempt on his life as he got out of a cab in east London. He was shot four times with a silenced pistol. He had been involved in a bitter dispute with two former business partners.

Alexander Perepilichnyy, November 2012

The businessman collapsed while running near his home in Weybridge, Surrey. His death was initially attributed to natural causes, but a pre-inquest hearing heard evidence that traces of a chemical that can be found in the poisonous plant gelsemium were later found in his stomach. Before his death, Perepilichnyy was helping a specialist investment firm uncover a $230m Russian money-laundering operation, a pre-inquest hearing was told. Hermitage Capital Management claimed that Perepilichnyy could have been deliberately killed for helping it uncover the scam involving Russian officials. A further pre-inquest hearing heard that he may have eaten a popular Russian dish containing the herb sorrel on the day of his death, which could have been poisoned. The inquest is continuing and is due to resume next month.

Boris Berezovsky, March 2013

The exiled billionaire was found hanged in an apparent suicide after he had spent more than decade waging a high-profile media battle against his one-time protege Putin. A coroner recorded an open verdict after hearing conflicting expert evidence about the way he died. A pathologist who conducted a postmortem examination on the businessman's body said he could not rule out murder.

Scot Young, December 2014

An associate of Berezovsky whom he helped to launder money, was found impaled on railings after he fell from a fourth-floor flat in Marylebone, central London. A coroner ruled that there was insufficient evidence that his death was suicide. But Young, who was sent to prison in January 2013 for repeatedly refusing to reveal his finances during a public divorce row, told his partner he was going to jump out of the window moments before he was found.

- In the UK, Samaritans can be contacted on 116 123. In the US, the National Suicide Prevention Lifeline is 1-800-273-8255.
- This article was amended on 8 March 2018 to make it clear that an inquest into the death of Alexander Perepilichnyy is continuing.

MCCAIN CONSPIRACIST SAY HIS BRAIN CANCER WAS FALSIFIED

President Trump displayed his innate grace and decency Saturday by spiking a White House statement honoring the late Sen. John McCain's life. Monday morning, the flag over the White House was (until criticism poured in) back to full staff, six days before protocol says it should have been. Even for Trump, this seemed churlish. Unless there is another explanation: John McCain is not dead. When McCain's family put out the news Friday that he had discontinued treatment for his terminal brain cancer, this was done 'To take media attention' from Senate candidate Kelli Ward, and, according to Ward herself, replace it with a 'Narrative that they hope is negative to me.' Ward had unsuccessfully challenged McCain in the 2016 Republican primary in Arizona, so it makes complete sense that, two years later, McCain would arrange his death to divert attention from Ward's bus tour. Furthermore, according to a 'Conspiracy Theory' network popular among some Trump boosters, when McCain supposedly died on Saturday, he did not succumb to cancer but took his own life to avoid being hauled off to Guantanamo Bay and put before a military tribunal for his longtime work helping Islamic State terrorists and others. (And before he died, he concealed his criminal ankle bracelet by wearing a medical boot on his leg.) Unless, of course, the suicide, like the cancer, was just a ruse. In that case, McCain will continue. During President Trump's rally on July 31, several attendees held or wore signs with the letter 'Q.' Here's what the QAnon 'Conspiracy Theory' is about.

So many lies. Heck, he's even lying in state! In death, as in life, McCain has a way of bringing out the loons. Undoubtedly the posthumous conspiracy theories would have amused him as much as anybody. He took particular delight in debunking 'Propaganda and crackpot conspiracy theories,' as he put it to Naval Academy midshipmen 10 months ago. No matter the evidence, 'Still the conspiracy theorists hock their wares,' he wrote in 2009, introducing a book refuting 9/11 conspiracy notions. 'They ignore the methods of science, the protocols of investigation and the dictates of logic. The conspiracy theorists chase any bit of information, no matter how flimsy, and use it to fit their preordained conclusions. They ascribe to the government, or to some secretive group, powers wholly out of proportion to what the evidence suggests. And they ignore the facts that are present in plain sight. We cannot let these tales go unanswered.'

Answering those tales is even more important at a time when the president amplifies and echoes them. In his love of truth, McCain was the anti-Trump. Trump rose to power with his "birther" conspiracy theory and the support of the Alex Jones crowd, and he has literally thrown open the doors of the White House to conspiracy theorists. Last Thursday, as the Daily Beast's Asawin Suebsaeng and Will Sommer reported, Trump hosted Lionel Lebron, a prominent conspiracy theorist, and posed with him in the Oval Office. Lebron is a 9/11 truther who believes Trump is fighting the deep state and globalist pedophiles and is a leading promoter of the very online network floating the notion McCain is alive or a suicide. Three days after his White House visit, Lebron tweeted an image of Trump crossing a swamp of Democrats, featuring racist images of Barack and Michelle Obama and the words 'Fire at will.' With the exception of Hillary Clinton, perhaps nobody stoked the conspiracy crowd's fevers like McCain. He was 'Songbird' McCain, a secret agent of the North Vietnamese who threw the 2008 election to Obama, covertly met with the leaders of Islamic State in Syria, secretively started the Robert S. Mueller III 'Witch hunt' against Trump and was "in bed with the Clinton Foundation" but turned against Clinton shortly before his death. A post on Sunday from the leader of a prominent conspiracy forum wrestled with whether McCain killed himself or surrendered: 'Suicide weekend? Hands up?... We are in control. BIG week ahead.' One wacky participant speculated, 'National Dog Day happens to be the day McCain's death announced. Coincidence?' Sorry, no. McCain died Saturday. National Dog Day was Sunday.

Weirdly, conspiracy theorist broadcaster Alex Jones accepted at face value McCain's death from brain cancer. 'I'm gonna take the high road because I think McCain was actually a twisted, compromised, tortured individual,' Jones said, calling McCain 'Leader of the deep state.' McCain would have had a ready rejoinder for these 'Deathers' — just as he did when he took the microphone in 2008 from the supporter who called Barack Obama an 'Arab'; ridiculed 'Chemtrail Kelli Ward' in 2016 for promoting the belief that jet contrails spread biological weapons and change weather; and denounced the "nutty conspiracy theory" in 2015 that accused him of staging Islamic State beheadings. McCain answered these nuts with calm reason. In memory of him, let's continue his fight until they, and their leader in the Oval Office, return to the crevices whence they came.

CIA KENNEDY ASSASSINATION CONSPIRACY THEORY

The CIA Kennedy assassination theory is a prominent John F. Kennedy assassination conspiracy theory. According to ABC News, the Central Intelligence Agency (CIA) is represented in nearly every theory that involves American conspirators. The secretive nature of the CIA and the conjecture surrounding high-profile political assassinations in the United States during the 1960s, has made the CIA a plausible suspect for some who believe in a conspiracy. Conspiracy theorists have ascribed various motives for CIA involvement in the assassination of President Kennedy, including Kennedy's refusal to provide air support to the Bay of Pigs invasion, his plan to cut the agency's budget by 20 percent, and the belief that he was weak on Communism.

Background

John F. Kennedy, the 35th President of the United States, was assassinated in Dallas, Texas, on November 22, 1963. Various agencies and government panels have investigated the assassination at length, drawing different conclusions. Lee Harvey Oswald is accepted by official investigations as the assassin, but he was murdered by Jack Ruby before he could be tried in a court of law. The discrepancies between the official investigations and the extraordinary nature of the assassination have led to a variety of theories about how and why Kennedy was assassinated. The House Select Committee on Assassinations (HSCA) concluded in 1979 that Oswald assassinated Kennedy, but that a conspiracy was probable. The committee did not implicate U.S. Intelligence agencies. Their conclusion was reached almost entirely because of the results of forensic analysis of a police dictabelt, which supposedly recorded the sound of a fourth bullet being fired in Dealey Plaza.

Origin

On March 1, 1967, businessman Clay Shaw, head of the International Trade Mart in New Orleans, was arrested and charged with conspiring to assassinate President John F. Kennedy by New Orleans District Attorney Jim Garrison. Three days later on March 4, the Italian left-wing newspaper Paese Sera published a story alleging that Shaw was linked to the CIA through his involvement in the Centro Mondiale Commerciale, a subsidiary of Permindex in which Shaw was a board member. According to Paese Sera, the CMC had been a front organization developed by the CIA for transferring funds to Italy for "illegal political-espionage activities" and had attempted to depose French President Charles de Gaulle in the early 1960s. On March 6, the newspaper printed other allegations about individuals it said were connected to Permindex, including Louis Bloomfield whom it described as 'An American agent who now plays the role of a businessman from Canada [who] established secret ties in Rome with Deputies of the Christian Democrats and neo-Fascist parties.' The allegations were retold in various newspapers associated with the Communist parties in Italy (l'Unità), France (L'Humanité), and the Soviet Union (Pravda), as well as leftist papers in Canada and Greece, prior to reaching the American press eight weeks later. American journalist Max Holland said that Paese Sera's allegations connecting Shaw to the CIA were what led to Garrison to implicate the CIA in a conspiracy to assassinate Kennedy.

Proponents and believers

Jim Garrison said anti-Communist and anti-Castro extremists in the CIA plotted the assassination of Kennedy to maintain tension with the Soviet Union and Cuba, and to prevent a United States withdrawal from Vietnam. James Douglass wrote in JFK and the Unspeakable that the CIA, acting upon the orders of conspirators with the 'Military industrial complex,' killed Kennedy and in the process set up Lee Harvey Oswald as a patsy. Like Garrison, Douglass stated that Kennedy was killed because he was turning away from the Cold War and pursuing paths of nuclear disarmament, rapprochement with Fidel Castro, and withdrawal from the war in Vietnam. Mark Lane, author of Rush to Judgment and Plausible Denial and the attorney who defended Liberty Lobby against a defamation suit brought by former CIA agent E. Howard Hunt has been described as a leading proponent of the theory that the CIA was responsible for the assassination of Kennedy. Others who believe the CIA was involved include authors Anthony Summers and John M. Newman. In 1977, the FBI released 40,000 files pertaining to the assassination of Kennedy, including an April 3, 1967, memorandum from Deputy Director Cartha DeLoach to Associate Director Clyde Tolson that was written less than a month after President Johnson learned from J. Edgar Hoover about CIA plots to kill Fidel Castro. According to DeLoach, LBJ aide Marvin Watson 'Stated that the President had told him, in an off moment, that he was now convinced there was a plot in connection with the assassination of President Kennedy. Watson stated the President felt that the CIA had had something to do with this plot.' When questioned in 1975, during the Church Committee hearings, DeLoach told Senator Richard Schweiker that he 'Felt that Watson's statement was sheer speculation.'

CONSPIRATORS AND EVIDENCE, SECOND OSWALD IN MEXICO CITY THEORY

Gaeton Fonzi was hired as a researcher in 1975 by the Church Committee and by the House of Representatives Select Committee on Assassinations in 1977. At the HSCA, Fonzi focused on the anti-Castro Cuban exile groups, and the links that these groups had with the CIA and the Mafia. Fonzi obtained testimony from Cuban exile Antonio Veciana that Veciana had once witnessed his CIA contact, who Fonzi would later come to believe was David Atlee Phillips, conferring with Lee Harvey Oswald. Through his research, Fonzi became convinced that Phillips had played a key role in the assassination of President Kennedy. Fonzi also concluded that, as part of the assassination plot, Phillips had actively worked to embellish Oswald's image as a communist sympathizer. He further concluded that the presence of a possible Oswald impersonator in Mexico City, during the period that Oswald himself was in Mexico City, may have been orchestrated by Phillips This evidence first surfaced in testimony given to the HSCA in 1978, and through the investigative work of independent journalist Anthony Summers in 1979.

Summers spoke with a man named Oscar Contreras who said that he met a man calling himself Lee Harvey Oswald, in Mexico City, in the fall of 1963. Contreras described 'Oswald' as 'maybe thirty-five years old, light-haired and fairly short' a description that did not fit the real Oswald. To Fonzi, it seemed too great a coincidence that Oswald would at random strike up a conversation regarding his difficulties in obtaining a Cuban visa with Contreras, a man who belonged to a pro-Castro student group and had contacts in the Cuban embassy in Mexico City. Fonzi's belief in a 'Second Oswald' directed by Phillips was strengthened by statements from other witnesses. On September 27, 1963, and again a week later, a man identifying himself as Oswald visited the Cuban embassy in Mexico City. Consular Eusebio Azcue testified to the HSCA that the real Oswald 'In no way resembled' the 'Oswald' to whom he had spoken to at length. Embassy employee Sylvia Duran also told Anthony Summers that the real Oswald she eventually saw on film 'Is not like the man I saw here in Mexico City.'

On October 1, 1963, the CIA issued a teletype to the FBI, the State Department, and the Navy, regarding Oswald's visits to Mexico City. The teletype was accompanied by a photo of a man identified as Oswald who in fact looked nothing like him. Also on October 1, the CIA recorded two tapped telephone calls to the Soviet embassy by a man identified as Oswald. The CIA transcriber noted that 'Oswald' spoke in 'Broken Russian.' The real Oswald was quite fluent in Russian. On November 23, 1963, the day after the assassination, FBI Director J. Edgar Hoover's preliminary analysis of the assassination included the following: The Central Intelligence Agency advised that on October 1st, 1963, an extremely sensitive source had reported that an individual identifying himself as Lee Oswald contacted the Soviet Embassy in Mexico City inquiring at to any messages. Special agents of this Bureau, who have conversed with Oswald in Dallas, Texas, have observed photographs of the individual referred to above and have listened to a recording of his voice. These special agents are of the opinion that the referred-to individual was not Lee Harvey Oswald. That same day, Hoover had this conversation with President Johnson.

JOHNSON: 'Have you established any more about the Oswald visit to the Soviet Embassy in Mexico in September?'

HOOVER: 'No, there's one angle that's very confusing for this reason. We have up here the tape and the photograph of the man at the Soviet Embassy, using Oswald's name. That picture and the tape do not correspond to this man's voice, nor to his appearance. In other words, it appears that there was a second person who was at the Soviet Embassy.'

Fonzi concluded it was unlikely that the CIA would legitimately not be able to produce a single photograph of the real Oswald as part of the documentation of his trip to Mexico City, given that Oswald had made five separate visits to the Soviet and Cuban embassies where the CIA maintained surveillance cameras.

Three tramps

The 'Three tramps' are three men photographed by several Dallas-area newspapers under police escort near the Texas School Book Depository shortly after the assassination of President Kennedy. The men were detained and questioned briefly by the Dallas police. They have been the subject of various conspiracy theories, including some that allege the three men to be known CIA agents. Some of these allegations are listed below. E. Howard Hunt is alleged by some to be the oldest of the tramps. Hunt was a CIA station chief in Mexico City and was involved in the Bay of Pigs Invasion. Hunt later worked as one of President Richard Nixon's White House Plumbers. Others believe that the oldest tramp is Chauncey Holt. Holt claimed to have been a double agent for the CIA and the Mafia and claimed that his assignment in Dallas was to provide fake Secret Service credentials to people in the vicinity. Witness reports state that there were one or more unidentified men in the area claiming to be Secret Service agents. Frank Sturgis is thought by some to be the tall tramp. Like E. Howard Hunt, Sturgis was involved both in the Bay of Pigs invasion and in the Watergate burglary.

In 1959, Sturgis became involved with Marita Lorenz. Lorenz would later claim that Sturgis told her that he had participated in a JFK assassination plot. In response to her allegations, Sturgis denied being involved in a conspiracy to kill Kennedy. In an interview with Steve Dunleavy of the New York Post, Sturgis said that he believed communist agents had pressured Lorenz into making the accusations against him. The House Select Committee on Assassinations had forensic anthropologists study the photographic evidence. The committee claimed that its analysis ruled out E. Howard Hunt, Frank Sturgis, Dan Carswell, Fred Lee Chapman, and other suspects. The Rockefeller Commission concluded that neither Hunt nor Frank Sturgis were in Dallas on the day of the assassination. Records released by the Dallas Police Department in 1989 identified the three men as Gus Abrams, Harold Doyle, and John Gedney.

E. Howard Hunt

Several conspiracy theorists have named former CIA agent and Watergate figure E. Howard Hunt as a possible participant in the Kennedy assassination and some, as noted before, have alleged that Hunt is one of the three tramps. Hunt has taken various magazines to court over accusations with regard to the assassination. In 1975, Hunt testified before the United States President's Commission on CIA activities within the United States that he was in Washington, D.C. on the day of the assassination. This testimony was confirmed by Hunt's family and a home employee of the Hunts. In 1976, a magazine called The Spotlight ran an article accusing Hunt of being in Dallas on November 22, 1963, and of having a role in the assassination. Hunt won a libel judgment against the magazine in 1981, but this verdict was overturned on appeal. The magazine was found not liable when the case was re-tried in 1985. In 1985, Hunt was in court again in a libel suit against Liberty Lobby. During the trial, defense attorney Mark Lane was successful in creating doubt among the jury as to Hunt's location on the day of the Kennedy assassination through depositions from David Atlee Phillips, Richard Helms, G. Gordon Liddy, Stansfield Turner, and Marita Lorenz, as well as through his cross examination of Hunt. In August 2003, while in failing health, Hunt allegedly confessed to his son of his knowledge of a conspiracy in the JFK assassination. However, Hunt's health improved, and he went on to live four more years.

Shortly before Hunt's death in 2007, he authored an autobiography which implicated Lyndon B. Johnson in the assassination, suggesting that Johnson had orchestrated the killing with the help of CIA agents who had been angered by Kennedy's actions as President. After Hunt's death, his sons, Saint John Hunt, and David Hunt, stated that their father had recorded several claims about himself, and others being involved in a conspiracy to assassinate President John F. Kennedy. In the April 5, 2007, issue of Rolling Stone, Saint John Hunt detailed a number of individuals purported to be implicated by his father, including Lyndon B. Johnson, Cord Meyer, David Phillips, Frank Sturgis, David Morales, Antonio Veciana, William Harvey, and an assassin he termed 'French gunman grassy knoll' who some presume was Lucien Sarti. The two sons alleged that their father cut the information from his memoirs to avoid possible perjury charges. According to Hunt's widow and other children, the two sons took advantage of Hunt's loss of lucidity by coaching and exploiting him for financial gain. The Los Angeles Times said they examined the materials offered by the sons to support the story and found them to be 'Inconclusive.'

David Sánchez Morales

Some researchers—among them Gaeton Fonzi, Larry Hancock, Noel Twyman, and John Simkin—believe that CIA operative David Morales was involved in the Kennedy assassination. Morales' friend, Ruben Carbajal, claimed that in 1973 Morales opened up about his involvement with the Bay of Pigs Invasion operation, and stated that 'Kennedy had been responsible for him having to watch all the men he recruited and trained get wiped out.' Carbajal claimed that Morales said, 'Well, we took care of that SOB, didn't we?' Morales is alleged to have once told friends, 'I was in Dallas when we got the son of a bitch, and I was in Los Angeles when we got the little bastard,' presumably referring to the assassination of President Kennedy in Dallas, Texas and to the later assassination of Senator Robert Kennedy in Los Angeles, California on June 5, 1968. Morales is alleged to have expressed deep anger toward the Kennedys for what he saw as their betrayal during the Bay of Pigs Invasion.

Frank Sturgis

In an article published in the South Florida Sun Sentinel on December 4, 1963, James Buchanan, a former reporter for the Pompano Beach Sun-Sentinel, claimed that Frank Sturgis had met Lee Harvey Oswald in Miami, Florida shortly before Kennedy's assassination.

Buchanan claimed that Oswald had tried to infiltrate the International Anti-Communist Brigade. When he was questioned by the FBI about this story, Sturgis claimed that Buchanan had misquoted him regarding his comments about Oswald. According to a memo sent by L. Patrick Gray, acting FBI Director, to H. R. Haldeman on June 19, 1972, "'Sources in Miami say he Sturgis is now associated with organized crime activities'. In his book, Assassination of JFK, published in 1977, Bernard Fensterwald claims that Sturgis was heavily involved with the Mafia, particularly with Santo Trafficante's and Meyer Lansky's activities in Florida.

George de Mohrenschildt

After returning from the Soviet Union, Lee Harvey Oswald became close friends with Dallas resident and petroleum geologist George de Mohrenschildt. De Mohrenschildt would later write an extensive memoir in which he discussed his friendship with Oswald. De Mohrenschildt's wife would later give the House Select Committee on Assassinations a photograph that showed Lee Harvey Oswald, standing in his Dallas backyard, holding two Marxist newspapers and a Carcano rifle, with a pistol on his hip. Thirteen years after the assassination, in September 1976, the CIA requested that the FBI locate De Mohrenschildt, in response to a letter De Mohrenschildt had written directly to his friend, CIA Director George H.W. Bush, appealing to Bush to stop the agency from taking action against him. Several television programs, including Jesse Ventura's 'Conspiracy Theories,' have alleged that De Mohrenschildt was Oswald's CIA handler but have offered little evidence.

On March 29, 1977, De Mohrenschildt stated during an interview with author Edward Jay Epstein that he had been ordered by CIA operative J. Walton Moore to meet Oswald. He also told Epstein that he would not have met Oswald had he not been ordered to do so. (In fact, de Mohrenschildt had met Oswald several times, from the summer of 1962 to April 1963.) That same day, De Mohrenschildt was informed by his daughter that a representative of the House Select Committee on Assassinations had stopped by, leaving a card, and intending to return that evening. De Mohrenschildt then committed suicide by shooting himself in the head shortly thereafter. De Mohrenschildt's wife later told sheriff's office investigators that her husband had been hospitalized for depression and paranoia in late 1976 and had tried to kill himself four times that year.

Role of Oswald

Findings by the Warren Commission and other federal investigations have conclusively ruled that Oswald either acted alone or conspired with others in the assassination, citing his actions in the years leading up to the event in support of that conclusion. Evidence of Oswald's pro-communist and radical tendencies include his defection to Russia, the New Orleans branch of the Fair Play for Cuba Committee he had organized, and also various public and private statements made by him espousing Marxism and extreme leftist ideologies. Other researchers have argued that his behavior was in fact a carefully-planned ruse as part of an effort by U.S. intelligence agencies to infiltrate subversive groups and conduct counter-intelligence operations in communist countries such as Russia and Cuba, and that his involvement in the assassination was instead that of an agent or informant of the government trying to expose the assassination plot.

Oswald himself claimed to be an innocent, denying all charges, and even declaring to reporters that he was 'Just a patsy.' He also insisted that the photos of him with a rifle had been faked, an assertion contradicted by statements made by his wife, Marina, who claimed to have taken the photos, and the analysis of photographic experts such as Lyndal L. Shaneyfelt of the FBI. In any case, less than 48 hours after his arrest Oswald was murdered, leaving many unanswered questions, and even fueling speculation by some as evidence of a cover-up. Oswald's role as FBI informant was investigated by Lee Rankin and others of the Warren Commission, but their findings were inconclusive. Several FBI employees had made statements indicating that Oswald was indeed a paid informant, but the commission was nonetheless unable to verify the veracity of those claims. FBI agent James P. Hosty reported that his office's interactions with Oswald were limited to dealing with his complaints about being harassed by the Bureau for being a communist sympathizer.

In the weeks before the assassination Oswald made a personal visit to the FBI's Dallas branch office with a hand-delivered letter which purportedly contained a threat of some sort but, controversially, Hosty destroyed the letter by order of J. Gordon Shanklin, his supervisor. Some researchers suggest that Oswald was an active agent of the Central Intelligence Agency, often pointing to the fact that he attempted to defect to Russia but was nonetheless able to return without difficulty even receiving a repatriation loan from the State Department as evidence of such. A former roommate of Oswald, James Botelho (who would later become a California judge stated in an interview with Mark Lane that he believed that Oswald engaged in an intelligence assignment in Russia, although Botelho made no mention of those suspicions in his testimony to the Warren Commission years earlier. Oswald's mother, Marguerite, often insisted that her son was recruited by an agency of the U.S. Government and sent to Russia. New Orleans District Attorney (and later judge) Jim Garrison, who in 1967 brought Clay Shaw to trial for the assassination of President Kennedy also held the opinion that Oswald was most likely a CIA agent who had been drawn into the plot to be used as a scapegoat, even going as far as to say that Oswald 'Genuinely was probably a hero'. Senator Richard Schweiker, a member of the U.S. Senate Select Committee on Intelligence remarked that 'Everywhere you look with Oswald, there're fingerprints of intelligence.'

Richard Sprague, interim staff director and chief counsel to the U.S. House Select Committee on Assassinations, stated that if he 'Had to do it over again,' he would have investigated the Kennedy assassination by probing Oswald's ties to the Central Intelligence Agency. In 1978, former CIA paymaster and accountant James Wilcott testified before the HSCA, stating that Lee Harvey Oswald was a 'Known agent' of the Central Intelligence Agency. Wilcott and his wife, Elsie (also a former employee of the CIA) later repeated those claims in a story by the San Francisco Chronicle. Despite its official policy of neither confirming nor denying the status of agents, both the CIA itself and many officers working in the region at the time (including David Atlee Phillips) have "unofficially" dismissed the plausibility of any CIA ties to Oswald. Robert Blakey, staff director and chief counsel for the U.S. House Select Committee on Assassinations supported that assessment in his conclusions as well.

Organized crime and a CIA conspiracy

Some conspiracy theorists have alleged a plot involving elements of the Mafia, the CIA, and the anti-Castro Cubans, including author Anthony Summers and journalist Ruben Castaneda. Castaneda wrote: 'Based on the evidence, it is likely that JFK was killed by a coalition of anti-Castro Cubans, the Mob, and elements of the CIA.' In his book, They Killed Our President, former Minnesota governor Jesse Ventura also concluded: 'John F. Kennedy was murdered by a conspiracy involving disgruntled CIA agents, anti-Castro Cubans, and members of the Mafia, all of whom were extremely angry at what they viewed as Kennedy's appeasement policies toward Communist Cuba and the Soviet Union.' Jack Van Lanningham, a prison cellmate of Mafia boss Carlos Marcello, claimed that Marcello confessed to him in 1985 to having organized Kennedy's assassination. Lanningham also claimed that the FBI covered up the taped confession which he said the FBI had in its possession. Robert Blakey, who was chief counsel for the House Select Committee on Assassinations, concluded in his book, The Plot to Kill the President, that Marcello was likely part of a Mafia conspiracy behind the assassination, and that the Mafia had the means, motive, and opportunity required to carry it out.

BLACK GENOCIDE

In the United States, black genocide refers to the genocide of African Americans both in the past and in the present. The decades of lynching's and long-term racial discrimination were first formally described as genocide by a now defunct organization, the Civil Rights Congress, in a petition to the United Nations in 1951. In the 1960s, Malcolm X accused the US government of engaging in genocide against black people, citing long-term injustice, cruelty, and violence by whites against blacks. Some accusations of genocide have been described as conspiracy theories. After President Lyndon B. Johnson pushed through his War on Poverty legislation including public funding of the Pill for the poor in the mid-1960s, family planning (birth control) was said to be "black genocide" at the first Black Power Conference held in July 1967. In 1970 after abortion was more widely legalized, some black militants named abortion specifically as part of the conspiracy theory. Most African-American women were not convinced of a conspiracy, and rhetoric about race genocide faded. However, in 1973, media revelations about decades of government-sponsored compulsory sterilization led some to say that this was part of a plan for black genocide. During the Vietnam War the increasing use of black soldiers in combat provided a basis for the accusation of a government supported "black genocide". In recent decades, the Disproportionately High Black Prison Population Has Been Cited In Support Of the Theory.

Slavery as Genocide

After World War II and following many years of mistreatment of African Americans by white Americans, the US government's official policies regarding the matter shifted significantly. The American Civil Liberties Union (ACLU) said in 1946 that negative international opinion about US racial policies brought pressure to bear on the US and that this was helping to alleviate the mistreatment 'Of racial and national minorities'. In 1948 President Harry S. Truman signed an order desegregating the military. Black citizens increasingly challenged existing ways of racial discrimination. Paul Robeson signed the We Charge Genocide petition. The United Nations (UN) was formed in 1945. The UN debated and adopted a Genocide Convention in late 1948, holding that genocide was the 'Intent to destroy, in whole or in part', a racial group. Based on the "in part" definition, the Civil Rights Congress (CRC), a group composed of African Americans with Communist affiliations, presented to the UN in 1951 a petition called 'We Charge Genocide'. The petition listed 10,000 unjust deaths of African Americans in the nine decades since the American Civil War. It described lynching, mistreatment, murder, and oppression by whites against blacks to conclude that the US government was conducting a genocide of African Americans, by refusing to address 'The persistent, widespread, institutionalized commission of the crime of genocide.'

The petition was presented to the UN convention in Paris by CRC leader William L. Patterson, and in New York City by the singer and actor Paul Robeson who was a civil rights activist and a Communist member of CRC. The Cold War raised American concerns about Communist expansionism. The CRC petition was viewed by the US government as being against America's best interests with regard to fighting Communism. The petition was ignored by the UN; many of the charter countries looked to the US for guidance and were not willing to arm the enemies of the US with more propaganda about its failures in domestic racial policy. American responses to the petition were various: Radio journalist Drew Pearson spoke out against the supposed 'Communist propaganda' before it was presented to the UN. Professor Raphael Lemkin, a Polish lawyer who had helped draft the UN Genocide Convention, said that the CRC petition was a misguided effort which drew attention away from the Soviet Union's genocide of Estonians, Latvians, and Lithuanians. The National Association for the Advancement of Colored People (NAACP) issued a statement saying that there was no black genocide even though serious matters of racial discrimination certainly did exist in America. Walter Francis White, leader of the NAACP, wrote that the CRC petition contained "authentic" instances of discrimination, mostly taken from reliable sources.

He said, 'whatever the sins of the nation against the Negro—and they are many and gruesome—genocide is not among them.' UN Delegate Eleanor Roosevelt said that it was "ridiculous" to characterize long term discrimination as genocide. The 'We Charge Genocide' petition received more notice in international news than in domestic US media. French and Czech media carried the story prominently, as did newspapers in India. In 1952, African-American author J. Saunders Redding traveling in India was repeatedly asked questions about specific instances of civil rights abuse in the US, and the CRC petition was used by Indians to rebut his assertions that US race relations were improving. In the US, the petition faded from public awareness by the late 1950s. In 1964, Malcolm X and his Organization of Afro-American Unity, citing the same lynching's and oppression described in the CRC petition, began to prepare its own petition to the UN asserting that the US government was engaging in genocide against black people. The 1964 Malcolm X speech "The Ballot or the Bullet" also draws from "We Charge Genocide".

Sterilization

Further information: Eugenics in the United States. Beginning in 1907, some US state legislatures passed laws allowing for the compulsory sterilization of criminals, mentally retarded people, and institutionalized mentally ill patients. At first, African Americans and white Americans suffered sterilization in roughly equal ratio. By 1945, some 70,000 Americans had been sterilized in these programs. In the 1950s, the federal welfare program Aid to Families with Dependent Children (AFDC) was criticized by some whites who did not want to subsidize poor black families. States such as North and South Carolina performed sterilization procedures on low-income black mothers who were giving birth to their second child. The mothers were told that they would have to agree to have their tubes tied or their welfare benefits would be cancelled, along with the benefits of the families they were born into. Because of such policies, especially prevalent in Southern states, sterilization of African Americans increased from 23% of the total in the 1930s and 1940s to 59% at the end of the 1950s and rose further to 64% in the mid-1960s. In mid-1973 news stories revealed the forced sterilization of poor black women and children, paid for by federal funds. Two girls of the Relf family in Mississippi, deemed mentally incompetent at ages 12 and 14, and also 18-year-old welfare recipient Nial Ruth Cox of North Carolina, were prominent cases of involuntary sterilization. Jet magazine presented the story under the headline 'Genocide.' Critics said these stories were publicized by activists against legal abortion

Systemic racism as genocide

Military history of African Americans and Racial discrimination against African Americans in the U.S. Military. African Americans pushed for equal participation in US military service in the first part of the 20th century and especially during World War II. Finally, President Harry S. Truman signed legislation to integrate the US military in 1948. However, Selective Service System deferments, military assignments, and especially the recruits accepted through Project 100,000 resulted in a greater representation of blacks in combat in the Vietnam War in the second half of the 1960s. African Americans represented 11% of the US population but 12.6% of troops sent to Vietnam.] Cleveland Sellers said that the drafting of poor black men into war was "a plan to commit calculated genocide". Former SNCC chairman Stokely Carmichael, black congressman Adam Clayton Powell, Jr. and SNCC member Rap Brown agreed. In October 1969, King's widow Coretta Scott King spoke at an anti-war protest held at the primarily black Morgan State College in Baltimore. Campus leaders published a statement against what they termed "black genocide" in Vietnam, blaming President Richard Nixon in the US as well as President Nguyễn Văn Thiệu and Vice President Nguyễn Cao Kỳ from South Vietnam.

Prison

Further information: Incarceration in the United States § Ethnicity, and Race and crime in the United States In 1969, H. Rap Brown wrote in his autobiography, Die Nigger Die!, that American courts 'Conspire to commit genocide' against blacks by putting a disproportionate number of them in prison. Political scientist Joy A. James wrote that "anti-black genocide" is the motivating force which explains the way that US prisons are filled largely with black prisoners.

Author and former prisoner Mansfield B. Frazier contends that the rumor in American ghettos 'That whites are secretly engaged in a program of genocide against the black race' is given 'A measure of validity' by the number of Black men of child-producing age who are imprisoned for crimes for which men of other races are not.

Birth control

A falling birth rate has been identified by some observers as harmful to a race of people; for instance, in 1905 Teddy Roosevelt said that it was "race suicide" for white Americans if educated white women continued to have fewer children. Certain African-American leaders also taught that political power came with greater population. In 1934, Marcus Garvey and his Universal Negro Improvement Association resolved that birth control constituted black genocide. The combined oral contraceptive pill, popularly known as "the Pill", was approved for US markets in 1957 as a medicine, and in 1961 for birth control. In 1962, civil rights activist Whitney Young told the National Urban League not to support birth control for blacks. Marvin Davies, leader of the Florida chapter of the NAACP, said that black women should reject birth control and produce more babies so that black political influence would increase in the future. Lyndon B. Johnson and Martin Luther King, Jr., agreed that birth control was beneficial to poor black families. The Pill was considered expensive by working class women; the first users were upper- and middle-class women. After President Lyndon B. Johnson, as part of his War on Poverty, obtained legislation in 1964 for government funding of birth control, Black militants became more concerned about a possible government-sponsored black genocide. Cecil B. Moore, head of the NAACP chapter in Philadelphia, spoke out against a Planned Parenthood program which was to establish a stronger presence in northern Philadelphia; the population in the targeted neighborhoods was 70% black. Moore said it would be "race suicide" for blacks to embrace birth control.

H. Rap Brown said that black genocide was based on four factors, including birth control. From 1965 to 1970, black militant males, especially younger men from poverty-stricken areas, spoke out against birth control as black genocide. The Black Panther Party and the Nation of Islam were the strongest voices. The Black Panther Party identified a number of injustices as contributing to black genocide, including social ills that were more serious in black populations, such as drug abuse, prostitution, and sexually transmitted disease. Other injustices included unsafe housing, malnutrition, and the over-representation of young black men on the front lines of the Vietnam War. Influential black activists such as singer/author Julius Lester and comedian Dick Gregory said that blacks should increase in population and avoid genocidal family planning measures. H. Rap Brown of the Student Nonviolent Coordinating Committee (SNCC) held that black genocide consisted of four elements: more blacks executed than whites, malnutrition in impoverished areas affected blacks more than whites, the Vietnam War killed more blacks than whites, and birth control programs in black neighborhoods were trying to end the black race. A birth control clinic in Cleveland, Ohio, was torched by black militants who said it contributed to black genocide. Black Muslims said that birth control was against the teachings of the Koran, and that the role of women in Muslim society was to produce children. In this context, the Black Muslims felt that birth control was a genocidal attack by whites. The Muslim weekly journal, Muhammad Speaks, carried many articles demonizing birth control.

In Newark, New Jersey, in July 1967, the Black Power movement held its first convention: the National Conference on Black Power. The convention identified several means by which whites were attempting the annihilation of blacks. Injustices in housing practices, reductions in welfare benefits, and government-subsidized family planning were named as elements of "black genocide". Ebony magazine printed a story in March 1968 which revealed that black genocide was believed by poor blacks to be the impetus behind government-funded birth control. Reverend Martin Luther King, Jr., was a strong proponent of birth control for blacks. In 1966, he was honored with the Margaret Sanger Award in Human Rights, an award based on the tireless birth control activism of Margaret Sanger, a co-founder of Planned Parenthood. King emphasized that birth control gave the black man better command over his personal economic situation, keeping the number of his children within his monetary means. In April 1968, Martin Luther King, Jr., was shot and killed. Charles V. Willie wrote in 1971 that this event marked the beginning of serious reflection among African Americans 'About the possibility of [black] genocide in America. There were lynchings, murders, and manslaughters in the past. But the assassination of Dr. King was too much. Many blacks believed that Dr. King had represented their best... If America could not accept Dr. King, then many felt that no black person in America was safe.' Angela Davis said that equating birth control with black genocide appeared to be 'An exaggerated, even paranoiac reaction.'

Black women were generally critical of the Black Power rejection of birth control. In 1968, a group of black radical feminists in Mt. Vernon, New York issued 'The Sisters Reply'; a rebuttal which said that birth control gave black women the 'Freedom to fight the genocide of black women and children,' referring to the greater death rate among children and mothers in poor families. Frances M. Beal, co-founder of the Black Women's Liberation Committee of the SNCC, refused to believe that the black woman must be subservient to the black man's wishes. Angela Davis and Linda LaRue reacted against the Black Power limitations directing women to serve as mothers producing 'Warriors for the revolution.' Toni Cade said that indiscriminate births would not bring the liberation of blacks closer to realization; she advocated the Pill as a tool to help space out the births of black children, to make it easier for families to raise them. The Black Women's Liberation Group accused "poor black men" of failing to support the babies they helped produce, therefore supplying young black women with reason to use contraceptives. Dara Abubakari, a black separatist, wrote that 'Women should be free to decide if and when they want children.' A 1970 study found that 80% of black women in Chicago approved of birth control, and that 75% of women in their child-bearing years were using it. A 1971 study found that a majority of black men and women were in favor of government-subsidized birth control. In Pittsburgh, Pennsylvania, a community struggle for and against a birth control clinic in the Homewood area of east Pittsburgh made national news.

Women in Pittsburgh had lobbied for a birth control clinic in the 1920s and were relieved in 1931 when the American Birth Control League (ABCL) established one. The ABCL changed its name in 1942 to Planned Parenthood. The Pittsburgh clinic initiated an educational outreach program to poor families in the Lower Hill District in 1956. This program was twinned into the poverty-stricken Homewood-Brushton area in 1958. Planned Parenthood considered opening another clinic there and conducted meetings with community leaders. In 1963 a mobile clinic was moved around the area. In December 1965, the Planned Parenthood Clinic of Pittsburgh (PPCP) applied for federal funding based on the War on Poverty legislation Johnson had promoted. In May 1966, the application was approved, and PPCP began to establish clinics throughout Pittsburgh, a total of 18 by 1967, 11 of these subsidized by the federal government and placed in poor districts. In mid-1966 the Pennsylvania state legislature held up family planning funds in committee. Catholic bishops gained media exposure for their assertion that

Pittsburgh birth control efforts were a form of covert black genocide. In November 1966, the bishops said that the government was coercing poor people to have smaller families. Some black leaders such as local NAACP member Dr. Charles Greenlee agreed with the bishops that birth control was black genocide.

Greenlee said Planned Parenthood was 'An honorable and good organization' but that the federal Office of Economic Opportunity was sponsoring genocidal programs. Greenlee said 'The Negro's birth rate is the only weapon he has. When he reaches 21 he can vote.' Greenlee targeted the Homewood clinic for closure; in doing so he allied with black militant William 'Bouie' Haden and Catholic prelate Charles Owen Rice to speak out against black genocide, and against PPCP's educational outreach program. Planned Parenthood's Director of Community Relations Dr. Douglas Stewart said that the false charge of black genocide was harming the national advancement of blacks. In July 1968, Haden announced he was willing to blow up the clinic to keep it from operating. The Catholic Church paid him a salary of $10,000, igniting an outcry in Pittsburgh media. Bishop John Wright was called a 'Puppet of Bouie Haden.' The PPCP closed the Homewood clinic in July 1968 and stopped its educational program because of concerns about violence. The black congregation of the Bethesda United Presbyterian Church issued a statement saying that accusations of black genocide were 'Patently false.' A meeting was scheduled for March 1969 to discuss the issue. About 200 women, mostly black, appeared in support of the clinic, and it was reopened.

This was seen as a major defeat for the black militant notion that government-funded birth control was black genocide. Other prominent black advocates for birth control included Carl Rowan, James L. Farmer, Jr., Bayard Rustin, Jerome H. Holland, Ron Dellums and Barbara Jordan. In the US in the 21st century, black people are most likely to be at risk of unintended pregnancy: 84% of black women of reproductive age use birth control, in contrast to 91% of Caucasian and Hispanic women, and 92% of Asian Americans. This results in black women having the highest rate of unintended pregnancy in 2001, almost 10% of black women giving birth between the ages of 15 to 44 had unintended pregnancies, which was more than twice the rate of white women. Poverty affects these statistics, as low-income women are more likely to experience disruption in their lives; disruption which affects the steady use of birth control. People in impoverished areas are more suspicious of the health care system, and they may refuse medical treatment and advice, especially for less-critical wellness treatments such as birth control.

Abortion

Slave women brought with them from Africa the knowledge of traditional folk birth control practices, and of abortion obtained through the use of herbs, blunt trauma, and other methods of killing the fetus or producing strong uterine cramps. Slave women were often expected to breed more slave children to enrich their owners, but some quietly rebelled. In 1856 a white doctor reported that a number of slave owners were upset that their slaves appeared to hold a 'Secret by which they destroy the fetus at an early age of gestation'. However, this folk knowledge was suppressed in the new American culture, especially by the nascent American Medical Association, and its practice fell away. After slavery ended, black women formed social groups and clubs in the 1890s to 'Uplift their race.' The revolutionary idea that a black woman might enjoy a full life without ever being a mother was presented in Josephine St. Pierre Ruffin's magazine The Woman's Era. Knowledge was secretly shared among clubwomen regarding how to find practitioners offering illegal medical or traditional abortion services. Working-class black women, forced more often into sex with white men, continued to find a need for birth control and abortion. Black women who earned less than $10 per day paid $50 to $75 for an illegal and dangerous abortion. Throughout the 20th century, 'Backstreet' abortion providers in black neighborhoods were also sought out by poor white women who wanted to rid themselves of a pregnancy.

Abortion providers who were black were prosecuted much more often than white ones. In the Tennessee General Assembly in 1967, Dorothy Lavinia Brown, MD, the first African-American woman surgeon and a state assemblywoman, was the first American to sponsor a proposed bill to fully legalize abortion. Though this early effort failed, abortion was made legal in various US states from 1967 to 1972. During this time, the Black Panthers printed pamphlets describing abortion as black genocide, expanding on their earlier stance regarding family planning. However, most minority groups stood in favor of the decriminalization of abortion; the New York Times reported in 1970 that more non-white women than white women died as a result of 'Crude, illegal abortions'. Legalized abortion was expected to produce fewer deaths of the mother. A poll in Buffalo, New York, conducted by the National Organization for Women (NOW), found that 75% of blacks supported the decriminalization of abortion. In the 1970s, Jesse Jackson spoke out against abortion as a form of black genocide. After the January 1973 Roe v. Wade Supreme Court decision made abortion legal in the US, Jet magazine publisher Robert E. Johnson authored an article called 'Legal Abortion: Is It Genocide Or Blessing In Disguise?' Johnson cast the issue as one which polarized the black community along gender lines: black women generally viewed abortion as a 'Blessing in disguise' but black men such as Reverend Jesse Jackson viewed it as black genocide. Jackson said he was in favor of birth control but not abortion. The next year, Senator Mark Hatfield, an activist against legal abortion, emphasized to Congress that Jackson "regards abortion as a form of genocide practiced against blacks.'

In Jet, Johnson quoted Lu Palmer, a radio journalist in Chicago, who said that there was inequity between the sexes: a young black man who helped create an unwanted pregnancy could go his 'Merry way' while the young woman involved was stigmatized by society and saddled with a financial and emotional burden, often without a safety net of caregivers to sustain her. Civil rights lawyer Florynce Kennedy criticized the idea that black women were needed to populate the Black Power revolution. She said that black majorities in the Deep South were not known to be hotbeds of revolution, and that limiting black women to the role of mothers was 'Not too far removed from a cultural past where Black women were encouraged to be breeding machines for their slave masters.' Tennessee Assemblywoman Dorothy Brown said black women "should dispense quickly the notion that abortion is genocide", rather, they should look to the earliest Atlantic slave traders as the root of genocide. Congresswoman Shirley Chisholm wrote in 1970 that the linking of abortion and genocide 'Is male rhetoric, for male ears.'

However, a link between abortion and black genocide has been claimed by later observers. Mildred Fay Jefferson, a surgeon, and an activist against legal abortion, wrote about black genocide in 1978, saying 'Abortionists have done more to get rid of generations and cripple others than all of the years of slavery and lynching.' In 2009, American pro-life activists in Georgia revived the idea that a black genocide was in progress. A strong response from this strategy was observed among blacks, and in 2010 more focus was placed on describing abortion as black genocide. White pro-life activist Mark Crutcher produced a documentary called Maafa

21 which criticizes Planned Parenthood and its founder Margaret Sanger, and describes various historic aspects of eugenics, birth control and abortion with the aim of convincing the viewer that abortion is black genocide. Pro-life activists showed the documentary to black audiences across the US. The film was criticized as propaganda and a false representation of Sanger's work. In March 2011, a series of abortion-as-genocide billboard advertisements were shown in South Chicago, an area with a large population of African Americans. From May to November 2011, presidential candidate Herman Cain criticized Planned Parenthood, calling abortion 'Planned genocide' and 'Black genocide'.

Analysis

In 1976, sociologist Irving Louis Horowitz published an analysis of black genocide and concluded that racist vigilantism and sporadic action by individual whites was to blame for the various statistics that show blacks suffering from higher death rates. Horowitz concluded that the US government could not be implicated as a conspirator, that there was no conspiracy to engage in concerted black genocide. Political scientist Joy A. James wrote in 2013 that the 'Logical conclusion' of American racism is genocide, and that members of the black elite are complicit, along with white Americans, in conducting black genocide.

OSAMA BIN LADEN DEATH CONSPIRACY THEORIES

The death of Osama bin Laden gave rise to various conspiracy theories, hoaxes, and rumors. These include the ideas that bin Laden had been dead for years or is still alive. Doubts about bin Laden's death were fueled by the U.S. military's supposed disposal of his body at sea, the decision to not release any photographic or DNA evidence of bin Laden's death to the public, the contradicting accounts of the incident with the official story on the raid appearing to change or directly contradict previous assertions, and the 25-minute blackout during the raid on bin Laden's compound during which a live feed from cameras mounted on the helmets of the U.S. special forces was cut off. On May 1, 2011, an image purporting to show a dead bin Laden was broadcast on Pakistani television. Although the story was picked up by much of the British press, as well the Associated Press, it was swiftly removed from websites after it was exposed as a fake on Twitter. On May 4, the Obama administration announced it would not release any images of Bin Laden's dead body.

The administration had considered releasing the photos to dispel rumors of a hoax, at the risks of perhaps prompting another attack by al Qaeda and of releasing very graphic images to people who might find them disturbing. Several photos of the aftermath of the raid were given to Reuters by an anonymous Pakistani security official, but though all appeared to be authentic, they were taken after the U.S. forces had left and none of them included evidence regarding bin Laden's fate. On May 6, it was reported that an al-Qaeda website acknowledged bin Laden's death. On May 11, Republican senator and Senate Armed Services Committee member Jim Inhofe stated he had viewed 'Gruesome' photographs of bin Laden's corpse, and later confirmed that the body 'Was him', adding, 'He's history'. On May 21, 2015, journalist Seymour Hersh published a report claiming that Pakistan had kept bin Laden under house arrest since 2006, that the U.S. had learned of bin Laden's location through a Pakistani intelligence official and not through tracking a courier, and that elements of the Pakistani military aided the U.S. in killing bin Laden. The White House denied Hersh's report.

Lack of physical evidence

The primary source of skepticism about the U.S. government's story has been its own refusal to provide any physical evidence to substantiate its claim. Although the Abbottabad raid has been described in great detail by U.S. officials, no physical evidence constituting actual proof of his death has been offered to the public, neither to journalists nor to independent third parties who have requested this information through the Freedom of Information Act (FOIA). Numerous organizations filed FOIA requests seeking at least a partial release of photographs, videos, and/or DNA test results, including The Associated Press, Reuters, CBS News, Judicial Watch, Politico, Fox News, Citizens United, and NPR. At the time of filing their FOIA request, The Associated Press said: This information is important for the historical record.

Burial at sea

Doubts about bin Laden's death were fueled by the U.S. military's disposal of his body at sea, though U.S. officials maintained that the burial was necessary because arrangements could not be made with any country to bury bin Laden within 24 hours, as dictated by Muslim practice. The Muslim practice has not always been followed by the U.S. in the past. For example, the bodies of Uday Hussein and Qusay Hussein, sons of Saddam Hussein, were held for 11 days before being released for burial. In that instance, however, several Iraqi cities were reluctant to grant a gravesite for Saddam Hussein's sons. The decision to bury bin Laden at sea was questioned by terrorists and by some 9/11 survivors and the relatives of the victims. Professor Peter Romaniuk of John Jay College described the burial at sea as a way to forestall further questions. He stated: 'Obviously they're going to be under pressure to show a body or produce further evidence, but this was a way of taking that issue off the table.' A stated advantage of a burial at sea is that the site is not readily identified or accessed, thus preventing it from becoming a focus of attention or "terrorist shrine".

In Pakistan

Senior Pakistani officials disseminated the theory that no firefight ever took place, and that whoever the U.S. forces captured, they executed him outside the compound, and took his body away on a helicopter. Hamid Gul, the former head of Pakistan's Inter-Services Intelligence (ISI), stated in an interview with CNN that he believed bin Laden had died many years ago, and that the official death story given out by the American media was a hoax. Furthermore, he thinks the American government knew about bin Laden's death for years, 'They must have known that he had died some years ago, so they were waiting. They were keeping this story on the ice, and they were looking for an appropriate moment and it couldn't be a better moment because President Obama had to fight off his first salvo in his next year's election as he runs for the presidential and for the White House and I think it is a very appropriate time to come out, bring this out of the closet.' Yet another scenario was reported in an article in the Urdu newspaper Ausaf, which quoted military sources as saying, 'Bin Laden has been killed somewhere else. But since the US intends to extend the Afghan war into Pakistan, and accuse Pakistan, and obtain a permit for its military's entry into the country, it has devised the assassination scenario.' Bashir Qureshi, who lives close to the compound where bin Laden was shot and whose windows were blown out in the raid, was dismissive. 'Nobody believes it. We've never seen any Arabs around here; he was not here.'

In Iran

A number of Iranians said they believed that bin Laden was working with the U.S. during the entire war on terror. Ismail Kosari, an Iranian MP, said that bin Laden 'Was just a puppet controlled by the Zionist regime in order to present a violent image of Islam after the September 11 attacks', and that his death 'Reflects the passing of a temporary US pawn, and symbolizes the end of one era and the beginning of another in American policy in the region'. Another MP, Javad Jahangirzadeh, said he believed that it was the U.S. that had conducted the terrorist attacks, and bin Laden was the main source of help. He stated, 'The West has been very pleased with bin Laden's operations in recent years. Now the West was forced to kill him in order to prevent a possible leak of information he had; information more precious than gold.' Iranian President Mahmoud Ahmadinejad said, 'I have exact information that bin Laden was held by the American military for some time... until the day they killed him he was a prisoner held by them,' in a live interview on Iranian state television.

In Turkey

Berkan Yashar, a Turkish politician, stated that bin Laden died of natural causes on June 26, 2006, and was buried and that Americans dug out bin Laden's body and displayed it, falsely telling the world that he was killed in an assault.

Seymour Hersh

On May 21, 2015, Pulitzer Prize winning journalist Seymour Hersh published a 10,000 word report and later a book -- The Killing of Osama bin Laden, challenging most aspects of the official account of Osama's death. Among other things, the report claims that the Pakistani Inter-Services Intelligence (ISI) had kept bin Laden under house arrest at Abbottabad since 2006, and that when the US discovered this Pakistani Army chief Pervez Kayani and ISI director Ahmad Shuja Pasha helped the U.S. in killing, not capturing bin Laden. Hersh's U.S. and Pakistani intelligence sources stated that the U.S. had learned of bin Laden's location through a "walk-in", a former ISI officer who came to the US embassy in Islamabad in 2010 seeking the $25 million reward, and not through tracking a courier. This claim had been previously reported by R.J. Hillhouse and was confirmed afterwards by NBC news.

The White House denied Hersh's report. Pakistani journalist Ahmed Rashid in the New York Review of Books finds the cooperation between the CIA and ISI that Hersh describes 'Inconceivable,' in part because 2011 was 'The worst year in US-Pakistan relations since the late 1980s' and 'Hatred and mistrust' between the CIA and ISI was 'Acute'—something Hersh does not mention in his article/book. Among the incidents that occurred in Pakistan in the months before the killing of bin Laden were the killing of two Pakistanis by Raymond Davis a CIA contractor; numerous death threats against the Islamabad CIA station chief after his name was leaked (purportedly by the ISI); the cessation of the issuing of visas for US officials, following which the entire US consulate in Lahore was shut down and moved to Islamabad over concerns about security; increased US anger over the refusal of Pakistan to exert pressure on the Taliban and Haqqani group; the death of 40 Pakistanis including many civilians and later 24 Pakistani soldiers from US drone strikes, the cut off of US supplies to Afghanistan by Pakistan.

Further adding to the implausibility of Hersh's theory, according to Rashid, is the unlikeliness that either the US would have 'Calmly accepted' Pakistan's hiding/protecting bin Laden, or that the dozens of Pakistani military, police, fire, and bureaucrats whose silence/complicity would have been required for a successful conspiracy would have cooperated with the American incursion. While there was little or no disapproval by the Pakistan public over Bin Laden's long residency in Pakistan, the US attack on the compound of bin Laden was so unpopular that just the failure of the military to detect and go after the US helicopters ignited outrage among the media, the public and the civilian government. Andrew Anthony in The Guardian called Hersh's theories 'Forceful but unconvincing.' Zach Dorman in the Los Angeles Times called Hersh's judgment 'Mixed, at best.' Rashid, Anthony, and Dorman were also skeptical of another theory expounded in Hersh's book that the Ghouta chemical attack that killed hundreds of Syrian civilians where instigated not by the Syrian government, but by rebels aided by Turkey working as agents provocateurs, blaming the Syrian government in hopes of forcing the Obama administration to enter the war against the government.

Internet

Facebook groups formed discussing a rumor, in what has been dubbed the 'Death hoax.' Some blogs theorized that the raid and killing were faked, in a conspiracy to attempt to deflect questions about President Obama's citizenship, or to boost Obama's approval ratings and guarantee his popularity during the 2012 U.S. presidential election.

Other Theories

In 2002, the FBI's top counter-terrorism official, Dale Watson, said, 'I personally think he; Osama bin Laden is probably not with us anymore.' Anti-war activist Cindy Sheehan stated, 'If you believe the newest death of OBL, you're stupid.' Sheehan further stated on her Facebook page, 'The only proof of Bin Laden being dead again that we were offered was Obama telling us that there was a DNA match between the man killed by the Navy SEALs and OBL. Even if it is possible to get DNA done so quickly, and the regime did have bin Laden DNA lying around a lab somewhere. Where is the empirical proof?'

On Russia Today, radio host Alex Jones claimed that bin Laden had been dead for nearly ten years, and that his body had been kept in liquid nitrogen so that it can be used as a propaganda tool at a future politically expedient time. In 2002, he claimed that an anonymous White House source had told him that bin Laden 'is frozen, literally frozen and that he would be rolled out in the future at some date'. In a separate interview in 2002, Steve Pieczenik told Jones that bin Laden had been dead for months. Jones also pointed to similar comments made by former Secretary of State Madeleine Albright in 2003, 'Yes we have been told by intelligence that they've got him, Bush may roll him out but because they exposed that at the election they didn't do it'. Jones further voiced doubts about the official story of bin Laden's death on his radio show telling his listeners, 'My friends, this is a complete and total hoax.'

The Iranian network Press TV interviewed Webster Tarpley and Stephen Lendman, who both doubted the official story of bin Laden's death. Tarpley said he believed bin Laden had been dead for a long time. He also claimed that the public was deceived by a staged announcement. Both Tarpley and Lendman suggested that Obama's announcement was also an excuse to involve the United States in wars with Pakistan and Middle Eastern nations. Andrew Napolitano, the host of the Fox Business program Freedom Watch, said bin Laden's death could not be verified and insinuated that Obama was using the death of bin Laden to save his 'Lousy presidency.' An article in Mediaite criticized Napolitano's remarks, opining that 'Such conspiracy talk is ultimately beneath Napolitano and his often enlightened discussions.'

Canadian deputy Leader of the Opposition and MP, Thomas Mulcair, stated in an interview with CBC Television that 'I don't think from what I've heard that those pictures of bin Laden's body exist.' His remarks were picked up by dozens of U.S. media outlets and criticized by various Canadian politicians. An official statement from the Taliban stated that the lack of photos or video footage is suspicious, as their own sources close to bin Laden had not confirmed or denied his death, and that 'When the Americans killed Mullah Dadullah, Taliban's chief military commander they publicly showed the footage.'

THE UNSOLVED DEATH OF A CONSPIRACY THEORIST

'Your boy's in trouble. If anything happens to me, investigate.' This was a text British conspiracy theorist Max Spiers sent to his mother just a few days before his death. Spiers had many investigations regarding government/military cover ups, extraterrestrial life/UFOs, etc. Spiers was enthusiastic about his research and believed in many conspiracy theories; he wanted to share his research with the world. On July 16, 2016, in Warsaw, Poland, Spiers was found dead on the sofa in a friend's apartment. Spiers was in Poland because he was scheduled to speak at a conference. Colleagues and friends of Spiers believed he was going to expose most of the information he knew regarding black magic involved in politics, his experience with extraterrestrial life, and how he believed he was being mined controlled. The idea of being abducted and examined by extraterrestrials was something Spiers believed he had experienced. He also believed he had supernatural powers since birth.

Throughout the years, Spiers had some drug issues. He was in an accident while he was living in the U.S and cracked his pelvis. He was given a prescription of opiate pain relief and later developed an opioid use disorder. When Spiers was no longer able to receive opiates, he used heroin. According to his actions during an interview, where Spiers appeared to be drugged, it seems he may have relapsed, but I have a theory about this I will get to later. When Spiers died on his friend's sofa, his friend had called for an ambulance. But when the paramedics arrived, they were unable to revive him. The Polish authorities then handed Spiers' body over the British authorities. The Polish police never conducted an autopsy; the British authorities, on the other hand, did. Mysteriously, they ruled that Spiers died of natural causes. Does vomiting amounts of black liquid seem natural? Not at all. The case was said to be closed, but Spiers' mother, Vanessa Bates, would not let the case die. Bates believed her son did not die of natural causes. Bates would investigate, as her son told her to in that text a few days before his death. When Bates was made aware of Spiers' death and was given her son's belongings, including his laptop, she discovered the laptop had been wiped clean. None of Spiers' research was found on the computer, nothing was left to indicate that this laptop belonged to Spiers' at all.

Bates believes her son was killed on purpose. It is not known by who exactly, but she believes someone or some group of people, wanted Spiers' research to remain a secret. When Bates was shown the video of Spiers' interview before his death, she believed she had seen him like this when he was using heroin. But why would Spiers all of a sudden relapse? Why would Spiers want to appear in this state and make himself seem less credible? I believe Spiers was drugged by a person or organization who wanted to hurt his credibility. Because who is going to believe someone who gets intoxicated before an interview? I think Spiers was made to look like this was so no one would believe a word of his theories, and what he had uncovered. I am not blaming the government for his death. But it is clear that Spiers was wanted to be kept quiet. And the only way to do that, was to have him dead. The investigation is still ongoing because Bates had urged for the real reason of her son's death.
And until we find out what exactly happened, the death of this conspiracy theorist, remains unsolved.

PRINCESS DIANA CONSPIRACY THEORIES: EIGHT REASONS PEOPLE BELIEVE THE CRASH IN PARIS WASN'T ALL IT SEEMS.

On the night of 31 August 1997, something terrible certainly happened: Princess Diana was killed in a fatal car crash in Paris, and the effects would be felt around the world. But that is where the consensus ends. For some people, what happened that night wasn't simply a tragic accident. Instead, it was the result of some kind of conspiracy, conducted secretly by agents of the British state or something else, they claim. Numerous reports, investigations and experts have all agreed with the official account of events: that Diana had been in a car driven by a man who was drunk, and that failing as well as other institutional ones allowed for the tragedy to happen. But others still believe that something more secretive and intentional happened that night. The conspiracy theories take a number of other forms, but all claim to point to the same fundamental belief: that someone wanted to kill Diana, and they helped orchestrate that night's fatal crash. Those conspiracies were so convincing and so widespread, helped by the Daily Express and Egyptian businessman Mohamed al-Fayed that the Met Police were forced to launch Operation Paget, an inquiry to establish whether there was any truth I the theories. It lasted years, cost millions of pounds – and found that the theories were entirely without foundation, and that all that happened that night was an incredibly unfortunate accident.

Diana's death didn't change the nature of the monarchy

The report examined 175 theories about what happened that night, some of them small and some of them profound. It found that none of them were true, still, however, those conspiracies rage. Here are ten of the things that makes people doubt the official story of events, as well as the truth about each of the claims.

Diana was pregnant

This, according to Mohamed al-Fayed, was the reason for the killing. Diana had become pregnant with his son's child, he said, and that idea was unpalatable to the British state. Mr. Fayed said that the royal family "could not accept that an Egyptian Muslim could eventually be the stepfather of the future King of England." And so, it plotted to kill her off. Discussion of a potential pregnancy came up even before Diana died. During a holiday in France a few weeks before, some newspapers speculated that she might be pregnant, and that speculation was buoyed up by mysterious comments Diana made about "a big surprise." But there was no sign of pregnancy during the post-mortem examination. Further tests on Diana's blood found there was no sign of pregnancy there, either. And there's no evidence even that Diana suspected she may be pregnant: numerous close friends and others said that her menstrual cycle was normal, that she was using contraception, and that she hadn't mentioned even the possibility of being pregnant to her confidantes.

Diana believed she was going to be killed by the establishment

The main motivating factor behind the conspiracies is the belief that Diana herself thought she was going to be killed. And that much, it appears, is true. Chief among them is a letter that was disclosed by Paul Burrell, Diana's one time butler, who said he had been given it for safekeeping. 'I am sitting here at my desk today in October, longing for someone to hug me and encourage me to keep strong and hold my head high. This particular phase in my life is the most dangerous. [...] is planning 'an accident' in my car, brake failure and serious head injury in order to make the path clear for Charles to marry,' it read. The letter appears eerily prescient. And, indeed, it had history: when Diana wrote the letter, she had experienced problems with her car, had voiced fears about them, and her bodyguard had died in an accident that she believed had been a conspiracy. Diana clearly had concerns about her safety: that much isn't a conspiracy theory. But there appears to be no official suggestion that she would actually be killed, even if there was animosity between some members of the royal family and Diana.

The paparazzi made the car crash intentionally

Photographers were blamed repeatedly and continue to be for Diana's death. The story caught on in part because it reflected a concern that had pursued Diana throughout her life: that the often prurient interest in her was causing her harm. This theory has three specific forms. The first alleges that the group of paparazzi chased and pushed Diana's Mercedes so that it could make the crash happen. The second argues that members of the paparazzi encouraged an environment where a crash could happen. The third suggests that the paparazzi accidentally created a situation that the conspirators exploited to kill the people in the car. The official investigation pointed out that the paparazzi aren't really a meaningful group: though they do the same job, they generally compete with each other for the best photo. Many of them work for different companies and do entirely different jobs, with some working as professional photojournalists. Official investigations have found that the Mercedes car that Diana was in does seem to have driven quickly in part to escape the photographers. But Operation Paget found that was the result of normal behavior by the paparazzi, and that they hadn't been participating in any criminal conspiracy.

Driver Henri Paul intentionally caused the crash

Henri Paul was the head of security at the Ritz Hotel in Paris. But conspiracy theorists believe that he was in the pay of at least one other organization: the security services in France or the UK, or both. People who doubt the official course of events say that its central claim about Mr. Paul being drunk at the time of the crash was not only false, but was a lie spread in the media to cover up the killing. And that was done in part by swapping his body with another person, so that the toxicological results would appear correct. There are a number of reasons people believe this. Mr. Paul did not seem to behave like he was drunk earlier on in the night, for instance. And beliefs about him being in the pay of security services come from the fact that he appeared to have more money than would be expected, and that some security offices have suggested they might have had a French source inside the hotel. But there's no evidence to suggest that either of those things contributed to the crash in any way other than the official account. Numerous tests showed that Mr. Paul's blood had alcohol in it – though there were mistakes made with the tests and repeated checks of those have certified that Mr. Paul had indeed been drinking.

There was something wrong with the Mercedes that Diana was travelling in

There is perhaps nothing more central to the conspiracy than the car that carried Diana, and which would eventually kill her. Conspiracy theorists claim that its route was blocked, that it was driving at an unusual speed, or that something had been tampered with in the car. Everything about the car appeared to be in order. People reported seeing different speeds – and the car was certainly driving fast that night but there was nothing unusual about the way it was driving. But a large part of the confusion here appears to emerge from the fact that it is simply too difficult to estimate speed. Witnesses who reported different things probably weren't wrong but it's exceedingly difficult to tell how fast something is going when you're outside of it, especially if you don't have anything to compare it to.

Bright flashes and strange vehicles were on the road

Numerous people reported seeing flashes as the car head into the tunnel where it would crash, flashes that were blamed for the crash itself. But the problem was that many people reported different flashes, at different times, from different places. There were a lot of flashes that night: the photographers following the car, and the light of the headlights of the vehicles. But none of them appear to have been malicious, or part of a conspiracy.

Diana's medical care was deliberately sabotaged

Conspiracy theorists believe that doctors allowed Diana to die, on purpose. By not treating her in the proper way, they stopped her from recovering. Most of this revolves around her treatment at the scene of the crash. If she had instead been taken to the nearest hospital and treated there, she may have survived, they say. Part of the belief in this theory comes from the fact that the French approach to emergency care is simply different from the UK. In France, emergency crews focus on giving treatment at the scene before moving a person to hospital; in the UK, it's about getting to the hospital sooner. As the writers of the Operation Paget report note, such a conspiracy would require a substantial number of expert doctors and other caregivers to both break their ethics and then lie about doing so. That didn't happen, they conclude. It's impossible to say whether or not there would have been more success if Diana was taken to hospital. But either way, doctors have said that it was almost impossible for her ever to survive her injuries.

Diana's bodyguard was killed off

Conspiracy theories around Diana circulated even when she was alive and, indeed, the Princess appeared to believe them. In 2004, US news channel NBC aired video showing Diana talking about an affair with Barry Mannakee, a former bodyguard who she described as 'The greatest love I've ever had'. 'But it was all found out and he was chucked out of royal protection. Then he was killed. I think he was bumped off,' she said in the tapes. Conspiracy theorists took up that claim and suggested there was a mysterious driver who had apparently helped orchestrate the car crash that Mr. Mannakee died in. He had been riding as a pillion passenger on a motorbike – that bike crashed into another car that was coming out of a junction, intentionally, according to some. Cons rumbled on and became a part of the same set of beliefs that animate theories about what really happened to Diana. But The Independent found after an investigation published weeks ago that the truth was just as tragic, but entirely accidental. The driver of the car had actually stopped immediately and then agreed to help out with the investigation, including giving a statement to Operation Paget.

THE DANNY CASOLARO PRIMER

13 reasons to doubt the official narrative surrounding his death

With an incomplete investigation, uncooperative agencies, and numerous outright lies, the journalist's death remains a mystery. The official version of events surrounding Danny Casolaro's death has been questioned since the beginning, but several recent revelations resulting from the release of government documents have undermined it. While there are still questions about Casolaro's death, there are over a dozen reasons to doubt the official conclusions.

1. Police tainted expert witness with leading video and withholding evidence

The claims of suicide typically cite the findings of the expert witness, Dr. Henry Lee, who had concluded that the scene and the evidence was all consistent with suicide. This finding was based in part off of a video 'Reenactment' of Casolaro's death which the Federal Bureau of Investigation refuses to release a copy of, without citing a FOIA exemption. The same police force was later found to have withheld critical evidence from the expert witness, the presence of towels that had been used to wipe up blood at the scene. The towels were thrown away.

2. The disappearing briefcase

Just before his death, Casolaro had a briefcase full of documents and notes. When his body was found, the briefcase was gone. At best, this indicates someone secretly found his body and removed the notes. At worst, it means someone else was there when he died.

3. Bua Report lied about a witness's existence

The Justice Department's Bua Report, which dismissed Casolaro's death as a suicide, not only failed to disclose one of the witnesses who saw the briefcase just before Casolaro's death, it falsely stated that the police found only one person who thought they'd seen the briefcase. A review of the handwritten police notes proves this wrong, as a second witness very clearly states that they saw, without doubt, a briefcase full of papers shortly before Casolaro died. The DOJ had these notes sealed.

4. Bua Report lied about a witness hearing threats

5. FBI lied to Congress

When Congress asked the FBI about Casolaro's death, the FBI responded with a claim that they hadn't looked into it. This was a lie.

6. FBI pressured agents to conclude suicide

More than half the FBI agents that did look into Casolaro's death 'Questioned the conclusion of suicide' and recommended further investigation, despite being aware that this was a threat to their careers.

7. 90 percent of the FBI file has gone missing

The FBI and DOJ can't seem to agree about the status of the file on Casolaro, with the DOJ claiming that more than 90 percent of it has gone missing.

8. Chief suspect threatened Casolaro

According to his ex-girlfriend, the chief suspect in Casolaro's death, Joseph Cuellar, had previously threatened Casolaro

9. DOJ ignored chief suspect's contradictory alibis

The chief suspect gave the DOJ two irreconcilable alibis for Casolaro's death. The DOJ ignored one of the alibis.

10. Chief suspect's final alibi isn't an alibi

The timeline of the chief alibi's suspect that the DOJ decided to publicize doesn't actually provide him with an alibi for Casolaro's death.

11. FBI said local police were uncooperative

When the FBI attempted to look into Casolaro's death, they were met with 'Almost complete resistance from the Martinsburg police and prosecutor's office.'

12. FBI said DOJ was uncooperative, withheld unredacted Bua Report

When an FBI Task Force requested a copy of the unredacted Bua Report from the DOJ, they were denied access to it, including the information most relevant to their investigation. No explanation appears to have been provided.

13. There was an unreported wiretap

Exemptions cited for withholding materials implies there was an undisclosed wiretap in the Casolaro investigation. Read more here. In short, the investigation was incomplete, with evidence being both withheld and fabricated. The FBI was under pressure to conclude that it was a suicide, but still questioned that. Both the police and the DOJ were uncooperative. Multiple lies were told. The chief suspect lied about his alibi, and ultimately doesn't have one that holds up. What, exactly, happened to Casolaro is still something of a mystery, but there are over a dozen reasons why the official investigation and the resulting explanation don't - and can't - answer the questions around his suicide.

LAS VEGAS SHOOTING WAS 'FALSE FLAG' OPERATION, INFOWARS FOUNDER CLAIMS

Blogpost reveals Jerad and Amanda Miller, who killed three on Sunday, were fans of conspiracy website hosted by Alex Jones The shooting of two Las Vegas police officers on Sunday morning at CiCi's pizza place was a 'False Flag' operation staged by the US government, according to Alex Jones, the talk radio host, conspiracy theorist and founder of the website InfoWars. But Jerad and Amanda Miller, the two alleged shooters, were actually vocal fans of InfoWars.com, and, more than that, as first revealed by Mother Jones, Jerad had as early as 2012 posted on the site about killing police officers. Miller's post, which is from May in that year, is titled 'The Police (To kill or not to kill)'. Miller discusses, at length, encounters he'd had with police officers, as well as the unfairness of being on probation. In the post, Miller said one particular experience made him feel like he had taken 'A trip back in time to Nazi Germany.' 'I do not wish to kill police,' he wrote. 'I understand that most of them believe they are doing the right thing.' But, he explained in the post, he felt he had little choice. 'I'm being pushed further and further into a corner,' Miller said. 'I am like a wild coyote. You corner me, I will fight to the death.'

The post concluded: 'So, do I kill cops and make a stand when they come to get me? I would prefer to die than sit in their jail.' In the comments underneath the post, his then fiancée Amanda wrote: 'Jerad, baby, I love you with all my heart and I'll stand behind you no matter what. It's true that it's not fair that I can't have a gun because you live with me.' At the time, the couple were living in Indiana, where a previous drug charge against Jerad prevented them from purchasing firearms. Jerad and Amanda Miller also frequently posted links to InfoWars to their Facebook pages. They appear to have been believers in a wide range of conspiracy theories and anti-government beliefs, including some championed by Jones. During his radio broadcast on Monday morning, Jones said that there was "so much proof" that the shooting was staged by the government that when he read about the event, his mind 'Exploded with hundreds of data points.'

The Cult of Nikola Tesla

The name of Nikola Tesla is associated with crazy conspiracy claims that have nothing to do with his real work. No personality in the history of science has been pushed further into the realm of mythology than the Serbian-American electrical engineer Nikola Tesla. He is, without a doubt, one of the true giants in the history of electromagnetic theory. As an inventor he was as prolific as they come, with approximately 300 patents having been discovered in at least 26 countries, but many more inventions as well that stayed within his lab and were never patented. As remarkable as were his talents was his personality: private, eccentric, possessed of extraordinary memory and bizarre habits, and with a headlong descent into mental illness during his later years. Tesla's unparalleled combination of genius and aberrance have turned him into one of the seminal cult figures of the day. As such, at least as much fiction as fact have swirled around popular accounts of his life, and devotees of conspiracy theories and alternative science hypotheses have hijacked his name more than that of any other figure. Today we're going to try and separate that fiction from the fact.

First, a very brief outline of his life; but in order to put it in the proper perspective, we have to first clear up a popular misconception. Tesla did not invent alternating current, which is what he's best remembered for. AC had been around for a quarter century before he was born, which was in 1856 in what's now Croatia. While Tesla was a young man working as a telephone engineer, other men around Europe were already developing AC transformers and setting up experimental power transmission grids to send alternating current over long distances. Tesla's greatest early development was in his mind: a rotary magnetic field, which would make possible an electric induction motor that could run directly from AC, unlike all existing electric motors, which were DC. At the time, AC had to be converted to DC to run a motor, at a loss of efficiency. Induction motors had been conceived before his birth, but none had ever been built. Tesla built a working prototype, but only two years after another inventor, Galileo Ferraris, had also independently conceived the rotary magnetic field and built his own working prototype.

Rightfully fearing that his own obscurity as a telephone engineer was hampering his efforts as an inventor, Tesla arranged to move to the United States. He did so in 1884, getting his famously ill-fated and short-lived job in Thomas Edison's laboratory. The tycoon George Westinghouse, who understood the potential of AC and induction motors and was actively seeking them, gratefully purchased some of Tesla's patents as soon as he learned about them. Royalties from Westinghouse fattened Tesla's wallet, and a number of highly public projects on which they collaborated made him a celebrity, including the 1893 illumination of the World's Fair with alternating current, and the subsequent creation of the Niagara Falls power plant. It was as a result of this windfall that Tesla set up his own laboratories and created his most intriguing inventions. Let's run through a list of some of the seemingly magical feats attributed to Tesla, beginning with:

Did Tesla invent X-rays?

Tesla did in fact accidentally create the first X-ray photographs in 1895, although inadvertently, when taking a picture of his friend Mark Twain with an early form of fluorescent tube light called a Geissler tube that, unbeknownst to Tesla, also emitted X-radiation. Before he could investigate further, his lab burned down, and he lost all that work. At nearly the same time, Wilhelm Röntgen announced his discovery of the X-ray. Later Tesla experimented with more powerful tubes to create stronger X-rays.

Did Tesla invent radio?

Generally, Tesla did beat Guglielmo Marconi to the demonstration of workable wireless communication and Tesla eventually won all the patent disputes (after his death), though Marconi is the one who shared a Nobel Prize for it. However, both men had been building upon theory and experimentation by dozens of other researchers going back nearly a full century. Patents for distinct types of wireless communication had begun to be filed by other inventors thirty years before either man. Tesla became famous for his radio controlled boat demonstration in 1896, but throughout 1895 and 1896, many inventors worldwide made all sorts of radio demonstrations, in Russia, India, the United States, and Europe. Tesla's contributions to radio were as good as anyone's, but they were hardly revolutionary in a field that was exploding at the time.

Did Tesla really sit in the middle of a room filled with lightning bolts?

Tesla spent two years in Colorado Springs where the El Paso Electric Company had agreed to give him free power. There he built the world's largest Tesla coil, the device most often associated with his name. A Tesla coil is a simple type of transformer, taking a low-voltage input and stepping it up to an exceedingly high voltage, even over several million volts. A large primary coil, into which the original low-voltage current is input, surrounds the base of a tightly-wound secondary coil sticking up in the air, like a big pole, and at the top is a metal torus. At full power, enough electrons are sent up that pole that they are forced to burst out into the atmosphere through the torus, creating the familiar lightning-like streamers that characterize Tesla coil demonstrations. Tesla posed for a famous publicity photograph that you've seen many times, of himself sitting in a chair inside his lab taking notes while the air all around him is filled with such streamers from his giant coil. This picture was, unfortunately, a double exposure. Among the actual cases of Tesla being ahead of his time was that his Colorado Springs coil had a third coil that increased the voltage through a process that we now call resonant rise. Resonant rise was not well understood until the 1970s.

Did Tesla cause a field of light bulbs 26 miles away to illuminate wirelessly?

He may or may not have; but it's almost certainly a myth. According to biographer John O'Neill, he did, but not quite as magically as is popularly depicted, and no supporting evidence has ever surfaced. Tesla's days at Colorado Springs were meticulously diarized, and no such experiment appears in them. Tesla discovered that the function served by the long inner coil could also be served by a different type of conductor, including the Earth itself. He took a Tesla coil and stuck its inner secondary coil into the ground. He input electricity to the primary coil, and this setup caused his current to be sent into the Earth. That current could be received by an identical setup, some 26 miles away, by receiving current from the primary coil. Wired to that receiver coil, he had an array of some 200 conventional incandescent light bulbs set out in a field.

So, although the light bulbs themselves were conventionally wired to a normal power source, that power was transmitted wirelessly. Whether this grand display ever happened or not (nobody has ever been able to duplicate it, despite many attempts), Tesla did record some of the calculations, and photographs do exist of very small scale experiments conducted locally at his lab — probably the closest he ever came. His idea for such a great distance as 26 miles relied on resonance to enhance the effect. He determined that the resonant frequency of the Earth's electromagnetic field was about 8 Hz. This frequency was rediscovered by science 50 years later when physicist Winfried Schumann predicted it while searching for ways to communicate with submarines.

Did Tesla create ball lightning?

Ball lightning, the very existence of which is dubious at best, beautifully illustrates the type of mythology that has been built up around Tesla. Many sources say he routinely created ball lightning in Colorado Springs, and there are even carefully edited quotes of Tesla's purporting to describe it. In fact, Tesla is not known to have ever mentioned ball lightning in any of his writing or speaking, and no record from his time is known to exist stating that he created, demonstrated, or knew about anything that could reasonably be called ball lightning despite intense rumormongering to the contrary, and despite a few mentions of 'Electric fireballs' in his writings which were about conventional matter burning normally. Tesla and ball lightning is pure mythology, consistent with cloaking a deified figure like Tesla with powers that seem almost magical.

Did Tesla plan to transmit power world-wide through the sky?

It was his ultimate plan, but the farthest he ever got was the partial construction of his famous tower at Wardenclyffe which was intended for wireless communication across the Atlantic. His worldwide wireless power system was theoretical only, employing the Schumann resonance to charge the Earth's ionosphere such that a simple handheld coil could receive electrical power for free anywhere, and everywhere, in the world. Tesla's idea was innovative, but innovative idea it remained, as debts mounted, and the tower was dismantled before it ever got to be used. Now that the nature of the ionosphere is much better understood, physicists now consider Tesla's concept unworkable, and no attempts to test it have ever worked. All sorts of conspiracy theories exist, for example that the HAARP research facility in Alaska is secretly a test of Tesla's worldwide power grid, or some sort of superweapon based on it. The profound differences between these systems become clear upon doing even the most basic of research.

Did Tesla invent a Death Ray?

Investment in Tesla's projects stopped with the advent of the Great Depression in the 1930s. During the final decade of his life, Tesla was essentially penniless and living in a New York hotel, consumed by what we think today was probably obsessive compulsive disorder. It was during this period and not earlier during his productive laboratory years that he openly spoke of having built and tested a Death Ray. None of Tesla's lab assistants ever corroborated this, and no papers, prototypes, or evidence have ever surfaced. He gave vague descriptions with only inadequate hints of what type of technology such a weapon might use. Whether this was mere showmanship to attract new investment, was a legitimate but unknown concept, or was only the ramblings of a deteriorating mind, will probably never be known.

Did the government seize all his notes upon his death?

Yes, they did. Tesla died in January of 1943, during some of the darkest hours of World War II. The war was going badly, and the American government was more than a little willing to bend the rules. The year before, nearly all Japanese Americans were imprisoned in an effort to prevent spying. So it wasn't that big of a stretch for the government, having heard his claims of a Death Ray, to employ a statute enacted during World War I that enabled an Alien Property Custodian to seize all assets of any enemy during wartime even though Tesla was an American citizen. They entered his New York hotel room and seized all his documents, which was all that remained of his life's work by that time. It wasn't very much, as Tesla's habit throughout his life was to keep plans in his head. It took the National Defense Research Committee's expert, Dr. John G. Trump, only three days to issue the following report.

Tesla's thoughts and efforts during at least the past 15 years were primarily of a speculative, philosophical, and somewhat promotional character often concerned with the production and wireless transmission of power; but did not include new, sound, workable principles, or methods for realizing such results. The hotel told them that Tesla had given them, as collateral in lieu of rent he could not afford, a piece of very dangerous equipment worth $10,000.

Trump collected it and reported:

...A multidecade resistance box of the type used for a Wheatstone bridge resistance measurements, a common standard item found in every electric laboratory before the turn of the century.

Appreciate the man, not the myth.

Hardly anything written about Nikola Tesla fails to exaggerate his inventions and deify the man. Factually wrong descriptions of his accomplishments are found all over the place. His name is broadly smeared by association with virtually every crank conspiracy theory on the planet. They want magically easy answers to complicated problems, and when they hear that Tesla invented such answers and that the government and industry suppressed them, they trumpet his name to the world. This group has become little more than a cult, an insult to the man and his accomplishments. However, Nikola Tesla was not to blame for any of that. Every reasonable textbook and history book on electromagnetic theory rightly confers upon him the enormous credit he fairly earned. Taking the trouble to learn about Tesla, about his unique personal history and about the reality of what his true contributions were, will always put you on firmer ground than accepting the untrue exaggerated or conspiratorial claims. Whenever you hear a good scientist's name co-opted and exploited by the promoters of crankery, you should always be skeptical

There are Hundreds more to research…..

12. *Drop My Shit Off At The Cleaners*

CLINTON BODY BAGS

Bill Clinton has quietly done away with several dozen people who possessed incriminating evidence about him. Multiple versions of lengthy lists of deaths associated with

Bill Clinton have been circulating online for about twenty years now. According to those lists, close to fifty colleagues, advisors, and citizens who were about to testify against the Clintons died in suspect circumstances, with the unstated implication being that Bill Clinton or his henchmen were behind each untimely demise. We shouldn't have to tell anyone not to believe this claptrap, but we will anyway. In a frenzied media climate where the Chief Executive couldn't boff a White House intern without the entire world finding out every niggling detail of each encounter and demanding his removal from office, are we seriously to believe the same man had been having double handfuls of detractors and former friends murdered with impunity? Don't be swayed by the number of names listed on screeds like this. Any public figure is bound to have a much wider circle of acquaintance than an ordinary citizen would. Moreover, the acquaintanceship is often one-sided: though many of the people enumerated on this list might properly claim to have 'Known' Clinton, he wouldn't know or remember having met a substantial number of them. "Body count" lists are not a new phenomenon. Lists documenting all the allegedly 'Suspicious' deaths of persons connected with the assassination of John F. Kennedy have been circulating for decades, and the same techniques used to create and spread the JFK lists have been employed in the Clinton version.

- List every dead person with even the most tenuous of connections to your subject. It doesn't matter how these people died, or how tangential they were to your subject's life. The longer the list, the more impressive it looks and the less likely anyone will be to challenge it. By the time readers find the underlying cause of the list, they'll be too weary to wonder what could possibly be relevant about the death of people such as Bill Clinton's mother's chiropractor.

- Play word games. Make sure every death is presented as "mysterious." All accidental deaths are to be labelled "suspicious," even though by definition accidents occur when something unexpected goes wrong. Every self-inflicted death discussed must include the phrase "ruled a suicide" to imply just the opposite. When an autopsy contradicts a "mysterious death" theory, dispute it; when none was performed because none was needed, claim that "no autopsy was allowed." Make liberal use of words such as 'allegedly' and 'supposedly' to dismiss facts you can't support or contradict with hard evidence.

- Make sure every inconsistency or unexplained detail you can dredge up is offered as evidence of a conspiracy, no matter how insignificant or pointless it may be. If an obvious suicide is discovered wearing only one shoe, ignore the physical evidence of self-inflicted death and dwell on the missing shoe. You don't have to establish an alternate theory of the death; just keep harping that the missing shoe "can't be explained."

- If the data doesn't fit your conclusion, ignore it. You don't have to explain why the people who claimed to have the most damaging goods on Bill Clinton (e.g., Gennifer Flowers, Paula Jones, Kathleen Willey, Linda Tripp, Monica Lewinsky, Kenneth Starr), walked around unscathed while dozens of bit players were supposedly bumped off. It's inconvenient for you, so don't mention it.

- Most important, don't let facts and details stand in your way! If you can pass off a death by pneumonia as a "suicide," do it! If a cause of death contradicts your conspiracy theory, claim it was "never determined." If your chronology of events is impossible, who cares? It's not like anybody is going to check up on this stuff …

Multiple versions of this 'Body count' list have been circulating online for two decades now. New victim names are routinely added, and old ones taken off, forming an endless variety of permutations. At this point, there is no one 'Official' list. But where did all this craziness start? In a 1994 letter to congressional leaders, former Rep. William Dannemeyer listed 24 people with some connection to Clinton who had died 'Under other than natural circumstances' and called for hearings on the matter. Dannemeyer's list of 'Suspicious deaths' was largely taken from one compiled by Linda Thompson, an Indianapolis lawyer who in 1993 quit her year-old general practice to run her American Justice Federation, a for-profit group that promotes pro-gun causes and various conspiracy theories through a shortwave radio program, a computer bulletin board, and sales of its newsletter and videos. Her list, called 'The Clinton Body Count: Coincidence or the Kiss of Death?' then contained the names of 34 people she believed had died suspiciously and who had ties to the Clinton family. Thompson admitted she had 'No direct evidence' of Clinton's killing anyone.

Indeed, she said the deaths were probably caused by "people trying to control the President" but refused to say who they were. Thompson said her allegations of murder 'Seem groundless only because the mainstream media haven't done enough digging.' Ah, but they had. If not before she put her list together, at least afterwards. Anyone who continues to state the mainstream media has given these claims short shrift is being disingenuous. Since 1994, various respected news outlets have been confronted with versions of the 'Clinton Body Count' list, run their own investigations of a few of the claims, and found nothing to substantiate what they looked into. Those investigations would culminate in yet another story about an oddball conspiracy rumor. But conspiracy theories don't die that easily. These 'Body count' lists and the many specious claims contained therein continue to circulate in cyberspace and beyond: yesterday's newspaper articles are forgotten with the next day's delivery, but e-mail lives forever.

James McDougal, Clinton's convicted Whitewater partner died of an apparent heart attack, while in solitary confinement. He was a key witness in Ken Starr's investigation. James McDougal, a key witness for Whitewater prosecutors when the investigation centered on an Arkansas land deal in which the president and McDougal were involved, had a pre-existing heart condition, and died of a heart attack on 8 March 1998 while in solitary confinement at the Federal Medical Center prison in Fort Worth. The ailing McDougal had been placed in solitary as punishment for failing to provide a urine sample for a drug test. On the day before his death and while still in his regular cell (where he had access to his heart medications), he had complained of dizziness, and while being processed for isolation he threw up. However, once in isolation, he did not ask for his medicines and appeared to guards 'Alert, well-oriented and absent any visible signs of distress' right up until his death. An investigation into the circumstances of his demise did not find evidence of foul play.

1.) Mary Mohane - former White House intern gunned down in a coffee shop. Nothing was taken. It was suspected that she was about to testify about sexual harassment at the White House. Former White House intern Mary Caitrin Mahoney, 25, manager of a Georgetown Starbucks, was killed along with two co-workers (Emory Allen Evans, 25, and Aaron David Goodrich, 18) on 6 July 1997 during a robbery of the shop. In March 1999, Carl Derek Havord

Cooper (29) of Washington was arrested and charged with these murders. Yes, it is unusual that three employees were killed in the course of a robbery during which nothing was taken. According to Cooper's 26 April 2000 guilty plea (he received life with no hope of parole), he went to the Starbucks to rob the place, figuring the receipts from the July 4 weekend would make for a fat take. He came in after closing, waved a .38, and ordered all three Starbucks employees into the back room. Once there, Mahoney made a run for it after Cooper fired a warning shot into the ceiling. She was ordered back to the room, but then went for the gun. Cooper shot her, then afterwards shot the other two employees. He left empty-handed, afraid the shots had attracted police attention. As regrettable as these three deaths were, this was nothing, but a case of a robbery gone wrong. And, right away, we have come to the first big lie of the 'Clinton Body Count' list.

Any unexplained death can automatically be attributed to President Clinton by inventing a connection between him and the victim. Mary Mahoney did once work as an intern at the White House, but so have hundreds of other people who are all still alive. There is no credible reason why, of all the interns who have served in the Clinton White House, Mahoney alone would be the target of a Clinton-directed killing. (Contrary to public perception, very few interns work in the West Wing of the White House or have any contact with the President. The closest most interns get to the chief executive is a single brief handshake or group photo.) The putative reason offered for Mahoney's slaying, that she was about to testify about sexual harassment in the White House, was a lie. This absurd justification apparently sprang from a hint dropped by Mike Isikoff of Newsweek just before the Monica Lewinsky scandal broke that a 'Former White House staffer' with the initial 'M' was about to talk about her affair with Clinton. We all know now, of course, that the 'Staffer' referred to was Monica Lewinsky, not Mary Mahoney. The conspiracy buffs maintained that White House hit men rushed out, willy-nilly, and gunned down the first female ex-intern they could find whose name began with 'M.'

2.) Vincent Foster - former White House Counsel, found dead of a gunshot wound to the head and ruled a suicide. He had significant knowledge of the Clintons' financial affairs and was a business partner with Hillary. If the Clintons are guilty of the crimes they are accused of by Larry, Vincent Foster would have detailed knowledge of those crimes. This laundry list of deaths always refers to someone taking his life as 'Ruled a suicide,' thus implying another conclusion of equal likelihood was capriciously dismissed by someone who had the power to do so. From here on, read 'Ruled a suicide' as 'an investigation was carried out and arrived at this ruling as the only reasonable conclusion.' White House deputy counsel Vince Foster committed suicide on the night of 20 July 1993 by shooting himself once in the head, a day after he contacted his doctor about his depression. A note in the form of a draft resignation letter was found in the bottom of his briefcase a week after his death. (Note that this letter was not, as is often claimed, a 'Suicide note;' it was Foster's outline for a letter of resignation.)

Foster cited negative Wall Street Journal editorials about him, as well as the much-criticized role of the counsel's office in the controversial firing of seven White House travel office workers. On 10 October 1997, special prosecutor Kenneth Starr released his report on the investigation into Foster's death, the third such investigation (after ones conducted by the coroner and Starr's predecessor, Robert B. Fiske) of the matter. The 114-page summary of a three-year investigation concluded that Foster shot himself with the pistol discovered in his right hand. There was no sign of a struggle, nor any evidence he'd been drugged or intoxicated or that his body had been moved. If Foster had been murdered or if unanswered questions about his death remained, Starr would have been the last person to want to conclude the investigation prematurely. Or are we to believe Kenneth Starr is part of the cover-up, too? And if we buy into this conspiracy theory, what are we expected to believe? That a group of professional killers capable of furtively carrying out dozens of murders all over the world shot Vince Foster, then clumsily dumped him in a park (after he had bled out), planted a gun he didn't own in his hand (without bothering to press his fingerprints onto it), amateurishly forged a suicide note (in several different handwritings), then expected the nation would believe his death was a suicide?

3.) C. Victor Raiser, II - former National Finance Co-Chairman of Clinton for President, and Montgomery Raiser, his son. Both died in a suspicious private plane crash in Alaska. No cause determined. Raiser was considered to be a major player on the Clinton team. All plane crashes are 'Suspicious,' because airplanes are supposed to stay in the air, and when they don't it's because something went terribly wrong. Pilot error and mechanical failure are by far the most common causes underlying any crash. The National Transportation Safety Board (NTSB) investigates every downed plane in the U.S., and though they might not always pin down the exact cause of a crash, they're generally fairly good about ruling out the use of explosives or mechanical tampering. If the NTSB doesn't find evidence of tampering or explosives, then that's not what downed the plane, and we're left with pilot error and mechanical failure as our choices. Raiser, his son, and three others died in a plane crash in Alaska on 30 July 1992 during a fishing trip. The pilot and another passenger survived and were hospitalized with severe burns. While the 'Body count' list claims 'No cause determined,' the NTSB reported otherwise: pilot error in a small plane flying in mountainous terrain during low visibility conditions led to the crash.

4.) Paul Tully - DNC Political Director, was found dead in a Little Rock hotel room. No cause was ever determined, and no autopsy was allowed. Tully was a key member of the damage control squad and came up with some of the Clinton strategies. Paul Tully died on 24 September 1992. Problem is, there wasn't anything the least bit unusual about his death, so whoever cooked up this list had to lie and claim that 'No cause was ever determined' and 'No autopsy was allowed.' However, an autopsy was performed, and Tully's cause of death was determined: a massive heart attack. (Not a surprising demise, given that Tully was extremely overweight, a heavy drinker, and a chain smoker.) According to Steve Nawojczyk, the Pulaski County coroner, 'An autopsy by the Arkansas medical examiner's office discovered advanced coronary artery disease.' He added that investigators found no evidence of external trauma to the body. Note again that the conspiracy buffs offer no putative reason for Tully's "killing" and would have us believe that Clinton ordered his chief strategist rubbed out while the most important election of his career was a little over a month away.

5.) Ed Willey - Clinton fund raiser. Found in the woods in Virginia with a gunshot wound to the head. Ruled a suicide. Ed Willey was a former Virginia state senator and a lawyer; his wife Kathleen was active in Democratic state politics, worked as a volunteer (including some fund-raising efforts) on behalf of the Clinton campaign in Virginia in 1992, and later served as a volunteer in the White House Social Office. Ed Willey's death was as clear cut a case of suicide as one is likely to find he was a desperate, unstable man who (along with his wife) spent money lavishly, stole $275,000 of a client's money, and was about half a million dollars in debt to the IRS. He took his own life on 29 November 1993, leaving behind a suicide note found by his wife reading: 'Saying I'm sorry doesn't begin to explain. I hope one day you will forgive me.' At the same time as Willey was killing himself, his wife was allegedly being groped by Bill Clinton. She said she'd gone to the Chief Executive looking for a job to help her family out of its fiscal crisis and found herself fending off his advances. Clinton admitted to the meeting but denied her version of what took place. Kathleen Willey testified in Paula Jones' sexual harassment suit against Clinton, but she never claimed that Clinton had her husband killed.

6.) Hershell Friday - Clinton fund-raiser. His plane exploded. Herschel Friday, an Arkansas lawyer who had been on the Clinton presidential campaign finance committee, died in an airplane accident on 1 March 1994. His plane did not 'Explode;' this accident was another case of pilot error that occurred when the 73-year-old Friday, at the plane's controls, crashed it during an attempted landing on a poorly-lighted private airfield at dusk on a dark and drizzly day.

7.) Jerry Parks - former security team member for Governor Clinton. Prior to his death he had compiled an extensive file on Clinton's activities. His family had reported being followed and his home broken into just before being gunned down at a deserted intersection. On 26 September 1993, Luther (Jerry) Parks was hit with ten bullets from a 9-mm semiautomatic handgun as he left a Mexican restaurant at the edge of Little Rock. His murder remains unsolved. Parks' security company guarded Clinton's campaign headquarters in 1992. Parks' son, Gary, asserted in Circle of Power and The Clinton Chronicles (both video products of Linda Thompson's American Justice Federation) that his father collected a secret file of Clinton's indiscretions, and that his father was using the file to try to blackmail the Clinton campaign. (He also claimed that Vince Foster knew of the file's existence.) Despite these allegations, the younger Parks never produced the mysterious file, and Clyde Steelman, a homicide sergeant with the Little Rock police force, dismissed Gary Parks' theories of his father's death as "unsubstantiated, nothing to grasp." A far more likely suspect in the murder was Jerry Parks' former partner, with whom Parks had quarreled bitterly.

8.) John Wilson - former Washington D.C. council member. Had ties to Whitewater. Died of a very suspicious hanging suicide. John Wilson was the chairman of the District of Columbia Council, and his suicide was far from 'Very suspicious,' Wilson had a long history of depression, was wrestling with marital problems, and had tried to kill himself on at least four other occasions. He finally succeeded on 19 May 1993. Upon his death, Wilson's wife said, 'His depression was an inherited problem; that he was able to contribute so much over the years in the face of his disability was a miracle.' Police said that he did not leave a note and that there were no signs of foul play. Wilson had absolutely nothing in common with Clinton other than that they worked in the same city (i.e., Washington, D.C.). The claim that Wilson had anything to do with the Whitewater real estate controversy is laughable.

9.) Kathy Ferguson - former wife of Arkansas State Trooper Danny Ferguson, the co-defendant with Bill Clinton in the Paula Jones lawsuit. Found dead in her living room of a gunshot wound to the head. Ruled a suicide. Interestingly, her packed suitcases seemed to indicate she was about to go somewhere. Kathy Ferguson killed herself with a gunshot to the right temple on 11 May 1994 at the home of her boyfriend, Bill Shelton. Their relationship had fallen on challenging times, with each accusing the other of having been unfaithful. Ferguson left behind a suicide note that read: 'I can't stay here any longer. Things will never be the same for us. I can't take that.' Close by was another note from Shelton questioning her relationship with another man, which Ferguson's daughter said her mother had been upset over? We found no mention of packed suitcases in any of the reports about Ferguson's death, but even if there were, it wouldn't be the least bit surprising. Is it so unusual that a woman might be thinking of moving out of the house of a boyfriend who had quarreled with her and challenged her fidelity?

10.) Bill Shelton - Arkansas state trooper and fiancé of Kathy Ferguson. Allegedly committed suicide by shooting himself at her grave. Shelton killed himself over Kathy Ferguson's grave on 12 June 1994, leaving a suicide note that was found beside his body. Just a month earlier he had quarreled with his girlfriend, accused her of cheating on him, and driven her to suicide. There was nothing mysterious about his death or his reasons for taking his life. And if the idea that the ex-wife of an Arkansas state trooper constitutes a Clinton 'Connection' weren't absurd enough, we're now offered the boyfriend of an ex-wife of an Arkansas state trooper.

11.) Gandy Baugh - attorney for Dan Lasater in a financial misconduct case. Supposedly jumped out the window of a tall building to commit suicide. News accounts stated that Gandy Baugh died 'At home' on 8 January 1994 without specifying the causes. 'Died at home' is a euphemism often employed in news articles and obituaries to avoid a direct mention of suicide, but we haven't found any definitive information about how Baugh died.

12.) Dr. Donald Rogers - dentist. Killed in a suspicious plane crash on his way to an interview with reporter Ambrose Evans-Pritchard to reveal information about Clinton. On 3 March 1994, the Cessna plane carrying a pilot, dentist, Donald Rogers, and two other passengers crashed. The pilot had earlier radioed in that he was experiencing electrical trouble and then lost radio contact. The NTSB's investigation of the crash found nothing 'Mysterious' about it: the plane's left generator had severely overheated and shut down, leaving the plane without electrical systems; the plane went down far off its planned route, and the pilot was good and lost at the time of the crash. No amount of digging has disclosed why a dentist would have such revelatory information about the President of the United States that a plane crash had to be arranged to bump him off.

13.) Stanley Huggins - lawyer investigating Madison Guaranty. Suicide. His extensive report has never been released. How anyone can confuse dying of pneumonia with suicide is beyond us. Huggins died on 23 June 1994, and according to Dr. Richard Callery, Delaware's top medical examiner, viral myocarditis and bronchial pneumonia killed Huggins. Lt. Joel Ivory of the University of Delaware police said his exhaustive investigation of Huggins's death turned up 'No sign at all of foul play.'

14.) Florence Martin - Accountant for the CIA and had information on the Barry Seal case. Three gunshot wounds to the head. On 23 October 1994, 69-year-old Florence Martin of Mabelle, Texas (40 miles from Wichita Falls), was murdered in her home by three gunshots to the head through a pillow. She wasn't an accountant for the CIA, though, she worked the graveyard shift at a convenience store in nearby Seymour and had lived in that area for decades. In 2012, Jack Wesley Melton was charged with Martin's murder. DNA found at the scene was matched to him, leading to his arrest.

15.) Suzane Coleman - reportedly had an affair with Clinton. Was seven months pregnant at the time she was found dead of a gunshot wound to the back of the head, ruled suicide? At the time of Susan Coleman's suicide, Bill Clinton was her law professor. In 1992 an overzealous supporter of George Bush hired investigators to probe this girl's 1977 suicide, and they found no evidence that she and Clinton had an affair. It was an old rumor and a baseless one, and even a determined attempt at muckraking turned up nothing to substantiate it.

16.) Paula Grober - Clinton's interpreter for the deaf. Traveled with Clinton from 1978 until her death in 1992 in a one-car accident. There were no witnesses. The accident that killed Paula Grober took place during the afternoon of 7 December 1992. Her car overturned at a curve in the highway, throwing her 33 feet from the vehicle. No one witnessed the accident. And again, no one has provided any explanation for what secrets about Clinton an interpreter might possess that would merit her murder.

17.) Paul Wilcher - attorney investigating corruption. He had investigated federal elections, drug and gun smuggling through Mena, the Waco incident, and had just delivered a lengthy report to Janet Reno. He died in his home of unknown causes. Wilcher's partially decomposed body was found seated on the toilet in his Washington, D.C., home on 22 June 1993, and his death was attributed to natural causes. According to the Washington Times, Wilcher 'Was investigating the theory of an 'October Surprise' conspiracy during the 1980 federal election campaign. He had been interviewing an inmate who claimed to have piloted George Bush to Paris so he could secretly seek to delay the release of 52 American hostages in Iran.' President Clinton, just a year into his first term, would hardly be likely to give up a key political advantage by bumping off someone who was supposedly about to dig up some major dirt on the opposition party.

18. Jon Parnell Walker — RTC investigator who mysteriously fell to his death from an apartment balcony. We have turned up no information about this man, not a report of his death nor of his being a Resolution Trust Corporation investigator. Various versions of this list state that his death took place on 15 August 1993 at the Lincoln Towers in Arlington, Virginia, but we've found no documentation of that.

19.) Ron Brown - former DNS Chairman, Commerce Secretary. Reported to have died in a plane crash, but new evidence reveals he may have been shot in the head. He was being investigated by a special investigator and was about to be indicted with 54 others. He spoke publicly of his willingness to 'Make a deal' with the prosecutors to save himself a few days before the fatal trip. He was not supposed to be on the flight but was asked to go at the last minute. (This count does not include the other business leaders and other passengers who died on this government-sponsored trade mission.) What 'New evidence'? Ron Brown and 34 others were killed in a plane crash in Croatia on 3 April 1996. The plane slammed into a mountain while on landing approach. There were no survivors. Much has been made of an x-ray of Brown's skull showing what supposedly looks like a round entry wound. Closer examination of Brown's skull by military officials revealed no bullet, no bone fragments, no metal fragments and even more telling, no exit wound. Simply imagining a scenario under which Ron Brown could have been shot takes one into the realm of the absurd. Was he shot in the head during the flight, in full view of thirty-four other witnesses? (If so, how did the shooters get off the plane?) Did the killers shoot him before the flight, then bundle his body into a seat (just like Weekend at Bernie's) and hope nobody noticed the gaping hole in his head? Or did Croatian commandos fortuitously appear on the scene to scale a mountain and pump a bullet into the head of an already-dead plane crash victim? An exhaustive Air Force investigation of the crash found that pilot error was to blame.

The aircrew made errors while planning and executing the mishap flight, which, when combined, were a cause of the mishap. During mission planning, the crew's review of the Dubrovnik approach failed to determine that it required two automatic direction finders, or ADFs, and that it could not be flown with the single ADF onboard their aircraft. Additionally, the crew improperly flight planned their route which added 15 minutes to their flight time. The pilots rushed their approach and did not properly configure the aircraft for landing prior to commencing the final segment of the approach. They crossed the final approach fix flying at 80 knots above final approach speed, and without clearance from the tower. As a result of the rushed approach, the late configuration, and a radio call from a pilot on the ground, the crew was distracted from adequately monitoring the final approach. The pilots flew a course 9 degrees left of the correct course. They also failed to identify the missed approach point and to execute a timely missed approach.

20.) Barbara Wise - Commerce Department secretary. Worked with Ron Brown and John Huang and had extensive knowledge of their activities. Found dead in her locked office the day after Thanksgiving. It was ruled a suicide. Interestingly, she was found partially clothed, bruised, and in a pool of blood. There was no pool of blood, and Barbara Wise's death was never ruled a suicide by anyone. She was discovered in her Commerce Department office on 29 November 1996 after having last been seen alive on 27 November 1996, the day before Thanksgiving. A thorough investigation uncovered no evidence of foul play or suicide. Wise had a history of frequent and severe health problems, including liver ailments, and her death was attributed to natural causes.

21.) Charles Meissner - Assistant Secretary of Commerce. John Huang was given a special security clearance by Meissner. Shortly thereafter, he died in the crash of a small plane. Charles Meissner died in the same plane crash that took the life of Ron Brown, the one in Croatia on 3 April 1996. Fourteen Commerce Department staffers died in that crash, Meissner, and Brown among them. We're now entering a long segment of the list wherein a number of deaths are tied to those of Don Henry and Kevin Ives, who were supposedly linked to Bill Clinton. All of this linkage is one big canard: Henry and Ives had nothing to do with Clinton; they were two young men who foolishly ripped off drugs from a dealer and were beaten to death in revenge. With no link between Clinton and Henry or Ives, the following eight entries collapse like a house of cards.

22 & 23.) Kevin Ives and Don Henry - Seventeen-year-old boys who apparently saw something related to drugs in Mena by accident late at night. Officially ruled an accidental death on the train tracks, but evidence shows they died before being placed on the tracks, one of a crushed skull and the other of a knife wound in the back. Henry and Ives were run over by a train on 23 Aug 1987. Dr. Fahmy Malak, Arkansas' former state medical examiner, ruled the deaths accidental, saying the teens fell asleep on the tracks after smoking marijuana. A 1988 Saline County grand jury determined the boys were murdered and their bodies afterwards laid on the tracks, but no other conclusions were reached, and no indictments were returned. A number of Malak's determinations had been challenged and overturned during his career. He certainly wasn't always a conscientious medical examiner, and his Ives and Henry rulings were only two of many such he botched. Getting back to the real meat of who killed the boys, we find nothing that ties Ives and Henry to Clinton. Though several of these lists will claim the boys accidentally stumbled onto a 'Protected' drug drop and were killed for it, there's no reason to believe even that. In a 25 May 1990 hearing before U.S. Magistrate Henry Jones Jr., Katherine Brightop said her ex-boyfriend Paul William Criswell told her that he and three other men were involved in the teenagers' deaths. Brightop said Criswell told her the boys tried to steal cocaine from

Callaway's home and they were caught and beaten to death before their bodies were placed on the tracks.

24.) Keith Koney - had information on the Ives and Henry deaths. Died in a motorcycle accident with reports of a high-speed car chased involved. 19-year-old Keith Coney died on 17 May 1988 when the motorcycle he was driving struck the back of a tractor-trailer. He was riding a motorcycle he'd stolen the day before. There were no reports of a high-speed car chase involved in his fatal traffic accident.

25.) Keith McKaskle - had information on the Ives and Henry deaths. Stabbed to death. In August 1989, Ronald Shane Smith was sentenced to ten years for the 10 November 1988 murder of Keith McKaskle. McKaskle had earlier expressed fears for his life, linking them to his knowing something about "the railroad track thing." Smith may have been paid to kill McKaskle, as a prison inmate said he had been approached and offered $4,000 to kill McKaskle himself.

26.) Gregory Collins - had information on the Ives and Henry deaths. Gunshot wound to the head. Greg Collins (25) of Bryant, Arkansas, was found shot in woods near Rosston on 2 December 1989. If he truly knew something about drug-related murders, that's reason enough for him to have been killed without any connection to Bill Clinton.

27.) Jeff Rhodes - had information on the Ives and Henry and McKaskle deaths. Tortured, mutilated, shot, body burned in a dumpster. In July 1989 Frank Pilcher was arrested for the April 1989 murder of Jeffrey Rhodes. Rhodes had earlier told his father he feared for his life because he'd witnessed a narcotics transaction. Rhodes was last seen alive on April 3. His body was discovered in a dumpster on April 19. He'd been shot twice in the head and his body was severely burned. The body was likely burned in an effort to destroy forensic evidence that would lead investigators to the murderer.

28.) James Milam - had information on the Ives and Henry deaths. He was decapitated. The coroner ruled death due to natural causes. This is my favorite entry. Remember that Arkansas medical examiner, the one I said wasn't always the most conscientious investigator on God's green earth? Yep, we're about to see him again. Fahmy Malak listed James Milam's cause of death as a perforated ulcer, adding that Milam's small dog afterwards ate the dead man's head, accounting for Milam's headless condition. Milam's daughter-in-law insisted Milam was murdered. She claimed Malak showed her photographs of the headless corpse, and the neck was cut clean. The Milam family has not attempted to legally challenge the ruling because of the expense, so we'll never know which way the cat jumps, ulcer, or murder. Whatever killed him, Milam died three months before the Ives and Henry murders. What are we supposed to believe here, that Clinton conspirators knocked off someone who "had information on the Ives and Henry deaths" three months before Ives and Henry actually died? Wow, talk about a preemptive strike!

29.) Jordan Kettleson - had information on the Ives and Henry deaths. Found shot in the front seat of his pickup truck. 21-year-old Jordan Kettleson died on 25 June 1990.

30.) Dr. Stanley Heard - Chair, National Chiropractic Health Care Advisory Committee. He personally treated Clinton's mother, stepfather, and brother. His personal small plane developed problems, so he rented another. Fire broke out in flight, and he crashed. Stanley Heard and Stephen Dickson died on 10 September 1993, when their Piper Turbo Lance II caught fire shortly after takeoff from Dulles airport and crashed. They'd attended a briefing that morning on the Clinton administration's health care plan. Dickson's plane had developed mechanical problems on the way to Washington the week before, so Dickson and Heard rented the Cherokee in St. Louis to make the trip. They rented a badly maintained plane, and it cost them their lives. Here is what the NTSB had to say about this crash. I've found nothing on the National Chiropractic Health Care Advisory that Heard supposedly chaired.

31.) Steve Dickson - attorney for Heard. Died in same plane crash.
Dickson attended the same briefing Heard did. We do not know if he was there as Heard's lawyer or for independent reasons.

32.) John Hillier - video journalist and investigator. He helped to produce the documentaries 'Circle of Power,' and 'The Clinton Chronicles.' He mysteriously died in a dentist's chair for no apparent reason. Again, we could find no record of this man's death or of his work. There have been a few dental chair deaths, but we turned up nothing on this one.

33.) Maj. Gen. William Robertson

34.) Col. William Densberger

35.) Col. Robert Kelly

36.) Spec. Gary Rhodes

37.) Steve Willis

38.) Robert Williams

39.) Conway LeBleu

40.) Todd McKeehan

41.) Sgt. Brian Haney

42.) Sgt. Tim Sabel

43.) Maj.William Barkley

44.) Capt. Scott Reynolds

* Above all former Clinton bodyguards who are dead.

Steve Willis, Robert Williams, Todd McKeehan, and Conway LeBleu were Alcohol, Tobacco and Firearms agents killed during the Waco confrontation on 28 February 1993. Brian Haney, Timothy Sabel, William Barkley, and Scott Reynolds died in a helicopter crash on 19 May 1993. These four were members of Marine Helicopter Squadron One, the unit responsible for transporting the President. They died when the Blackhawk helicopter they had taken out for a maintenance-evaluation flight crashed. There was no evidence of sabotage. Clinton had set foot in the aircraft on only one occasion, two months earlier, when he traveled from the White House to the USS Theodore Roosevelt. Jarrett Robertson, William Densberger, Robert Kelly, and Gary Rhodes all died on 23 February 1993 when their Army UH-60 Blackhawk helicopter crashed on landing in Weisbaden, Germany. A jury later found that the pilots were not at fault, but that the helicopter 'Entered into an uncontrollable right turn caused by a design defect.'

45.) Gary Johnson - former attorney for Larry Nichols, severely beaten and left for dead. Again, we could find nothing on this incident or even this man's life.

46.) Dennis Patrick - had millions of dollars laundered through his account at Lasater & Co. without his knowledge. There have been several attempts on his life, all unsuccessful. It's hard to know what to say about this one. Though we found credible reference to Patrick's life having been in danger a few times, we were unable to trace back to news reports on the original incidents. Without seeing them, we're not confident in stating an opinion on whether or not those attempts took place. Patrick was a client of Lasater, albeit a reluctant one. He was asked to open an account there, he refused, one was opened for him anyway, and he was handed 'Profits" from one transaction for his part in allowing whatever was going on to take place. Again, someone who got involved with drug dealers ended up in trouble. In this case, an otherwise upstanding man took money he knew to be dirty to keep quiet about what his account was being used for. If was subsequently chased by drug dealers who didn't want the details of the transactions to come too light, was that all that surprising?

47.) L.J. Davis - reporter. While investigating the Clinton scandals he was attacked in his hotel room and his notes were taken. He survived. Davis said he had awakened in his hotel room with a big bump on his head. He soon admitted having drunk at least four martinis that night. No pages were missing from his notebook, and he had no idea how he ended up on the floor. 'I certainly wasn't about to conclude that somebody cracked me on the head,' Davis said at the time.

48.) Larry Nichols - former marketing director of ADFA. Responsible for bringing forth more evidence and witnesses on Clinton corruption than any other source. Very public about his claims against Clinton. He has suffered six beatings, arrest on trumped up charges, and a near arrest. In 1988 Larry Nichols, then a marketing director for the Arkansas Development Finance Authority, was fired from his job for making hundreds of calls to the Nicaraguan contras from his office. In 1990 he filed a lawsuit against Clinton claiming the then-Governor of Arkansas and others made him the scapegoat in a misappropriation-of-funds charge that cost him his job. In that suit he also tossed in claims of extramarital affairs, naming five women Clinton was supposed to have chased across the sheets. Nichols withdrew his lawsuit in 1992 and issued a round of apologies to everyone involved. He admitted what he'd said had been an attempt to destroy the Governor by innuendo.

Nichols has since changed his tune yet again, and has returned to making allegations against Clinton, always being careful to stop just short of asserting Clinton is involved in various murders and other crimes Nichols points to as 'Suspicious.' Since his dismissal from the AFDA, Nichols has made a career of peddling anti-Clinton books and tapes to the lunatic fringe. Take anything claimed about or by this man with a huge grain of salt. Now, ask yourself: how many people with whom you were acquainted have died mysteriously or violently in the past 10 years. The bottom line on this piece of e-lore? It's a badly worked laundry list dressed up to appear significant. The promised damning connections to the Chief Executive are missing, with innuendo misinformation offered up in their place. Nothing ties Clinton to any of these deaths, something this list (and others of its ilk) conveniently glosses over.

What evidence is offered that would compel a rational person to believe there was Clinton involvement in any of these deaths? Clinton was acquainted with some people who died, that's about all one can make of this list. Indeed, that's far more than can be made of a number of the entries, specifically, that of Ives and Henry and all those supposedly tied to theirs. Though it's clear from digging through numerous newspaper articles there was a thriving and dangerous drug culture in Little Rock, how or why this should be connected to Bill Clinton is left unanswered. Regrettably, Little Rock is akin to numerous other large cities: it has its share of drug dealers, murders, and violence. It also has one very famous citizen. And that's about as much of a connection as anyone can make. Whereas a typical private citizen has a much smaller circle of acquaintance, those in public office come into contact with a great many people over the course of their careers. It is therefore not unusual to find at least a few accidental deaths, homicides, and suicides among any politician's list of contacts. (For example, a "body count" list exists for George Bush.)

A number of suicides are enumerated in this list. Suicide is far from an unusual mode of demise. It claims 32,000 lives in the U.S. every year, and it's the 9th leading cause of death. It is indeed a rare person who does not know someone who died by his own hand. Deaths by airplane crash account for a number of entries on the list. Again, this is not all that surprising. Every year many small planes crash in the United States, and some of those crashes result in fatalities. As mentioned above, the National Transportation Safety Board investigates every one of them, to determine both the cause of the accident as well as to gather data that will help prevent future tragedies. The agency does a thorough job of looking into the circumstances surrounding each downed plane. To describe any of the plane crash deaths on this list as 'Suspicious' is to suggest the NTSB was part of a cover-up. There have been a couple of unsolved murders (Jerry Parks, Kevin Ives, and Don Henry), but there have also been deaths by natural causes that have been tossed into the mix willy-nilly simply to boost the body count. (As we said earlier, how can anyone claim a death by pneumonia was a suicide?) All the best lies make sure to mix a bit of truth in with them, and the few genuinely unsolved murders work to cloak the many less credible claims in an aura of plausibility. Don't be overly bemused by them, study each entry on its own merits.

One final question to ask yourself before falling for any Clinton Body Count list: If the Chief Executive was having people bumped off left, right, and center, why aren't Monica Lewinsky and Linda Tripp on this list? At the time of Mary Mahoney's death, a death this list hints was ordered by Clinton, neither Tripp nor Lewinsky were the high-profile household names they now are; they were complete unknowns. It would be another six months before information about them would explode into the news. If the President were in the habit of having those dangerous to his presidency put in the ground, why didn't he order these deaths?

On April 8, QAnon posted two messages linking the Clintons and the CIA to the plane crash of John F. Kennedy Jr and how his death cleared the path for Hillary Clinton to start her political career by running unopposed by any major Democratic rival for the newly available US Senate seat for New York. If the Clintons were involved in the death of JFK Jr it would be ironic since Bill Clinton sought to find out who killed President Kennedy just before his inauguration in January 1993, presumably to avoid a similar fate. The answers he received later helped Hillary Clinton launch her political career. It's worth repeating that QAnon represents several figures associated with U.S. military intelligence that are working through the Trump White House to release sensitive information to help expose and overcome the power of the Deep State through covert operations. Hence QAnon's posts opens the reader to the rarefied world of actionable U.S. military intelligence. Furthermore, QAnon's posts reveal the thinking of military intelligence officials about leading political figures such as the Clintons and agencies such as the CIA. We are now ready to closely examine what QAnon had to say about JFK Jr: The first two lines of the post reveal that Donald Trump had a relationship with JFK Jr.

This is not that surprising since there are photos showing Trump and Kennedy together at his exclusive Mar-a-Lago club on Feb 29, 1996. The fact that they were probably friends is significant in that Trump would likely be highly motivated to have the truth come out about what really happened. The next line in the post refers to the Kennedy's plane crash on July 16, 1999, which killed him, his wife and sister-in-law. The crash happened soon after JFK Jr had told two friends that he was planning to run for the U.S. Senate seat that had become available after the retirement of Daniel Patrick Moynihan. Only months before the crash, Hillary Clinton had declared her candidacy for the Senate seat, but was running into criticism for being a carpetbagger since she and Bill Clinton were not New York residents. According to a New York Daily News story published on July 20, 1999, JFK, Jr., was secretly planning to run for the Senate seat despite Hillary having already declared her candidacy. Given a 1997 private poll showing that 'John F. Kennedy Jr. was by far the state's most popular Democrat.' it's highly likely that he would have succeeded. Kennedy's entry into the Senate seat race would have denied Hillary the start she was seeking to her political career just before Bill's impending Presidential retirement.

QAnon was clearly linking the plane crash to the start of Hillary's political career. While some may consider this to be mere coincidence, QAnon's next post suggested something sinister had in fact happened. The link was to a January 1956 document in the CIA's reading room that discussed an Earth Satellite Program that was linked to Guided Missiles and CIA operations. CIA Director Allen Dulles was mentioned as a part of the program. QAnon was implying that that JFK Jr's plane crash was linked in some way to this or a similar advanced aerospace program, the CIA and Dulles. The Dulles connection is highly significant since there is much documentation linking him directly to the 1963 assassination of President John F. Kennedy. More specifically, there is a Memorandum containing a set of eight policy directives drafted by Dulles on behalf of a mysterious committee called Majestic 12 (MJ-12) in charge of advanced aerospace programs. One of the eight directives, Project Environment, gave cryptic authorization for the assassination of any public official that threatened Majestic 12 operations.

DRAFT – DIRECTIVE REGARDING PROJECT ENVIRONMENT

When conditions become non-conducive for growth in our environment and Washington cannot be influenced any further, the weather is lacking any precipitation … it should be wet. Dr Robert Wood, who is the foremost expert in analyzing MJ-12 documents using forensic methods, has concluded that the partially burned document is an assassination directive. In an interview discussing the burned document, he pointed out that the cryptic phrase 'It should be wet' originates from Russia, where the phrase 'Wet works' or 'Wet affairs' denotes someone who had been killed and is drenched with blood. In the book, Kennedy's Last Stand, I analyzed the testimonies, circumstances and documents supporting the conclusion that Dulles had arranged for the MJ-12 directives to be applied to the Kennedy administration in general, and to President Kennedy in particular. The CIA's Counter Intelligence chief, James Jesus Angleton, was given the authority to carry out the MJ-12 directives, as documented in a leaked November 12, 1963, Memorandum released only 10 days before Kennedy's assassination.

The Top Secret Memorandum instructed the then Director of the CIA, John McCone, to share all classified UFO information with NASA, in order to fulfill its requirement as outlined in National Security Action Memorandum (NSAM) 271. In short, the two memoranda Kennedy issued on November 12, 1963, would ensure that access to classified UFO files would be extended to more government agencies, ultimately resulting in direct Presidential access. Such direct access had been denied to President Kennedy by McCone's predecessor, Allen Dulles, who retired as CIA Director in November 1961, but likely continued on in his other position as head of the MJ-12 Committee as suggested in the eight MJ-12 Policy Directives. It's feasible that the MJ-12 Directives drafted by Dulles and approved by the MJ-12 Committee were used not only for the 1963 assassination of President Kennedy, but also for the removal of his son, 36 years later. There have been many questions raised about Kennedy's plane crash and whether or not it was simply due to his inexperience as a pilot, compounded by marital and financial problems, as suggested in an official report by the National Transportation Safety Board.

Was the report a cover up for the plane being shot down or sabotaged in a targeted assassination conducted by the CIA? This is exactly what QAnon appears to be suggesting. So why would the CIA want to help Hillary Clinton attain public office, and was this related in any way to Dulles' mysterious MJ-12 Directives? To get an answer, we can begin with the Clintons involvement in a CIA run drug operation out of Mena, Arkansas during Bill's governorship.

There have been multiple witnesses and documents showing how then Governor Clinton was protecting and facilitating the Mena CIA operation. In late 2017, a movie based on real events was released showing how a former TWA airline pilot, Barry Seal, was recruited by the CIA to a covert operation out of Mena, Arkansas, which involved illegal arms and drug running, and how Governor Clinton protected the entire operation.

More damning is the testimony and documents supplied by Roger Morris, an investigative journalist, who exposed the full extent of Clinton's involvement in the CIA drug running program, and Seal's involvement. In a book, interviews and documentary, Morris revealed how the thousands of documents and many witnesses in his investigation were never published by the mainstream media or investigated by the FBI or the U.S. Congress. The reason why Morris' investigative efforts got nowhere is that the drug money was used by the CIA to finance MJ-12 operations secretly conducted throughout the US in the development of advanced aerospace programs. Many UFO sightings were in fact advanced aerospace vehicles that were part of secret space programs under development by the US Air Force and Navy, with the help of major aerospace corporations. Having shown his usefulness in the CIA drug running operation at a state level, the MJ-12 group cleared the path for Clinton to become President so he could do the same at a national level. Just before beginning his first term on January 20, 1993, President-Elect Clinton made a very strange request to close family friend and lawyer Webster Hubbell:

'If I put you over there in justice I want you to find the answer to two questions for me: One, who killed JFK. And two, are there UFOs.' According to Hubbell, who described the incident in his memoirs, Friends in High Places, 'Clinton was dead serious.' Hubble said that he was unsuccessful in finding satisfactory answers. He was eventually forced to resign as Associate Attorney General due to the Whitewater political scandal and was jailed in July 1995 for 18 months. The Clintons quickly learned, because of what had happened to Hubble, that the Deep State, through the CIA and mysterious policy groups like Majestic 12, had great power. Despite all his power as President, Clinton could not thwart the Deep State's plans.

The Clintons decided to end their efforts to get answers to questions concerning JFK's assassination and what lay behind the UFO phenomenon. This was despite them knowing that the CIA drug running operations was secretly funding highly classified aerospace programs. By the end of Bill's Presidency, the CIA's 'Unofficial' black budget was estimated to be as much as one trillion dollars annually, which was more than double the Pentagon's budget at the time. The Clintons had become a critical part of the CIA/MJ-12 operations at both state and national levels during Bill's political career. As Bill's Presidency wound down, Hillary's political career offered another opportunity for a compliant and heavily compromised political leader that would support the CIA's illicit fund raising for secret MJ-12 operations. Secret deals were subsequently struck, and the CIA/MJ-12 (aka Deep State) supported Hillary's rise to political power, and the New York Senate Seat was planned to be her launching pad for high political office.

Consequently, when JFK Jr was on the verge of publicly declaring that he was going to run for the Senate seat, not only did he threaten Hillary's nascent political career, but he also threatened the carefully crafted plans for future CIA funding of MJ-12 operations. Consequently, the same or a similar policy directive to Project Environment, which had been used to assassinate President Kennedy, could now be used against JFK Jr for his threat to MJ-12 operations. QAnon's posts linking JFK Jr's 1999 plane crash with Hillary Clinton and the CIA are certainly a bombshell. Close examination of the history of the Clintons and CIA secret Deep State actors such as MJ-12 provides a powerful rationale for why JFK Jr was perceived as a threat and assassinated in a plane crash made to look like an accident.

SETH RICH: HOW A YOUNG MAN'S MURDER ATTRACTED CONSPIRACY THEORIES

The unsolved death of a Democratic Party operative became political when conspiracy theories took off on social media. Now, nearly two years later, one simple question has been left unanswered: who killed Seth Rich? In the early hours of 10 July 2016, Seth Rich was making his way home from a night out in Washington DC. The 27-year-old was a digital campaigner with the Democratic Party, and he lived in the Bloomingdale area of the city, home to many young politicos hoping to make it big in the nation's capital. Seth was chatting to his girlfriend as he ambled the few miles home from his favorite bar. At 4:19 a.m. he told her he was almost at the door and had to go. Second later, gunshots rang out. Seth was found lying on the ground a block from his apartment. He had two bullet holes in his back and his watch, wallet and phone were all found on him. There were signs of a struggle. Seth's hands and face showed bruising. He died shortly thereafter. The Washington police say that Seth's murder was a street robbery gone wrong. The case remains unsolved.

But unlike most other murders, Seth's death soon became a national story, as conspiracy theorists latched on in the fevered atmosphere of the 2016 presidential election. The timing of the murder and the fact that he had worked for a political party instantly raised eyebrows. Just weeks after his death, Wikileaks published 20,000 emails obtained from Democratic National Committee computers via an anonymous source. Seth's death became the subject of a series of conspiracy theories. Depending on the politics of those speculating, Seth was killed by the Clintons or assassinated by Russian agents. Various theories called him a closet Bernie Sanders fan, an undercover Republican leaking secrets to Putin's Russia, or a patriot killed by a corrupt establishment. These theories - which were based on little or no evidence - began in the corners of the internet on obscure websites and blogs, but spread rapidly to Reddit, Facebook, and Twitter. Eventually some of them made it into mainstream news - and were seized upon by supporters of Donald Trump to aid their own political ends. It was this chain of events that we sought to unpick in our film Conspiracy Files: Murder in Washington.

Who was Seth Rich?

Pablo Manriquez was a colleague of Seth's working for the communications team at the Democratic National Committee (DNC). He remembers Seth as an earnest young American patriot and a loyal and committed Democrat. He told us, 'There's a photo of him in an American flag, sort of head to toe, shirt, and pants, - that wasn't an ironic fashion statement. He loved America, he believed in the Democratic Party and that was central to understanding Seth.' Pablo remembers when he first heard the theories that began to circulate about Seth's death. 'I saw somebody post something to the effect of - 'is it true what they're saying about Seth on Facebook?' he said. 'The story just erupted, and it was just his Facebook profile picture and his DNC headshot that just filled my news stream. That was the first big red flag that this was going to be a really bad thing.' It started with a single post on Twitter. A Bernie Sanders-supporting Twitter account connected the murder with a lawsuit filed by Sanders supporters against the

DNC. Shortly thereafter, the conspiracies really began to take root on the online message board Reddit. Links to local news stories about Seth's murder were posted, suggesting Seth was killed for leaking DNC emails. The theories then spread from Reddit and the anonymous 4Chan message board to Twitter and Facebook. 'Stories like this will start on fringe sites - and then they will be pushed on social media by conspiracy-minded groups particularly on the alt-right, but not exclusively,' says Ben Nimmo, a fellow at the Atlantic Council's Digital Forensic Research Lab.

Political football

Despite the turmoil within the Democratic Party as a result of the leak, just four days after the emails were published, Hilary Clinton was nominated for president. And so began the last stage of the most brutal Presidential election campaign in living memory. It wasn't long before those on the right saw Seth's death as a useful campaigning tool. Roger Stone is a right wing political operative who at one time worked for the Nixon White House and refers to himself as a dirty tricks specialist. He started tweeting about Seth Rich. Anna Merlan, who is writing a book about 'Conspiracy Theories,' says that 'Stone was tapping into a wider right-wing theory that the Clintons have had people killed. Roger Stone was part of a group of far right figures in the 90s who basically suggested that Bill Clinton was running a drug cartel out of Arkansas and having his political opponents killed to cover it up. He coined the term 'Clinton Body Count,' and Hilary became embroiled in that.' The growing conspiracy theories received a further boost when Wikileaks founder Julian Assange appeared on Dutch TV and strongly implied that Seth had been the whistleblower behind the email leak. 'What Julian Assange was an accelerant to this very small slow-burning fire,' Merlan says. Soon afterwards, Wikileaks posted a tweet offering a cash reward for anyone who could help solve the murder. Many people interpreted that as an implicit confirmation that Seth Rich had been their source. In reality, nobody knows to this day if this was the case. Assange has consistently refused to confirm or deny that Seth or anyone else was the organization's source.

Second wind

The conspiracy theories picked up a second wind when attention turned to alleged links between President Trump and Russia. 'The implication was that if Seth Rich had been the leaker it can't have been Russia that leaked the emails to Wikileaks,' says Ben Nimmo. The case gathered pace after it emerged that wealthy Republican donor Ed Butowsky had hired private investigator Rod Wheeler to investigate. Wheeler was also a Fox News contributor and former police detective. His findings appeared on the Fox News website and one of its main presenters, Sean Hannity, turned his attention to the story. Hannity used his Twitter feed to demand a Congressional investigation. The Russian Embassy in London even weighed in. It emerged that Butowsky, and Wheeler met Donald Trump's press secretary at the time, Sean Spicer, to discuss the story. However, the original Fox News piece soon fell apart and was retracted by the network. Rod Wheeler is currently suing Fox and Butowsky for defamation claiming they misquoted him. Seth Rich's family have also launched legal action against Fox and Butowsky. Seth Rich's mother Mary Rich told the US TV show Good Morning America, '

They never called us to check any facts. They took a rumor and ran with it. We lost his body the first time, and the second time we lost his soul,' she said. Nimmo says that the case shows how social media can push conspiracies from the fringes into the mainstream. "There have always been conspiracy theories, but when they have always been passed by word of mouth in small circles, they never really have impact," he says. "Now you can now spread that around the internet, and you won't find many people in a single physical location who buy into it, but you will find enough people in enough different locations that you can give it the impression of having a substantial belief group."

THE MURDER OF KEVIN IVES AND DON HENRY

The apparent murder in Saline County in 1987 of seventeen-year-old Kevin Ives and sixteen-year-old Don Henry has spurred ongoing controversy, including conspiracy theories tying their deaths to a drug-smuggling scandal. The case was the subject of journalist Mara Leveritt's award-winning book The Boys on the Tracks. On Sunday, August 23, 1987, at around 4:00 a.m., the bodies of the two boys were spotted by the crew of a Union Pacific locomotive near Crooked Creek trestle in Alexander (Pulaski and Saline counties). The bodies were lying between the tracks, wrapped in a pale green tarp; there was a gun nearby. The train was unable to avoid running over the bodies. The train's crew immediately reported the incident to railroad officials and to local law enforcement at Benton (Saline County), where the train had come to a full stop. By 4:40 a.m., local and state police had arrived at the scene and begun investigating. At first, local officials treated the incident like an apparent suicide despite the objections of the train crew. Reportedly, no tarp was found by the police, but they did take in a shattered .22 caliber rifle as evidence. Best friends Kevin Ives and Don Henry had been out hunting late on Saturday night, August 22, but when they could not be found the next morning, their parents began searching for them. The spot where their bodies were found was about a mile from the home of Henry's family in Alexander. On Monday, local officials contacted the Ives and Henry families after the two boys had been identified conclusively through dental records. The story was covered statewide and soon went national. State officials—including the state medical examiner, Dr. Fahmy Malak—ruled the boys' death as an apparent suicide despite the fact that all four parents disputed the ruling.

A week after Ives and Henry were buried, their parents were summoned to the office of state medical examiner. Malak said that these were 'Two accidental deaths due to THC intoxication;' THC is a component of marijuana. Malak's theory was that the two boys had smoked enough marijuana that they simply fell asleep on the tracks that night before being run over. Local authorities did not question Malak's findings, but the parents were motivated to conduct their own investigations. According to Leveritt, Malak was accused by his own staff of keeping "outdated crime lab stationery" on which he allegedly falsified findings in autopsy reports just before certain cases went to court. Moreover, the hospital where the boys were taken and examined kept no records of their presence there. The hospital clerk told an investigator, per Leveritt, "That's why the families were not billed." However, a medical report found by an EMT at the tracks that night noted that the boys' blood "looked like it lacked oxygen," raising questions about whether Ives and Henry were already dead when the train hit them. In March 1988, the parents announced that Dr. James Garriot of San Antonio, Texas, had given a second opinion on Malak's findings.

Garriot concluded that it was highly unlikely for any amount of THC exposure to have the effects that Malak had alleged and that the only truly reliable test for the presence of drugs in the boys' systems, mass spectrometry, had not been performed. Another toxicologist, Dr. Arthur

J. McBray of North Carolina, said that Malak's conclusions were 'Very bizarre,' and that he had never heard of anyone becoming unconscious from exposure to any amount of THC. However, Saline County sheriff James H. Steed Jr. repeatedly told the Benton Courier that there was nothing at the tracks that night to suggest that it was nothing more than a 'Strange accident.' Linda Ives, mother of Kevin Ives, criticized Steed's administration in a letter she had published in the Benton Courier. After that, Dan Harmon, the parents' lawyer, made a deal with Steed in February 1988: If the parents would withdraw their criticism of Steed and support him, they would get the investigation they had wanted all along. Six months after the incident, a three-day-long hearing was held in the Saline County Courthouse in Benton, with the Ives and Henry families hoping to get a new ruling.

With the help of lawyers Dan Henry and Richard Garrett, Malak's ruling of 'Accidental' death was overturned, but the result was hardly definitive. On February 26, 1988, five days after the hearing, the cause of the boys' deaths was changed from 'Accidental' to 'Undetermined.' Following the discovery of new information after a second autopsy of the two boys' bodies by Georgia medical examiner Dr. Joseph Burton, the case was put before a grand jury in April 1988. That May, an editorial in the Benton Courier posited the possibility that the boys may have been murdered. A month after that, the grand jury ruled their deaths a 'Probable homicide.' Before leaving Arkansas, Burton told Garrett that, per his calculations, the two boys had 'Smoked only one or two joints of marijuana before their deaths.'

NBC's hit show Unsolved Mysteries featured a segment on the case in the fall of 1988. When asked about his thoughts on the case by host Robert Stack, Garrett alleged that the boys 'Saw something they shouldn't have seen, and it had to do with drugs.' Despite the grand jury's announcement that the boys' deaths may have been related to drug trafficking, Sheriff Steed refused to allow any funds to aid in the investigation. Steed had also lied about where he had sent the boys' clothes for examination. Per Leveritt, Steed sent the clothes to the Arkansas State Crime Lab, not to the Federal Bureau of Investigation (FBI) as he was supposed to do. Steed was not reelected as county sheriff following his involvement with the case. The focus of the investigations turned toward allegations that their deaths had something to do with drug trafficking, and some additional people were thought to be connected to the deaths or to have information—people who knew each other and supposedly knew things about what Leveritt calls the county's 'Drug underworld.'

Two days after Steed lost the election, Keith McKaskle, one of Harmon's informants in the case who was asked by Harmon to take aerial photographs of the crime scene, was murdered. McKaskle was also a well-known manager of a local club on the Saline County–Pulaski County line. On January 22, 1989, twenty-six-year-old Greg Collins, who had been called to testify before the grand jury, died from three shotgun blasts to the face. In addition, just weeks before, Collins's friend Keith Coney, who was also called to testify to the grand jury, died in a motorcycle accident. By March 1989, another recipient of a subpoena to appear before the grand jury, Daniel 'Boonie' Bearden, had disappeared. Another death supposedly connected with the case was that of twenty-one-year-old Jeffrey Edward Rhodes, whose body was found in a landfill in April 1989. The deaths were ruled homicides in March 1990 after yet another investigation, but, per the Arkansas Gazette, there were no reported arrests.

On September 10, 1991, four years after the deaths of Kevin Ives and Don Henry, the announcement of Malak's resignation appeared in the Arkansas Gazette. With Governor Bill Clinton's presidential campaign beginning around the same time, some alleged that Malak had made a deal with Clinton, but Malak repeatedly denied the accusations. In 1994, The Clinton Chronicles, a propaganda video purporting to connect Bill Clinton to various crimes, was released. The deaths of Ives and Henry were among those to which Bill Clinton was supposedly connected. The Clinton Chronicles advanced the conspiracy theory that, while governor of Arkansas, Clinton had a connection to a scandal involving large shipments of cocaine, guns, and money from Central America passing through Arkansas at the Mena Intermountain Municipal Airport. It further speculated that the two boys had been murdered after stumbling upon a shipment moving through Saline County that night in August 1987.

Harmon, who had represented the Ives and Henry parents, was convicted of racketeering, conspiracy, extortion, and drug possession with intent to distribute in 1997. Leveritt says in her book that his conviction and the resulting eleven-year prison sentence handed down in 1998 proved to the boys' parents at least, that their sons' deaths 'Had occurred in an environment of local corruption.' Despite the exhaustive collection of details that Leveritt provides in the book, she offers no answers to the questions it raises. The case remains unsolved. In August 2016, a new lawsuit was filed by Linda Ives citing a violation of the Freedom of Information Act by local and federal officials, or "stonewalling," in relation to the boys' deaths. On November 15, 2017, a federal judge ordered three defendants in the suit, the Executive Office of U.S. Attorneys, the Drug Enforcement Administration, and the Department of Homeland Security to turn over for private review documents that had formerly been redacted; the judge dismissed several other agencies from the suit, including the Central Intelligence Agency, the U.S. State Department, the FBI, the Arkansas State Police, the Saline County Sheriff's Office, and the Bryant Police Department. It was reported in February 2018 that former World Wrestling Federation wrestler Billy Jack Haynes had recorded a video testimony in which he claimed to have witnessed the murders of Ives and Henry while providing security for a drug trafficking drop in 1987.

ANTHONY BOURDAIN SLAMMED HILLARY CLINTON AND 'GROPEY, DISGUSTING' BILL CLINTON IN NEWLY RELEASED INTERVIEW

In an interview, published more than a month after his death, Anthony Bourdain called former President Bill Clinton a 'Gropey, grabby disgusting' person and slammed the Clintons for how they handled the Monica Lewinsky scandal. The celebrity chef and 'Parts Unknown' host, who hanged himself in a French hotel in June, sat down with journalist Maria Bustillos from the magazine Popula before his death. The sit-down was published on Sunday. Bourdain, one of the most outspoken supporters of the #MeToo movement, told the magazine it was shameful how the Clintons handled the scandal involving Lewinsky.

'Bill Clinton, look, the bimbo eruptions, it was fucking monstrous. That would not have flown today,' Bourdain said about the scandal. 'Bill Clinton is a piece of shit. Entitled, rapey, gropey, grabby, disgusting, and the way that he and Hillary destroyed these women and the way that everyone went along, and, and are blind to this!' Bourdain slammed the Clintons for how they handled the political sex scandal. The 61-year-old went on to say it was 'Unforgivable' the way the couple had shut down the accusers. 'The way they efficiently dismantled, destroyed, and shamelessly discredited these women for speaking their truth,' he said. When asked if Clinton should have been kicked out of the office, Bourdain said no. 'I would look at this way. I would never under any circumstances vote for Bill Clinton today,' Bourdain told the magazine. 'But I think impeaching the guy over Lewinsky was ridiculous. Particularly given today.' Bourdain said it was 'Unforgivable' how the Clintons handled the scandal involving Monica Lewinsky and other accusers. He added, 'It was the shaming, discrediting, undermining the women that made both of them unsuitable for any future endeavors. I don't think they should've pulled him from office.'

HOLLYWOOD STARS DEFEND ASIA ARGENTO AFTER SHE'S BULLIED FOLLOWING ANTHONY BOURDAIN'S DEATH

Bourdain also said he was frustrated by Hillary Clinton's reaction to the allegations against Harvey Weinstein, but when he tweeted as such, he said his words were twisted. 'I was really disappointed with the statement. But even by expressing that, the way that my comment was turned, very neatly, suddenly I wasn't expressing disappointment in her statement; I was blaming her for Harvey Weinstein's crimes. The way that turned very nicely was a good bit of artistry and deeply frightening to me and really, really…' he said. When speaking about Weinstein, the celebrity chef detailed how he wants the film producer to die. 'My theory of how he goes is, uh, he's brushing his teeth in a bathroom, he's naked in his famous bathrobe, which is flapping open, he's holding his cell phone in one hand because you never know who on the Weinstein board has betrayed him recently, and he's brushing his teeth,' Bourdain said. Bourdain added that he imagines Weinstein getting a 'Massive fucking stroke,' before falling backwards into a bathtub. 'He finds himself, um, with his robe open feet sticking out of the tub, and in his last moments of consciousness as he scrolls through his contacts list trying to figure out who he can call, who will actually answer the phone,' the celebrity chef said. 'And he dies that way, knowing that no one will help him and that he is not looking his finest at time of death,' Bourdain said.

ANTHONY BOURDAIN, CNN HOST AND CELEBRITY CHEF, CAUSE OF DEATH REVEALED

The TV host also spoke about his daughter Ariane, his relationship with girlfriend Asia Argento and how he would vote for Barack Obama despite finding him 'Very unconvincing in public.' 'Asia said this to me. Children create themselves independently of us. All you can do is show, like in my case, my daughter feels loved. She knows she's loved. She has good self-esteem. Very important,' Bourdain said. Anthony Bourdain often spoke out against Harvey Weinstein. He detailed how he envision how the fallen movie mogul will die. Bourdain was found unresponsive on June 8 in the bathroom of a luxury hotel in the small town of Kaysersberg. He was in France working on an upcoming episode of 'Parts Unknown.'

FROM WHITEWATER TO BENGHAZI: A CLINTON-SCANDAL PRIMER

In a letter on Sunday, FBI Director James Comey wrote that newly discovered emails do not change the FBI's prior conclusion that Hillary Clinton should not be charged with a crime. That's FBI Director James Comey's new message to Congress and, by extension, the American public on Sunday. A little over a week ago, Comey shook the presidential election with a letter to the chairs of several congressional committees, announcing that the FBI had found a new tranche of emails pertinent to its investigation into Hillary Clinton's use of a private email server while secretary of state. The emails came from an unrelated case, he said, since widely reported to be an investigation into alleged sexts to a teenager from Anthony Weiner, whose estranged wife is a top Clinton aide—and there was no timeline for finishing the review. Campaign, which seized on the matter as proof of Clinton's bad judgment. Her poll numbers, as well as her favorability figures and Democratic enthusiasm, sagged. New leaks began dripping out of the FBI on a daily basis, along with allegations that the bureau was trying to tip the election toward Trump. The Clinton campaign demanded that Comey say more, but no information was forthcoming. But in a new letter on Sunday, Comey revealed that FBI agents had been working 'Around the clock' to look at the emails.

'During that process, we reviewed all of the communications that were to or from Hillary Clinton while she was Secretary of State,' Comey wrote. 'Based on our review, we have not changed our conclusions that we expressed in July with respect to Secretary Clinton.'

In other words, it was all much ado about nothing. Comey's recommended in July was that although Clinton had been 'Extremely careless' with classified information, there was no grounds for charging her with a crime. Put more bluntly, the FBI altered the course of the presidential campaign for what amounts to a fire drill. This doesn't mean the email story is gone entirely. On Friday, a new release showed that in at least one case Clinton forwarded emails to her daughter, Chelsea Clinton, that the government now labels classified. The chain in question was released on November 4, as part of the ongoing release of Clinton's emails from her time as secretary of state. The messages appeared to be related to climate talks in Copenhagen in December 2009, although they were redacted so that it is impossible to tell. They were sent to an email address that Chelsea Clinton used under an alias, "Diane Reynolds." It was not marked classified at the time. The emails and the private server through which they operated have been a defining story of the Clinton campaign. In March 2015, The New York Times first reported on Clinton's use of a private email address and a private server during her time at Foggy Bottom.

The story has dogged Clinton ever since, raising questions about her judgment and trustworthiness. While polls showed Clinton's lead over Trump narrowing slightly before Comey's first letter, on October 28, the news brought on near panic among Democrats. Clinton's polling fell further, and her favorability tumbled, and so did enthusiasm among Democrats. Clinton's struggles to generate enthusiasm among her voters, and to bring up her favorability, have contributed to a still-tight race over a rival, Donald Trump, who has committed multiple errors that would have been lethal for practically any other candidacy. The emails represent something of a classic Clinton scandal. Although the House investigation turned up no evidence of wrongdoing on her part with respect to the attacks themselves, it was during that inquiry that her private-email use became public. This is a pattern with the Clinton family, which has been in the public spotlight since Bill Clinton's first run for office in 1974.

Something that appears potentially scandalous on its face turns out to be innocuous, but an investigation into it reveals different questionable behavior. The canonical case is Whitewater, a failed real-estate investment Bill and Hillary Clinton made in 1978. Although no inquiry ever produced evidence of wrongdoing, investigations ultimately led to President Clinton's impeachment for perjury and obstruction of justice. With Hillary Clinton the Democratic nominee for president, every Clinton scandal, from Whitewater to the State

Department emails will be under the microscope. (No other American politicians—even ones as corrupt as Richard Nixon, or as hated by partisans as George W. Bush have fostered the creation of a permanent multimillion-dollar cottage industry devoted to attacking them.) Keeping track of each controversy, where it came from, and how serious it is, is no small task, so here's a primer. We'll update it as new information emerges.

THE CLINTONS' PRIVATE EMAIL SERVER

What? During the course of the Benghazi investigation, New York Times reporter Michael Schmidt learned Clinton had used a personal email account while secretary of state. It turned out she had also been using a private server, located at a house in New York. The result was that Clinton and her staff decided which emails to turn over to the State Department as public records and which to withhold; they say they then destroyed the ones they had designated as personal.

When? 2009-2013, during Clinton's term as secretary. Who? Hillary Clinton; Bill Clinton; top aides including Huma Abedin How serious is it? Very serious. A May report from the State Department inspector general is harshly critical of Clinton's email approach, but Loretta Lynch announced on July 6 that the Justice Department would not pursue criminal charges, removing the threat of an indictment that could be fatal to her campaign. On October 28, the FBI announced is it reviewing a new tranche of emails that turned up in an unrelated investigation, but it did not offer any other details on the scope. In any case, the scandal will remain a millstone around her neck forever. Comey's damning comments about her conduct— "Although we did not find clear evidence that Secretary Clinton or her colleagues intended to violate laws governing the handling of classified information, there is evidence that they were extremely careless in their handling of very sensitive, highly classified information"—will reverberate throughout the campaign. Also unresolved is the question of whether Clinton's server was hacked. You can read the FBI report here.

Clinton's State Department Emails

Secretary of State Hillary Clinton checks her phone on board a plane from Malta to Tripoli, Libya. What? Setting aside the question of the Clintons' private email server, what's actually in the emails that Clinton did turn over to State? While some of the emails related to Benghazi have been released, there are plenty of others covered by public-records laws that are still in the process of being vetted for release. When? 2009-2013 How serious is it? Serious. While the contents of emails revealed so far has been more eyerolly than scandalous, the bigger problem is the revelation that dozens of email chains contained information that was classified at some level. In one case, Clinton forwarded information to her daughter, Chelsea Clinton that while not marked classified at the time, is now considered to be. Meanwhile, some emails remain to be seen. The State Department, under court order, is slowly releasing the emails she turned over, but there are other emails that she didn't turn over, which have surfaced through court battles.

Benghazi

A man celebrates as the U.S. Consulate in Benghazi burns on September 11, 2012. What? On September 11, 2012, attackers overran a U.S. consulate in Benghazi, Libya, killing Ambassador Chris Stevens and three other Americans. Since then, Republicans have charged that Hillary Clinton failed to adequately protect U.S. installations or that she attempted to spin the attacks as spontaneous when she knew they were planned terrorist operations. She testifies for the first time on October 22. When? September 11, 2012-present. How serious is it? With the June 28 release of the House committee investigating Benghazi, this issue is receding. That report criticized security preparations at the American facility in Benghazi as well as stations elsewhere, but it produced no smoking guns or new accusations about things Clinton could have done the night of the attacks. Although some conservatives will likely continue to assail her, the biggest damage is likely to be iterative, the highly damaging private-email story was revealed during the course of the House inquiry. The August revelation of up to 30 new, unreleased emails suggested some new information, but it turned out there was only one truly new message, a flattering personal note from an ambassador.

Conflicts of Interest in Foggy Bottom

What? Before becoming Clinton's chief of staff, Cheryl Mills worked for Clinton on an unpaid basis for four months while also working for New York University, in which capacity she negotiated on the school's behalf with the government of Abu Dhabi, where it was building a campus. In June 2012, Deputy Chief of Staff Huma Abedin's status at State changed to "special government employee," allowing her to also work for Teneo, a consulting firm run by Bill Clinton's former right-hand man. She also earned money from the Clinton Foundation and was paid directly by Hillary Clinton. In a separate case, ABC News reports that a top Clinton Foundation donor named Rajiv Fernando was placed on State's International Security Advisory Board. Fernando appeared significantly less qualified than many of his colleagues and was appointed at the behest of the secretary's office. Internal emails show that State staff first sought to cover for Clinton, and then Fernando resigned two days after ABC's inquiries. Judicial Watch released documents that show Doug Band, a Foundation official, trying to put a donor in touch with a State Department expert on Lebanon and to get someone a job at Foggy Bottom.

Who? Both Cheryl Mills and Huma Abedin are among Clinton's longest-serving and closest aides. Abedin remains involved in her campaign (and she's also married to Anthony Weiner). When? January 2009-February 2013. How serious is it? This is arcane stuff, to be sure. There are questions about conflict of interest—such as whether Teneo clients might have benefited from special treatment by the State Department while Abedin worked for both. To a great extent, this is just an extension of the tangle of conflicts presented by the Clinton Foundation and the many overlapping roles of Bill and Hillary Clinton.

Sidney Blumenthal

Blumenthal takes a lunch break while being deposed in private session of the House Select Committee on Benghazi. (Jonathan Ernst / Reuters / Zak Bickel / the Atlantic) What? A former journalist, Blumenthal was a top aide in the second term of the Bill Clinton administration and helped on messaging during the bad old days. He served as an adviser to Hillary Clinton's 2008 presidential campaign, and when she took over the State Department, she sought to hire Blumenthal. Obama aides, apparently still smarting over his role in attacks on candidate Obama, refused the request, so Clinton just sought out his counsel informally. At the same time, Blumenthal was drawing a check from the Clinton Foundation. When? 2009-2013. How serious is it? Only mildly. Some of the damage is already done. Blumenthal was apparently the source of the idea that the Benghazi attacks were spontaneous, a notion that proved incorrect and provided a political bludgeon against Clinton and Obama. He also advised the secretary on a wide range of other issues, from Northern Ireland to China, and passed along analysis from his son Max, a staunch critic of the Israeli government (and conservative bête noire). But emails released so far show even Clinton's top foreign-policy guru, Jake Sullivan, rejecting Blumenthal's analysis, raising questions about her judgment in trusting him.

The Speeches

What? Since Bill Clinton left the White House in 2001, both Clintons have made millions of dollars for giving speeches. When? 2001-present. Who? Hillary Clinton; Bill Clinton; Chelsea Clinton. How serious is it? Intermittently dangerous. It has a tendency to flare up, then die down. Senator Bernie Sanders made it a useful attack against her in early 2016, suggesting that by speaking to banks like Goldman Sachs, she was compromised. There have been calls for Clinton to release the transcripts of her speeches, which she has declined to do, saying if every other candidate does, she will too. For the Clintons, who left the White House up to their ears in legal debt, lucrative speeches—mostly by the former president—proved to be an effective way of rebuilding wealth. They have also been an effective magnet for prying questions. Where did Bill, Hillary, and Chelsea Clinton speak? How did they decide how much to charge? What did they say? How did they decide which speeches would be given on behalf of the Clinton Foundation, with fees going to the charity, and which would be treated as personal income? Are there cases of conflicts of interest or quid pro quos—for example, speaking gigs for Bill Clinton on behalf of clients who had business before the State Department?

The Clinton Foundation

A brooch for sale at the Clinton Museum Store in Little Rock, Arkansas
What? Bill Clinton's foundation was actually established in 1997, but after leaving the White House it became his primary vehicle for … well, everything. With projects ranging from public health to elephant-poaching protection and small-business assistance to child development, the foundation is a huge global player with several prominent offshoots. In 2013, following Hillary Clinton's departure as secretary of State, it was renamed the Bill, Hillary, and Chelsea Clinton Foundation.

When? 1997-present

Who? Bill Clinton; Hillary Clinton; Chelsea Clinton, etc.

How serious is it? If the Clinton Foundation's strength is President Clinton's endless intellectual omnivorousness, its weakness is the distractibility and lack of interest in detail that sometimes come with it. On a philanthropic level, the foundation gets decent ratings from outside review groups, though critics charge that it's too diffuse to do much good, that the money has not always reached its intended recipients, and that in some cases the money doesn't seem to have achieved its intended purpose. The foundation made errors in its tax returns it has to correct. Overall, however, the essential questions about the Clinton Foundation come down to two, related issues. The first is the seemingly unavoidable conflicts of interest: How did the Clintons' charitable work intersect with their for-profit speeches? How did their speeches intersect with Hillary Clinton's work at the State Department? Were there quid-pro-quos involving U.S. policy? Did the foundation steer money improperly to for-profit companies owned by friends? The second, connected question is about disclosure. When Clinton became secretary, she agreed that the foundation would make certain disclosures, which it's now clear it didn't always do. And the looming questions about Clinton's State Department emails make it harder to answer those questions. The Wall Street Journal reports that the FBI was probing the investigation, though it's unclear what its status is.

The Bad Old Days

What is it? Since the Clintons have a long history of controversies, there are any number of past scandals that continue to float around, especially in conservative media: Whitewater. Troopergate. Paula Jones. Monica Lewinsky. Travelgate. Vince Foster's suicide. Juanita Broaddrick. When? 1975-2001. Who? Bill Clinton; Hillary Clinton; a brigade of supporting characters. How serious is it? The conventional wisdom is that they're not terribly dangerous. Some are wholly spurious (Foster). Others (Lewinsky, Whitewater) have been so exhaustively investigated it's hard to imagine them doing much further damage to Hillary Clinton's standing. In fact, the Lewinsky scandal famously boosted her public approval ratings. But the January 2016 resurfacing of Juanita Broaddrick's rape allegations offers a test case to see whether the conventional wisdom is truly wise or just conventional. On May 23, Donald Trump released a video prominently highlighting Broaddrick's accusation.

13. It's the Grand Wizard Charlie Brown

Thirty years after the dust had settled on the fields of Waterloo, a poisonous anti-Semitic pamphlet circulated in Europe, claiming the Rothschild family had accrued its vast wealth on the back of Wellington's triumph. The 'facts' were entirely made up. In the summer of 1846, a political pamphlet bearing the ominous signature 'Satan' swept across Europe, telling a story which, though lurid and improbable, left a mark that can be seen to this day. The pamphlet claimed to recount the history of the richest and most famous banking family of the time, the Rothschilds and its most enduring passage told how their vast fortune was built upon the bloodshed of the battle of Waterloo, whose bicentenary falls this year.

Here is the story that 'Satan' told.

Nathan Rothschild, the founder of the London branch of the bank, was a spectator on the battlefield that day in June 1815 and, as night fell, he observed the total defeat of the French army. This was what he was waiting for. A relay of fast horses rushed him to the Belgian coast, but there he found to his fury that a storm had confined all ships to port. Undaunted, 'Does greed admit anything is impossible?' asked Satan, he paid a king's ransom to a fisherman to ferry him through wind and waves to England. Reaching London 24 hours before official word of Wellington's victory, Rothschild exploited his knowledge to make a killing on the Stock Exchange. 'In a single coup,' announced the pamphlet, 'He gained 20 million francs.' Beyond all doubt this tale was anti-Semitic in intent. Satan was in reality a left-wing controversialist called Georges Dairnvaell, who made no attempt to hide his loathing for Jews and the Rothschilds in particular. Though they had been little known in 1815, by 1846 the Rothschilds had become the Rockefellers or the Gates's of their age, their name a byword for fabulous wealth. Nathan himself had died in 1836 and so could not rebut the claims. Every aspect of Dairnvaell's tale, the ruthlessness, the guile, the greed – represents a derogatory racial stereotype, and he was writing at a moment when such attitudes were having one of their periodic surges of popularity in Europe.

The story was also false, Nathan Rothschild was not at Waterloo or even in Belgium at the time. There was no Channel storm. And he made no great killing on the stock market. Yet the Satan pamphlet, translated into many languages and reprinted many times, gave this legend such a grip on history that, albeit often in modified or diluted forms, references to it can still be found today both in popular culture and in scholarly works. Versions appear in a Hollywood film of 1934 and the 2009 Sebastian Faulks novel A Week in December; in past editions of the Dictionary of National Biography and Encyclopedia Britannica; in Elizabeth Longford's acclaimed 1970s biography of the Duke of Wellington; and (with a very different analysis) in Niall Ferguson's authorized history of the Rothschilds. Perhaps more predictably, the story provided the plot for a Nazi film of 1940 entitled The Rothschilds: Shares in Waterloo, and the tale can be read on many anti-Semitic websites.

How does a crude racist smear endure for so long? More importantly, how has it survived as a supposed sub-plot of history – towards which even the most respected writers have felt obliged to nod – when it is one of those myths that, on being challenged with inconvenient facts, simply adjusts its form? For example, when it was finally accepted that Nathan Rothschild was definitely not at Waterloo, the story changed: the banker was in London, but had made elaborate preparations to get the news first, either by special messenger or pigeon post. An additional twist was added. Once he knew Wellington had won, Rothschild was said to have deliberately provoked a collapse of the stock market by spreading false rumors of a defeat, so allowing him to pick up shares at rock-bottom prices and double his profits later, after official news of the victory had sent the markets soaring. Was there any truth to this revised version, or to any of the other variants that have surfaced over the years? We will come to that. The legend has had innocent uses.

For example, the former CIA chief Allen Dulles repeated it in a 1963 book on espionage as he wanted to illustrate the value of early information. Other writers have adopted the tale simply as a good yarn, without any anti-Semitic intent. Even the Rothschild family, always deeply uncomfortable with the story, has tried to domesticate it. Their preferred version glosses over any alleged profits and stresses that Nathan's first action on hearing of the victory had been that of any good citizen of the time: he informed the government. (This was the version Elizabeth Longford embraced.) All the while, error and trickery were hampering attempts to separate the myth from the facts. What apparent evidence was there? For many years, historians cited a line from the London Courier newspaper dated 20 June 1815, two days after the battle and a day before official news of the victory arrived. It stated simply, 'Rothschild has made great purchases of stock.' On the face of it, this supported the legend, but there is a problem: those words do not appear in surviving copies of that day's Courier.

Instead, it now appears that the purported quotation originated in the writings of a Scottish historian, Archibald Alison, in 1848, two years after the Satan pamphlet was published. Further backing for the legend came in the form of an entry in the 1815 diary of a young American visitor to London, James Gallatin. On the day of Waterloo, he writes of great public anxiety over events in Belgium, adding: 'They say Monsieur Rothschild has mounted couriers from Brussels to Ostend and a fast clipper ready to sail the moment something is decisive on the battlefield one way or the other.' Once again, this is not what it seems. The Gallatin diary was exposed in 1957 as a fake cooked up late in the 19th century long after the Satan story had gained currency.

The first modern attempt to challenge the myth was made in the 1980s by a Rothschild – Baron Victor, a retired scientist and public servant who wrote a book about his ancestor Nathan. It was Victor who identified the powerful role played by the Satan pamphlet, and he debunked many of the dafter allegations. But he also discovered in the Rothschild archives a document that muddied the water. This was a letter written to Nathan Rothschild by a bank employee in Paris about a month after Waterloo, and it included the statement, 'I am informed by Commissary White you have done well by the early information which you had of the victory gained at Waterloo.' Proof, it seemed, that the legend had some foundation in fact. There matters have stood since the 1980s, and in those years the old legend has enjoyed a new lease of life online, while historians and writers have continued to pay it lip service. But fresh evidence has now surfaced which allows us finally to put this story in its proper context.

Newspapers published in the week of Waterloo make it clear that the first person to bring authentic news of the victory at Waterloo to London was not Nathan Rothschild; rather, it was a man who had learnt of it in the Belgian city of Ghent and made a dash to England. This shadowy figure identified only as 'Mr. C of Dover,' was telling his story freely in the City from the morning of Wednesday 21 June at least 12 hours before the official news arrived. It was published in at least three newspapers that afternoon. We also know that a news report written that Wednesday evening referred to Nathan Rothschild receiving a letter from Ghent reporting a victory and passing his news to the government, though this was noted alongside reports of two other, similar letters.

So, while it is confirmed that Rothschild had early news, he was not the only one. Did Rothschild have time to buy shares? Apparently, but in the thin market of the period, it could not have been enough to accumulate holdings sufficient to earn him the millions that Dairnvaell wrote of. Nor did he manipulate the market to double his gains, for, contrary to legend, there was no slump in prices that Wednesday. Nathan Rothschild may have 'Done well' from his purchases when stocks rose sharply following the confirmation of the victory, but his gains were dwarfed by those of numerous rival investors who, without any advantage of early information, had bought key government securities earlier, more cheaply and in quantity. Two hundred years on from Waterloo, then, not much is left of Satan's tale. It's just possible to see the factual elements upon which a vivid myth was built Nathan Rothschild did have early information and it seems he did buy shares. But it was only by taking these facts out of their relatively humdrum context and adding a heap of falsehoods on top relays of horses, storms in the channel, pigeon post, and market manipulation that a narrative of any interest was fashioned. There is no doubt why that was done, to smear the Rothschilds and Jews generally. Perhaps this bicentenary year of Waterloo would be a good time to recognize that smear for what it is.

DECONSTRUCTING THE ROTHSCHILD CONSPIRACY

Today we're going to point our skeptical eye at the famous Rothschild banking family, and the multitudinous conspiracy theories surrounding them. Just about every conspiracy theory website that presumes the world's government's act in willing concert under the guidance of some secret council points the finger at the Rothschilds. We're going to take a modern-day look at this mysterious family, see who they really are and what they really do, and see exactly what evidence there is that shows that they are actually directing world affairs. Why would superpowers such as the United States, Russia, and China willingly give up their sovereignty, conducting wars and exerting control over markets according to instructions from above? The answer, according to the believers, is money. Driven by their quest for money, the Rothschilds have been said to assassinate US Presidents, and to create virtually every war since the 1800s in order to finance both sides. Some say the Rothschilds (who are Jewish) caused the Holocaust, while others say they were the true power behind the creation of Israel. They would, and continue, to do anything for money. In fact, one of the earliest and most influential Rothschilds, Nathan, is claimed to have said.

'I care not what puppet is placed upon the throne of England to rule the Empire on which the sun never sets. The man who controls Britain's money supply controls the British Empire, and I control the British money supply.'

The Rothschilds' whole story is one of money, and it began in the 18th century. Their history is perhaps largely responsible for the modern belief that Jews control the world's money supply, which is not entirely unrooted in fact. Throughout Christian Europe, it was common for institutionalized anti-Semitism to prohibit Jews from owning property; so Jewish businesspeople had no choice but to work in the fields of commerce and finance, where money could be kept liquid and easily transferred or hidden. By denying Jews the stability of property ownership, Christians unwittingly forced Jews of the day into great financial expertise. The greatest of these financial adepts was Mayer Amschel Rothschild, born in 1744 in a Jewish slum of Frankfurt. Not much is known about his early life, as his was one of tens of thousands of marginalized, outcast families. But once he came of age he became an apprentice at a small bank in Hamburg, where he learned the trade.

Returning to Frankfurt at the age of 19, he offered his own banking services in a modest way, beginning with trading of rare coins and related investments. He was energetic, clever, and most of all he was charismatic. And he was smart, seeking out wealthy clientele, and associating with nobility whenever he could. By the age of 40, he had consolidated his most important business contact: the Landgrave William, the Elector of Hesse, one of only a tiny number of nobles empowered to elect the Holy Roman Emperor. When William was younger, he had engaged in the trading of rare coins with Mayer's father, and so the two had always known one another. When William inherited his own father's massive fortune, his friendship with Mayer Rothschild gave Mayer the ability to begin conducting larger international transactions.

This was the point at which the Rothschild name became first involved with the manipulation of money behind the scenes of wars. Mayer was a firm believer in family business, and insisted on using his own sons, by then he had five as his business partners. What he did next became the model for many powerful Jewish financiers who followed: He installed each of his five sons as his agents in the five major financial centers of Europe: the eldest Amschel Mayer Rothschild in Frankfurt, Salomon Mayer Rothschild in Vienna, Nathan Mayer Rothschild in London, Calmann Mayer Rothschild in Naples, and the youngest Jakob Mayer Rothschild in Paris. One of Mayer's earliest transactions was the start of the pseudohistory and hyperbole surrounding everything Rothschild. Napoleon was on the march through Europe, and the popular version of the story claims that William gave the entirety of his fortune to Mayer to protect it from being seized by Napoleon. Mayer was able to hide the money by sending it to his son Nathan in London.

The London Rothschild office had to spend it somewhere, and loaned it to the British crown, in order to finance the British armies fighting Napoleon in Spain and Portugal in the Peninsular War. In fact, all William gave to Mayer were some important papers. Nathan had already long managed the bulk of William's money, and much of it was already invested with the British Crown. William was no stranger to such transactions; his father had gained much of that wealth in the first place through the financing of Britain's war on the American colonies, a few decades earlier. Nevertheless, the Rothschilds' savvy investments of William's money paid off handsomely, netting sufficient interest that their own wealth eventually exceeded that of their original nest-egg client. This marked the birth of the Rothschild banking dynasty. Four of Mayer's five sons had sons of their own, most of whom were sent to other financial centers to head new offices. By Mayer's edict, family members intermarried with first and second cousins, keeping the company sealed tight against outsiders. At their height, the Rothschilds' wealth, if it had been pooled, would have been the largest single fortune in world history. Europe was littered with dozens of staggering mansions owned by family members. Throughout the 19th century, N M Rothschild and Sons in London filled the role now held by the International

Monetary Fund, stabilizing the currencies of major world governments. They profited heavily, but they also provided a crucial international service.

World Wars I and II, the costs of which exceeded the abilities of either the Rothschilds or any other banks to finance and resulted in the creation of the International Monetary Fund, marked the end of this part of the Rothschilds' business. In addition, Nazi Germany devastated the Austrian Rothschilds and seized all of their assets. The family members escaped to the United States, but lost their entire fortunes to the Nazis, including a number of palaces and a huge amount of artwork. The banks' sizable assets became the property of Nazi Germany, and this is the only seed of truth to the claim that the Rothschilds 'Funded the Holocaust.' By the time of the state of Israel's creation in the late 1940s, there were hundreds of Rothschild descendants, many still in banking or asset management, many in philanthropy, and many in unrelated businesses. Some Rothschilds supported Israel; some were passionately opposed. The idea of a single unified Rothschild establishment was long gone.

No doubt many financial institutions were involved in Israel's early days, some were Rothschild banks, many more were not. It is this twisting and spinning of ordinary events into dark powerful deeds that characterizes much of the Rothschild conspiracy claims. Case in point: At the 1815 Battle of Waterloo, Rothschild couriers were able to deliver news of the British victory to Nathan a full day ahead of government messengers. Nathan bought bonds at a low price that was fluctuating with uncertainty and did very well the next day when official news came, and prices rose. The conspiracy theory version states that Nathan first dumped bonds on the market to fool other investors into thinking he had news that the battle was lost, and through this ruse, multiplied the family fortune. In fact, there is no historical record of this prior to a 1940 German movie called Die Rothschilds Aktien auf Waterloo, described as 'The Third Reich's first anti-Semitic manifesto on film.' The truth is that the Rothschild bank was already heavily invested betting on a protracted war, and this short-term gain on bonds merely offset a long-term loss.

One of their most famous transactions came in 1825, when England's unregulated banks all went into crisis due to poor management of interest rates. Nathan Rothschild had earlier bought huge amounts of gold from the struggling Bank of England at a fire sale price and sold it to the French national bank. When the Bank of England suffered a liquidity crisis as depositors clamored for their funds, the bank was able to borrow that same money back from Nathan, and thus averted disaster. Virtually every conspiracy website claims that this is how the Rothschilds 'Took over the Bank of England.' No. They gave them a loan, which was paid back. In later years one Rothschild descendant sat on the Bank of England's board for a time, but by no logic can it be defended that their 1825 transaction constituted 'Taking them over'.

In fact, that famous quote from Nathan Rothschild about "controlling the British money supply" turns out to be a fabrication. I found no original source for the quote at all, though it's repeated in dozens of conspiracy books and on tens of thousands of conspiracy websites. I did a thorough search of all available newspaper archives from Nathan's lifetime, and had some friends check various university library systems. No such quote appears in the academic literature. After such a thorough search, I feel confident stating that he never made such a statement. But the quote doesn't appear to be completely made up by the conspiracy theorists. It's most likely a revised and restyled version of this quote attributed to Nathan's father, the original Mayer Rothschild.

'Give me control of a Nation's money supply, and I care not who makes its laws. But like the longer, more specific quote from Nathan, even this one turns out to be apocryphal. Author G. Edward Griffin did manage to track it down, though. He found that this saying was'

Quoted by Senator Robert L. Owen, former Chairman of the Senate Committee on Banking and Currency and one of the sponsors of the Federal Reserve Act, National Economy, and the Banking System, (Washington, D.C.: U.S. Government Printing Office, 1939), p. 99. This quotation could not be verified in a primary reference work. However, when one considers the life and accomplishments of the elder Rothschild, there can be little doubt that this sentiment was, in fact, his outlook and guiding principle. And this is certainly true. In Rothschild's day, before banking regulation and antitrust laws existed, it was indeed possible for small groups to gain controlling interests in enough financial institutions that it could be argued that they "controlled" a nation's money supply. Evidently the Senator made up the quote to support whatever speech he was making and attributed it to a famous name to give it some clout. Some claim the Rothschilds own half the world's wealth. If they do, it's only in the same way that you do. Anyone with an interest-bearing bank account owns shares in whatever funds their bank invests in. Those funds own shares in other funds and public companies, and so on.

At some level, virtually every financial entity owns, and is owned by, any other entity, in every country. The notion that anyone could 'Control the world's finances' is ludicrous. There is no longer any such thing as a monolithic House of Rothschild with connections to any significant number of all the scores of today's independent Rothschild business ventures. The closest thing is Rothschilds Continuation Holdings AG, a Swiss company that manages interests in many Rothschild-founded institutions. There are no longer any Rothschild family members on its board (the last having retired in 2011), though about eight Rothschilds are believed to own stakes in it (like many holding companies, it's privately held, so its records are not public). Its other owners include Rabobank and Hong Kong based Jardine Matheson Holdings. The Rothschild funds it manages now focus on mergers and acquisitions. Make no mistake, it's a large and successful company; but with billions in assets, it's a relatively small fish in the sea of world financial institutions with trillions in assets, including Deutsche Bank, Mitsubishi UFJ Financial Group, HSBC Holdings, BNP Paribas, Japan Post Bank, Crédit Agricole Group, Barclays PLC, Industrial & Commercial Bank of China, Royal Bank of Scotland Group, JP Morgan Chase & Co., and many others.

Anyone trying to point the finger at the scattered Rothschilds as 'Controlling' world banks has an awfully tall order. That little factoid is about 100 years out of date. By my analysis, the Rothschilds are best thought of not as an evil shadow conspiracy, but as a great success story of rags to riches, Jewish slum to financing the defeat of Napoleon. The price of gold is fixed twice a day by five members of the London Bullion Association: Barclays Capital, Deutsche Bank, Scotiabank, HSBC, and Societe Generale, and they conduct their twice-daily meeting over the telephone. Today this is mere financial necessity, but until 2004, it was also a century-old tradition as great as the ringing of the bell at the New York Stock Exchange. The five distinguished representatives included a Rothschild, and they met in person in a paneled room at the London office of N M Rothschild & Sons. That ritual is now a thing of the past, as is the power of the world's greatest financial dynasty.

GOOD OLE' UNCLE KRAMPUS...

Kill a man and you're a Murderer.

Kill many and you're a Conqueror.

Kill them all and you're a GOD…

Jacob Rothschild is Guilty of the Conspiracy against All Humankind…

Many people do not believe that conspiracy exists. My interest in conspiracies arose when I found out that they exist in the case of the destruction of my homeland Yugoslavia. World media presented the destruction of Yugoslavia as an internal conflict amongst the Yugoslav people; this depiction was just a facade. The essence of the breakup of Yugoslavia was rooted in the colonization of the country. In 1990, the western republics, Slovenia and Croatia, elected parties that supported capitalism. Previously ruling communists won the Serbian election. As a result, Serbia impeded on the pro-Western reforms in Yugoslavia. I realized that the Western politicians and media supported the pro-Western republics and accused the Serbs for all of the problems Yugoslavia entered. This bias was the result of a conspiracy that aimed to alienate people and weaken them politically and economically, which is exactly what happened. The conspirators got power over the whole territory of the former Yugoslavia and cheaply took resources that were built by all the people of Yugoslavia. People realize that injustice happens around the world. Many media accuse the corporations that rule the world and produce injustice, but they do not blame the people who rule the corporations. In that way the media accept that nothing can be done against these rulers. Conspirators like such media because they spread general apathy in society.

I have recognized that the allegations against corporations are useless and that it is necessary to find people who benefit from the ruling of the corporations in order to be able to stop them. Ten years ago, I wondered, who might have such great power that they could destroy Yugoslavia? Through investigation, I came to the conclusion that all roads lead to the Rothschild family, although they are very unexposed. The Rothschild family secretly governs the Western world, and so no one could hold them responsible for it. No one could remove them from power. Is that not the goal of conspiracy? At that time, I noticed that many religious people believed that doomsday is approaching and speculated on the identity of the Antichrist. They suspected

George Soros, Prince Charles, and even the Pope. I tried to take advantage of the interest of Christians and suggested in the article 'Has the Antichrist Come?' Written in 2003, that Jacob Rothschild could be the Antichrist. By the nineteenth century, the Rothschild family had already become the richest family in the world. Lord Byron presented the family in his poem "Don Juan," canto 12/5, written in the old year of 1823.

Who hold the balance of the World? Who reign?
O'er congress, whether royalist or liberal?
Who rouse the shirtless patriots of Spain?
(That make old Europe's journals "squeak and gibber" all)
Who keep the World, both old and new, in pain?
Or pleasure? Who make politics run glibber all?
The shade of Buonaparte's noble daring? –
Jew Rothschild, and his fellow-Christian, Baring.

Then began the industrial revolution and the blossoming of colonialism where the Rothschilds certainly became even richer; but then they withdrew from the public arena. Why did they do this? After conquering the Western world, as expected, they wanted to conquer the entire world. Taking into account that rulers were often unpopular, and for this they could even pay with their heads, the Rothschilds have decided to conquer the world secretly. And they have succeeded. Today, they barely place on the list of the richest men in the world. One could get the impression that they lost wealth in the last two hundred years but there is no supporting evidence. On the contrary, I believe that the Rothschilds have never been richer or more powerful than today. How can the Rothschilds increase their wealth and influence in the world while decreasing their visibility? The Rothschilds, as the richest people in the world, have cleverly come to idea to make contracts with poor agents who then represent them in the ownership of companies. As a reward, these people usually receive about 15% ownership as a gift, in order to incentivize their work, while the rest belongs to the Rothschilds. These people were immediately able to buy mansions, yachts, and planes. They are incredibly grateful for it, loyal to the Rothschilds, and do their best not to disappoint them. Such contracts are mutually very beneficial.

An example, after the arrest of Mikhail Khodorkovsky for tax evasion in the oil company 'Yukos' in Russia, there appeared a risk that his stocks would be seized. Control over Mikhail Khodorkovsky's shares of 'Yukos' were transferred to Lord Jacob Rothschild. Source is the article from 'The Washington Times,' November 2, 2003: 'Arrested oil tycoon passed shares to banker'. Oddly, the article cannot be found in the archives of the publishing house any more but fortunately, a copy of the article is available on the web page 'Action Report Online.' The significance of this article lies in the fact that it shows Jacob Rothschild as a real majority owner of the company 'Yukos.' In this case, greed has forced Jacob Rothschild to act erroneously because for the first time, it was uncovered that he hides his own wealth behind other people and, most interestingly, he uncovered it on his own. It should be added that the value of these shares exceeds the entire wealth of the whole Rothschild family, according to Forbes. This means that the wealth and power of the Rothschild family is presented falsely. Why?

Can we assume that the Rothschild model of hiding their wealth behind Khodorkovsky was applied to the other families throughout history? Of course, we can. The Rothschilds were the richest people in the world long before the wealthy families Rockefeller, Morgan, Buffet, and others appeared. The Rothschilds have most likely sponsored the rise of these families in a similar fashion to Khodorkovsky. The Banking Monopoly states: 'During WWI, JP Morgan was thought to be the richest man in the US, but after his death it was discovered that he was only a lieutenant of the Rothschild's. Once Morgan's 'Will' was made public, it was discovered that he owned only 19% of JP Morgan companies '. David Icke writes in Children of the Matrix, that the Rockefellers and Morgans were just "gofers" for the European Rothschilds. Political Vel Craft argues.

'Warren Buffett Is Rothschild's Front Man in the United States.' None of these articles provides evidence that the Rothschilds contracted Rockefeller, Morgan, Buffet, and others to represent them in the ownership and management of the world's biggest companies because the contracts that regulate their relationship are secret and as such are inaccessible to the public. But the articles provide beyond a reasonable doubt that something like that is more than possible. In this way, the Rothschild family most likely controls the largest banks, the most profitable companies, and the most influential media. They are united in a single hierarchical organization that has predominant financial power, which brings them political power and controls all power centers in the Western world. In such a manner, the Rothschilds most likely manage the Western world, although they are not in politics nor on the lists of the world' richest. If there were two centers of such power, then they would have fought for dominance and through their strife we would know who they are, but there is no such thing. The absence of such conflicts tells me with complete certainty that the Rothschild family has monopoly power in the Western world. Therefore, we can hold the Rothschilds accountable for almost everything in the western world. This article will do that to a large extent.

Jacob Rothschild hides his power so much that he does not hesitate to use any means to present himself as a humble philanthropist. An insinuation: A photo of Jacob Rothschild taken by mistake in his home, Waddesdon Manor in England, with the 'Richest' man in the world, Warren Buffett, and California Governor Arnold Schwarzenegger, has recognized Jacob Rothschild as a very influential man. That is most likely why Jacob Rothschild decided to present Warren Buffett as a great philanthropist and himself as a man surrounded by such people. I think that Jacob Rothschild was behind Warren Buffett's statement that he intends to donate 85% of his wealth to charity. Of course, in this case, this wealth belongs to Jacob Rothschild. The source: Reuters. Recently, David Rockefeller decided to sell 37% of his Wealth Advisory and Asset Management Group to Jacob Rothschild for an undisclosed sum. Source: Financial Services. It's no surprise they cooperate well, but this is not the problem here. When people buy something they usually need to pay taxes. According to the law, there are some exceptions and buying corporations is one of them. In this particular case even issuing a bill is not necessary. Why is the law so convenient to those who purchase corporations?

The Rothschilds have such a huge financial power that they could easily redeem all the worth of the stock exchange. In addition, they offer investments to independent companies that the companies could hardly refuse. If the owners of the companies accept the terms of the investment, they may even retain control of their companies. It is critical for the Rothschilds that they are cooperative. If these companies oppose the Rothschilds they run into problems. A huge campaign comes to mind that was supposed to split Microsoft in two because of the allegedly unacceptable monopoly that the company had in the world. The majority owner Bill Gates started playing bridge with Warren Buffet on which occasion Buffet probably explained to Gates the importance of "cooperativeness" in the Western world. I believe that Bill Gates accepted and since then there was no pressure to split Microsoft any more. The same happens with entire countries. Saudi Arabia has been cooperative with the Rothschilds and therefore nobody touches it. The Rothschilds do not care what oil company exploits oil in the world as long as it belongs to them. If it does not, then the people who control the oil lose their power or even their lives like Muammar Gaddafi and Saddam Hussein.

I do not claim that the Rothschilds have organized the killing of those people. No, their deaths were a side product of the Rothschild's need to control oil in the world. I do not claim either that the Rothschilds wanted to steal the oil. It will still belong to Iraq and Libya. But the Rothschilds will bring to power obedient people contrary to Muammar Gaddafi and Saddam Hussein. Thus, the Rothschilds will establish control over these countries and then of course over their oil. No one else has such power. The Rothschilds are able to achieve this goal because they are invisible and cannot be held accountable. One of the most important agents of the Rothschild family is George Soros. By portraying himself as a "great benefactor," he helped the reforms in Eastern Europe and donated to these countries one billion dollars through his organization "Open Society." The name he gave his organization is at least shamelessly hypocritical because he is one of the prominent members of the most closed society. He is a pirate who wounded many countries and peoples as a result of his greed. William Engdahl wrote about it in his article: The Secret Financial Network Behind 'Wizard' George Soros.

The article also presents Soros' connection with the Rothschilds. Can you who do not believe in conspiracies explain why Soros has donated one billion dollars? Here is my explanation. It was not a gift but a big scam by which the agents of the Rothschild family's secret organization took the properties of Eastern European countries. I have no evidence. But if you think that the pirate Soros donated one billion dollars to the countries of Eastern Europe to let independent people get rich, then the Rothschild's conspiracy has successfully formed the way you think. By giving donations to Eastern Europe, Soros promoted capitalism as an ideal system financed parties and media, and corrupted politicians. That allowed other agents of the Rothschild's to step in in organized manner and buy the state ownerships in these countries. That is how an investment of one billion dollars returned trillions. This is the only proper way to interpret Soros' philanthropy. It was organized crime. Some local people in these countries got rich as well, but they are agents who run the Rothschild companies and generally work for commissions.

The governments of East European countries received assistance from representatives of the West, binding them to follow the policy of Western countries. If some government of the East European countries opposes the policies imposed from the West then that country experiences rebellion against the government. The President of Ukraine, Viktor Yanukovich was dismissed by violent revolution because he tried to build a closer relationship with Russia. This was an overly complex operation that funded the revolution in Ukraine, which has misguided the world about occurrences in Ukraine by controlled media, which has forced the leaders of the world to support a violent change of government in Ukraine. Who could have an interest and the power to achieve it? Only the Rothschilds. Russia opposes the aggressive policy of the West and therefore the West increasingly attacks it. I believe that this is the beginning of the third major aggression against Russia after Napoleon and Hitler. I do not think it would be an armed war between America and Russia because both sides know they cannot win. The battles will be performed by economic and political exhaustion and will last until one of the parties gives up.

The Russians defeated Napoleon and Hitler, and I believe they might defeat Rothschild as well, primarily because they are moral contrary to the corrupt West and therefore stronger. It would take years, if not decades, of exhausting struggle, during which the countries will stagnate, and people will suffer. The Rothschild family decides for whom people vote in the elections in the US and in all influenced countries around the world by investing copious amounts of money to political parties that are most suitable to them and by promoting them through the media they control. In the end, it does not matter to them who will win because they finance, through their agents, all influential parties that follow their interests around the world. Thus, they ensure that the policy that suits them would be accepted wherever liberal democracy exists. In the previous presidential elections in the US in 2012, both the dominant parties have spent around a billion dollars. There were more candidates for the presidential position, but the Americans did not even know they exist. Where is the democracy? This is a hidden dictatorship of the Rothschild family. It very rarely happens that things do not work out as the Rothschilds predict. But it does happen. On the way of conquering the world, the Rothschilds met resistance from the Serbs. Serbs resisted the Rothschild family in the attack on Yugoslavia for ten years.

The Rothschilds lost patience and decided to break the resistance by way of military aggression of NATO pact on Yugoslavia. Only the Rothschilds can organize an aggression against a sovereign country without consequences because no one can connect them to this aggression. Only Rothschild can mobilize all the western media to justify this aggression through lies. This has backed the support of the world nations for aggression against Yugoslavia. Only Rothschild can benefit from it. US President Bill Clinton, as the highest authority of NATO, was supposed to command the aggression against Yugoslavia. He knew that such a command would be criminal because it did not have permission from the UN. Therefore, Clinton persistently refused to issue such a command even though the Rothschilds pressured him for years. Then the Rothschild agents set up the Lewinsky case and blackmailed him with impeachment if he refused the aggression against Yugoslavia. Only the Rothschilds can blackmail the US President in such a manner.

President Clinton of course preferred his position more than the lives of thousands of people and commanded the attack on Yugoslavia. Immediately after his approval, the Lewinsky case was completely forgotten. Please see the chronology at CNN. But it's not all. Clinton got a 500 million dollar donation to build his library in Little Rock, Arkansas. May it be the reward for the attack on Yugoslavia? I wrote excessively about the war in Yugoslavia in the article "My debt to Yugoslavia." I am deeply convinced that an investigation against US President Bill Clinton for the criminal aggression on Yugoslavia would lead to Jacob Rothschild. But who can sue President Clinton? The successful aggression on Yugoslavia encouraged the Rothschilds to go further in conquering the world. Thus, in turn came Iraq and Afghanistan, countries rich with minerals. These states were independent and that is something the Rothschild family certainly wanted to change.

To make it easier to accomplish they chose George W. Bush for the US President because he was completely on their side as opposed to President Clinton. For the aggression on Afghanistan and Iraq they needed the support of the people. It was found in the terrorist attack in New York on 9/11/2001. I think the Rothschilds would wait way too long for such an opportunity so that I believe they made it happened much sooner by the help from their Muslim allies which the terrorists did not know about. There is an open suspicion that Saudi Arabia had their fingers in it. President Bush immediately accused Afghanistan and Iraq for the terrorist attack even though he had no proof. He gave the ultimatum to Afghanistan and Iraq which they could not accept and ordered the aggression against these countries. Practically only the Rothschilds can control the American government, only they could benefit from the occupation of Iraq and Afghanistan, only they are able to launch the aggression, and only they could establish a puppet government there. Only they could have profited from these wars.

In order to hide their responsibility if something went wrong, they cunningly sought reserve culprits for the wars. They could not find anyone else but the US government itself. Therefore, they formed the conspiracy theory that claims the Bush administration carried out the attack on the twin towers in New York 9/11/2001 in order to obtain a pretext for attacks on Iraq and Afghanistan. This is nonsense. President Bush did not have the operational ability to derive a significant personal benefit from the aggression on Iraq and Afghanistan. I am sure President Bush did not know about that because he was surprised and reacted very awkwardly when he heard that the planes hit the World Trade Center. But numerous experts who claim that building number 7 was demolished with explosives were found and they accused the US government. This conspiracy theory is presented a lot in the media which would not be possible without the support of the Rothschild family that controls the media. I am an architect and I know that the steel structure is extremely sensitive to high temperatures and rapidly loses its loading weight capacity when it is exposed to fire, as opposed to concrete structures.

Building number seven was burning on low floors almost all day collapsing under the heavy load of the building, which looks like a demolition. The same thing happened to the twin skyscrapers. With such conspiracies the Rothschilds deceive people. The accusation against the US government does not bother the Rothschilds at all, because it serves to carry the burden of all the evil that the Rothschilds commit. Some indication exists which presents the possibility that the Rothschilds bypassed the president, helped the terrorists in the United States achieve their goal, and obstructed the investigation to bring additional suspicion to the US government. Thus, they remove any possible doubt from themselves.

The Rothschilds support false conspiracy theories because they invalidate the credibility of real conspiracies. Many people write about the evil Rothschilds even though often they do not have evidence. The Rothschilds have never sued any such writers because such trials would have brought negative attention. Instead of it, they clean themselves from all the evil they cause by being crafty. You may not believe it, but they alone accuse themselves of the stupid conspiracies. Yes they are doing it. Example: Before it's News recently published: 'Rothschild Takes Down Malaysian Airliner MH370 to gain rights to the Semiconductor Patent – Getting Rid of Those Who Stood In His Way!' What a stupidity! It is equally absurd as if they are accused of stealing food from a grocery store. The authors of such texts should be afraid the Rothschilds might sue them for slander. Of course, unless the Rothschild's agents hired them to author such articles. Such articles can bring benefits to the Rothschilds because by its shallowness devaluate the real accusations.

Unconvincing conspiracy theories create the opposite effect, so that people dismiss conspiracy theories as impossible in today's 'Democratic society.' And that is a part of the Rothschild's conspiracy as well. With such articles, the Rothschilds become innocent people who suffer unjust accusations in the eyes of the world. Therefore, the Rothschild themselves help distribute such articles. Media today deliberately indoctrinate people by imposing misinformation and shallow values, because misinformed and stupid people are obedient and cannot resist. On the other hand, nobody investigates the real conspiracy. In the TV broadcast, Democracy Now on 33.2007, the U.S. General Wesley Clark said that immediately after 9/11, the Pentagon planned attacks on Afghanistan, Iraq, Syria, Lebanon, Libya, Somalia, Sudan, and Iran. Is not that enough proof that there is a conspiracy? Clark is a true whistleblower because he unadvisedly betrayed the criminal action by the U.S. authorities. The U.S. Army General's statement has not awakened any interest in the U.S. judiciary or the media. On the other hand, I am not sure if whistleblowers Assange and Snowden have said anything that is not known, but still they are persecuted by the American justice system. Why? Because the U.S. justice and the media are controlled by the Rothschild family.

The media have a purpose to remove public interest from the factual issues by imposing endless useless public discussions. Assange and Snowden are victims created exactly for that purpose. If what they have revealed did not fit to big capital, you would not know that they exist. To return to the US aggression on Iraq and Afghanistan; if you physically attack a man you will most likely end up in jail; if you attack Iraq and Afghanistan, kill hundreds of thousands of people to steal their resources, nothing will happen. It cannot be like this. Given that I am very well versed with the aggression against Yugoslavia, I recognized in the criminal aggression against Iraq and Afghanistan the handwriting of the Rothschild family. Have you ever asked yourself why the President of the US may be impeached for cheating on his wife but cannot be impeached for the criminal aggression against Iraq? I am deeply convinced that the investigation against US President George W Bush for the criminal aggression on Iraq would lead to Jacob Rothschild. But who can sue President George W Bush?

In order to decrease the dissatisfaction of the people in the United States due to bad policies of George W. Bush, the Rothschild family, aided by their agent David Rockefeller, chose the young and intelligent Barack Obama for the US presidential position. I read somewhere that David Rockefeller, agent of the Rothschild family, first congratulated Barack Obama on his victory long before the election. Barack Obama as a humane man, attracted the American left and tried to remove the problems that the right wing Bush administration built in America. But he is not strong enough to succeed in doing so. Just before the nomination for the presidency, Obama graduated Harvard law. People who complete university must be obedient followers of authority otherwise they would not be able to complete their studies. The Rothschilds knew that they could relatively easily manipulate young Obama and that is why they chose him. The Rothschilds made from an exemplary law student who believes that everyone is innocent until a court proves him guilty, a criminal and murderer.

Obama signed an order for the predatory arrest of Osama Bin Laden that resulted in his cruel murder. He spat on his own diploma. Why has he done this? He felt pressure from the media and the U.S. government officials that surrounded him. They are all controlled by the Rothschilds because otherwise they could not be in the position they hold. No one has convinced me that Osama Bin Laden had anything to do with the terrorist actions that are attributed to him. If you noticed, all the media's gravest charges have been proved only by putting his picture on the television screen. It is possible that the death was the silencing of a man who was wrongly accused and who could tell an uncomfortable truth in court. America, pressured by the Rothschilds, kills people around the world with the excuse that in this way they fight terrorism, spread democracy and human rights. That is a lie; this is only about the discipline of disobedient countries. Obama sends drones that kill people in Afghanistan daily under the pretext that it prevents terrorism and spreads democracy. This is terrorism. Could you imagine Afghan drones flying over the United States and killing people because America is an undemocratic and terrorist state? The biggest crime of President Barack Obama was the aggression against Libya. I am deeply convinced that the investigation against US President Barack Obama for the criminal aggression on Libya, would lead to Jacob Rothschild. But who can sue President Barack Obama?

On the way to conquering the world, the Rothschilds certainly want to conquer Russia. The newly elected President of the United States Donald Trump, in his election campaign, promised reconciliation with Russia, because cooperation is the best solution for both countries. With such statements he could not gain the support of the Rothschilds. The victory of President Trump shows that the Rothschilds are still not omnipotent. President Trump during the election campaign announced the crackdown on lobbying by 'Global elite,' which is synonymous with the Rothschilds. He should launch an investigation against Rothschild based on facts which beyond a reasonable doubt accuse Rothschild of the conspiracy against America and humankind. But the Rothschilds leave no traces behind their covert operations, so that it would be difficult to prove the accusation against them. In addition, it would require President Trump to clash with the corrupt US administration and powerful people who draw benefits from the existing system. It suggests to me that President Trump will not take the risk of opening an investigation against the Rothschilds. This means that nothing significant can be changed.

It can be expected with great certainty that the Rothschilds will pressure President Trump to follow their policies. They will try to bribe him, and if they fail, they will look for Trumps flaws, such as they found with Clinton in the Monica Lewinsky case. It will not be difficult to achieve knowing Trump's peculiar character. Trump has already showed weakness in keeping election promises before entering the White House. So, a variant of continuing conflict between Russia and America is more likely than cooperation. Sometimes leaders lose their lives through violence. Knowing what kind of power the Rothschild family possess, if I were in the position of public attorney I would ask the Rothschild family if they know something about the unsolved murders of Presidents John Kennedy, Salvador Allende, Olof Palme, Slobodan Milosevic, and others. For this, of course, there has to exist political will. If it appears, I believe that the Rothschilds would get scared of such an investigation and would stop creating the criminal policies of society. I believe that this would immediately reduce the problems in the world. Other heads of "developed" Western countries are also either corrupted or incompetent because other people have no access to such positions.

The Rothschilds founded the Bilderberg group. It is a private organization that openly recruits and ideologically directs leaders of the Western world. No wonder that the presidents of Great Britain, France, Italy, and Turkey have recently adopted rebels in Syria as legal representatives of the government. This is a crime. These rebels were secretly created and financed by the Rothschild family with the goal to take control over Syria. That is how the Rothschild family replaces disobedient governments of independent countries. Thus, gaining control of all the resources of this world that they do not have yet under control. And since they are fully invisible no one can stop them in that.

A few years ago, I saw on a YouTube video, which could not be found anymore, that the Israeli Prime Minister Netanyahu said: "Do not worry us control the U.S. government." An intelligent man cannot afford such an arrogant statement if the process of the enslavement of American society is not completed. However, Netanyahu did not tell the truth because Israel does not control the U.S. government, but rather the Rothschild family does. The Rothschilds control the US parliament as well through the AIPAC (The American Israel Public Affairs Committee). If any senator or representative of the people opposes the Rothschilds, they will not be politicians anymore because AIPAC has the power to dismiss disobedient politicians and they know it. The American laws have been created in a way that suits the rich for centuries. No wonder why those who purchase corporations are not required to pay taxes.

America is a colony of the Rothschilds. This is indirectly confirmed by the National Security Advisor to President Jimmy Carter, Zbigniew Brzezinski. He recently said, "I do not think there is an implicit obligation for the United States to follow like a stupid mule whatever the Israelis do. I think that the United States has the right to have its own national security policy." This sentence shows all the weakness of the US administration to the power the Rothschilds possess. The Rothschilds control the judicial departments of Western countries as well. They have established the International court in Hague to judge the nations that oppose them. So that is why the Serbs are punished. Just recently, the judgments were made by which the Croatian generals Gotovina and Markač and Kosovar politician Hardinaj were declared innocent in the war in Yugoslavia while the Serbian general Tolimir received a life sentence of imprisonment. The civil war in Yugoslavia produced equal evil on all sides. General Tolimir is no guiltier than the other three people. The judgments are crimes of the corrupted court. Serbian President Slobodan Milosevic was killed in Hague.

As the court had no evidence against him, the tension of the four-year stressful trial and most likely inadequate medical treatment for his ailing heart killed him. Vojislav Šešelj, president of the Serbian Radical Party, was in jail in the Hague tribunal for ten years without the judgment. That court is a crime itself and a shame for today's society. Judges from all over the world judge at this court and that means that judges all over the world are corrupt and that there is no justice anywhere. James Bissett, former Canadian ambassador to Yugoslavia claimed that George Soros, the agent of the Rothschild family, funded the International Court in Hague. This means that the Serbs were tried by the same man who attacked them. It says to me that the family Rothschild has an impact not only on governments around the world but also on the judiciary. The family Rothschild should be charged for the evil they produces but this, of course, is not possible with a corrupt judiciary. Besides, no one knows that he is responsible for it and therefore he produce the evil in the world uninterruptedly.

In short, power corrupts, and as long as there is power over people, there will be corruption.

The conspiracy has absorbed science as well. Sometime early this year, I watched the video from the conference of 'The Institute for New Economic Thinking.' In this video, George Soros has called upon all economic schools, including Marxist, to contribute to finding a way out of the economic crisis. The call is not sincere because if it were, they would analyze the economic ideas I offered to them, but they had no such intention. They do not want to solve the economic crisis because it suits them better than the release from the economy crisis. What's that all about? The crisis of capitalism is not based on a lack of production, but on the lack of purchasing power of people. If the big businesses cared about bringing the economy out of the crisis, they need only to find a way for people to earn more. For this reason, I drafted the article Let's Remove Unemployment where I offered shortening working hours proportionally to the unemployment rate. In this way, the ratio of jobs to workers would be equal. That would establish a fair market of work where the salaries of workers and profits of employers would be justly regulated.

In such an economy, the owners of companies would have to attract workers by increasing wages. The increased purchasing power of workers would increase the trade of goods and services and that would bring businesses higher profits and would pull capitalism out of the crisis. But it would also reduce the economic dependence of workers on businesses. That would free workers from fear of their economic future. Workers would no longer be interested in fighting wars for the interests of big business around the world, for example. Big business is not interested in making money because it already has all the money; it has an interest in controlling the people and its best bet is during a crisis. And that is the main reason the economics crises exist. All economic crises, including the U.S. Great Depression are incurred through financial interest rate manipulation of the Rothschild family. Webster Griffin Tarpley wrote about that. Through economic crisis, the Rothschilds force independent entrepreneurs to bankruptcy and cheaply take their wealth. So Rothschilds wider circle of people depend on their power. Then workers, because of fear for their own future, silently accept unfairly low wages and their own powerlessness. And if they rebel against the injustice that is happening to them, they at best can oust government but that can change nothing.

The policy controlled by the big business remains the same. The shortening of working hours proportionally to the unemployment rate should be the first idea to come to the mind of an independent thinker in order to reduce the suffering of workers and improve the economy and society. But such an idea is nowhere to be seen. Why? Because it is forbidden by the conspiracy of the Rothschild family. Such an idea would start a transformation of society towards a better socio-economic system. That is why such an idea cannot be heard at universities or in media. None of the media, including those on the left, wanted to publish my article "Let's Remove Unemployment." Why? Because most of them are controlled by big business and the rest are indoctrinated by imposed knowledge. The indoctrinated people do not believe that such a simple measure can fix society and economy in the first place because they've never heard for it. An idea that does not have access to the public cannot be accepted by political parties either. So, the cycle of powerlessness never ends.

But why did Soros call the Marxists when he knew that they were the greatest enemies of capitalism? Then I realized that they are not afraid of Marxists. Probably half the professors of sociology in the Western world are Marxists. They openly teach Marxist philosophy in universities, which would not have been possible if Marxism could undermine capitalism in any way. I am deeply convinced that the Rothschilds consciously manipulate the Marxist-oriented professors by putting them on the wrong path. This way, they reduce the possibility of an appearance of a good left-social system that could defeat capitalism. I wrote about it in the article The Failures of Marxism and the Right Path to Socialism and Communism. This conspiracy has been established a long time ago. Apparently Lenin returned to Russia from exile with suitcases full of money. The reason? Russian Czar Nicholas Romanov angered the Rothschilds with his support of the American government in a conflict with the Bank of England. Besides, the Russian Czar allegedly repaid the debt to the international bankers and did not want to continue to borrow money from them. That was enough for the Rothschilds to finance the revolution. Exactly the same thing is happening to Syria right now.

This is possible only because no one can imagine that the Rothschild family is behind all of it. They realize their interests through financing of crimes because no one can connect the crimes with them. The Rothschilds have imposed a system of education that makes people stupid. I am not exaggerating. Such an education helps them to stay in power and rule over society. How did they do it? They have been supporting mistaken scientists for centuries who develop wrong or insufficiently right knowledge, and by the help from politics which they also control, they have imposed such knowledge to the system of education. Almost all social scientists may belong to such a group including Karl Marx. Sigmund Freud is a supported carrier of unsuccessful theory of psychoanalysis, which is largely rejected. The philosopher Friedrich Nietzsche was supported in developing a wrong philosophy from the standpoint of creating a good society. Less well-known Bell, Weinberg, and Hammersmith are supported in the development of the theory of homosexuality registered in genetic code. I've shown that this theory is wrong in the article 'Homosexuality.' These scientists have become authorities mostly by the help of the Rothschilds.

University students have been forced to accept the incorrect or not enough correct knowledge of such authorities if they want to pass exams. Intellectuals who have accepted such knowledge became incompetent and could not find an escape from the problems of society. The best students of the wrong or insufficiently correct sciences became the most influential people in society and then spread false knowledge. In this way the Rothschilds have produced helpless and useless sciences. I wrote more about it in the article My Clash with Sciences. Scientists who are deeply indoctrinated with false knowledge cannot improve the world; nor understand or accept progressive ideas. That is the reason the world cannot move forward. Conspiracy has affected food production as well. In my article "Epilogue ", I wrote that indications exist that the Rothschild family deliberately poisons people with food in order to produce food cheaply and make more profits. Thus, also hire medical and pharmaceutical industries more, over which they have control too. Furthermore, health care and pharmaceutical industry are not keen enough to treat people honestly, because healthy people are not spending money on medical treatment.

There are indications that the Rothschilds deliberately poison people with food to reduce the Earth's population. William Engdahl in his book 'Seeds of Destruction' states that the expansion of genetically modified crops and food all over the world today, have reached that scope that can and must be proclaimed as 'Genocide, crimes against humanity.' The conspiracy of the Rothschild family has reached every pore of today's society. Only cooperative people, those who follow the interests of big business have access to the media and are in influential positions in society. They are obedient because they are corrupted by their positions in society and by the markedly high living standards that the system gives to them. People believe that these corrupted individuals deserve everything because of their arduous work and skills, but this is not true. They are only pawns of the people who actually run society.

But that is not all, the Rothschilds control their opposition as well. They corrupt fighters for justice who publicly confront the existing system but do nothing to change it. They took control over the 'Occupy' movement. Also, they like to support indoctrinated fighters for justice who are unable to make progress. Noam Chomsky, for example, is an honest fighter for justice, but has his fight helped humankind? Has he offered a solution that might improve the situation around the world? He has not. And so, the Rothschilds must love his contribution to the betterment of humankind. While people who might improve society, like me for example, do not have financial support, do not have access to universities, media, or politics, and cannot help. Every day you can see all kinds of published nonsense but my philosophy, which defines the bright future of humanity, has no access anywhere. Everything is based on a deep conspiracy. People who believe media and follow fighters for 'Justice,' actually work in favor of their own powerlessness.

The conspiracy is completely hidden so that public does not know anything about it. It is possible that only Jacob Rothschild has access to the entire conspiracy. He has far more power than any emperor in the history of humankind, but nobody knows it. I believe that his wife thinks he is just a successful businessman. Even his son Nathaniel until recently did not know how powerful his father was. When he learned that he would inherit his power, he suddenly transformed from an irresponsible adventurer to a highly successful 'Independent' businessman. Of course, a narrow circle of his family were acquainted with the conspiracy, as well as several other family members, including of course, David Rockefeller, who rules in the name of Rothschild over the United States. In the hierarchy below them no one, I repeat no one, I believe not even Soros, knows how powerful Jacob Rothschild really is. That is why the conspiracy remains undiscovered. So then how have I discovered how powerful Jacob Rothschild is?

Around the turn of the millennium, I became convinced that the Rothschilds rule the Western world by studying various documents over the Internet. Many documents and the genealogy of the Rothschild family suggests that the London branch manages the whole family. A variety of statements, articles, and documents indicate that Jacob is the head of the London branch. That is how I realized that Jacob Rothschild is the secret ruler of the western world. He suits the role perfectly as a quiet man mostly known for his love of arts and flowers. This image is of course built up so that no one would have thought that he could be the leader of a global conspiracy. I have no solid evidence against Jacob Rothschild because it is impossible to collect it without the help of governments. State governments are corrupted, incompetent, or afraid of the power of corporations so that they have no intention to search for the evidence and accuse Jacob Rothschild. Anyway, by finishing my research, I concluded that there might be only a 0.1% chance that he is not at the head of the conspiracy hierarchy, and a 0% chance that he is not among the top five. He is certainly guilty for the conspiracy against humankind.

The situation in the world is only getting worse and so I have decided to act. It makes no sense to attack presidents, governments, and corporations under media accusations of evil in the world because they are only highlighted puppets Jacob Rothschild has managed and protected. This article is not proof against the Rothschilds, but it provides sufficient information and explanations that beyond a reasonable doubt can and should invite public prosecutors to launch an investigation against the Rothschilds. But this requires political will which corrupted governments do not have. Therefore, the dire situation in the world does not change. This article has a task to inform people about what is happening in the world, and I expect the unsatisfied people to exert political pressure on their governments to launch an investigation against the Rothschilds. Or to choose new governments that will show the courage to initiate such an investigation. Once the Rothschild family is accused of crime it will be stopped. Then the evil in the world will be stopped as well.

14. Operation Northwoods

In March 1962, the US Joint Chiefs of Staff submitted preliminary plans to the US Secretary of Defense that included attacking an American military base and launching terrorist attacks in American cities. These and other incidents, under the code name Operation Northwoods, were 'False Flag' operations, that is, incidents the US would stage in such a way that blame would fall on Castro's Cuba. In response to Cuba's 'Aggression,' the United States would then be justified in a massive invasion of Cuba, ridding the Western Hemisphere of a Communist outpost 90 miles off the coast of Florida.

Under the Umbrella of the Cuban Project-After the CIA-supported Bay of Pigs Invasion failed miserably in April 1961, the US started to develop the Cuban Project, an umbrella of covert operations to 'Help Cuba overthrow the Communist regime' by October 1962. Organized by President Kennedy's brother, Attorney General Robert Kennedy and the CIA, the Cuban Project was also known as Operation Mongoose. Operation Northwoods was one of 33 plans that were considered under Operation Mongoose; other plans included tainting Fidel Castro's clothes with thallium salts so his beard would fall out and spraying hallucinogens in the broadcast studio before Castro gave a televised speech.

Operation Northwoods contained nine 'Pretexts to justify US military intervention in Cuba.'

(1) Provoke a Cuban military response

The best outcome would be to harass or trick the Cubans into believing an attack was imminent, so they actually attacked US forces first.

(2) Stage a Cuban Attack on Guantanamo

Friendly uniformed Cubans could be used to attack the US Guantanamo Bay Naval Base in southeastern Cuba, including actually firing mortars into the base and damaging some infrastructure. Meanwhile, aircraft on the ground inside the base could be sabotaged and burned and a ship sunk in the harbor entrance. "Attacking" Cubans would be captured and mock funerals held for their American victims. The US would respond by attacking Communist Cuban artillery and mortar emplacements near Guantanamo to be followed by large scale military operations.

(3) 'Remember the Maine'

In a reference to the battleship Maine which mysteriously blew up in Havana Harbor in 1898 contributing to start of the Spanish-American War, a "Remember the Maine" incident could be staged. An unmanned ship could be blown up, preferably near Havana or Santiago with many Cuban witnesses. Cuban vessels and aircraft investigating the burning ship would then appear to be involved in the "attack." US air/sea rescuers protected by US fighters would evacuate the non-existent crew and casualty lists would be published in US newspapers, fanning national outrage.

(4) Stage Cuban Terrorist Attacks on American Soil

A coordinated Cuban terrorist plot could be manufactured by staging attacks in Florida cities and Washington (DC), including setting off bombs. Cuban refugees could be targeted and, for maximum publicity, actually wounded in the process. A "boatload" of Cubans seeking refuge in the US could be targeted by the "Cuban terrorists" (at the time, about 2,000 Cubans were fleeing Cuba each week). The sinking of their boat could be simulated or real.

(5) Stage a Cuban Attack on a Neighbor

As an example, B-26 Medium Bombers and C-46 Transports could be disguised as Cuban military aircraft and make cane-field burning runs against the Dominican Republic dropping Soviet incendiaries. Radio traffic could lead to planted "Cuban" arms shipments on Dominican beaches.

(6) Fake MiGs

It would take about three months to create reasonable facsimiles of Cuban MiGs. These would be flown by US pilots to harass civil aircraft (ordinary American passengers would become witnesses that Cuban MiGs flew at them), attack shipping and destroy unmanned US aircraft.

(7) Staged Hijackings

Staged hijacking of civil aircraft and shipping could be made to appear to be condoned by Cuba.

(8) Stage the Shooting Down of a Civil Airliner

Two civil airliners could be painted with identical identifications. One would be converted to a drone and hidden at Eglin Air Force Base in the Florida Panhandle, while the other would become a chartered flight full of hand-picked "college students" bound for Venezuela or some other country which would require overflying Cuban airspace. Somewhere south of Florida, the two planes would rendezvous where the one with passengers would descend and proceed to Eglin AFB where the passengers would be evacuated. The drone would then continue on the filed flight plan until it was over Cuba where it would begin broadcasting a Mayday distress signal that it was under attack by Cuban MiGs. Shortly thereafter, a radio signal would detonate the aircraft.

(9) Stage Shooting Down a US Fighter

A series of exercises including four or five F-101 fighters would occur on a frequent basis whereby they would string themselves out and approach Cuba, turn back before the 12-mile limit and return home. After this routine has been established, a previously briefed pilot would take up position as the tail end plane and gradually fall further and further behind. When near Cuba he would broadcast that he was being attacked by Cuban MiGs and was going down. He would drop to extremely low altitude and proceed to a secure base. Meanwhile, a submarine or boat would disperse F-101 parts, including a parachute, about 15 miles off the Cuban coast.

Chairman of the Joint Chiefs of Staff, General Lyman Lemnitzer
United States Army (b. Aug 29, 1899, d. Nov 12, 1988), Chairman of the Joint Chiefs of Staff (1960 - 1962), Supreme Allied Commander, Europe (1963 - 1969)

Operation Northwoods Sent to the Secretary of Defense

All these incidents were discussed by the Joint Chiefs of Staff and compiled into Operation Northwoods under the subject 'Justification for US Military Intervention in Cuba (Top Secret)' with the recommendation that any overt or covert military operations be assigned to the Joint Chiefs of Staff. The paper was specifically NOT to be forwarded to commanders of unified or specific commands, US officers in NATO or the Chairman of the US Delegation to the UN Military Staff Committee. The proposal, signed by Chairman of the Joint Chiefs of Staff, General Lyman Lemnitzer, was sent to Defense Secretary Robert McNamara on March 13, 1962. President Kennedy meets with General Curtis Lemay and reconnaissance pilots in the Oval Office. This is not the meeting described in the text, but a later meeting during the Cuban Missile Crisis (October 1962). Three days later, a meeting was held in the Oval Office to discuss 'Guidelines for Operation Mongoose,' including plans proposed in Operation Northwoods. Among those attending were several generals, including General Lemnitzer, Attorney General Robert Kennedy and President John Kennedy. When General Lemnitzer told the President of the plans to create plausible pretexts that would allow full military retaliation, President Kennedy personally rejected them, stating bluntly that "we were not discussing the use of US military force." Of the four divisions to be used in the military "response," Kennedy told Lemnitzer that none of them would be available as they might be needed elsewhere.

Aftermath

A few months later, Kennedy removed Lemnitzer as Chairman of the Joint Chiefs of Staff. American military leaders thought Kennedy was going soft on Cuba and Kennedy's mistrust of his generals grew, culminating in the Cuban missile crisis in October 1962 when the Joint Chiefs of Staff unanimously agreed that a full-scale invasion of Cuba was the only solution and Kennedy overrode them. Lemnitzer' S career was not over, however. In November 1962 he was appointed as Commander of US European Command. Just two months later, in January 1963, General Lemnitzer was appointed Supreme Allied Commander Europe of NATO, where he served until July 1969.

Operation Northwoods Released to Public

President John F. Kennedy was assassinated on November 22, 1963. Operation Northwoods was made public in 1997 as part of a series of documents released by the John F. Kennedy Assassination Records Review Board and put online in April 2001.

THE TRUTH ABOUT TONKIN

Questions about the Gulf of Tonkin incidents have persisted for more than 40 years. But once-classified documents and tapes released in the past several years, combined with previously uncovered facts, make clear that high government officials distorted facts and deceived the American public about events that led to full U.S. involvement in the Vietnam War. On 2 August 1964, North Vietnamese patrol torpedo boats attacked the USS Maddox (DD-731) while the destroyer was in international waters in the Gulf of Tonkin. There is no doubting that fact. But what happened in the Gulf during the late hours of 4 August and the consequential actions taken by U.S. officials in Washington—has been seemingly cloaked in confusion and mystery ever since that night. Nearly 200 documents the National Security Agency (NSA) declassified and released in 2005 and 2006, however, have helped shed light on what transpired in the Gulf of Tonkin on 4 August. The papers, more than 140 of them classified top secret, include phone transcripts, oral-history interviews, signals intelligence (SIGINT) messages, and chronologies of the Tonkin events developed by Department of Defense and NSA officials. Combined with recently declassified tapes of phone calls from White House officials involved with the events and previously uncovered facts about Tonkin, these documents provide compelling evidence about the subsequent decisions that led to the full commitment of U.S. armed forces to the Vietnam War.

Raids and Patrols in the Tonkin Gulf

In early 1964, South Vietnam began conducting a covert series of U.S.-backed commando attacks and intelligence-gathering missions along the North Vietnamese coast. Codenamed Operations Plan (OPLAN) 34A, the activities were conceived and overseen by the Department of Defense, with the support of the Central Intelligence Agency, and carried out by the South Vietnamese Navy. Initial successes, however, were limited; numerous South Vietnamese raiders were captured, and OPLAN 34A units suffered heavy casualties. In July 1964, Lieutenant General William C. Westmoreland, commander of the U.S. Military Assistance Command, Vietnam, shifted the operation's tactics from commando attacks on land to shore bombardments using mortars, rockets, and recoilless rifles fired from South Vietnamese patrol boats. The U.S. Navy, meanwhile, had been conducting occasional reconnaissance and SIGINT-gathering missions farther offshore in the Tonkin Gulf.

Destroyers carried out these so-called Desoto patrols. After missions in December 1962 and April of the next year, patrols were scheduled for 1964 in the vicinity of OPLAN 34A raids. In fact, one of the patrols' main missions was to gather information that would be useful to the raiders. A top-secret document declassified in 2005 revealed the standing orders to the Desoto patrols: 'Locate and identify all coastal radar transmitters, note all navigation aids along the DVR's [Democratic Republic of Vietnam's] coastline, and monitor the Vietnamese junk fleet for a possible connection to DRV/Viet Cong maritime supply and infiltration routes.' The United States was playing a dangerous game. The South Vietnamese conducted OPLAN 34A raids and the U.S. Navy's Desoto patrols could be perceived as collaborative efforts against North Vietnamese targets. In reality, there was no coordination between the forces conducting the operations.

Daylight Attack on a Destroyer

On 28 July, the Maddox sortied from Taiwan end route to her Desoto patrol station. Specially equipped with a communications intercept van and 17 SIGINT specialists, she was to patrol in international waters off the North Vietnamese coast, from the demilitarized zone (DMZ) north to the Chinese border. On the night of 30-31 July, the destroyer was on station in the Gulf of Tonkin when a 34A raid was launched against Hon Me Island. From two boats, South Vietnamese commandos fired machine guns and small cannon at the island's radar and military installations. At the same time, two other South Vietnamese commando boats carried out a similar attack against Hon Ngu Island, more than 25 miles to the south. After observing North Vietnamese patrol torpedo boats pursuing the vessels that had attacked Hon Me, the Maddox withdrew from the area. Nevertheless, when later queried by NSA headquarters, the destroyer indicated she had been unaware of the OPLAN raid on the island. That ignorance set the stage for a showdown between North Vietnamese forces and the U.S. Navy eavesdropping platform.

By 1 August, the destroyer had returned to the area and was back on patrol. In the early hours of the next day, Maddox communication technicians intercepted SIGINT reports of North Vietnamese vessels getting under way, possibly intent on attacking the destroyer. On board the ship, Commander, Destroyer Division 192, Captain John J. Herrick ordered the vessel out to sea, hoping to avoid a confrontation. But at 1045, he reversed orders, turning the Maddox back toward the coast, this time to the north of Hon Me Island. Weather conditions were clear, and seas were calm. At 1440, the destroyer detected three North Vietnamese patrol boats approaching her position from the west. Aware of North Vietnamese intent from the earlier SIGINT message, Captain Herrick ordered gun crews to open fire if the fast-approaching trio closed to within 10,000 yards of the destroyer, and at about 1505 three 5-inch shots were fired across the bow of the closest boat. In return, the lead vessel launched a torpedo and veered away.

A second boat then launched two 'Fish' but was hit by gunfire from the destroyer. Re-engaging, the first PT boat launched a second torpedo and opened fire with her 14.5-mm guns, but Maddox shell fire heavily damaged the vessel. Overhead, meanwhile, four F8 Crusaders that the Maddox had called in earlier from the USS Ticonderoga (CVA-14) were rapidly approaching. One of the pilots, Navy Commander James Stockdale, commanding officer of VF-

51, recalled that they passed over the unscathed Maddox at 1530, minutes after the 22-minute surface engagement had ended. All of the enemy boats were heading northwest at about 40 knots, two in front of the third by about a mile. The destroyer was retiring to the south. Stockdale and the other pilots, with orders to 'Attack and destroy the PT boats,' made multiple firing runs on the enemy vessels. The two lead boats maneuvered evasively but were nevertheless heavily damaged. The third was left dead in the water and burning.

Fighting Phantoms on 4 August

The next day, the Maddox resumed her Desoto patrol, and, to demonstrate American resolve and the right to navigate in international waters, President Lyndon B. Johnson ordered the USS Turner Joy (DD-951) to join the first destroyer on patrol off the North Vietnamese coast. That night, the South Vietnamese staged more OPLAN 34A raids. Three patrol craft attacked a security garrison at Cua Ron (the mouth of the Ron River) and a radar site at Vine Son, firing 770 rounds of high-explosive munitions at the targets. North Vietnamese installations had been attacked four separate times in five days. On the morning of 4 August, U.S. intelligence intercepted a report indicating that the communists intended to conduct offensive maritime operations in the Gulf of Tonkin. In contrast to the clear conditions two days earlier, thunderstorms and rain squalls reduced visibility and increased wave heights to six feet. In addition to the difficult detection conditions, the Maddox's SPS-40 long-range air-search radar and the Turner Joy's SPG-53 fire-control radar were both inoperative. 9   That night, Herrick had the two ships move out to sea to give themselves maneuver space in case of attack.

The Maddox nevertheless reported in 2040 that she was tracking unidentified vessels. Although the U.S. destroyers were operating more than 100 miles from the North Vietnamese coastline, the approaching vessels seemed to come at the ships from multiple directions, some from the northeast, and others from the southwest. Still other targets appeared from the east, mimicking attacking profiles of torpedo boats. Targets would disappear, and then new targets would appear from the opposite compass direction. Over the next three hours, the two ships repeatedly maneuvered at high speeds to evade perceived enemy boat attacks. The destroyers reported automatic-weapons fire; more than 20 torpedo attacks; sightings of torpedo wakes, enemy cockpit lights, and searchlight illumination; and numerous radar and surface contacts. By the time the destroyers broke off their 'Counterattack,' they had fired 249 5-inch shells, 123 3-inch shells, and four or five depth charges.

Commander Stockdale was again in the action, this time alone. When his wingman's aircraft developed trouble, Stockdale got permission to launch solo from the Ticonderoga. He arrived overhead at 2135. For more than 90 minutes, he made runs parallel to the ships' course and at low altitude (below 2,000 feet) looking for the enemy vessels. He reported later, 'I had the best seat in the house to watch that event and our destroyers were just shooting at phantom targets—there were no PT boats there . . . there was nothing there but black water and American firepower.' Captain Herrick also began to have doubts about the attack. As the battle continued, he realized the 'Attacks' were actually the results of 'Overeager sonar operators' and poor equipment performance. The Turner Joy had not detected any torpedoes during the entire encounter, and Herrick determined that the Maddox's operators were probably hearing the ship's propellers reflecting off her rudder during sharp turns. The destroyer's main gun director was never able to lock onto any targets because, as the operator surmised, the radar was detecting the stormy sea's wave tops.

By 0127 on 5 August, hours after the 'Attacks' had occurred, Herrick had queried his crew and reviewed the preceding hours' events. He sent a flash (highest priority) message to Honolulu, which was received in Washington at 1327 on 4 August, declaring his doubts, 'Review of action makes many reported contacts and torpedoes fired appear doubtful. Freak weather effects on radar and overeager sonar men may have accounted for many reports. No actual visual sightings by MADDOX. Suggest complete evaluation before any further action taken.'

Confusion in Washington

Messages declassified in 2005 and recently released tapes from the Lyndon Baines Johnson Library reveal confusion among the leadership in Washington. Calls between the Joint Chiefs of Staff; the National Military Command Center; headquarters of the Commander in Chief, Pacific; and Secretary of Defense Robert McNamara were frequently exchanged during the phantom battle. Vietnam was 12 hours ahead of Washington time, so the "attacks" in the evening of 4 August in the Gulf of Tonkin were being monitored in Washington late that morning. In Hawaii, Pacific Fleet Commander-in-Chief Admiral U. S. Grant Sharp was receiving Captain Herrick's reports by flash message traffic, not voice reports. At 0248 in the Gulf, Herrick sent another report in which he changed his previous story: Certain that original ambush was bonafide.

Details of action following present a confusing picture. Have interviewed witnesses who made positive visual sightings of cockpit lights or similar passing near Maddox. Several reported torpedoes were probably boats themselves which were observed to make several close passes on Maddox. Own ship screw noises on rudders may have accounted for some. At present cannot even estimate number of boats involved. Turner Joy reports two torpedoes passed near her. McNamara phoned Sharp at 1608 Washington time to talk it over and asked, 'Was there a possibility that there had been no attack?' Sharp admitted that there was a 'Slight possibility;' because of freak radar echoes, inexperienced sonar men, and no visual sightings of torpedo wakes. The admiral added that he was trying to get information and recommended holding any order for a retaliatory strike against North Vietnam until 'We have a definite indication of what happened.'

Other intelligence supported the belief that an attack had occurred. An intercepted SIGINT message, apparently from one of the patrol boats, reported, 'Shot down two planes in the battle area. We sacrificed two comrades, but all the rest are okay. The enemy ship could also have been damaged.' Amid all the other confusion and growing doubt about the attack, this battle report was a compelling piece of evidence. In 1723 in Washington, Air Force Lieutenant General David Burchinal, the director of the Joint Staff, was watching the events unfold from the National Military Command Center when he received a phone call from Sharp. He admitted that the new SIGINT intercept 'Pins it down better than anything so far.' McNamara considered the report, coupled with Admiral Sharp's belief the attack was authentic, as conclusive proof. At 2336, President Johnson appeared on national television and announced his intent to retaliate against North Vietnamese targets: 'Repeated acts of violence against the armed forces of the United States must be met not only with alert defense, but with positive reply. The reply is being given as I speak to you tonight.' Back on board the Ticonderoga, Commander Stockdale had been ordered to prepare to launch an air strike against the North Vietnamese targets for their 'Attacks' of the previous evening.

Unlike Captain Herrick, Stockdale had no doubt about what had happened, 'we were about to launch a war under false pretenses, in the face of the on-scene military commander's advice to the contrary.' Despite his reservations, Stockdale led a strike of 18 aircraft against an oil storage facility at Vinh, located just inland of where the alleged attacks on the Maddox and Turner Joy had occurred. Although the raid was successful (the oil depot was completely destroyed and 33 of 35 vessels were hit), two American aircraft were shot down; one pilot was killed and the second captured. On 7 August, Congress, with near unanimity, approved the Gulf of Tonkin Resolution, which President Johnson signed into law three days later. Requested by Johnson, the resolution authorized the chief executive to 'Take all necessary measures to repel any armed attack against the forces of the United States and to prevent further aggression.' No approval or oversight of military force was required by Congress, essentially eliminating the system of checks and balances so fundamental to the U.S. Constitution. On hearing of the authorization's passage by both houses of Congress, the delighted President remarked that the resolution 'Was like Grandma's nightshirt. It covers everything.'

Analysis of the Evidence

Historians have long suspected that the second attack in the Gulf of Tonkin never occurred and that the resolution was based on faulty evidence. But no declassified information had suggested that McNamara, Johnson, or anyone else in the decision-making process had intentionally misinterpreted the intelligence concerning the 4 August incident. More than 40 years after the events, that all changed with the release of the nearly 200 documents related to the Gulf of Tonkin incident and transcripts from the Johnson Library. These new documents and tapes reveal what historians could not prove: There was not a second attack on U.S. Navy ships in the Tonkin Gulf in early August 1964. Furthermore, the evidence suggests a disturbing and deliberate attempt by Secretary of Defense McNamara to distort the evidence and mislead Congress. Among the most revealing documents is a study of the Gulf of Tonkin incidents by NSA historian Robert J. Hanyok. Titled 'Skunks, Bogies, Silent Hounds, and the Flying Fish:

The Gulf of Tonkin Mystery, 2-4 August 1964,' it had been published in the classified Cryptological Quarterly in early 2001.

Hanyok conducted a comprehensive analysis of SIGINT records from the nights of the attacks and concluded that there was indeed an attack on 2 August but the attack on the 4th did not occur, despite claims to the contrary by President Johnson and Secretary McNamara. According to John Prados of the independent National Security Archive, Hanyok asserted that faulty signals intelligence became 'Vital evidence of a second attack and [Johnson and McNamara] used this claim to support retaliatory air strikes and to buttress the administration's request for a Congressional resolution that would give the White House freedom of action in Vietnam.' Almost 90 percent of the SIGINT intercepts that would have provided a conflicting account were kept out of the reports sent to the Pentagon and White House. Additionally, messages that were forwarded contained 'Severe analytic errors, unexplained translation changes, and the conjunction of two messages into one translation.' Other vital intercepts mysteriously disappeared. Hanyok claimed that 'The overwhelming body of reports, if used, would have told the story that no attack occurred.'

The historian also concluded that some of the signals intercepted during the nights of 2 and 4 August were falsified to support the retaliatory attacks. Moreover, some intercepts were altered to show different receipt times, and other evidence was cherry picked to deliberately distort the truth. According to Hanyok, 'SIGINT information was presented in such a manner as to preclude responsible decision makers in the Johnson Administration from having the complete and objective narrative of events of 04 August 1964.' And what about the North Vietnamese battle report that seemed to provide irrefutable confirmation of the attack? On further examination, it was found to be referring to the 2 August attacks against the Maddox but had been routinely transmitted in a follow-up report during the second 'Attack.' The North Vietnamese were oblivious to the confusion it would generate. What should have stood out to the U.S. leadership collecting all the data of these attacks was that, with the exception of the battle report, no other SIGINT 'Chatter' was detected during the attacks on 4 August? In contrast, during the 2 August attack NSA listening posts monitored VHF communications between North Vietnamese vessels, HF communications between higher headquarters in Hanoi and the boats, and communication relays to the regional naval station. None of these communications occurred on the night of 4 August.

The Defense Secretary's Role

Subsequently, Secretary McNamara intentionally misled Congress and the public about his knowledge of and the nature of the 34A operations, which surely would have been perceived as the actual cause for the 2 August attack on the Maddox and the apparent attack on the 4th. On 6 August, when called before a joint session of the Senate Foreign Relations and Armed Services committees to testify about the incident, McNamara eluded the questioning of Senator Wayne Morse (D-OR) when he asked specifically whether the 34A operations may have provoked the North Vietnamese response. McNamara instead declared that 'Our Navy played absolutely no part in, was not associated with, and was not aware of, any South Vietnamese actions, if there were any.' Later that day, Secretary McNamara lied when he denied knowledge of the provocative 34A patrols at a Pentagon news conference. When asked by a reporter if he knew of any confrontations between the South and North Vietnamese navies, he responded: 'No, none that I know of. . .. They operate on their own. They are part of the South Vietnamese Navy . . . operating in the coastal waters, inspecting suspicious incoming junks, seeking to deter and prevent the infiltration of both men and material.' Another reporter pressed the issue, 'Do these [patrol boats] go north, into North Vietnamese waters?' McNamara again eluded the question, 'They have advanced closer and closer to the 17th parallel, and in some cases, and I think they have moved beyond that in an effort to stop the infiltration closer to the point of origin.'

In reality, McNamara knew full well that the 34A attacks had probably provoked the 2 August attacks on the Maddox. On an audio tape from the Johnson Library declassified in December 2005, he admitted to the President the morning after the attacks that the two events were almost certainly connected, 'And I think I should also, or we should also at that time, Mr. President, explain this OPLAN 34-A, these covert operations. There's no question but what that had bearing on it. On Friday night, as you probably know, we had four TP [sic] boats from South Vietnam, manned by South Vietnamese or other nationals, attack two islands, and we expended, oh, 1,000 rounds of ammunition of one kind or another against them. We probably shot up a radar station and a few other miscellaneous buildings. And following 24 hours after that with this destroyer in the same area undoubtedly led them to connect the two events. . ..' Intelligence officials realized the obvious. When President Johnson asked during a 4 August meeting of the National Security Council, 'Do they want a war by attacking our ships in the middle of the Gulf of Tonkin?'

CIA Director John McCone answered matter-of-factly, 'No, the North Vietnamese are reacting defensively to our attacks on their offshore islands . . . the attack is a signal to us that the North Vietnamese have the will and determination to continue the war.' Johnson himself apparently had his own doubts about what happened in the Gulf on 4 August. A few days after the Tonkin Gulf Resolution was passed, he commented, 'Hell, those damn, stupid sailors were just shooting at flying fish.' Can the omission of evidence by McNamara be forgiven? Within time, the conflict in Vietnam would likely have occurred anyway, given the political and military events already in motion. However, the retaliatory attack of 5 August marked the United States' first overt military action against the North Vietnamese and the most serious escalation up to that date. The Tonkin Gulf Resolution, essentially unchallenged by a Congress that believed it was an appropriate response to unprovoked, aggressive, and deliberate attacks on U.S. vessels on the high seas, would open the floodgates for direct American military involvement in Vietnam. McNamara's intentional distortion of events prevented Congress from providing the civilian oversight of military matters so fundamental to the congressional charter. Some historians do not let the Johnson administration off so easily. Army Colonel H. R. McMaster, author of the highly acclaimed 1997 book Dereliction of Duty, accused Johnson and McNamara of outright deception:

To enhance his chances for election, [Johnson] and McNamara deceived the American people and Congress about events and the nature of the American commitment in Vietnam. They used a questionable report of a North Vietnamese attack on American naval vessels to justify the president's policy to the electorate and to defuse Republican senator and presidential candidate Barry Goldwater's charges that Lyndon Johnson was irresolute and "soft" in the foreign policy arena. For his part, McNamara never admitted his mistakes. In his award-winning 2003 video memoirs Fog of War, he remained unapologetic and even bragged of his ability to deceive, 'I learned early on never answer the question that is asked of you. Answer the question that you wish had been asked of you. And quite frankly, I follow that rule. It's a particularly good rule.' We may never know the whole truth behind the Tonkin events and the motivations of those involved. However, it is important to put what we do know into context. The administration's zeal for aggressive action, motivated by President Johnson's election worries, created an atmosphere of recklessness and overenthusiasm in which it became easy to draw conclusions based on scanty evidence and to overlook normally prudent precautionary measures. Without the full picture, Congress could not offer the checks and balances it was designed to provide. Subsequently, the White House carried the nation into the longest and one of the costliest conflicts in our nation's history.

PEARL HARBOR MEMO SHOWS US WARNED OF JAPANESE ATTACK

On the 70th anniversary of Pearl Harbor, the attack that propelled America into the Second World War, a declassified memo shows that Japanese surprise attack was expected It was described by President Franklin D. Roosevelt as 'A date that will live in infamy', a day on which the slaughter of 2,400 US troops drew America into Second World War and changed the course of history. Now, on the 70th anniversary of Japan's devastating bombardment of the US Pacific Fleet at Pearl Harbor, Hawaii, evidence has emerged showing that President Franklin D. Roosevelt was warned three days before the attack that the Japanese empire was eyeing up Hawaii with a view to 'Open conflict.' The information, contained in a declassified memorandum from the Office of Naval Intelligence, adds to proof that Washington dismissed red flags signaling that mass bloodshed was looming and war was imminent. 'In anticipation of possible open conflict with this country, Japan is vigorously utilizing every available agency to secure military, naval and commercial information, paying particular attention to the West Coast, the Panama Canal and the Territory of Hawaii,' stated the 26-page memo.

Dated December 4, 1941, marked as confidential, and entitled 'Japanese intelligence and propaganda in the United States,' it flagged up Japan's surveillance of Hawaii under a section headlined 'Methods of Operation and Points of Attack.' It noted details of possible subversives in Hawaii, where nearly 40 per cent of inhabitants were of Japanese origin, and of how Japanese consulates on America's west coast had been gathering information on American naval and air forces. Japan's Naval Inspector's Office, it stated, was 'Primarily interested in obtaining detailed technical information which could be used to advantage by the Japanese

Navy.' 'Much information of a military and naval nature has been obtained,' it stated, describing it as being 'Of a general nature' but including records relating to the movement of US warships.

The memo, now held at the Franklin D. Roosevelt Presidential Library and Museum in upstate New York, has sat unpublicized since its declassification 26 years ago. Its contents are revealed by historian Craig Shirley in his new book 'December 1941: 31 Days that Changed America and Saved the World.' Three days after the warning was delivered to the White House, hundreds of Japanese aircraft operating from six aircraft carriers unleashed a surprise strike on the US Navy's base at Pearl Harbor, wiping out American battleships, destroyers, and air installations. A total of 2,459 US personnel were killed and 1,282 injured. Conspiracy theorists have long claimed that Roosevelt deliberately ignored intelligence of an imminent attack in Hawaii, suggesting that he allowed it to happen so that he would then have a legitimate reason for declaring war on Japan. Up to that point, public and political opinion had been against America's entry into what was seen largely as a European war, despite Roosevelt's private support for the Allies' fight against the so-called Axis - Germany, Italy, and Japan.
But Mr. Shirley said, 'Based on all my research, I believe that neither Roosevelt nor anybody in his government, the Navy or the War Department knew that the Japanese were going to attack Pearl Harbor. There was no conspiracy.' 'This memo is further evidence that they believed the Japanese were contemplating a military action of some sort, but they were kind of in denial because they didn't think anybody would be as audacious to move an army thousands of miles across the Pacific, stop to refuel, then move on to Hawaii to make a strike like this.'

As with the September 11 terrorist attacks in 2001, US leadership was guilty of a "failure of imagination" in its inability to translate warning signs into a specific prediction of the horror that lay ahead, he said. Roosevelt declared war on Japan the day after the blitz on Pearl Harbor. Japan, Germany, and Italy reciprocated with their own declarations, but America's involvement in the war turned the tide against the Axis powers and ultimately led the Allies to victory. Americans, who a year previously had been assured by Roosevelt that they would not be sent to fight foreign wars, suddenly found their fates transformed. The US military swelled, with 16 million heading off to war, and women took on new and more widespread roles in the workforce, and in the military. Washington became a global power base, and the War Powers

Act gave the president supreme executive authority. The 'America First' movement, which had lobbied against the country's entry into the war and at its peak had 800,000 members, disbanded within days.

'December 7, 1941 was the powder-keg that changed the world. It changed America instantly from an isolationist country on the morning of December 7 to an internationalist country on the morning of December 8,' said Mr. Shirley. The 70th anniversary of the tragedy at Pearl Harbor is being marked with a week of commemorative events in Hawaii. They culminate on Wednesday in a minute's silence and a ceremony of remembrance overlooking the wreck site of the USS Arizona, which sank with the loss of 1,177 lives. Of the 29,000 survivors who joined the Pearl Harbor Survivors Association following its foundation in 1958, only ten per cent are still alive, most aged in their late 80s and beyond. With so few left, and most unable to travel to reunions or help with the group's administration, the PHSA will close down after the anniversary. 'It's going to be a poignant moment. Eventually we're all going to be gone,' said Duane Reyelts of St Augustine, Florida, who was a 19-year-old signalman aboard the USS Oklahoma when it was bombed at Pearl Harbor. He will turn 90 later this month, but still has vivid memories of waking in his bunk after working the midnight watch, when the ship's warning system sprang to life with the order: "All hands man your battle stations." Seconds later, a torpedo hit with a thunderous explosion. He could hear vast amounts of water pouring in below, and eight more torpedoes.

The ship turned over, forcing him to scramble up a wall to escape. 'I happened to be small enough to get out of a porthole. When I got out, I was sitting on the bottom of the ship, and I couldn't believe what I was seeing: planes were attacking and the whole harbor seemed to be on fire. Bodies in the water, smoke, screams.' he said. He hesitated to jump in the water but had no choice as a stream of machine-gun fire rained around him from the aircraft overhead. He swam to the USS Maryland, where he joined a line of sailors hauling ammunition. 'The Navy and armed forces must have had notification that something could happen; being a signalman on the bridge and being on lookout, which was something we were told - if you see a periscope out there, it may not be ours. But we never really imagined an assault of this nature,' he said. He will re-tell his story once more during a remembrance service aboard a US Navy vessel on Wednesday, when the ashes of Pearl Harbor veterans who have died during the last year will be scattered at sea. 'Those of us who are left try to tell our stories as much as possible, not just for history's sake but because America needs to be kept alert today,' he said. 'America needs to remember the lessons of Pearl Harbor.'

OKLAHOMA CITY BOMBING: 20 YEARS LATER, KEY QUESTIONS REMAIN UNANSWERED

Timothy McVeigh and Terry Nichols faced three trials and a vast FBI investigation, but many details of their attack remain unexplained. Twenty years ago, on 19 April 1995, a disaffected veteran named Timothy McVeigh drove a Ryder truck stuffed with explosives into downtown Oklahoma City and destroyed a federal office building, killing 168 people, including 19 children, and maiming hundreds of others. That much we know. We also know that, within 90 minutes of the bombing, McVeigh was pulled over near the Kansas border and arrested, alone, at the wheel of a glaringly improbable getaway car, an ancient, spluttering rust bucket of a Mercury sedan with no license plates, which made him a sitting duck for any passing highway patrolman. How could such a callous, carefully planned attack have come to such an incongruously slapdash end? After a vast investigation headed by the FBI, three trials mounted against McVeigh and his co-conspirator, Terry Nichols, and an avalanche of court documents, there is still no definitive answer to that question.

Perhaps the most striking thing about the Oklahoma City bombing – by far the most destructive act perpetrated by a home-grown assailant against fellow Americans – is not how much we've learned over the past 20 years but rather how much we still do not know. Despite the government's insistence that the case has been solved, we don't know the exact origin of the plot or how many people carried it out. The federal indictment against McVeigh and Nichols – the latter fronted the money and did most of the bomb's construction for McVeigh – made specific mention of "others unknown," and when their trials were almost over, the presiding judge publicly urged the FBI and other law enforcement agencies to keep investigating.

The plea fell largely on deaf ears.

We don't know how McVeigh and Nichols learned to build a fertilizer bomb of such size and power. (Neither received more than rudimentary explosives training when they served together in the Army, and their early experiments with smaller devices were haphazard at best.) We don't know the identities of the other people seen with McVeigh on the morning of the bombing – only that more than 20 eyewitnesses were unanimous in telling the FBI he was not alone. There is no ready explanation for a different Ryder truck seen by witnesses at McVeigh's motel in Kansas and at the state park where the bomb was assembled in the week leading up to the bombing; no explanation for the other people seen inside McVeigh's motel room during the same period; no satisfactory explanation of the fact that two people were seen renting the bomb truck on 17 April, neither of them entirely fitting McVeigh's description.

An examination of the official investigative files on the Oklahoma City bombing, about one million pages of material, does little to bolster the assertion of Frank Keating, a former FBI agent who was Oklahoma governor in 1995 that "two evil men did this, and two evil men paid". Rather, it does the opposite. The impression, confirmed by the memories of front-line investigators and lawyers who prosecuted the case but did not speak independently about it for many years, is of leads left dangling or shut down instead of being pursued with the FBI's customary vigor. Obvious suspects were offered deals by government prosecutors, usually but not always in exchange for their testimony. Others slithered down the priority list until they were lost or forgotten. Half a dozen rightwing radicals fingered as possible suspects by government informants or by fellow anti-government warriors were not questioned about the bombing, even when it became clear they had lied about their whereabouts on 19 April.

Oklahoma: the day homegrown terror hit America

A bigger issue, which would re-emerge in the wake of the 9/11 attacks, was chronic interagency rivalry. In 1995, the FBI and the Bureau of Alcohol, Tobacco, and Firearms (ATF) were both monitoring the radical far right, but trust between the two was at rock bottom following a disastrous ATF raid two years earlier on a religious compound outside Waco, Texas, and an ensuing FBI-led siege that ended with the place burning to the ground. More than 80 people died. In early 1995, the ATF didn't tell the FBI it had an informant inside a remote community in eastern Oklahoma, that the informant had reported talk of bombings, and that the

ATF afraid of triggering another Waco had decided to pull the informant out rather than act on her information. McVeigh telephoned the community, Elohim City, two weeks after the informant was shut down, and there are multiple indications he came visiting days later in search of recruits. John Magaw, who was ATF director in 1995, said in a 2010 interview with me that if the informant had been kept on, the bomb plot may have been thwarted.

The FBI, meanwhile, had its own troubled history with Elohim City. Since influential players in both agencies were reluctant to open that can of worms, it remained largely unopened – to the fury of investigators, including Danny Defenbaugh, who ran the task force for more than two years. 'When you get agencies working together in a joint Task Force, they should be holding hands, not keeping their fingers crossed behind their backs,' Defenbaugh said. "Sometimes dealing with other players in this is like pulling teeth from a toothless tiger." The Justice Department felt pressure to win what was turning into a frustratingly circumstantial case, especially against McVeigh. Prosecutors knew McVeigh was guilty and were quite sure it was his idea to park the truck bomb directly beneath the daycare center at the Alfred P Murrah federal building. Their challenge, though, was to prove it without raising significant questions about others they could not catch, or whose involvement they could not demonstrate beyond a reasonable doubt.

And so, a month into the investigation, the desire to keep looking for other suspects or sniff around places like Elohim City started giving way to a contrary impulse not to overcomplicate the story or give ammunition to the defense at trial. Even as the government struggled to find conclusive evidence that McVeigh had been at the key locations in the bomb plot, or had been there with nobody but Nichols, his role was expanded in the official narrative from leading suspect to solo mastermind. 'If you convicted him McVeigh but did not get the death penalty, which would not be okay,' said Scott Mendeloff, one of the McVeigh prosecutors. 'We could not lose this … It was like a pressure cooker.'

They did not lose.

An unrepentant McVeigh chose in the end to speed up his own death sentence. He waived his right to further appeals, reinforced the government's 'Mastermind' theory of the bombing with a self-aggrandizing book-length account to two reporters, and went to the execution chamber in 2001. It's not just conspiracy theorists who doubt McVeigh dreamed up the plot by himself and carried it out with just Terry Nichols for help. Larry Mackey, the No 2 prosecutor against McVeigh and the lead prosecutor against Nichols, has acknowledged his team did not entirely believe it, either. 'If you had said to us, 'Anybody in the room 100% confident that McVeigh was alone, raise your hand,' we would have all kept our hands in our laps,' Mackey told me in 2010. But if the official narrative of the bombing is incomplete or wrong, what really happened? One thing the prosecutors stripped away at trial was the vital context of the radical anti-government movement, which in the early 1990s was in ferment over what it saw as crypto-fascist government tactics at Waco and at a mountainside siege at Ruby Ridge, Idaho, in which a government sharpshooter killed the wife of a survivalist holding her 14-month-old baby in her arms.

In 1992, a propagandist named Louis Beam, described by a senior ATF investigator as 'The most dangerous man in America' gave a speech to fellow radicals calling for 'A thousand points of resistance'. It was time, he said, 'To fertilize the tree of liberty with the blood of both patriot and tyrant' (a line almost identical to the slogan McVeigh had on his t-shirt when he was arrested). Beam advocated the formation of small, secretive cells that would carry out attacks at the direction, but without the specific knowledge, of the movement leadership. In 1994, Beam told a career criminal named Roy Byrd, who later told the FBI that 'Something big' would happen in Oklahoma City, Denver, or Dallas on 19 April 1995, the second anniversary of the fire that ended the Waco siege. 'They've got some kid who's going to do something,' Beam reportedly said.

The original plan, according to several sources, including an FBI informant, had been to blow up not the Murrah building but the federal courthouse next door. The two buildings shared an underground garage and McVeigh's crew was supposed to plant the bomb there, much as Ramzi Yousef had planted a fertilizer bomb beneath the World Trade Center in New York two years earlier, an attack McVeigh had studied and vowed to improve upon. The Ryder truck was first seen downtown around 8am, 50 minutes before McVeigh later claimed to have arrived, but could not get into the garage because the truck was too tall – a clamorous miscalculation confirmed to the Guardian by both senior government sources and members of the radical far right. There followed a nerve-wracking hour in which people and vehicles associated with the Ryder truck were spotted several times around downtown and adjoining neighborhoods. Plan B was, apparently, to park the truck in an alley between the federal courthouse and the

Old Post Office building, site of Oklahoma's main bankruptcy court. But the truck had to back out of the alley, said multiple sources, because a US Marshals Service truck was already there dropping off a prisoner. Parking the bomb in the handicapped spot directly below the daycare center was Plan C and as far as anyone can tell, McVeigh's idea alone. If, as seems likely, McVeigh was left suddenly alone at this point, the 18-year-old Mercury Marquis may have been the only car available to him. Everything about it, including the missing license plates and the propaganda materials left on the front passenger seat, suggest it was meant to be kept close to the bomb site and provide a 'Signature' for the attack. It became a getaway car only as a desperation measure.

America's forgotten tragedy

Who were the other people seen with McVeigh? We don't know, although members of McVeigh's subculture have certainly pointed fingers at residents of Elohim City; at a chemist living in the Arizona desert whom McVeigh tried to recruit; and at a white supremacist punk rocker-turned-bank robber named Kevin McCarthy, who lied twice to the FBI about his whereabouts on 19 April but whose information was not shared with the bombing task force because he was being relied upon as a government witness in the bank robbery case. We also don't know the identities of the original John Does One and Two, the people who rented the bomb truck under an alias in Junction City, Kansas, and whose sketches were circulated widely in the days after the bombing. The FBI could never convincingly show how McVeigh got to the rental shop himself from a McDonald's where he was captured on surveillance tape shortly before the time stamp on the rental agreement.

It's possible that whoever did rent the truck played no further part in the conspiracy. What we do know is that the government showed little interest in answering these questions once the case against McVeigh and Nichols was set. The Clinton administration wanted convictions and 'Closure.' The FBI director Louis Freeh was engaged in a war of attrition against many of his own senior investigators over personality clashes. Some of the FBI's best and brightest were either distracted or prevented from doing what should have been the crowning job of their careers. Oklahoma City has come to be overshadowed, of course, by the even bigger atrocities of 9/11 and all the geopolitical earthquakes that have followed. It is, in many ways, America's forgotten tragedy, and that constitutes a failure in and of itself.

MARCH 11, 2004, IN MADRID: WAS IT REALLY AN ISLAMIST ATTACK?

A series of bombings plunged Madrid into mourning five years ago. The Spanish legal system concluded that this operation, attributed first to ETA and then to Al Qaeda, was Islamist inspired, though not linked with international networks. The Spanish press, led by the newspaper El Mundo, today is calling into question that conclusion, which was of obvious political character. As in the cases of the September 11th attacks in the U.S., or those in Bali, Casablanca, and London, we will take a look at an analysis of the issue. - 192 dead and 1,800 injured. The Madrid attack represents an authentic trauma for Spanish society, above all because the controversy over the real perpetrators of the attack has not yet ended. On March 11, 2004, around 7:40 in the morning, ten bombs exploded on four trains in the space of a few minutes. The date appears to have been carefully selected because the events took place just three days before the general elections in which the People's Party (of the political right) of outgoing President José María Aznar was presented as the favorite.

The suspicions of the press and of the majority of Spaniards turned immediately to ETA, the Basque nationalist group, against which the outgoing prime minister had preached a policy of force. But with the arrest of a group of Moroccan suspects on the eve of elections, the suspicions of the public were redirected towards al Qaeda. The attack might have been in retaliation for Spain's participation in the war against Iraq, although autopsies showed that it had not been a suicide attack. The subsequent insistence of the Aznar government in condemning ETA was interpreted as the result of a campaign calculation and in the elections of March 14 victory went to the Socialist Party of Jose Luis Zapatero. Three weeks later, on April 3, seven North African suspects 'committed suicide' by blowing up the apartment in which police had surrounded them. The investigative proceedings then lasted more than two years until the opening of the trial for the bombings in February 2007. The courts upheld the theory of an

Islamist attack, but the alleged organizers of the attack were acquitted. Only one defendant was found guilty of having planted bombs on the trains and most of the 29 defendants were convicted of being members of Jihadist groups, not for being involved in the attack.

The appeals trial upheld that ruling in July 2008. In Spain, an intense controversy continues even now around the attack, designated as "11-M". The foreign press has essentially abstained from reporting the polarization of the Spanish media on the topic. Spain's two main newspapers, in fact, take starkly opposing viewpoints when addressing the terrorist attacks of March 11. According to El Pais (center-left Atlanticist newspaper), there are no legitimate doubts about the Islamist theory, while for El Mundo (center-right nationalist newspaper) the Islamist theory is nothing more than a police set-up. The journalist most representative of the advocates of this nationalist view is undoubtedly Luis del Pino, who works for Libertad Digital, the leading online newspaper in Spain, and also the author of several books and documentaries on the subject for TeleMadrid. Other media, more willing to try to discredit than to initiate a rational debate, consider the position of Luis Del Pino a conspiracy theory or 'Consparanoia.'

Division exists even among skeptics who oppose the theory of an Islamist attack. Some incriminate ETA while others suspect the secret services of Spain as well as of foreign nations. Our article does not take up the issue of the real perpetrators of the attack but rather is limited to showing that the official version is false. Given that the Spanish justice system has endorsed the theory of an Islamist attack, it is essential to begin by laying out this theory. As incredible as it may seem, the evidence that supposedly confirms the theory cannot stand up to rigorous analysis. And the suspicious behavior of certain elements of the police forces clearly indicates the existence of an intent to sabotage the investigation. All the information contained in this article comes from the Spanish media cited above and from official court documents, such as the formal accusation, hearings from the trial, and the verdict.

The Islamist trail

The theory of an Islamist attack is the final conclusion of an investigation that developed out of two tracks. We will present here the progress of that investigation, emphasizing the evidence accepted by the Spanish courts. The first track of the investigation begins with a bomb that did not explode. Three of the bombs placed in the trains were defective and failed to explode. So very soon after the attack, it was known that the bombs had been concealed in bags or backpacks. On the morning of March 11th, explosives specialists neutralized two of them by controlled explosions. But no one noticed the third backpack and it was set aside with the victims' possessions. It was upon inventorying these possessions that the backpack containing the bomb was found, in the police station of suburban Vallecas during the night of March 11th and 12th. That bomb, known as 'The Vallecas backpack,' consisted of 10 kilograms of 'Goma-2 Eco' dynamite, shrapnel, a detonator, and a cell phone that should have triggered the explosion via its alarm setting. The phone contained a SIM card which, when it was tracked through the sales network, made it possible to determine where it had been sold. The tracking led to a telephone store in Madrid belonging to a Moroccan, Jamal Zougam. Based on those elements, the police arrested Zougam, two of his employees and two Indians who had allegedly sold the phone.

Those arrests came on March 13, the eve of the elections. The media announced the arrests and gave wide coverage to photos of the suspects. During the following days, several passengers on the metro said they had seen the detainees on the bombed trains. Finally, the inconsistency of the testimonies led to the release of four of the five suspects several weeks later. Zougam remained in prison because the testimonies against him seemed more solid. The other track that serves as a starting point for the investigation are revelations by Rafa Zouhier, a petty drug dealer from Morroco and an informant for the Guardia Civil (the second largest police force in Spain). A few days after the attack this individual told police in a taped telephone conversation that he harbored strong suspicions about a man named Jamal Ahmidan, alias 'El Chino.' El Chino is another Moroccan petty drug dealer and Zouhier had put him in contact with a gang from Asturias (a region of northern Spain) suspected of smuggling, among other things, explosives originally intended for mining activities.

One member of that gang, Emilio Trashorras, confirmed to the police that he had provided El Chino with Goma-2 Eco explosives, an assertion corroborated by a young gypsy who participated in the transaction. Moreover, communications among various members of El Chino's gang were being intercepted as part of an investigation into drug trafficking, and the recordings confirm that the persons concerned had traveled to Asturias. The two tracks of investigation lead to completely different individuals. On one hand, Zougam, and on the other, El Chino and his gang. No personal links have been found between the two. The only connection comes from seven SIM cards whose numbers appear during tracking of phone marketing networks. And they are connected to El Chino because the telephone carrier Amena said that the cards were activated for the first time the day before the attack in the antenna reception area that covers El Chino's house.

Apparently, the explosives were found in that house and the bomb preparation took place in that same location. No activity was ever generated from the seven SIM cards after their activation, which seems to indicate that they might have been used to detonate the bombs. This is how the link was established between Zougam and El Chino's gang. Around noon on April 3, three weeks after the bombing, police finally located El Chino's gang in an apartment in Leganés outside Madrid. Upon discovering the presence of the police, the suspects refused to surrender and opened fire. At the end of the day, the GEO (Special Operations Group of the Spanish police) launched an assault to try to capture the members of the terrorist group. The intelligence services warned the police that the besieged suspects had made several telephone calls in which they announced their intent to commit suicide. The police forced open the apartment door and an explosion occurred that killed the 7 suspects and a GEO police officer. Amid the rubble of the apartment were found Goma-2 Eco explosives, some documents, and a video claiming responsibility for the attack, but the people featured in the video were not identifiable due to masks they were wearing. Like El Chino, most of the seven dead were petty drug dealers. The rest were members of radical Islamist circles. The trial sentence concluded that these people set the bombs, with the participation of Zougam, and planned to commit other attacks in the region of Granada, where they had rented an apartment. A certain amount of secondary evidence supports the conclusions of that investigation.

Among the exhibits is a Renault Kangoo van which was the first crucial element found during the investigation and its discovery led to numerous controversies. This vehicle was discovered in the parking lot of the Alcala subway station, where all the trains that exploded had passed on March 11. An attendant in the neighborhood said that on the morning of March 11 he had seen three suspicious individuals loitering around the Kangoo. They were essentially masked with scarves and hats and one of them walked to the subway station carrying a bag.

Towards the end of the morning, the police opened the van and inspected it. Two dogs trained to detect explosives checked the Kangoo without finding anything suspicious. Upon discovering that it was on a list of stolen vehicles, the van was taken to a police location. There, after a new inspection, 7 detonators appeared in the van, along with a fragment of Goma-2 Eco explosive wrapped up under a seat and, most importantly, an audio cassette with a recording of the Koran, which would have a decisive impact on Spanish public opinion. The trial verdict concluded that the objective of the terrorist group was to impose Islamic law in Europe by force and that the group was inspired by Al Qaeda, while not being actually linked to that organization.

The cracks in the verdict

We have just presented here all the important pieces of evidence that served as the basis of the Islamist attack theory. All, nevertheless, are plagued by suspect elements, as we will see as we analyze them again one by one. The primary physical evidence relates to one of the bombs that did not explode on March 11, the one that appeared in the backpack in Vallecas. Serious suspicions of fabrication exist, however, with regards to its composition and with regard to the circumstances in which the discovery occurred. In the first place, the bomb did not explode because of a cable that simply was not connected. The explosives expert in charge of deactivating it testified in court that this "shoddy piece of work" did not match the complexity of the rest of the device. There is also an essential difference between the composition of this bomb and those that did explode. The Vallecas backpack contained 640 grams of screws and nails intended to serve as shrapnel. However, autopsies revealed that none of the victims had been struck by metal projectiles. And, according to the police who handled them, the two bombs defused on the morning of March 11 contained no such projectiles. What motivated the terrorists to put shrapnel in just one of the bombs? And finally, the circumstances of the discovery of the Vallecas backpack are unclear.

During the trial, explosives experts explained that they had searched all the objects left in the train cars four times and confirmed that it was impossible that the found bomb had been among them. Its origin is even more doubtful because the abandoned objects, among which the bomb was purportedly found, were moved 3 times throughout the day of March 11, not always under the best surveillance, and ended up at the Vallecas police station, contrary to what the judge had ordered. If one adds to this the conflicting testimony about when it was discovered, the fact that the bomb was not mentioned in the inventories of abandoned objects, and the fact that there are no photos of the bomb before the time that it was dismantled, the inconsistency of such evidence becomes clear. Notwithstanding all this, the court used it as a key element in rendering its verdict. The investigation into the telephone marketing network concluded that the SIM card found in the backpack in Vallecas had been on sale in Zougam's store. On what was the investigation based to reach that conclusion? Before their sale to a customer in a store, SIM cards usually pass through the hands of three or four intermediaries.

But only the initial brokers list on their invoices the identification number of each SIM card sold. Subsequent brokers only record the total number of SIM cards. In this case, there is no invoice showing that the SIM card in question was sold to Zougam. The only thing that allows one to reach that conclusion is the testimony of his supplier, who says he remembers specifically the sale of that SIM card among hundreds of other cards. Let us accept, nevertheless, that fact as sufficient proof and continue examining the course of the investigation. The fact of having sold a SIM card does not make the seller responsible for any possible criminal use that the buyer might make of that card. But Zougam had appeared as a witness in a previous investigation about Islamist terrorists. It would seem that was the only motive for his arrest on March 13, given that no witness had described him nor had identified him before that date. A re-analysis of Zougam's behavior up until his arrest shows that apparently he committed a series of truly incredible indiscretions. In the first place, he used a SIM card on sale in his own store to make the Vallecas bomb.

Secondly, he left that SIM card in the phone even though it was not necessary to use its alarm clock function. And, thirdly, he continued his normal activity until the day of his arrest on the afternoon of March 13, despite the fact that all of Spain had known since the morning of March 12 that police had dismantled one of the bombs. From that moment on, Zougam had to know that the investigators were in possession of a SIM card that would lead to him. But he did not try to hide or flee. The incoherence of that behavior leads to doubts about his guilt. The media gave wide publicity to the arrests of March 13 and to photos of the suspects. Passengers from the attacked trains spontaneously showed up to testify about the suspects seen on trains on March 11. Some of these testimonies implicate Zougam and constitute the only evidence of his involvement in the attack. There is also in this case an incredibly inconsistent piece of evidence, in relation to the seriousness of the facts.

The first problem is the spreading of Zougam's picture across the media, thereby preventing testimonies from complying with a fundamental rule: memory must not be influenced by other images seen after the events. Moreover, some witnesses did not agree as to the trip that Zougam allegedly made on the trains, with contradictions regarding his description, how he was dressed or stating that he placed a bag in a place where no bomb exploded. Finally, the verdict of October 2007 only takes into account 3 testimonies incriminating Zougam. In the appeals trial of July 2008, the court invalidated one of those 3 testimonies because the witness had given his statement to the investigative judge rather than before the court, where he had not even been convoked, and a fact which prevented Zougam's defense from questioning him despite already existing doubts about his statement. For example, according to that witness, the suspect got off the train, onto the platform, and then returned to the same train car through the door that connected to the other car, all strangely indiscreet behavior for someone who is planting bombs. There are, therefore, only two statements accusing Zougam, and these come from two Romanian friends who were traveling together. The first came forward as a witness three weeks after the bombings.

At that moment, her description of the suspect is very brief: a person 1 meter 80 centimeters tall, of average build, and carrying a handbag. Without further details. But that same description becomes more precise days later when the police show her a series of photos among which she recognizes Zougam: shoulder-length hair, a rather thick nose, a goatee, lower lip thicker than upper, etc. It is reasonable to ask then if what this witness is describing is what she saw in the photograph rather than what she remembered. In addition, her statements continued to change with regard to other details, such as the position of the car in the train. After a year, the witness recalled that the suspect had pushed her, justifying in that way why she remembered his face, and then saying for the first time that she was traveling with a friend, who thus became the second accusing witness against Zougam.

Why did an entire year pass without her mentioning the friend who was traveling with her? Why did that other witness wait a year before coming forward? What could this new witness still remember after all this time? Can her testimony be considered as independent of that of her friend? And it is precisely on the basis of these two dubious declarations that the only guilty finding for the carrying out of the bombings on March 11 was reached. For his part, Zougam always denied any involvement in the bombings. All the others who allegedly planted bombs on April 3 died in the explosion of the Leganés apartment, three weeks after the attacks. An important consequence of the deaths of these individuals is that the investigation did not reconstruct the exact role of each one in the carrying out the attack, thus focusing attention on those accused. The court acknowledged in its ruling that it ignored which of these 7 individuals were involved in placing the bombings and where they did it.

This contrasts with the case of Zougam, clearly accused of having placed the bombs on the train that exploded at the Santa Eugenia station. Considering the difficulties involved in maintaining the records of the accusation against Zougam, one might think that the lack of information [about the people killed in Leganés] was paradoxically beneficial to those attempting to prove the guilt of those 7 suspects since it avoided any contradiction with reality. The investigation then focused on demonstrating that the death of those in the Leganés apartment was a suicide, a suicide that was used as proof of the fanaticism of the suspects, while the discovery of documents which claimed responsibility for the attack among the ruins of the apartment was interpreted as a posthumous confession. The circumstances under which that apartment was discovered, just at the time when the 7 suspects were inside, remain unclear. For a long time, the police spoke of a shootout in the street between several of its officers and a gang of North Africans. The incident allegedly resulted in a chase that led the gang to take refuge in the apartment in Leganés.

But this episode later disappears from the official version to make way for another explanation. According to this version, the police reviewed the list of calls from a suspect phone belonging to the terrorist cell. By calling one of the numbers on that list, the police made contact with a property owner who claimed to have rented an apartment in Leganés to a group of Arabs about a month prior. That is the version of the apartment's discovery mentioned in the verdict, in which the story of the chase is totally ignored. The police then surrounded the apartment on the afternoon of April 3. Around 9 PM, the GEO began the assault in a hasty manner, according to members of that group. But before gaining entrance, the apartment blew up, killing its 7 occupants and a GEO member. Due to the condition of the bodies, it was necessary to use fingerprints or DNA during the identification process. The investigation concluded that it was a group suicide, but the suicidal nature of the explosion was not as clearly established as verdict stated.

Before the assault by the GEO and the explosion, neighbors had heard gunshots, shouting and even Arabic chants coming from the apartment. But no one clearly saw the suspects. And there were no fingerprints or any sign of bullet impacts that should exist there after an exchange of gunfire. The decisive argument supporting the theory of suicide is that the suspects allegedly had communicated by telephone with their families during the siege to say goodbye. During the trial, the only family member called as a witness to those phone calls was the brother of one of the 7 suspects, Abdenabi Kounjaa. This witness testified that he could not recognize the voice of his brother during the call, and that he did not think it was him, which is why he immediately alerted the police and did not call back to convince his brother not to commit suicide. That testimony casts serious doubt on the authenticity of the calls, especially if one considers that no other family was summoned to the trial as a witness.

The investigative file contains 3 successive reports on those calls but provides no further clarification of the matter. Each report contradicts the previous one in various aspects: the phones used, the identity of certain recipients of calls, and the number of calls made to some recipients. So many differences justify doubts about the reliability of such information. Did the suspects really commit suicide? What circumstances brought about the presence of those individuals in that apartment? By April 3, the media had already been announcing for 4 days that they were being sought and their pictures had already been disclosed. In that context, for all of them to meet in an apartment outside Madrid, instead of escaping each by his own means, was extremely imprudent. And why would these criminals, who had just committed a massive crime, wait for the police to evacuate the entire neighborhood before blowing up their apartment? The inconsistencies do not end there. Anyone interested in the movements of suspects from the time of the attack to the moment of their suicide will learn, for example, that El Chino was partying with his wife's family 8 days after the attack, in the same house where he allegedly built the bombs.

The very profile of most of the members of the cell does not correspond to a radical Islam that allegedly led them to perpetrate the massacre and later to commit suicide. Four of them were petty criminals linked to the world of drug trafficking, a fact not very compatible with Islam. El Chino lived with a native Spaniard, who wore flimsy clothes, and their son went to Catholic school. The death of the other 7 suspects allowed, in any case, the reconstruction of a scenario without going into too much detail, and without the accused being able to contradict it. Moreover, journalists who have had access to the investigative file have cast doubt on the above connection and between the 7 suicides and Zougam. According to these journalists, there is nothing in the documents provided by the phone company Amena to indicate that the seven SIM cards in question had been put into use at the home of El Chino. The defense brought up that problem during the trial without the Amena employees who had been invited to testify as experts responding to it.

The last major element in favor of the Islamist attack theory is the Renault Kangoo van. The verdict stated that several members of the terrorist cell, without specifying exactly who, used the van to arrive at the subway with their bombs. Therefore, the court did not take into account the evidence given during the trial itself by the dog handler who participated in the inspection of that vehicle. In effect, although the dog handler recognized the possibility of a small piece of explosive being overlooked, that same expert stated that the handling of bags with dozens of kilograms of explosives would have left a trace of odor inside the vehicle, traces that his dog would have detected. Question from Zougam's defense attorney, 'In the event that the van had been transporting 50 or 30 kilos of explosives, would the dog have detected that smell? Yes, he would have detected it, he would have immediately, because explosive residues remain, and the dog would have detected it.' Then another lawyer asked whether the dog would have detected the smell if the explosive would have been particularly well packaged. The witness replied that the handling of such a large amount of explosive always leaves a smell. Furthermore, the attendant who brought the Kangoo van to the attention of the police stated that he thought the individuals were Eastern Europeans, and the metro station employee who sold a ticket to one of the individuals claimed he spoke without an accent.

Regarding this point, once again the behavior of the suspects is surprising. Why attract attention by turning to the ticket saleswoman with their faces almost masked instead of buying the ticket at a vending machine? Why run the risks of using a stolen vehicle without changing the license plates? And why did the terrorists abandon that vehicle, in particular leaving detonators, explosives and clothing inside it? According to the indictment, that clothing contained DNA samples of suspects, but the verdict did not take into account that evidence. So many unexplained aspects of the supporting evidence cause the Islamist attack theory to lose all credibility. This is especially so considering that this article does not mention all of them. In his book Les Dessous du Terrorisme, Gerhard Wisnewski shows, for example, the inconsistency in the various Islamist claims of responsibility for the attack. In accepting the thesis of Islamist responsibility, the Spanish court concluded to a surprising extent that these contradictions were not significant.

The shadow of the police

Is there other evidence to support the theory of an Islamist attack or to steer the investigation in another direction? The problem is that key elements of the investigation have been neglected in a manner that is, to say the least, disturbing. First, the train cars where the bombs exploded were destroyed just two days after the attack. Why was it necessary to eliminate the 'Crime scene' so quickly? In 2006, a subway train that had suffered an accident in Valencia was kept for 2 years because of the needs of the investigation. The court acknowledged in its ruling that answers would have been found to address many doubts if the coaches had been preserved for a longer time. The most important of those doubts has to do with the nature of the explosive used. The analysis of the chemicals deposited on the objects located near the explosions would have provided key information for the investigation. However, no one knows yet exactly what it was that exploded on the trains, as was acknowledged in the verdict. We see here why it was not possible to determine the type of explosive used. The first was negligence in selecting the agency that performed the analysis of the samples. The responsibility for that analysis was put into the hands of bomb disposal specialists, whose laboratories have only rudimentary methods for analysis of explosive substances. Under usual procedure, forensic police would have had to ensure the analysis, precisely because they have far more advanced methods. The results of the forensic analysis were also very imprecise.

The report submitted to the investigative judge indicated the presence of 'Generic components of dynamite' in the samples. But it does not specify the type of dynamite. Was it Titadyne, Goma-2 Eco? Even more surprisingly, it does not even include the list of chemical components found. Faced with so much uncertainty, the court ended up ordering a new expert analysis at the time the trial began in 2007. Unfortunately, the new expert analysis had to use the already analyzed samples, since they could not collect new samples due to the previously mentioned destruction of the trains. The experts complained about the small number of samples kept by police and the contamination of these samples due to serious negligence in the course of the previous analysis. Finally, their findings do not shed more light on the type of explosive used given that those findings include a list of products that do not correspond to the makeup of TNT. At the end of this entire process, there was great interest in the anticipated testimony of the director of the laboratory of bomb deactivation specialists to answer questions about the work she had delivered in March 2004. But she testified that she did not have the chromatography media in which the chemical elements appeared, nor did she even have the documents in which they had made notes during the carrying out of their analysis. Nevertheless, she shocked the court when she recited for the first time the precise listing of chemical compounds found, explaining that she had never turned over that list because no one had explicitly asked for it.

The imprecision of the analysis report had led to such a huge controversy in Spain during the 3 years between the attack and the testimony of the director of the laboratory that her explanation was laughable. What credence can be given to that list, first mentioned after 3 years and which corresponds to the composition of Goma-2 Eco dynamite? To the question of the explosives must be added the doubts that led to the statements of the chief of the bomb-dismantling specialists who oversaw operations on March 11. Upon seeing the damage, the bombs had caused, the chief of the specialists stated that visible tearing of the structures of the train cars was characteristic of high power explosives, of a military type, not of dynamite. It is important to remember that certain military explosives leave no chemical traces at the scene of an explosion, which make them exceedingly difficult to detect. Another source of doubt is the location of the bombs as reconstructed in the formal accusation. According to that document, most of the bags, which contained 10 kilograms of explosives, were not hidden but, for example, had been left between two front seats situated face to face next to a window, or in the baggage area, or beside the trash receptacle, or under a folding seat (which should have closed). Only one bomb was hidden under a non-folding seat.

Why didn't the terrorists try to better hide the handbags? And how is it possible that such heavy bags, abandoned in such visible places, did not attract the attention of the passengers? To answer these questions, several journalists expressed the hypothesis that the bombs were very much smaller and made not with dynamite but rather with high-powered explosives. The Goma-2 Eco dynamite found in the Kangoo van, in the Vallecas backpack, and in the Leganes apartment does not prove that the same explosive was used to blow up the trains. The suspicions about these facts suggest that these were items intended to divert attention from the crime scene, in other words, away from the trains. A final example of negligence: the recordings of conversations among police patrols would have helped to clarify the issue of the chase that allegedly took place in Leganés. But when the judge asked for these recordings, the police said they had not been preserved. More serious than these acts of negligence is the existence of strong suspicions of falsification of various elements of the investigation. We have already mentioned the Vallecas backpack, the Kangoo van and the goodbye phone calls by the Leganés suicides. But there are other elements whose fabrication is so obvious that not even the verdict took them into account, such as, for example, the telephone conversations of Rabei Osman, an Egyptian who lived in Italy. Italian police recorded and translated his conversations in 2004, and in one of them this individual allegedly takes responsibility for organizing the attacks.

During the trial, new translations requested by the defense showed that the sentences in which Osman takes credit for organizing the attack were simply invented by the Italian translators. The Spanish court was therefore obliged to absolve him of all ties to the attack, after he had been presented as the brains of the Islamist group. The verdict does not name an organizer of the attack, a fact which provoked the indignation of victims' associations, who filed an appeal. But the most notorious fabrication of the investigation is a Skoda Fabia car that police found near the Alcala metro station, 20 meters from where the Kangoo van was found. That discovery was made on June 13, 2004, in other words, 3 months after the attacks. This second vehicle allowed the strengthening of the argument that the 7 or 8 terrorists arrived in Alcala by car, and it also bore traces of DNA from one of those killed in Leganés. Nevertheless, many observers doubt that a vehicle parked so close to the Kangoo van would have been able to go unnoticed for 3 months, even more so considering that its registration number is not even mentioned in records collected on March 11. That piece of evidence thus remained in limbo until June 2005 when police delivered the testimony of a Chilean prisoner to the investigative judge. This man claimed to have stolen the Skoda and subsequently to have sold it in October 2003 to one of those killed in Leganés. But this evidence was once again discredited in March 2006, when a journalist from El Mundo revealed the testimony of a security guard in a suburb of Madrid where the Skoda was abandoned in November 2003.

According to this new witness, the vehicle was improperly parked for 3 weeks and received numerous parking violations, until it disappeared. By verifying that testimony through the records of the parking violations, it was discovered that the Skoda had been involved in various crimes such as street robberies. These crimes were committed between September and October 2003, a period during which the car was supposedly in possession of the Chilean. But until then the police, as well as the Chilean, had totally concealed those facts from the investigative judge. When he tried again to examine the South American prisoner, the judge learned that he had been extradited to Chile without anyone having notified him of the fact. To all these contradictions must be added the inconsistency of the behavior of the terrorists. To commit one of the worst attacks that has ever been seen in Europe they were unable to produce anything better than to use a stolen car, involved in a whole series of crimes, which had been abandoned in the street for a time, which had various parking violations, and on which it did not even occur to them to change the license plates.

The court therefore had no choice but to remove the Skoda from the list of elements of proof in its verdict. Moreover, the DNA found on that likely fabricated evidence raises doubts as to the traces of DNA found on clothing so 'Conveniently' abandoned by the suspects in this case. Take, finally, some examples of suspected falsification of testimony. Emilio Trashorras confirmed that police had asked him to invent the episode according to which it was he who provided the explosives to El Chino. This witness thought he would enjoy the status of protected witness and that he would have no more problems with the law. For his part, the witness Hassan Serroukh told the investigative judge that his statement to police had been falsified. That testimony described Zougam as a religious fanatic, something that Serroukh claims he never said. Acts of negligence and suspected fabrications are among the many suspicious police actions that appear in the investigation which followed the attack. But suspicions are heightened even further upon examining the preparations for the attack as presented in the verdict. Two key players in the attack were informants for the security forces. The first, Zouhier, put the terrorist cell in contact with an explosives trafficker. The investigation revealed that the Civil Guard, which controlled this informant, called him two days before the attack.

The second, Trashorras, is nothing less than the actual explosives trafficker. He had several telephone conversations with his police contact the day before, the day after and two days after having placed the explosives in the hands of El Chino. But that police contact maintains Trashorras told him nothing about that fact. In addition, the mobile phones used in the manufacture of the bombs were unlocked at a location belonging to a policeman of Syrian origin, Maussili Kalaji. What a coincidence that all these terrorist collaborators have been linked to the police! And above all, what "luck" that none of them were turned in by these police before they committed the crime. Apparently, the terrorists also were lucky in terms of the surveillance they were subjected to by the police. As recorded in police records, since January 2003 the police had been closely monitoring an Islamist group which included several of the terrorists who would later die in Leganés.

In sum, this group was regularly under surveillance on 81 days spread between January 2003 and February 2004. This monitoring appears to have intensified during the first half of February 2004, but ceased abruptly on February 17, that is, eleven days before the operation to deliver the explosives, and twenty-four days before the attack itself. The same good luck will later accompany the two accomplices of the terrorist cell whose telephone conversations were being intercepted in the course of an investigation into drug trafficking. The phone taps were suspended abruptly on March 12, the day after the attack. Let's consider the first example in which the silhouette of the police is visible behind the terrorists. After the explosion of the apartment in Leganés, several documents regarding ETA appear among the ruins. It was determined after the fact that these documents came from the neighboring apartment, which was partly destroyed. That other apartment was occupied by a policeman who - one more coincidence - specialized in fighting terrorism.

All these suspicious behaviors, before and after the attack, linked to the obvious inconsistency of the Islamist theory, suggest that the real culprits were under the protection of the state apparatus. It must be emphasized, however, that only a reopening of the investigation can determine whether those suspicions are founded. By revealing evidence that shatters the official version and absolves the alleged organizers, the trial has done nothing more than confirm the extreme fragility of the theory of an Islamist attack. In any case, in the political context, the court did not attempt to precisely establish the facts. It had to conclude that José María Aznar's accusations against ETA were unfounded, as had already been decided by the broadest of juries, the voters. At the same time, the court had to conclude that the accusations by neo-cons against al Qaeda were also unfounded, something which the new government of Jose Luis Zapatero had already decided. The court determined that the initial evidence had been fabricated to falsely accuse the Basque organization ETA but declined to go further in terms of the manipulations carried out by certain elements of the police. The court chose, not surprisingly, to content itself with the hypothesis with which it had been presented and which was the only one that could restore social calm: the hypothesis of Islamist responsibility without links to al Qaeda.

NOW THE TRUTH EMERGES: HOW THE US FUELED THE RISE OF ISIS IN SYRIA AND IRAQ

The war on terror, that campaign without end launched 14 years ago by George Bush, is tying itself up in ever more grotesque contortions. On Monday, the trial in London of a Swedish man, Bherlin Gildo, accused of terrorism in Syria, collapsed after it became clear British intelligence had been arming the same rebel groups the defendant was charged with supporting. The prosecution abandoned the case, apparently to avoid embarrassing the intelligence services. The defense argued that going ahead with the trial would have been an 'Affront to justice' when there was plenty of evidence the British state was itself providing 'Extensive support' to the armed Syrian opposition. That didn't only include the 'Non-lethal assistance' boasted of by the government (including body armor and military vehicles), but training, logistical support, and the secret supply of "arms on a massive scale." Reports were cited that MI6 had cooperated with the CIA on a "rat line" of arms transfers from Libyan stockpiles to the Syrian rebels in 2012 after the fall of the Gaddafi regime. Clearly, the absurdity of sending someone to prison for doing what ministers and their security officials were up to themselves became too much. But it's only the latest of a string of such cases. Less fortunate was a London cab driver Anis Sardar, who was given a life sentence a fortnight earlier for taking part in 2007 in resistance to the occupation of Iraq by US and British forces. Armed opposition to illegal invasion and occupation clearly doesn't constitute terrorism or murder on most definitions, including the Geneva Convention.

But terrorism is now squarely in the eye of the beholder. And nowhere is that more so than in the Middle East, where today's terrorists are tomorrow's fighters against tyranny and allies are enemies, often at the bewildering whim of a western policymaker's conference call. For the past year, U.S., British and other western forces have been back in Iraq, supposedly in the cause of destroying the hyper-sectarian terror group Islamic State (formerly known as al-Qaida in Iraq). This was after Isis overran huge chunks of Iraqi and Syrian territory and proclaimed a self-styled Islamic caliphate. The campaign isn't going well. Last month, Isis rolled into the Iraqi city of Ramadi, while on the other side of the now nonexistent border its forces conquered the Syrian town of Palmyra. Al-Qaida's official franchise, the Nusra Front, has also been making gains in Syria. Some Iraqis complain that the US sat on its hands while all this was going on. The

Americans insist they are trying to avoid civilian casualties and claim significant successes. Privately, officials say they don't want to be seen hammering Sunni strongholds in a sectarian war and risk upsetting their Sunni allies in the Gulf. A revealing light on how we got here has now been shone by a recently declassified secret US intelligence report, written in August 2012, which uncannily predicts and effectively welcomes the prospect of a 'Salafist principality' in eastern Syria and an al-Qaida-controlled Islamic state in Syria and Iraq. In stark contrast to western claims at the time, the Defense Intelligence Agency document identifies al-Qaida in Iraq (which became Isis) and fellow Salafists as the "major forces driving the insurgency in Syria" – and states that 'Western countries, the Gulf states and Turkey' were supporting the opposition's efforts to take control of eastern Syria.

Raising the 'Possibility of establishing a declared or undeclared Salafist principality,' the Pentagon report goes on, 'This is exactly what the supporting powers to the opposition want, in order to isolate the Syrian regime, which is considered the strategic depth of the Shia expansion (Iraq and Iran).'

American forces bomb one set of rebels while backing another in Syria

Which is pretty well exactly what happened two years later. The report isn't a policy document. It's heavily redacted and there are ambiguities in the language. But the implications are clear enough. A year into the Syrian rebellion, the US and its allies weren't only supporting and arming an opposition they knew to be dominated by extreme sectarian groups; they were prepared to countenance the creation of some sort of 'Islamic state' despite the 'Grave danger' to Iraq's unity as a Sunni buffer to weaken Syria. That doesn't mean the US created Isis, of course, though some of its Gulf allies certainly played a role in it – as the US vice-president, Joe Biden, acknowledged last year. But there was no al-Qaida in Iraq until the US and Britain invaded. And the US has certainly exploited the existence of Isis against other forces in the region as part of a wider drive to maintain western control. The calculus changed when Isis started beheading westerners and posting atrocities online, and the Gulf States are now backing other groups in the Syrian war, such as the Nusra Front. But this US and western habit of playing with jihadi groups, which then come back to bite them, goes back at least to the 1980s war against the Soviet Union in Afghanistan, which fostered the original al-Qaida under CIA tutelage. It was recalibrated during the occupation of Iraq, when US forces led by General Petraeus sponsored an El Salvador-style dirty war of sectarian death squads to weaken the Iraqi resistance. And it was reprised in 2011 in the Nato-orchestrated war in Libya, where Isis last week took control of Gaddafi's home town of Sirte.

In reality, U.S. and western policy in the conflagration that is now the Middle East is in the classic mould of imperial divide-and-rule. American forces bomb one set of rebels while backing another in Syria, and mount what are effectively joint military operations with Iran against Isis in Iraq while supporting Saudi Arabia's military campaign against Iranian-backed Houthi forces in Yemen. However confused US policy may often be, a weak, partitioned Iraq and Syria fit such an approach perfectly. What's clear is that Isis and its monstrosities won't be defeated by the same powers that brought it to Iraq and Syria in the first place, or whose open and covert war-making has fostered it in the years since. Endless western military interventions in the Middle East have brought only destruction and division. It's the people of the region who can cure this disease – not those who incubated the virus.

'Black Flags,' Tracing the Birth of Isis

In the last month, terror attacks that left 130 dead in Paris and 43 dead in Beirut and took down a Russian airliner with 224 people aboard have made the entire world horribly aware that the Islamic State not only seeks to establish a caliphate in Syria and Iraq, but also is beginning to export its monstrous savagery abroad. Although the Islamic State has been in the headlines for only two years, and its metastasis has been alarmingly swift, the seeds of the group in its many incarnations were planted many years ago, as Joby Warrick's gripping new book, 'Black Flags,' makes clear. Mr. Warrick, a reporter for The Washington Post and the author of the 2011 best seller 'The Triple Agent,' has a gift for constructing narratives with a novelistic energy and detail, and in this volume, he creates the most revealing portrait yet laid out in a book of Abu Musab Al-Zarqawi, the founding father of the organization that would become the Islamic State (also known as ISIS or ISIL).

In 'Black Flags,' Mr. Zarqawi comes across as a kind of Bond villain, who repeatedly foils attempts to neutralize him. He was a hard-drinking, heavily tattooed Jordanian street thug (well versed in pimping, drug dealing and assault), and when he found religion, he fell for it hard, having a relative slice off his offending tattoos with a razor blade. He traveled to Afghanistan in 1989 to wage jihad; during a stint in a Jordanian prison, he emerged as a leader known and feared for his ruthlessness as an enforcer among Islamist inmates. He began thinking of himself as a man with a destiny, and in the aftermath of the American invasion of Afghanistan in 2001, he set up a small training camp in Iraq's northeastern mountains, near the Iranian border. At this point, Mr. Zarqawi was just a small-time jihadist. But then, Mr. Warrick writes, "in the most improbable of events, America intervened," declaring — in an effort to make the case for ousting Saddam Hussein that 'This obscure Jordanian was the link between Iraq's dictatorship and the plotters behind the September 11, 2001, terrorist attacks.'

As C.I.A. analysts well knew, this assertion was false; in retrospect, it would also have the perverse effect of turning Mr. Zarqawi into 'An international celebrity and the toast of the Islamist movement.' Weeks later, when United States troops invaded Iraq, this newly famous terrorist 'Gained a battleground and a cause and soon thousands of followers.' Accused by the Bush administration of being in league with Saddam Hussein, Mr. Zarqawi would use the Americans' toppling of the dictator to empower himself. He was a diabolical strategist, and he quickly capitalized on two disastrous decisions made by the Americans (dissolving the Iraqi Army and banning Baath Party members from positions of authority), which intensified the country's security woes and left tens of thousands of Iraqis out of work and on the street. Soon, former members of Mr. Hussein's military were enlisting in Mr. Zarqawi's army; others offered safe houses, intelligence, cash, and weapons.

While the Bush White House was debating whether there even was an insurgency in Iraq, Mr. Zarqawi was helping to direct the worsening violence there, orchestrating car and suicide bombings and shocking beheadings. He also used terrorism to change the battlefield, fomenting sectarian hatred between the Shiites and the disenfranchised and increasingly bitter Sunnis, guaranteeing more chaos, and discrediting the electoral process. Mr. Zarqawi's penchant for ultraviolence had won him his favorite moniker, 'The sheikh of the slaughterers,' but by mid-2005, his bloodthirstiness and killing of Shiite innocents worried Al Qaeda's leadership, which warned him that 'The mujahed movement must avoid any action that the masses do not understand or approve.' After many narrow escapes, Mr. Zarqawi was finally killed by a United States airstrike in June 2006, and over the next few years, the United States managed to decimate much of his organization.

Still, dangerous embers remained, and they would burst into flames under the group's new leader, Abu Bakr al-Baghdadi, who shared Mr. Zarqawi's taste for gruesome violence, and who had built up a valuable network of supporters while serving time in Camp Bucca, a United States-controlled prison known as a 'Jihadi university' for its role in radicalizing inmates. The sectarianism of the Iraqi Prime Minister Nuri Kamal al-Maliki drove increasingly marginalized Sunnis into the embrace of the Islamic State, a dynamic hastened by the withdrawal of American troops in 2011. Meanwhile, in Syria, the chaos of civil war created perfect conditions for the Islamic State's explosive growth and a home base for its self-proclaimed caliphate.

REVIVING THE 'CHEMICAL WEAPONS' LIE: NEW US-UK CALLS FOR REGIME CHANGE, MILITARY ATTACK AGAINST SYRIA

Here it comes again. As the enemies of peace continue to pressure a new US President into deeper war commitments overseas, and as Washington's Deep State works relentlessly opposing Russian moves in Syria at every turn, the war drums have started again, beating harder than ever now, clamoring for a new US-led attack on Syria. This morning we saw the familiar theme emerge, and just in time to provide a convenient backdrop to this week's Brussels' 'Peace Talks' and conference on 'Syria's Future.' The US-led 'Coalition' prepares to make its end-run into Syria to 'Retake Raqqa,' and impose its Safe Zones in order to partition Syria, more media demonization of the Syrian government appears to be needed by the West. On cue, the multi-billion dollar US and UK media machines sprung into overdrive this morning over reports based primarily from their own 'activist' media outlets. Aleppo Media Center and others embedded in the Al Nusra-dominated terrorist stronghold of Idlib, Syria, alongside their media counterpart the UK-based Syrian Observatory for Human Rights (SOHR) funded by the UK and EU, are all now claiming that the Syrian and Russian Airforces have launched a chemical weapons airstrike killing civilians in Idlib.

In their report today entitled, 'Syria conflict: 'Chemical attack' in Idlib kills 58', the BBC is also alleging in their report that Sarin gas was used. The alleged "chemical airstrikes" are said to have taken place in the town of Khan Sheikhoun, about 50km south of the city of Idlib. Predictably, the BBC and other similar reports by CNN, have triggered a wave of 'Consensus condemnation' and indignation by the usual voices, the UN's Staffan de Mistura, Francois Hollande, and, of course, UK Foreign Secretary Boris Johnson, who said that President Bashar al-Assad 'Would be guilty of a war crime' if it somehow be proven that his 'regime' was responsible. 'Bombing your own civilians with chemical weapons is unquestionably a war crime and they must be held to account,' he said (reported by BBC). But is the mainstream media's version of events what actually happened?

The BBC claims in their article that, 'Opposition activists said Syrian government or Russian warplanes carried out the strikes.' This claim should be checked against any Russian air sorties scheduled for the same period. As of this morning, Russia's defense ministry has stated that it had not carried out any air strikes the area. The problem here is that the BBC and others are not only taking 'Opposition activists' reports of a chemical attack at face value, but they are also elevating claims that the Syrian and Russian Airforces were then later hitting the medical clinics who were treating the survivors: 'Later, aircraft fired rockets at local clinics treating survivors, medics and activists said.' Expectedly, as with past claims of 'Chemical attacks,' the notorious US-UK funded 'NGO,' the White Helmets have already played a central role in scripting the narrative for this latest chemical attack. As with so many other previous reports on Syria, the BBC, CNN, and AP's reporting relies exclusively on 'Opposition activists' and 'Opposition media agencies,' including the 'Pro-opposition' Step News agency,' the Edlib Media Center (EMC), and 'Opposition journalists' like photographer Hussein Kayal, as well as an unnamed 'AFP news agency journalist.' The unnamed 'AFP journalist' is particularly interesting, as it seems to be the source of a key portion of the BBC's version of events.

'An AFP news agency journalist saw a young girl, a woman and two elderly people dead at a hospital, all with foam still visible around their mouths.' The journalist also reported that the same facility was hit by a rocket on Tuesday afternoon, bringing down rubble on top of doctors treating the injured. However, as you read further down the BBC report, the story gets less certain, as the story becomes very loose: 'The source of the projectile was not clear, but the EMC and the opposition Local Co-ordination Committees (LCC) network said warplanes had targeted several clinics.' After their source, the SOHR refused to say which 'Chemical' was supposedly dropped, the BBC quickly moved in to fill in the blanks by framing the story that the Syrian-Russian Airforces had launched a 'Sarin Attack.' 'The SOHR said it was unable to say what exactly was dropped. However, the EMC and LCC said it was believed to be the nerve agent Sarin, which is highly toxic and considered 20 times as deadly as cyanide.'

At no point in its reporting does the BBC ever express any skepticism that maybe their 'activist' sources could be providing false or misleading information. Ultimately, these reports can be used to trigger renewed calls by Western officials for military strikes against the 'Syrian Regime' which was exactly what happened today after these news stories were circulated. Within a few hours after these reports circulated, Congressman Adam Kinzinger (R, Illinois) came on CNN with Wolf Blitzer who asked Kinzinger directly: What can be done to remove this regime? Kinzinger then replied by calling outright for US airstrikes to 'Take out the Assad Regime in Syria,' including "cratering their airstrips so no planes can take off" and creating a 'No Fly Zone' over Syria. These statements, as bombastic as they may sound, are serious and should not be taken casually. The problem is they are based on a series of lies.

Of course, Kinzinger was followed on-air by John McCain protesting against US Secretary of State Rex Tillerson's recent comments this week that, 'The Syrian people should be able to choose their own (political) future,' effectively holding the overwhelming majority of Syrian in contempt for supporting their government. CNN Senior Middle East correspondent Arwa Damon also chimed in with Blitzer from New York, and without any real evidence presented as to what has happened and who is to blame, she swiftly concluded that the Idlib "chemical attack" was the work of 'the regime' and that America cannot stand back idly and do nothing, and how this would show a "lack of humanity," The BBC does briefly mention an alternative report, but carefully tried to discredit it in the court of political opinion by labelling it as from 'Pro-Government journalists,' stated here.

'Pro-government journalists later cited military sources as saying there had been an explosion at an al-Qaeda chemical weapons factory in Khan Sheikhoun that was caused either by an air strike or an accident.'

This story of Syria striking a munitions facility is just as likely, if not more so, than the current conspiracy making the rounds in the Western mainstream and Gulf media, and was actually reported by TASS news agency out of Moscow on April 4th, but rather than follow-up on this, the BBC, CNN and the mainstream chorus have immediately written it off and opted instead to pursue the narrative which will allow them to expedite the military escalation which they have expressed on record since at least 2013. If this were a criminal prosecution, the rebel-terrorist-coalition axis has the overwhelming primary motive, as well as expressed intent to escalate documented on countless occasions. So why is there no rational line of inquiry here? As expected, the UN affiliated chemical weapons watchdog, the OPCW, quickly announced they were 'Seriously concerned' about the alleged chemical attack, and that they were now 'Gathering and analyzing information from all available sources.' One hopes that this will entail more than just looking at 'Activist' or White Helmets material being circulated on the US and western media. Incredibly, Kinzinger also said on national TV with CNN that people should ignore any stories which DO NOT implicate the Syrian government waged chemical attacks against its own people in East Ghouta in 2013 and that these should be dismissed as 'Fake news' put out by 'The Russians and the FSB.' By this statement, Kinzinger is essentially saying that award-winning American journalists Seymour Hersh and Robert Parry are akin to being Russian agents. Many in Official Washington pose the fallacious argument that 'Obama failed to enforce the Red Line in Syria, and let Assad get away with it (in 2013)'.

If we go by the actual facts (see research bibliography below) of the 2013 Ghouta incident, then Assad never crossed the 'Red Line,' but the US and Gulf-backed 'Rebels' absolutely did. These are the same 'rebels which Adam Kinzinger himself travelled to northern Syria circa 2013-2014 to provide his personal assurances that these terrorist fighters would be receiving US weapons and TOW missiles which arguably, is responsible for extended the life of this needless proxy war in Syria. So based on the facts of the Ghouta chemical incident, Rep. Kinzinger is actually wrong and lying in his capacity as a high-ranking House Committee member and doing so with no accountability from CNN whilst broadcasting to a national audience in the United States. The result of this is millions of Americans and politicians are left misinformed of notable events – once again, led by misinformation into another war. This is the fundamental problem with mainstream media's own fake news, it leads to wars, many of them illegal, and always waged on false pretenses. In 2013, the US and UK went on an all-out propaganda blitz to try and implicate the Syrian Government in advance of war votes in both Washington and London. The campaign failed.

QANON CORROBORATES HAWAII MISSILE ATTACK & HUNT FOR ROGUE CIA SUBMARINE

On February 11, the anonymous whistleblower 'Qanon' posted information that corroborates claims that a false flag ballistic missile attack was launched against Hawaii on January 13, and that a submarine linked to the CIA is currently being hunted by the U.S. and other regional military forces, QAnon has quickly grown in popularity since first appearing in late October, 2017 discussing the 'Coming storm' of revelations, document dumps, trials, events, etc., linked to Trump White House pledges to 'Drain the Swamp'. Today QAnon has an estimated audience of millions who closely follow his/her posts. Major media sources such as Newsweek have published overly critical stories attempt to dismiss QAnon as just the latest incarnation of unsubstantiated right wing conspiracy theories. QAnon's cryptic style of communication involves questions, links, photos, acronyms, and codes, which are used as breadcrumbs for the reader to learn about highly classified efforts underway by White Hats in the government/military opposed to Deep State corruption and human rights abuses in the U.S. and around the world. The most telling official document that substantiates QAnon's claims to date is an extraordinary Executive Order passed by President Trump on December 21, 2017, declaring a national emergency, and freezing the financial assets of anyone involved in human rights abuses and corruption anywhere around the world.

The mainstream media has strangely ignored Trump's 'Executive Order Blocking the Property of Persons Involved in Serious Human Abuse or Corruption,' and its deep significance, especially given what QAnon has previously stated. If Trump's Executive Order were indeed targeting the Deep State, it's not surprising that it would provoke a strong reaction by powerful groups suddenly cut off from their financial assets. That's where the ballistic missile alert on the morning of January 13 in Hawaii becomes relevant. As discussed in three previous articles (see here, here, and here), there have been a number of whistleblowers, witnesses and analysts who have all said the missile alert was genuine, and not a false alarm at all, as public officials contend. QAnon followed the Hawaii missile alert the next day warning about an upcoming week of false flag attacks by the Deep State. This implied that the Hawaii incident was part of a series of false flag attacks, and not a false alarm. Since January 14, however, QAnon has not said much to cast light on the Hawaii ballistic missile alert. That is until February 11 when QAnon provided a long post referring to a recent false flag missile attack intended to start a war.

The relevant post appears below and the section of comments relevant to the Hawaii missile alert is highlighted in red. It is worth examining QAnon's questions in light of what has been previously learned about the Hawaii missile alert and Trump's December 21 Executive Order. QAnon wrote. Ask yourself, who is trying to start a war? The most obvious answer is those targeted by Trump's Executive Order. Individuals and groups responsible for human rights abuses and corruption in the U.S. and globally, have the most to lose if their financial assets are frozen. QAnon then wrote: Ask yourself, if a missile were launched by rogue actors, what would be the purpose? The purpose would be to create a false flag attack where blame would be pinned on a credible state actor capable of launching a ballistic missile that could hit Hawaii: North Korea. The "rogue actors" really responsible for the attack, would thereby have created a scenario where the U.S. military would have been forced to respond.

QANON NEXT POINTEDLY ASKS: ASK YOURSELF, WHAT WOULD/SHOULD IMMEDIATELY START A WAR?

We know from World War II history that the December 7, 1941, surprise attack on Pearl Harbor, Hawaii, home of the U.S. Pacific Fleet, was the catalyst for America entering the war. The next day, the U.S. Congress overwhelmingly voted to declare war on the Empire of Japan. QAnon is here telling us that a successful nuclear missile attack on Pearl Harbor would have triggered a similar War Declaration by the U.S. Congress against the alleged perpetrator. North Korea. Were the 'Rogue actors' behind the attack, also hoping that an unsuccessful nuclear missile attack, in the event the missile was shot down, would also trigger war? This possibility arises from what an anonymous Hickham Air Force Base fusion analyst says he overheard after the missile was shot down. In a post to a website protecting the anonymity of posters, s/he said, Most significant here is what the analyst says he overheard a Federal Investigator and a Hawaii state official say about Trump's refusal to order a retaliation 'That this demonstrated weakness in the Trump admin and a refusal to protect the people.' QAnon's next question is especially important for identifying who was behind the missile Hawaii attack, ask yourself 'Would the Public understand the following statement: Rogue actors (Clowns/US former heads of State) initiated a missile launch in order to 'Force' the US into a WAR/conflict against X?' QAnon has previously referred to the CIA as "Clowns in Action," and has described former Presidents Bush (Snr), Clinton and Obama as Deep State/CIA assets. In short, 'Clowns' is QAnon's code word for the CIA.

In a previous article, I provided documentary evidence supporting insider claims that the CIA's clandestine services division created a shadowy Navy with its own aircraft, ballistic missile carrying submarines, and even an aircraft carrier battle group that all together comprises a 'Dark Fleet.' QAnon is quite clear that s/he is referring to the famed 1990 movie, 'The Hunt for Red October'. The plot of the movie described how the major powers were all hunting for a rogue Soviet submarine equipped with ballistic nuclear weapons whose captain and officers wished to defect with their new stealth technology. QAnon's repeated references to Red October is telling us that a similar scenario is currently occurring with the U.S. and other major world powers all seeking a rogue CIA submarine equipped with ballistic nuclear missiles and advanced stealth technology.

Rather than the captain and crew wishing to defect however, the CIA submarine may be seeking a new opportunity to launch a false flag attack designed to precipitate a major regional war. While QAnon remains controversial in the major media, multiple sources have claimed s/he is authentic and deserves serious consideration. Many alternative media sites closely follow QAnon's information including Dr. Jerome Corsi who has become the resident Infowars.com expert on QAnon. QAnon's references to a recent missile attack by rogue actors wishing to start a major war needs to be considered with what we know about the January 13 Hawaii missile alert. QAnon is telling us that it was not a false alarm, and that it was a genuine attempt to start a major war by pinning the blame for a contrived nuclear attack, successful or not, on North Korea. The CIA linked submarine involved is apparently still at large, and capable of attempting further false flag attacks using ballistic nuclear missiles.

TRUMP EXECUTIVE ORDER TARGETS DEEP STATE & OPENS DOOR TO FULL DISCLOSURE

Something very profound happened in the U.S. on December 21 with the passage of President Donald Trump's 'Executive Order Blocking the Property of Persons Involved in Serious Human Rights Abuse or Corruption'. The order declared a state of national emergency concerning human rights and corruption and named specific individuals and organizations that would have their bank accounts and assets frozen regardless of where in the world the abuses had occurred. While the mainstream media has largely ignored Trump's Executive Order, the alternative media has been paying close attention. Many have noted the Executive Order is far more significant than what it appears to be on the surface. Rather than just freezing the financial resources of foreign citizens linked to the Russian sphere of influence, as it superficially appears to do, it is really targeted at members of the 'Deep State' (aka Cabal or Illuminati) that have been involved in human trafficking, pedophilia, and systemic corruption all over the planet. The language of the Executive Order is incredibly open ended in terms of how international corruption and human rights abuses threaten US national security.

'I, DONALD J. TRUMP, President of the United States of America, find that the prevalence and severity of human rights abuse and corruption that have their source, in whole or in substantial part, outside the United States, such as those committed or directed by persons listed in the Annex to this order, have reached such scope and gravity that they threaten the stability of international political and economic systems…The United States seeks to impose tangible and significant consequences on those who commit serious human rights abuse or engage in corruption, as well as to protect the financial system of the United States from abuse by these same persons. I therefore determine that serious human rights abuse and corruption around the world constitute an unusual and extraordinary threat to the national security, foreign policy, and economy of the United States, and I hereby declare a national emergency to deal with that threat.'

Its annex identifies key individuals and organizations, several of whom are clearly associated with Russia. The Executive Order is linked to the Global Magnitsky Human Rights Accountability Act that emerged from the murder of a prominent dissident exposing human rights abuses and corruption in Russia. This linkage can easily lead readers into falsely believing that the Executive Order is solely intended to target corrupt Russian officials, and corruption and human rights abuses by countries in Russia's sphere of influence. Yet, as a number of alternative media sources point out, Trump's Executive Order goes well beyond the Russian sphere of influence. It is really targeting the Deep State and fulfilling his 2016 campaign pledge to 'Drain the swamp'. For example, Jim Stone, a freelance journalist, writes: The executive order is presented as a national emergency up front, right in the beginning. At first it reads like he's going after foreigners which are named directly in an annex at the end. That's not what this is. The first part of the order only cements the second part of the order, to prevent American criminals from running away to foreign countries and being supported by foreigners.

To sum this up:

No swamp critter can accept help from another swamp critter in getting away ... Child traffickers and other human rights abuses are covered, the stealing of and misuse of government funds is covered, all items are covered for foreigners and U.S. citizens, any foreigners who have assets in the U.S. that have done anything against the U.S. for the purpose of supporting the American swamp will have those assets seized, anyone in violation of anything in this executive order will have their assets seized.... . An anonymous whistleblower using the pseudonym MegaAnon says that the Executive Order has led to many powerful members of the Deep State waking up with no financial resources. Guess what? The Swamp's financials 'Froze over' while they all slept last night, y'all. It's gonna be a Loooooong Christmas break for them... they were all broke before sunrise ... This covers kids/humans, drugs, arms/guns, WMD's, chemicals, Uranium, organs, etc. Now if you want to know who in our swamp woke up with frozen accounts, foundations, 'Charities,' side businesses and shell orgs/LLC's, etc. dig into the annex list...

The Executive Order and the language it uses really does mark a momentous event. Quite simply, it marks a transfer of political power from the Deep State to the U.S. military in terms of who is really in control of the U.S. Republic. It's no secret that Donald Trump has surrounded himself with senior military officers who share his desire to 'Drain the swamp.' His Chief of Staff, John Kelly, is a retired four star USMC general; his Secretary of Defense, James Mattis, is also a retired four star USMC general; his National Security Advisor, James McMaster, is an active duty three star US Army general; his head of the National Security Agency, Mike Rogers, is an active duty four star Navy Admiral; the head of the Secret Service, Randolph Alles is a retired two star Marine General; and the list goes on. The role of Admiral Mike Rogers is particularly significant since he broke ranks with the US intelligence community back in late 2016 to warn Trump about a Deep State effort to undermine and even prevent him from coming into power by spying on his transition team. While Trump was President-elect, Rogers traveled to Trump Tower on November 17, 2016, to warn him of the Deep State plans. The next day, the Washington Post reported on a recommendation by the Intelligence Community and Pentagon in October 2016 to sack Rogers. President Obama's Director of National Intelligence, James Clapper, and the Secretary of Defense, Ashton Carter, reportedly were dissatisfied with Rogers performance, including his visit to Trump.

In a move apparently unprecedented for a military officer, Rogers, without notifying superiors, traveled to New York to meet with Trump on Thursday at Trump Tower. That caused consternation at senior levels of the administration, according to the officials, who spoke on the condition of anonymity to discuss internal personnel matters. CIA Director John Brennon was a key player in the effort to remove Rogers as illustrated by the Washington Post story which is the traditional official news outlet promoting CIA interests. To his credit, President Obama did not take action against Rogers. Now more than a year after these back stage maneuverings, Rogers remains at the helm of the NSA closely monitoring the global activities of the Deep State and advising Trump and his National Security team. This has been especially significant when it came to the Central Intelligence Agency which has long been the key U.S. institution in funding and enforcing the will of the Deep State. In particular, the CIA's Clandestine Services and Counterintelligence divisions were instrumental in creating an unofficial 'Black budget' for funding highly classified projects and operations ever since the CIA's creation in 1947.

These two branches of the CIA have long been the secret enforcers of Deep State as best illustrated in the Kennedy Assassination. James Jesus Angleton, chief of the CIA's Counterintelligence office, played a direct role, while Richard Helms (Deputy Director of Plans) provided covert support for the operation. Trump's elevation of former congressman, Mike Pompeo, to become CIA Director was intended to bring the CIA under direct Presidential authority. Pompeo was, however, effectively sidelined from exercising any real power over the CIA's covert operations. It was Pompeo's more balanced approach to US-Russia relations that earned him the enmity of shadowy CIA groups. The situation dramatically changed on Saturday November 18, when a number of USMC helicopters flew over the CIA's Headquarters in Langley, Virginia. A former FBI agent, Hal Turner confirmed through credible sources that the helicopters had 'Buzzed' the CIA HQ for roughly 30 minutes. The intent was clear, the USMC was threatening the CIA's clandestine services division to get on board with the Trump administration or else. This is not the first time that the CIA has been intimidated by a US President threatening to unleash the US military against it.

In 1958, President Eisenhower threatened the CIA's Area 51 facilities in Nevada with invasion by the US First Army stationed at Colorado if the CIA did not fully disclose all its classified programs there. In a May 2013 video interview, a former CIA operative revealed what he heard Eisenhower tell his boss to relay to the mysterious MJ-12 Committee in charge of the Area 51 facility, for which the CIA provided operational security. The clearest sign that the CIA is now firmly under Trump's control is President Putin thanking President Trump and Pompeo for thwarting a planned terrorist attack against a prominent St. Petersburg cathedral. A December 17 Kremlin Press Release stated: Vladimir Putin thanked Donald Trump for the information passed on by the United States' Central Intelligence Agency (CIA) that helped detain the terrorists who plotted to set off explosions at Kazan Cathedral in St Petersburg and other public places in the city. The information received from the CIA was enough to locate and detain the criminals.

The Russian President asked the US President to convey his appreciation to the Central Intelligence Agency director and the operatives of US intelligence services who received this information. It is unprecedented for a Russian Head of State to publicly thank the CIA. The underlying message was clear, the CIA was now under the control of White Hats in the U.S. national security system and Putin was very grateful. What we are witnessing with Trump's December 21 Executive Order is the final act of a well thought out plan to sideline the Deep State, 'Drain the swamp', and reinstate direct Presidential authority over the U.S. national security system. Effectively, we are witnessing a handover of real power from the Deep State to the U.S. military via Donald Trump as Commander in Chief.

What is particularly noteworthy in the Executive Order is that this transfer of power is being done quietly behind the scenes with little mainstream attention. Key figures in the Deep State are finding their global financial resources frozen and are being secretly detained via sealed indictments that now have worldwide impact due to Trump's Executive Order. By late November, there were over four thousand sealed federal indictments being tracked by alternative news journalists such as Hal Turner. Many of these are being enforced by Special Operations Command personnel that are going around the planet arresting key Deep State figures. All this leads to the question, what does all this mean for a seven decades-long suppression of the truth regarding extraterrestrial life and technology, the existence of a breakaway German colony in Antarctica, and the existence of multiple secret space programs? The way in which the Executive Order has been crafted for a specific target, and quietly enforced is that the U.S. military is wanting to keep much of what is occurring off the public radar.

The primary reason for doing so is clearly to minimize disruption to the U.S. political system while the transfer of power takes place. Once the transfer process is complete, we can expect some of the sealed indictments being publicly revealed, and Trump publicly declaring victory in his effort to 'Drain the swamp.' We can expect a lot of unexpected retirements by indicted individuals who are currently making plea deals to escape imprisonment. Individuals involved in the most egregious human rights abuses such as child trafficking, will highly likely be publicly exposed and tried. As the transfer of power process moves forward, we can expect that more of the truth about secret space programs, Antarctica and extraterrestrial life will be disclosed. Based on how the U.S. military is dealing with key figures from the Deep State, it can be predicted that disclosure will take place in a gradual manner that does not disrupt the social fabric of US and stability of the global community. Disclosure is inevitable, but with the U.S. military now increasingly in charge of the American end of the process, disclosure is likely to happen in a series of gradual steps that culminate in sweeping changes all across the planet as advanced technologies involving zero-point energy, antigravity propulsion and holographic healing are strategically released.

While removal of the Deep State and its corrosive global influence through human rights abuses and corruption is a welcome development, the outsized behind-the-scenes influence of the U.S. military in the Trump administration is a cause for concern in the long term. Predictably, disclosures that will occur throughout the remainder of the Trump administration will promote US national security interests largely defined through a military mindset. President Eisenhower's greatest lament over the way classified projects involving advanced technologies were being managed in the U.S. was that excessive secrecy cut out the best people from the decision making process. Only full disclosure will prevent a similar problem from arising in the future where a new Deep State emerges, one dominated by military interests, with control over advanced technologies, which it uses to dominate the rest of humanity. Full disclosure is essential for humanity transitioning from an insular planet dominated either by criminal syndicates or a military mindset, into to a more informed peaceful planetary society worthy of becoming a full member of a galactic community.

US SPECIAL FORCES ARREST SATANIC PEDOPHILE GROUP – THE ANTARCTICA CONNECTION

According to a retired FBI and career military source, US Special Forces acting under the authority of the Department of Defense and with other global military authorities have been arresting members of a satanic pedophile group that has infiltrated multiple levels of government in the United States, European Union, and other national governments. The numbers of individuals associated with the global pedophile group according to the source, who chooses to remain anonymous, has greatly exceeded what the military had expected. The retired FBI/military source shared a six page report of what the Special Forces had discovered with secret space program whistleblower, Corey Goode. Goode says that he has known the source since 2008 when they met in several courses organized by the Department of Homeland Security. In a personal skype communication, Goode shared certificates of two courses he says he attended with the source who sat by him, and where they had 'A conversation about conspiracies, ET/UFO/SSP' Goode's long association with the source and his military/law enforcement background supports the reliability of the information he passed on to Goode. On August 9, Goode released an update about what his FBI/military source had told him.

He begins by describing the history of his relationship with his FBI/Military source: I have recently had meetings with a highly placed contact. I met him in the FEMA Mass Casualties response course when I was still in the Texas State Guard. He stopped talking to me when I began Cosmic Disclosure. He suddenly contacted me again right after the elections had concluded. He shared a cluster of Intel with me before going dark again… Until now. Goode's secret space program disclosures through his Cosmic Disclosure show with David Wilcock beginning in July 2015, led to his FBI/military source backing away from Goode, presumably for him sharing extremely sensitive military information about secret space programs. For those who have followed Goode's information, he says that in early 2016, he was abducted multiple times by personnel from a US Air Force run secret space program that were trying to find the sources that were leaking him sensitive military information.

Apparently, the USAF run program determined that Goode's information was accurate and coming from off-planet sources. The senior USAF officer running Goode's interrogations,

'Sigmund' then began sharing sensitive information with Goode about Antarctica and arranged for him to give briefings to select aerospace officials. In return, the USAF space program wanted to learn what Goode's off planet sources were telling him. Shortly after the positive change in his relationship with the USAF Secret Space Program, Goode's FBI/military source began sharing information again. Goode wrote about what his source had told him immediately after the election of President Donald Trump: I had reported that there were teams of US Special Forces that were conducting domestic surveillance and investigations of a satanic group that had infiltrated all aspects of government agencies and the military.

These Special Forces teams have been in place since the middle of the election cycle. Apparently, a week ago, a new level had been reached in these Special Forces arrests whereby what was occurring needed to be publicly shared. Goode had a six page report read to him by his FBI/military source and wrote: He gave me this report about a week ago and contacted me again stating it was important to get some of it out to the public. I was informed that a secret report on how pervasive these infiltrations are is more shocking than what was expected. Strangely, this report also had notes from several secret grand juries that are active right now in D.C. The report states that the conspiracy involves the majority of powerful people in within the UN, EU, US, State and local (City) power structures. These government organization are completely complicit in what is going on. All the way down to local Post Offices and Police Offices. I have to tell you; this was a very creepy report.

These military investigators have expressed their shock and anger to their superiors as well as their desire to take them down. They report that it is so systemic that they are at a loss of how to counter and defeat these people without a military coup, which would involve US Special Forces and trusted 'Military Contractors' that come from Alliance countries (And are already in place in the US). Goode goes on to reveal that some Special Forces have been summarily executing some of these satanic pedophiles, and have been taken off the investigation, Some of these Special Forces Investigators have been removed from the investigation because they are highly suspected as being involved in torturing and killing some of these low level 'Pedo-Gate' suspects. The scope of this cult takeover of government is shocking to even the people that think they have seen it all. They can't figure out how the government was infiltrated to such a degree. In our skype communication, Goode added.

366

'Most of these SF teams have been directly involved in investigations of crimes against humanity in places we would all recognize…. They have 'Seen it all' in other countries and are shocked at what is occurring in the West under their noses.' Goode's information is well supported by the research of authors such as John Decamp who wrote about the Franklin Cover-up, which detailed pedophile rings abusing children that compromised senior politicians in federal and state governments. More recently, Robert David Steele, a retired CIA/USMC official has also been speaking about the high level pedophile groups that have infiltrated many governments. In a related development, Goode shared in our skype conversation that he has also been warned to back off his disclosures about military research and development activities in Antarctica, I received another warning for US (Everyone I work with) to NOT report on the R&D or Space Port facilities in Antarctica….

Info on Ancient Civilizations is fair game, info on the R&D Facilities is deemed too sensitive to report. If we continue to report on this topic they will attack us relentlessly and make it impossible to get any of the other information out. Goode also shared that the R&D facilities on Antarctica are massive in scale and activity. He was told that "the 'Dulce Base' stories are nursery rhymes compared to what is going on there." Most disturbing is the extensive collaboration with a Reptilian extraterrestrial group called the Draconians in Antarctica. He said:

Dracos work with people on the base and oversee the operations of the bases. They work along with humans in the lower levels while people on the upper levels never see or hear about them. In a detailed 18,000 word report on the Dulce Base written on September 25, 2003, I covered the extensive human rights abuses occurring there, and the involvement of Draconian Reptilians. It is therefore not that surprising that the same thing, albeit on a much larger scale, is occurring in Antarctica. The extensive collaboration occurring in Antarctica at secret industrial bases with Draconians underscores the importance of dealing with global pedophile rings. These rings have been claimed to be the means by which children are covertly taken to these Draconian controlled bases and abused. In his August 9 update, Goode emphasizes the importance of a global meditation scheduled for August 21 at 11:11 am Pacific Coast Time. The meditation will coincide with a conference being organized at Mount Shasta where Goode and I will be speaking. The meditation is a particularly good way to begin mobilizing global support for what US Special Forces are doing to help remove heavily compromised individuals from positions of authority and stop the systematic abuse of children. [Update 8/10/17 – Note that the Posse Comitatus Act which bars the US military from performing domestic law enforcement has several exceptions. 'An exception exists for military personal engaged in support roles for the Joint Special Operations Command.' This exception confirms that US Special Forces can indeed arrest US citizens in domestic operations sanctioned by JSOC, just as Corey Goode's source has claimed].

MIL·I·TAR·Y-IN·DUS·TRI·AL COM·PLEX
/ˈMILə͵TERĒ INˈDƏSTRĒƏL ͵KÄMˈPLEKS, ˈKÄMPLEKS/
Noun

      Noun: military-industrial complex; plural noun: military-industrial complexes
      1.   A country's military establishment and those industries producing arms or other military materials, regarded as a powerful personal stake.

The military-industrial complex is a nation's military establishment, as well as the industries involved in the production of armaments and other military materials. In his 1961 farewell address, U.S. President Dwight D. Eisenhower famously warned the public of the nation's increasingly powerful military-industrial complex and the threat it posed to American democracy. Today, the United States routinely outspends every other country for military and defense expenditures.

EISENHOWER AND THE MILITARY

A retired five-star general in the U.S. Army, Dwight D. Eisenhower had served as commander of Allied forces during World War II and directed the D-Day invasion of France in 1944. Eisenhower's two terms as U.S. president (1953-61) coincided with an era of military expansion unlike any other in the nation's history. Rather than draw down its troops, as it had after World War II, the U.S. military kept a large standing army after the Korean War ended in 1953 and maintained a prominent level of military preparedness due to the ongoing Cold War between the United States and the Soviet Union. Private companies that after past wars had gone back to civilian production kept manufacturing armaments, producing increasingly sophisticated weapons in an arms race with the Soviets. Despite—or perhaps because of—his own experience with war, Eisenhower worried about the nation's military growth, and the escalation of the Cold War, throughout his presidency. He tried to cut budgets for military services during his presidency, upsetting many in the Pentagon EBSITE As one Eisenhower biographer, David Nichols, told the Associated Press in 2010, 'The military wanted a lot more than he was willing to give them. It frustrated the Army. He thought about it all the time.'

Eisenhower's Farewell Address

Eisenhower didn't coin the phrase 'Military-industrial complex,' but he did make it famous. On January 17, 1961, three days before John F. Kennedy was inaugurated as his successor, Eisenhower delivered a farewell address in a TV broadcast from the Oval Office. 'In the councils of government, we must guard against the acquisition of unwarranted influence, whether sought or unsought, by the military-industrial complex,' the 34th president warned. 'The potential for the disastrous rise of misplaced power exists and will persist.' According to Eisenhower, the 'Conjunction of an immense military establishment and a large arms industry is new in the American experience,' and he feared it would lead to policies that would not benefit Americans as a whole, like the escalation of the nuclear arms race at great cost to the nation's well-being. In addition to the Department of Defense and private military contractors, Eisenhower and his advisers also implicitly included members of Congress from districts that depended on military industries in the military-industrial complex. Though dangerous, Eisenhower considered the military-industrial complex necessary to deter Soviet Union from aggression against the United States and its allies. But he urged his successors in government to balance defense and diplomacy in their relations with the Soviet Union, saying: 'We must learn how to compose differences not with arms, but with intellect and decent purpose.'

Military-Industrial-Congressional Complex?

Some have claimed that Eisenhower intended to say 'Military-industrial-congressional complex,' in order to explicitly call out Congress for its role in the growth of the military industry, but that he struck out the final term at the last minute to avoid offending lawmakers.

But according to James Ledbetter, author of Unwarranted Influence: Dwight D. Eisenhower and the Military-Industrial Complex, evidence points away from this theory: A draft of the speech dated almost a month before it was delivered included the phrase 'Military-industrial complex' intact. Still, it was clear Eisenhower, and his advisers did see at least some members of Congress playing a role in the dangers the military-industrial complex posed to the public. Eisenhower and his fellow conservatives also viewed the growth of the military-industrial complex as part of a broader expansion of federal power that began with President Franklin D. Roosevelt and the New Deal.

Military-Industrial Complex Today

Since Eisenhower delivered it in 1961, his farewell speech has come to be a touchstone for those with concerns about unchecked military expansion, and the continuing close ties between private military contractors, members of the military establishment and the federal government. The United States regularly spends far more on its military than any other country, though its defense spending is usually a relatively small percentage of the nation's total gross domestic product (GDP), compared with some other countries. According to a 2014 report by the Council of Foreign Relations, in the years after World War II, national defense spending as a percentage of GDP ranged from a high of 15 percent in 1952 (during the Korean War) to a low of 3.7 percent in 2000. Military spending rose sharply again the following year, after the 9/11 terrorist attacks led to the U.S. government declaring a global war on terrorism. Military expenditures, which are included in the discretionary spending category in the federal budget, include a base budget for the U.S. Department of Defense as well as additional spending on Overseas Contingency Operations (OCO) and the Global War on Terror (GWOT). In fiscal year 2016, according to the Pew Research Center, the U.S. government spent some $604 billion on national defense, which made up 15 percent of its total spending of about $3.95 trillion. By contrast, a two-year budget deal passed by Congress and signed by President Donald Trump in February 2018 approved some $716 billion for defense spending in fiscal year 2019, compared with $605 in non-defense domestic spending.

Systemic-Conspiracy as Social Pathology

Military-Industrial Complexity Theory and the Abstraction of War Systemic-conspiracy is one of six research streams at The Abs-Tract Organization, and this is the first of a series of blog posts on it. This stream is a companion to Evolutionary Globalization. For a draft research essay providing more background depth, see Towards a Theory of Conspiracy: Analyzing Hidden Power in Globalization Processes. You can't talk about conspiracy (theory) without understanding 'Systemic-Conspiracy.' Yet most of the commentary on conspiracy theory skips over depth and reduces it to pointing out absurd speculation and ignoring the actual complexity. Late 2016, the NY Times lamented 'The Paranoid Style in American Politics Is Back.' Wired magazine mocks, 'To Make Your Conspiracy Theory Legit, Just Find an 'Expert." Most recently, Conspiracy Theorists Have a Fundamental Cognitive Problem, Say Scientists.

A better mode of analysis is more relevant than ever, as The Guardian reports that we may be "entering a golden age of the conspiracy theory" because of the 'post-truth' era of Trump. The paradoxical and unprovable nature of these issues forces people to default to one side—paranoid or skeptic—without any real resolution. But debasing conspiracy theory to its most cartoonish form is a disservice to critical inquiry into systemic-conspiracy. The typical critique goes that conspiracy theory is a delusion, a result of apophenia, and the tendency to see connections in random patterns (think constellations or Rorschach tests). This is part of it, but to reduce it to simply debunking is a disservice to the truth that conspiracy theory attempts to represent. For a well-cited overview and discussion of conspiracy theory (and some ontology of real conspiracy), see Daniël Verhoeven's 'Conspiracy Theories'… a long history and a new trend." In academia, the study of the conspiracy-tinted view of globalization even has its own subfield of 'Popular geopolitics.' But neither pundits nor tin-foil hat theorists are readily armed with the proper sociological theory, so I hope to inform about that here. Those closest to breaking the dark and inconvenient truths about our political world work at outlets like The Intercept or TruthDig. They cover the daily beat of what I call systemic-conspiracy. And it is with those audiences that I would think this concept will resonate the most deeply.

I must stress here that my purpose is not to prove conspiracy theories, or even indulge them necessarily, but to examine how 'Systemic-Conspiracy' is the inherent 'Evil' omnipresent in the system, manifesting intentional and systemic conspiracies, which we are all both victims and enablers of. This is relevant and convergent with Jordan Peterson's oft-repeated warning that we all have the potential for totalitarian fascism in us; to participate in systems of violence. Systemic-conspiracy is sociologically latent, which is arguably the major lesson of the 20th century. The term 'Systemic-Conspiracy' is needed to function as a counterpoint to 'Conspiracy Theory.' Rather than conspiracies being just anomalous events orchestrated by particular people, I wish to invert to way people think about them, to understand that history/society itself is a sort of conspiracy, depending on your perspective (i.e., slave vs. master). My fundamental contention is that understanding the world through the lens of actual conspiracy and systems theory can be more true than false.

Time and whistleblowing has moved watershed cases out of the realm of conspiracy theory into historical fact (and political contest). When this happens the 'truth conditions' immediate change and consequently it breaks into public consciousness so people can process it openly. Edward Snowden's NSA revelations represent a clear example, on a number of levels. Similarly, the JASTA legal initiative brings the complexity of terrorism and the fraudulence of the 9/11 Commission Report into clear focus. Andrew Cockburn wrote recently "Will the 9/11 case finally go to trial?" And the bulk of evidence, including documents released 75 years after the event, confirm that the Reichstag fire was most likely a false flag. As if we need to go into specific cases though, especially to prove the existence of systemic-conspiracy, which is inherent in the system. The extensions of US foreign policy and operations of intelligence agencies are by definition institutional conspiracies, often directly contradicting the 'official story,' international law, and the prerogatives of free and open democracy. But ironically, all of that is in the name of open society, so we have a deeper problem, and now it has a name: systemic-conspiracy.

'Systemic-Conspiracy'

The term 'Systemic-Conspiracy' refers to 'The system' and the structural conditions that create incentives and pressures to participate, knowingly or unknowingly, in systems of power that have definite malicious intent, negative externalities, objectionable consequences, often illegal methods, and not to mention conspiratorial aspects and appearances. Our concern is with the path-dependence and social complexity that make war inevitable or at least make it seem inevitable and justifiable when it is actually an economic imperative (a business decision) for some people. I coin the term "systemic-conspiracy" to describe the abstract and (ir-) rational nature of war, whether overt or covert, abstract or concrete, wherever it is present. Not only war, but the pathological tendencies of capitalism and markets to sponsor conflict and invest in social control, and then to hide and obscure the process. It is in part a function of the rules of the system and of human nature.

The former we can and must change; the latter we must evolve. 'Systemic-Conspiracy' can be viewed as a high-level abstraction based on a large set of devastating practices that 'Over-determine' the problem and institutionalize conspiracy. These concepts include tacit collusion, moral hazard, politicized issue, politicization of science, spin (propaganda), doublespeak, media manipulation, disinformation, manufactured controversy, manufacturing consent, noble lie, post-truth politics, electoral fraud, full-spectrum dominance, externality, war profiteering, militarism, white-collar crime, whitewashing, price fixing, perverse incentives, rent-seeking, dirty hands, cronyism, the iron law of oligarchy, covert operation, cover-up, and of course false flag, to name just a few. The sum-total of these practices guarantee that not only will there be profit made off undesirable consequences but that the crimes will be covered and protected by effective corporate self-defense strategies.

'Systemic-Conspiracy' produces conspiratorial outcomes and sows the rational distrust of elites and institutions. But it is hard to see clearly because we are not typically exposed directly to these confusing and terrifying anti-social practices, or the obscure concepts that explain them. Systemic-conspiracy is thus an abstract synthesis, compression, and simplification of these complex phenomena. The war-on-drugs and the war-on-terror are blatant Orwellian manifestations of systemic-conspiracy, but also paradoxical because they purport to defend the peace and freedom that we enjoy. In truth the military and law enforcement serve vital functions, but under systemic-conspiracy they create more problems than they solve, and a minority profit from it. And yet, the system also employs the obedience of many decent well-intentioned people, so it is difficult to attribute malice and agency to the horrific effects. Integral to this theory is Hannah Arendt's concept of the 'Banality of evil;' the idea that ordinary people, following orders, can collectively commit the most atrocious acts. We do jobs for money, and it makes a lot of people do things they don't want to.

Employees are inclined to follow policies and not question them, and for the most part they are trusting the reasons for why things the way they are, but this is a large grey area where systemic-conspiracy precipitates. Let's look at the most obvious and indisputable object of conspiracy theory, and the best example of its systemic nature: the military–industrial-(etc.) complex. I add the 'etc.' placeholder because over the 50 some odd years since being named, it has grown to include the mainstream media, academia, congress, sports, entertainment, pharma, oil, law, and prisons, among other sectors of the economy. So, let's not pretend for a second this isn't a thing and hasn't been studied thoroughly.

Over-stretching the metaphor has even been criticized by one of the initial critics (Parenti), in that prisons don't remotely match the military budget, nor will they produce any related 'Technological and industrial spin-off,' but he is missing the point of their complicity, which is why I want to re-define it. The original concept 'military-industrial complex' refers to monetary relationships between the government, the military, and the defense industrial base. It is a type of 'Iron triangle,' defined as; 'The closed, mutually supportive relationships that often prevail in the United States between the government agencies, the special interest lobbying organizations, and the legislative committees or subcommittees with authority over a particular functional area of government policy.'

This arrangement is inherently prone to moral hazards and rent seeking, as shown by recurrent scandals and abuses of power. My moderately deep literature review shows that the 'complex' extends far beyond the initial 'military-industrial' identity which Eisenhower warned against at the end of his presidency. Like the octopus metaphor that conspiracy theory invokes, its tentacles have reached into academia, media, congress, pharma, entertainment, and more. It is particularly important to note that that this growth has happened despite a public warning by a former president of the United States; it is a testament to the power of denial, and of systemic-conspiracy. Systemic-conspiracy should be considered not just 'Systemic' but also 'Systematic' in that can be methodically or done according to a plan. The modern military-industrial complex is the bastard child of the global rape that was World War 2, and it came of age during 'The Cold War' which oversaw proxy wars all over the globe and the prospect of nuclear annihilation. Although it was 'systematic,' WW2 is not considered a 'Conspiracy' in any conventional sense, and nor was the Cold War, although WW2 was a conspiracy in the sense of Germany having a more-or-less secret plan to take over the world.

More accurately, it was a systemic-conspiracy par excellence in that all of the resources of the system were organized around pathological beliefs and dedicated the literal 'dead end' of genocide and world war. It required the support and participation of its own mass society. The Cold War increased the systematization of war, while decreasing the body count. As you can see from this relatively cursory overview, conspiracy, the ridiculed subject of conspiracy theory, is in fact very real as a systemic pathology. And in fact, almost everyone plays some unwitting role in it. Systemic-conspiracy can be actualized in various forms, such as organized crime and corruption, institutional racism (via vicious abstraction) and mass incarceration, exploitation, and extortion (which deepens economic inequality), the dumbing down of democracy (anti-intellectualism), and co-option of governance by corporations (regulatory capture). Even simple alienation could be considered an expression of the oppressive weight of systemic-conspiracy. It is a way to describe the built-in features of our social, economic, religious, and political systems that force to live and act in a system that has hidden effects of exploitation and oppression.

This is different from a naturally emergent hierarchy and class structure, which systemic-conspiracy manipulates and exacerbates to its pathological limits. More prime examples are easy to identify slavery is a systemic-conspiracy, as it becomes normalized and openly practiced, while the grotesque truth of it is hidden. Rather than being the evil brainchild of a couple of whispering individuals, slavery was an institution which an individual could scarcely challenge. It was all based on vicious lies, yet it became a prevailing dogma of a Western civilization. It's easy for us to look back in retrospect and condemn it, but more difficult to understand how it was happening in the moment. The concept of systemic-conspiracy holds that at any given time in history there are systemic injustices that are taken for granted and may not be salient to the population being abused at that time. Slaves didn't sign-up for slavery, but they were denied the very knowledge to articulate the crisis they were in. Even in retrospect, it may not be fully understandable. But the more we study it, the more we reveal how abstract and complex the problem is. We cannot atone for slavery until the modern war-on-drugs is understood as an extension of it. The preconditions for revolution are that the oppressed group develops a "class consciousness" and becomes aware of their collective exploitation. But this is only part of it, as most black people already know exactly what I'm talking about, yet the oppression continues; the system blocks. This is why knowledge interventions are as critical as a matter of policy. Think tanks that do not extol this fact are guilty by association with systemic-conspiracy.

The Third-Wave of Conspiracy Research

The way in which I analyze conspiracy reflects a third "turn" in the scholarship on conspiracy theory. The first paradigm is based on the groundbreaking work of Richard Hofstader in The Paranoid Style in American Politics (an essay and then book, circa 1964). This approach is psychopathological, which describes the paranoid mentality as a form of cognitive fundamentalism. The second turn is socioethnographical, which highlights the validity of 'Social facts' from the perspective of the believer/conspiracist. The third wave of conspiracy scholarship describes what I call systemic-conspiracy, which acknowledges that the social structure and 'system' itself is pathological, in ways that obstruct consensus and social justice, producing both intentional and unintentional negative consequences. Rather than just 'shit happening' (as Pete Mandik would have it, in his article 'Shit Happens' 2007), the actions and protocols in systemic-conspiracy very much correspond to what the conspiracy theory is speculating about, although often not directly. The term systemic-conspiracy has been used before, but only in the context of describing conspiracy theories. Barkun classifies a systemic type of conspiracy theory but is not theorizing systemic-conspiracy itself. For example, the Catholic Church is cited as coveting global ambitions (which many organizations do benignly). But I would say a better example of systemic-conspiracy within the Catholic Church is the systematic cover-up of pedophilia. For decades it was maintained in the realm of conspiracy theory, hiding the sick truth, but now we know unequivocally the deep dark extent.

Similarly, systemic-conspiracy theories about Jews, Freemasons, and Communists project a sinister agency on to their agendas which engenders xenophobia, but it is not at all fair to charge the entire organization with conspiracy. It is certainly not true that 'Jews' rule the world, or even the media, but Israel's forceful occupation of Palestine and the corresponding 'regime of truth' that justifies it is another prime example of 'Systemic-Conspiracy.' One conspiracy researcher describes how 'Conspiracy' no longer refers to a secret plot led by a handful of insiders, but rather a 'Broad array of social controls' institutionalized in a 'Large organization, technology, or system, a powerful and obscure entity so dispersed that it is the antithesis of the traditional conspiracy' (Melley, 2000). Another agrees in that 'Conspiracy Theory' makes more sense in terms of informational networks of power where potentialities for agency and secrecy dynamically meet (Dean, 2000, paragraph 10). This new discourse of systemic-conspiracy also gives way to new subfields, such as the study of 'State crimes against democracy' (SCAD), which is an empirical alternative to conspiracy theorizing (deHaven-Smith 2010, 797). SCADs occur where the interests of national security intersect with domestic Presidential politics (806). SCADs are a unique form of political corruption in that they employ 'Political, military, and/or economic elites at the very highest levels of the social and political order' (795).

Along these lines, Noam Chomsky divides terrorism into 'Retail,' as practiced by non-state actors, and 'Wholesale,' as carried out by states, the latter of which being the dominant form. I would describe most of Chomsky's work as exposing 'Systemic-Conspiracy,' which is ironic because he eschews conspiracy theory. Chomsky considers conspiracy theory antithetical to 'institutional analysis,' which emphasizes institutional factors and downplays individual agency. The institutional approach relies on scholarship and mainstream media reports to track the behavior of officially known institutions. This is why academics might rightly consider a number of conspiratorial allegations unsubstantiated by the media as illogical or irrational, or quite simply, impossible. Chomsky rejects that these alleged conspiracies are possible in an institutional setting, and that it is the structure that would ensure "propagandists" emerge to 'Conceal the actual workings of power.' This approach is in contrast to the "French School" of institutional analysis which centers on exposing the unseen forms of power that prescribe behavior and organizational protocols, of which Michel Foucault was affiliated.

With respect to 9/11, this deconstructive approach is continued in Baudrillard's The Spirit of Terrorism and Ward Churchill's On the Justice of Roosting Chickens. The latter essay (in) famously attributed some systemic guilt to the victims in the WTC: 'As for those in the World Trade Center… Well, really, let's get a grip here, shall we? True enough, they were civilians of a sort. But innocent? Gimme a break. They formed a technocratic corps at the very heart of America's global financial empire, the 'Mighty engine of profit' to which the military dimension of U.S. policy has always been enslaved and they did so both willingly and knowingly. Recourse to 'Ignorance,' a derivative, after all, of the word 'Ignore' counts as less than an excuse among this relatively well-educated elite. To the extent that any of them were unaware of the costs and consequences to others of what they were involved in and in many cases excelling at it was because of their absolute refusal to see. More likely, it was because they were too busy braying, incessantly and self-importantly, into their cell phones, arranging power lunches and stock transactions, each of which translated, conveniently out of sight, mind and smelling distance, into the starved and rotting flesh of infants. If there was a better, more effective, or in fact any other way of visiting some penalty befitting their participation upon the little Eichmanns inhabiting the sterile sanctuary of the twin towers, I'd really be interested in hearing about it.'

The United States is the largest purveyor of state terror in the world, and this fact gives rise to the allegations that 9/11 is, as David Macgregor describes, 'Machiavellian state terror.' This refers to terror initiated by actors other than those suspected (potentially within the state) in order to advance the ruling agenda. And this is not even considering the odious money flows to non-state terrorists, bravely discussed by Loretta Napoleoni in The Intricate Economics of Terrorism. In The Ghosts of State Terror, Richard Jackson analyzes the reasons for a conspiracy of silence around state terror. Jackson's first order critique of the study of terrorism is that the actor based definition of terrorism excludes state culpability, the research focus has a political bias, and the discourse rejects the weight of empirical evidence of state terrorism. His second critique is that ignorance of state terrorism in academic discourse serves to facilitate state hegemony, legitimize foreign and domestic policy discourse to the public, and defer awareness of the terroristic tendencies of states. Jackson's most pressing insight is how deconstructing the dominant narrative gives rise to 'Alternative and potentially emancipatory forms of knowledge and practice.' The emergence of new discourses that analyze narratives of state terror and conspiracy can help to rehabilitate the governmentality of the state. But as Jeffrey Sluka explains in Death Squad: The Anthropology of State Terror, it is dangerous for the anthropologist to study state terror in his country of origin. Given that the United States is arguably the global leader and hegemon, this poses unprecedented challenges for exposing 'Systemic-Conspiracy' within.

'We were set up to fail' write the 9/11 Commission co-chairs Thomas Kean and Lee Hamilton, through inadequate funding and an unrealistic mandate, among other obstructions. This quote fully fuels conspiracy theories but does not seem to vindicate academic inquiries. But the attraction of alternate explanations has persisted in non-paranoid minds. Top counter-terrorism advisor to the Bush and Clinton administrations, Richard Clarke, continues to assert that the CIA covered its duplicitous relationship with some of the hijackers. And we now know from the '28 pages' withheld from the Commission report, Saudi officials were involved. Moreover, WikiLeaks disclosures (of Stratfor emails) revealed that Bin Laden's corpse was not dumped at sea, as officially reported, but rather was taken back to the US. So, it would seem that the truth must be somewhere in between the conspiracy theory and the 'Official narrative.' The critical discourse of systemic-conspiracy is about challenging the status-quo which tends to foreclose awareness of certain illegal state and corporate practices. We must update our language and discourse to "systemic-conspiracy" if possible. The term military-industrial complex now seems a bit anachronistic, to say the least.

But more important is to understand and reverse the tumorous growth of the leviathan and our complicity in it. In principle, pragmatic 'Conspiracy theory' attempts to make this dark reality salient, but the discourse itself has in part been co-opted and neutralized by 'Systemic-Conspiracy.' As the news article links at the top are indicative of, public intellectuals are quick to weigh in and flex their critique against a crazy straw person versions of conspiracy theory. It doesn't help that the performative right-wing-nut Alex Jones, who occasionally raises legitimate concepts such as the 'Police state' or the very name of his platform; 'Information warfare' is a very polarizing and partisan conspiracist. He is not just a conspiracy theorist, but now a minion of Trump and a wildly rich business man in his own right. Instead of draining the swamp Trump is hosting tiki-torch pool parties in it, Jones is serving cocktails, while the systemic-conspiracy marches on.

Abstraction in 'Systemic-Conspiracy'

Not a far-off representation of some abstract global influencers Abstraction is our core research stream out of six because it is present in all the others. Systemic-conspiracy is very abstract, and the problem of it is also one of violent abstraction. Not to mention, abstraction is invaluable for depicting and schematizing networks and systems. To show this, in my articles on abstraction I have touched on a number of topics that correspond to systemic conspiracy, and vice-versa. Vicious Abstraction and Systemic Racism discusses how racism becomes mystified and systemic via republican political strategy, coincidently through a process of misrepresentation called 'vicious abstraction.' The war-on-drugs, which finds the most support among republicans, is a systemic-conspiracy as it mobilizes a large workforce to carry out unjust laws, which in fact were designed to suppress people of color and hippies. The post The Abstract Empire of Global Capital touches on conspiracy in several ways.

The term comes from George Soros, who is also a subject of 'Conspiracy Theory.' The global expansion of capital has conspiratorial effects, disrespecting democratic will and violating borders unapologetically, all while increasing wealth inequality. Finance itself is heavily dependent on 'Abstraction.' And the remedy to this conspiracy is in my view what H.G. Wells called 'The Open Conspiracy.' Perhaps most importantly, The Abstract Society defines 'The system' which is instrumental to the concept of systemic-conspiracy as an abstracting entity. The post reviews the book of the same name and outlines the negative pressures and alienation effects of our highly advanced mass society in the 20th century and beyond. The latter two articles also both reference the abstraction of 'Money,' the deprivation of which is used as a means of control, producing the effect of conspiracy. All three articles are replete with references to abstraction, clarifying the concept and the implications for systemic-conspiracy. In order to understand systemic-conspiracy, we have to understand this depth of abstraction.

For the purposes of The Abs-Tract Organization, on the think tank and policy front relating to systemic-conspiracy, it is important to consider three more of our articles: The Role of Think Tanks in Meta-Governance, The US Policy Environment and Political Climate Change, and Think Tank Knowledge vs. Corporate Power. These articles outline how knowledge and policy have themselves become corrupted, which I'm implying is by the extension of this conspiracy logic. It is a very abstract conspiracy indeed when it's operating at the level of discourse. The systemic problems we face are all meta-problems requiring meta-solutions. I believe that if we can agree on the diagnosis of the bigger picture, we can formulate macro policy solutions. The most abstract idea out there that defeats systemic-conspiracy is this one: to counter the military-industrial complex, we should invest in the peace–industrial complex. In his stunning 13-min talk 'What is the Peace-Industrial Complex?' Idriss Aberkane calls war a 'Parasite' and advocates 'Weapons of mass construction' as an antidote to the pointless commitment to war. Aberkane very eloquently redefines superpower as the projection of construction (which elicits love) rather than destruction (which elicits hate).

The irony is that the peace-industrial complex is actually more functional and profitable, so the transition to it is incentivized. Imagine a peace-industrial complex as large and well-funded as the military one, if you even can… But the utter stupidity of systemic-conspiracy by which we are collectively arrested is so powerful, that real change is written off as a pipe-dream. The intractability and absurdity of it all was highlighted when the authoritarian dictator of North Korea Kim Jong-un owned President Trump by aptly calling him a 'Dotard,' going viral on twitter, at once humanizing Kim a little and making him all the more threatening. All conspiracy theories aside, Business Insider put together this very abstract network graph of Bilderberg members. The point is not that they control everything, but that they are embedded in systems of control. These are business people playing with a sort of Ouija board of global governance. Given their large salaries and bonuses, they are also paid not to know certain things, like how they are instrumental in systemic-conspiracy, and how it co-opts their conscience. They are insulated and made ignorant of the deep critique of capitalism, as it threatens their position and status. Thus, they can wash their dirty hands and pardon themselves of any wrongdoing. They are also disincentivized to speak out or change the current system. Instead, they funnel money to aesthetically 'Progressive' projects that have little real impact.

Agnotology

What you don't know can you kill you. Agnotology is a nascent field that emphasizes the cultural production of ignorance as an anti-epistemological force. It provides great insight into state secrecy and social epistemology. In Agnotology: 'The Making and Unmaking of Ignorance,' the authors (also editors) of the volume, Proctor and Schiebinger, make the case that ignorance is under theorized and that their new term goes a long way in rectifying it. Ironically, we are ignorant of our own ignorance. In the book, Peter Galison's empirically reflects this observation estimate that the amount of data classified is 5–10 times greater than the open literature publicly accessible. Moreover, Proctor echoes the Socratic wisdom that knowledge of one's own ignorance is a necessary prerequisite for intellectual enlightenment. Considering this, Agnotology contributes substantial and needed insight to theories of knowledge. Proctor divides ignorance into three types: native state (common form; innocence; naiveté), lost realm (forgotten; selective; missed), and strategic ploy ('strategies to deceive'). It is primarily the last type that concerns us when dealing with conspiracy.

Examples of strategic ploy ignorance are found in trade secrets, the tobacco industry, and military secrecy. Trade secrecy is legitimized because it is concerned with intellectual property as capital that drives business and economics. However, other forms of secrecy are more nefarious as they obscure truths vital to the public in order to advance their own interests. The truth about the lethality of smoking was stalled for nearly half a century through the concerted 'manufacture of doubt' Likewise, for even longer the scientific consensus on climate change has been marginalized and obstructed by conservatives. Post 9/11, the Bush regime has also implemented an array of draconian legislative measures including the Patriot Acts resulting in scandals such as NSA wiretapping and extraordinary rendition, among others. Another potentially dangerous form of strategic ploy ignorance production is the state-secrets privilege. The executive can annul any lawsuits or investigations if disclosure of information pertaining to the case can potentially threaten national security.

A notable case involved FBI whistleblower Sibel Edmonds, whose appeals to expose evidence of FBI internal security breaches and a cover-up were blocked by the invocation of the state secrets privilege. Similarly, the disclosure of 'Top Secret' information, such as Daniel Ellsberg's Pentagon Papers, is extremely dangerous and considered treasonous. However, exposing the crimes also reveals how dysfunctional the government really is. It is marginally productive to describe these issues outside the context of systemic-conspiracy. The cases of climate change and tobacco-harm denial plainly reveal the systematic distortion of science and policy, and the manipulation of public opinion. And with Agnotology, denial is truly the operative word. The successful suppression of these cases from the dominant news narrative is yet another testament to the power of a systemic faceless enemy. The systemic-conspiracy is not one that explicitly engages a few people, but one that implicitly engages many people in subtle and banal ways. Awareness in a new broader context makes it more salient.

Meta-Marxism

'In the social production of their life, men enter into definite relations that are indispensable and independent of their will; these relations of production correspond to a definite stage of development of their material forces of production.,' Marx, a Contribution to the Critique of Political Economy The above quote is made in the context of defining historical materialism, the cornerstone of Marx's scientific worldview. The rest of the quote goes on to explain the relationship between the material and economic conditions of a society and how that shapes social consciousness (in order to, I might add, justify the economic methods of productivity, be it slavery or otherwise). I'm cutting it because I want to reapply this excerpt to systemic-conspiracy, in how people are compelled and incentivized into conditions and relationships that they would not otherwise choose. The military-industrial complex pays well, and it's funded by tax-payers who aren't. Systemic-conspiracy is unabashedly Marxist analysis. It has to be, as they are both so critically interested in power, social structure, capitalism, and the relationship between elites and masses. This approach is rooted in the Frankfurt school's critical theory, which examined the Holocaust in real time and analyzed it retrospectively.

The Marxian philosophy of history (historical materialism) also dovetails with the study systemic-conspiracy and evolutionary globalization, so it is integral to our approach here. This is going to raise the hackles of those allergic to terms like Marxism, postmodernism, atheism, and communism. But metamodernism immunizes against this irrational skepticism. Moreover, we are not adding neo- or post- prefixes, but meta-. Marx may turn off conservatives, but systemic-conspiracy is a bipartisan meta-issue if there ever was one, and those who turn a blind eye to it will be shown on the wrong side of history. It is established that both major US political parties are co-opted by corporate interests. The war machine is a business's first and foremost, and this fact cannot be evaded. That does not mean that all military are bloodthirsty, but contractors do have perverse incentives and ludicrous expenses. Nor does it mean we are calling for communist revolution, but a political paradigm shift is necessary. Our intent is to lay the theory bare, so that the analysis of systemic-conspiracy can speak for itself, and a new policy consensus can form. The defense industry is invested in its own survival, when it should be committed to its own "planned obsolescence."

Summary

'Systemic-conspiracy' is the malicious, sinister, impersonal features of "the system" that manifest in power structures, which then have criminal and counterproductive effects against innocent people. In the broadest sense, it is so widespread that it applies from the horrors of totalitarian war down to the absurdities of ab-gimmicks. It projects the appearance of conspiracy, is systemic and secretive in the form of tacit-collusion, as well as conceals actual micro-conspiracies. It is analogous to The Matrix, which is everywhere watching and controlling you, fating you and others to a slavish existence. Think of what purpose it ultimately serves that Call of Duty is one of the most successful video games of all time. I will take Goat Simulator over war games any day, thank you very much. There is banality and complexity all the way through systemic-conspiracy, but the common thread is a decisively pathological meta-ethic: the war mentality; us vs. them. Every little moral aberration of ours becomes amplified when is plugged into the system. There are ripple effects that turn into shockwaves down the line, and throughout time. In order to see systemic-conspiracy properly both in the past and present, we have to abstract up to the highest level of analysis. We can, for the purpose of analysis, ignore agency and focus on the system itself; on the contradictions and antinomies that compel us to engage in conflict rather than resolution. By definitively exposing the dysfunctional structure of the 'systemic conspiracy,' we can more effectively embrace demilitarization policies and put war out of business.

ELON MUSK'S VAST OIL CONSPIRACY ENDS WITH SAUDI BILLIONS

Elon Musk has always hated the fossil-fuel industry. His stated mission for Tesla Inc. is to hasten its demise, and more than once he's blamed the 'Unrelenting and enormous' power of oil interests for sabotaging his efforts. But now, in his bid to take Tesla private, Musk is courting billions of oil dollars. After a week of playing coy about who he's been trying to enlist to help buy out Tesla's publicly traded shares, Musk revealed at least one potential partner: Saudi Arabia. It's hard to think of a more perfect symbol of Big Oil and its money than a sovereign wealth fund created by the world's biggest oil exporter. Musk said in a blog post on Monday that he's been in talks with Saudi Arabia 'Going back almost two years.'

How Saudi's Stake in Tesla Could Help Musk Go Private: Quick Take

Constructing the appearance of a high-stakes struggle between Tesla and the fossil-fuel industry has always been key to Tesla's brand strategy. In the age of global warming, Musk has argued over and over again, you're either part of the solution with civilization hanging in the balance or you're the problem. Every time he unveils a new Tesla product be it a battery for your home or an expensive sports car, he's careful to lay out the case for how it helps the worldwide transition to sustainable energy. The idea that oil money was arrayed against him made buying his products seem like choosing a side in an epochal struggle. By now it's clear, however, that the battle lines can't be quite so neatly drawn. Some of the very parties Musk has been condemning as threats to the planet want to be seen as part of the solution, too.

An Oil Conspiracy Theory

To get a sense of Musk's distrust of the fossil-fuel industry, you don't have to go back far. In an email to his workforce in June, Musk alleged attempts by a former employee, later identified as Martin Tripp, to 'Sabotage' the company. The letter described 'A lengthy list of organizations that want Tesla to die,' including, Musk said, the oil industry. Tripp has since filed a whistle-blower complaint with the SEC claiming Tesla made misstatements to investors and is seeking $1 million in damages from Musk's public condemnation.

From Musk's email:

The oil and gas companies, the wealthiest industry in the world, they don't love the idea of Tesla advancing the progress of solar power and electric cars. Don't want to blow your mind, but rumor has it that those companies are sometimes not super nice. Then there are the multitude of big gas/diesel car company competitors. If they're willing to cheat so much about emissions, maybe they're willing to cheat in other ways? With Musk's new disclosures about his talks with Saudi Arabia, it's clear that this email was written long after he knew one of the biggest pools of oil money was interested in financing, not destroying, his company. This wasn't an isolated suggestion that oil was out to get him. A month earlier, Musk had attacked the credibility of journalists by arguing that the media industry was beholden to fossil-fuel advertisers. Musk's solution was to threaten to launch a website, pravduh.com that would let user's rate journalists and their editors as a way to correct for the corrupting influence of oil money.

These examples stretch back years. In 2013, while opening a Tesla showroom in London, he decried attacks by the oil industry on electric vehicles and climate science. 'It's kind of like the battle against big tobacco in the old days, and how they'd run all these ads about how tobacco's no problem,' he said. In May 2016, just weeks after Tesla unveiled its Model 3 electric car, Musk was especially critical of the oil industry. 'It is quite worrying, the future of the world,' he said. 'We need to appeal to the people and educate them to sort of revolt against this and to fight the propaganda of the fossil fuel industry, which is unrelenting and enormous.' Four months later, Tesla accused a former executive from an oil-and-gas services company, Todd Katz, of impersonating Musk in an email to get confidential data about the company. Tesla alleged he was part of an effort to undermine cleaner transportation. The Kingdom Tower in Riyadh, Saudi Arabia.

Making Peace with Oil Money

The fossil-fuel industry, just like the media Musk likes to attack, has never been the monolith he made it out to be. Yes, oil companies have at times lobbied to protect their business and pushed the politics of climate change away from stringent regulation. But some of the biggest innovations and sources of funding for climate solutions have also come from Big Oil. Take the lithium-ion battery at the core of all Tesla vehicles. That technology was first developed by a chemist at Exxon in the 1970s. Even today, at a time when electric vehicles are poised to cut demand for oil, there are tens of thousands of electric-vehicle charging stations across Europe owned and operated by Royal Dutch Shell Plc, Engie SA and Statoil ASA. That's why it's not totally surprising to learn from Musk's blog post on Monday that Saudi Arabia's sovereign wealth fund first approached him in early 2017. The Saudi Public Investment Fund, or PIF, recently accumulated an almost 5 percent stake and is interested in taking the company private, as Bloomberg News first reported Sunday. The Saudis aren't even the only ones putting oil money to work for Tesla: The Norwegian sovereign-wealth fund, created by that country's oil wealth, held 0.48 percent of Tesla's stock at the end of 2017.

While Saudi Arabia's economy is built on crude exports, the government has acknowledged that the source of its prosperity is also doing environmental harm and can't continue forever. Diversification is central to the kingdom's Vision 2030 program. The country is already investing in solar power, smart cities, and the future of transportation. Saudi Arabia hopes to sell shares of the state oil company, Saudi Aramco, to help expand its sovereign wealth fund to eventually control more than $2 trillion. It makes sense that a portion of that money would find its way to electric vehicles, which are forecast to increase from global sales of 1.1 million last year to 30 million by 2030, according to Bloomberg New Energy Finance. A bigger investment to help take Tesla private would hand some part of the operating control of the world's biggest electric-car maker over to one of the world's top oil producers. That's the kind of shadowy influence that Tesla's chief executive officer might have once framed as a threat. But with traditional automakers researching battery technology to compete with Tesla, and oil states pouring money into Musk's vision, it's starting to seem like a vast electric-vehicle conspiracy is underway.

THE BEST SPACEX CONSPIRACIES ABOUT THE FALCON HEAVY LAUNCH

Did Elon Musk pull off the perfect murder? And other things conspiracy theorists are wondering. On Tuesday, SpaceX made history with the successful flight of the Falcon Heavy, the most powerful operational rocket in the world. I was on site to watch it happen and it looked pretty real to me, but not everyone was convinced. Even SpaceX CEO Elon Musk acknowledged how fake the whole thing seemed. 'You can tell it's real because it looks so fake,' Musk said at a press conference after the launch. 'We'd have way better CGI if it were fake.' Still, in a time-honored tradition that dates back to the moon landings, conspiracies about what really happened on the Falcon Heavy flight abound. I dove down the rabbit hole inhabited by SpaceX truthers to find out how the wool could've been pulled over my eyes.

THEORY: ELON MUSK COMMITTED THE PERFECT MURDER

All right so let's look at the facts: We have an eccentric billionaire determined to colonize other planets. Said billionaire has created the most powerful operational rocket in the world. At the last minute, the billionaire announces that his own personal car, loaded with a dummy pilot, will be placed on top of the rocket, and launched into a billion-year orbit around the sun. No one at SpaceX apparently knew about the plan to launch the car and dummy pilot before the billionaire tweeted it out. Something doesn't add up. This sounds like a caricature of an early-franchise Bond villain because on some level Musk is a caricature of an early-franchise Bond villain, but the circumstances surrounding the launch had some asking: Did Elon Musk just commit the perfect murder In a popular post on the Shower Thoughts subreddit, user 'halo3kings' suggested that Musk got away with the perfect murder by sending a body to Mars. Musk said the spacesuit didn't contain any sensors, which is kind of fishy, wouldn't you want to get some data about how the suit performs in the empty vacuum of space? Probably, unless that suit contained a human body. A more gruesome variant of the conspiracy theory claims that someone is drugged and alive in the suit, adding a dark irony to the 'Don't Panic' sign on the car's dash. But what about the car itself? Was Musk involved in a hit and run and needed to dump the evidence? Are there still more bodies in the trunk?! I guess we'll never know….

THEORY: THE ROADSTER DEPLOYMENT NEVER HAPPENED

A quick trawl through the #FakeX hashtag on Twitter and YouTube will yield dozens of theories about how the deployment of Musk's Tesla roadster into interplanetary space never happened. Compared to the murder theory, these theories are a bit more banal and tend to crop up around most SpaceX/NASA launches. Of course, there's the omnipresent theory that the whole thing was CGI and that the flash as the payload was released into space was actually an accidental camera flash at a CGI studio.

THE 'DIAL MUSK FOR MURDER' SPACEX FALCON HEAVY CONSPIRACY

As one of the richest (net worth of $20.9 billion, listed by Forbes as the 53rd richest person in the world) and most powerful (21st on the Forbes list of The World's Most Powerful People) people in the world, Tesla and SpaceX CEO Elon Musk is no stranger to controversies and conspiracies, especially when it comes to SpaceX launches and his deep interest in traveling to and colonizing Mars. UFO watchers seem to find UFOs at many SpaceX launches, including the ill-fated explosion on the launch pad in 2016 and this week's successful launch of the Falcon Heavy rocket, whose payload was a Tesla Roadster with a dummy astronaut in the driver's seat that was sent on a mission to Mars (although that seems to have changed – more on this later). But nothing beats the conspiracy theory floated on reddit and other Internet sites suggesting that the entire launch may have been a cover-up for a murder! 'Elon Musk launched a car into space with a dummy in a spacesuit in the driver's seat. The idea is that the dummy is actually a corpse, hidden in plain sight on international news, and nobody will ever be able to find the person he killed.' Wait a minute, you say. That certainly sounds plausible … as well as a great plot for a murder mystery. And the plot thickens.

'THE REAL CORPSE IS IN THE TRUNK.'

Whoa! The Roadster's trunk is definitely big enough for a corpse. But who would Elon Musk want dead so badly that he would create such an elaborate murder scheme? That's when the conspiracy starts to unravel. Suggestions range from Elon's space and World's Richest Man rival Jeff Bezos (he's still alive) to actress Amber Heard (she's still alive) to John Wick (you realize he's not real, don't' you?) to Musk himself, he's not dead but alive in the car heading to his 'Home' planet while a clone takes his place here.
All together now… Really?

Well, there was that UFO spotted during the Falcon Heavy launch, right? As with most launches these days, UFOs spotted at liftoff are probably news or security drones. Something in the video feed from the Roadster in orbit was suspected to be space debris. And, despite the fact that it was Musk's rocket, the launch took place using a NASA facility and was heavily inspected by NASA and government officials. If you don't think these people are tough, ask Mad Mike Hughes. Stepping back a bit, why would someone like Musk commit a murder he needed to cover up? Most celebrity murderers are impulsive killers or jilted lovers, think boxing promoter Don King, Oscar Pistorius, O.J. Simpson, or Phil Spector. Does Musk act or talk like someone with something sinister to hide? Why not just send another probe to track down the Roadster, pull it over and inspect the driver and the trunk? (Sounds like the first episode of CSI: Mars.) That's where Musk does sound a little evasive, stating that the rocket overshot the trajectory to send the car around the Sun before flinging it to Mars and it will instead end up in the asteroid belt, possibly even approaching the dwarf planet Ceres. That is, IF it survives that long. While Musk said it would be orbiting Mars for billions of years, most scientists think cosmic radiation will destroy the Tesla and its contents, sinister or not, within a year. Do you think that may have been Musk's idea all along? Conspiracy or not (and the needle seems too buried deep in NOT territory), kudos to Musk and SpaceX for getting the world interested in launches and space travel again.

CONSPIRACY THEORISTS ARE CONVINCED THAT THE NEXT SPACEX LAUNCH HAS SOMETHING TO DO WITH NIBIRU

We have barely begun 2018 and we've already got another Nibiru story to deal with. The mysterious planet, also known as Planet X, was supposedly set to destroy the entire Earth on at least four occasions in 2017 but nothing materialized. Some conspiracy theorists remain certain that Nibiru will appear in our solar system in the next 12 months and bring about the end of days - but now there is also a theory that someone is trying to prevent it. That someone is none other than Elon Musk and his space exploration company SpaceX, who are due to launch a new aircraft onboard a Falcon 9 rocket today. Little is known about the Zuma satellite, but it is being launched in connection with the US government via a deal with the aerospace and defense company Northrop Grumman. Space.com report that Zuma will go into a low-Earth orbit after taking off from the Cape Canaveral Air Force Station in Florida. The launch was delayed twice last year but SpaceX confirmed on Twitter that they are now targeting a launch on Sunday. Team at the Cape completed additional propellant loading tests today. Extreme weather slowed operations, but Falcon 9 and the Zuma spacecraft are healthy and go for launch—now targeting January 7 from Pad 40 in Florida.

Due to the secrecy surrounding this launch, theorists are now very suspicious about its actual intentions. In true conspiracy fashion, they have put two and two together and determined that the launch definitely has something to do with Nibiru. A post from October on the conspiracy website Someone's Bones claimed that Musk had been collaborating with the government in order to destroy Nibiru and that he is obsessed with the theory. According to the website, an anonymous source said: Elon is secretly obsessed with Nibiru, I've known him for ten years; I know how the man thinks. The government promised him 'life after Nibiru' if he got onboard with their program and promised to keep it all hush hush. That's why all the payloads are classified; they deal with scientific instruments created to better gauge Nibiru's time line and the effects that will imperil our planet once it crosses. Granted, I don't know all the details, but I know what I've been told, by Elon and others, and from what I've learned privately. The source also claims that Musk has been working with the government and NASA to gather intelligence on a brown dwarf star and seven other planets that 'Intersect the inner solar system every 3,600 years give or take.'

They go on to add:

Elon has met with high ranking military and civilian officials several times during the last two months. There's a reason the government is enlisting public help for money and secrecy.

DO YOU KNOW WHY OBAMA KILLED THE SHUTTLE PROGRAM?

Because too many questions were being asked about what exactly those orbiters are doing up there. It is highly unlikely that this launch has anything to do with Nibiru, a planet which has been labelled a hoax by NASA, or that Obama killed the shuttle program to kill speculation about it. If it is true then hopefully the mission is a success, and we won't have to listen to these ridiculous theories anymore.

PLANET X NIBIRU IS HEADING TOWARDS EARTH AND WILL END ALL LIFE

A NASA paper suggests that Planet Nibiru does exist, and it could have deadly consequences for the planet. The Nibiru cataclysm, a conspiracy theory? The Nibiru cataclysm is a supposed disastrous encounter between the Earth and a large planetary object from outside our solar system. Is it just a conspiracy theory? A NASA paper which was originally published in 1988 is said to reveal that there is a mysterious unnamed planet beyond the tiny ice planet of Pluto. It is believed by many that the Planet X referred to by NASA could be the fabled Planet Nibiru which many thinks could be the initiator of a major, imminent apocalyptic event for the people of Earth.

The cataclysmic event will be caused by the sheer force of gravitational strength

The study in question concerned observations on gravitational influences on a group of celestial objects which were referred to as 'Extreme trans-Neptunian objects' (ETNOs). Planet X or Planet Nibiru was said to be much larger than Earth and has a considerably longer orbital period. Best estimates by NASA suggested that the orbital period of the planet spanned a remarkable three thousand six hundred years.

Planet "X" Nibiru also was known as Planet Nine

This previously concealed study has suggested too many people that NASA and the United States government have been aware of the presence of Planet Nibiru for many years and that they are also away from the catastrophic effects its gravitational power could have for life on planet Earth. The secret NASA files apparently reveal that Planet Nine has disrupted the orbits of other planets in its orbital period and that it is imminently about to enter a disruptive passage into the inner solar system. Currently, it is thought that the planet is emitting waves of 'Plasmatic energy particles' which will eventually come to disrupt the core flows of Earth. This disruption is likely to trigger huge and catastrophic changes in the Earth's climate. It is thought that the effects of the Planet Nibiru can already be felt on Earth in the form of increased seismic and volcanic activity, bizarre weather patterns and an uptick in natural disasters. Disturbingly, it is believed that this freak meteorological activity will become much worse before coming to a head at the end of the year.

Planet Nibiru which will cause a pole shift

It is thought that this cataclysmic event will be caused by the sheer force of gravitational strength by Planet Nibiru which will cause a pole shift on the planet Earth. This will lead to approximately two-thirds of the human population being wiped out. It is also estimated that a further two-thirds of those who survive will perish over the next six months due to starvation and exposure to the elements. It is said that this has been common knowledge among NASA personnel and officers within the Pentagon and the CIA for quite some time. However, these government agencies have elected to keep this information concealed from the public in a bid to subdue the panic that this event will undoubtedly cause.

1. Zecharia Sitchin, Ancient Astronauts and Planet X Nibiru

2. Zecharia Sitchin was a Russian-American author of books proposing an explanation for human origins involving ancient astronauts.

Comet Elenin and Nibiru

Some have decided that comet Elenin, which will enter our inner solar system and pass nearest Earth in October 2011, is actually Nibiru. Even then, though, scientists say Elenin will come no closer than 100 times farther than the distance from Earth to the moon.

Overview

Caltech researchers have found mathematical evidence suggesting there may be a 'Planet X' deep in the solar system. This hypothetical Neptune-sized planet orbits our sun in a highly elongated orbit far beyond Pluto. The object, which the researchers have nicknamed 'Planet Nine,' could have a mass about 10 times that of Earth and orbit about 20 times farther from the sun on average than Neptune. It may take between 10,000 and 20,000 Earth years to make one full orbit around the sun. The announcement does not mean there is a new planet in our solar system. The existence of this distant world is only theoretical at this point and no direct observation of the object nicknamed have been made. The mathematical prediction of a planet could explain the unique orbits of some smaller objects in the Kuiper Belt, a distant region of icy debris that extends far beyond the orbit of Neptune. Astronomers are now searching for the predicted planet.

In Depth

In January 2015, Caltech astronomers Konstantin Batygin and Mike Brown announced new research that provides evidence of a giant planet tracing an unusual, elongated orbit in the outer solar system. The prediction is based on detailed mathematical modeling and computer simulations, not direct observation. This large object could explain the unique orbits of at least five smaller objects discovered in the distant Kuiper Belt. 'The possibility of a new planet is certainly an exciting one for me as a planetary scientist and for all of us,' said Jim Green, director of NASA's Planetary Science Division. 'This is not, however, the detection or discovery of a new planet. It's too early to say with certainty there's a so-called Planet X. What we're seeing is an early prediction based on modeling from limited observations. It's the start of a process that could lead to an exciting result.' The Caltech scientists believe Planet X may have has a mass about 10 times that of Earth and be similar in size to Uranus or Neptune. The predicted orbit is about 20 times farther from our sun on average than Neptune (which orbits the sun at an average distance of 2.8 billion miles). It would take this new planet between 10,000 and 20,000 years to make just one full orbit around the sun (where Neptune completes an orbit roughly every 165 years).

When was it discovered?

Planet X has not yet been discovered, and there is debate in the scientific community about whether it exists. The prediction in the Jan. 20 issue of the Astronomical Journal is based on mathematical modeling.

What is its Name?

Batygin and Brown nicknamed their predicted object 'Planet Nine,' but the actual naming rights of an object go to the person who actually discovers it. The name used during previous hunts for the long suspected giant, undiscovered object beyond Neptune is 'Planet X.' If the predicted world is found, the name must be approved by the International Astronomical Union. Planets are traditionally named for mythological Roman gods.

Why Do They Think It's There?

Astronomers studying the Kuiper Belt have noticed some of the dwarf planets and other small, icy objects tend to follow orbits that cluster together. By analyzing these orbits, the Caltech team predicted the possibility that a large, previously undiscovered planet may be hiding far beyond Pluto. They estimate the gravity of this potential planet might explain the unusual orbits of those Kuiper objects.

What's next?

Astronomers, including Batygin and Brown, will begin using the world's most powerful telescopes to search for the object in its predicted orbit. Any object that far away from the sun will be very faint and hard to detect, but astronomers calculate that it should be possible to see it using existing telescopes. 'I would love to find it,' says Brown. 'But I'd also be perfectly happy if someone else found it. That is why we're publishing this paper. We hope that other people are going to get inspired and start searching.' 'Anytime we have an interesting idea like this, we always apply Carl Sagan's rules for critical thinking, which include independent confirmation of the facts, looking for alternate explanations, and encouraging scientific debate,' said Green. "If Planet X is out there, we'll find it together. Or we'll determine an alternate explanation for the data that we've received so far.

'Now let's go explore.'

15. The HAARPIEST HAARP…

HAARP: Secret Weapon Used For Weather Modification and Electromagnetic Warfare

Weather modification will become a part of domestic and international security and could be done unilaterally… It could have offensive and defensive applications and even be used for deterrence purposes. The ability to generate precipitation, fog, and storms on earth or to modify space weather, and the production of artificial weather all are a part of an integrated set of technologies which can provide substantial increase in US, or degraded capability in an adversary, to achieve global awareness, reach, and power. (US Air Force, emphasis added. Air University of the US Air Force, AF 2025 Final Report, and the HAARP facility in Gakona Alaska was closed down in 2014. The Recent IPCC Climate Change report quite deliberately fails to identify the instruments of weather warfare. Michel Chossudovsky, Global Research, October 14, 2018

'It isn't just conspiracy theorists who are concerned about HAARP. The European Union called the project a global concern and passed a resolution calling for more information on its health and environmental risks. Despite those concerns, officials at HAARP insist the project is nothing more sinister than a radio science research facility.'

— Quote from a TV documentary on HAARP by the Canadian Broadcasting Corporation (CBC). HAARP (High Frequency Active Auroral Research Program) is a little-known, yet critically important U.S. military defense program which has generated quite a bit of controversy over the years in certain circles. Though denied by HAARP officials, some respected researchers allege that secret electromagnetic warfare capabilities of HAARP are designed to forward the US military's stated goal of achieving full-spectrum dominance by the year 2020. Others go as far as to claim that HAARP can and has been used for weather modification, to cause earthquakes and tsunamis, to disrupt global communications systems, and more. Major aspects of the program are kept secret for alleged reasons of 'National security.' Yet there is no doubt that HAARP and electromagnetic weapons capable of being used in warfare do exist. According to the official HAARP website, 'HAARP is a scientific endeavor aimed at studying the properties and behavior of the ionosphere, with particular emphasis on being able to understand and use it to enhance communications and surveillance systems for both civilian and defense purposes.' The ionosphere is the delicate upper layer of our atmosphere which ranges from about 30 miles (50 km) to 600 miles (1,000 km) above the surface of the Earth. The HAARP website acknowledges that experiments are conducted which use electromagnetic frequencies to fire pulsed, directed energy beams in order to 'Temporarily excite a limited area of the ionosphere.' Some scientists state that purposefully disturbing this sensitive layer could have major and even disastrous consequences. Concerned HAARP researchers like Dr. Michel Chossudovsky of the University of Ottawa and Alaska's Dr. Nick Begich (son of a US Congressman) present evidence suggesting that these disturbances can even cause tsunamis and earthquakes.

Selected Articles: Weather Modification as US Military Strategy?

Two key major media documentaries, one by Canada's public broadcasting network CBC (see below) and the other by the History Channel (below), reveal the inner workings of

HAARP in a most powerful way. The very professionally researched CBC documentary includes this key quote:

'It isn't just conspiracy theorists who are concerned about HAARP. In January of 1999, the European Union called the project a global concern and passed a resolution calling for more information on its health and environmental risks. Despite those concerns, officials at HAARP insist the project is nothing more sinister than a radio science research facility.' The actual wording at bullet point 24 in this telling document states that the EU 'Considers HAARP by virtue of its far-reaching impact on the environment to be a global concern and calls for its legal, ecological and ethical implications to be examined by an international independent body before any further research and testing.' This reveling document further states that the EU regrets the repeated refusal of the U.S. government to send anyone to give evidence on HAARP. For an even more detailed and revealing 45-minute History Channel documentary on HAARP and other secret weapons used for electromagnetic warfare. Below are two quotes from the History Channel documentary:

'Electromagnetic weapons … pack an invisible wallop hundreds of times more powerful than the electrical current in a lightning bolt. One can blast enemy missiles out of the sky, another could be used to blind soldiers on the battlefield, still another to control an unruly crowd by burning the surface of their skin. If detonated over a large city, an electromagnetic weapon could destroy all electronics in seconds. They all use directed energy to create a powerful electromagnetic pulse.'

'Directed energy is such a powerful technology it could be used to heat the ionosphere to turn weather into a weapon of war. Imagine using a flood to destroy a city or tornadoes to decimate an approaching army in the desert. The military has spent a huge amount of time on weather modification as a concept for battle environments. If an electromagnetic pulse went off over a city, basically all the electronic things in your home would wink and go out, and they would be permanently destroyed.'

History Channel Documentary

For those who still doubt that such devastating secret weapons have been developed, here is an intriguing quote from an article in New Zealand's leading newspaper, the New Zealand Herald: 'Top-secret wartime experiments were conducted off the coast of Auckland to perfect a tidal wave bomb, declassified files reveal. United States defense chiefs said that if the project had been completed before the end of the war, it could have played a role as effective as that of the atom bomb. Details of the tsunami bomb, known as Project Seal, are contained in 53-year-old documents released by the Ministry of Foreign Affairs and Trade.'

If the military secretly developed a weapon which could cause a tsunami over half a century ago, what kind of advanced deadly weapons might be available now? And why is it that the general public still doesn't know about secret weapons developed over 50 years ago? To understand why the media isn't covering these overly critical issues, click here. Clearly the military has the capability to cause a tsunami and likely to cause earthquakes and hurricanes, as well. It's time for us to take action to spread the word on this vital topic. Having interpreted to for top generals in my work as a language interpreter with the US Department of State, I learned that military planners are always interested in developing the most devastating weapons possible. Yet these weapons are kept secret as long as possible, allegedly for reasons of national security. The many layers of intense secrecy both in the military and government result in very few people being aware of the gruesome capabilities for death and destruction that have been developed over the years. There are many examples of major defense projects kept successfully out of the public's eyes for years and even decades.

The massive Manhattan Project (development of the first atomic bomb) is one such example. The building of an entire city to support the project in Oak Ridge, Tennessee was successfully kept secret even from the state's governor. The stealth bomber was kept top secret for many years, and the public still has no way of knowing its full capabilities. It is through the use of the highly organized military and intelligence services that the power elite of our world, working in cooperation with key allies in government and corporate ownership of the media, are able to carry out major cover-ups and secret operations like those involved with HAARP. Some researchers have raised questions about the possible involvement of HAARP in major disasters like the earthquake in Haiti, Indonesian tsunami, and hurricane Katrina. Could these have been HAARP experiments gone awry? Might they even have been caused by rogue elements which gained control of this devastating technology? Of course, disasters like this happen regularly on a natural basis, yet if you begin to research, there is some high strangeness around some of these disasters. The evidence is inconclusive, yet with the known and unknown major destructive capabilities of this weapon, significant questions remain.

A Terrifying Look at the Control of Weather Warfare -- A Look at HAARP – Getting' Preachy Wit It...

We shall take a basic look at the technology involved in controlling the weather. We shall try to take a simple look so you can understand a most complex scientific subject. The New World Order is coming! Are you ready? Once you understand what this New World Order really is, and how it is being gradually implemented, you will be able to see it progressing in your daily news!! The idea behind Weather Control is simple when you think about it simply. When you see and experience a strong thunderstorm, with a lot of lightning and thunder, what fact about this storm strikes you the most? Are you not impressed by the powerful display of energy that you witness? Energy is the primary ingredient behind nature's storms. Therefore, you must believe that, just perhaps, if energy is the most dominant outward factor in all kinds of storms, then energy might be the key factor in creating such storms in the first place.

Energy, Energy, Energy, Energy, Energy, Energy

So, you ask, how much energy is required to create, and then direct, storms? The answer to that question depends upon many factors but let us tell you how much capability has been built into the newly created power transmission station in remote Alaska. These power transmission towers are not your typical towers, as they are designed to generate power in such a way that it is beamed up into the ionosphere in tremendous quantities.

'The $30 million [Pentagon] project, euphemistically named HAARP (High Frequency Active Auroral Research Program), is made to beam more than 1.7 gigawatts (billion watts) of radiated power into the ionosphere -- the electrically charged layer above Earth's atmosphere. Put simply, the apparatus is a reversal of a radio telescope -- just transmitting instead of receiving. It will 'boil the upper atmosphere'. After [heating] and disturbing the ionosphere, the radiations will bounce back onto the earth in for form of long waves which penetrate our bodies, the ground, and the oceans.' Let us allow Dr. Begich explain this concept. '... This invention provides the ability to put unprecedented amounts of power in the Earth's atmosphere at strategic locations and to maintain the power injection level, particularly if random pulsing is employed, in a manner far more precise and better controlled than heretofore accomplished by the prior art ....'

'... The goal is to learn how to manipulate the ionosphere on a grander scale than the Soviet Union could do with its similar facilities. HAARP would be the largest ionospheric heater in the world, located in a latitude most conducive to putting Eastlund's invention into practice.' Furthermore, from this northern latitude, the energy could be aimed into the ionosphere so that it would bounce back down to the earth so it would come down wherever the scientists wanted it to come down. The secret was to learn how and where to aim it to hit the earth where they wanted it to hit, creating the type of disaster or weather they desired. In a nutshell, this is the nucleus of the expertise just recently acquired to control the weather. By pouring measured energy that has been focused into certain parts of the ionosphere, scientists can create all kinds of storms like hurricanes, thunderstorms, floods, tornadoes, and drought.

In NEWS1198, 'U.N. Treaty Proves Weather Control Is Real', we report news articles that Malaysia actually contracted with a Russian Weather Modification company to create a hurricane that would be directed close enough to clear the smoke and smog from Malaysia's cities without actually coming on to land to create devastation. This Russian company delivered, and Malaysia had clear skies. Our information also tells us that, not only can hurricanes be created, but they can also be dismantled should scientists so desire. And they certainly can be driven on the ocean much like we drive our cars on roadways. Therefore, one has to ask why American scientists have allowed unprecedented hurricanes, like Andrew, to ever come on shore. Why are American scientists allowing extensive damage and lives lost to recent unprecedented storms, since they have the capability to keep these storms away from us? Doesn't our own American Government have our best interests at heart?

Keep that thought in mind as we examine still more aspects of this HAARP technology that is pouring such enormous quantities of energy into our upper atmosphere. Research quickly found that this technology could be used in ways other than just to control the weather. They discovered they had stumbled upon a weapon which could be used most effectively, to destroy, destroy, and destroy some more, with the vast majority of the peoples of the world completely unaware of what was happening to them. After all, most people today still believe that the control of the basic weather of this planet is out of the control of mankind.

Christians believe only God can control the weather, and we take great comfort in this belief. After all, we know that Earth is a small planet hurtling through an empty, cold, and inhospitable space at over 60,000 miles per hour. Most of us instinctively know that we can only trust an Omnipotent and All Wise God to control the basic operating systems of planet earth. If we even thought that man, with all his inherent wickedness, could seize control of the basic operating systems of earth, and the entire earth could be ruined by man's deliberate wickedness or by his lack of understanding of the power he has now placed in his hand, we would see panic on a scale unimagined before! Do not misunderstand: Earth could be destroyed, made unfit for human habitation, by mistakes accidentally created. The New Age scientists of 'Angels Don't Play This HAARP' are worried about just this type of accidental damage to earth. They are worried that the following damage might be done to this earth, some of which might render this planet uninhabitable. If you are a Christian that literally believes the Scriptures, you know that God will not allow this planet to become inhabitable, as He will not allow man to completely destroy what God has created and declared good.

However, we also know that the Book of Revelation foretells unprecedented destruction that God either directs or allows, that 'Destroys the sinners out of the land' [Isaiah 13:9-13]. God judges wicked man at the same time as He is cleansing the earth to prepare for the arrival of Jesus Christ to begin His Millennial reign. We are extremely interested in the fact that many of the "lying signs and wonders" of the Antichrist can be staged by the technology of HAARP. Further, many of the physical acts of judgment contained in the Book of Revelation, and parallel passages in the Major and Minor Prophets, can be created by this HAARP technology. Given the desperately wicked heart of man, perhaps the most damage God could do would be to allow man to get unprecedented ability and power in his grasp, and then move His Holy Spirit out of the way to allow man to treat other men as his wicked heart would direct!

- We find it very interesting that God's wording in the Book of Revelation seems to back up this interpretation that God may allow man to possess technological power that he could use against other men, according to the wickedness of his heart. Look at the wording of some of these passages. The word, 'Given,' in each of these Scriptures is Strong's #G1325, 'Didomi', which means "to give", to 'Grant', and to 'Receive'. In other words, these Scriptures are saying that God is going to allow the men of Antichrist to receive abilities that they never possessed before. These abilities will then be used to bring God's Judgments upon this wicked earth and its rebellious people.

- Revelation 6:4-5 -- This passage foretells the next horse that rides out of Heaven after Antichrist rides, symbolizing his appearance on the earth. 'And there went out another horse that was red: and power was given to him that sat thereon to take peace from the earth, and that they should kill one another: and there was given unto him a great sword.' In this instance, mankind will receive the ability to wage unprecedented warfare upon the inhabitants of the earth.

- Revelation 6:8 -- This passage foretells that man will be given unprecedented ability to kill other men with unprecedented means. 'And I looked and behold a pale horse: and his name that sat on him was Death, and Hell followed with him. And power was given unto them over the fourth part of the earth, to kill with sword, and with hunger, and with death, and with the beasts of the earth.' We shall demonstrate that HAARP technology can wield this kind of weapon upon the peoples of the earth.

- Revelation 13:5 -- Antichrist is given unprecedented ability by God to reign with a degree of wickedness and audacity never seen in history. 'And there was given unto him a mouth speaking remarkable things and blasphemies; and power was given unto him to continue forty and two months.' While HAARP cannot give the Antichrist such a great mouth, it can give him the ability to project his speeches all over the world, where people can see his image in the sky above them, speaking to them in their own language!

- Revelation 13:7 -- Antichrist is given the ability to slaughter the saints of God. 'And it was given unto him to make war with the saints, and to overcome them: and power was given him over all kindred's, and tongues, and nations.' I find it highly instructive that the same unprecedented ability which God is going to allow Antichrist to rule mankind and slaughter the saints of God is the same type of unprecedented technological ability God is going to give man in these other passages.

- Revelation 16:8-9 -- HAARP can create this scourge of heat from the Sun! 'And the fourth angel poured out his vial upon the sun; and power was given unto him to scorch men with fire. And men were scorched with extreme heat, and blasphemed the name of God, which hath power over these plagues.' I find it highly instructive that, while the last part of this passage says God retains power over these plagues, the first part of the passage says that God is going to 'Give' unto wicked men unprecedented powers by which other men are going to be judged! In other words, while God is allowing Satan to reveal unprecedented ability to human scientists to inflict death and suffering on wicked man, God retains ultimate control.

- Now, let us examine some of the concerns of these New Age scientists of the damage HAARP can inflict upon the earth. HAARP can:

- Create Earthquakes on demand wherever and whenever you wish on the earth. 'The planetary-scale engineers tried to replace a ten by forty kilometer section of the ionosphere with a 'Telecommunications shield' of 350,000 copper needles tossed into orbit ... when the military sent up a band of tiny copper wires into the ionosphere to orbit the planet so as to 'reflect radio waves and make reception clearer', we had the 8.5 Alaska earthquake and Chile lost a good deal of its coast. That band of copper wires interfered with the planetary magnetic field.'

- Manipulate Global Weather Systems, changing weather patterns, rainfall, drought

- Earth going wild in its rotation, possibly spinning out of control

- Redirecting Jet Streams

- Redirecting flow of Electrojet Stream

- Magnifying and focusing sunlight, called 'Skybusting'. This process could burn holes in the protective ozone layers, thus allowing intense sunlight to pour through, burning mankind severely. Look at Revelation 16:8, quoted above

- Mind Control. Using extremely low frequency bombardment at just the same frequency as the human brain operates, you can change a person's thoughts or emotions. God help us all when and if wicked men achieves finesse with this weapon!

- HAARP can create nuclear-sized explosions without radiation! This process is protected by patent 4,873,928. This might be the 'Great sword' being wielded by the forces of Antichrist in Revelation 6:4. With this weapon, you could attack targets with nuclear-sized explosions without having to deliver nuclear warheads on missiles, or on aircraft, or any carrier!! This development could render all military calculations about how to defend against an enemy's attack completely useless.

- Suddenly, my mind lights up like a lightbulb! Suddenly, I understand why the Russian and American negotiators were suddenly able to reach agreement on the destruction of so many warheads and missiles. Each side even allowed inspection teams to oversee the destruction of actual warheads and missiles. The world felt very much safer. However, warheads carried on missiles are obsolete!! If both sides can create nuclear-sized explosions without radiation by HARRP-type radio transmitting towers, you would not need missiles to carry warheads. How can you defend against a nuclear-sized attack that is being initiated by silent, invisible ELF radio waves? How do you defend against a nuclear-sized attack when it is being initiated by ELF radio waves that are being generated on enemy territory, fly up to the ionosphere above his territory, and then bounce back down to your territory to create the explosion! Clearly, the world has entered an entirely new world of warfare that no one has even conceived let alone thought through very well.

- Furthermore, this subject brings us to the next capability of HAARP and like radio wave technology. These ELF radio transmitters can throw up an impenetrable shield against incoming missiles, aircraft, or anything trying to get through our airspace! Then, why are we attempting to perfect an anti-missile missile that can actually hit another missile in flight? Why is the American military moving rapidly in conjunction with the Israeli military to bring this more effective anti-missile missile to Israel so as to better protect against Syrian and Egyptian missiles? They probably don't want very many people knowing that we possess this type of effective missile shield over any battlefield, either strategic or tactical. When the Arabs engage the Israelis in this next war, they just might be shocked at the type of weapons that are annihilating them! The existence of this type of military capability is also the reason we are allowing the Arab governments to buy American weaponry to fight Israel in this next war. The Arabs don't understand that the Israeli military and we have taken a quantum leap forward in destructive, killing, and annihilating capability!

In fact, has the infantryman finally been made obsolete in warfare?

The greatest concern of New Age scientist Nick Begich, in his book, 'Angels Don't Play This HAARP,' is that scientists and the military are so very arrogant in their ignorant, reckless use of focused energy into the ionosphere. Military scientists talk about 'Kicking this thing in high gear to see what would happen'! This attitude is complete arrogance. What if they set off an unintended reaction in the atmosphere that cannot be controlled or stopped? Indeed, I think some of the judgments foretold in the Book of Revelation might come from this type of major miscalculation by scientists.

16. *AAARR'… There be Pirates on them thar Waters!!!*

'Deception is a state of mind and the mind of the State.' – James Jesus Angleton (Mother of the CIA) of the most infamous secret societies in the world is known as the American order of Skull and Bones that was founded in 1832 at Yale University. The order is also known as

'Bones,' and members are called 'Bonesmen' who are some of the world's most powerful elites such as President George HW Bush, his son George W. Bush, and current U.S. Secret of State, John Kerry to name a few. The secrecy behind the order was confirmed by George W. Bush who wrote in his autobiography, 'In my senior year I joined Skull and Bones, a secret society; so secret, I can't say anything more.' Two Bonesmen, George W. Bush and John Kerry had both been Presidential candidates in the 2004 elections, when Kerry was asked what it meant that he and Bush were both Bonesmen; former Presidential candidate John Kerry said, "Not much, because it's a secret." George Bush eventually won his second term and continued his war campaign in Iraq.

The order was incorporated in 1856 by General William Huntington Russell, and Alphonso Taft who became Secretary of War under President Grant in 1876. The numerical value of this year is 1+8+7+6 = 22, and the numerical motto for Skull and Bones is 322, or 3 x's 22 which you will see below is not a coincidence. In numerology, the number 22 is often called the Master Builder. The Phoenician-Hebrews possess 22 books, and their alphabet is made up of 22 letters, which was created to compose the Word of God. The Kabbalah teaches us that the letters of the Hebrew alphabet are the building blocks of universe. The underlying occult scientific significance of the number 22 in science would represent the bones of the skull, of which there are twenty-two. 8 form the cranium, or braincase, and 14 are associated with the face. Our brains are what we use to think, reason, and come to know the divine or God.

The 22 letters of the Hebrew alphabet created to compose the Word of God is our 22 boned skull, and the place where we receive the light to become illuminated, or enlightened beings. Hence, to be like Saint John and have our own Revelation. This is why I believe Skull and Bones had chosen the number 22 as the master builders of a New World Order (NWO). This fact would be validated by Bonesmen, former CIA director and President, George HW Bush; who in the video below taken from National television, makes no bones about their Apocalyptic plans for a New World Order. Please keep in mind that this speech of biblical proportions was done on 9-11-1991, and it was exactly 10 years later to the day that the U.S. suffered an attack on the World Trade Center Towers. Shortly thereafter his son George W. Bush would begin the war in Iraq. Now I would like to theorize about the number 66 and the connection to the Skull and Bones numerical motto of 322… In the bible, the Number 66 is the numerical value of the Wheel from the Hebrew Galgal, which is remarkably similar to the word.

Google; meaning a wheel, whirl, whirlwind, or simply Chaos. The meaning of Gal, Gul, or Gull is to trick or to cheat. The word 'Curse' is used 66 times in the Old Testament. 'As for the wheels, it was cried unto them in my hearing, O wheel.' – Ezekiel 10.13This chaos of tricks may be indicative of the CIA domestic counter terrorism plan founded under Skull and Bones member, James Jesus Angleton who was called the 'Mother of the Central Intelligence Agency.' Angleton was solely responsible for a domestic espionage project called Operation 'Chaos,' and had coined the phrase, 'Deception is a state of mind and the mind of the State.' Hence, from this point forward the CIA would play a vital role in creating chaos both domestically and abroad, or 'Ordo Ab Chao' which is the motto of the 33rd degree of Scottish Rite Freemasonry.

FREEMASONS

The 'Classical' European secret society clearly borrowed its organizational model from Freemasonry, which itself originated from the guilds and brotherhoods of Scottish and English masons. The official birth of Freemasonry is conventionally set at 1717, the foundation date of the Grand Lodge of London, which in 1723 issued what, after its author, became known as the Constitutions of James Anderson. These regulations were not meant to formulate a particular doctrine, but to delineate a free space in which fraternal tolerance allowed for interesting and pleasant company. As in the guilds, the (almost exclusively male) members of the new lodges passed through a series of initiations to ascending degrees of apprentice, journeyman, and master. The building trade had become merely symbolic; the candidate was seen as a rough stone that had to be polished. The lodges were endowed with a considerable autonomy and engaged in various activities, most often in the fields of charity, education, and merry socializing.

Because of the substantial cost of membership, they recruited disproportionally from the better-off. Members were held to secrecy, but as the illustration shows, this in no way excluded public demonstrations. In England Freemasonry soon became a successful and respectable institution. The movement spread both to the English colonies and the Continent. Here, however, the authorities, fearing moral, religious, or political troubles, were much more reserved than in liberal England. The Continental lodges were frequently suspected of oppositional or unorthodox tendencies, which was of course mostly a matter of definition. The Catholic Church condemned Freemasonry in 1738, the first of many occasions. Its popularity rose quickly nonetheless, aided in part by the creation of new 'systems' that offered more than three degrees and, perhaps, a hint of hidden knowledge or a special experience. In France, on the eve of the Revolution, one in twenty city dwellers was a Freemason. This helps to explain why after the 'fall of Throne and Altar' the lodges became suitable candidates for the role of scapegoat.

Freemasonry Explained: A Guide to the Secretive Society

When did it begin, is it a religion, and are its members' identities kept secret? Freemasonry models itself upon the fraternities of medieval stonemasons who would use secret words and symbols to recognize each other's

When did Freemasonry begin?

The first grand lodge, established to govern Freemasonry in England and Wales, was formed in 1717, during a meeting at a pub in the City of London called the Goose and Gridiron. At that time there were four lodges in the city. But in Scotland, a masonic lodge in Edinburgh has records to show that it has been in existence since at least 1599. During the early 18th century, Freemasonry spread quickly to Europe and the colonies.

Two Freemasons' lodges set up at Westminster are continuing to operate. Why are they so secretive?

Freemasonry's guiding metaphor is the craft of stonemasonry: it models itself upon the fraternities of medieval stonemasons who would use secret words and symbols to recognize each other's legitimacy, and so protect their work from outsiders. During some periods of history, Freemasons have been persecuted by the Nazis, for example and have needed to go underground to survive. But there are persistent suspicions that Freemasons also remain secretive in order to conceal the way in which they can assist each other in business and the workplace.

Is there any substance to these claims?

Such rumors are very rarely substantiated, and masons are expected to swear an oath that they will not be involved in 'any act that may have a tendency to subvert the peace and good order of society, by paying due obedience to the laws of any state.' But parliament's home affairs select committee heard that in 1995, the Lancashire police authority was obliged to pay £70,000 to a father and son who were assaulted and then arrested and prosecuted after stumbling on a masonic dinner being hosted by a lodge dominated by police officers. The committee heard that a police officer who investigated the fracas was a mason, as was the manager of the hotel where the dinner took place.

Is Freemasonry a religion?

No, it is a secular movement, although new members are expected to acknowledge a belief in a God-like superior being, often called the Grand or Great Architect of the Universe. Anyone believing in a single deity may be admitted. Rudyard Kipling, who was a member of a masonic lodge in Lahore, wrote a number of poems about his fellow masons who were Muslims, Hindus, Sikhs, and Jews. In theory, all discussion of religion and politics is prohibited within lodges.

Are the identities of all Freemasons kept secret?

No, individual masons can declare themselves if they wish, and the names of senior officers of the brotherhood in England and Wales can be found in a masonic year book. The grand master is the Duke of Kent. Prince Philip, the Duke of Edinburgh, is a member of a navy lodge. Others who have declared their membership in recent years include the Rev Jesse Jackson, the former astronaut Edwin 'Buzz' Aldrin and musician Rick Wakeman. However, a great many masons do not disclose their membership outside the brotherhood.

JESUITS

In addition to Freemasonry, European secret societies had a second organizational model: the Jesuit Order or, rather, the image constructed by its numerous opponents. Right from the beginning in 1540, the Jesuits caused suspicion even among coreligionists, and were accused of hypocrisy, fanaticism, and ambition. As missionary 'soldiers of the Pope' they became a symbol of the supranational pretensions of the Catholic Church; and since some of them had at one time defended tyrannicide, the violent death of any prince was invariably laid at their feet. The history of the Monita secreta mirrors the development of their reputation. A falsification first published in Cracow in 1614 and endlessly reprinted even today, the pamphlet was presented as the revelation of the secret instructions of the order known only to its leaders. A new version that appeared later in the century focused on how the Jesuits consciously and systematically strove for world domination. In this and other ways, they were increasingly depicted as a secret society with distinctly 'Modern' traits - and one that was, moreover, exceedingly successful, even to the point where it became a source of inspiration for its enemies.

The Monita played a role when the Societas Jesu was forbidden in Portugal in 1759. In less than a decade, France, Spain, Naples, and Parma followed suit, and in 1773 Pope Clemens XIV disbanded the order. Yet among its opponents, initial joy was soon replaced by the fear that it was surreptitiously regrouping, making something that had been partly secret entirely invisible. In the German-speaking lands, voices were raised to suggest that the Jesuits were behind the organization of secret societies fighting Protestantism and the Enlightenment; and soon they were said to have infiltrated the lodges and conquered Freemasonry from the inside. This drew the attention of Count Mirabeau (1749-1791), the future president of the French National Assembly and himself a Mason, who discussed the German secret societies after a visit to Prussia in 1786-1787. He compared the Jesuits to the (already suppressed) Order of the Illuminati, stressing their value as an example; and in this, he not only followed in the footsteps of the first Illuminatus, but at the same time prefigured many a nineteenth-century conspirator.

ILLUMINATI

In 1776 Adam Weishaupt (1748-1830), professor of Canon Law at the University of Ingolstadt, founded a secret society that (after discarding the names of Perfectibilists and Order of the Bees) became known as the Order of the Illuminati. By attracting prominent members, it aimed to obtain important positions in society and thus to establish a moral regime that would lead all citizens back to the original state of liberty and equality. To this end, Weishaupt designed a graded organization based on elements taken from Freemasonry and the Jesuit Order (as he perceived it) and headed by a few higher degrees whose very existence was to remain unknown. Only this invisible inner circle was acquainted with the aims of the order; the lower degrees, whose understanding was deemed insufficient, were persuaded that fewer radical goals were pursued. The Illuminati tried to seize control of certain Masonic lodges to use them for propaganda and recruitment, a method that was to prove popular with many nineteenth-century revolutionaries. Due in large part to the efforts of Baron Adolph von Knigge (1752-1796), the future author of an immensely popular book of manners, Über den Umgang mit Menschen, and the organization succeeded in the first half of the 1780s in expanding from Bavaria to the rest of Germany.

It numbered between 1000 and 2000 members, among them several princes as well as intellectuals such as Goethe, Herder, and Pestalozzi. Yet it was discovered and outlawed in 1785, even though the official publication of many of its programs and other documents generated much publicity for its ideas. The Originalschriften exposed the Illuminati as living proof of how the Enlightenment conspired against the existing order and hence prepared the way for them to be accused, after the earthquake of the French Revolution, of being its subterranean cause. In 1797 the former Jesuit Augustin de Barruel (Mémoires pour servir à l'histoire du Jacobinisme) and the Scottish physicist John Robison (Proofs of a Conspiracy against All the Religions and Governments of Europe) published the two best known outlines of this conspiracy theory. In the years of bewildering revolution and unprecedented warfare their argument made a deep and lasting impression.

CARBONARI

Napoleon's slow fall in 1813-1815 left many European regions in an unstable situation: a simple return to the ancien régime was impossible, yet there were no viable alternatives in sight. As a result, the years of 1815-1830 were marked by a virtually uninterrupted series of political assassinations, military conspiracies, and popular revolts in Spain, France, a number of German and Italian states, Greece, Russia, the Netherlands, and Poland; and as a matter of course, the names of secret societies were linked to all of those events. Pride of place was given to the Carbonari of the kingdom of the Two Sicilies. This was due to the time they had existed (going back to just after the French occupation of Naples in 1806), their size (it was really a large movement, which even included priests in spite of the interdict by the Church), and the almost perfect image of the romantic rebel they evoked. The origins of the 'coal-burners' remained obscure, but there was a clear similarity to the graded organization and initiation rites of Freemasonry, which to conservatives had been the instrument of choice of the Illuminati in bringing about the French Revolution. This impression was only confirmed when the Carbonari actually came to play a vital role in the Italian insurrections of 1820-1821. Ever since, the term carbonaro was used to designate a revolutionary conspirator all over Europe. We know several program documents of the Carbonari. Their rules were quickly translated into French by Edme-Théodore Bourg (1785-1852), a one-time secretary to Napoleon's marshal Berthier, who wrote under the name of Saint-Edme. His text is much the same as the Italian version published by Alessandro Luzio in IL processo Pellico-Maroncelli (1903).

BURSCHENSCHAFTEN

On March 23, 1819, the popular German writer August von Kotzebue was killed in Mannheim as a 'Traitor to the fatherland' by a student of Theology, Carl Ludwig Sand (1795-1820). Kotzebue, who was also a Russian consul, had sharply denounced the Burschenschaften, the new student associations that after the expulsion of the French had come to demand a free and Christian unified German state (and which had burned Kotzebue's Geschichte des deutschen Reichs together with the Code Napoléon at the Wartburg festival of 1817). Sand was a member of the original or Urburschenschaft in Jena, of its inner circle (engere Verein), and of the Unbedingten (Uncompromising Ones), a secret radical group founded by Carl Follen. Kotzebue's assassination triggered the convocation of a conference of the German Confederation at Karlsbad (Karlovy Vary), which in August 1819 issued a series of decrees against 'demagoguery' and established a Central Commission of Investigation in Mainz. The Commission would contribute substantially to institutionalizing the concept of 'secret society' and spreading the notion that dangerous groupings lurked everywhere.

Another contribution came from Sand's friend Johannes Wit (or Witt, 1799-1863), a Dane by birth, who assumed the name of Wit von Dörring, after his stepfather. Wit's biography is as rich in riddles as adventures. At first a member of the Unbedingten, he abandoned his revolutionary ideas after 1820, or that's what he later said. His actual behavior made him extremely hard to judge, as on his travels all over Europe he switched with apparent ease from conservative to radical circles and back. Yet, since he combined a meddlesome nature with an inflated ego and found himself repeatedly in highly ambivalent circumstances, he ended up being mistrusted by both the revolutionaries and the police. During (and indeed also before) his years of imprisonment in five countries, he gave the authorities extensive and sensational, but unreliable information on the radical underground. Much of this he subsequently published in many volumes of memoirs, which are the source of a number of myths and half-truths that may still be encountered today. Later in life he advocated abstinence, protected orphans, and headed an official Austrian press agency that never materialized

GRAND FIRMAMENT

Gioacchino (Giovacchino) Prati (1790-1863), who spent most of his life as an exile, and a poor one at that, was born in the Trentino, studied in Vienna, Landshut, and Milan, and became a medical doctor and a lawyer. During his study he was already engaged in various secret societies, but his revolutionary activity really took shape after he fled (probably because of debts) to Chur, Switzerland, in 1816. There, with the German exiles Carl Follen and Wilhelm Snell, he established a political triumvirate that tried to link French, German, and Italian organizations in a European underground center. This fitted well with the efforts of Filippo Buonarroti (1761-1837), an Italian-French revolutionary whose experience went back to the conspiracy of Gracchus Babeuf in 1796 and whom Prati greatly admired. Living in Geneva since 1806, Buonarroti frequently attempted to submit other secret societies to his own in order to steer them on the right path. In the early 1820s, this fed into speculations, both in revolutionary and police circles, about the existence of one over-arching revolutionary committee, the Grand Firmament, with its seat in Paris or Geneva. Though nothing indicates that the project of a 'secret International' ever attained any substance, the Holy Alliance took it quite seriously.

It put increased pressure on Switzerland, which was increasingly considered a 'failed state' because of the many fugitives it harbored. In 1823 the Swiss finally gave in: Buonarroti was forced to move to Brussels, where in 1828 he published his Conspiration pour l'Egalité on the events of 1796, and Prati departed for London, where he would become an ardent adherent of Saint-Simonism. It should be noted that their position had become all the more compromised after Alexandre Andryane (1797-1863), one of Buonarroti's lieutenants, had been arrested in Milan in January 1823 with letters and documents intended for Italian acquaintances. This gave the Austrian police a wealth of information on the Sublimes Maîtres Parfaits, and proof of the existence of a conspiracy. Andryane was condemned to death, but his sentence was modified to life imprisonment in the castle of Spielberg at Brünn (Brno). In 1832 he was pardoned. He returned to France and wrote two volumes of memoirs, which went through several printings, but are not always to be trusted. Still, his tale provides a glimpse of how Buonarroti recruited the members of his secret societies and what went on at their meetings.

FRANCE

The July Revolution of 1830 brought an end to the French Restoration, but not to the monarchy - nor, consequently, to the republican secret societies, some of whose programs began to include social-revolutionary elements. Auguste Blanqui (1805-1881) perhaps contributed more than anyone to the amalgamation of the two traditions, putting the radical-liberal tactics of a semi-military coup d'état at the service of his communist ideas. For him, secret societies were an almost natural way of association, and he even tried to lead them from the dozens of prisons where he spent more than half of his adult life. In 1834, with Armand Barbès and Martin Bernard, he organized the Société des Familles, and after its discovery, the Société des Saisons. The name reflects the structure: the Society of the Seasons was constructed of units of seven people, who formed a Week, four Weeks formed a Month, and so on. On May 12, 1839, the organization attempted an insurrection in Paris. It was unsuccessful, and in the course of the following months all of the most important participants were arrested and brought before the courts in two groups. In the first case, Barbès was condemned to death, and in the second, Blanqui; yet both sentences were changed to life imprisonment. The proceedings of the court cases were published as a book - one of many ways in which the doings of secret societies became known to the public at large.

GERMANY

Since migrants usually need protection more than others, in an environment where their status is often contested, they have always been great founders of secret societies all over the world. Some of the best researched among them are the organizations founded by German artisans in Paris and Switzerland in the second quarter of the nineteenth century. Perhaps the most Conspiracy famous one originated when the public German People's Association (Deutsche Volksverein) in Paris was transformed in the spring of 1834 into the League of Outlaws (Bund der Geächteten), which took a Carbonari-like form. The writer Jacob Venedey (1805-1871), who had fled to France in 1833, and the lawyer Theodor Schuster were the most important leaders. Venedey later withdrew from radical circles, although he was still on the left in the German Parliament that gathered in Frankfurt after the Revolution of 1848.The members of the League of Outlaws, which extended its influence to a few German cities, drew inspiration from French communism as outlined in Filippo Buonarroti's formulation of the ideas of Gracchus Babeuf. Early in 1834, the German People's Association had already translated a text of Charles Teste, in which this companion of Buonarroti had given his own interpretation of the 'Declaration of the Rights of Man and of the Citizen'. Together with the Creed of an Outlaw, published around the same time, Teste's pamphlet would constitute the political program of the secret organization. After a few years, the League of Outlaws split. Most members joined the new League of the Just (Bund der Gerechten), from which the Communist League (Bund der Kommunisten) sprang in 1827.

RUSSIA

When the Polytechnicum, as the Eidgenössische Technische Hochschule was then known, became one of the first institutions of higher education in Europe to admit women, in the early 1870s dozens of young Russian women flocked to Zurich, most often to study medicine. They met the radical Russian exiles who had fled there before, and when Tsar Alexander II ordered them to return to Russia in 1873, they took home the fight for social justice. Some of the former students, most of them around twenty years old, established the Allrussian Social-Revolutionary Organization, also known as the Moscow Circle. They tried to introduce socialist ideas to the factories, but were soon rounded up, and were accused in 1877 in what became known as the Trial of the Fifty. The government brought the case in order to discredit the accused, but its intention backfired: especially the defense of Sof'ya Bardina (1852-1883) made a deep impression and set an example for others. That this was not necessarily peaceful was demonstrated by Vera Zasulich, who less than a year after the trial shot the chief of the St Petersburg police.

Most Russians in Zurich shared the ideas of either Pyotr Lavrov, who stressed the importance of propaganda, or Mikhail Bakunin, who considered a popular revolution inevitable. Bakunin also played a prominent role in the international workers' movement and, in his double quality of Russian and conspirator, had become a target of criticism by Karl Marx and Friedrich Engels. Yet, from the point of view of the East, the combination of Russia with secret societies was obvious rather than strange, as Pyotr Tkachov (1844-1886) explained in reply to an article by Engels. Tkachov, who, from his stay at the University of St Petersburg in 1861 to his flight to Switzerland in 1873, had alternated revolutionary activity with prison, belonged to neither of the two Zurich groups. In his opinion (which had earned him the sobriquet 'Russian Jacobin') equality was an ideal that could only be realized in Russia by means of a strictly organized revolutionary elite that would seize power in the state. Tkachov's posthumous reputation is partly based on his youthful remark, publicized by Albert Camus, that the real renewal of society can only be obtained by liquidating everyone above the age of twenty-five.

UNITED STATES

The United States shows how migrants often take their own model of a secret society with them. The fraternity derived from English Freemasonry, publicly known yet secret, was particularly popular. From the mid-nineteenth until well into the twentieth century, some tens of millions of men (and far fewer women) were members of fraternal orders, which as a matter of fact often also functioned as insurance companies. Among the numerous new organizations that sprang up after the Civil War was the Ku Klux Klan (from the Greek kuklos, circle), founded in Tennessee in 1866, but disbanded after a few violent years. In part as a result of the success of Birth of a Nation, the movie by D.W. Griffith, the Klan was resurrected in 1915 and, after the US entered WW I, evolved into a militant white enemy of Catholics, Blacks, Jews, strikers, and others deemed un-American. In the mid-1920s it counted some 3 million members, but by the end of the decade membership was closer to 100,000, and the mass movement dwindled to a sect. The Irish migrants to the coal fields of Pennsylvania in the mid-nineteenth century imported a different tradition. Since 1760 the Irish countryside had had underground organizations, whose members were over time called Whiteboys, Ribbonmen, or Molly Maguires, who were engaged in intermittent fights against the landowners. In Pennsylvania, amid the more skilled English and Welsh miners, the Irish clearly were at the bottom of the social scale.

When they tried to defend themselves against deteriorating Labor conditions after the Civil War, their old organizational traditions resurfaced in the framework of the local lodges of the Ancient Order of Hibernians, an Irish-American brotherhood that normally followed the English pattern. Economic developments, efforts to establish a trade union, tensions among the Catholic Irish due to the Church's aversion to secret societies, the customary toughness of the mining region - these and other elements contributed to a growing climate of violence, for which the Molly Maguires were blamed. The Philadelphia & Reading Railroad, which had acquired many of the mines, hired the Pinkerton Detective Agency, one of whose agents, James McParlan, infiltrated the group under the alias of McKenna. From the mid-1870s, this resulted in arrests, trials, and 20 death sentences. For Allan Pinkerton, the Mollies were part of a success story that gave his agency a name and provided the material for a sensational book.

ASIA

In the course of the nineteenth century Europe's colonial powers increasingly often discovered the existence of 'secret societies' in their colonies. The name was applied to remarkably diverse groupings. To take a famous example, in the second part of the eighteenth century, local migrants in South China created mutual benefit societies, which for assorted reasons were soon persecuted by the authorities. Thus, the Heaven and Earth Society (Tiandihui), as the groups were collectively known, acquired an anti-Manchu, nationalist, or even revolutionary reputation. Together with thousands of Chinese migrants, their organizational form spread throughout Southeast Asia and came to the attention of British and Dutch officials. Some of them perceived a similarity to Freemasonry or believed that the kongsis could play a role in administering the Chinese communities. In the long run, however, most officers looked askance at their activities, many of which were criminalized with the development of colonial legislation. In spite (or because) of this, the Triads continued to expand and easily outlived colonialism. Moreover, they became hugely popular in the Western imagination for sharing a fascination for the Shaolin monastery and the martial arts with Bruce Lee. Associated in popular culture with Indiana Jones were the Thugs or Stranglers from central India.

In the 1820s William Sleeman, an officer of the British East India Company, began systematically to collect certain murder stories that sounded pretty unusual. His research persuaded him he was on the trail of a secret brotherhood that ritually strangled travelers as sacrifices to their goddess Kali. Sleeman's grandson later calculated that the Thugs had caused 40,000 victims a year over several centuries, but what is certain is that between 1826 and 1848 about 4,500 people were tried for Thuggee, 500 of whom were hanged. The startling nature of Sleeman's discovery caused a sensation in Europe, thanks also to the fictionalized Confessions of a Thug from the pen of Philip Meadows Taylor (1839). Eugène Sue (1804-1857) used the topic for Le Juif errant, whose serialized publication in le Constitutionnel in 1844-1845 quintupled the print run of the paper. This may have been due to the main character, Rodin, a cunning, proverbial Jesuit, who attempts to rob a Protestant family of an old inheritance - the novel appeared during a new round of commotion concerning the Societas Jesu - but it certainly helped that he had a Dutch merchant in Batavia hire the Thugs for some special operations.

PRECURSORS

In the course of the nineteenth century, European interest in secret societies not only expanded across countries due to the blossoming of ethnography, but also in time, with new disciplines such as the history of religion discovering a rich past. Egyptian, Greek, and other ancient 'mystery religions' attracted much attention, being linked to a long literary-utopian tradition. One remarkable example was the organization of the Pythagoreans, legendary already in Antiquity, as painted by Sylvain Maréchal (1750-1803). In 1796 this poet had been involved in the conspiracy of Gracchus Babeuf against the Directory, which tried to get political affairs in France on a new track after the fall of Robespierre. At the end of his imaginary tale of the voyages of Pythagoras written a few years later, Maréchal has the Greek philosopher summarize the rules of his school, in which secrecy was always highly valued. The first and last law of our association, Pythagoras says, is the return to the original state when everything was held in common - thus formulating the very principle of Babeuf's program. Old, yet non-imaginary tales of travel also proved of sudden interest. Olfert Dapper (1635? -1689), of Amsterdam, for instance, writing about the kingdom of Kquoja in present-day Sierra Leone, was the first one to mention the secret societies of men and women that are known as Poro and Sande. Not every anthropologist is happy with the use of the term 'secret society' in this context, but the tradition is stubborn. Dapper himself never traveled; for this part of his work, he probably relied on an eyewitness, perhaps the Dutch merchant Samuel Blommaert, a director of the West India Company. It is likely, though, that the illustrations in his book, often reproduced as genuine, were the fruit of his publisher's imagination.

Literature

The literature on secret societies is immense and of extremely unequal quality. The dozen titles below are therefore entirely unrepresentative. These are all interesting books based on thorough archival research, which throw light on important aspects of the phenomenon.

- Maurice Agulhon, Pénitents et Franc-Maçons de l'ancienne Provence: essai sur la sociabilité méridionale, Paris: Fayard, 1968 (IISH call number: 32/40) Demonstrates how the more well-off members of the old religious fraternities switched to the more restricted secular lodges in the eighteenth century; and stimulated academic interest in Freemasonry to such an extent that its bibliography is now hopelessly out-of-date. For an update, see Pierre-Yves Beaurepaire, L'Espace des Franc-Maçons (2003).

- Johann Joachim Christoph Bode, Journal von einer Reise von Weimar nach Frankreich im Jahr 1787, ed Hermann Schüttler, Neuried: ars una, 1994 (IISH call number: 2006/661) The rediscovered diary of a prominent Illuminatus, whose trip to Paris figures in the conspiracy literature as a crucial step in the launch of the French Revolution. With extensive notes and an introduction by a major specialist.

- J.M. Roberts, The Mythology of the Secret Societies, London: Secker & Warburg, 1972 (IISH call number: 74/50) A now classic study, the first to place the European secret societies of the Restoration in perspective, throwing doubt on both their effectiveness and the danger they posed.

- Ferdinand de Bertier, Souvenirs inédits d'un conspirateur: Révolution, Empire et première Restauration, ed Guillaume de Bertier de Sauvigny, Paris: Tallandier, 1990 (IISH call number: 2006/8360). The memoirs of a royalist conspirator against Napoleon, who joined Freemasonry in order to learn how to build a Catholic secret society, the Chevaliers de la Foi. Edited by a historian of the Restoration who happens to be a descendant of the author. Vito Dicara, Elite di periferia: conflitti locali e carboneria a Caltagirone tra monarchia amministrativa e guerra independentista, Caltanissetta: Ed Lussografica, 2004 (IISH call number: 2006/8372) A detailed study of Carbonaro life in the political and social context of a small Sicilian town.

- Pierre-Arnaud Lambert, La Charbonnerie française 1821-1823: du secret en politique, Lyon: Presses universitaires de Lyon, 1995 (IISH call number: 1997/2865) Written by a political scientist, who naturally relied on Alan Spitzer's Old Hatreds and Young Hopes (1971), this book compares the Charbonnerie to other French, German, and Italian secret societies. Unusually, it pays serious attention to such documents as their rules, which tend to be neglected in favor of program documents.

- Geoffrey Cubitt, The Jesuit Myth: conspiracy theory and politics in nineteenth-century France, Oxford: Clarendon, 1993 (IISH call number: 1994/811) Inventory and analysis of the anti-Jesuit conspiracy theories that formed the progressive counterpart to certain conservative views on Freemasonry and were never absent from the political debate in nineteenth-century France and several other countries.

- David MacKenzie, Violent Solutions: revolutions, nationalism, and secret societies in Europe to 1918, Lanham, MD etc. University Press of America, 1996 (IISH call number: 1997/5211) The greatest authority on the notorious Black Hand puts this

Serbian secret society in a European perspective emphasizing, alongside Greek and Russian examples, the parallels from the history of Italian and German unification.

- Kevin Kenny, Making Sense of the Molly Maguires, New York etc. Oxford University Press, 1998 (IISH call number: 1999/1159). A study of the organization of the Irish miners in Pennsylvania in the third quarter of the nineteenth century, which for the first time calls attention to the traditions existing in the Irish counties from which the migrants came.

- Dian H. Murray, in coll with Qin Baoqi, The Origins of the Tiandihui: the Chinese Triads in legend and history, Stanford, CA: Stanford University Press, 1994 (IISH call number: 1999/1495) A comparative historiographic study of how the perception of the renowned Chinese secret societies developed, in China and elsewhere. At the same time, an excellent introduction to the social-historical work of David Ownby (1996) and the historical-anthropological analysis of Barend ter Haar (1998).

- Helmut Möller, Ellic Howe, Merlin Peregrinus: vom Untergrund des Abendlandes, Würzburg: Königshausen + Neumann, 1986 (IISH call number: 2006/8375) The story of Theodor Reuss (1855-1923), who from anarchist exile developed into the animating force of the Ordo Templis Orientis and was remarkable even among the many adventurers who at the turn of the nineteenth to twentieth century explored the boundaries of Western civilization.

- Maria Carlson, 'No Religion Higher than Truth': a history of the theosophical movement in Russia, 1875-1922, Princeton, NJ: Princeton University Press, 1993 (IISH call number: 1993/2251) Like the English Theosophical Society, studied by Joy Dixon in Divine Feminine (2001), its Russian sister organization was in many respects a secret society run by women; and even more than its English example the Russian movement had a profound influence on modern art.

17. One Giant Step for Man, One Giant Fucking Lie Bro!!!

The U.S. Military Has Been In Space from the Beginning

While the proposed branch of the armed forces may be controversial, the history of the so-called 'Space Force' is longstanding. The words 'Space Force' conjure up images of plastoid-alloy-clad soldiers firing ray guns at aliens, but military activities in space aren't just science fiction. The U.S. military has been involved with space since the beginning, just, perhaps, not under that name. Today, Vice President Mike Pence revealed that the administration hopes to have Space Force ready to fly by 2020 during a speech at the Pentagon. The proposal still needs congressional approval, but White House officials have steadily been pushing forward without the support of Congress. Initial moves to establish a U.S. Space Command (a combatant unit dedicated to defending space) could start by the end of the year. That would require pulling space experts from across all branches of the military and creating an office dedicated to developing space weapons and acquiring satellites. Pence also announced a new civilian position, Assistant Secretary of Defense for Space that would oversee the establishment of the Space Force. In June, during a meeting of the National Space Council at the White House, President Donald Trump spoke on the subject. 'My administration is reclaiming America's heritage as the world's greatest space-faring nation. The essence of the American character is to explore new horizons and to tame new frontiers. But our destiny, beyond the Earth, is not only a matter of national identity, but a matter of national security,' he announced. 'It is not enough to merely have an American presence in space. We must have American dominance in space.'

Yet if the idea is to ensure the military is involved in space, a dedicated space force may not be needed; the military has been in space since space was a place you could be in. As early as 1915, the newly established National Advisory Committee for Aeronautics (NACA) was dominated by military personnel and industry executives. NACA laboratories helped develop many technologies that ended up in military aircraft during World War II. After that, NACA worked with the Air Force to develop planes capable of supersonic flight. It then moved on to working on ballistic missile designs and in the 1950s began developing plans for manned flight. In 1958, a year after the U.S.S. R's launch of the first ballistic missile and Sputnik satellite kick started the Space Race, NACA was rolled into the newly created NASA, a civilian agency which had a broader mandate, more power, and more resources. Clinton Parks at Space.com reports that the civilian nature of NASA was never a given. Senate Majority Leader Lyndon Johnson wanted to establish a space agency to make sure the United States controlled space militarily. President Eisenhower didn't want a space agency at all, believing it was a waste of money. Eventually, the two compromised, creating a civilian agency after Johnson was convinced space wasn't just a potential battlefield, but that a platform for scientific and technological advancement that would be a huge boon for the U.S. and commercial interests.

The establishment of NASA did not mean an end for the U.S. military in space, though many of its projects among the stars were and still are classified. In fact, during the 1960s, the U.S. Air Force ran a parallel staffed space program to the one run by NASA, even designing an orbiting 'Laboratory' and selecting a class of 17 astronauts. Though it ran for six years, the program was cancelled in 1969 and no Air Force astronauts were launched (that we know of). In 1982, the Air Force Space Command was officially established, and today employs 35,000 people. The agency works on cybersecurity, launches satellites and other payloads for the military and other government agencies, monitors ballistic missile launches and orbiting satellites and runs a military GPS system. And of course, there's plenty of things they do that we don't know about. For instance, it's well documented that the Air Force has two X-37B space planes, including one that returned to Earth last year after two years in orbit, though what it was doing is unknown.

And NASA and the military also maintain a strong relationship. Over the decades, the vast majority of NASA astronauts have been military service members. During the heyday of the space shuttle, NASA would routinely ferry classified payloads into orbit for the Department of Defense among other projects the agencies have collaborated on. As for the President's directive to create a new space force, Alex Ward at Vox reports that it may not be valid. Constitutionally, only Congress has the authority to 'Raise and support armies.' The last branch to be created, the Air Force, was created by an act of Congress in 1947. Todd Harrison, director of the aerospace security project at the Center for Strategic and International Studies tells Patrick Kelley at Roll Call that 'The President can't create a new military service on his own. There's going to have to be legislation.' What's more, the military seems resistant to the idea of separating out a Space Force from the Air Force. Secretary of Defense Jim Mattis, for one, has gone on the record opposing the creation of a space force. Last summer, when a Space Corps proposal was floated in Congress, Mattis wrote in a letter that it would add an 'Additional organizational and administrative tail' and excess layers of bureaucracy to military operations.

At the time, the White House also called the establishment of a space branch 'Premature.' Officials from the Air Force also went on record saying the move would add costs and unnecessary layers of bureaucracy to current space operations and that they would rather space operations become more integrated into the Air Force's mission. That's not to say the U.S. military isn't focusing on potential threats in space. Military analyst Lt. Col. Rick Francona tells Euan McKirdy at CNN that military leaders definitely have an eye on the sky. 'I hate the term 'the final frontier' but (space) is the ultimate high ground. Space doesn't dominate one small geographic area, it dominates continents, oceans,' he says. 'Most military thinkers know this is the battle space of the future.' Deborah Lee James, Air Force secretary during the Obama administration, agrees, pointing out that many critical satellites and communications devices necessary for modern warfare are located in space, and that other nations, China, and Russia in particular, are making moves to control the region around Earth. 'Space is no longer a peaceful domain,' she told Ward last July. 'There is a real possibility that a conflict on Earth could bleed into space.'

Classified Shuttle Missions: Secrets in Space

STS-39 Mission - Specialist Charles L. Veach monitors an AFP-675 panel on Discovery's aft flight deck. The space shuttle was NASA's primary option for transporting astronauts to Earth orbit between 1981 and 2011. The five shuttles that went into space flew 135 missions. Crews deployed satellites, conducted experiments, and studied the Earth. A handful of the missions were classified, and little is known about these secret missions, even 30 years after the fact. Joint operations in the early days of the space shuttle program, some of the missions were run jointly by NASA and the military. This was in part because the National Reconnaissance Office had successfully requested the shuttle's payload bay, the part of the shuttle that carried satellites be carried into space, be enlarged to accommodate large military satellites, according to Air & Space Magazine. NRO also wanted polar shuttle missions, since polar missions make it possible to see the Earth's entire surface below (as opposed to equatorial missions, which are limited.) The Air Force went as far as to create a launch pad in Vandenberg, California for polar-orbiting space shuttle missions, but after the Challenger incident, plans to use the pad were permanently mothballed. After the Challenger disaster on Jan. 28, 1986, U.S. policy changed to allow the Department of Defense to use expendable, unscrewed rockets again. Classified shuttle flights continued with payloads that could not be shifted to the Titan IV rocket, the magazine added. The astronauts encountered considerable challenges in keeping information secret since the shuttle did not have secure information channels, and their movements and training operations had to be somehow kept separate in a normally open public agency. Here is some of what we know about the missions with DOD.

STS-4 Columbia (Launched June 27, 1982) - The classified payload was known as Cryogenic Infrared Radiance Instrument for Shuttle (CIRRIS), which was supposed to test infrared sensors for a future surveillance satellite called Teal Ruby, according to America Space. The lens cap on CIRRIS failed to open, and the experiment failed. America Space added that Teal Ruby ended up being cancelled after the Challenger incident, which delayed shuttle flights by several years. 'Teal Ruby was first shifted onto STS-39 and finally cancelled,' the publication said. 'By the time STS-39 lifted off in April 1991, it carried not Teal Ruby … but an updated version of CIRRIS. Apparently, by the time it would have been ready to launch, the Teal Ruby technology considered 'Advanced' in the late 1970s, would be virtually obsolete, because sensor technology was advancing rapidly.'

STS-51C Discovery (Launched Jan. 24, 1985) - Little is known about STS-51C's payload officially besides this terse line on the NASA website: 'The U.S. Air Force Inertial Upper Stage (IUS) booster was deployed and met the mission objectives.' Multiple sources suggest that the satellite deployed was called Magnum/ORION ELINT, a signals intelligence program about which little is known. Before launch, no pre-flight commentary was available until nine minutes before liftoff, a first in the shuttle program.

STS-51J Atlantis (Launched Oct. 3, 1985) - Two Defense Satellite Communications System satellites were released on this mission, according to NASA. The system is intended to support secure data and voice transmissions for military users from across the globe.

STS-62A Discovery (Cancelled) - This mission was supposed to be the first one using the Air Force pad in Vandenberg, Calif., but it was cancelled after the Challenger explosion. Its main mission was to put Teal Ruby into orbit, according to NASASpaceflight.com.

STS-27 Atlantis (Launched Dec. 2, 1988) - It's probable that the crew released a satellite called ONYX, which had radar on board capable of observing targets on the ground through any kind of weather or cloud cover. According to Air&Space Magazine, one of the satellite's antenna dishes did not open and the crew possibly, although it's not confirmed officially, did a spacewalk to fix the issue.

STS-28 Columbia (Launched Aug. 8, 1989) - Air&Space Magazine reports that STS-28 hauled the Satellite Data System spacecraft into orbit; SDS was supposed to relay imagery from other military satellites. The magazine got confirmation on this from an Air Force officer, who was not named in the story.

STS-33 Discovery (Launched Nov. 22, 1989) - NASA's website simply says this was a Department of Defense mission. The payload has not been confirmed.

STS-36 Atlantis (Launched Feb. 28, 1990) - There are many theories as to what STS-36 carried, but nothing has been officially confirmed. The shuttle's ground track took it as high as 62 degrees, which is a record for the shuttle program.

STS-38 Atlantis (Launched Nov. 15, 1990) - NASA's website only says that this was a Department of Defense mission. No confirmed information about the payload is available.

STS-39 Discovery (Launched April 28, 1991) - The Air Force partially declassified this mission before launch. The unclassified payload was known as Air Force Program-675 (AFP-675), which was an updated version of CIRRIS. According to NASA, the classified payload 'Consisted of Multi-Purpose Release Canister (MPEC),' but no further information appears to be available.

STS-53 Discovery (Launched Dec. 2, 1992) - The main payload for this mission remains classified, with little information about what it could be.

What Does Trumps Space Force Mean For The Secret Space Force? What's going on in Space?

An unclassified Department of Defense document, one of many, shows high interest from the United States to weaponize space, as well as detonate weapons in outer space. It's from the 1950's, and for those who've looked into space matters over the years, it comes as no surprise at all that Donald Trump is announcing a new branch of the military, a United States Space Force. But there is also something confusing, a secret space force in existence long before Trump came into office. Whoever they are, they must really not like that Trump would bring attention to these efforts... But who knows, politics has become nothing, but a tool used by the Deep State so it's hard to tell what's really going on. Ultimately, the human race can evolve past the need for such a system, one that's corrupt and serves the human race no purpose or platform to move forward. To complement that, we have testimony from a number of high ranking military whistle-blowers who have said some pretty unbelievable things, like Colonel Ross Dedrickson, a man who had a long stint with the US Atomic Energy Commission, saying that the US actually tried to detonate a nuclear weapon on the moon for testing, and that this was 'Not acceptable to the extraterrestrials.' We'll get to that later... The point is, there is a good chance we've been in outer space, and the militarization of it has been in the works or, to some extent, has probably already been accomplished. This is the stuff black budgets are made of restricted access programs (SAPs) that have no oversight from Congress. Some today refer to them as 'unacknowledged special access programs.'

This idea gained even more traction several years ago when the largest (publicly disclosed) military computer hack of all time took place. What type of information is hidden from the public? You will have to ask Gary Mckinnon. In 2002 the U.S. government charged and arrested Gary for the hack. So, what did Gary find? He found a list of non-terrestrial off-world officers of rank. He was unable to tell if they represented the Air Force, Navy, or Army. He also found multiple pictures of UFOs and lists of fleet-to-fleet transfers of materials from ship to ship... Whatever that means. You can watch an interview with Gary in this article we published years ago, it's where the quotes above come from. Even comments made not long ago from the recently retired Aerospace Director at Lockheed Martin, Steven Justice, have raised some eye-brows of what kind of technology is out there. Prior to Trump speaking out, The House Armed Services Committee voted to split the US Air Force, which will lead to the creation of the US Space Corps. This would make America the only nation with a branch of military dedicated to space, as far as we know. Let's not forget about the already existing United Air Force Space Command. This would, therefore, be the first new military branch created in the U.S. since 1947.

'This is an issue the subcommittee has studied for months, and I can't even tell you how many meetings with space experts and leaders [Democratic Rep.] Jim [Cooper] and I have had on this subject,' Rep. Mike Rogers (R-AL), Chairman of the House Armed Services Subcommittee on Strategic Forces stated.

According to IFL Science, "The subcommittee believes this move will help the US maintain their strategic advantage in space. But not all members of the committee were equally pleased with this as the mark-up (proposed legislation before it is passed) was only discussed in a couple of meetings." Why The Plans To Weaponize Space? Remember the big Wikileaks release of emails? One in particular to John Podesta by astronaut Dr. Edgar Mitchel stated,

Dear John. Because the War in Space race is heating up, I felt you should be aware of several factors as you and I schedule our Skype talk. Remember, our nonviolent ETI from the contiguous universe are helping us bring zero point energy to Earth. They will not tolerate any forms of military violence on Earth or in space. The following information in italics was shared with me by my colleague Carol Rosin, who worked closely for several years with Wernher von Braun before his death. Carol and I have worked on the Treaty on the Prevention of the Placement of Weapons in Outer Space, attached for your convenience. You can read the rest of the email straight from Wikileaks here, and also download the documents attached on the website. It's interesting because he mentions Carol Rosin, the first female corporate manager of Fairchild Industries. A space and missile defense consultant who has worked with various corporations, government departments, and intelligence communities, she worked closely with Wernher Von Braun shortly before his death, specifically on the subject of space-based weapons.

According to her,

I met the late Dr Wernher Von Braun in early 74, at that time Von Braun was dying of cancer, but he assured me that he would live a few more years in order to tell me about the game that was being played, that game being the effort to weaponize space, to control Earth from space and space itself. He asked me to be his spokesperson, to appear on occasions when he was too ill to speak, and I did. And what he asked me to do was to educate decision makers and the public about why we shouldn't be putting weapons into space . . . and what the alternatives are, how we could be building a cooperative space system. What was most interesting to me, was a repetitive sentence that he said to me over and over again. . .. And that was the strategy that was being used to educate the public and decision makers, and the scare tactics, the spin that was being put on the weapons system. And that was how we identify an enemy. The enemy at first he said, the enemy against whom we're going to build a space based weapons system . . . First the Russians are going to be considered the enemy . . . then terrorists would be identified and that was soon to follow . . . then we were going to identify third world crazies, we now call them nations of concern. . .. The next enemy was asteroids . . . and against asteroids we're going to build space based weapons. And the funniest one of all, was against what he called aliens, extraterrestrials that would be the final card. And over, and over, and over during the four years that I knew him and was giving his speeches for him, he would bring up that last card. 'And remember Carol, the last card is the alien card. We're going to have to build space based weapons against aliens,' and all of it, he said, is a lie.

This wouldn't come as a surprise, terrorism, and the entire war on terror has been a fabrication in a large sense, a script, events created to justify the infiltration of other countries.

'I spent 33 years and four months in active military service and during that period I spent most of my time as a high class muscle man for Big Business, for Wall Street and the bankers. In short, I was a racketeer, a gangster for capitalism. I helped make Mexico and especially Tampico safe for American oil interests in 1914. I helped make Haiti and Cuba a decent place for the National City Bank boys to collect revenues in. I helped in the raping of half a dozen Central American republics for the benefit of Wall Street. I helped purify Nicaragua for the International Banking House of Brown Brothers in 1902-1912. I brought light to the Dominican Republic for the American sugar interests in 1916. I helped make Honduras right for the American fruit companies in 1903. In China in 1927 I helped see to it that Standard Oil went on its way unmolested. Looking back on it, I might have given Al Capone a few hints. The best he could do was to operate his racket in three districts. I operated on three continents.' Smedley D. Butler, War is a Racket: The Antiwar Classic by One of America's Most Decorated Soldier

Are we going to see the same thing with space? Why do we have to militarize everything? The truth is, we don't, and our consciousness is simply used to allowing those with that type of intention to do so. If there already exists a secret space program, run by 'A shadowy government with its own Air Force, its own Navy, its own fundraising mechanism' that has 'The ability to pursue its own ideas of the national interest, free from all checks and balances, and free from the law itself,' words expressed by Senator Daniel Inouye.

The recently unclassified but secretive Advanced Aerospace Threat Identification Program was funded $22 million from 2008 to 2011, with the vast majority of the funding going to Bigelow Airspace. That's a company conveniently owned by one of Reid's friends and donors, Robert Bigelow, though the program was also approved by since-deceased Senators Ted Stevens and Daniel Inouye. That $22 million enabled contractors to build a low-key Nevada warehouse for what they claimed was unidentified artifacts obtained from UFOs, as well as compile witness accounts. I also covered this story in more detail in this article titled, The US Government Just Admitted to Recovering Materials from UFOs- Recently Robert stated that he knows we are not alone, and that intelligent extraterrestrials are visiting us. If there is already a secret government and a secret space force operating in space, what is Trump doing here? Is he disrupting this force?

Above Majestic Producer Reveals Secret Space Program Disclosures & Document Dumps Imminent

Corey Goode, producer of the bestselling Above Majestic documentary, released a major update on November 17 concerning a new insider that he has privately met and vetted. The insider is a retired surgeon with 30 years' experience in a major branch of the US military and used the pseudonym 'Bones' after revealing his true identity. Goode says that after he met Bones about a year ago, he subsequently put Bones in touch with his other insider sources, including 'Sigmund,' another pseudonym used by former senior officer in a USAF run secret space program. Sigmund first met Goode in early 2016, when he was leading interrogations of Goode's information, which included classified information about the USAF program, which Goode calls the Military Industrial Complex Secret Space Program (MIC-SSP). Sigmund eventually had to go on the run from the Cabal/Deep State after confirming Goode's claims of a far more technologically advanced Navy run space program, Solar Warden. Sigmund eventually began working with the Secret Space Program (SSP) Alliance – a broad alliance of defectors from rival secret space programs and Solar Warden – who rescued him.

According to Goode, Bones passed on two hard drives with numerous digital files to Sigmund revealing details of the "Dark Fleet," which is a German run secret space program that originated out of their hidden Antarctica bases and alliance with a group of Reptilians called Dracos. After agreements were reached between the Germans and the Eisenhower Administration in the 1950's, the Germans were able to infiltrate all aspects of the US military industrial complex as Goode has previously explained. After the treaty was signed and the joint Secret Space Programs began in earnest, things quickly got out of hand and the Nazi Break Away group won the race to infiltrate and take over the other side. They soon controlled every aspect of the U.S. from the Financial System, The Military Industrial Complex, and soon after, all three branches of the government itself. Goode summarized what Bones told him regarding the classified name of the Dark Fleet which has still not been publicly revealed: When I asked him which program he was involved in, he looked me straight in the eyes and told me the actual classified program name. He then said, "I think you have been referring to this program as 'Dark Fleet.'

I was shocked to hear the actual name of this program dropped so freely. After arranging a meeting between Sigmund and Bones where the latter handed over digital files on the two hard drives, Goode described what Sigmund told him in an early morning meeting on November 17, 2018, at Lunar Operations Command, a former German moon base now controlled by the MIC-SSP: We sat there as Sigmund talked about the new intelligence they had received about the Dark Fleet. He went on to give a nearly 3-hour summary on what was found on the two hard drives that Bones had given them. Sigmund was visibly excited and stated 'We have everything! Their infrastructure, their lists of assets going back 80 years and where they are located. We now know of Dark Fleet bases in over a dozen different star systems as well as on the Earth and have the joint agreements and battle plans that the Dark Fleet had signed with the Draco's and an insectoid race as well as non-aggression pacts with other ET Groups.' I asked Goode today why Sigmund was able to travel safely to Lunar Operations Command (LOC) when the Cabal/Deep State was after him through their own space program that Goode has called the Interplanetary Corporate Conglomerate (ICC), which controls the LOC. He replied:

It is a joint facility and control is with ICC, but different programs think classified ppl from their own projects run everything. You have levels of SSP coming in and out. They timeshare the assets at the LOC's. Only middle brass ever see's the ppl that run the bases and the ppl that cycle in or are lower SSP's only have access to the middle brass, etc. Goode went on to state that the digital files Bones gave to Sigmund had enabled the SSP Alliance, working in tandem with the Earth Alliance (a consortium of White Hats in every major nation on the planet) to identify all Dark Fleet operatives, and subject them to sealed indictments and future arrests. Sigmund stated that they now had everything they needed to intercept Dark Fleet assets on every continent on Earth. They have now identified every Dark Fleet agent and double agent on the planet and how they have infiltrated the ICC and MIC SSP Programs. He was confident that they now had enough information to pass to the Earth Alliance for future indictments. Among the more than 60,000 sealed cases currently found in judicial records, the vast majority involve indictments, which will lead to arrests when unsealed.

Some of the looming arrests, according to Goode, involve Dark Fleet assets. It's furthermore worth pointing out that the Executive Order issued by Donald Trump on December 21, 2017, allows the confiscation of property of all those involved in human rights abuses and international corruption. This has allowed Trump's military backed government to systematically strip the Dark Fleet/Deep State of their financial assets, which were used to control the planet. What's particularly noteworthy is Goode's claim that all Dark Fleet assets in the solar system and even adjacent start systems, will be confiscated and handed over to White Hats who will ensure that these are eventually used for the benefit of all humanity. He wrote:

The SSP Alliance is also confident that they now have actionable intelligence on every ICC, Dark Fleet, Solar Warden and Intergalactic League of Nations base and asset in the galaxy and are ready once the action begins. I am told this will assure that the entire extra planetary infrastructure that has been built in secret will be available for use by a new system that has been outlined. This is a post-disclosure plan that a minority in the Earth Alliance has put a lot of planning into. Essentially, Goode is here stating that the new system will be something along the lines of 'Star Fleet' in the Star Trek series, whose creator Gene Rodenberry had been secretly briefed about the Navy's secret space program. Finally, Goode said that the SSP and Earth Alliance plan to use him for future disclosure dumps: He [Sigmund] went on to say that they are gathering information to release through me at a future date.

I was told that after this information was compiled it would then be given to me to disclose in a way that is beneficial to the SSP Alliance. I was also informed that at about the same time that I am cleared to drop the Dark Fleet information that I should also be cleared to release the information from my meeting at the LOC Alpha, Bravo & Charley, and the tour of ancient alien ruins within the Moon itself. Some of the information will be disclosed in documentaries similar to Above Majestic: The Implications of a Secret Space Program, which the SSP Alliance believes is an excellent way of disclosing the truth. Most importantly, the SSP Alliance is committed to full disclosure and wants to make a partial disclosure impossible: The SSP Alliance plan is unchanged, they plan to make a partial disclosure impossible and find a way to Full Disclosure thus delivering the entire 'SSP Infrastructure' to all of humanity on equal terms.

Goode shared with me additional information today explaining that Bones is not alone in sharing information about the Dark Fleet: BONES & 5 of his team of leakers, all between the ages of 68-82 were brought into protective custody by the SSP Alliance not long after the meeting where Bones handed over the 2 drives…. They had tons of videos of old timers giving death bed confessions and testimony on what they did in DF. I am told it is incredibly detailed and disturbing stuff. He also pointed out that the Dark Fleet (DF) and the ICC are concerned over the prospects of more defections as this information is revealed, and people are subject to sealed indictments and their financial assets confiscated. The ICC and DF know we received this Intel and are very worried. This intel release was approved because it would cause more of them to defect as there is a rumor that more and more of the DF assets have defected from the DF but have not joined SSP Alliance, it is speculated that they are trying to go rogue with their own program and assets that is totally broken away from our solar systems infrastructure At this stage some will ask whether there is any documentary evidence supporting any of Goode's incredible claims, especially his assertion that he will be used as a conduit for future document releases? Actually, there is. Goode was the person who first released two Unclassified for Official Use Only Defense Intelligence Reference Documents (DIRD), which were commissioned in 2007 by the forerunner to the Advanced Aerospace Threat Identification Program. The two documents are titled "Traversable Wormholes, Stargates, and Negative Energy" and "Warp Drive, Dark Energy, and the Manipulation of Extra Dimensions," the first was authored by Dr. Eric Davis, and the second co-authored by Dr. Richard Obousy and Davis.

In fact, Dr Davis confirmed the authenticity of the documents released by Goode, in a June 24, 2018, appearance on Coast to Coast radio, where he said: … that 2 or 3 of these papers had been "leaked" onto the Internet, by 'Someone on the beltway.' The beltway is a highway that encircles Washington. A reference to 'Inside the beltway' means matters of importance to US government officials; lobbyists; and government contractors. While most UFO researchers are reluctant to discuss Goode's role in releasing the DIRD documents, and instead point to less controversial sources such as Tom DeLonge's To The Stars Academy, and George Knapp's, iTeam, the fact is that out of 38 DIRD documents known to have been written, only three to date have been officially released, two by Goode, and one by Knapp's iTeam. What Goode's public release of the two DIRD papers conclusively show is that he does have high level access to genuine insiders with documents they have been authorized to release through him. This helps raise confidence in the accuracy of what Goode has revealed about Bones and Sigmund regarding the Dark Fleet, and the prospects for full disclosure through future document releases similar to the DIRD articles, and documentaries such as Above Majestic.

Conspiracy Theory Follows Call For 'Space Force'

Q: Did President Donald Trump call for the creation of a 'Space force' to fight off an 'Alien attack'?

A: No. The president did request exploration of a 'Space force,' but it is unrelated to extraterrestrial activity.

On June 18, President Donald Trump called for the creation of a 'Space force' a new branch of the military in addition to the Army, Air Force, Navy, Marines, and Coast Guard. By that afternoon, a conspiracy theory website had combined Trump's request with a made-up claim that the president had spoken with aliens and feared an 'Alien attack.' Outlandish? Yes. But the site called Truth Unsealed is run by a man who has a YouTube channel with more than 60,000 subscribers and a website dedicated to peddling the thoroughly debunked 'Pizzagate' conspiracy theory. That infamous conspiracy theory drove Edgar Maddison Welch to take an AR-15 rifle into the Comet Ping Pong pizza shop in Washington D.C., where he fired shots on Dec. 4, 2016. The alien story says in part:

Truth Unsealed, June 18:

Since assuming office on January 20, 2017, Trump has periodically exchanged messages with intelligent extraterrestrial life forms who, according to White House Press Secretary Sarah Huckabee Sanders, have provided him with advice and guidance on a multitude of issues including an impending attack from another world. 'They know he's an excellent negotiator, probably the best our planet has to offer and that's why they've elected to speak with him,' Secretary Sanders told a handful of reporters during an off-camera briefing on Wednesday. While Sanders could not comment on the extent or frequency of the encounters, she said President Trump is 'extremely humbled' to be the first head of state to make contact with alien life. Those two paragraphs are lifted, almost word-for-word, from a September 2017 story on a satirical website, Real News Right Now. We spoke with Robert Shooltz, the 35-year-old who runs the website and authored the satirical story under the pen name, R. Hobbus J.D. He explained that the idea behind it was to joke that the president would get policy ideas from aliens. 'It's a silly thing,' he said. Shooltz described himself as a moderate who leans left. He said he cast a write-in vote for Bernie Sanders in the 2016 general election.

Shooltz said he finds 'It upsetting' when his stories that are meant to poke fun at public figures, such as Trump, get picked up and misused by other websites. But, ultimately, he puts the responsibility of recognizing made-up claims on readers and he does not include a satire disclaimer on his website. Instead, he drops subtle hints that the site is a spoof, like listing the "Stephen Glass Distinction in Journalistic Integrity" among his awards — Stephen Glass was a writer for the New Republic who left the magazine in disgrace after it was revealed that he had fabricated many of his stories. While most of the story on the conspiracy theory site was taken from Shooltz's spoof, the part about Trump's call for a "space force" is true. Recognition of the importance of space for national security goes at least as far back as 2001, when a commission headed by Donald Rumsfeld who became the secretary of defense that year, issued a report recommending extensive enhancement of the military's operation in space.

'We know from history that every medium, air, land, and sea has seen conflict. Reality indicates that space will be no different,' the commission wrote in its report. 'Given this virtual certainty, the U.S. must develop the means both to deter and to defend against hostile acts in and from space.' More recently, since Trump took office, Defense Secretary James Mattis noted in his prepared remarks for his confirmation hearing that, 'While our military maintains capable land, air, and sea forces, the cyber and space domains now demand an increasing share of our attention and investment.' Also, in January, the Department of Defense issued its National Defense Strategy for 2018 in which it anticipated that space and cyberspace would become 'Warfighting domains.' And, on March 13, the president floated the idea of creating a new branch of the military to focus on space during a speech in California, saying, 'I was saying it the other day, because we're doing a tremendous amount of work in space; I said: 'Maybe we need a new force. We'll call it the space force.' And I was not really serious, and then I said: 'What a great idea. Maybe we'll have to do that.''

The Real Reasons We Haven't Had Full Disclosure Yet

First, I'd like to point out that many major governments, including the British, Australian, and Russian governments, have made their information regarding UFOs fully available to the public… the public just can't be bothered going through the legal processes necessary to access that information. As for the media having access to that information… well, who says they don't? But the media (except for YouTube) is controlled by the Illuminati, and the Illuminati are conspiring with evil ETs to enslave the human race, so of course the media will always deny the existence of ETs (the Illuminati don't want you to know what they're up to). NASA (the anagram really stands for Never a Straight Answer) knew about the possibility of ET life before they saw any evidence of it and decided in advance that if they should discover such evidence, they would hide it. Their reasoning went as follows: 'Anthropological files contain many examples of societies, sure of their place in the universe, which have disintegrated when they had to associate with previously unfamiliar societies, expounding different ideas, and different life ways. Others, that survived such an experience, usually did so by paying the price of changes in values and attitudes and behavior.' This is a quote from page 215 of the Brookings Report, on which the original NASA charter was based. What the report (at least this section of it) is basically saying, is that the discovery of extraterrestrials, or even their artifacts, could cause the end of civilization as we know it?

I don't personally believe this, but it's what NASA thinks. Their reasoning is faulty, because it seems based on the "disintegration" of Native American society, after it was exposed to European colonists. The error in this logic is that when Europeans came to America, they came as invaders and conquerors. It was not mere knowledge of the Europeans, and their superior technology, which destroyed the society of the American Indians. It was the European invaders use of their superior technology (guns) to deliberately kill the Indians and terrorize them into submission that destroyed their culture. Even saying that their culture has been 'Destroyed' is an overstatement, because in many small towns on reservations throughout the US today, the American Indian culture survives, despite determined efforts to wipe it out (by various methods) over hundreds of years. The mere knowledge that ETs exist will not harm us, and there is no evidence, that when ETs choose to reveal themselves to us, they will come as conquerors and invaders, as the European colonists of America did. Hundreds of Hollywood movies depicting ETs as conquerors and invaders are not evidence, that this is what they are like. NASA seems guilty of anthropomorphizing ETs: of accusing those of thinking like humans do.

NASA seems to assume that because we (humans) used our superior technology to conquer, ETs must do the same. But this assumption must base on the further assumption that ETs do not already have the technology to conquer us. Otherwise, we have to ask: If ETs want to conquer us, and they have the technology, why haven't they done it already? And this is precisely the question we should ask before we go assuming that ETs have hostile intentions towards us. Every book I've read on ETs (and I've read dozens) suggests that some ETs have technology thousands, or even millions of years ahead of ours, and if this is true, they could have conquered our planet at any time. A civilization just a million years older than ours (given that the universe is 15 billion years old, it is highly possible, if not likely, that many such civilizations exist) could easily have conquered Earth hundreds of thousands of years ago, when our ancestors were just cavemen, incapable of putting up any resistance whatsoever. But they didn't and they haven't, so there's no reason to suppose they will. Do you really think they're holding back because they're afraid of us? Of our weapons technology? Didn't you read the part where I said their technology is thousands, if not millions, of years ahead of ours? Movies such as Independence Day, which depict humans having a chance to fight back, against an extraterrestrial invasion, are completely unrealistic. In the event of a real ET invasion, we would have as much chance of fighting back as cavemen would have against nuclear weapons. The only thing stopping ETs from invading us is they don't want to.

So, NASA's argument against revealing their knowledge of ETs to the public is rubbish, but as long as they cling to it, NASA will never tell the public the truth about ETs. But the real drivers of this conspiracy of denial, are power and money. Whoever has access to, and control over ET technologies, has power over those who don't have such technologies, and can make money by limiting others' access to those technologies. The Illuminati have mind control technologies (supplied by their ET allies), but of course they don't want us to know about that, because if enough people did know about it, it would be a threat to the Illuminati's power, and their plans for world domination. Similarly, the Illuminati have a large fleet of Alien Reproduction Vehicles (ARVs, reverse-engineered from captured Alien space craft, and indistinguishable from the real thing, unless you look very closely), but if enough people knew about this, they could never use these ARVs to stage a false alien invasion of Earth.

The Illuminati have been planning just such a False Flag attack for decades now, in order to create such a panic that the human race will endorse a One World Government, which will, of course, be controlled by the Illuminati. The Illuminati end game is to stage a false flag 'Alien' invasion of Earth, so that they can unite all the governments and armies of the world under Illuminati rule. If the Illuminati can condition us to see ETs as evil 'Alien' invaders, though depicting them as such through films, we are unlikely to question the reality of a false (staged by the Illuminati) 'Alien' invasion. The Illuminati could continue the 'Invasion' as long as they wished, by using their fleet of ARVs to attack hapless civilians around the world. Because ARVs are indistinguishable from real ET craft (except to those with inside knowledge), most people would be deceived, and would beg the Illuminati to save them.

The Illuminati would thus be in control of both sides of this 'War': the United Earth Military (or some such), and the 'Alien invaders,' and they could continue the war as long as it suited their purpose. That purpose being, to terrorize the unsuspecting majority of humans, so that they will accept the Illuminati (possibly by now calling themselves the United Earth Government; they never call themselves by their real name) as saviors and rulers, without question. We (at least those of us who didn't know what was really happening) would then willingly give the Illuminati (in the guise of the United Earth Government) a free hand to implement whatever draconian measures they deemed "necessary" to end the 'Alien threat.'

The Illuminati have other, sinister motives, for making sure you never find out about the extraterrestrial technologies in their possession. ET craft are powered by Zero Point energy: an unlimited, clean, renewable energy source that would completely negate the need for fossil fuels. Even worse, (from the Illuminati's point of view), Zero Point generators could be made from such cheap, commonly available materials, that anyone could make one in their back yard (if they only knew how to assemble the materials in the correct way). Widespread knowledge and use of Zero Point technology would spell the end of the fossil fuel industry, and the end of Illuminati world domination, via control of the world's energy supplies. The Illuminati will do everything in their power to make sure this doesn't happen. And their power is considerable. The fossil fuel industry, (which the Illuminati own) is worth around $600 trillion globally. $600 trillion buys a lot of power to corrupt and silence anyone who threatens to reveal zero point energy to the world. If you ever build your own over-unity energy device (over-unity means the device produces more energy than it consumes) be incredibly careful who you tell about it. If the Illuminati find out, they might offer to buy you out.

They'd offer enough money to set you up for life, and not surprisingly, this works on most people. Which is why the US patents office has over 5,000 patents on over-unity energy technologies… none of which have been put into use. The Illuminati buy your technology so they can patent it and bury it. Heaven forbid, it should ever fall into the right hands: the hands of someone who might use it to liberate the world from the fossil industry. But what if you were that person, and you did have a vision of ending fossil fuels, and providing clean, free energy for all. What if you weren't willing to sell out on that vision, no matter how much money you were offered? Then, the Illuminati would destroy your workshop, your technology, and all your research (usually by burning it). They might beat you up, or even take you away for torture. If none of this was enough to silence you, they might threaten your family and friends, and even make good on these threats. If even that didn't shut you up, they'd kill you. There is an extensive list of scientists who have "disappeared" and had their workshops burned, after they created over-unity devices.

Another technology, which could change the world as much as Zero Point energy, is anti-gravity (reverse-engineered from the propulsion systems of ET spacecraft). A human designed anti-gravity ship would be just like a real ET flying saucer: working equally well for travel within the Earth's atmosphere, for inter-planetary travel, or inter-stellar travel. The widespread use of this technology would make wheeled vehicles obsolete, putting the (largely Illuminati owned) car industry out of business, and striking the fossil fuel industry a crippling blow. The benefits for the human race would be near-instantaneous travel from one point on Earth, to any other point on Earth; the ability to travel between planets in seconds (because anti-gravity drives enable FTL travel); travel between stars in minutes; and travel between galaxies in hours. Can you imagine what the world would be like, if such technology were available to the average human being… not just a wealthy handful? The Illuminati can imagine this, and it is their worst nightmare… they will do everything in their power to stop this from happening.

Here's why. If everyone had access to their own flying saucer, humans would spread across the galaxy very quickly. We wouldn't be limited to just one planet anymore, which would make it impossible for the Illuminati to control us: if we didn't like planets under Illuminati control, we could just go to other planets; maybe even start our own colonies on other planets or asteroids. FTL (faster-than-light) travel would put thousands of planets and asteroids within easy reach. And all of the resources of those planets and asteroids would be within easy reach, as well. We would have unlimited freedom, with infinite abundance: the resources of the entire universe at our disposal. There'd be no more need for money, which has been the Illuminati's primary means of controlling us for thousands of years. If we could break that shackle, we'd be free of the Illuminati forever.

Best of all, if we had FTL travel, we could finally take our rightful place in intergalactic society, amongst all the benevolent alien races who have been waiting so long for us to join them. If their civilizations are thousands, or even millions of years ahead of ours, then some of them may possess galactic empires spanning thousands of planets. With these beings as our allies and trading partners, we would truly have infinite abundance, and infinite freedom, as a species, to learn, grow, and explore. Freedom, as individuals, to live our lives any way we want, without the Illuminati (in the guise of governments, banks, corporations, and fossil fuel/power companies) telling us what to do. But, like I said, this is the Illuminati's worst nightmare. Why do you think they won't allow space travel? Why do you think we haven't been to Mars yet? Why do you think we haven't even been back to the Moon in 50 years?! It's simple. As long as we're confined to just one planet, the Illuminati can control us, like sheep in a pen. I think we're ready to break out of that pen (have been for decades, actually) and become a star faring race. But first we must find a way to remove the boot of the Illuminati from our collective throats.

Partial Disclosure and Competing Secret Space Programs

A secret space program run by the U.S. Air Force with the support of the National Security Agency, Defense Intelligence Agency, and the National Reconnaissance Office, has concluded that Corey Goode's testimony of multiple secret space programs with interstellar spacecraft using temporal drive technologies is not disinformation. This is among the most recent claims of Goode in a December 11 update about information he recently acquired as a result of his abduction and interrogation by what he describes as a Military Industrial Complex Secret Space Program (MIC-SSP) comprising the above U.S. military intelligence entities. In a previous abduction incident in late September, Goode described a senior USAF officer in charge of his chemical interrogation who told Goode that they believed he was spreading disinformation from a rogue Special Access Program. On October 26, Goode was abducted for a third time by this MIC-SSP, which he states is not advanced as the U.S. Navy's 'Solar Warden', and other secret space programs he has previously described in interviews and reports.

He claims that the senior USAF officer in charge of the vehicle he was taken to, which he dubbed 'Sigmund,' revealed that analysis of data from the two prior abductions has led to the conclusion that Goode is telling the truth after all. Sigmund said that the tests first confirmed a key aspect of Goode's testimony, which is that he has traveled to off planet locations: The lab results once again confirmed that I had been in the approximate off-planet locations I had claimed. The MIC space program people do not have any intelligence suggesting I had ever actually visited these locations. I was never a part of their program. This led to the Sigmund concluding that he was being deliberately misled by his superiors about the existence of more advanced programs to his own: My tests proved, beyond any shadow of doubt, that there was much more to the secret space program than he knew. As a high-ranking superior officer, this naturally came as quite a shock to him. He was led to believe that he had access to all relevant compartments of the UFO cover-up. Goode describes how it is possible that a USAF space program would not be aware of other secret space programs, including the Navy's Solar Warden, despite having craft capable of interplanetary travel in our solar system: The MIC SSP has at least two large space stations in earth's orbit as well as a number of manned satellites. They are roughly circular in shape and are large space stations with enough facilities for many people to work in various labs and so forth.

The above descriptions suggest something similar to a 1952 design by Dr. Werner Von Braun. Goode continued to describe other technologies belonging to the MIC SSP: They are also reported to possess floating aircraft carriers that look exactly the same as what we saw in The Avengers and Captain America: The Winter Soldier. They have craft that can travel around our solar system, as well as other stealth-looking varieties. This technology makes them feel that if anything else was going on in our solar system, they would be able to see it. When they see the crafts from other programs, or of any of a number of ET races, they are simply told that these are ours. They are told that they are not on a need-to-know basis about that particular program and not to speak about their sighting with anyone…. The MIC SSP are told that we cannot travel outside our solar system… This is due to gravitational and energetic conditions at the boundary of our heliosphere that any escape impossible with their current technology. This helps confirm that advanced antigravity craft are revealed through movies such as Captain America: The Winter Soldier in a "soft disclosure" process.

Goode describes the belief system that MIC-SSP holds about extraterrestrial life:

They believe that any ETs have long since come and gone from our solar system, other than time travelers from Earth's own future who have developed the technology to come back and visit us. They believe that some of these future humans now look like Grays due to evolutionary changes from living underground for thousands of years. Goode recalled a conversation he had with "Gonzales" (a pseudonym used by a liaison to the Secret Space Program Alliance), who describes the reason why there was no attempt to stop Goode being abducted by MIC SSP: Gonzales stated that he was sorry he couldn't share some of the details before about why I was being abducted and interrogated. He stated that this was part of an operation that was seeding information into the ranks of this MIC SSP. Apparently many of them are disillusioned and questioning whether or not they were indeed at the top of the intelligence totem pole as they had been led to believe…. These individuals were now in a state of mind that led many of them to believe that there was much more going on in "the programs" than they had been led to believe. Gonzales revealed that allowing Sigmund to extract the information from Goode about the Solar Warden and other SSPs would lead to Sigmund changing his view that Goode, Gonzales, and others were part of an Unacknowledged Special Access Program that had gone rogue and was releasing classified information.

This had led to Sigmund and the MIC-SSP hunting operatives of the Secret Space Program Alliance (such as Gonzales) for interrogation: Sigmund was causing a LOT of problems for the SSP Alliance. He was hunting them down as traitors, pretty much. Once he got this recent info from me, he then turned and has been asking a lot of angry questions from his superiors. So that mission seems to be accomplished for now. Goode's information here is incredibly significant since it shows how overly compartmentalized the world of unacknowledged Special Access Programs is, where one compartment is not informed about another, even though they are both performing deep space operations. Importantly, Goode added that his interrogations would have a beneficial in terms of plans for partial disclosure: He [Gonzales] stated that if this information gets to the right people within the MIC SSP it could hinder the wider plans of doing a partial disclosure of their program. It has been confirmed through Wikileaks that a partial UFO disclosure initiative was being prepared through rock Star

Tom DeLonge, who is being helped by two retired USAF Generals along with senior corporate officials such as the head of Lockheed Martin's Skunkworks. The plan was to release information about the USAF/DIA/NSA/NRO space program with Earth orbiting space stations and antigravity TR-3B spacecraft capable of limited interplanetary operations.

Partial disclosure would be designed to hide the existence of more advanced space programs that use interstellar technologies with temporal drives and have been implicated in various abuses including human slave trade in space. Partial disclosure would essentially be a 'Limited hangout' operation to hide the truth by revealing the existence of the less advanced USAF secret space program. Goode and the Secret Space Program Alliance has been advocating 'Full disclosure' of all programs and of extraterrestrial life since late 2014. It appears that his military abductions have led to key leaders in the USAF secret space program finally learning the truth about themselves being deceived about the full scope of what is happening in space. This will add to the pressure for full disclosure and limit the prospects of a limited disclosure narrative being implemented.

Age Regression Used In Secret Space Programs Confirmed As Scientifically Feasible

Due to recent breakthroughs in genetic research, the claims of three whistleblowers, who say they underwent an age-regression process in secret space programs, have become that much more plausible. The whistleblowers, Corey Goode, Randy Cramer, and Michael Relfe, all say that they were age-regressed to become 20 years younger at the end of their respective tours of duty in secret space programs. Recently, geneticists have identified the genes that control the aging process, and in stunning experiments, the results of which have been released in peer reviewed scientific journals, have demonstrated that they were able to reverse the aging process to varying degrees of success. The results of these experiments make it plausible that the three whistleblowers did indeed undergo an age-regression process using classified medical technologies in secret space programs, as they claimed. The lead genetic scientist in the publicly announced age reversal studies is Dr. David Sinclair, who discussed in an interview the results of his genetic experiments first conducted on mice: We've discovered genes that control how the body fights against ageing and these genes, if you turn them on just the right way, they can have immensely powerful effects, even reversing ageing – at least in mice so far… We fed them a molecule that's called NMN, and this reversed ageing completely within just a week of treatment in the muscle, and now we're looking to reverse all aspects of ageing if possible. He explained how this process could also be done safely for humans:

We've gone from mice into early human studies actually. There have been some clinical trials around the world, and we're hoping in the next few years to know if this will actually work in people as well ... They show that the molecules that extend lifespan in mice are safe in people. Professor Sinclair went on to say in his interview that drugs based on the nicotinamide mononucleotide (NMN) molecule could be successfully developed "to restore youthfulness in human cells." Sinclair's view that NMN based drugs will eventually be developed for safe use by humans is stunning in its implications. He may well be in the midst of developing the fabled elixir of life, which accounts for him quickly being elevated into the world's 100 most influential people according to Time Magazine. It's important to point out that Sinclair's pioneering genetic research is open source and unclassified.

This means that is highly likely, if not almost certain, that classified research in the field of age reversal/regression technology is far more advanced than anything achieved by Sinclair and his peers. In several private interviews with William Tompkins, a former U.S. Naval Intelligence operative who subsequently worked with leading aerospace contractors for more than four decades, he revealed that he worked on a classified study developed by the company, TRW, on age regression drugs from 1967-1971. Tompkins said that he first came across the development of age-regression technologies when he participated in the debriefings of U.S. Navy spies, from 1942 to 1945, at the Naval Air Station, San Diego. These spies revealed the existence of age-regression studies that were then secretly underway in Nazi Germany.

At the time, Tompkins job was to distribute briefing packets to U.S. companies and think tanks with expertise in the areas used by the Nazis for developing their breakthrough technologies. Tompkins said that the Massachusetts Institute of Technology (MIT) was among the academic research centers delivered briefing packets by him. Therefore, it is possible that scientists at MIT have been aware of the Nazi age-regression studies since 1942! Significantly, Sinclair's breakthrough in age-regression studies was achieved while he was a post-doctoral fellow at MIT under Dr. Leonard Guarente at M.I.T. Was this merely coincidence, or was

Sinclair helped or encouraged while at MIT to develop the insights into the age reversal potential of genetic manipulation? Recently, Tompkins has privately disclosed to me that classified 'Age-regression' drugs have been developed. He says these drugs have been used for some time in the '20 year and back' tours of duty in secret space programs.

This is consistent with the age-regression process described by Goode, Cramer and Relfe, which involved medication administered to them over a two week period where they were physically immobilized. Even more recently, Tompkins says the drugs have been refined so that they can be used for more extensive age-regression periods. For example, reversing a 90 year old back to where s/he has the physical body of a 27 year old is now possible. Tompkins says that there is a covert U.S. Navy sanctioned disclosure process underway to release these age-regression technologies into the public sector. It is, therefore, possible that Sinclair's research may have been stimulated by this covert Navy initiative during his time at MIT. At the very least, Sinclair's pioneering age-reversal experiments and identification of the NMN molecule that can be used for developing "age-regression" drugs means that the claims of Goode, Cramer and Relfe no longer appear so outlandish, and are indeed scientifically feasible.

Top Aerospace Designer Blows Whistle on Secret Us Navy Space Battle Fleets

Over a 12 year period beginning in 1951, William Tompkins worked for an above Top Secret think tank within the Douglas Aircraft Company designing kilometer-long antigravity spacecraft covertly requested by the U.S. Navy. Now aged 92, Tompkins has come forward to expose the secret projects he worked on in his newly released autobiography, Selected by Extraterrestrials: My life in the top secret world of UFOs, think-tanks, and Nordic secretaries. Tompkins supports his claims with numerous documents including two designs he completed for space battle cruisers and space carriers that would decades later become the backbone of U.S. Navy Space Battle Groups. Tompkins was given the job at the "Advanced Design" Douglas think tank, due to exceptional skills he exhibited in his war time service with Navy Intelligence from 1942-1945. Significantly, during his service at San Diego's Naval Air Station, Tompkins directly participated in intelligence debriefings of Navy agents embedded within Nazi Germany's most secret aerospace facilities during and immediately after World War II.

In his autobiography, Tompkins describes what the Navy spies had found:

The Navy agents (spies) in Germany discovered what all those "out of this world" aliens gave Hitler: UFOs, antigravity propulsion, beam weapons, extended life, and plenty of mind-controlled willing girls programs. The reptilians made a deal with the Third Reich SS giving them this big box full of toys in exchange for letting Hitler enslave the rest of the planet. Over his four years with Navy Intelligence, Tompkins helped in the covert distribution of data from Nazi Germany's two distinct secret space programs to Douglas Aircraft Company, along with other select aerospace companies and universities that had the scientific expertise to understand what the Nazis were doing. When Tompkins joined Douglas Aircraft Company in 1950, it had already formed its Advanced Design think tank to design antigravity space craft.

Once Tompkins moved over to Advanced Design in 1951, he was specifically tasked to design a variety of antigravity space vehicles, using his knowledge of Naval Intelligence gathered from Nazi Germany and his own talent for technical detailing. Tompkins describes his two superiors at the Advanced Design Think Tank: I reported directly to Dr [Wolfgang] Klemperer and Elmer Wheaton, the V.P. of engineering who wore two hats. He was V.P. of all the classified missile and space-systems programs. Unknown to 99.9%, Wheaton was V.P. of the above top secret compartmentalized extraterrestrial threats research Think Tank, too, sometimes referred to as Advanced Design. Further, Tompkins relates the covert way in which the Navy went about making design requests to Advanced Design: After receiving our unsolicited proposal for star ships [the Navy put out a sole source request for a proposal for exploratory star mission vehicles…]. Actually, we didn't even get an RFP (Request for Proposal); it was just slipped in under the floor door to our Advanced Design…. on the envelope it only said: 'To Whom it may concern.'

Tompkins says that he approached his work by studying the mission parameters for the requested future space battle groups. He then was able to produce designs that would allow the Navy to fulfill its future space missions. Creating the configuration of a Naval Space Battle Group comprising kilometer-long vehicles from the mission parameters he had been given, Tompkins explains: I redefined a standard Naval space battle group complement, stating that it would consist of one 2.5 kilometer spacecraft carrier, with a two-star on board as flag, three to four 1.4k heavy space cruisers, four to five 1k space destroyers, two 2k space landing assault ships for drop missions, two 2k space logistic support ships, and two 2k space personal transports. Tompkins writes about two Navy star ship designs completed at the Douglas think tank and includes the documents in his autobiography: The figures following show two original drawings of naval spacecraft carriers and battle cruisers that were visualized in Advanced Design, in 1954, from dozens of alternate configurations. Scale modes of these kilometer-long craft were subsequently made.

The first design is for the 1.4 km battle cruiser.

The second design is for the 2.5 km long spacecraft carrier.

Tompkins later worked for TRW, General Dynamics and other aerospace companies that were working on different classified aspects of the space battle cruisers and carriers being secretly built by the U.S. Navy. More of this information will be released in future volumes of his autobiographical accounts. After his initial designs of the space carriers were completed in the early 1960s, Tompkins claims that it took nearly a decade for detailed architectural plans to be developed, enabling official construction to begin. Consequently, building began in the 1970's and the first operational space carriers were deployed in the 1980's, under a highly classified space program called Solar Warden. Tompkins' claim corroborates the testimony of other secret space program whistleblowers who state that the Solar Warden Program became operational in the 1980's under President Reagan.

Eventually, there were eight space carrier battle groups that were built for the U.S. Navy in the 1980's and 1990's, according to Tompkins. How credible is Tompkins extraordinary testimony? To support his claims, Tompkins includes several documents in his autobiography. These include copies of two separate passes he received to enter and leave the San Diego Naval Air Station with up to three packages. These packages contained the alleged secret data provided by the Navy agents that was being distributed by Tompkins to select corporations. The passes were signed by the head of Naval Intelligence at the Naval Air Station, Admiral Rick Obatta. These documents provide hard evidence that Tompkins was indeed acting as a courier for Naval Intelligence during World War II, as he claimed. As for what was in the packages that Tompkins was carrying, he has supplied a copy of his mission statement that provides an answer. His mission orders confirm that he was authorized to work as a 'Disseminator of Aircraft Research and Information.' This is compelling documentary evidence that the packages Tompkins was carrying contained classified Naval intelligence on advanced aircraft designs, which include those developed in Nazi Germany.

In addition to the documents presented in his book, there is further confirmation of Tompkins' background in advanced aerospace programs. Tompkins employment, at Douglas Aircraft from 1950 to 1963, has been verified by another former Douglas Aircraft Company employee, Dr. Robert Wood. Dr. Wood worked for 43 years at Douglas Aircraft (which later merged to form McDonnell Douglas) and was able to confirm Tompkins thorough knowledge of senior company officials such as Elmer Wheaton and Dr. Klemperer. Dr. Wood was so impressed with Tompkins detailed testimony that he decided to assist him by becoming the editor of his autobiography. A March 26, 1941, article in the Evening Outlook newspaper of Santa Monica shows Tompkins explaining his ship models to Navy Captain G.C. Gearing, Commandant of the 11th Naval District in San Diego.

Finally, Tompkins phenomenal design abilities were publicly recognized by Navy officials back in 1941, who made statements to the national press about his highly detailed models of previously classified naval battle groups. This led to Tompkins being recruited into Navy Intelligence in 1942. The documents that Tompkins has supplied in support of his testimony, confirm that he had the skills, background, and employment history to have worked on large antigravity spacecraft that were secretly designed under contract to the U.S. Navy, while he was employed at Douglas Aviation from 1950 to 1963. Tompkins testimony impressively corroborates the core claims made by Corey Goode and other independent whistleblowers about the secret space programs examined in the book, Insiders Reveal Secret Space Programs and Extraterrestrial Alliances (2015).

After the publication of Selected by Extraterrestrials in December 2015, Tompkins received a copy of Insiders Reveal Secret Space Programs from Dr. Robert Wood. In subsequent phone conversations, Tompkins stated that much of information that he read in Insiders Reveal Secret Space Programs, which is substantially based on disclosures made by Corey Goode, is accurate. During Tompkins long career with U.S. Navy Intelligence and the aerospace industry, he compiled an impressive collection of documents that substantiate his testimony and background. Some of these can be found in his book, Selected by Extraterrestrials. According to Tompkins, the U.S. Navy had corporate contractors design kilometer-long antigravity spacecraft in the 1950s to early 1960s, with construction beginning in the 1970s, leading to their deployment in the 1980s. His documentary support of these claims is substantive and compelling. Tompkins testimony and documents provide powerful evidence that in the 1980's and 1990's, the U.S. Navy did indeed covertly deploy eight space carrier battle groups in a top secret space program called Solar Warden.

Secret Mars Colonies Trade With Up To 900 Extraterrestrial Civilizations

An inspection tour of a secret Mars colony that took place less than two months ago, on June 20, is the focus of episode seven of Gaia TV's Cosmic Disclosure. Secret space program whistleblower, Corey Goode, had earlier released a detailed report of the incident on June 22. In the Cosmic Disclosure interview with David Wilcock, Goode summarizes key aspects of the tour, as well as giving more details about the alleged trading conducted by a secret space program, the Interplanetary Corporate Conglomerate, with up to 900 extraterrestrial civilizations. Upon arrival at the base located in Mars' southern hemisphere, Goode described seeing a parked dart-shaped space vehicle that belonged to the Interplanetary Corporate Conglomerate (ICC). Goode claims that these vehicles are among the most advanced spacecraft produced by the ICC Space Program. One of the dart-shaped vehicles had been captured by the NASA live stream of the International Space Station. It was docked with the Space Station and the incident has still not been satisfactorily explained by NASA.

Goode says that such incidents are staged by a "Secret Space Program Alliance" to help prepare Earth's population for the major disclosures that lie ahead. Goode also described the underground rail system that used vitrified rock for the walls of the tunnels that crisscrossed between the facilities all across Mars. He described the tunnels as looking like ripple-like glass. Wilcock explained how classified tunnel boring equipment has to pause periodically to create reinforced ring sections, which give the tunnels the rippled look. Underground bases researcher, Richard Sauder, has described how such advanced tunneling equipment works: Nuclear subterrenes work by melting their way through the rock and soil, actually vitrifying it as they go, and leaving a neat, solidly glass-lined tunnel behind them. The heat is supplied by a compact nuclear reactor that circulates liquid lithium from the reactor core to the tunnel face, where it melts the rock. In the process of melting the rock the lithium loses some of its heat.

It is then circulated back along the exterior of the tunneling machine to help cool the vitrified rock as the tunneling machine forces its way forward. The cooled lithium then circulates back to the reactor where the whole cycle starts over. In this way the nuclear subterrene slices through the rock like a nuclear powered, 2,000 degree Fahrenheit (1,100 Celsius) earthworm, boring its way deep underground. Glass-like tubes have been photographed by NASA's Mars Global Surveyor orbiter, which has led to speculation that they were tunnels of some kind, built by giant worms or some other method. Goode's experiences at the Mars facility makes clear that these glass-like tubes are in fact part of a secret Mars-wide rail transportation network.

One of the most astounding aspects of the inspection tour is the claim that the Interplanetary Corporate Conglomerate (ICC) trades with at least 900 different extraterrestrial civilizations. Goode and Lt Col Gonzales (a pseudonym used by another eyewitness yet to reveal himself) were shown an optical neurological device that was designed to interface with technologies that was immensely popular on spacecraft. Goode expressed his surprise at how far the ICC has gone in developing advanced technologies that were being requested by a number of extraterrestrial civilizations. Goode's surprise is something that many in the general public are highly likely to share upon learning the truth about the different secret space programs, and their interactions with up to 900 extraterrestrial civilizations.

What is especially helpful for those investigating Goode's credibility is being able to compare his recollection of the Mars inspection tour in the Cosmic Disclosure interview, and the report he wrote on June 22. Comparing testimonies is a remarkably familiar technique used by investigators wanting to confirm whether a person is lying or not. That's why police investigators will get witnesses to repeat their recollections again and again. What is especially significant here is that writing and speaking utilize different hemispheres of the brain. While Goode's written report uses more of his analytical left brain functions, the verbal report uses the more intuitive right brain functions. If he were lying or fabricating his story in any way, there would be inconsistencies. I found, however, no inconsistency between the earlier written report and Goode's verbal recollection of the Mars inspection tour.

Goode's narration of the incident appears to be a sincere recollection of experiences that genuinely occurred, rather than trying to recall something that had been contrived. Goode briefly touches upon a number of other issues in his Cosmic Disclosure interview regarding stasis-being giants who were mistakenly thought by global elites (Cabal/Illuminati) to be their returning gods. In addition, he gives more details about NSA documents that were taken by Edward Snowden that have finally been decrypted and will soon be released in a massive document dump. This is an episode of Cosmic Disclosure that you really don't want to miss!

Mission to Mars Investigates Claims of Slave Labor at Secret Corporate Base

Corey Goode today released a report about an inspection tour he claims was held on Mars on June 20 that he attended along with others from a Secret Space Program Alliance. He describes how he was first picked up from his home by a blue/indigo sphere that belongs to a group of advanced extraterrestrial visitors called the 'Sphere Being Alliance,' which have appointed him to be their delegate at all meetings involving Earth's secret space programs. The sphere took Goode to a secret base on the moon called Lunar Operations Command where he met with a Lt Colonel Gonzales, the delegate representing a Secret Space Program Alliance wanting to fully disclose to the world the truth about extraterrestrial life and advanced technologies. Goode describes how he and Gonzales were each assigned a security team of two Intuitive Empath (IE) assistants (a position Goode previously held for 20 years when he served in the Solar Warden Space program from 1987 to 2007). Goode and Gonzales were accompanied on the trip to Mars by a representative of the Interplanetary Corporate Conglomerate (ICC). The ICC evolved out of a consortium of companies such as Lockheed Martin, Northrup Grumman, Boeing Corporations etc., that create the advanced technologies used by the five secret space programs that emerged in the post-World War 2 era.

Goode says that the trip took 30 minutes which is longer than the few minutes it normally takes to travel to Mars since it is currently on the opposite side of the sun. The total current distance is approximately 250 million miles apart (~420 million km) which means that

Goode's transport shuttle averaged a staggering ¾ the speed of light. Conventional rocket propelled craft would take up to 260 days to make the same journey. What immediately caught my attention was what Goode said about the roof of the shuttle craft as it left the LOC: As we lifted off and flew through the bay doors that opened we could see the surface of the moon grow distant quickly and then the earth through the transparent panels in the walls of the vessel. We then went to speed and the panels changed to an opaque color. This is very similar to what Randy Cramer (aka Captain Kaye) described seeing when he was first taken to Mars by a shuttle from Lunar Operations Command back in 1987: Interestingly enough, the feeling inside the vehicle when he pulled out of the hangar bay and positioned himself at whatever distance he was from the earth, whatever perfect distance they wanted so that when the visual array came on, and the ceilings became a projection of what the vehicle was seeing in front of it. … You really had a sense that we were all hovering in space in these chairs, staring out at Earth, getting our big look for the last time, and it was awe-inspiring.

It absolutely stands out as one of the most amazing moments in my entire life. Goode describes the terms that had been agreed to between the representatives of the ICC and the Secret Space Program Alliance Council for what would happen once they reached Mars: Gonzales again told the ICC Representative that we appreciated them agreeing to the terms of allowing us to bring the armed security, choosing the site of the conference once in orbit, the tours and allowing us to bring one family of our choosing back with us to question and to either provide sanctuary to or allow to return to their home colony depending on the families wishes. I sat and listened since I had not been a part of the negotiations and hoped to overhear something new from the process.

Upon arrival at Mars, Gonzales was given by the ICC representative a list of ICC facilities on Mars in the northern hemisphere that would be suitable for the base inspection. Gonzales instead requested a location in the southern hemisphere which greatly concerned the ICC representative who at first denied its existence. Gonzales insisted that the base existed according to fresh intelligence. The ICC then contacted his superiors and said it would take an hour to prepare the base for the inspection. After arriving at the southern hemisphere base Goode described the instructions they were given of what they would be able to discuss with the base inhabitants: The ICC representative then told us what the subject of that conversation was going to be. He was carefully watching our reactions as he gave us a summary of what to expect from the base commander. He stated that the people at this facility were here for generations and that they were under the impression for decades now that the earth had been through some sort of cataclysm and was no longer inhabitable.

He said that we are being asked to not throw off the social dynamics of the facility by revealing that this was not the case or that any of us were from the surface of Earth. Goode and Gonzales then met the base commander who told them the following about the primary mission of the facility which was described as a multi-decades social experiment: As we entered, the base commander gave us the storyline about the people not knowing that the earth was still thriving and that this wasn't anything to do with any slavery theories being promoted by the SSP Alliance but was a complex 'Social experiment.' It was stressed that we needed to be careful not to contaminate a multi-decades long experiment that will help humanity. I looked at Gonzales and he rolled his eyes at me as this was being said. The base commander then stated that the "main hall" was being setup for the conference and that we would be taken on a tour of the industrial plant first that was 8 kilometers away via an underground train. He said after the conference we would then tour the colony and meet the people, see their living conditions, and ask a family if they would be willing to leave with us.

Goode then described how he inadvertently revealed that he was from Texas to one of the base security team who presumably had been told that the Earth's surface had been devastated in some cataclysm. This led to a growing commotion among the base's security team and led to their replacement: It was at about this time that another monorail train arrived with many more security personnel. They told us to halt, and they separated the security team that was with us, disarmed them and escorted them to the trains and left. A new security team was assigned to us and the ICC representative that obviously had an "ear wig" (communication device in his ear) told us that we were not to communicate with the security team unless it was to do with something security related.

Goode next describes how he, Gonzales and their security team were next taken to a large conference hall and saw many of the colonists and their leaders who made a presentation about the advanced technologies produced at the facility, and the exopolitical agreements that had been reached with up to 900 different extraterrestrial civilizations: We were brought into the "main hall" that looked like an area that people are brought in for daily propaganda and there were a large number of ICC leadership members present who were bustling about as well and it was difficult to count how many were there. They sat us down and put on a 'Dog and Pony Show' on a large 'Smart-glass screen' that showed all sorts of technologies that they produce, what they procure in trade for those technologies and stated that they had ongoing trade agreements with almost 900 civilizations and did occasional trade with far more than that. They showed all sorts of spacecraft and spacecraft components that some groups integrate into their own technologies and also discussed the exopolitical agreements they had made with groups that pass through our sector on a regular basis using the nearby natural portal systems that are a part of the "cosmic web." Goode then describes an incident that led to him, Gonzales and their security team being detained by the base commander.

It began with the family that was chosen to accompany Goode and his companions back for a debriefing away from the facility: It was now time for Gonzales to give the ICC representative the choice of the family we were to take back with us. He gave the number of a certain family's dwelling that was an alpha numeric number outside their door and 15 minutes later a man, woman, teenage son, and pre-teen daughter showed up with a small bag in each of their hands. They seemed kind of stoic and nervous. This was to be expected but they seemed off to me. .. When the door was closed Gonzales turned to the people and told them they were safe and that he would not betray their good faith. He said that "We know that there is another member of your family that is not present," the father said, "How could you know that?" Gonzales motioned to our security personnel and said that "our people have abilities." The family then clammed up and would not talk. Gonzales became upset and said he would straighten this out and he and the two security personnel assigned to him left the vessel.

Goode says that the base commander became irate when challenged by Gonzales and was thrown into a detention cell and was soon joined by Goode and his two man security team. Along the way, Goode described what he saw: 'As we walked back through the rows of cells we saw quite a lot of people in various psychological stages of psychological distress locked up.' Fearing the worst from the base commander that Gonzalez described as a 'Tyrant and a total megalomaniac,' Goode revealed how the blue/indigo spheres belonging to the Sphere Alliance rescued them: It wasn't a minute later that we saw our blue/indigo orb friends zipping through the walls of the cell, one for each of us. They danced around for a couple seconds and the other SSP personnel who had never traveled this way backed against the wall. Gonzales explained how the transportation works and then we each followed the SOP and were soon back at the LOC room where I was transported at the beginning of this journey.

Now safe at the Lunar Operations Command, Gonzales told Goode that mission had provided good intelligence about ICC operations on Mars: He stated that the ICC's goal was propaganda and that since the recent reports that were released to the public about the slave trade and labor going on by the ICC that they have been extremely upset and worked-up about information being public that was never supposed to be so.

The inspection of the Mars ICC facility described in Goode's report helps confirm that slave labor conditions do indeed exist at these facilities where civilians are psychologically manipulated and physically abused by tyrannical base leaders who tolerate no dissent. The advanced technologies produced at these covert Mars facilities appear to be a valuable commodity in trade agreements with an extraordinarily high number of extraterrestrial civilizations – up to 900 if the ICC representative is correct. The existence of secret bases on Mars and elsewhere in the solar system, controlled by a corporate conglomerate trading advanced technologies produced by human workers in slave labor conditions for interstellar trade is certainly a cause for great concern. There appears to be minimal accountability or oversight of such facilities and the base commanders running them.

To date Goode has not provided any hard evidence or documents supporting his extraordinary claims. Lt Col. Gonzales is yet to publicly come forward to confirm his participation or identity. There are however important similarities in the testimonies of Goode and Randy Cramer which helps confirm that a secret space program with bases on Mars does indeed exist. Goode has said that there are plans for future document dumps that will substantiate his claims. For now, Goode claims that his revelations will help the public prepare for the full extent of the shocking disclosures to come. If Goode's testimony is accurate, as I believe it is, it is comforting to know that secret corporate bases on Mars and elsewhere are being investigated by a Secret Space Program Alliance that wants to disclose slave labor practices to the world and launch trials against those responsible. It's only through a full disclosure of secret space programs that the people responsible for "crimes against humanity "can be exposed and brought to justice.

Extraterrestrial Contact: International Law & Crimes against Humanity

On June 15, a legal scholar released a provocative article in Space Review analyzing international legal norms and rights that would apply to visiting extraterrestrial life. The Space Review article comes less than a month after a bill (The Space Act) was passed by the U.S. House of Representatives dealing with U.S. and international law as it applies to commercial activities in space. 'Legal implications of an encounter with extraterrestrial intelligence' is a very timely article due to international efforts to update commercial space laws, especially as it is becoming more likely than ever that eventually extraterrestrial life or artifacts will be encountered by national space programs, if they haven't been already! The Space Review article helps identify key issues about how to regard commercial activities in space that result from agreements with extraterrestrial life.

In the case that some of these agreements violate international legal norms, then would this make such agreements valid or invalid? This is especially important since there have been testimonies by whistleblowers claiming that agreements have already been reached with alien visitors in secret space programs that allegedly involve crimes against humanity. The author of 'Legal implications of an encounter with extraterrestrial intelligence,' Babak Hassanabadi says that one of the first legal issues to resolve is whether extraterrestrials have the same 'Human rights' as the rest of us. He writes: In a world first, a court in Argentina issued a historic and unprecedented ruling that favors the rights of an orangutan held in captivity. Sandra the orangutan was granted legal action so she may be transferred to a habitat in keeping with her development…. These developments with regard to assigning human-like rights for terrestrial nonhuman animals leaves no doubt for inferring that extraterrestrial intelligent life forms, at least in terrestrial legal systems' point of view, will enjoy rights equal to their human counterparts. Hassanabadi's point is a fair one.

If humanity is prepared to recognize an orangutan as having human rights, then we would do the same for extraterrestrials, even if they looked like Chewbacca, the Wookie from

Star Wars. Hassanabadi discusses what kind of laws would apply to alien visitors: Although it seems very unlikely that technologically advanced aliens would recognize the political boundaries of our nation-states, if a spacecraft with aliens onboard landed anywhere on Earth, and they do not carry any political mission to make contact with humans, legally speaking they would be subject to the territorial jurisdiction in which they have entered unless otherwise collectively agreed upon by the international legal community.

If extraterrestrials land in New York City for example, then the laws of the Empire State and U.S. Federal laws would apply. In 1969, NASA passed a federal regulation dealing with 'Extra-terrestrial Exposure'. The 'Extraterrestrial Exposure Law' offers a legal precedent for the detention and indefinite imprisonment of any individual who comes into contact with extraterrestrials. Presumably, extraterrestrials themselves could also be detained and quarantined under this little known NASA regulation that while officially withdrawn, created a legal precedent for its future use. May the Force be with any law enforcement officer trying to quarantine a Wookie? Hassanbadi recommends another approach to local or national laws being applied to extraterrestrials: The best approach would be to assign the aliens the same legal rights that foreign diplomats enjoy while they are on mission in foreign countries.

That is, if extraterrestrials come to Earth in small or large numbers and reside temporarily or permanently, their laws and traditions among themselves should remain out of human legal intervention and judgment. Basically, we would treat extraterrestrial visitors like the New York City authorities treat foreign diplomats. They have immunity from prosecution if they misbehave but can be expelled for major crimes. Mayor Bill de Blasio stands an impressive 6' 5" (196 cm) so an alien Wookie might do as he's told if he was asked to leave. Who would conduct negotiations with extraterrestrials? After examining a number of international protocols and treaties, Hassanabadi concludes the logical choice is the United Nations and its Secretary General: To be certain, any negotiation with extraterrestrial intelligent life forms will be the most urgent global challenge of human history and no institution other than the United Nations (including its specialized organs) is more legitimate and accepted by consensus to take the lead in representing the human civilization.... we can conclude that from the point of view of international law that the UN Secretary General is the best candidate to sit at the negotiation table with extraterrestrial intelligent life forms if we meet them here on our planet.

Fortunately, the United Nations Headquarters is in New York City, so Bill de Blasio would be on hand if a Wookie tried to intimidate Ban Ki-moon who stands a mere 5' 8" (175 cm). Hassanabadi raises a critical observation about any agreements reached with alien visitors: [I]f aliens travel to Earth to conclude any kind of pact, treaty, or agreement on behalf of their civilization with human civilization in general or—very unlikely but not impossible—with single nation-states on Earth, then existing international law shall prevail. In other words, the provisions of Vienna Convention about the law of treaties along with the principles of the charter of United Nations ought to be observed by human signatories of such interplanetary legal document. Here again, the diplomatic rights of the alien negotiating team should be upheld by their human political counterparts. For most of the general public, such a point seems obvious and is no great cause for concern given the widespread view that we have yet to make contact with extraterrestrial life.

Future agreements would presumably be done under the close scrutiny of a world public and media transfixed by the possibilities of humanity joining galactic society. According to many whistleblowers, however, secret agreements have already been reached with extraterrestrial visitors. Surely such secret agreements would be null and void if they weren't announced or ratified by national legislatures one might protest. Not so according to Hassanabadi's legal analysis. Even agreements signed in secret between duly appointed national representatives without completion of the full ratification process – these are called 'Executive Agreements,' are valid under international law due to the 'Vienna Convention about the law of treaties.' A possibility that Hassanabadi didn't examine is what happens if these secret agreements with aliens violate international law? What if there are future, or even past, agreements where humans are secretly taken away in an off-world slave trade? After all, during the 18th and 19th centuries, there were many agreements between colonial powers and local African elites that were accepted as valid under international commercial law at the time that made the slave trade possible.

Could something analogous happen or be happening in space where secret commercial space laws make it possible for a form of galactic human slave trade to happen? Dan Sherman worked for the US Air Force and the National Security Agency as an electronic communications expert for 12 years. He says he discovered agreements had been reached with aliens who were abducting people and taking them into space and reporting back to the NSA. Niara Terela Isley is a former US Air Force radar tracking operator who reveals that she was taken between eight and ten times to a moon base by a secret space program operating from the vicinity of Area 51 where she was briefly assigned. She claims the moon base was guarded by Reptilian beings that used human workers in slave labor conditions. Corey Goode claims to have served in a secret space program for 20 years. He says he witnessed and was briefed about humans being forced to work as slave labor in secret corporate bases on Mars, and even being sold off to aliens in other solar systems in a galactic slave trade.

Slavery is recognized as a "crime against humanity" and identified as such in a number of international treaties such as the Rome Statute that led to the creation of the International Criminal Court (ICC) in 2002. Here's what the ICC has to say about slavery as a crime against humanity, 'Crimes against humanity' include any of the following acts committed as part of a widespread or systematic attack directed against any civilian population, with knowledge of the attack ... enslavement; deportation or forcible transfer of population; ... sexual slavery; enforced disappearance of persons... other inhumane acts of a similar character intentionally causing great suffering or serious bodily or mental injury. If secret agreements have been reached with extraterrestrial visitors that involve slavery, then these agreements clearly violate international law, and are not protected under the 'Vienna Convention about the law of treaties.'

Consequently, signatories and those carrying out such agreements would be committing crimes against humanity and be subject to prosecution under the International Criminal Court. The idea of extraterrestrials reaching secret agreements with national representatives that violate international law and commit crimes against humanity may not be an abstract possibility to be debated by Hassanabadi and legal scholars. It is, according to Goode, Isley and others whistleblowers that served in or learned about classified space programs, a reality that has been happening behind the scenes for several decades now. Allegedly, there's a flourishing slave trade and humanity will have to deal with the awful truth once the cover-up of extraterrestrial life is disclosed. If a Wookie has been involved in such an illegal human slave trade program, then all bets are off Mayor de Blasio – off to the International Criminal Court he goes!

Update – 6/20/15: I posted a comment to Babak Hassanabadi's Space Review article notifying him about the above article and received the following reply: 'Dear Dr. Salla, Thank you very much for your comment and also I appreciate your very meticulous article 'Extraterrestrial contact: international law & crimes against humanity' …. I totally agree with you that legal doctrines ought to be supplemented by evidential facts otherwise they will remain abstract and useless. But abstract theories might become extremely helpful if they shed light on how to deal with consequences of the situations all of which now may seem unlikely but if happen may cause tremendous chaos and uncertainty. As you truly pointed out in your thought article, in case any secret deal with aliens is made by governments that contradicts he generally accepted principles of international law, such agreement is doomed to be invalid. In such a case, International Criminal Court will have the jurisdiction to trial the persons in charge of making such a treaty or agreement due to committing crimes against humanity or other major offenses the court has jurisdiction over to adjudicate.

Mysterious Government Time Travel Programs and Assassinations

Conspiracies of nefarious government plots and shadow projects seem to never get old. The idea that beneath the veneer of what we can see or are shown there are dark deeds and secret experiments into realms beyond our current understanding going on is alluring, often irresistible, and never ceases to amaze, entertain, and incite debate, spawning countless conspiracy theories ranging from the plausible to the absurd. Among the plethora of government conspiracy theories, one cannot get much more bizarre than top secret time travel experiments and the potential consequences for whistle-blowers of these shady programs, and here we will look at some very peculiar accounts indeed. By far one of the most outrageous and flat-out bonkers accounts of a secret government-run time travel program comes to us from Seattle, Washington-based attorney Andrew D. Basiago, who in 2004 came forth with a mind-bogglingly weird tale. Basagio claimed that the government had long been involved with a top secret operation he called 'Project Pegasus,' which apparently was an umbrella term for a wide variety of strange experiments, involving things such as teleportation, inter-dimensional doorways, and of course time-travel, and which he explained thus:

Project Pegasus was the classified, defense-related research and development program under the Defense Advanced Research Projects Agency (DARPA) in which the US defense-technical community achieved time travel on behalf of the US government – the real Philadelphia Experiment.

According to Basagio, much of the mysterious project revolved around particularly time travel, especially its potential applications and studying the effects it had on the human body. To this effect he claims that children were often recruited into the program, because it was believed that they were more resilient to any negative effects of these temporal shifts. Indeed, Basagio himself claims that he was one of these children, and that he was involved with these experiments from the age of 7, after which he stayed there from the years 1968 to 1972. It was claimed that the government had several different versions of a time machine, with varying degrees of effectiveness. The most promising was apparently a machine based on alleged plans designed by the famed inventor Nicola Tesla himself, retrieved from his New York apartment after his death in 1943. This fantastic machine supposedly featured two 8-foot-tall 'Elliptical booms,' between which was funneled what Basagio called 'Radiant energy,' which could supposedly bend the fabric of space and time. The machine would conjure up a shimmering wall of light, which a user could enter to pass into a 'Vortal tunnel' and be whisked off to different eras.

Using such technology, Basagio says the government had him participate in several different experiments, which included a few time jumps. Two of these jumps purportedly concerned the former president of the United States, Abraham Lincoln. In one case, Basagio apparently jumped back to November 19, 1863, where he appeared at Gettysburg, Pennsylvania, the day just before Lincoln was to give his famous Gettysburg Address. Basagio says that in order to blend in at his destination he had been dressed in period clothes, disguised as a bugle boy, but that his shoes had been too big. Thinking that the ruse wouldn't work because of the oversized shoes, he claims that he had then wandered away from the crowd, and that he was photographed at the time. On a few occasions Basagio says that he was sent back to the Ford Theater on the night of Lincoln's assassination, at one point even running across his own time-traveling self. Although he did not witness the assassination himself, he does claim to have heard the shot ring out and the subsequent panic and commotion from the crowd.

Overall, Basagio claims he made around 8 time jumps utilizing several different technologies, such as the Tesla machine, a "plasma confinement chamber," and a 'Jump room.' Rather than time-travel as many may perceive it, Basagio has said that it was more like branching out into alternate realities and timelines, of which he has explained: It was like they were sending us to slightly different alternative realities on adjacent timelines. As these visits began to accumulate, I twice ran into myself during two different visits. After the first of these two encounters with myself occurred, I was concerned that my cover might be blown. Unlike the jump to Gettysburg, in which I was clutching a letter to Navy Secretary Gideon Welles to offer me aid and assistance in the event I was arrested, I didn't have any explanatory materials when I was sent to Ford's Theatre. This technology has been refined and developed since its earlier days, claims Basagio, and he has related that at first there were some accidents, including a child who came through one of these portals without his legs. However, it is apparently safe now, and Basagio has said that one of the reasons he has come forward with this information is because he believes it to be something the public has a right to know about, and that teleportation or time travel technology could be used for the good of mankind.

It is all very much in the vein of a sci-fi film and should probably be taken with a healthy grain of salt, as this is the same man who claims that he also made several teleportation jumps to a secret base on Mars, accompanied by none other than Barack Obama himself. It is a damn strange and interesting yarn, though. When it comes to time travel, why should the U.S. government have all the fun? The United Kingdom has also allegedly dabbled in such technologies, and this has been brought forward as recently as June of 2018, by a mysterious anonymous man who claims to have been in the employ of the British government. During his time there, he claims that he volunteered to test out time travel technology. During the experiment, he says he was paid €200,000 for the purpose of jumping forward in time to the year 2365 in order to learn about the future. The man said of the government's use of time travel: People in the Government aren't exactly sure how things work; paradoxes can happen. All they know is that time travel is possible, and we've figured out ways of doing it. I can tell you for a fact that time travel does exist within factions of the British Government. So, what did he see there in the future, you may find yourself asking? Well, the man claims that he materialized from his time jump atop a very tall futuristic skyscraper, although he is unsure of what city it was.

All around him were swarms of all manner of flying vehicles, as well as buildings that were of a unique slanted design, which soared up to dizzying heights into the sky, and most bizarrely of all, strange robots and beings that may have been aliens. He said of the fantastical sight that met him thus: On top of the skyscraper, I saw various flying cars and modes of transportation that were travelling right by me. There were very long ones and very short ones, there were buses and cars, and I remember seeing a much higher form of air traffic above that, including aeroplanes that I have never seen before. I remember receiving a few strange looks from people in the cars that were looking at me. The buildings were all slanted for some reason. They were very tall, much taller than you would see in New York or Los Angeles. I remember seeing robots, humans and what appeared to be aliens. I don't know if they were genetically modified humans or if they were aliens – but I remember seeing strange creatures with large eyes and almond-shaped heads. There were also very regular looking humans that you would think were any average Joe today – but they were wearing very strange clothing.

Altogether the man claims to have spent 6 days in the future, which he describes as 'The most memorable of my life. I had an amazing time.' During his conversations with the people of the future he says that he told them what year he was from and that they were not surprised at all, informing him that time travel would become widely used from the year 2028. It's another very weird account, and whether it is real or not it is quite entertaining at the very least. With such shadowy top secret projects, one may wonder what these governments think about these whistleblowers inconveniently coming forward with this classified information. Are they ignored? Are they trailed by mysterious agents like the Men in Black? According to one man, they face the risk of extermination and assassination. In July of 2018, a man calling himself simply "Noah" came forward to claim that he was a time traveler employed by an unnamed government, although he does have an American accent. According to Noah, he is from the year 2030, and was sent back with some colleagues on some unspecified mission.

Sometime during the mission, he says, there was an accident, and they were subsequently intentionally stranded in the year 2018 due to their 'Incompetence,' after which they apparently became somehow separated. The whole bizarre story apparently came out under hypnosis, with a video of the whole thing posted online to a channel called 'Apex TV.' During the very odd interview, Noah claims that World War III will break out with North Korea, and that the government routinely strands in time or kills those who screw up or tell of what is really going on with time travel. In the video, a spaced-out looking Noah gives quite a cryptic account of events, and during the bizarre interview tells the hypnotist of this: I know them enough that they will come and kill you guys if you said anything about this. I know how to keep my own. They would kill you fast. Trust me. It's all your fault though. The government killed time travelers that spoke out. And I knew they wouldn't be able to fend for themselves.

I still can't believe I got away with it. It is uncertain what any of this really means, and one is left to wonder if this is a hoax, the product of a delusional imagination festering within a perhaps very troubled individual, or if he really is a time traveler. In the end there is no evidence to prove any of it either way, and that is the problem with all of these cases. Here we have looked at tales of dark government conspiracies and stories of time travel and the consequences of coming out with it, and it is all overly dramatic and entertaining, but it ends up just being that- amusing stories, without any basis in verifiable truth. Are world governments secretly engaging in secretive time travel projects, even silencing those who come forward? Probably not, but then again that is what they would want us to think, isn't it?

Andrew Basiago Involved In Project Pegasus Time Travel Program

We live in a strange time, where uncertainty about the future is at an all-time high – political systems are in disarray, technology will either prove to be our savior or undoing, and weather patterns are chaotic. There is however, one man who claims to have visited the past and future, during which he delivered dire messages to deceased presidents and gained Intel from our future government. Having been involved in a CIA time travel program called Project Pegasus, Andrew Basiago has prescient knowledge to save humanity as we know it, and he is running for president of the United States.

DARPA Project Pegasus

According to Basiago, between 1962-'72 the U.S. government ran a clandestine operation called Project Pegasus. The program led to the successful development of a number of highly advanced technologies allowing for teleportation, physical time travel, and holographic time travel. He claims the program was run jointly by the CIA and DARPA, and was used to contact former presidents, teleport to Mars, and maintain a rapport with extraterrestrials. Beginning when he was just a child, Basiago was selected from a group of psychically gifted children to become a time traveling liaison who would go on to meet historical and future dignitaries, as well as various extraterrestrial entities. Basiago says his father had previously worked for the Ralph M. Parsons Engineering Corporation, where he helped develop the technology. When Basiago was brought to participate in his first 'Jump,' he says his father had already been time traveling for years at the Curtiss-Wright Corporation in New Jersey. It was here where he was first exposed to the portal he would later use to teleport through time and space. The portal itself, Basiago describes as two parentheses-shaped booms that were 8 feet tall and spaced about 10 feet apart. He describes the computer configuration from which the portal was being controlled as rudimentary and plugged into the wall with a power cord that will look more fitting if it lead to a lathe or drill press – ironic for a machine capable of tearing the space-time continuum.

Andrew Basiago Gettysburg Jump

Upon activation, this time-traversing machine created a 'Vortal tunnel' from radiant energy that was capable of bending the fabric of reality. This radiant energy was discovered by Nikola Tesla, whose schematic was posthumously discovered by the government in his New York apartment in 1943. The technology was parlayed into what Basiago calls a plasma confinement chamber which a user jumps into before being transported to a different moment or place in time. His first journey teleported him to the state capital of New Mexico, though he remained in the same time period. Later in his life he says he was able to corroborate the capital building as a common location involved in the program from a woman who said she saw people materialize there. He continued this training by traveling just a few hours back in time to get used to the sensation. Eventually, he would travel back to Abraham Lincoln's Gettysburg address, Washington's tent during the Revolutionary War, and even to the time of Jesus. He says the government had a desire to check the veracity of the historical accounts of these three figures, due to their significance and the fact that they have been written about extensively. Basiago says he also traveled to the future, to the year 2045, where he was transported to a building made of emerald and tungsten steel. There he was given a miniature canister of microfilm to be brought back to the '70s, which contained a wealth of knowledge of every historical event up until then. Apparently, not everything is digitized in the future.

Andy 2016 and Beyond

You may have heard about Basiago not too long ago, when he made waves in the media claiming Barack Obama had been a part of the same teleportation/time travel program as he. This even solicited a response from the White House, which adamantly denied the claim, though Basiago maintains his position. According to Basiago, Obama went by the name Barry Soetero and was initially teleported to Mars at the age of 19. Soetero was sent on his interplanetary mission to communicate with Martian animals and the extraterrestrials living on the red planet. He claimed in a 2012 speech that he has definitive photographic evidence of intelligent life there from a picture of a Martian purportedly carving a rock with a handsaw on the planet's surface. This past election, Basiago unfortunately didn't make it past the primaries, though he has future knowledge that sometime between now and 2028, he will either be elected president or vice president. He says this information was divulged to him from members with career associations in the CIA.

In the 2016 election, Basiago was unable to get his name on the ballot in all 50 states due to the exorbitant cost of running in a presidential election. He says it would have cost $5 million and he couldn't produce the money, therefore he ran as an independent, write-in candidate. Basiago has another decade to fulfill his prophecy of landing in one of the top two positions in the White House, with his next campaign poised for the 2020 election. Unlike other candidates, Basiago has posted an unbelievably detailed layout of his presidential platform and the 100 policies he intends to enact once he is elected. These unwavering guidelines promise to usher in a new era of truth, reform, and innovation in America. Much of this platform is predicated on progressive policies like investing in public education, green energy, net neutrality, and religious tolerance. Judging his candidacy on these aspects alone, he might fit in with most far-left progressive ideologies. Though, the primary pillars of his candidacy are set on revealing what he believes to be the government's biggest secret: time travel. The first measure Basiago might enact upon taking office: declassify and reveal all technology related to quantum transportation and America's history of time travel technology. This would include the chronovisor, the holographic teleportation machine he says he used to speak to George Washington.

Although he says time travel for every citizen would create a universe way too chaotic, Basiago believes everyone should have access to teleportation – it would solve many of our transportation shortcomings. Next up, presidential honesty. Basiago wants all former presidents who are still alive to come forth and admit they were given previous knowledge of their destinies. They all knew they were picked specifically to become president, so it's time for them to come clean. The government would also have to disclose to the American public that they've been blinded from an ongoing and longstanding extraterrestrial presence, which began when we first developed and used atomic weapons. According to Basiago, the use of atomic weapons creates a tear in the fabric of space-time, of which there is nothing worse we could be doing to the universe in the eyes of extraterrestrial civilizations. Could Basiago really have time traveled throughout history via a clandestine government program called Project Pegasus? We may never know. But in today's political climate, there have been a number of unforeseen revelations and disclosures that might have seemed absurd in the past. If we vote Andy 2020 we may find out.

18. *And The Runner Up is…*

The Ever-Growing List of Admitted 'False Flag' Attacks

Presidents, Prime Ministers, Congressmen, Generals, Spooks, Soldiers and Police admit to 'False Flag' Terror. In the following instances, officials in the government which carried out the attack (or seriously proposed an attack) admit to it, either orally, in writing, or through photographs or videos:

(1) Japanese troops set off a small explosion on a train track in 1931, and falsely blamed it on China in order to justify an invasion of Manchuria. This is known as the 'Mukden Incident' or

the 'Manchurian Incident.' The Tokyo International Military Tribunal found, 'several of the participators in the plan, including Hashimoto [a high-ranking Japanese army officer], have on various occasions admitted their part in the plot and have stated that the object of the 'Incident' was to afford an excuse for the occupation of Manchuria by the Kwantung Army ….' And see this, this, and this.

(2) A major with the Nazi SS admitted at the Nuremberg trials that – under orders from the chief of the Gestapo – he and some other Nazi operatives faked attacks on their own people and resources which they blamed on the Poles, to justify the invasion of Poland.

(3) The minutes of the high command of the Italian government – subsequently approved by Mussolini himself – admitted that violence on the Greek-Albanian border was carried out by Italians and falsely blamed on the Greeks, as an excuse for Italy's 1940 invasion of Greece.

(4) Nazi general Franz Halder also testified at the Nuremberg trials that Nazi leader Hermann Goering admitted to setting fire to the German parliament building in 1933, and then falsely blaming the communists for the arson.

(5) Soviet leader Nikita Khrushchev admitted in writing that the Soviet Union's Red Army shelled the Russian village of Mainila in 1939 – while blaming the attack on Finland – as a basis for launching the "Winter War" against Finland. Russian president Boris Yeltsin agreed that Russia had been the aggressor in the Winter War.

(6) The Russian Parliament, current Russian president Putin and former Soviet leader Gorbachev all admit that Soviet leader Joseph Stalin ordered his secret police to execute 22,000 Polish army officers and civilians in 1940, and then falsely blamed it on the Nazis.

(7) The British government admits that – between 1946 and 1948 – it bombed 5 ships carrying Jews attempting to flee the Holocaust to seek safety in Palestine, set up a fake group called 'Defenders of Arab Palestine', and then had the psuedo-group falsely claim responsibility for the bombings (and see this, this, and this).

(8) Israel admits that in 1954, an Israeli terrorist cell operating in Egypt planted bombs in several buildings, including U.S. diplomatic facilities, then left behind 'Evidence' implicating the Arabs as the culprits (one of the bombs detonated prematurely, allowing the Egyptians to identify the bombers, and several of the Israelis later confessed) (and see this and this). The U.S. Army does not believe this is an isolated incident. For example, the U.S. Army's School of Advanced Military Studies said of Mossad (Israel's intelligence service), 'Ruthless and cunning. Has capability to target U.S. forces and make it look like a Palestinian/Arab act.'

(9) The CIA admits that it hired Iranians in the 1950's to pose as Communists and stage bombings in Iran in order to turn the country against its democratically-elected prime minister.

(10) The Turkish Prime Minister admitted that the Turkish government carried out the 1955 bombing on a Turkish consulate in Greece – also damaging the nearby birthplace of the founder of modern Turkey – and blamed it on Greece, for the purpose of inciting and justifying anti-Greek violence.

(11) The British Prime Minister admitted to his defense secretary that he and American president Dwight Eisenhower approved a plan in 1957 to carry out attacks in Syria and blame it on the Syrian government as a way to effect regime change.

(12) The former Italian Prime Minister, an Italian judge, and the former head of Italian counterintelligence admit that NATO, with the help of the Pentagon and CIA, carried out terror bombings in Italy and other European countries in the 1950s through the 1980s and blamed the communists, in order to rally people's support for their governments in Europe in their fight against communism. As one participant in this formerly-secret program stated: 'You had to attack civilians, people, women, children, innocent people, unknown people far removed from any political game. The reason was quite simple. They were supposed to force these people, the Italian public, to turn to the state to ask for greater security' ... so that 'A state of emergency could be declared, so people would willingly trade part of their freedom for the security' (and see this) (Italy and other European countries subject to the terror campaign had joined NATO before the bombings occurred). And watch this BBC special. They also allegedly carried out terror attacks in France, Belgium, Denmark, Germany, Greece, the Netherlands, Norway,

Portugal, the UK, and other countries. The CIA also stressed to the head of the Italian program that Italy needed to use the program to control internal uprisings. 'False Flag' attacks carried out pursuant to this program include – by way of example only:

- The murder of the Turkish Prime Minister (1960)
- Bombings in Portugal (1966)
- The Piazza Fontana massacre in Italy (1969)
- Terror attacks in Turkey (1971)
- The Peteano bombing in Italy (1972)
- Shootings in Brescia, Italy, and a bombing on an Italian train (1974)
- Shootings in Istanbul, Turkey (1977)
- The Atocha massacre in Madrid, Spain (1977)
- The abduction and murder of the Italian Prime Minister (1978) (and see this)
- The bombing of the Bologna railway station in Italy (1980)
- Shooting and killing 28 shoppers in Brabant County, Belgium (1985)

(13) In 1960, American Senator George Smathers suggested that the U.S. launch 'A 'False attack made on Guantanamo Bay which would give us the excuse of actually fomenting a fight which would then give us the excuse to go in and [overthrow Castro]'.

(14) Official State Department documents show that, in 1961, the head of the Joint Chiefs and other high-level officials discussed blowing up a consulate in the Dominican Republic in order to justify an invasion of that country. The plans were not carried out, but they were all discussed as serious proposals.

(15) As admitted by the U.S. government, recently declassified documents show that in 1962, the American Joint Chiefs of Staff signed off on a plan to blow up American airplanes (using an elaborate plan involving the switching of airplanes), and also to commit terrorist acts on American soil, and then to blame it on the Cubans in order to justify an invasion of Cuba. See the following ABC news report; the official documents; and watch this interview with the former Washington Investigative Producer for ABC's World News Tonight with Peter Jennings.

(16) In 1963, the U.S. Department of Defense authored a paper promoting attacks on nations within the Organization of American States – such as Trinidad-Tobago or Jamaica – and then falsely blaming them on Cuba.

(17) The U.S. Department of Defense also suggested covertly paying a person in the Castro government to attack the United States: 'The only area remaining for consideration then would be to bribe one of Castro's subordinate commanders to initiate an attack on Guantanamo.'

(18) A U.S. Congressional committee admitted that – as part of its 'Cointelpro' campaign, the FBI had used many provocateurs in the 1950s through 1970s to carry out violent acts and falsely blame them on political activists.

(19) A top Turkish general admitted that Turkish forces burned down a mosque in Cyprus in the 1970s and blamed it on their enemy. He explained: 'In Special War, certain acts of sabotage are staged and blamed on the enemy to increase public resistance. We did this in Cyprus; we even burnt down a mosque.' In response to the surprised correspondent's incredulous look the general said, 'I am giving an example.'

(20) A declassified 1973 CIA document reveals a program to train foreign police and troops on how to make booby traps, pretending that they were training them on how to investigate terrorist acts: The Agency maintains liaison in varying degrees with foreign police/security organizations through its field stations ….
CIA provides training sessions as follows:

   a. Providing trainees with basic knowledge in the uses of commercial and military demolitions and incendiaries as they may be applied in terrorism and industrial sabotage operations.

   b. Introducing the trainees to commercially available materials and home laboratory techniques, likely to be used in the manufacture of explosives and incendiaries by terrorists or saboteurs.

c.Familiarizing the trainees with the concept of target analysis and operational planning that a saboteur or terrorist must employ.

d.Introducing the trainees to booby trapping devices and techniques giving practical experience with both manufactured and improvised devices through actual fabrication. The program provides the trainees with ample opportunity to develop basic familiarity and use proficiently through handling, preparing, and applying the various explosive charges, incendiary agents, terrorist devices and sabotage techniques.

(21) The German government admitted (and see this) that, in 1978, the German secret service detonated a bomb in the outer wall of a prison and planted 'Escape tools' on a prisoner, a member of the Red Army Faction, which the secret service wished to frame the bombing on.

(22) A Mossad agent admits that, in 1984, Mossad planted a radio transmitter in Gaddaffi's compound in Tripoli, Libya which broadcast fake terrorist transmissions recorded by Mossad, in order to frame Gaddaffi as a terrorist supporter. Ronald Reagan bombed Libya immediately thereafter.

(23) The South African Truth and Reconciliation Council found that, in 1989, the Civil Cooperation Bureau (a covert branch of the South African Defense Force) approached an explosives expert and asked him "to participate in an operation aimed at discrediting the ANC [the African National Congress] by bombing the police vehicle of the investigating officer into the murder incident", thus framing the ANC for the bombing.

(24) An Algerian diplomat and several officers in the Algerian army admit that, in the 1990s, the Algerian army frequently massacred Algerian civilians and then blamed Islamic militants for the killings (and see this video; and Agence France-Presse, 9/27/2002, French Court Dismisses Algerian Defamation Suit Against Author).

(25) In 1993, a bomb in Northern Ireland killed 9 civilians. Official documents from the Royal Ulster Constabulary (i.e., the British government) show that the mastermind of the bombing was

a British agent, and that the bombing was designed to inflame sectarian tensions. And see this and this.

(26) The United States Army's 1994 publication Special Forces Foreign Internal Defense Tactics Techniques and Procedures for Special Forces – updated in 2004 – recommends employing terrorists and using 'False Flag' operations to destabilize leftist regimes in Latin America. False flag terrorist attacks were carried out in Latin America and other regions as part of the CIA's 'Dirty Wars.' And see this.

(27) Similarly, a CIA "psychological operations" manual prepared by a CIA contractor for the Nicaraguan Contra rebels noted the value of assassinating someone on your own side to create a 'Martyr' for the cause. The manual was authenticated by the U.S. government. The manual received so much publicity from Associated Press, Washington Post and other news coverage that – during the 1984 presidential debate – President Reagan was confronted with the following question on national television: At this moment, we are confronted with the extraordinary story of a CIA guerrilla manual for the anti-Sandinista contras whom we are backing, which advocates not only assassinations of Sandinistas but the hiring of criminals to assassinate the guerrillas we are supporting in order to create martyrs.

(28) A Rwandan government inquiry admitted that the 1994 shoot down and murder of the Rwandan president, who was from the Hutu tribe – a murder blamed by the Hutus on the rival Tutsi tribe, and which led to the massacre of more than 800,000 Tutsis by Hutus – was committed by Hutu soldiers and falsely blamed on the Tutis.

(29) An Indonesian government fact-finding team investigated violent riots which occurred in 1998 and determined that 'Elements of the military had been involved in the riots, some of which were deliberately provoked'.

(30) Senior Russian Senior military and intelligence officers admit that the KGB blew up Russian apartment buildings in 1999 and falsely blamed it on Chechens, in order to justify an invasion of Chechnya (and see this report and this discussion).

(31) As reported by the New York Times, BBC and Associated Press, Macedonian officials admit that in 2001, the government murdered 7 innocent immigrants in cold blood and pretended that they were Al Qaeda soldiers attempting to assassinate Macedonian police, in order to join the 'War on terror'. Luring foreign migrants into the country, executing them in a staged gun battle, and then claiming they were a unit backed by Al Qaeda intent on attacking Western embassies. Macedonian authorities had lured the immigrants into the country, and then – after killing them – posed the victims with planted evidence – 'Bags of uniforms and semiautomatic weapons at their side' – to show Western diplomats.

(32) At the July 2001 G8 Summit in Genoa, Italy, black-clad thugs were videotaped getting out of police cars and were seen by an Italian MP carrying 'Iron bars inside the police station'. Subsequently, senior police officials in Genoa subsequently admitted that police planted two Molotov cocktails and faked the stabbing of a police officer at the G8 Summit, in order to justify a violent crackdown against protesters.

(33) The U.S. falsely blamed Iraq for playing a role in the 9/11 attacks – as shown by a memo from the defense secretary – as one of the main justifications for launching the Iraq war. Even after the 9/11 Commission admitted that there was no connection, Dick Cheney said that the evidence is 'Overwhelming' that al Qaeda had a relationship with Saddam Hussein's regime, that Cheney "probably" had information unavailable to the Commission, and that the media was not 'doing their homework' in reporting such ties. Top U.S. government officials now admit that the Iraq war was really launched for oil … not 9/11 or weapons of mass destruction. Despite previous 'Lone wolf' claims, many U.S. government officials now say that 9/11 was state-sponsored terror; but Iraq was not the state which backed the hijackers. (Many U.S. officials have alleged that 9/11 was a false flag operation by rogue elements of the U.S. government; but such a claim is beyond the scope of this discussion. The key point is that the U.S. falsely blamed it on Iraq, when it knew Iraq had nothing to do with it.). (Additionally, the same judge who has shielded the Saudis for any liability for funding 9/11 has awarded a default judgment against Iran for $10.5 billion for carrying out 9/11 … even though no one seriously believes that Iran had any part in 9/11.)

(34) Although the FBI now admits that the 2001 anthrax attacks were carried out by one or more U.S. government scientists, a senior FBI official says that the FBI was actually told to blame the Anthrax attacks on Al Qaeda by White House officials (remember what the anthrax letters looked like). Government officials also confirm that the white House tried to link the anthrax to Iraq as a justification for regime change in that country. And see this.

(35) According to the Washington Post, Indonesian police admit that the Indonesian military killed American teachers in Papua in 2002 and blamed the murders on a Papuan separatist group in order to get that group listed as a terrorist organization.

(36) The well-respected former Indonesian president also admits that the government probably had a role in the Bali bombings.

(37) Police outside of a 2003 European Union summit in Greece were filmed planting Molotov cocktails on a peaceful protester.

(38) In 2003, the U.S. Secretary of Defense admitted that interrogators were authorized to use the following method: 'False Flag': Convincing the detainee that individuals from a country other than the United States are interrogating him." While not a traditional false flag attack, this deception could lead to former detainees attacking the country falsely blamed for the interrogation.

(39) Former Department of Justice Lawyer John Yoo suggested in 2005 that the US should go on the offensive against al-Qaeda, having 'Our intelligence agencies create a false terrorist organization. It could have its own websites, recruitment centers, training camps, and fundraising operations. It could launch fake terrorist operations and claim credit for real terrorist strikes, helping to sow confusion within al-Qaeda's ranks, causing operatives to doubt others' identities and to question the validity of communications.'

(40) Similarly, in 2005, Professor John Arquilla of the Naval Postgraduate School – a renowned US defense analyst credited with developing the concept of 'Netwar', called for western intelligence services to create new 'Pseudo gang' terrorist groups, as a way of undermining

'Real' terror networks. According to Pulitzer-Prize winning journalist Seymour Hersh, Arquilla's 'Pseudo-gang' strategy was, Hersh reported, already being implemented by the Pentagon, 'Under Rumsfeld's novel approach, I was told, US military operatives would be permitted to pose abroad as corrupt foreign businessmen seeking to buy contraband items that could be used in nuclear-weapons systems. In some cases, according to the Pentagon advisers, local citizens could be recruited and asked to join up with guerrillas or terrorists... The new rules will enable the Special Forces community to set up what it calls 'action teams' in the target countries overseas which can be used to find and eliminate terrorist organizations. 'Do you remember the right-wing execution squads in El Salvador?' the former high-level intelligence official asked me, referring to the military-led gangs that committed atrocities in the early nineteen-eighties. 'We founded them, and we financed them,' he said. 'The objective now is to recruit locals in any area we want. And we aren't going to tell Congress about it.' A former military officer, who has knowledge of the Pentagon's commando capabilities, said, 'We're going to be riding with the bad boys.'

(41) United Press International reported in June 2005: U.S. intelligence officers are reporting that some of the insurgents in Iraq are using recent-model Beretta 92 pistols, but the pistols seem to have had their serial numbers erased. The numbers do not appear to have been physically removed; the pistols seem to have come off a production line without any serial numbers. Analysts suggest the lack of serial numbers indicates that the weapons were intended for intelligence operations or terrorist cells with substantial government backing. Analysts speculate that these guns are probably from either Mossad, or the CIA. Analysts speculate that agent provocateurs may be using the untraceable weapons even as U.S. authorities use insurgent attacks against civilians as evidence of the illegitimacy of the resistance.

(42) In 2005, British soldiers dressed as Arabs were caught by Iraqi police after a shootout against the police. The soldiers apparently possessed explosives and were accused of attempting to set off bombs. While none of the soldiers admitted that they were carrying out attacks, British soldiers and a column of British tanks stormed the jail they were held in, broke down a wall of the jail, and busted them out. The extreme measures used to free the soldiers – rather than have them face questions and potentially stand trial – could be considered an admission.

(43) Undercover Israeli soldiers admitted in 2005 to throwing stones at other Israeli soldiers so they could blame it on Palestinians, as an excuse to crack down on peaceful protests by the Palestinians.

(44) Quebec police admitted that, in 2007, thugs carrying rocks to a peaceful protest were actually undercover Quebec police officers (and see this).

(45) A 2008 US Army special operations field manual recommends that the U.S. military use surrogate non-state groups such as 'Paramilitary forces, individuals, businesses, foreign political organizations, resistant or insurgent organizations, expatriates, transnational terrorism adversaries, disillusioned transnational terrorism members, black marketers, and other social or political 'Undesirables." The manual specifically acknowledged that U.S. special operations can involve both counterterrorism and "Terrorism" (as well as "transnational criminal activities, including narco-trafficking, illicit arms-dealing, and illegal financial transactions.")

(46) The former Italian Prime Minister, President, and head of Secret Services (Francesco Cossiga) advised the 2008 minister in charge of the police, on how to deal with protests from teachers and students: He should do what I did when I was Minister of the Interior … infiltrate the movement with agents provocateurs inclined to do anything …. And after that, with the strength of the gained population consent … beat them for blood and beat for blood also those teachers that incite them. Especially the teachers. Not the elderly, of course, but the girl teacher's yes.

(47) An undercover officer admitted that he infiltrated environmental, leftwing, and anti-fascist groups in 22 countries. Germany's federal police chief admitted that – while the undercover officer worked for the German police – he acted illegally during a G8 protest in Germany in 2007 and committed arson by setting fire during a subsequent demonstration in Berlin. The undercover officer spent many years living with violent "Black Bloc" anarchists

.

(48) Denver police admitted that uniformed officers deployed in 2008 to an area where alleged 'Anarchists' had planned to wreak havoc outside the Democratic National Convention ended up

getting into a melee with two undercover policemen. The uniformed officers didn't know the undercover officers were cops.

(49) At the G20 protests in London in 2009, a British member of parliament saw plain clothes police officers attempting to incite the crowd to violence.

(50) The oversight agency for the Royal Canadian Mounted Police admitted that – at the G20 protests in Toronto in 2010 – undercover police officers were arrested with a group of protesters. Videos and photos (see this and this, for example) show that violent protesters wore remarkably similar boots and other gear as the police and carried police batons. The Globe and Mail reports that the undercover officers planned the targets for violent attack, and the police failed to stop the attacks.

(51) Egyptian politicians admitted (and see this) that government employees looted priceless museum artifacts 2011 to try to discredit the protesters.

(52) Austin police admit that 3 officers infiltrated the Occupy protests in that city. Prosecutors admit that one of the undercover officers purchased and constructed illegal "lock boxes" which ended up getting many protesters arrested.

(53) In 2011, a Colombian colonel admitted that he and his soldiers had lured 57 innocent civilians and killed them – after dressing many of them in uniforms – as part of a scheme to claim that Columbia was eradicating left-wing terrorists. And see this.

(54) Rioters who discredited the peaceful protests against the swearing in of the Mexican president in 2012 admitted that they were paid 300 pesos each to destroy everything in their path. According to Wikipedia, photos also show the vandals waiting in groups behind police lines prior to the violence.

(55) A Colombian army colonel has admitted that his unit murdered 57 civilians, then dressed them in uniforms and claimed they were rebels killed in combat.

(56) On November 20, 2014, Mexican agent provocateurs were transported by army vehicles to participate in the 2014 Iguala mass kidnapping protests, as was shown by videos and pictures distributed via social networks.

(57) The highly-respected writer for the Telegraph Ambrose Evans-Pritchard says that the head of Saudi intelligence – Prince Bandar – recently admitted that the Saudi government controls 'Chechen' terrorists.

(58) Two members of the Turkish parliament, high-level American sources and others admitted that the Turkish government – a NATO country – carried out the chemical weapons attacks in Syria and falsely blamed them on the Syrian government; and high-ranking Turkish government admitted on tape plans to carry out attacks and blame it on the Syrian government.

(59) The Ukrainian security chief admits that the sniper attacks which started the Ukrainian coup were carried out in order to frame others. Ukrainian officials admit that the Ukrainian snipers fired on both sides, to create maximum chaos.

(60) Burmese government officials admitted that Burma (renamed Myanmar) used false flag attacks against Muslim and Buddhist groups within the country to stir up hatred between the two groups, to prevent democracy from spreading.

(61) Israeli police were again filmed in 2015 dressing up as Arabs and throwing stones, then turning over Palestinian protesters to Israeli soldiers.

(62) Britain's spy agency has admitted (and see this) that it carries out "digital false flag" attacks on targets, framing people by writing offensive or unlawful material … and blaming it on the target.

(63) The CIA has admitted that it uses viruses and malware from Russia and other countries to carry out cyberattacks and blame other countries.

(64) U.S. soldiers have admitted that if they kill innocent Iraqis and Afghanis, they then 'Drop' automatic weapons near their body so they can pretend they were militants.

(65) Similarly, police frame innocent people for crimes they didn't commit. The practice is so well-known that the New York Times noted in 1981:

So common … There's a Name for It

The use of the bully's trick is so common that it was given a name hundreds of years ago. "False flag terrorism" is defined as a government attacking its own people, then blaming others in order to justify going to war against the people it blames. Or as Wikipedia defines it: 'False Flag; operations are covert operations conducted by governments, corporations, or other organizations, which are designed to appear as if they are being carried out by other entities. The name is derived from the military concept of flying false colors; that is, flying the flag of a country other than one's own. False flag operations are not limited to war and counter-insurgency operations and have been used in peace-time; for example, during Italy's strategy of tension.

Leaders Throughout History Have Acknowledged False Flags:

A history of false flag attacks used to manipulate the minds of the people! 'In individuals, insanity is rare; but in groups, parties, nations, and epochs it is the rule.'
— Friedrich Nietzsche

'Terrorism is the best political weapon for nothing drives people harder than a fear of sudden death.'
– Adolph Hitler

'Why of course the people don't want war … But after all it is the leaders of the country who determine the policy, and it is always a simple matter to drag the people along, whether it is a democracy, or a fascist dictatorship, or a parliament, or a communist dictatorship … Voice or no voice, the people can always be brought to the bidding of the leaders. That is easy. All you

have to do is to tell them they are being attacked and denounce the pacifists for lack of patriotism and exposing the country to danger. It works the same in any country.'
– Hermann Goering, Nazi leader.

'The easiest way to gain control of a population is to carry out acts of terror. The public will clamor for such laws if their personal security is threatened.'
– Josef Stalin.

There Is No American 'Deep State'

Experts on Turkish politics say the use of that term misunderstands what it means in Turkey—and the ways that such allegations can be used to enable political repression. Over the last week, the idea of a 'Deep state' in the United States has become a hot concept in American politics. The idea is not new, but a combination of leaks about President Trump and speculation that bureaucrats might try to slow-walk or undermine his agenda have given it fresh currency. A story in Friday's New York Times, for example, reports, 'As Leaks Multiply, Fears of a 'Deep State' in America.' It's an idea that I touched on in discussing the leaks. While there are numerous examples of activity that has been labeled as originating from a "deep state," from Latin America to Egypt, the most prominent example is Turkey, where state institutions contain a core of diehard adherents to the secular nationalism of Mustafa Kemal Ataturk, which is increasingly being eroded by the government of Recep Tayyip Erdogan.

Turkey has seen a series of coups, stretching back to 1960, as well as other activity attributed to a deep state. It's tempting to view the leaks about General Michael Flynn and other matters as a push to undermine the Trump presidency, though well short of coup, and therefore to compare it to the Turkish deep state. Some progressives have expressed a hope that bureaucracy might serve as a check on Trump, though they have generally avoided calling this a deep state. But Trump's defenders, both in Congress and on the fringe right, have employed the term, as have centrist observers and leftist critics of the national-security state. Trump has not yet used the phrase, but it seems like only a matter of time before it pops up in some late-night or early-morning tweet.

Are Deep-State Leakers Defending Democracy or Corroding It?

Trump Suddenly Takes a Stand against Russia. But experts on Turkey are not so quick to follow suit. They see a couple of problems with the analogy. First, it's not a precise application of the term; it portrays any sort of resistance to the regime as a 'Deep state,' failing to isolate what truly makes the shadowy structures in places like Turkey different. Second, a review of Turkish politics over the last decade shows the dangers in allowing a deep state to become a real menace in the mind of the public. 'Be careful playing with the deep-state idea, because it can so easily get out of control that it becomes a monster that helps whoever's in charge curb freedom and intimidate dissidents, because it's such a nebulous concept,' said Soner Cagaptay, who directs the Turkish Research Program at the Washington Institute for Near East Policy. 'You don't have to prove that it exists. Once the notion is out there, and the public starts to believe it, anybody can be attached to it.'

It's all well and good to argue that there are similarities between the Turkish deep state and American resistance to Trump. There are even some shared elements, like the presence of a corps of career government employees who see themselves as the last line of defense for longstanding national values against an insurgent president seeking to tear them down. It's also interesting that members of the military have seemed wary of Trump, warning of the importance of NATO and pushing back on reported plans to bring back torture—just as the military is the bastion of secularism in Turkey. As Cagaptay puts it, Turkey has historically had three checks on government power, two democratic (the courts and the media) and a third undemocratic: the military. These superficial similarities threaten to overshadow some of the deeper differences, though. Zeynep Tufekci, a Turkish sociologist and writer at the University of North Carolina, tweeted a string of criticisms about the analogy Friday morning. 'Permanent bureaucracy and/or non-electoral institutions diverging with the electoral branch is not that uncommon even in liberal democracies,' she wrote. 'In the Turkey case, that's not what it means. There was a shadowy, cross-institution occasionally *armed* network conducting killings, etc. So, if people are going to call non electoral institutions stepping up leaking stuff, fine. But it is not 'deep state' like in Turkey.' Omer Taspinar, who teaches at the National Defense University, took a similar position. 'The Deep State was a kind of criminal organization,' he said.

'It was not the judiciary, the civil society, the media, or the bureaucrats trying to engage in checks and balances against a legitimately elected government. What we're witnessing in the U.S., it's basically the institutional channels.' The Turkish deep state, historically, was willing to use violence to achieve its ends, and held close ties to organized crime. The resistance against Trump has involved leaking of government information—something that is sometimes criminal, and occasionally prosecuted, but is meaningfully different from killing or beating opponents. The fact that the deep state in Turkey was known for lawlessness and criminality meant that it was disliked by a wide range of factions there, from liberals to the religious, more conservative factions that the military repeatedly slapped down as they gained power. That began to change with the rise of Recep Tayyip Erdogan. Erdogan had previously been banned from government for violating rules against Islamist politics, but he returned in a more moderate guise, becoming prime minister in 2003. (He became president in 2014.) Erdogan learned to use the idea of deep state as a cudgel against it.

'It became such common currency that it allowed Erdogan's AKP government to cripple Turkey's democratic checks and balances, including media and courts, many of whose members Erdogan connected to this alleged deep state and then locked up during a set of trials collectively known as Ergenekon,' said Cagaptay, who writes about Erdogan's power grab in a forthcoming book The New Sultan. Those trials began in 2008. Erdogan started small: He first arrested 'People who looked like they were bad apples: Former military officials, connected to loan sharks, and everybody applauded that,' Cagaptay said. Then the investigation expanded. The murder of a prominent journalist was pinned on the deep state; then a substantial portion of Turkey's active-duty generals and admirals were accused. The trials effectively crippled the military, even though they were based largely on flimsy evidence. The indictment basically said, 'It is such a good plot, and it is hidden, because nothing that the deep state does is ever transparent,' Cagaptay said.

Once the military was neutralized, Erdogan was in a strong position. The army had removed prime ministers who got too ambitious in the past, but they were no longer in a position to do so. (The failed coup in July 2016 further affirmed just how weakened the military was.) "The Ergenekon case was the pivotal moment in Erdogan's undermining of Turkish democracy, because he used it then to go after courts and media, intellectuals, business people, pretty much anybody who did not support his political agenda," Cagaptay said. By the time a Turkish court overturned all 275 Ergenekon convictions in 2016, it didn't matter: The damage to institutions was done, and Erdogan had consolidated his grip on power. That's the danger of the deep-state analogy, and the danger of trying to operate a deep state: It is liable to facilitate its own destruction. It can place some real restraints on a government, up to a point. But if a leader can convince the public that it exists and is a real threat, he can manipulate that threat into empowering himself, undercutting the values that the deep state had pretended to safeguard. And it is a perfect foil for a demagogue. 'I think Erdogan's agenda was not eliminating it, it was taking it over,' Cagaptay said. 'Turkey has not become more liberal, freer after 15 years of Erdogan. Ironically, Turkey has become not freer after the elimination of the deep state. It has become less free.'

Cagaptay, like Tufekci and Taspinar, argued the American analogy was a bad one. But even if that is true, allegations of a deep state could be an effective foil for Trump, just as they have been for Erdogan. 'It's such a catchy concept because it helps explain so much,' Cagaptay said. 'If you want to explain inefficiency, it's not inefficiency but it's a deep state. Why did the U.S. government fail in a certain policy? Oh, it's because the deep state wanted it to fail, not because it was bad execution, or bad policy, or combination of both.' These are all good reasons to hesitate before labeling resistance to Trump, whether in the form of bureaucratic obstruction or leaks to the press, as the work of an American deep state. There is the important caveat that if the national-security state truly were plotting to topple a duly elected president, in the manner of past Turkish coups, that would be as serious a danger to the republic as anything that Trump could do.

Unfortunately, it is the practice of the national-security state, like the deep state, to work in darkness and obscurity, but there is also no evidence yet to support such a vast conspiracy—and recalling how Erdogan used lack of evidence as proof of nefarious behavior, it's important to move cautiously in assigning motives. The tale of Erdogan and the deep state may have a great deal to teach Americans about the deep state, but it might also teach some lessons about Trump. Consider the trio of checks and balances on the Turkish government: the media, the courts, and the deep state. Trump spent generous portions of his bizarre, rambling press conference on Thursday railing against both the media and the courts, working to undermine their credibility and influence as a check on his policies, an echo of the way Erdogan has railed against them in Turkey. The U.S. may not have a 'Real Deep State,' but that doesn't mean the U.S. president can't borrow his tactics from countries that do.

19. To be or Not to Covid-19

COVID-19 misinformation

COVID-19 misinformation refers to misinformation and 'Conspiracy Theories' about the scale of the COVID-19 pandemic and the origin, prevention, diagnosis, and treatment of the disease COVID-19, which is caused by the virus SARS-CoV-2. False information, including intentional disinformation, has been spread through social media, text messaging, and mass media. False information has been propagated by celebrities, politicians, and other prominent public figures. Multiple countries have passed laws against 'Fake news,' and thousands of people have been arrested for spreading COVID-19 misinformation. The spread of COVID-19 misinformation by governments has also been significant.

Commercial frauds have claimed to offer at-home tests, supposed preventives, and 'Miracle' cures. Several religious groups have claimed their faith will protect them from the virus. Without evidence, some people have claimed the virus is a bioweapon accidentally or deliberately leaked from a laboratory, a population control scheme, the result of a spy operation, or the side effect of 5G upgrades to cellular networks.

The World Health Organization (WHO) declared an 'Infodemic' of incorrect information about the virus that poses risks to global health. While belief in conspiracy theories is not a new phenomenon, in the context of the COVID-19 pandemic, this can lead to adverse health effects. Cognitive biases, such as jumping to conclusions and confirmation bias, may be linked to the occurrence of conspiracy beliefs. In addition to health effects, harms resulting from the spread of misinformation and endorsement of conspiracy theories include increasing distrust of news organizations and medical authorities as well as divisiveness and political fragmentation.

On 30 January 2020, the BBC reported on the developing issue of conspiracy theories and bad health advice regarding COVID-19. Examples at the time included false health advice shared on social media and private chats, as well as conspiracy theories such as the outbreak being planned with the participation of the Pirbright Institute. On 31 January, The Guardian listed seven instances of misinformation, adding the conspiracy theories about bioweapons and the link to 5G technology, and including varied false health advice.

In an attempt to speed up research sharing, many researchers have turned to preprint servers such as arXiv, bioRxiv, medRxiv, and SSRN. Papers are uploaded to these servers without peer review or any other editorial process that ensures research quality. Some of these papers have contributed to the spread of conspiracy theories. The most notable case was an unreviewed preprint paper uploaded to bioRxiv which claimed that the virus contained HIV 'Insertions.' Following objections, the paper was withdrawn. Preprints about COVID-19 have been extensively shared online and some data suggest that they have been used by the media almost 10 times more than preprints on other topics.

According to a study published by the Reuters Institute for the Study of Journalism, most misinformation related to COVID-19 involves 'Various forms of reconfiguration, where existing and often true information is spun, twisted, recontextualised, or reworked'; less misinformation 'Was completely fabricated'. The study also found that 'Top-down misinformation from politicians, celebrities, and other prominent public figures,' while accounting for a minority of the samples, captured a majority of the social media engagement. According to their classification, the largest category of misinformation (39%) was 'Misleading or false claims about the actions or policies of public authorities, including government and international bodies like the WHO or the UN'.

In addition to social media, television and radio have been perceived as sources of misinformation. In the preliminary stages of the COVID-19 pandemic in the United States, Fox News adopted an editorial line that the emergency response to the pandemic was politically motivated or otherwise unwarranted, and presenter Sean Hannity claimed on-air that the pandemic was a 'Hoax" (he later issued a denial). When evaluated by media analysts, the effect of broadcast misinformation has been found to influence health outcomes in the population. In a natural experiment (an experiment that takes place spontaneously, without human design or intervention), two similar television news items that were shown on the Fox News network one month apart in 2019 were compared.

One item reported the effects of COVID-19 more seriously, while a second item downplayed the threat of COVID-19. The study found that audiences who were exposed to the news item downplaying the threat were statistically more susceptible to increased COVID-19 infection rates and death. In August 2021, television broadcaster Sky News Australia was criticized for posting videos on YouTube containing misleading medical claims about COVID-19. Conservative talk radio in the US has also been perceived as a source of inaccurate or misleading commentary on COVID-19. In August and September 2021, several radio hosts who had discouraged COVID-19 vaccination, or expressed skepticism toward the COVID-19 vaccine, subsequently died from COVID-19 complications, among them Dick Farrel, Phil Valentine, and Bob Enyart.

Misinformation on the subject of COVID-19 has been used by politicians, interest groups, and state actors in many countries for political purposes: to avoid responsibility, scapegoat other countries, and avoid criticism of their earlier decisions. Sometimes there is a financial motive as well. Multiple countries have been accused of spreading disinformation with state-backed operations in the social media in other countries to generate panic, sow distrust, and undermine democratic debate in other countries, or to promote their models of government.

A Cornell University study of 38 million articles in English-language media around the world found that US President Donald Trump was the single largest driver of the misinformation. Analysis published by National Public Radio in December 2021 found that as American counties showed higher vote shares for Trump in 2020, COVID-19 vaccination rates significantly decreased, and death rates significantly increased. NPR attributed the findings to misinformation.

Misinformation regarding virus origin

Investigations into the origin of COVID-19, the consensus among virologists is that the most likely origin of the SARS-CoV-2 virus to be natural crossover from animals, having spilled-over into the human population from bats, possibly through an intermediate animal host, although the exact transmission pathway has not been determined. Most new infectious diseases begin this way and genomic evidence suggests an ancestor virus of SARS-CoV-2 originated in horseshoe bats.

An alternative hypothesis under investigation, deemed unlikely by the majority of virologists given a lack of evidence, is that the virus may have accidentally escaped from the Wuhan Institute of Virology in the course of standard research. A poll in July 2021 found that 52% of US adults believe COVID-19 escaped from a lab.

Unsubstantiated speculation and conspiracy theories related to this topic have gained popularity during the pandemic. Common conspiracy theories state that the virus was intentionally engineered, either as a bio-weapon or to profit from the sale of vaccines. According to the World Health Organization, genetic manipulation has been ruled out by genomic analysis. Many other origin stories have also been told, ranging from claims of secret plots by political opponents to a conspiracy theory about mobile phones. The Pew Research Center found, for example, that one in three Americans believed the new coronavirus had been created in a lab; one in four thought it had been engineered intentionally. The spread of these conspiracy theories is magnified through mutual distrust and animosity, as well as nationalism and the use of propaganda campaigns for political purposes.

The promotion of misinformation has been used by American far-right groups such as QAnon, by rightwing outlets such as Fox News, by former US President Donald Trump and also other prominent Republicans to stoke anti-China sentiments and has led to increased anti-Asian activity on social media and in the real world. This has also resulted in the bullying of scientists and public health officials, both online and in-person, fueled by a highly political and oftentimes toxic debate on many issues. Such spread of misinformation and conspiracy theories has the potential to negatively affect public health and diminish trust in governments and medical professionals.

The resurgence of the lab leak and other theories was fueled in part by the publication, in May 2021, of early emails between National Institute of Allergy and Infectious Diseases (NIAID) director Anthony Fauci and scientists discussing the issue. Per the emails in question, Kristian Andersen (author of one study debunking genomic manipulation theories) had heavily considered the possibility, and emailed Fauci proposing possible mechanisms, before ruling out deliberate manipulation with deeper technical analysis. These emails were later misconstrued and used by critics to claim a conspiracy was occurring. However, despite claims to the contrary in some US newspapers, no new evidence has surfaced to support any theory of a laboratory accident, and the majority of peer-reviewed research points to a natural origin. This has parallels in previous outbreaks of novel diseases, such as HIV, SARS and H1N1, which have also been the subject of allegations of laboratory origin.

Wuhan lab origin

One early source of the bio-weapon origin theory was former Israeli secret service officer Dany Shoham, who gave an interview to The Washington Times about the biosafety level 4 (BSL-4) laboratory at the Wuhan Institute of Virology. A scientist from Hong Kong, Li-Meng Yan, fled China and released a preprint stating the virus was modified in a lab rather than having a natural evolution. In an ad hoc peer-review (as the paper was not submitted for traditional peer review as part of the standard scientific publishing process), her claims were labelled as misleading, unscientific, and an unethical promotion of 'Essentially conspiracy theories that are not founded in fact.' Yan's paper was funded by the Rule of Law Society and the Rule of Law Foundation, two non-profits linked to Steve Bannon, a former Trump strategist, and Guo Wengui, an expatriate Chinese billionaire. This misinformation was further seized on by the American far-right, who have been known to promote distrust of China. In effect, this formed 'A fast-growing echo chamber for misinformation.' The idea of SARS-CoV-2 as a lab-engineered weapon is an element of the Plandemic conspiracy theory, which proposes that it was deliberately released by China.

The Epoch Times, an anti-Communist Party of China newspaper affiliated with Falun Gong, has spread misinformation related to the COVID-19 pandemic in print and via social media including Facebook and YouTube. It has promoted anti-China rhetoric and conspiracy theories around the coronavirus outbreak, for example through an 8-page special edition called 'How the Chinese Communist Party Endangered the World', which was distributed unsolicited in April 2020 to mail customers in areas of the United States, Canada, and Australia. In the newspaper, the SARS-CoV-2 virus is known as the 'CCP virus', and a commentary in the newspaper posed the question, 'Is the novel coronavirus outbreak in Wuhan an accident occasioned by weaponizing the virus at that [Wuhan P4 virology] lab?' The paper's editorial board suggested that COVID-19 patients cure themselves by 'Condemning the CCP' and 'maybe a miracle will happen'. In response to the propagation of theories in the US of a Wuhan lab origin, the Chinese government promulgated the conspiracy theory that the virus was developed by the United States army at Fort Detrick.

Gain-of-function research

One idea used to support a laboratory origin invokes previous gain-of-function research on coronaviruses. Virologist Angela Rasmussen writes that this is unlikely, due to the intense scrutiny and government oversight gain-of-function research is subject to, and that it is improbable that research on hard-to-obtain coronaviruses could occur under the radar. The exact meaning of 'Gain of function' is disputed among experts.

In May 2020, Fox News host Tucker Carlson accused Anthony Fauci of having 'Funded the creation of COVID' through gain-of-function research at the Wuhan Institute of Virology (WIV). Citing an essay by science writer Nicholas Wade, Carlson alleged that Fauci had directed research to make bat viruses more infectious to humans. In a hearing the next day, US senator Rand Paul alleged that the US National Institutes of Health (NIH) had been funding gain-of-function research in Wuhan, accusing researchers including epidemiologist Ralph Baric of creating 'Super-viruses.' Both Fauci and NIH Director Francis Collins have denied that the US government supported such research. Baric likewise rejected Paul's allegations, saying his lab's research into cross-species transmission of bat coronaviruses did not qualify as gain-of-function.

A 2017 study of chimeric bat coronaviruses at the WIV listed NIH as a sponsor; however, NIH funding was only related to sample collection. Based on this and other evidence,

The Washington Post rated the claim of an NIH connection to gain-of-function research on coronaviruses as 'Two Pinocchio's,' representing 'Significant omissions and/or exaggerations.'

Accidental release of collected sample

Another theory suggests the virus arose in humans from an accidental infection of laboratory workers by a natural sample. Unfounded online speculation about this scenario has been widespread. In March 2021, an investigatory report released by the WHO described this scenario as 'Extremely unlikely' and not supported by any available evidence. The report acknowledged, however, that the possibility cannot be ruled out without further evidence. The investigation behind this report operated as a joint collaboration between Chinese and international scientists. At the release briefing for the report, WHO Director-General Tedros Adhanom Ghebreyesus reiterated the report's calls for a deeper probe into all evaluated possibilities, including the laboratory origin scenario. The study and report were criticized by heads of state from the US, the EU, and other WHO member countries for a lack of transparency and incomplete access to data. Further investigations have also been requested by some scientists, including Anthony Fauci and signatories of a letter published in Science.

Since May 2021, some media organizations softened previous language that described the laboratory leak theory as 'Debunked' or a 'Conspiracy Theory'. On the other hand, scientific opinion that an accidental leak is possible, but unlikely, has remained steady. A number of journalists and scientists have said that they dismissed or avoided discussing the lab leak theory during the first year of the pandemic as a result of perceived polarization resulting from Donald Trump's embrace of the theory.

Stolen from Canadian lab

Some social media users have alleged that COVID-19 was stolen from a Canadian virus research lab by Chinese scientists. Health Canada and the Public Health Agency of Canada said that this had 'No factual basis. The stories seem to have been derived from a July 2019 CBC news article stating that some Chinese researchers had their security access to the National Microbiology Laboratory in Winnipeg, a Level 4 virology lab, revoked after a Royal Canadian

Mounted Police investigation. Canadian officials described this as an administrative matter and said there was no risk to the Canadian public.

Responding to the conspiracy theories, the CBC stated that its articles 'Never claimed the two scientists were spies, or that they brought any version of a coronavirus to the lab in Wuhan.' While pathogen samples were transferred from the lab in Winnipeg to Beijing on 31 March 2019, neither of the samples contained a coronavirus. The Public Health Agency of Canada has stated that the shipment conformed to all federal policies, and that the researchers in question are still under investigation, and thus it cannot be confirmed nor denied that these two were responsible for sending the shipment. The current location of the researchers under investigation by the Royal Canadian Mounted Police has also not been released. In a January 2020 press conference, NATO secretary-general Jens Stoltenberg, when asked about the case, stated that he could not comment specifically on it, but expressed concerns about 'Increased efforts by the nations to spy on NATO allies in different ways'.

Accusations by China

According to The Economist, conspiracy theories exist on China's internet about COVID-19 being created by the CIA in order to 'Keep China down'. According to an investigation by ProPublica, such conspiracy theories and disinformation have been propagated under the direction of China News Service, the country's second largest government-owned media outlet controlled by the United Front Work Department. Global Times and Xinhua News Agency have similarly been implicated in propagating disinformation related to COVID-19's origins. NBC News however has noted that there have also been debunking efforts of US-related conspiracy theories posted online, with a WeChat search of 'Coronavirus is from the U.S.' reported to mostly yield articles explaining why such claims are unreasonable.

On 12 March 2020, two spokesmen for the Chinese Ministry of Foreign Affairs, Zhao Lijian and Geng Shuang, alleged at a press conference that Western powers may have 'Bio-engineered' COVID-19. They were alluding that the US Army created and spread COVID-19, allegedly during the 2019 Military World Games in Wuhan, where numerous cases of influenza-like illness were reported. A member of the U.S. military athletics delegation based at Fort

Belvoir, who competed in the 50mi Road Race at the Wuhan games, became the subject of online targeting by netizens accusing her of being 'Patient zero' of the COVID-19 outbreak in Wuhan, and was later interviewed by CNN, to clear her name from the 'False accusations in starting the pandemic'.

In January 2021, Hua Chunying renewed the conspiracy theory from Zhao Lijian and Geng Shuang that the SARS-CoV-2 virus originating in the United States at the U.S. biological weapons lab Fort Detrick. This conspiracy theory quickly went trending on the Chinese social media platform Weibo, and Hua Chunying continued to cite evidence on Twitter, while asking the government of the United States to open up Fort Detrick for further investigation to determine if it is the source of the SARS-CoV-2 virus. In August 2021, a Chinese Foreign Ministry spokesman repeatedly used an official podium to elevate the Fort Detrick's origin unproven idea. According to a report from Foreign Policy, Chinese diplomats, and government officials in concert with China's propaganda apparatus and covert networks of online agitators and influencers have responded, focused on repeating Zhao Lijian's allegation relating to Fort Detrick in Maryland, and the 'Over 200 U.S. bio labs' around the world.

Accusations by Russia

On 22 February 2020, US officials alleged that Russia is behind an ongoing disinformation campaign, using thousands of social media accounts on Twitter, Facebook, and Instagram to deliberately promote unfounded conspiracy theories, claiming the virus is a biological weapon manufactured by the CIA and the US is waging economic war on China using the virus.

Accusations by other countries

According to Washington, DC-based nonprofit Middle East Media Research Institute, numerous writers in the Arabic press have promoted the conspiracy theory that COVID-19, as well as SARS and the swine flu virus, were deliberately created and spread to sell vaccines against these diseases, and it is 'Part of an economic and psychological war waged by the U.S. against China with the aim of weakening it and presenting it as a backward country and a source of diseases'. Accusations in Turkey of Americans creating the virus as a weapon have been reported and a YouGov poll from August 2020 found that 37% of Turkish respondents believed the US government was responsible for creating and spreading the virus.

Reza Malekzadeh, Iran's deputy health minister, rejected bioterrorism theories. An Iranian cleric in Qom said Donald Trump targeted the city with coronavirus 'To damage its culture and honor.' Reza Malekzadeh, Iran's deputy health minister and former Minister of Health, rejected claims that the virus was a biological weapon, pointing out that the US would be suffering heavily from it. He said Iran was hard-hit because its close ties to China and reluctance to cut air ties introduced the virus, and because early cases had been mistaken for influenza. The theory has also circulated in the Philippines[e] and Venezuela. An October 2020 Globsec poll of Eastern European countries found that 38% of respondents in Montenegro and Serbia, 37% of those in North Macedonia, and 33% in Bulgaria believed the USA deliberately created COVID-19.

Jewish origin

In the Muslim world, Iran's Press TV asserted that 'Zionist elements developed a deadlier strain of coronavirus against Iran.' Similarly, some Arab media outlets accused Israel and the United States of creating and spreading COVID-19, avian flu, and SARS. Users on social media offered other theories, including the allegation that Jews had manufactured COVID-19 to precipitate a global stock market collapse and thereby profit via insider trading, while a guest on Turkish television posited a more ambitious scenario in which Jews and Zionists had created COVID-19, avian flu, and Crimean–Congo hemorrhagic fever to 'Design the world, seize countries, and neuter the world's population'. Turkish politician Fatih Erbakan reportedly said in a speech, 'Though we do not have certain evidence, this virus serves Zionism's goals of decreasing the number of people and preventing it from increasing, and important research expresses this.' Israeli attempts to develop a COVID-19 vaccine prompted negative reactions in Iran. Grand Ayatollah Naser Makarem Shirazi denied initial reports that he had ruled that a Zionist-made vaccine would be halal, and one Press TV journalist tweeted that 'I'd rather take my chances with the virus than consume an Israeli vaccine.' A columnist for the Turkish Yeni Akit asserted that such a vaccine could be a ruse to carry out mass sterilization.

Muslims spreading virus

In India, Muslims have been blamed for spreading infection following the emergence of cases linked to a Tablighi Jamaat religious gathering. There are reports of vilification of Muslims on social media and attacks on individuals in India. Claims have been made that Muslims are selling food contaminated with SARS-CoV-2 and that a mosque in Patna was sheltering people from Italy and Iran. These claims were shown to be false. In the UK, there are reports of far-right groups blaming Muslims for the pandemic and falsely claiming that mosques remained open after the national ban on large gatherings.

In the United States

An alert by the US Federal Bureau of Investigation regarding the possible threat of far-right extremists intentionally spreading COVID-19 mentioned blame being assigned to Jews and Jewish leaders for causing the pandemic and several statewide shutdowns.

In Germany

Flyers have been found on German tram cars, falsely blaming Jews for the pandemic.

In Britain

According to a study carried out by the University of Oxford in early 2020, nearly one-fifth of respondents in England believed to some extent that Jews were responsible for creating or spreading the virus with the motive of financial gain.

Population-control scheme

According to the BBC, Jordan Sather, a YouTuber supporting the QAnon conspiracy theory and the anti-vax movement, has falsely claimed that the outbreak was a population-control scheme created by the Pirbright Institute in England and by former Microsoft CEO Bill

Gates. Piers Corbyn was described as 'Dangerous' by physician and broadcaster Hilary Jones during their joint interview on Good Morning Britain in early September 2020. Corbyn described COVID-19 as a 'Psychological operation to close down the economy in the interests of mega-corporations" and stated "vaccines cause death'.

5G mobile-phone networks

Openreach engineers appealed on anti-5G Facebook groups, saying they are not involved in mobile networks, and workplace abuse is making it difficult for them to maintain phone lines and broadband. In February 2020, BBC News reported that conspiracy theorists on social media groups alleged a link between COVID-19 and 5G mobile networks, claiming that the Wuhan and Diamond Princess Outbreaks were directly caused by electromagnetic fields and by the introduction of 5G and wireless technologies. Conspiracy theorists have alleged that the pandemic was a cover-up for a 5G-related illness. In March 2020, Thomas Cowan, a holistic medical practitioner who trained as a physician and operates on probation with the Medical Board of California, alleged that COVID-19 is caused by 5G. He based this on the claims that African countries had not been affected significantly by the pandemic and Africa was not a 5G region. Cowan also falsely alleged that the viruses were waste from cells that were poisoned by electromagnetic fields, and that historical viral pandemics coincided with major developments in radio technology.

The video of Cowan's claims went viral and was recirculated by celebrities, including Woody Harrelson, John Cusack, and singer Keri Hilson. The claims may also have been recirculated by an alleged 'Coordinated disinformation campaign,' similar to campaigns used by the Internet Research Agency in Saint Petersburg, Russia. The claims were criticized on social media and debunked by Reuters, USA Today, Full Fact and American Public Health Association executive director Georges C. Benjamin. Cowan's claims were repeated by Mark Steele, a conspiracy theorist who claimed to have first-hand knowledge that 5G was in fact a weapon system capable of causing symptoms identical to those produced by the virus. Kate Shemirani, a former nurse who had been struck off the UK nursing registry and had become a promoter of conspiracy theories, repeatedly claimed that these symptoms were identical to those produced by exposure to electromagnetic fields.

Steve Powis, national medical director of NHS England, described theories linking 5G mobile-phone networks to COVID-19 as the 'Worst kind of fake news'. Viruses cannot be transmitted by radio waves, and COVID-19 has spread and continues to spread in many countries that do not have 5G networks. There were 20 suspected arson attacks on phone masts in the UK over the 2020 Easter weekend. These included an incident in Dagenham where three men were arrested on suspicion of arson, a fire in Huddersfield that affected a mast used by emergency services, and a fire in a mast that provides mobile connectivity to the NHS Nightingale Hospital Birmingham. Some telecom engineers reported threats of violence, including threats to stab and murder them, by individuals who believe them to be working on 5G networks. On 12 April 2020, Gardaí and fire services were called to fires at 5G masts in County Donegal, Ireland. The Gardaí were treating the fires as arson. After the arson attacks, British Cabinet Office Minister Michael Gove said the theory that COVID-19 virus may be spread by 5G wireless communication is 'Just nonsense, dangerous nonsense as well'. Telecommunications provider Vodafone announced that two Vodafone masts and two it shares with O2, another provider, had been targeted.

By 6 April 2020, at least 20 mobile-phone masts in the UK had been vandalized since the previous Thursday. Because of the slow rollout of 5G in the UK, many of the damaged masts had only 3G and 4G equipment. Mobile-phone and home broadband operators estimated there were at least 30 incidents where engineers maintaining equipment were confronted in the week up to 6 April. As of 30 May, there had been 29 incidents of attempted arson at mobile-phone masts in the Netherlands, including one case where 'Fuck 5G' was written. There have also been incidents in Ireland and Cyprus. Facebook has deleted messages encouraging attacks on 5G equipment. Engineers working for Openreach, a division of British Telecom, posted pleas on anti-5G Facebook groups asking to be spared abuse as they are not involved with maintaining mobile networks. Industry lobby group Mobile UK said the incidents were affecting the maintenance of networks that support home working and provide critical connections to vulnerable customers, emergency services, and hospitals. A widely circulated video showed a woman accusing employees of broadband company Community Fibre of installing 5G as part of a plan to kill the population.

Of those who believed that 5G networks caused COVID-19 symptoms, 60% stated that much of their knowledge about the virus came from YouTube. In April 2020, YouTube announced that it would reduce the amount of content claiming links between 5G and COVID-19. Videos that are conspiratorial about 5G that do not mention COVID-19 would not be removed, though they might be considered 'Borderline content' and therefore removed from search recommendations, losing advertising revenue. The discredited claims had been circulated by British conspiracy theorist David Icke in videos (subsequently removed) on YouTube and Vimeo, and an interview by London Live TV network, prompting calls for action by Ofcom. It took YouTube on average 41 days to remove Covid-related videos containing false information in the first half of 2020.

Ofcom issued guidance to ITV following comments by Eamonn Holmes about 5G and COVID-19 on This Morning. Ofcom said the comments were 'Ambiguous' and 'Ill-judged' and they 'Risked undermining viewers trust in advice from public authorities and scientific evidence". Ofcom also found local channel London Live in breach of standards for an interview it had with David Icke. It said that he had 'Expressed views which had the potential to cause significant harm to viewers in London during the pandemic.'

On 24 April 2020, The Guardian revealed that Jonathan Jones, an evangelical pastor from Luton, had provided the male voice on a recording blaming 5G for deaths caused by COVID-19.He claimed to have formerly headed the largest business unit at Vodafone, but insiders at the company said that he was hired for a sales position in 2014 when 5G was not a priority for the company and that 5G would not have been part of his job. He had left Vodafone after less than a year. A tweet started an internet meme that Bank of England £20 banknotes contained a picture of a 5G mast and the SARS-CoV-2 virus. Facebook and YouTube removed items pushing this story, and fact checking organizations established that the picture is of Margate Lighthouse and the 'Virus' is the staircase at the Tate Britain.

American scientist selling virus to China

In April 2020, rumors circulated on Facebook, alleging that the US Government had 'Just discovered and arrested' Charles Lieber, chair of the Chemistry and Chemical Biology

Department at Harvard University for 'Manufacturing and selling' the novel coronavirus (COVID-19) to China. According to a report from Reuters, posts spreading the rumor were shared in multiple languages over 79,000 times on Facebook. Lieber was arrested on 28 January 2020, and later charged with two federal counts of making an allegedly false statement about his links to a Chinese university, unrelated to the virus. The rumor of Lieber, a chemist in an area entirely unrelated to the virus research, developing COVID-19 and selling it to China has been discredited.

Meteor origin

In 2020, a group of researchers that most notably included Edward J. Steele and Chandra Wickramasinghe, the foremost living proponent of panspermia, claimed in ten research papers that COVID-19 originated from a meteor spotted as a bright fireball over the city of Songyuan in Northeast China on 11 October 2019 and that a fragment of the meteor landed in the Wuhan area, which started the first COVID-19 outbreaks. However, the group of researchers did not provide any direct evidence proving this conjecture. In an August 2020 article, Astronomy.com called the meteor origin conjecture 'So remarkable that it makes the others look boring by comparison'.

NCMI intelligence report

In April 2020, ABC News reported that, in November 2019, 'U.S. intelligence officials were warning that a contagion was sweeping through China's Wuhan region, changing the patterns of life and business and posing a threat to the population'. The article stated that the National Center for Medical Intelligence (NCMI), had produced an intelligence report in November 2019 which raised concerns about the situation. The director of the NCMI, Col. R. Shane Day said 'Media reporting about the existence/release of a National Center for Medical Intelligence Coronavirus-related product/assessment in November 2019 is not correct. No such NCMI product exists.'

PCR testing

In reality, the reverse transcription PCR test for SARS-CoV-2 is extremely sensitive to the virus and testing laboratories have controls in place to prevent and detect contamination. However, the tests only reveal the presence of the virus and not whether it remains infectious. Social-media posts have falsely claimed that Kary Mullis, the inventor of polymerase chain reaction (PCR), said that PCR testing for SARS-CoV-2 does not work. Mullis, who received the Nobel Prize in Chemistry for the invention of PCR, died in August 2019 before the emergence of the SARS-CoV-2 virus and never made these statements. Several posts claim Mullis said, 'PCR tests cannot detect free infectious viruses at all,' that PCR testing was designed to detect any non-human DNA, or the DNA and RNA of the person being tested, or that the process of DNA amplification used in PCR will lead to contamination of the samples.

A video of a 1997 interview with Mullis has also been widely circulated, in which Mullis says PCR will find 'Anything'; the video description asserts that this means PCR cannot be used to reliably detect SARS-CoV-2. A claim attributed to the Swiss Federal Office of Public Health that PCR testing is fraudulent became popular in the Philippines and remains a widespread belief. According to a report from AFP, research associate Joshua Miguel Danac of the University of the Philippines' National Institute of Molecular Biology and Biotechnology debunked the claim, calling PCR tests "the gold standard for diagnosis". Fake testing and perception of fake testing remains a problem in the Philippines.

Misreporting of morbidity and mortality numbers

Correctly reporting the number of people who were sick or who had died was difficult, especially during the earliest days of the pandemic. In China, the Chinese under-reporting during early 2020. Leaked documents show that China's public reporting of cases gave an incomplete picture during the initial stages of the pandemic. For example, on 10 February 2020, China publicly reported 2,478 new confirmed cases. However, confidential internal documents that later leaked to CNN showed 5,918 new cases on 10 February. These were broken down as 2,345 confirmed cases, 1,772 clinically diagnosed cases and 1,796 suspected cases.

Nurse whistleblower

On 24 January 2020, a video circulated online appearing to be of a nurse named Jin Hui in Hubei, describing a far direr situation in Wuhan than reported by Chinese officials. However, the BBC said that contrary to its English subtitles in one of the video's existing versions, the woman does not claim to be either a nurse or a doctor in the video and that her suit and mask do not match the ones worn by medical staff in Hubei.

The video claimed that more than 90,000 people had been infected with the virus in China, that the virus could spread from one person to 14 people (R0 = 14) and that the virus was starting a second mutation. The video attracted millions of views on various social media platforms and was mentioned in numerous online reports. The claimed R0 of 14 in the video was noted by the BBC to be inconsistent with the expert estimation of 1.4 to 2.5 at that time. The video's claim of 90,000 infected cases was noted to be 'Unsubstantiated'.

Alleged leak of death toll by Tencent

On 5 February 2020, Taiwan News published an article claiming that Tencent may have accidentally leaked the real numbers of death and infection in China. Taiwan News suggested that the Tencent Epidemic Situation Tracker had briefly showed infected cases and death tolls many times higher of the official figure, citing a Facebook post by 38-year-old Taiwanese beverage store owner Hiroki Lo and an anonymous Taiwanese netizen. The article, referenced by other news outlets such as the Daily Mail and widely circulated on Twitter, Facebook and 4chan, sparked a wide range of conspiracy theories that the screenshot indicates the real death toll instead of the ones published by health officials. Justin Lessler, associate professor at the Bloomberg School of Public Health, claims the numbers of the alleged 'Leak' are unreasonable and unrealistic, citing the case fatality rate as far lower than the 'Leaked information'. A spokesman for Tencent responded to the news article, claiming the image was doctored, and it features 'False information which we never published.'

Mass cremation in Wuhan

On 8 February 2020, a report emerged on Twitter claiming that data showed a massive increase in sulfur emissions over Wuhan, China. The Twitter thread then claimed the reason was due to the mass cremation of COVID-19 victims. The story was shared on multiple media outlets, including Daily Express, Daily Mail, and Taiwan News. Snopes debunked the misinformation, pointing out that the maps used by the claims were not real-time observations of sulfur dioxide (SO2) concentrations above Wuhan. Instead, the data was a computer-generated model based on historical information and forecast on SO2 emissions. A story in The Epoch Times on 17 February 2020 shared a map from the Internet that falsely alleged massive sulfur dioxide releases from crematoriums during the COVID-19 pandemic in China, speculating that 14,000 bodies may have been burned. A fact check by AFP reported that the map was a NASA forecast taken out of context.

Decline in cellphone subscriptions

There was a decrease of nearly 21 million cellphone subscriptions among the three largest cellphone carriers in China, which led to misinformation that this is evidence for millions of deaths due to COVID-19 in China. The drop is attributed to cancellations of phone services due to a downturn in the social and economic life during the outbreak. In the US, accusations have been made of under-reporting, over-reporting, and other problems. Necessary data was corrupted in some places, for example, on the state level in the United States. The public health handling of the pandemic has been hampered by the use of archaic technology (including fax machines and incompatible formats), poor data flow and management (or even no access to data), and general lack of standardization and leadership. Privacy laws hampered contact tracing and case finding efforts, which resulted in under-diagnosis and under-reporting.

Allegations of inflated death counts

In August 2020, President Donald Trump retweeted a conspiracy theory alleging that COVID-19 deaths are systematically overcounted, and that only 6% of the reported deaths in the United States were actually from the disease. This 6% number is based on only counting death certificates where COVID-19 is the sole condition listed. The lead mortality statistician at the CDC's National Center for Health Statistics said that those death certificates likely did not include all the steps that led to the death and thus were incomplete. The CDC collects data based on case surveillance, vital records, and excess deaths. A FactCheck.org article on the issue reported that while 6% of the death certificates included COVID-19 exclusively as the cause of death and 94% had additional conditions that contributed to it, COVID-19 was listed as the underlying cause of death in 92% of them, as it may directly cause other severe conditions such as pneumonia or acute respiratory distress syndrome. The U.S. experienced 882,000 'Excess deaths' (i.e., deaths above the baseline expected from normal mortality in previous years) between February 2020 and January 2022, which is somewhat higher than the officially recorded mortality from COVID-19 during that period (835,000 deaths). Analysis of weekly data from each U.S. state shows that the calculated excess deaths are strongly correlated with COVID-19 infections, undercutting the notion that the deaths were primarily caused by some factor other than the disease.

Misleading Johns Hopkins News-Letter article

On 22 November 2020, a study by Genevieve Briand (assistant director for the master's program in Applied Economics at JHU) was published in the student-run Johns Hopkins News-Letter claiming to have found 'No evidence that COVID-19 created any excess deaths'. The study was later retracted after it was used to promote conspiracy theories on right-wing social media accounts and misinformation websites, but the presentation was not removed from YouTube, where it had been viewed more than 58,000 times as of 3 December 2020. Briand compared data from spring 2020 and January 2018, ignoring expected seasonal variations in mortality and unusual peaks in the spring and summer of 2020 compared to previous spring and summer months. Briand's study failed to account for the total excess mortality from all causes reported during the pandemic, with 300,000 deaths associated with the virus per CDC data. Deaths per age group were also shown as a percentage rather than as raw numbers, greatly underestimating the effects of the pandemic given large population sizes. The study also suggested that deaths attributed to cardiac and respiratory diseases in infected persons were incorrectly categorized as deaths due to COVID-19. This view fails to recognize that those with such conditions are more vulnerable to the virus and therefore more likely to die from it. The retraction of Briand's study went viral on social media under false claims of censorship.

Misinformation targeting Taiwan

On 26 February 2020, the Taiwanese Central News Agency reported that copious amounts of misinformation had appeared on Facebook claiming the pandemic in Taiwan was out of control, the Taiwanese government had covered up the total number of cases, and that President Tsai Ing-wen had been infected. The Taiwan fact-checking organization had suggested the misinformation on Facebook shared similarities with mainland China due to its use of simplified Chinese characters and mainland China vocabulary. The organization warned that the purpose of the misinformation is to attack the government.

In March 2020, Taiwan's Ministry of Justice Investigation Bureau warned that China was trying to undermine trust in factual news by portraying the Taiwanese government reports as fake news. Taiwanese authorities have been ordered to use all possible means to track whether the messages were linked to instructions given by the Chinese Communist Party. The PRC's Taiwan Affairs Office denied the claims, calling them lies, and said that Taiwan's Democratic Progressive Party was 'Inciting hatred' between the two sides. They then claimed that the 'DPP continues to politically manipulate the virus.' According to The Washington Post, China has used organized disinformation campaigns against Taiwan for decades.

Nick Monaco, the research director of the Digital Intelligence Lab at Institute for the Future, analyzed the posts and concluded that the majority appear to have come from ordinary users in China, not the state. However, he criticized the Chinese government's decision to allow the information to spread beyond China's Great Firewall, which he described as 'Malicious.' According to Taiwan News, nearly one in four cases of misinformation are believed to be connected to China. On 27 March 2020, the American Institute in Taiwan announced that it was partnering with the Taiwan FactCheck Center to help combat misinformation about the COVID-19 outbreak.

Misrepresented World Population Project map

In early February 2020, a decade-old map illustrating a hypothetical viral outbreak published by the World Population Project (part of the University of Southampton) was misappropriated by a number of Australian media news outlets (and British tabloids The Sun, Daily Mail and Metro) which claimed the map represented the COVID-19 pandemic. This misinformation was then spread via the social media accounts of the same media outlets, and while some outlets later removed the map, the BBC reported, on 19 February, that a number of news sites had yet to retract the map.

'Casedemic'

COVID-19 deniers use the word casedemic as a shorthand for a conspiracy theory holding that COVID-19 is harmless and that the reported disease figures are merely a result of increased testing. The concept is particularly attractive to anti-vaccination activists, who use it to argue that public health measures, and particularly vaccines, are not needed to counter what they say is a fake epidemic. David Gorski writes that the word casedemic was seemingly coined by Ivor Cummins, an engineer whose views are popular among COVID-19 deniers in August 2020. The term has been adopted by alternative medicine advocate Joseph Mercola, who has exaggerated the effect of false positives in polymerase chain reaction (PCR) tests to construct a false narrative that testing is invalid because it is not perfectly accurate (see also § PCR testing, above). In reality, the problems with PCR testing are well-known and accounted for by public health authorities. Such claims also disregard the possibility of asymptomatic spread, the number of potentially-undetected cases during the initial phases of the pandemic in comparison to the present due to increased testing and knowledge since, and other variables that can influence PCR tests.

Spreading the Disease

Early in the pandemic, little information was known about how the virus spreads, when the first people became sick, or who was most vulnerable to infection, serious complications, or death. During 2020, it became clear that the main route of spread was through exposure to the virus-laden respiratory droplets produced by an infected person. There were also some early questions about whether the disease might have been present earlier than reported; however, subsequent research disproved this idea.

California herd immunity in 2019

In March 2020, Victor Davis Hanson publicized a theory that COVID-19 may have been in California in the fall of 2019 resulting in a level of herd immunity to at least partially explain differences in infection rates in cities such as New York City vs Los Angeles. Jeff Smith of Santa Clara County stated that evidence indicated the virus may have been in California since December 2019. Early genetic and antibody analyses refute the idea that the virus was in the United States prior to January 2020.

Patient Zero

In March 2020, conspiracy theorists started the false rumor that Maatje Benassi, a US army reservist, was 'Patient Zero' of the pandemic, the first person to be infected with COVID-19. Benassi was targeted because of her participation in the 2019 Military World Games at Wuhan before the pandemic started, even though she never tested positive for the virus. Conspiracy theorists even connected her family to the DJ Benny Benassi as a Benassi virus plot, even though they are not related, and Benny had also not had the virus.

Surface and fomite transmission

Early in the pandemic it was claimed that COVID-19 could be spread by contact with contaminated surfaces or fomites—even though this is an uncommon transmission route for other respiratory viruses. This led to recommendations that high-contact surfaces (like playground equipment or school desks) be frequently deep-cleaned and that certain items (like groceries or mailed packages) be disinfected. Ultimately, the US CDC concluded that the likelihood of transmission under these scenarios was less than 1 in 10,000. They further concluded that handwashing reduced the risk of exposure to COVID-19, but surface disinfection did not.

Resistance/susceptibility based on ethnicity

There have been claims that specific ethnicities are more or less vulnerable to COVID-19. COVID-19 is a new zoonotic disease, so no population has yet had the time to develop population immunity. Beginning on 11 February 2020, reports quickly spread via Facebook, implied that a Cameroonian student in China had been completely cured of the virus due to his African genetics. While a student was successfully treated, other media sources have indicated that no evidence implies Africans are more resistant to the virus and labeled such claims as false information. Kenyan Secretary of Health Mutahi Kagwe explicitly refuted rumors that 'Those with black skin cannot get Coronavirus,' while announcing Kenya's first case on 13 March. This false myth was cited as a contributing factor in the disproportionately high rates of infection and death observed among African Americans.

There have been claims of 'Indian immunity,' that the people of India have more immunity to the COVID-19 virus due to living conditions in India. This idea was deemed 'Absolute drivel' by Anand Krishnan, professor at the Centre for Community Medicine of the All India Institute of Medical Sciences (AIIMS). He said there was no population immunity to the COVID-19 virus yet, as it is new, and it is not even clear whether people who have recovered from COVID-19 will have lasting immunity, as this happens with some viruses but not with others. Iran's Supreme Leader Ayatollah Ali Khamenei claimed the virus was genetically targeted at Iranians by the US, giving this explanation for the pandemic having seriously affected Iran. He did not offer any evidence. A group of Jordanian researchers published a report claiming that Arabs are less vulnerable to COVID-19 due to a genetic variation specific to those of Middle East heritage. This paper had not been debunked by November 2020.

Xenophobic blaming by ethnicity and religion

UN video warns that misinformation against groups may lower testing rates and increase transmission. COVID-19-related xenophobic attacks have been made against individuals with the attacker blaming the victim for COVID-19 on the basis of the victim's ethnicity. People who are considered to look Chinese have been subjected to COVID-19-related verbal and physical attacks in many other countries, often by people accusing them of transmitting the virus. Within China, there has been discrimination (such as evictions and refusal of service in shops) against people from anywhere closer to Wuhan (where the pandemic started) and against anyone perceived as being non-Chinese (especially those considered African), as the Chinese government has blamed continuing cases on re-introductions of the virus from abroad (90% of reintroduced cases were by Chinese passport-holders). Neighboring countries have also discriminated against people seen as Westerners.

People have also simply blamed other local groups like pre-existing social tensions and divisions, sometimes citing reporting of COVID-19 cases within that group. For instance, Muslims have been widely blamed, shunned, and discriminated against in India (including some violent attacks), amid unfounded claims that Muslims are deliberately spreading COVID-19, and a Muslim event at which the disease did spread has received far more public attention than many similar events run by other groups and the government. White supremacist groups have blamed COVID-19 on non-whites and advocated deliberately infecting minorities they dislike, such as Jews.

Bat soup consumption

Some media outlets, including Daily Mail and RT, as well as individuals, disseminated a video showing a Chinese woman eating a bat, falsely suggesting it was filmed in Wuhan and connecting it to the outbreak. However, the widely circulated video contains unrelated footage of a Chinese travel vlogger, Wang Mengyun, eating bat soup in the island country of Palau in 2016. Wang posted an apology on Weibo, in which she said she had been abused and threatened, and that she had only wanted to showcase Palauan cuisine. The spread of misinformation about bat consumption has been characterized by xenophobic and racist sentiment toward Asians. In contrast, scientists suggest the virus originated in bats and migrated into an intermediary host animal before infecting people. South Korean 'Conservative populist' Jun Kwang-hun told his followers there was no risk to mass public gatherings as the virus was impossible to contract outdoors. Many of his followers are elderly.

Lifetime of the virus

Misinformation has spread that the lifetime of SARS-CoV-2 is only 12 hours and that staying home for 14 hours during the Janata curfew would break the chain of transmission. Another message claimed that observing the Janata curfew would result in the reduction of COVID-19 cases by 40%.

Mosquitoes

It has been claimed that mosquitoes transmit COVID-19. There is no evidence that this is true. COVID-19 is likely to spread through small droplets of saliva and mucus.

Contaminated objects

A fake Costco product recall notice circulated on social media purporting that Kirkland-brand bath tissue had been contaminated with COVID-19 (meaning SARS-CoV-2) due to the item being made in China. No evidence supports that SARS-CoV-2 can survive on surfaces for prolonged periods of time (as might happen during shipping), and Costco has not issued such a recall. A warning claiming to be from the Australia Department of Health said COVID-19 spreads through petrol pumps and that everyone should wear gloves when filling up petrol in their cars. There were claims that wearing shoes in one's home was the reason behind the spread of COVID-19 in Italy.

Cruise ships as safe havens

Claims by cruise-ship operators notwithstanding, there are many cases of coronaviruses in hot climates; some countries in the Caribbean, the Mediterranean, and the Persian Gulf are severely affected. In March 2020, the Miami New Times reported that managers at Norwegian Cruise Line had prepared a set of responses intended to convince wary customers to book cruises, including 'Blatantly false' claims that COVID-19 'Can only survive in cold temperatures, so the Caribbean is a fantastic choice for your next cruise', that 'Scientists and medical professionals have confirmed that the warm weather of the spring will be the end of the Coronavirus', and that the virus 'Cannot live in the amazingly warm and tropical temperatures that your cruise will be sailing to'. Flu is seasonal (becoming less frequent in the summer) in some countries, but not in others. While it is possible that COVID-19 will also show some seasonality, this has not yet been determined. When COVID-19 spread along international air travel routes, it did not bypass tropical locations. Outbreaks on cruise ships, where an older population lives in close quarters, frequently touching surfaces which others have touched, were common. It seems that COVID-19 can be transmitted in all climates. It has seriously affected many warm-climate countries. For instance, Dubai, with a year-round average daily high of 28.0 Celsius (82.3 °F) and the airport said to have the world's most international traffic, has had thousands of cases.

Breastfeeding infants

While commercial companies that make breastmilk substitutes promote their products during the pandemic, the WHO and UNICEF advise that women should continue to breastfeed during the COVID-19 pandemic even if they have confirmed or suspected COVID-19. Current evidence indicates that it is unlikely that COVID-19 can be transmitted through breast milk.

Sexual transmission and infertility

Corona virus can persist in men's semen even after they have begun to recover, although the virus cannot replicate in the reproductive system. Chinese researchers who found the virus in the semen of men infected with COVID-19, claimed that this opened up a small chance the disease could be sexually transmitted, though this claim has been questioned by other academics since this has been shown with many other viruses such as Ebola and Zika. A team of Italian scholars said in a paper it released in March that 11 of 43 men who recovered from infections, or one-quarter of the test subjects, were found to have either azoospermia (no sperm in semen) or oligospermia (low sperm count). Mechanisms through which infectious diseases affect sperm is roughly divided into two categories. One involves viruses entering the testes, where they attack spermatogonia. The other involves high fever exposing the testes to heat and thereby killing sperm.

Prevention

People tried many different things to prevent infection. Sometimes the misinformation was false claims of efficacy, such as claims that the virus could not spread during religious ceremonies, and at other times the misinformation was false claims of inefficacy, such as claiming that alcohol-based hand sanitizer did not work. In other cases, especially with regard to public health advice about wearing face masks during the COVID-19 pandemic, additional scientific evidence resulted in different advice over time.

Efficacy of hand sanitizer, antibacterial soaps

Washing in soap and water for at least 20 seconds is the best way to clean hands. The second-best is a hand sanitizer that is at least 60% alcohol. Claims that hand sanitizer is merely 'Antibacterial not antiviral,' and therefore ineffective against COVID-19, have spread widely on Twitter and other social networks. While the effectiveness of sanitizer depends on the specific ingredients, most hand sanitizer sold commercially inactivates SARS-CoV-2, which causes COVID-19. Hand sanitizer is recommended against COVID-19, though unlike soap, it is not effective against all types of germs. Washing in soap and water for at least 20 seconds is recommended by the US Centers for Disease Control (CDC) as the best way to clean hands in most situations. However, if soap and water are not available, a hand sanitizer that is at least 60% alcohol can be used instead, unless hands are visibly dirty or greasy. The CDC and the Food and Drug Administration both recommend plain soap; there is no evidence that antibacterial soaps are any better, and limited evidence that they might be worse long-term.

Public use of face masks

The U.S. Surgeon General Jerome Adams urged people to wear face masks and acknowledged that it is difficult to correct earlier messaging that masks do not work for the general public. Authorities, especially in Asia, recommended wearing face masks in public early in the pandemic. In other parts of the world, authorities made conflicting (or contradictory) statements. Several governments and institutions, such as in the United States, initially dismissed the use of face masks by the general population, often with misleading or incomplete information about their effectiveness. Commentators have attributed the anti-mask messaging to attempts at managing mask shortages caused by initial inaction, remarking that the claims went beyond the science, or were simply lies

In February 2020, U.S. Surgeon General Jerome Adams tweeted 'Seriously people—STOP BUYING MASKS! They are NOT effective in preventing general public from catching

#Coronavirus;' he later reversed his position with increasing evidence that masks can limit the spread of COVID-19. On 12 June 2020, Anthony Fauci (a key member of the White House Coronavirus Task Force) confirmed that the American public were told not to wear masks from the beginning, due to a shortage of masks, and then explained that masks do actually work. Some media outlets claimed that neck gaiters were worse than not wearing masks at all in the COVID-19 pandemic, misinterpreting a study which was intended to demonstrate a method for evaluating masks (and not actually to determine the effectiveness of diverse types of masks).

The study also only looked at one wearer wearing the one neck gaiter made from a polyester/spandex blend, which is not sufficient evidence to support the claim about gaiters made in the media. The study found that the neck gaiter, which was made from a thin and stretchy material, appeared to be ineffective at limiting airborne droplets expelled from the wearer; Isaac Henrion, one of the co-authors, suggests that the result was likely due to the material rather than the style, stating that 'Any mask made from that fabric would probably have the same result, no matter the design.' Warren S. Warren, a co-author, said that they tried to be careful with their language in interviews, but added that the press coverage has 'Careened out of control' for a study testing a measuring technique.

There are false claims spread that the usage of masks causes adverse health-related issues such as low blood oxygen levels, high blood carbon dioxide levels, and a weakened immune system. Some also falsely claimed that masks cause antibiotic-resistant pneumonia by preventing pathogenic organisms to be exhaled away from the body.

Individuals have speciously claimed legal or medical exemptions to avoid complying with mask mandates. Individuals have, for instance, claimed that the Americans with Disabilities Act (ADA; designed to prohibit discrimination based on disabilities) allows exemption from mask requirements. The United States Department of Justice (DOJ) responded that the Act 'Does not provide a blanket exemption to people with disabilities from complying with legitimate safety requirements necessary for safe operations.' The DOJ also issued a warning about cards (sometimes featuring DOJ logos or ADA notices) that claim to 'Exempt' their holders from wearing masks, stating that these cards are fraudulent and not issued by any government agency. On 31 July 2020, Filipino President Rodrigo Duterte said those who did not have cleaning supplies could use gasoline as a disinfectant to clean their masks, 'for people who don't [have Lysol], drench it in gasoline or diesel ... just find some gasoline and dip your hand with the mask in it.' His spokesman, Harry Roque, later corrected him.

Alcoholic beverages

Contrary to some reports, drinking alcohol does not protect against COVID-19, and can increase health risks (short term and long term). Drinking alcohol is ethanol; other alcohols, such as methanol, which causes methanol poisoning, are acutely poisonous, and may be present in badly prepared alcoholic beverages. Iran has reported incidents of methanol poisoning, caused by the false belief that drinking alcohol would cure or protect against COVID-19; alcohol is banned in Iran, and bootleg alcohol may contain methanol. According to Iranian media in March 2020, nearly 300 people have died and more than a thousand have become ill due to methanol poisoning, while Associated Press gave figures of around 480 deaths with 2,850 others affected. The number of deaths due to methanol poisoning in Iran reached over 700 by April. Iranian social media had circulated a story from British tabloids that a British man and others had been cured of COVID-19 with whiskey and honey, which combined with the use of alcohol-based hand sanitizers as disinfectants, led to the false belief that drinking high-proof alcohol can kill the virus.

Similar incidents have occurred in Turkey, with 30 Turkmenistan citizens dying from methanol poisoning related to COVID-19 cure claims. In Kenya, in April 2020, the Governor of Nairobi Mike Sonko came under scrutiny for including small bottles of the cognac Hennessy in care packages, falsely claiming that alcohol serves as 'Throat sanitizer' and that, from research, it is believed that 'Alcohol plays a key role in killing coronavirus'. In July 2020, the president of Belarus, Alexander Lukashenko, recommended drinking vodka to prevent COVID-19.

Warm or hot drinks

There were several claims that drinking warm drinks at a temperature of around 30 °C (86 °F) protects one from COVID-19, most notably by Alberto Fernández, the president of Argentina said, 'The WHO recommends that one drink many hot drinks because heat kills the virus.' Scientists commented that the WHO had made no such recommendation, and that drinking hot water can damage the oral mucosa. These false claims mostly spread out across social media and in Latin American countries.

Vegetarian immunity

Claims that vegetarians are immune to COVID-19 spread online in India, causing '#NoMeat_NoCoronaVirus' to trend on Twitter. Such claims are allegedly false.

Religious protection

A number of religious groups have claimed protection due to their faith. Some refused to stop practices, such as gatherings of large groups that promoted the transmission of the virus. In Israel, some Ultra-Orthodox Jews initially refused to close synagogues and religious seminaries and disregarded government restrictions because 'The Torah protects and saves,' which resulted in an eight-fold faster rate of infection among some groups.

In South Korea, the River of Grace Community Church in Gyeonggi Province spread the virus after spraying salt water into their members' mouths in the belief that it would kill the virus, while the Shincheonji Church of Jesus in Daegu where a church leader claimed that no Shincheonji worshipers had caught the virus in February while hundreds died in Wuhan, later caused the biggest spread of the virus in the country. In Tanzania, President John Magufuli, instead of banning congregations, urged the faithful to go to pray in churches and mosques in the belief that it will protect them. He said that COVID-19 is a devil, therefore 'cannot survive in the body of Jesus Christ; it will burn' (the 'Body of Jesus Christ' refers to the Christian church).

Despite the COVID-19 pandemic, on 9 March 2020, the Church of Greece announced that Holy Communion, in which churchgoers eat pieces of bread soaked in wine from the same chalice, would continue as a practice. The Holy Synod said Holy Communion 'Cannot be the cause of the spread of illnesses, with Metropolitan Seraphim saying the wine was without blemish because it represented the blood and body of Christ, and that 'Whoever attends Holy Communion is approaching God, who has the power to heal.' The Church refused to restrict

Christians from taking Holy Communion, which was supported by several clerics, some politicians, and health professionals. The Greek Association of Hospital Doctors criticized these professionals for putting their religious beliefs before science. A review of the medical publications on the subject, published by a Greek physician, claims that the transmission of any infectious disease through the Holy Communion has never been documented. This controversy divided the Greek society, the politics, and medical experts.

The Islamic missionary movement Tablighi Jamaat organised Ijtema mass gatherings in Malaysia, India, and Pakistan whose participants believed that God would protect them, causing the biggest rise in COVID-19 cases in these and other countries. In Iran, the head of Fatima Masumeh Shrine encouraged pilgrims to visit the shrine despite calls to close the shrine, saying that they 'Consider this holy shrine to be a place of healing.' In Somalia, myths have spread claiming Muslims are immune to the virus.

Tobacco

In 2020, small observational studies were discussed on social media and other outlets in which tobacco smoking was shown to be protective against SARS-CoV-2 infections. In April 2020, researchers at a Paris hospital noted an inverse relationship between smoking and COVID-19 infections, which led to an increase in tobacco sales in France. These results were at first so astonishing that the French government initiated a clinical trial with transdermal nicotine patches. Clinical reviews of available information are clear, however, that smoking in fact leads to an increased chance of COVID-19 infections, and that smokers generally experience much more severe respiratory symptoms.

Cocaine

Cocaine does not protect against COVID-19. Several viral tweets spread around Europe and Africa, purporting that snorting cocaine would sterilize one's nostrils of SARS-CoV-2 particulates. In response, the French Ministry of Health released a public service announcement debunking this claim, saying 'No, cocaine does NOT protect against COVID-19. It is an addictive drug that causes serious side effects and is harmful to people's health.' The World Health Organization also debunked the claim.

Helicopter spraying

In Sri Lanka, the Philippines and India, it has been claimed that one should stay at home on particular days when helicopters spray 'COVID-19 disinfectant' over homes. No such spraying has taken place, nor is it planned, nor, as of July 2020, is there any such agent that could be sprayed.

Vibrations

The notion that the vibrations generated by clapping during March 2020 Janata curfew would kill the virus was debunked by the media. Amitabh Bachchan was heavily criticized for one of his tweets, which claimed vibrations from clapping and blowing conch shells as part of the Janata Curfew would have reduced or destroyed COVID-19 potency as it was Amavasya, the darkest day of the month.

Food

In India, fake news circulated that the World Health Organization warned against eating cabbage to prevent COVID-19 infection. Claims that the poisonous fruit of the Datura plant is a preventive measure for COVID-19 resulted in eleven people being hospitalized in India. They ate the fruit, following the instructions from a TikTok video that propagated misinformation regarding the prevention of COVID-19.

Vitamin D

In February 2020, claims that Vitamin D pills could help prevent COVID-19 circulated on social media in Thailand. In May 2020, the Centre for Evidence-Based Medicine, while noting that 'Current advice is that the entire population of the UK should take vitamin D supplements to prevent vitamin D deficiency', found 'No clinical evidence that vitamin D supplements are beneficial in preventing or treating COVID-19'. Vitamin D promotion has gained traction amongst anti-vaccinationists, who wrongly say it can be taken as an alternative to getting vaccinated against COVID-19. A preprint of a journal article from Indonesia purporting to show a beneficial effect of vitamin D for COVID-19 went viral across social media, and was cited several times in mainstream academic literature, including in a recommendation from NICE. Subsequent investigation, however, found none of the authors seemed to be known of at the hospitals listed as their affiliations, suggesting the paper was entirely fraudulent.

Vaccines

General misinformation related to vaccination and immunization and Vaccine hesitancy. Anti-vaccination activists and other people in many countries have spread a variety of unfounded 'Conspiracy Theories' and other misinformation about COVID-19 vaccines based on misunderstood or misrepresented science, religion, exaggerated claims about side effects, a story about COVID-19 being spread by 5G, misrepresentations about how the immune system works and when and how COVID-19 vaccines are made, and other false or distorted information. This misinformation has proliferated and may have made many people averse to vaccination. This has led to governments and private organizations around the world introducing measures to encourage vaccination such as lotteries, mandates, and free entry to events, which has in turn led to further misinformation about the legality and effect of these measures themselves.

Hospital conditions

Some conservative figures in the United States, such as Richard Epstein, downplayed the scale of the pandemic, saying it has been exaggerated as part of an effort to hurt President Trump. Some people pointed to empty hospital parking lots as evidence that the virus has been exaggerated. Despite the empty parking lots, many hospitals in New York City and other places experienced thousands of COVID-19-related hospitalizations. In the course of 2020, conspiracy theorists used the #FilmYourHospital hashtag to encourage people to record videos in seemingly empty, or sparsely populated hospitals, in order to prove that the pandemic was a 'Hoax'.

Treatment

Widely circulated posts on social media have made many unfounded claims of treatment methods of COVID-19. Some of these claims are scams, and some promoted methods are dangerous and unhealthy.

Herbal treatments

Various national and party-held Chinese media heavily advertised an 'Overnight research' report by Wuhan Institute of Virology and Shanghai Institute of Materia Medica, Chinese Academy of Sciences, on how shuanghuanglian, an herb mixture from traditional Chinese medicine (TCM), can effectively inhibit COVID-19. The report led to a purchase craze of shuanghuanglian. The president of Madagascar Andry Rajoelina launched and promoted in April 2020 an herbal drink based on an Artemisia plant as a miracle cure that can treat and prevent COVID-19 despite a lack of medical evidence. The drink has been exported to other African countries. Based on in-vitro studies, extracts of E. purpurea (Echinaforce) showed virucidal activity against coronaviruses, including SARS-CoV-2. Because the data was experimental and solely derived from cell cultures, antiviral effects in humans have not been elucidated. As a result, regulatory agencies have not recommended the use of Echinacea preparations for the prophylaxis and treatment of COVID-19.

Vitamin C

During the COVID-19 pandemic, vitamin C was the subject of more FDA warning letters than any other quack treatment for COVID-19.

Common cold and flu treatments

In March 2020, a photo circulated online showing a 30-year-old Indian textbook that lists aspirin, antihistamines, and nasal spray as treatments for coronavirus diseases. False claims spread asserting that the book was evidence that COVID-19 started much earlier than reported and that common cold treatments could be a cure for COVID-19. The textbook actually talks about coronaviruses in general, as a family of viruses. A rumor circulated on social media posts on Weibo, Facebook and Twitter claiming that Chinese experts said saline solutions could kill COVID-19. There is no evidence for this. A tweet from French health minister Olivier Véran, a bulletin from the French health ministry, and a small speculative study in The Lancet Respiratory Medicine raised concerns about ibuprofen worsening COVID-19, which spread extensively on social media. The European Medicines Agency and the World Health Organization recommended COVID-19 patients keep taking ibuprofen as directed, citing lack of convincing evidence of any danger.

Cow dung and urine

Indian political activist Swami Chakrapani and Member of the Legislative Assembly Suman Haripriya claimed that drinking cow urine and applying cow dung on the body can cure COVID-19. In Manipur, two people were arrested under the National Security Act for social media posts which said cow urine and dung did not cure the virus. (They were arrested under Section 153 of the Indian Penal Code for allegedly promoting enmity between distinct groups on grounds of religion, race, place of birth, residence, language, etc. and acts prejudicial to maintenance of harmony). WHO's chief scientist Soumya Swaminathan criticized politicians incautiously spreading such misinformation without evidence.

2-Deoxy-D-glucose

A drug based on 2-deoxy-D-glucose (2-DG) was approved by the Drugs Controller General of India for emergency use as adjunct therapy in moderate to severe COVID-19 patients. The drug was launched at a press conference with a false claim that it was approved by the World Health Organization. It was developed by the DRDO along with Dr. Reddy's Laboratories, who stated in a press release, that the drug 'Helps in faster recovery of hospitalized patients and reduces supplemental oxygen dependence.' The Wire as well as The Hindu noted that the approval was based on poor evidence; no journal publication (or preprint) concerning efficacy and safety are yet available.

Traditional Chinese Medicine (TCM) prescriptions

Since its third version, the COVID management guidelines from the Chinese National Health Commission recommends using Traditional Chinese medicines to treat the disease. In Wuhan, China Central Television reported that local authorities have pushed for a set of TCM prescriptions to be used for every case since early February. One formula was promoted at the national level by mid-February. The local field hospitals were explicitly TCM-oriented. According to state media, as of 16 March 2020, 91.91% of all Hubei patients have used TCM, with the rate reaching 99% in field hospitals and 94% in bulk quarantine areas. In March 2020, the online insert of the official People's Daily, distributed in The Daily Telegraph, published an article stating that Traditional Chinese medicine 'Helps fight coronavirus'.

Chloroquine and hydroxychloroquine

There were claims that chloroquine was used to cure more than 12,000 COVID-19 patients in Nigeria. On 11 March 2020, Adrian Bye, a tech startup leader who is not a doctor, suggested to cryptocurrency investors Gregory Rigano and James Todaro that 'Chloroquine will keep most people out of hospital'. (Bye later admitted that he had reached this conclusion through 'Philosophy' rather than medical research.) Two days later, Rigano and Todaro promoted chloroquine in a self-published article that claimed affiliation with the Stanford University School of Medicine, the National Academy of Sciences, and the Birmingham School of Medicine, the three institutions mentioned that they had no links to the article, and Google removed the article for violating its terms of service.

Ivermectin

Early in the COVID-19 pandemic, laboratory research suggested Ivermectin might have a role in preventing or treating COVID-19. Online misinformation campaigns and advocacy boosted the drug's profile among the public. While scientists and physicians largely remained skeptical, some nations adopted Ivermectin as part of their pandemic-control efforts. Some people, desperate to use Ivermectin without a prescription, took veterinary preparations leading to shortages of supplies of Ivermectin for animal treatment leading to the FDA tweeting 'You are not a horse' to draw attention to the issue. Subsequent research failed to confirm the utility of Ivermectin for COVID-19, and in 2021 it emerged that many of the studies demonstrating benefit were faulty, misleading, or fraudulent. Nevertheless, misinformation about Ivermectin continued to be propagated on social media and the drug remained a cause célèbre for anti-vaccinationists and conspiracy theorists.

Dangerous treatments

Some QAnon proponents, including Jordan Sather and others, have promoted gargling 'Miracle Mineral Supplement' (actually chlorine dioxide, a chemical used in some industrial applications as a bleach that may cause life-threatening reactions and even death) as a way of preventing or curing the disease. The Food and Drug Administration has warned multiple times that drinking MMS is 'Dangerous' as it may cause 'Severe vomiting' and 'Acute liver failure.' Twelve people were hospitalized in India when they ingested the poisonous thornapple (Datura stramonium AKA Jimsonweed) after seeing the plant recommended as a 'coronavirus home remedy' in a TikTok video. Datura species contain many substances poisonous to humans, mainly through anticholinergic effects.

Silver

In February 2020, televangelist Jim Bakker promoted a colloidal silver solution, sold on his website, as a remedy for COVID-19; naturopath Sherrill Sellman, a guest on his show, falsely stated that it 'Hasn't been tested on this strain of the coronavirus, but it's been tested on other strains of the coronavirus and has been able to eliminate it within 12 hours'. The US Food and Drug Administration and New York Attorney General's office both issued cease-and-desist orders against Bakker, and he was sued by the state of Missouri over the sales. The New York Attorney General's office also issued a cease-and-desist order to radio host Alex Jones, who was selling silver-infused toothpaste that he falsely claimed could kill the virus and had been verified by federal officials, causing a Jones spokesman to deny the products had been sold for the purpose of treating any disease. The FDA later threatened Jones with legal action and seizure of several silver-based products if he continued to promote their use against COVID-19.

Mustard oil

The yoga guru Ramdev claimed that one can treat COVID-19 by pouring mustard oil through the nose, causing the virus to flow into the stomach where it would be destroyed by gastric acid. He also claimed that if a person can hold their breath for a minute, it means they are not suffering from any type of coronavirus, symptomatic or asymptomatic. Both these claims were found to be false.

Untested treatments

U.S. president Donald Trump suggested at a press briefing on 23 April 2020 that disinfectant injections or exposure to ultraviolet light might help treat COVID-19. There is no evidence that either could be a viable method. Misinformation that the government is spreading an 'Anti-corona' drug in the country which? During Janata curfew, a stay-at-home curfew enforced in India, went viral on social media. Following the first reported case of COVID-19 in Nigeria on 28 February, untested cures and treatments began to spread via platforms such as WhatsApp. In March 2020, the US Federal Bureau of Investigation arrested actor Keith Lawrence Middlebrook for wire fraud with a fake COVID-19 cure.

Spiritual healing

Another televangelist, Kenneth Copeland, claimed on Victory Channel during a program called 'Standing against Coronavirus,' that he can cure television viewers of COVID-19 directly from the television studio. The viewers had to touch the television screen to receive the spiritual healing.

Organ trafficking

In India, baseless rumors spread saying that people were being taken to care centers and killed to harvest their organs, with their bodies then being swapped to avoid suspicion. These rumors spread more quickly through online platforms such as WhatsApp, and resulted in protests, attacks against healthcare workers, and reduced willingness to seek COVID-19 testing and treatment.

Simpson's prediction

Claims that The Simpsons had predicted the COVID-19 pandemic in 1993, accompanied by a doctored screenshot from the show (where the text "Corona Virus" was layered over the original text 'Apocalypse Meow', without blocking it from view), were later found to be false. The claim had been widely spread on social media.

Virus remains in body permanently

It has been wrongly claimed that anyone infected with COVID-19 will have the virus in their bodies for life. While there is no curative treatment, most infected people recover from the disease and eliminate the virus from their bodies.

Efforts to combat misinformation

On 2 February 2020, the World Health Organization (WHO) described a 'Massive Infodemic', citing an over-abundance of reported information, which was false, about the virus that 'Makes it hard for people to find trustworthy sources and reliable guidance when they need it'. The WHO stated that the high demand for timely and trustworthy information has incentivized the creation of a direct WHO 24/7 myth-busting hotline where its communication and social media teams have been monitoring and responding to misinformation through its website and social media pages. The WHO specifically debunked several claims as false, including the claim that a person can tell if they have the virus or not simply by holding their breath; the claim that drinking substantial amounts of water will protect against the virus; and the claim that gargling salt water prevents infection.

Social media

In early February 2020, Facebook, Twitter, and Google announced that they were working with WHO to address misinformation on their platforms. In a blog post, Facebook stated that it would remove content flagged by global health organizations and local authorities that violate its content policy on misinformation leading to 'Physical harm.' Facebook is also giving free advertising to WHO. Nonetheless, a week after Trump's speculation that sunlight could kill the virus, The New York Times found '780 Facebook groups, 290 Facebook pages, nine Instagram accounts and thousands of tweets pushing UV light therapies', material which those companies declined to remove from their platforms. On 11 August 2020, Facebook removed seven million posts with misinformation about COVID-19. At the end of February 2020, Amazon removed more than a million products that claimed to cure or protect against COVID-19 and removed tens of thousands of listings for health products whose prices were 'Significantly higher than recent prices offered on or off Amazon', although numerous items were 'Still being sold at unusually soaring prices' as of 28 February.

Millions of instances of COVID-19 misinformation have occurred across multiple online platforms. Other researchers monitoring the spread of fake news observed certain rumors started in China; many of them later spread to Korea and the United States, prompting several universities in Korea to start the multilingual 'Facts Before Rumors' campaign to evaluate common claims seen online. The proliferation of such misinformation on social media has led to workshops for the application of machine learning resources to detect misinformation. In addition, the divisive nature of the issue, being mired in existing political tensions, has led to online bullying of scientists.

Wikipedia

The media have praised Wikipedia's coverage of COVID-19 and its combating the inclusion of misinformation through efforts led by the English-language Wikipedia's WikiProject Medicine, among other groups. From May 2020, Wikipedia's consensus for the COVID-19 pandemic page has been to 'Not mention the theory that the virus was accidentally leaked from a laboratory in the article.' WHO began working with Wikipedia to provide much of its infographics and reports on COVID-19 to help fight misinformation, with plans to use similar approaches for fighting misinformation about other infectious diseases in the future?

Newspapers and scholarly journals

Initially, many newspapers with paywalls lowered them for some or all their COVID-19 coverage. Many scientific publishers made scientific papers related to the outbreak unrestricted access. The scientific publishing community, while intent on producing quality scholarly publications, has itself been negatively impacted by the infiltration of inferior or false research leading to the retraction of several articles on the topic of COVID-19, as well as polluting valid and reliable scientific study, bringing into question the reliability of research undertaken. Retraction Watch maintains a database of retracted COVID-19 articles.

Podcasts

In January 2022, 270 US healthcare professionals, scientists and professors wrote an open letter to Spotify complaining that podcast host Joe Rogan had a 'Concerning history of broadcasting misinformation, particularly regarding the Covid-19 pandemic' and describing him as a 'Menace to public health'. This was in part due to Rogan platforming and promoting the conspiracy theories of Robert W. Malone who was one of two recent guests on The Joe Rogan Experience who compared pandemic policies to the holocaust. The letter described the interview as a 'Mass-misinformation events of this scale have extraordinarily dangerous ramifications.' The Joe Rogan Experience is one of the world's most popular podcasts, with an audience of millions. The Malone episode was removed from YouTube due to violation of the site's misinformation policy; the letter urged Spotify to adopt a medical misinformation policy.

Government censorship

In many countries, censorship was performed by governments, with 'Fake news' laws being enacted to criminalize certain types of speech regarding COVID-19. Often, people were arrested for making posts online. In March 2020, the Turkish Interior Ministry reported 93 suspects and 19 arrests of social media users whose posts were 'Targeting officials and spreading panic and fear by suggesting the virus had spread widely in Turkey and that officials had taken insufficient measures'. In April 2020, Iran's military said that 3600 people had been arrested for 'Spreading rumors' about COVID-19 in the country. In Cambodia, at least 17 individuals who expressed concerns about the spread of COVID-19 were arrested between

January and March 2020 on 'Fake news' charges. In April 2020, Algerian lawmakers passed a law criminalizing 'Fake news' deemed harmful to 'Public order and state security'.

In the Philippines, China, India, Egypt, Ethiopia, Bangladesh, Morocco, Pakistan, Saudi Arabia, Oman, Iran, Vietnam, Laos, Indonesia, Mongolia, Sri Lanka, Kenya, South Africa, Cote d'Ivoire, Somalia, Mauritius, Zimbabwe, Thailand, Kazakhstan, Azerbaijan, Montenegro, Serbia, Malaysia, Singapore, and Hong Kong, people have been arrested for allegedly spreading false information about the COVID-19 pandemic. The United Arab Emirates has introduced criminal penalties for the spread of misinformation and rumors related to the outbreak. Myanmar blocked access to 221 news websites, including several leading media outlets. In the United States, some elected officials aided the spread of misinformation. On 3 January 2022, Congressman Troy Nehls entered a full transcript of the Malone interview on The Joe Rogan Experience into the Congressional Record in order to circumvent what he said was censorship by social media.

Scams

The WHO has warned of criminal scams involving perpetrators who misrepresent themselves as representatives of the WHO seeking personal information from victims via email or phone. Also, the Federal Communications Commission has advised consumers not to click on links in suspicious emails and not to give out personal information in emails, text messages or phone calls. The Federal Trade Commission has also warned on charity scams related to the pandemic, and has advised consumers not to donate in cash, gift cards, or wire transfers. Cybersecurity firm Check Point stated there has been a significant increase in phishing attacks to lure victims into unwittingly installing a computer virus under the guise of emails related to COVID-19 containing attachments. Cyber-criminals use deceptive domains such as 'cdc-gov.org' instead of the correct 'cdc.gov,' or even spoof the original domain so it resembles specific websites. More than 4,000 domains related to COVID-19 have been registered.

Police in New Jersey, United States, reported incidents of criminals knocking on people's doors and claiming to be from the CDC. They then attempt to sell products at inflated prices or otherwise scam victims under the guise of educating and protecting the public from COVID-19. Links that purportedly direct to the Johns Hopkins University COVID-19 map, but instead direct to a false site that spreads malware, have been circulating on the Internet. Since the passage in March 2020 of the CARES Act, criminals have taken advantage of the stimulus bill by asking people to pay in advance to receive their stimulus payment. Because of this, the IRS has advised consumers to only use the official IRS COVID-19 web address to submit information to the IRS (and not in response to a text, email, or phone call). In response to these schemes, many financial companies, like Wells Fargo and LoanDepot, as well as health insurers, like Humana, for example, have posted similar advisories on their websites.

SARS 'CONSPIRACY THEORY'

The SARS conspiracy theory began to emerge during the severe acute respiratory syndrome (SARS) outbreak in China in the spring of 2003, when Sergei Kolesnikov, a Russian scientist, and a member of the Russian Academy of Medical Sciences, first publicized his claim that the SARS coronavirus is a synthesis of measles and mumps. According to Kolesnikov, this combination cannot be formed in the natural world and thus the SARS virus must have been produced under laboratory conditions. Another Russian scientist, Nikolai Filatov, head of Moscow's epidemiological services, had earlier commented that the SARS virus was probably man-made. However, independent labs concluded these claims to be premature since the SARS virus is a coronavirus, whereas measles and mumps are paramyxoviruses. The primary differences between a coronavirus and a paramyxovirus are in their structures and method of infection, thus making it implausible for a coronavirus to have been created from two paramyxoviruses.

The widespread reporting of claims by Kolesnokov and Filatov caused controversy in many Chinese internet discussion boards and chat rooms. Many Chinese believed that the SARS virus could be a biological weapon manufactured by the United States, which perceived China as a potential threat. The failure to find the source of the SARS virus further convinced these people and many more that SARS was artificially synthesized and spread by some individuals and even governments. Circumstantial evidence suggests that the SARS virus crossed over to humans from Asian palm civets, 'Civet cats,' a type of animal that is often killed and eaten in Guangdong, where SARS was first discovered.

Supporters of the conspiracy theory suggest that SARS caused the most serious harm in mainland China, Hong Kong, Taiwan and Singapore, regions where most Chinese reside, while the United States, Europe and Japan were not affected as much. However, the highest mortality from SARS outside of China occurred in Canada where 43 died. Conspiracist further take as evidence the idea that, although SARS has an average mortality rate of around 10% around the world, no one died in the United States from SARS. However, there were only 8 confirmed cases out of 27 probable cases in the US (10% of 8 people is less than 1 person). Regarding reasons why SARS patients in the United States experienced a relatively mild illness, the U.S. Centers for Disease Control has explained that anybody with fever and a respiratory symptom who had traveled to an affected area was included as a SARS patient in the U.S., even though many of these were found to have had other respiratory illnesses.

Tong Zeng, an activist with no medical background, authored the book The Last Defense Line: Concerns about the Loss of Chinese Genes, published in 2003. In the book, Zeng suggested researchers from the United States may have created SARS as an anti-Chinese bioweapon after taking blood samples in China for a longevity study in the 1990s. The book's hypothesis was a front-page report in the Guangzhou newspaper Southern Metropolis Daily. Coronaviruses similar to SARS have been found in bats in China, suggesting they may be their natural reservoir.

THE LONG, STRANGE HISTORY OF BILL GATES POPULATION CONTROL CONSPIRACY THEORIES

Anti-vaccine protesters in Melbourne, Australia on May 10, 2020. Three months into the global pandemic, Bill Gates has displaced George Soros as the chief bogeyman of the right. In April, dozens of Texans crowded around Infowars host Alex Jones at an anti-shutdown demonstration in Austin, Texas, chanting 'Arrest Bill Gates.' A New York-based tech nonprofit falsely rumored to be working with the Bill and Melinda Gates Foundation to implant vaccine microchips in people received so many death threats that it contacted the FBI. And a White House petition demanding the billionaire's foundation be investigated for 'Medical malpractice and crimes against humanity' amassed half-a-million signatures in three weeks. Gates, who has announced that his $40 billion-foundation will shift its 'Total attention' to fighting COVID-19, has been accused of a range of misdeeds, from scheming to profit off a vaccine to creating the virus itself. On April 8, Fox News host Laura Ingraham and Attorney General Bill Barr speculated about whether Gates would use digital certificates to monitor anyone who got vaccinated.

Accusations that Bill Gates has sinister plans to control or experiment on the public under the guise of medical charity date back at least a decade, in part to an obscure political fight in Ghana. A Christian Right broadcaster, Brannon Howse of 'Worldview Watch,' warned that Gates and the 'Medical globalist deep state' were using the crisis to regulate people's fertility depending on their worldview, through 'Procreation tickets' and microchips. On Instagram, anti-vaccination activist Robert F. Kennedy, Jr., posted a video featuring a '1984' style audience listening to Gates, with text declaring that the Microsoft Corp. co-founder 'Is conducting global social and medical experimentation,' via the World Health Organization. The New York Times noted that misinformation about Gates has become 'The most widespread of all coronavirus falsehoods' trending online. But while these themes have fed the imagination of QAnon, Pizzagate and anti-vaccination proponents since January, conspiracy theories involving Gates actually have a much longer history. Accusations that he has sinister plans to control or experiment on the public under the guise of medical charity date back at least a decade, including to an obscure and different political fight in Ghana.

A New War over Birth Control in Africa

In 2010, a former staffer with a government health initiative in Ghana made a shocking claim: a project partially funded by the Gates Foundation had tested the contraceptive Depo-Provera on unsuspecting villagers in the remote region of Navrongo, as part of an illicit 'Population experiment.' The woman making the charge was the Ghanaian-born, U.S.-educated communications officer for another Gates-funded initiative by the Ghanaian government and Columbia University to use mobile phones to improve health care access for rural women and children. She had previously attempted to sue her employer for a multi-million dollar settlement when, after repeated clashes with her boss, her contract wasn't renewed. The lawsuit fizzled, but with help from a small U.S. nonprofit called the Rebecca Project for Human Rights, she shopped a series of stories to Ghana's tabloid press. The Depo-Provera story caused a national scandal.

Although it was denounced by Ghanaian health professionals and traditional leaders as libelous, the Navrongo project hadn't tested any medications, so many death threats were directed at the project that some staff had to be evacuated across the Burkina Faso border.

The new narrative was that Gates was waging 'Chemical warfare on poor women' in a neocolonial effort to suppress African births. The episode would mark the opening shot in a new war over birth control in Africa. It also reflected an evolution in the U.S. anti-abortion movement's strategy in which it started to co-opt the language of women's and civil rights used by progressives. There were fewer bloody fetus posters and more talk about how abortion and contraception violated women's safety and impeded racial justice. Anti-abortion groups hired black activists and highlighted uglier aspects of the history of reproductive health care in particular, the courting of the eugenics movement by Planned Parenthood founder Margaret Sanger in the early part of the 20th century. A right-wing documentary, Maafa 21: Black Genocide in 21st Century America, used a Swahili word that refers to the holocaust of African enslavement to denounce Planned Parenthood as racist. Billboards in Atlanta and Manhattan carried messages like, 'The most dangerous place for an African American is in the womb.' And federal and state legislators proposed a series of bills banning race- and sex-selective abortions in order to insinuate that abortion providers deliberately target communities of color.

Thinly sourced research from a small nonprofit, The Rebecca Project, suggested a massive international conspiracy, led by the Gates Foundation, to push dangerous contraceptives on poor black women as a means of decreasing African births. As black feminists pointed out, these groups cared little for women's or civil rights in general, or black women's well-being in particular. (A 2009 U.S. House bill titled the 'Susan B. Anthony and Frederick Douglass Prenatal Nondiscrimination Act' was co-sponsored by a champion of the Confederate flag.) But the strategy exploited the real and painful history of medical abuses against people of color in the U.S., from compulsory or coercive sterilization campaigns from the 1910s to '60s (including the sterilization of a third of all Puerto Rican mothers between 20 and 49 years old by 1965) to unsafe contraceptives marketed to poor women of color from the 1970s to '90s. And the legacy of those abuses could be profound. One 2016 study found that the notorious Tuskegee Study, wherein hundreds of black men were left with untreated syphilis so U.S. government researchers could track the progress of the disease, led to such mistrust of the medical establishment that it reduced the life expectancy of a generation of black men by more than a year.

The Rebecca Project, a small, Washington-based nonprofit focused on issues disproportionately affecting women of color, hadn't been involved on either side of the abortion fight. But in 2011, the group released a thinly-sourced report titled 'Non-Consensual Research in Africa: The Outsourcing of Tuskegee,' outlining what it claimed was a series of unethical U.S.-backed medical experiments in Africa. Some of the examples were documented stories of legitimate concern, for instance, HIV-positive women in southern Africa had been pressured into sterilization procedures by local health care entities. The report attempted to link them to shakier allegations of USAID funding being used for coercive sterilization campaigns in other countries. But the report's real target, it seemed, was the Gates-backed health initiative in Navrongo. Later, the report's lead author would suggest that people involved with the project should be charged with attempted genocide.

The report had numerous factual problems. Its author, the Rebecca Project's chief financial officer, Kwame Fosu also hadn't disclosed a significant conflict of interest: The employee who'd leveled the charges against the Ghana project was the mother of his child. The fallout wound up splitting the organization, as one of its founders and several staff departed, taking with them all the Rebecca Project's funding. Left with the group's name, Fosu doubled down on his conspiratorial claims. In 2013, Fosu published another report, 'Depo-Provera: Deadly Reproductive Violence Against Women.' Drawing heavily on unnamed sources, paranoid accusations and the rhetoric of right-wing anti-abortion groups, this report used the Ghana story to anchor claims of a massive international conspiracy, led by the Gates Foundation, to push dangerous contraceptives on poor black women as a means of decreasing African births and advancing "population control ideology." Fosu brought the Rebecca Project into alliance with a network of conservative Catholic nonprofits, like C-Fam and the Population Research Institute (PRI) that had long focused on fighting reproductive rights in developing nations or at the United Nations.

Rebecca Project for Justice

(A portion of the title page from The Rebecca Project for Justice's 2013 report.)

His new allies began publicizing Fosu's claims to a large audience of conservative activists, arguing that he had uncovered the smoking gun confirming their long-held suspicions. As the head of PRI put it, 'The population controllers will stop at nothing to stop African women from having children.' By 2014, the Rebecca Project was focusing full-time on the scourge of Depo-Provera. At the same time, the Gates Foundation was undertaking a new mission to radically expand contraceptive access to women in Africa, including with a new, low-dose adaptation of Depo-Provera. The foundation's family planning campaign had already drawn predictable backlash from religious groups. But as U.S. anti-abortion groups and websites circulated the Rebecca Project's allegations, the opposition was no longer dominated by complaints that Gates was tempting African women to defy their faith. The new narrative was that Gates was waging 'Chemical warfare on poor women' in a neocolonial effort to suppress African births.

Soon, powerful figures across Africa were making similar claims, undermining vital public health projects in the process. In 2014, Zimbabwe's Registrar General, Tobaiwa Mudede — the official responsible for overseeing the country's dubious elections, warned women to avoid modern contraceptives because they caused cancer and were a Western ploy to limit African population growth. In 2015, Mudede told parliamentarians, 'Western countries are bent on curtailing the population of the darker races of the world.' According to a parliamentary committee, Mudede's campaign panicked Zimbabwean women, who flooded into clinics to have contraceptive implants removed. Recently, these claims have grown to suggest that a Gates-backed vaccine against COVID-19 in which the foundation has invested $300 million, could be a stealth attack on African populations. In Kenya, all 27 members of the nation's Conference of Catholic Bishops declared that a WHO/UNICEF campaign to administer neonatal tetanus vaccines to women of childbearing age was really 'A disguised population control program.' According to the bishops, the vaccines were laced with a hormone that would cause repeated miscarriages and eventual sterility.

The same conservative Catholic network the Rebecca Project had allied itself with published numerous stories amplifying the bishops' accusations and casting doubt on the government's response. The Kenyan Parliament was forced to have the vaccine tested repeatedly. But by the time the claims were debunked, priests around Kenya had already instructed their congregants to refuse the vaccine. Back in the U.S., Fosu also worked with C-Fam to lobby delegates from African nations, with some success. After a meeting of the Commission on the Status of Women, a regional grouping of African countries released an unprecedented statement expressing concerns over 'Harmful contraceptives,' echoing specific claims by Fosu and his allies. The next month, at the Commission on Population and Development, delegates couldn't agree on an outcome document for the first time in the commission's 48 years, the result, conservative advocates claimed, of African and other developing nations' frustration with 'The profusion of references to population control, adolescent sexual activity, abortion, and comprehensive sexuality education.'

Undermining Confidence in a Coronavirus Vaccine

The Rebecca Project has long since faded into obscurity. But the current attacks on Gates and his foundation are now broadcasting the same themes to a massive global audience. In April, Trump boosters Diamond & Silk vowed they would never take a vaccine created by Gates because he'd sought to make Africans 'Guinea pigs.' (This claim was helped along by erroneous media reporting that falsely suggested Gates planned to test his vaccine in South Africa.) 'I have a problem receiving any vaccine from any entity, especially anybody like Bill Gates who pushed for population control. The same thing that Margaret Sanger pushed for,' Diamond said. 'Abortions! Genocide!' Silk explained. In response to these and other conspiracy theories, including their contention that the virus was a 'Plandemic,' Fox Nation reportedly cut ties with the pair. But Diamond and Silk weren't alone.

Conservative commentator Candace Owens tweeted in April that 'Vaccine-criminal Bill Gates' had used 'African & Indian tribal children to experiment w/ non-FDA approved drug vaccines.' Last week, she declared 'That under no circumstances will I be getting any #coronavirus vaccine that becomes available. Ever. No matter what.' In the U.S. alone, nearly a third of Americans say they'll refuse a coronavirus vaccine. An Infowars video suggested that Gates was the successor of eugenicist population controllers from Sanger to Nazi collaborators and asked whether viewers would 'Allow your government to impose forced vaccines.' In a viral sermon, Rev. Danny Jones, the pastor of a 250-member Georgia church, predicted that

Gates would use vaccines to usher in a new world order under which Christians might be forced to accept biometric tattoos.

On Twitter, hundreds of posts claimed that the billionaire had publicly said that vaccines could be used to lower the population by 10% to 15%. This was an old misrepresentation of Gates' suggestion that increasing vaccination rates in the developing world could slow population growth, since families in which more children survive to adulthood might have fewer children overall. Doctored photographs falsely suggesting the Gates Foundation runs a 'Center for Human Population Reduction' spread so widely that both Reuters and Snopes published articles debunking them. Anti-vaxxer and Pizzagate proponents began sharing old C-Fam articles as proof that Gates 'Thinks There Are Too Many Africans.' And the White House petition resurrected the old Kenyan controversy, informing new believers that Gates has 'Already been credibly accused of intentionally sterilizing Kenyan children through the use of a hidden HCG antigen in tetanus vaccines.'

By Saturday, the Gates-population control narrative had made its way onto conservative network One American News, quoting an anti-social distancing protester who charged, 'This is not about COVID or about a virus. This is about gaining control over the human race and limiting population.' Anti-Gates theories have resurfaced in Africa, as well. Unfounded rumors that Gates had bribed Nigerian lawmakers to pass a compulsory vaccination bill sparked a legislative investigation there. African Twitter influencers posted threads linking him not just to population control but the entire history of colonialist medical violence. One described the foundation's family planning work 'As genocide in Sub-Saharan Africa." Another suggested that Gates would turn to 'Toxic Covid-19 vaccines' to depopulate South Africa next, since it had become 'Clear that this Depo is not working fast enough.'

Nancy Rosenblum, author of 'A Lot of People are Saying: The New Conspiracism and the Assault on Democracy,' said that some people may simply see the proliferation of these conspiracy narratives as a vehicle to advance their agenda, exploiting the swirling outrage around Gates to introduce fringe arguments to a much larger audience. To Quassim Cassam, author of the book 'Conspiracy Theories,' the anti-Gates attacks reflect a larger global trend towards populism, characterized by profound distrust of the establishment and experts. 'If you say it's Gates or big corporations who are responsible for developing coronavirus via 5G, these are all ways of expressing anti-elitist sentiment,' Cassam said. 'They're fantasies, but they're fantasies that give expression to real things in their lives.' The potential impact of such fantasies could be dire. The legacy of medical abuses against people of color helped give rise to HIV/AIDS conspiracy theories, Rosenblum noted, from claims that it was a government-crafted bioweapon to charges that life-saving medications were poison. After the latter theory was adopted by South Africa's former president, Thabo Mbeki, Harvard University researchers found it was responsible for more than 330,000 unnecessary deaths.

The Gates Foundation has already committed $300 million to fighting the coronavirus and finding a vaccine. Tens of millions of that sum are dedicated to ensuring that vaccines are distributed in poor countries. Conspiracy theories suggesting an eventual vaccine is part of a nefarious plot could leave many of the world's most vulnerable at greater risk; in the U.S. alone, a late April survey found, nearly a third of Americans say they'll refuse a vaccine. Of course, the same side that is accusing Gates of planning an imminent eugenicist attack is also loudly pushing to reopen the economy, even though this will almost undoubtedly come at the cost of thousands of lives, overwhelmingly people of color. Rather than reckon with that reality, Republican leaders have argued that 'There are more important things than living' and the public will 'Have to accept' massive new casualties.

Wisconsin's chief justice dismissed superclusters of infection in the minority-staffed meatpacking industry as distinct from the threat posed to 'Regular folks.' One local California official mused that allowing the virus to 'Run rampant' through the ranks of the homeless, the old, the sick and the poor, represents a 'Natural' process of culling the 'Herd' that could lighten Social Security and health care burdens and free up jobs and housing. Against this backdrop, right-wing claims of eugenics or population control begin to seem not just disingenuous, but like the most amoral form of projection.

20. American Communist Party

The Communist Party USA, officially the Communist Party of the United States of America (CPUSA), is a communist party in the United States established in 1919 after a split in the Socialist Party of America following the Russian Revolution. The history of the CPUSA is closely related to the American labor movement and communist parties worldwide. Initially operating underground due to the Palmer Raids starting in the First Red Scare, the party was influential in American politics in the first half of the 20th century and played a prominent role in the labor movement from the 1920s through the 1940s, becoming known for opposing racism and racial segregation after sponsoring the defense for the Scottsboro Boys in 1931. Its membership increased during the Great Depression, and they played a key role in the Congress of Industrial Organizations.

The CPUSA subsequently declined due to events such as World War II, the beginning of the Cold War, the second Red Scare, and the influence of McCarthyism. Its opposition to the Marshall Plan and the Truman Doctrine was unpopular, with its endorsed candidate Henry A. Wallace under-performing in the 1948 presidential election. Its support for the Soviet Union increasingly alienated it from the rest of the left in the United States in the 1960s. The CPUSA received significant funding from the Soviet Union and crafted its public positions to match those of Moscow. The CPUSA also used a covert apparatus to assist the Soviets with their intelligence activities in the United States and utilized a network of front organizations to shape public opinion. The CPUSA opposed glasnost and perestroika in the Soviet Union and as a result major funding from the Communist Party of the Soviet Union ended in 1989.

Charter for a local unit of the CPUSA dated October 24, 1919

For the first half of the 20th century, the Communist Party was influential in various struggles for democratic rights. It played a prominent role in the labor movement from the 1920s through the 1940s, having a major hand in founding most of the country's first industrial unions (which would later use the McCarran Internal Security Act to expel their communist members) while also becoming known for opposing racism and fighting for integration in workplaces and communities during the height of the Jim Crow period of racial segregation. Historian Ellen Schrecker concludes that decades of recent scholarship offer 'A more nuanced portrayal of the party as both a Stalinist sect tied to a vicious regime and the most dynamic organization within the American Left during the 1930s and '40s'. It was also the first political party in the United States to be racially integrated. By August 1919, only months after its founding, the Communist Party claimed 50,000 to 60,000 members. Members also included anarchists and other radical leftists. At the time, the older and more moderate Socialist Party of America, suffering from criminal prosecutions for its antiwar stance during World War I, had declined to 40,000 members. The sections of the Communist Party's International Workers Order (IWO) organized for communism around linguistic and ethnic lines, providing mutual aid and tailored cultural activities to an IWO membership that peaked at 200,000 at its height. Subsequent splits within the party have weakened its position.

During the Great Depression, many Americans became disillusioned with capitalism, and some found communist ideology appealing. Others were attracted by the visible activism of Communists on behalf of a wide range of social and economic causes, including the rights of African Americans, workers and the unemployed. The Communist Party played a significant role in the resurgence of organized labor in the 1930s. Still others, alarmed by the rise of the Falangists in Spain and the Nazis in Germany, admired the Soviet Union's early and staunch opposition to fascism. Party membership swelled from 7,500 at the start of the decade to 55,000 by its end. Party members also rallied to the defense of the Spanish Republic during this period after a nationalist military uprising moved to overthrow it, resulting in the Spanish Civil War (1936–1939). The Communist Party of the Soviet Union, along with leftists throughout the world, raised funds for medical relief while many of its members made their way to Spain with the aid of the party to join the Lincoln Brigade, one of the International Brigades.

The Communist Party's early labor and organizing successes did not last. As the decades progressed, the combined effects of the second Red Scare, McCarthyism, Nikita Khrushchev's 1956 'Secret Speech' denouncing the previous decades of Joseph Stalin's rule and the adversities of the continued Cold War mentality, steadily weakened the party's internal structure and confidence. Party membership in the Communist International and its close adherence to the political positions of the Soviet Union made the party appear to most Americans as not only a threatening, subversive domestic entity, but also as a foreign agent fundamentally alien to the American way of life. Internal and external crises swirled together, to the point where members who did not end up in prison for party activities tended either to disappear quietly from its ranks or to adopt more moderate political positions at odds with the party line. By 1957, membership had dwindled to less than 10,000, of whom some 1,500 were informants for the FBI. The party was also banned by the Communist Control Act of 1954, which still remains in effect although it was never really enforced.

The party attempted to recover with its opposition to the Vietnam War during the civil rights movement in the 1960s, but its continued uncritical support for an increasingly stultified and militaristic Soviet Union further alienated it from the rest of the left-wing in the United States, which saw this supportive role as outdated and even dangerous. At the same time, the party's aging membership demographics and calls for 'Peaceful coexistence' failed to speak to the New Left in the United States. With the rise of Mikhail Gorbachev and his effort to radically alter the Soviet economic and political system from the mid-1980s, the Communist Party finally became estranged from the leadership of the Soviet Union itself. In 1989, the Soviet Communist Party cut off major funding to the American Communist Party due to its opposition to glasnost and perestroika. With the dissolution of the Soviet Union in 1991, the party held its convention and attempted to resolve the issue of whether the party should reject Marxism–Leninism. The majority reasserted the party's now purely Marxist outlook, prompting a minority faction which urged social democrats to exit the now reduced party. The party has since adopted Marxism–Leninism within its program. In 2014, the new draft of the party constitution declared, 'We apply the scientific outlook developed by Marx, Engels, Lenin, and others in the context of our American history, culture, and traditions'.

The 30th National Convention was held in Chicago in 2014

The Communist Party is based in New York City. From 1922 to 1988, it published Morgen Freiheit, a daily newspaper written in Yiddish. For decades, its West Coast newspaper was the People's World, and its East Coast newspaper was The Daily World. The two newspapers merged in 1986 into the People's Weekly World. The People's Weekly World has since become an online only publication called People's World. It has since ceased being an official Communist Party publication as the party does not fund its publication. The party's former theoretical journal Political Affairs is now also published exclusively online, but the party still maintains International Publishers as its publishing house. In June 2014, the party held its 30th National Convention in Chicago. The party announced on April 7, 2021, that it intended to run candidates in elections again, after a hiatus of over thirty years. Steven Estrada, who is running for city council in Long Beach, is one of the first candidates to run as an open member of the CPUSA again (although Long Beach local elections are non-partisan).

Beliefs

According to the constitution of the party adopted at the 30th National Convention in 2014, the Communist Party operates on the principle of democratic centralism, its highest authority being the quadrennial National Convention. Article VI, Section 3 of the 2001 Constitution laid out certain positions as non-negotiable. Struggle for the unity of the working class, against all forms of national oppression, national chauvinism, discrimination, and segregation, against all racist ideologies and practices, ... against all manifestations of male supremacy and discrimination against women, ... against homophobia and all manifestations of discrimination against gays, lesbians, bisexuals, and transgender people.

Among the points in the party's 'Immediate Program' are a $15/hour minimum wage for all workers, national universal health care and opposition to privatization of Social Security. Economic measures such as increased taxes on 'The rich and corporations', 'Strong regulation' of the financial industry, 'Regulation and public ownership of utilities' and increased federal aid to cities and states; opposition to the Iraq War and other military interventions; opposition to free trade treaties such as the North American Free Trade Agreement (NAFTA); nuclear disarmament and a reduced military budget; various civil rights provisions; campaign finance reform including public financing of campaigns; and election law reform, including instant runoff voting.

Bill of Rights; Socialism

The Communist Party emphasizes a vision of socialism as an extension of American democracy. Seeking to 'Build socialism in the United States based on the revolutionary traditions and struggles' of American history, the party promotes a conception of 'Bill of Rights Socialism' that will 'Guarantee all the freedoms we have won over centuries of struggle and also extend the Bill of Rights to include freedom from unemployment' as well as freedom 'From poverty, from illiteracy, and from discrimination and oppression.' Reiterating the idea of property rights in socialist society as it is outlined in Karl Marx and Friedrich Engels's Communist Manifesto (1848), the Communist Party emphasizes.

Many myths have been propagated about socialism. Contrary to right-wing claims, socialism would not take away the personal private property of workers, only the private ownership of major industries, financial institutions, and other large corporations, and the excessive luxuries of the super-rich. Rather than making all wages entirely equal, the Communist Party holds that building socialism would entail 'Eliminating private wealth from stock speculation, from private ownership of large corporations, from the export of capital and jobs, and from the exploitation of large numbers of workers.'

Living standards

Among the primary concerns of the Communist Party are the problems of unemployment, underemployment, and job insecurity, which the party considers the natural result of the profit-driven incentives of the capitalist economy. Millions of workers are unemployed, underemployed, or insecure in their jobs, even during economic upswings and periods of 'recovery' from recessions. Most workers experience long years of stagnant and declining real wages, while health and education costs soar. Many workers are forced to work second and third jobs to make ends meet. Most workers now average four different occupations during their lifetime, many involuntarily moved from job to job and career to career. Often, retirement-age workers are forced to continue working just to provide health care for themselves and their families. Millions of people continuously live below the poverty level; many suffer homelessness and hunger.

Public and private programs to alleviate poverty and hunger do not reach everyone and are inadequate even for those they do reach. With capitalist globalization, jobs move from place to place as capitalists export factories and even entire industries to other countries in a relentless search for the lowest wages. The Communist Party believes that 'Class struggle starts with the fight for wages, hours, benefits, working conditions, job security, and jobs. But it also includes an endless variety of other forms for fighting specific battles: resisting speed-up, picketing, contract negotiations, strikes, demonstrations, lobbying for pro-labor legislation, elections, and even general strikes.' The Communist Party's national programs considers workers who struggle 'Against the capitalist class or any part of it on any issue with the aim of improving or defending their lives' part of the class struggle.

Imperialism and war

The Communist Party maintains that developments within the foreign policy of the United States as reflected in the rise of neoconservatives and other groups associated with right-wing politics have developed in tandem with the interests of large-scale capital such as the multinational corporations. The state thereby becomes thrust into a proxy role that is essentially inclined to help facilitate 'Control by one section of the capitalist class over all others and over the whole of society.' Accordingly, the Communist Party holds that right-wing policymakers such as the neoconservatives, steering the state away from working-class interests on behalf of a disproportionately powerful capitalist class, have 'Demonized foreign opponents of the U.S., covertly funded the right-wing-initiated civil war in Nicaragua, and gave weapons to the Saddam Hussein dictatorship in Iraq. They picked small countries to invade, including Panama and Grenada, testing new military equipment and strategy, and breaking down resistance at home and abroad to U.S. military invasion as a policy option.'

From its ideological framework, the Communist Party understands imperialism as the pinnacle of capitalist development: the state, working on behalf of the few who wield disproportionate power, assumes the role of proffering "phony rationalizations" for economically driven imperial ambition as a means to promote the sectional economic interests of big business. In opposition to what it considers the ultimate agenda of the conservative wing of American politics, the Communist Party rejects foreign policy proposals such as the Bush Doctrine, rejecting the right of the American government to attack 'Any country it wants, to conduct war without end until it succeeds everywhere, and even to use 'tactical' nuclear weapons and militarize space. Whoever does not support the U.S. policy is condemned as an opponent. Whenever international organizations, such as the United Nations, do not support U.S.

government policies, they are reluctantly tolerated until the U.S. government is able to subordinate or ignore them.'

Juxtaposing the support from the Republicans and the right-wing of the Democratic Party for the Bush administration-led invasion of Iraq with the many millions of Americans who opposed the invasion of Iraq from its beginning, the Communist Party notes the spirit of opposition towards the war coming from the American public. Thousands of grassroots peace committees were organized by ordinary Americans ... neighborhoods, small towns and universities expressing opposition in countless creative ways. Thousands of actions, vigils, teach-ins, and newspaper advertisements were organized. The largest demonstrations were held since the Vietnam War. 500,000 marched in New York after the war started. Students at over 500 universities conducted a Day of Action for 'Books not Bombs.'

Over 150 anti-war resolutions were passed by city councils. Resolutions were passed by thousands of local unions and community organizations. Local and national actions were organized on the Internet, including the 'Virtual March on Washington DC'.... Elected officials were flooded with millions of calls, emails, and letters. In an unprecedented development, large sections of the US labor movement officially opposed the war. In contrast, it took years to build labor opposition to the Vietnam War. ... For example, in Chicago, labor leaders formed Labor United for Peace, Justice and Prosperity. They concluded that mass education of their members was essential to counter false propaganda, and that the fight for the peace, economic security and democratic rights was interrelated. The party has consistently opposed American involvement in the Korean War, the Vietnam War, the First Gulf War and the post-September 11 conflicts in both Iraq and Afghanistan. The Communist Party does not believe that the threat of terrorism can be resolved through war.

Women and minorities

Robert G. Thompson and Benjamin J. Davis leaving the courthouse during the Smith Act trials of Communist Party leaders in 1949–1958. The Communist Party Constitution defines the U.S. working class as 'Multiracial and multinational. It unites men and women, young and old, gay, and straight, native-born and immigrant, urban and rural. We are employed and unemployed, organized, and unorganized, and of all occupations – the vast majority of our society.' The Communist Party seeks equal rights for women, equal pay for equal work and the protection of reproductive rights, together with putting an end to sexism. The party's ranks include a Women's Equality Commission, which recognizes the role of women as an asset in moving towards building socialism.

Historically significant in American history as an early fighter for African Americans' rights and playing a leading role in protesting the lynchings of African Americans in the South, the Communist Party in its national program today calls racism the 'Classic divide-and-conquer tactic.' From its New York City base, the Communist Party's Ben Davis Club and other Communist Party organizations have been involved in local activism in Harlem and other African American and minority communities. The Communist Party was instrumental in the founding of the progressive Black Radical Congress in 1998, as well as the African Blood Brotherhood. Historically significant in Latino working class history as a successful organizer of the Mexican American working class in the Southwestern United States in the 1930s, the Communist Party regards working-class Latino people as another oppressed group targeted by overt racism as well as systemic discrimination in areas such as education and sees the participation of Latino voters in a general mass movement in both party-based and nonpartisan work as an essential goal for major left-wing progress.

The Communist Party holds that racial and ethnic discrimination not only harms minorities but is pernicious to working-class people of all backgrounds as any discriminatory practices between demographic sections of the working class constitute an inherently divisive practice responsible for 'Obstructing the development of working-class consciousness, driving wedges in class unity to divert attention from class exploitation, and creating extra profits for the capitalist class.' The Communist Party supports an end to racial profiling. The party supports continued enforcement of civil rights laws as well as affirmative action.

Environment

The Communist Party notes its commitment to participating in environmental movements wherever possible, emphasizing the significance of building unity between the environmental movement and other progressive tendencies. The Communist Party's most recently released environmental document the CPUSA National Committee's '2008 Global Warming Report' takes note of the necessity of "major changes in how we live, move, produce, grow, and market". These changes, the party believe, cannot be effectively accomplished solely on the basis of profit considerations. They require long-term planning, massive investment in redesigning and re-engineering, collective input, husbanding resources, social investment in research for long-term sustainability, and major conservation efforts. ... Various approaches blame the victims. Supposedly the only solution is to change individual consumer choices since people in general are claimed to cause the problem. But consumers, workers, and poor people don't have any say in energy plant construction, in decisions about trade or plant relocation or job export, in deciding on tax subsidies to polluting industries like the oil industry.

Supporting cooperation between economically advanced and less economically developed nations in the area of environmental cooperation, the Communist Party stands in favor of promoting 'Transfer from developed countries to developing countries of sustainable technology, and funds for capital investment in sustainable agriculture, energy, and industry. We should support efforts to get the developed nations to make major contributions to a fund to protect the rainforests from devastation.' The Communist Party opposes drilling in the Alaska National Wildlife Refuge, the use of nuclear power until and unless there is a safe way to dispose of its waste and it conceives of nuclear war as the greatest possible environmental threat.

Religion

The Communist Party is not against religion, but instead regards positively religious people's belief in justice, peace, and respectful relations among peoples. To build good relations with supporters of religion, the party has its own Religious Commission.

Geography

The Communist Party garnered support in particular communities, developing a unique geography. Instead of a broad nationwide support, support for the party was concentrated in different communities at contrasting times, depending on the organizing strategy at that moment.

Before World War II, the Communist Party had relatively stable support in New York City, Chicago and St. Louis County, Minnesota. However, at times the party also had strongholds in more rural counties such as Sheridan County, Montana (22% in 1932), Iron County, Wisconsin (4% in 1932), or Ontonagon County, Michigan (5% in 1934). Even in the South at the height of Jim Crow, the Communist Party had a significant presence in Alabama. Despite the disenfranchisement of African Americans, the party gained 8% of the votes in rural Elmore County. This was mostly due to the successful bi-racial organizing of sharecroppers through the Sharecroppers' Union.

Unlike open mass organizations like the Socialist Party or the NAACP, the Communist Party was a disciplined organization that demanded strenuous commitments and frequently expelled members. Membership levels remained below 20,000 until 1933 and then surged upward in the late 1930s, reaching a peak of 66,000 in 1939. The party fielded candidates in presidential and many state and local elections not expecting to win but expecting loyalists to vote the party ticket. The party mounted symbolic yet energetic campaigns during each presidential election from 1924 through 1940 and many gubernatorial and congressional races from 1922 to 1944. The Communist Party organized by districts that did not coincide with state lines, initially dividing the country into 15 districts identified with a headquarters city with an additional "Agricultural District". Several reorganizations in the 1930s expanded the number of districts.

Relations with other groups

United States labor movement; May Day parade with banners and flags, New York. The Communist Party has sought to play an active role in the labor movement since its origins as part of its effort to build a mass movement of American workers to bring about their own liberation through socialist revolution.

Soviet funding and espionage

From 1959 until 1989, when Gus Hall condemned the initiatives taken by Mikhail Gorbachev in the Soviet Union, the Communist Party received a substantial subsidy from the

Soviets. There is at least one receipt signed by Gus Hall in the KGB archives. Starting with $75,000 in 1959, this was increased gradually to $3 million in 1987. This substantial amount reflected the party's loyalty to the Moscow line, in contrast to the Italian and later Spanish and British Communist parties, who's Eurocommunism deviated from the orthodox line in the late 1970s. Releases from the Soviet archives show that all national Communist parties that conformed to the Soviet line were funded in the same fashion. From the Communist point of view, this international funding arose from the internationalist nature of communism itself as fraternal assistance was considered the duty of communists in any one country to give aid to their allies in other countries. From the anti-Communist point of view, this funding represented an unwarranted interference by one country in the affairs of another. The cutoff of funds in 1989 resulted in a fiscal crisis, which forced the party to cut back publication in 1990 of the party newspaper, the People's Daily World, to weekly publication, the People's Weekly World.

Somewhat more controversial than mere funding is the alleged involvement of Communist members in espionage for the Soviet Union. Whittaker Chambers alleged that Sandor Goldberger also known as Josef Peters, who commonly wrote under the name J. Peters headed the Communist Party's underground secret apparatus from 1932 to 1938 and pioneered its role as an auxiliary to Soviet intelligence activities. Bernard Schuster, Organizational Secretary of the New York District of the Communist Party, is claimed to have been the operational recruiter and conduit for members of the party into the ranks of the secret apparatus, or 'Group 'A' line.' Stalin publicly disbanded the Comintern in 1943. A Moscow NKVD message to all stations on September 12, 1943, detailed instructions for handling intelligence sources within the Communist Party after the disestablishment of the Comintern.

There are a number of decrypted World War II Soviet messages between NKVD offices in the United States and Moscow, also known as the Venona cables. The Venona cables and other published sources appear to confirm that Julius Rosenberg was responsible for espionage. Theodore Hall, a Harvard-trained physicist who did not join the party until 1952, began passing information on the atomic bomb to the Soviets soon after he was hired at Los Alamos at age 19. Hall, who was known as Mlad by his KGB handlers, escaped prosecution. Hall's wife, aware of his espionage, claims that their NKVD handler had advised them to plead innocent, as the Rosenbergs did, if formally charged.

It was the belief of opponents of the Communist Party such as J. Edgar Hoover, longtime director of the FBI; and Joseph McCarthy, for whom McCarthyism is named; and other anti-Communists that the Communist Party constituted an active conspiracy, was secretive, loyal to a foreign power and whose members assisted Soviet intelligence in the clandestine infiltration of American government. This is the traditionalist view of some in the field of Communist studies such as Harvey Klehr and John Earl Haynes, since supported by several memoirs of ex-Soviet KGB officers and information obtained from the Venona project and Soviet archives.

At one time, this view was shared by the majority of the Congress. In the 'Findings and declarations of fact' section of the Subversive Activities Control Act of 1950 (50 U.S.C. Chap. 23 Sub. IV Sec. 841), it stated. The Communist Party, although purportedly a political party, is in fact an instrumentality of a conspiracy to overthrow the Government of the United States. It constitutes an authoritarian dictatorship within a republic ... the policies and programs of the Communist Party are secretly prescribed for it by the foreign leaders ... to carry into action slavishly the assignments given.... The Communist Party acknowledges no constitutional or statutory limitations.... The peril inherent in its operation arises [from] its dedication to the proposition that the present constitutional Government of the United States ultimately must be brought to ruin by any available means, including resort to force and violence ... its role as the agency of a hostile foreign power renders its existence a clear present and continuing danger.

In 1993, experts from the Library of Congress traveled to Moscow to copy previously secret archives of the party records, sent to the Soviet Union for safekeeping by party organizers. The records provided an irrefutable link between Soviet intelligence and information obtained by the Communist Party and its contacts in the United States government from the 1920s through the 1940s. Some documents revealed that the Communist Party was actively involved in secretly recruiting party members from African American groups and rural farm workers. Other party records contained further evidence that Soviet sympathizers had indeed infiltrated the State Department, beginning in the 1930s. Included in Communist Party archival records were confidential letters from two American ambassadors in Europe to Roosevelt and a senior State Department official. Thanks to an official in the Department of State sympathetic to the party, the confidential correspondence, concerning political and economic matters in Europe, ended up in the hands of Soviet intelligence.

Counterintelligence

In 1952, Jack and Morris Childs, together codenamed SOLO, became FBI informants. As high-ranking officials in the American Communist Party, they informed on the CPUSA for the rest of the Cold War, monitoring the Soviet funding. They also traveled to Moscow and Beijing to meet USSR and PRC leadership. Jack and Morris Childs both received the Presidential Medal of Freedom in 1987 for their intelligence work. Morris's son stated, 'The CIA could not believe the information the FBI had because the American Communist Party had links directly into the Kremlin.' According to intelligence analyst Darren E. Tromblay, the SOLO operation, and the Ad Hoc Committee, were part of 'Enveloping geopolitical awareness' by the FBI about factors such as the Sino-Soviet split. The Ad Hoc Committee was a group within CPUSA that circulated a pro-Maoist bulletin in the voice of a 'Dedicated but rebellious comrade.' Allegedly an operation, it caused a schism within the CPUSA.

Criminal prosecutions

When the Communist Party was formed in 1919, the United States government was engaged in prosecution of socialists who had opposed World War I and military service. This prosecution was continued in 1919 and January 1920 in the Palmer Raids as part of the First Red Scare. Rank and file foreign-born members of the Communist Party were targeted and as many as possible were arrested and deported while leaders were prosecuted and in some cases sentenced to prison terms. In the late 1930s, with the authorization of President Franklin D. Roosevelt, the FBI began investigating both domestic Nazis and Communists. In 1940, Congress passed the Smith Act, which made it illegal to advocate, abet, or teach the desirability of overthrowing the government.

In 1949, the federal government put Eugene Dennis, William Z. Foster and ten other Communist Party leaders on trial for advocating the violent overthrow of the government. Because the prosecution could not show that any of the defendants had openly called for violence or been involved in accumulating weapons for a proposed revolution, it relied on the testimony of former members of the party that the defendants had privately advocated the overthrow of the government and on quotations from the work of Marx, Lenin, and other revolutionary figures of the past. During the course of the trial, the judge held several of the defendants and all of their counsel in contempt of court. All of the remaining eleven defendants were found guilty, and the Supreme Court upheld the constitutionality of their convictions by a 6–2 vote in Dennis v. United States, 341 U.S. 494 (1951). The government then proceeded with the prosecutions of more than 140 members of the party.

Panicked by these arrests and fearing that the party was dangerously compromised by informants, Dennis and other party leaders decided to go underground and to disband many affiliated groups. The move heightened the political isolation of the leadership while making it nearly impossible for the party to function. The widespread support of action against communists and their associates began to abate after Senator Joseph McCarthy overreached himself in the Army–McCarthy hearings, producing a backlash. The end of the Korean War in 1953 also led to a lessening of anxieties about subversion. The Supreme Court brought a halt to the Smith Act prosecutions in 1957 in its decision in Yates v. United States, 354 U.S. 298 (1957), which required that the government prove that the defendant had actually taken concrete steps toward the forcible overthrow of the government, rather than merely advocating it in theory.

African Americans

The Communist Party played a significant role in defending the rights of African Americans during its heyday in the 1930s and 1940s. The Alabama Chapter of the Communist Party USA played an important role in organizing the unemployed Black workers, the Alabama Sharecroppers' Union, and numerous anti-lynching campaigns. Further, the Alabama chapter organized many young activists that would later go on to be prominent members in the civil rights movement, such as Rosa Parks. Throughout its history many of the party's leaders and political thinkers have been African Americans. James Ford, Charlene Mitchell, Angela Davis and Jarvis Tyner, the current executive vice chair of the party, all ran as presidential or vice presidential candidates on the party ticket. Others like Benjamin J. Davis, William L. Patterson,

Harry Haywood, James Jackson, Henry Winston, Claude Lightfoot, Alphaeus Hunton, Doxey Wilkerson, Claudia Jones and John Pittman contributed in important ways to the party's approaches to serious issues from human and civil rights, peace, women's equality, the national question, working class unity, socialist thought, cultural struggle and more. African American thinkers, artists, and writers such as Claude McKay, Richard Wright, Ann Petry, W. E. B. Du Bois, Shirley Graham Du Bois, Lloyd Brown, Charles White, Elizabeth Catlett, Paul Robeson, Gwendolyn Brooks, and many more were one-time members or supporters of the party, and the Communist Party also had a close alliance with Harlem Congressman Adam Clayton Powell Jr. The party's work to appeal to African Americans continues to this day. It was instrumental in the founding of the Black Radical Congress in 1998.

Gay rights movement

One of the most prominent sexual radicals in the United States, Harry Hay, developed his political views as an active member of the Communist Party. Hay founded in the early 1950s the Mattachine Society, America's second gay rights organization. However, gay rights was not seen as something the party should associate with organizationally. Most party members saw homosexuality as something done by those with fascist tendencies (following the lead of the Soviet Union in criminalizing the practice for that reason). Hay was expelled from the party as an ideological risk. In 2004, the editors of Political Affairs published articles detailing their self-criticism of the party's early views of gay and lesbian rights and praised Hay's work. The Communist Party endorsed LGBT rights in a 2005 statement. The party affirmed the resolution with a statement a year later in honor of gay pride month in June 2006.

United States peace movement

The Communist Party opposed the United States involvement in the initial stages of World War II (until June 22, 1941, the date of the German invasion of the Soviet Union), the Korean War, the Vietnam War, the invasion of Grenada and American support for anti-Communist military dictatorships and movements in Central America. Meanwhile, some in the peace movement and the New Left rejected the Communist Party for what it saw as the party's bureaucratic rigidity and for its close association with the Soviet Union. The Communist Party was consistently opposed to the United States' 2003–2011 war in Iraq. United for Peace and Justice (UFPJ) includes the New York branch of the Communist Party as a member group, with Communist Judith LeBlanc serving as the co-chair of UFPJ from 2007 to 2009.

China in America

Most Americans probably don't realize that one of the greatest threats to our national and economic security has already infiltrated nearly every aspect of our society, the influence of the Chinese Communist Party (CCP). Backed by considerable financial largesse and run through harmless-sounding front organizations, the CCP is aggressively limiting free speech on American college campuses, co-opting and corrupting American politicians and businesses, stealing invaluable American research and development, and undermining the very foundations of our democratic republic. Ensuring prosperity and sovereignty in the next century demands that we recognize and confront the CCP's propaganda, influence, and subversion wherever it is found, and it is found nearly everywhere one looks. This is not mere hyperbole or speculation; it is very real, and it is happening right now. In 2020, FBI Director Christopher Wray warned, 'We've now reached the point where the FBI is opening a new China-related counterintelligence case about every 10 hours.' Think about that, a new case every 10 hours. That's nearly 17 a week, 17 complex counterintelligence cases resulting from China's activities in the United States.

Let's look at what's happening on college campuses. China is spreading its propaganda through the innocuous-sounding Confucius Institutes, academic front organizations that, according to a bipartisan report from the Senate's Permanent Subcommittee on Investigations, are completely controlled by the Chinese Communist Party. Active on more than 100 college campuses, these 'Institutes' are outposts of propaganda for the CCP. In exchange for resources and academic programs such as language education, Confucius Institutes exert incredible pressure and leverage over universities, threatening to pull their funding to ensure that some topics like Taiwan, Tibet, Falun Gong, and the Uyghurs are off-limits.

The CCP is stealing invaluable intellectual property through its "Thousand Talents Program," co-opting researchers and scientists with the promise of financial gain for the benefit of the People's Liberation Army and state-owned or state-linked businesses. In June 2020, Charles Lieber, chair of Harvard's Department of Chemistry and Chemical Biology, was indicted for his involvement in this program which, through the Wuhan Institute of Technology, provided him a $50,000 monthly stipend, more than $150,000 in living expenses, and more than $1.5 million to establish a laboratory back in China, all of which he failed to disclose. Congressman Eric Swalwell (D-Calif.) is the latest example of the CCP's slow, methodical efforts to gain access to influential politicians and sensitive information. Rep. Swalwell was targeted by a Chinese national named Fang Fang, or Christine Fang, who worked to get close to centers of political power through a classic 'Honeypot' operation. While it does not appear, she received any classified information, the personal habits, schedules, thoughts, and opinions of public officials would all be invaluable to an intelligence officer, if not now, then certainly in the future.

Rep. Swalwell is not alone. A driver for Sen. Dianne Feinstein (D-Calif.) is believed to have worked for China's Ministry of State Security for 20 years. In that trusted position, he would have been privy to countless phone conversations, in-car discussions, and other forms of "chatter," all of which would be a goldmine for Chinese intelligence. Beijing is working aggressively, and with some success, to co-opt American intelligence officers. In August 2017, CIA officer Alexander Yuk Ching Ma, 67, was arrested along with a relative (also a CIA officer) for conspiring to send classified information to the People's Republic of China. In 2004 an FBI counterintelligence agent pleaded guilty for concealing a 20-year relationship with a suspected Chinese double agent — a woman he initially recruited.

What the Chinese Communist Party is doing goes well beyond cultural outreach and diplomatic engagement. It is a holistic campaign of malign influence designed to disarm our democracy's protective antibodies and weaken our republic. It is about corrupting people and institutions to ensure that they self-censor, avoid sensitive topics and promote Beijing's talking points. It is about threatening American businesses with boycotts, as happened with the NBA, to ensure that the companies don't support Taiwan or Hong Kong, and certainly don't discuss the imprisonment of millions of Uyghurs. It is about classic intelligence operations that seek to undermine American intelligence and security operations overseas. It is about peddling Chinese propaganda masked as legitimate journalism, such as the China Daily inserts you may have seen in your local papers. Our future economic security and national security depend on confronting the Chinese Communist Party's campaign of influence wherever it is found. If we fail to do so today, we will cede our sovereignty and our future, and that of our children, to Beijing and that's something that isn't worth any price.

The Socialist Threat

As the far-left congresswomen known as the Squad celebrated their overwhelming victories in Democratic primaries earlier this year, far-sighted radical strategists were plotting to achieve their long-range goal, a socialist America governed by, in the words of the Marxist group Socialist Alternative, 'A tested Marxist leadership.' For those who say it can't happen here, there are warning signs aplenty. In New York, Representative Alexandria Ocasio-Cortez did not just turn back her well-known Latina challenger, CNBC anchor Michelle Caruso-Cabrera, and she crushed her, winning 74.6 percent of the vote. Representative Rashida Tlaib easily defeated Detroit City Council president Brenda Jones, 66.3 percent to 33.7 percent. Ilhan Omar won her Minnesota primary against a well-funded Antone Melton-Meaux with 57.4 percent. In each case, the socialists defeated liberal Democrats who were attractive, organized, and had plenty of money. It didn't matter, an overwhelming majority of Democratic primary voters endorsed the OAC-Tlaib-Omar vision of a socialist America, including the multitrillion-dollar Green New Deal.

This was only some of the evidence of a revolutionary shift in the Democratic Party that is on its way to becoming the Socialist Party. Three senior Democrats in the House of Representatives lost their seats to AOC-like candidates. Representative Lacy Clay of Missouri, a 20-year incumbent, lost to Cori Bush, a Black Lives Matter leader. Representative Eliot Engel of New York, chairman of the House Foreign Affairs Committee, was defeated by progressive school Principal Jamaal Bowman. Representative Dan Lipinski of Illinois, one of the very few pro-life Democrats in Congress, lost to leftist challenger Marie Newman.

What Americans Must Know About Socialism

The grassroots efforts of Democratic Socialists of America (DSA) and similar left-wing groups are paying significant dividends. In New York, five statewide candidates for the General Assembly who had been endorsed by DSA all won their primaries. Several had come-from-behind victories because of absentee ballots—a key socialist initiative. At least two self-described democratic socialists not endorsed by DSA also won statewide races. They ran on platforms that included the Green New Deal, single-payer health care, criminal justice reform, housing for New York State's 70,000 homeless, affordable housing for the poor, and new taxes on the rich and Wall Street to pay for all of it. Their goal, as set forth in campaign literature, is to 'Advance a vision for a socialist world.'

Socialists found receptive voters across the country. In Philadelphia, democratic socialist Nikil Saval won the Democratic primary for the state senate. Summer Lee, the first Black woman to represent southwestern Pennsylvania in the state senate, won reelection with 75 percent of the vote.

In Montana, six 'Berniecrats,' backed by Our Revolution, a progressive political action committee, won their primaries. San Francisco elected Chesa Boudin, son of the leftist militants, its district attorney. In the California primary, exit polls revealed that 53 percent of Democrats viewed socialism 'Favorably.' In Texas, Democratic voters in the primary approved of socialism by 56 percent, a 20-point margin over capitalism. Socialism is indeed riding a wave of momentum when more Texans than Californians view it favorably. Socialists are building on the remarkable candidacy of Senator Bernie Sanders, who raised more money than any other candidate in 2020 (an estimated $200 million), enlisted an unprecedented army of volunteers, and won the Iowa caucuses and the primaries in New Hampshire and Nevada. But he was unable to overcome the still-powerful Democratic establishment, which rallied behind former vice president Joe Biden.

Socialist strategists are calculating how best to push the Democratic Party farther to the left. Writing in Jacobin, Curt Ries argues that socialists need stronger institutions on the left, especially more militant labor unions. Ries, who worked in the Sanders campaign, points out that only three smaller unions backed Sanders. He also claims that socialists need more activist organizations like DSA, Our Revolution, and the Sunrise Movement, along with more independent media like Democracy Now! And Jacobin. Socialists need 'Class-struggle elections,' argues Ries that pit the people against the ruling class and focus on 'The greed and corruption of capitalism.' Socialists believe, he said, that with the multiple crises in the economy, government, and public health, now is the time to push for a world where 'All people can live with dignity, security, and freedom.'

The Socialist Alternative has called for the formation of a new left party with 'A clear socialist program and a tested Marxist leadership.' The Call, a publication run by Bread and Roses, a caucus of Marxist organizers, has declared, echoing Karl Marx, that American workers need 'A mass working class party.' The Sunrise Movement, a youth-led leftist climate group, has cautioned that a workers' party should not be an 'Immediate' goal. But those on the far left agree that a workers' party is 'A crucial strategic goal for the socialist movement.' These radicals clearly see themselves as a revolutionary vanguard like the Bolsheviks of 1917, prepared to strike when the moment is ripe to bring down a weakened political and economic structure. Although they are comparatively few, DSA has a membership of about 70,000, they are committed. They have helped to elect a number of national and local candidates. According to the polls, the mood of the country is favorable to radical solutions such as free education, free health care, and the Green New Deal, which would eliminate oil, coal, and natural gas as energy sources.

Writing in Javelin, DSA strategist Jared Abbott refers to a great debate that will take place between pragmatists and idealists on the left. Should socialists adopt a strategy of coalition-building with Democrats and others on the left? Or follow a strategy of confrontation with Democrats, running their own candidates and building a combative class-centered left-wing organization? Resolution of the debate depends in large measure on our national leadership. A Democratic president and a Democratic Congress would strengthen the pragmatists' call for collaboration. A Republican president with a Republican Senate would enhance the idealists' strategy of confrontation.

Given the electoral gains cited above, are we certain that a socialist America is impossible, especially when 70 percent of Millennials say they would vote for a socialist? We cannot depend on someone else to step forward. We must go on the offensive, disseminating the truth about socialism and the free-enterprise alternative. We must point out that socialism has never worked anywhere, most recently in Venezuela and in past years in Israel, India, and Great Britain. We must show that it is based on the failed prophecies of a delusional economist named Karl Marx, who predicted two centuries ago that capitalism would wither away, that socialism would mean the end of private property and of small businesses, of which there are now 30 million in America.

Further, we must explain that, thanks to free enterprise, one billion people left poverty and a new middle class has formed around the world—that capitalism not socialism has brought greater wealth and more freedom to more people than any other economic system in history. Unlike the rights that Thomas Jefferson wrote about in the Declaration of Independence, these facts are not self-evident. We must present them untiringly and defend them ceaselessly. The alternative, losing our country to so-called democratic socialists is unthinkable.

21. *Agenda 21*

Agenda 21 is a non-binding action plan of the United Nations with regard to sustainable development. It is a product of the Earth Summit (UN Conference on Environment and Development) held in Rio de Janeiro, Brazil, in 1992. It is an action agenda for the UN, other multilateral organizations, and individual governments around the world that can be executed at local, national, and global levels. One major objective of the Agenda 21 initiative is that every local government should draw its own local Agenda 21. Its aim initially was to achieve global sustainable development by 2000, with the "21" in Agenda 21 referring to the original target of the 21st century.

Structure

Agenda 21 is grouped into 4 sections:

Section I: Social and Economic Dimensions is directed toward combating poverty, especially in developing countries, changing consumption patterns, promoting health, achieving a more sustainable population, and sustainable settlement in decision making.

Section II: Conservation and Management of Resources for Development includes atmospheric protection, combating deforestation, protecting fragile environments, conservation of biological diversity (biodiversity), control of pollution and the management of biotechnology, and radioactive wastes.

Section III: Strengthening the Role of Major Groups includes the roles of children and youth, women, NGOs, local authorities, business and industry, and workers; and strengthening the role of indigenous peoples, their communities, and farmers.

Section IV: Means of Implementation includes science, technology transfer, education international institutions, and financial mechanisms.

Development and evolution

The full text of Agenda 21 was made public at the UN Conference on Environment and Development (Earth Summit), held in Rio de Janeiro on 13 June 1992, where 178 governments voted to adopt the program. The final text was the result of drafting, consultation, and negotiation, beginning in 1989 and culminating at the two-week conference.

Rio+5 (1997)

In 1997, the UN General Assembly held a special session to appraise the status of Agenda 21 (Rio +5). The Assembly recognized progress as 'Uneven' and identified key trends, including increasing globalization, widening inequalities in income, and continued deterioration of the global environment. A new General Assembly Resolution (S-19/2) promised further action.

Rio+10 (2002)

The Johannesburg Plan of Implementation, agreed to at the World Summit on Sustainable Development (Earth Summit 2002), affirmed UN commitment to 'Full implementation' of Agenda 21, alongside achievement of the Millennium Development Goals and other international agreements.

Agenda 21 for culture (2002)

The first World Public Meeting on Culture, held in Porto Alegre, Brazil, in 2002, came up with the idea to establish guidelines for local cultural policies, something comparable to what Agenda 21 was for the environment. They are to be included in various subsections of Agenda 21 and will be carried out through a wide range of sub-programs beginning with G8 countries.

Rio+20 (2012)

In 2012, at the United Nations Conference on Sustainable Development the attending members reaffirmed their commitment to Agenda 21 in their outcome document called 'The Future We Want'. Leaders from 180 nations participated.

Sustainable Development Summit (2015)

Agenda 2030, also known as the Sustainable Development Goals, was a set of goals decided upon at the UN Sustainable Development Summit in 2015. It takes all of the goals set by Agenda 21 and re-asserts them as the basis for sustainable development, saying, 'We reaffirm all the principles of the Rio Declaration on Environment and Development...' Adding onto those goals from the original Rio document, a total of 17 goals have been agreed on, revolving around the same concepts of Agenda 21; people, planet, prosperity, peace, and partnership.

Implementation

The Commission on Sustainable Development acts as a high-level forum on sustainable development and has acted as preparatory committee for summits and sessions on the implementation of Agenda 21. The UN Division for Sustainable Development acts as the secretariat to the Commission and works 'Within the context of' Agenda 21. Implementation by member states remains voluntary, and its adoption has varied.

Local level

The implementation of Agenda 21 was intended to involve action at international, national, regional, and local levels. Some national and state governments have legislated or advised that local authorities take steps to implement the plan locally, as recommended in Chapter 28 of the document. These programs are often known as 'Local Agenda 21' or 'LA21'. For example, in the Philippines, the plan is 'Philippines Agenda 21' (PA21). The group, ICLEI-Local Governments for Sustainability, formed in 1990; today its members come from over 1,000 cities, towns, and counties in 88 countries and is widely regarded as a paragon of Agenda 21 implementation. Europe turned out to be the continent where LA21 was best accepted and most implemented. In Sweden, for example, four small- to medium-sized municipalities in the southeast of Sweden were chosen for a 5-year study of their Local Agenda 21 (LA21) processes a Local Agenda 21 initiative.

Regional levels

The UN Department of Economic and Social Affairs' Division for Sustainable Development monitors and evaluates progress, nation by nation, towards the adoption of Agenda 21, and makes these reports available to the public on its website. The Rio+10 report identified over 6400 local governments in 113 countries worldwide that were engaged in Local Agenda 21 (LA21) activities, a more than three-fold increase over less than five years. 80% = 5120 of these local governments, were located in Europe. A significant increase has been noted in the number of countries in which one or more LA21 processes were underway.

Australia

Australia is a signatory to Agenda 21 and 88 of its municipalities subscribe to ICLEI, an organization that promotes Agenda 21 globally. Australia's membership is second only to that of the United States.

Africa

In Africa, national support for Agenda 21 is strong and most countries are signatories. But support is often closely tied to environmental challenges specific to each country; for example, in 2002 Sam Nujoma, who was then President of Namibia, spoke about the importance of adhering to Agenda 21 at the 2002 Earth Summit, noting that as a semi-arid country, Namibia sets a lot of store in the United Nations Convention to Combat Desertification (UNCCD). Furthermore, there is little mention of Agenda 21 at the local level in indigenous media. Only major municipalities in sub-Saharan African countries are members of ICLEI. Agenda 21 participation in North African countries mirrors that of Middle Eastern countries, with most countries being signatories but little to no adoption on the local-government level. Countries in sub-Saharan Africa and North Africa generally have poorly documented Agenda 21 status reports. [citation needed] By contrast, South Africa's participation in Agenda 21 mirrors that of modern Europe, with 21 city members of ICLEI and support of Agenda 21 by national-level government.

United States

The national focal point in the United States is the Division Chief for Sustainable Development and Multilateral Affairs, Office of Environmental Policy, Bureau of Oceans and International Environmental and Scientific Affairs, U.S. Department of State. A June 2012 poll of 1,300 United States voters by the American Planning Association found that 9% supported Agenda 21, 6% opposed it, and 85% thought they didn't have enough information to form an opinion.

Support

The United States is a signatory country to Agenda 21, but because Agenda 21 is a legally non-binding statement of intent and not a treaty, the United States Senate did not hold a formal debate or vote on it. It is therefore not considered to be law under Article Six of the United States Constitution. President George H. W. Bush was one of the 178 heads of government who signed the final text of the agreement at the Earth Summit in 1992, and in the same year Representatives Nancy Pelosi, Eliot Engel and William Broomfield spoke in support of United States House of Representatives Concurrent Resolution 353, supporting implementation of Agenda 21 in the United States.

Created by Executive Order 12852 in 1993, the President's Council on Sustainable Development (PCSD) is explicitly charged with recommending a national action plan for sustainable development to the President. The PCSD is composed of leaders from government and industry, as well as from environmental, labor, and civil rights organizations. The PCSD submitted its report, "Sustainable America: A New Consensus", to the President in early 1996. In the absence of a multi-sectoral consensus on how to achieve sustainable development in the United States, the PCSD was conceived to formulate recommendations for the implementation of Agenda 21. Executive Order 12852 was revoked by Executive Order 13138 in 1999. The PCSD set 10 common goals to support the Agenda 21 movement:

1. Health and the environment
2. Economic Prosperity
3. Equity
4. Conservation of nature
5. Stewardship
6. Sustainable communities
7. Civic engagement
8. Population
9. International responsibility
10. Education.

In the United States, over 528 cities are members of ICLEI, an international sustainability organization that helps to implement the Agenda 21 and Local Agenda 21 concepts across the world. The United States has nearly half of the ICLEI's global membership of 1,200 cities promoting sustainable development at a local level. The United States also has one of the most comprehensively documented Agenda 21 status reports. In response to the opposition, Don Knapp, U.S. spokesman for the ICLEI, has said 'Sustainable development is not a top-down conspiracy from the U.N., but a bottom-up push from local governments.'

Opposition

Anti-Agenda 21 theories have circulated in the U.S. Some Tea Party movement activists and others promoted the notion that Agenda 21 was part of a UN plot to deny property rights, undermine U.S. sovereignty, or force citizens to move to cities. Activists believed that the non-binding UN resolution was 'The linchpin in a plot to subjugate humanity under an eco-totalitarian regime.' The conspiracy had its roots in anti-environmentalist ideology and opposition to land-use regulation. Agenda 21 fears have played a role in opposition to local government's efforts to promote resource and land conservation, build bike lanes, and construct hubs for public transportation. The non-profit group ICLEI – Local Governments for Sustainability USA was targeted by anti-Agenda 21 activists. In 2012 Glenn Beck co-wrote a dystopian novel titled Agenda 21 based in part on concepts discussed in the UN plan. In the same year, fears of Agenda 21 'Went mainstream' when the Republican National Committee adopted a platform resolution stated that 'We strongly reject the U.N. Agenda 21 as erosive of American sovereignty.'

Several state and local governments have considered or passed motions and legislation opposing Agenda 21. Most such bills failed, 'Either dying in committee, getting defeated on the statehouse floor or in the case of Missouri's 2013 bill getting vetoed by the governor.' In Texas, for example, broadly worded legislation that would prohibit any governmental entity from accepting from or granting money to any 'Nongovernmental or intergovernmental organization accredited by the United Nations to implement a policy that originated in the Agenda 21 plan' was defeated because it could have cut off funding for groups such as 4-H, the Boy Scouts of America, and the Texas Wildlife Association.

In Arizona, a similarly sweeping bill was introduced in the Arizona State Legislature seeking to mandate that the state could not 'Adopt or implement the creed, doctrine, or principles or any tenet' of Agenda 21 and to prohibit the state 'Implementing programs of, expending any sum of money for, being a member of, receiving funding from, contracting services from, or giving financial or other forms of aid to" an array of sustainability organizations. The bill, which was opposed by the state chamber of commerce and the mayor of Phoenix, was defeated in 2012. Alabama was one state that did adopt an anti-Agenda 21 resolution, unanimously passing in 2012 a measure to block 'Any future effort to 'Deliberately or inadvertently infringe or restrict private property rights without due process, as may be required by policy recommendations originating in, or traceable to 'Agenda 21.'"

Far right-wing groups, including the John Birch Society, assert that Agenda 21 is part of a scheme using environmental protection as a cover to impose a worldwide dictatorship. During her 2014 U.S. Senate campaign, Joni Ernst promoted a conspiracy theory claiming Agenda 21 would force Iowa farmers off their land and into the cities.

Europe

The Rio+10 report identified 5120 of local governments in Europe having a 'Local Agenda 21'. As most Europeans live in about 800 cities of +50.000 inhabitants, it is fair to say that just about all EU cities, communes and villages have a local Agenda 21.

Case in point:

By 1997 70% of UK local authorities had committed to Agenda 21. Many, such as the London Borough of Enfield, employed Agenda 21 officers to promote the program.

Sweden reported that 100% of the municipalities had adopted LA21 by 2002.

France, whose national government, along with 14 cities, is a signatory, promotes nationwide programs in support of the goals of Agenda 21.

Baltic nations formed the Baltic 21 coalition as a regional expression of Agenda 21.

STEALING LAND AND SMART CITIES

Darwin City Council installed a network of hundreds of new devices across the center of the city last year. This web of 'Smart' lights, environmental sensors and video cameras is designed to give the council more power to monitor and manage urban places and the people who occupy them. The council says the A$10 million 'Switching on Darwin' project is 'Delivering smart technology to encourage innovative solutions and enhance community life'. We argue it is better seen as a project of surveillance and control, which is embedded in a long history of settler-colonial urbanism.

Intensified surveillance

Journalists and community members alike worried about the project. The scale and rapid rollout of the project, some argued, meant it would erode Darwinians' privacy through intensified surveillance. The introduction of new digital surveillance measures in Darwin poses particular concerns for already marginalized groups, as ANU sociologists Gavin Smith and Pat O'Malley have pointed out. The most affected are likely to be Aboriginal and Torres Strait Islander people, who are already disproportionately targeted, criminalized, and incarcerated. The Darwin project also occurs in the context of the federal government's plan to develop northern Australia. This development agenda has been criticized for, among other things, its lack of interest in the Indigenous people who are the traditional owners of much of the land.

Privacy concerns dismissed

Two of the chief concerns for Switching on Darwin critics were the possible use of facial recognition software and the potential involvement of Chinese tech company Huawei. Darwin's lord mayor dismissed criticisms as the baseless concerns of 'Conspiracy Theorists.' He also gave advice to people worried about privacy: 'Don't get a license, give away your credit cards, and get out of Facebook.' Compared with the slick sales pitch that usually accompanies smart city projects, the lord mayor's blunt approach is more like the strident accusations of "fake news" that are now common in political discourse.

The logic of 'Smart cities'

But if we dig a little deeper, the lord mayor's comments reveal a set of assumptions about "smart cities" that animate conversations about how cities should work in Australia. First, that digital technologies typically in the form of solutions and services bought from companies outside government are a necessary part of 'Vibrant' and 'Liveable' 'World cities.' Second, that privacy and surveillance issues are unfortunate byproducts of technological progress but are outweighed by their benefits. And finally, that technologies are straightforward non-political ways to change cities.

For governments and corporations, the vision of the smart city means a generic 'Public' enjoys more convenience, planners enjoys more information and efficiency, and politicians enjoy more growth and security. It's an enticing vision, but it is built on faulty assumptions. This vision assumes smart systems are simply a matter of technocratic management or corporate outsourcing and focuses on the supposedly unprecedented "disruption" of emerging technologies. In doing this, it overlooks important connections between the operations of smart urbanism and much older practices of colonial control.

Smart urban systems function in remarkably similar ways, for similar purposes and with similar outcomes. For example, the high-tech, data-driven systems that police now use to identify and assess people, like the New South Wales Police Force's Suspect Targeting Management Plan, disproportionately target the same exact marginalized groups who have always been subjected to over-policing, in this case young and/or Aboriginal people. But now these decisions can be hidden and justified by algorithmic analysis. Existing power dynamics and structural inequalities cannot be erased by installing some new digital systems and declaring that the future city has arrived. Instead, the new systems can make these dynamics harder to see and at the same time entrench them more deeply.

Captured cities

In practice, the smart city is vastly different from the vision. It is better understood as the captured city. As a model for urban governance, the captured city takes the capabilities offered by smart systems and puts them to work in surveillance and control. Often this includes importing tools and ideas from military intelligence into police departments, and extending methods of colonial control, such as welfare restrictions in Aboriginal communities to the population at large. The city and its inhabitants are thus 'Captured,' both by surveillance that collects data and by authorities who control territory. What happens to the captured city then will be shaped by the context in which the smart urban systems are deployed. There is no reason to believe things will be different now because the boosters of smart urbanism drop a few buzzwords and make some lofty promises. Indeed, these technologies equip the state with even better tools to monitor and control its population, often by design. We've heard it all before, every time a tech executive or venture capitalist makes promises to fulfil the techno-utopian dream of disruption.

Darwin is not alone

Darwin is well on its way to becoming a captured city, but it is not alone. As all levels of government across Australia seek smarter ways of governing, examples of similar urban technologies being used in policing and control are springing up around the country. These projects include a police scheme to target people who they believe may commit crimes in future in Sydney (which disproportionately affects Aboriginal people), 'Crime Prevention Through Environmental Design' guidelines in Brisbane and facial recognition systems in Perth. These examples demonstrate how the perceived neutrality of smart city technology uses stories about progress, modernity, and innovation to entrench and disguise existing urban injustices. Ultimately, the 'Smart city' in Australia is best understood not as a break with older, analogue modes of governing urban space, but as a continuation of the settler-colonial project of displacement, enclosure, and control. Coming to a city near you.

'FAKE" MEDIA COVERAGE

Fake news, real coverage: How 'Conspiracy Theories' spread through media and politics, half of the American public believes in a popular conspiracy theory. Take the idea that compact fluorescent light bulbs are a form of mind control, the U.S. government was behind the terrorist attack on 9/11, or any number of theories connected to big political names, and someone believes it. While there's a stereotype attached to people who believe in conspiracy theories, the reality is much different. 'Often what you find is a bunch of regular people who face circumstances in their lives that put them in a situation where they're seeking out answers to puzzling questions. It's harder to say, 'I have no idea what's going on' than it is to say, 'I have a specific idea that these people are the problem," said graduate student Jordan Foley.

PhD candidate Jordan Foley

Foley's background in mass communication and rhetoric, combined with experience on the debate team at Wake Forest University where he received his master's degree, gives him a clever idea of how a particular idea can become convincing. Now, as a doctoral candidate in the School of Journalism and Mass Communication (SJMC) at UW–Madison, Foley's focus has turned to the ways that information spreads throughout online and mainstream media, winding up in the minds and hearts of people in the U.S. Examining this idea provides more understanding into how people came to know about conspiracy theories, believe them, and spread them.

For his dissertation, Foley investigates how conspiracy theories circulate after mass shootings. Existing research identifies the type of people that tend to believe conspiracy theories, such as those who already experience more stress and anxiety, or who tend to be more skeptical of official narratives. Others are affected by a traumatic life event such as losing a loved one in a terrorist attack and then find conspiracy theories credible in their search for answers. However, Foley said there was little focus on how these ideas are transmitted in the first place. 'A mass shooting shifts news coverage for, almost, weeks,' Foley said. 'With that media attention, there's a lot more opportunity for groups and organizations and voices to make their way into that conversation.'

Using machine learning algorithms to sift through internet posts, news articles, and other text around different mass shootings, Foley plans to analyze how today media ecology is contributes to spreading conspiracy narratives. Recently, Foley and colleagues at SJMC including graduate students Yini Zhang, Aman Abhishek, Josephine Lukito, Jiyoun Suk, Sang Jung Kim, and Zhongkai Sun published a paper using similar machine learning techniques to see how social media conversations changed after a mass shooting. They found that mass shootings with certain features – such as a higher number of casualties or children as victims – got more attention on Twitter. While gun control sentiments were more common after these shootings, the gun rights discourse stayed constant whether or not conversations about shootings were active on the social platform. Additionally, they found that shootings with a higher percentage of African American victims got less attention than those with lower percentages, Foley said.

With his dissertation, Foley will track conspiratorial claims such as that certain mass shootings were staged. After the Sandy Hook school shooting, conspiracy theories that the victims were paid actors circulated on social media platforms like Twitter, Facebook, and Reddit. Foley noted that media reporting errors, such as incorrectly identifying the shooter because he was carrying his brother's ID card gave fodder to those who were spreading these narratives. It's a timely topic, as the U.S. grapples with the proliferation of fake news and misinformation. The constant developments in the conversation around misinformation also make Foley's research challenging. Recently, Twitter, Facebook, and Instagram banned conspiracy theorist Alex Jones, among whose many claims was that Sandy Hook shooting victims were child actors. This development means that Foley has to search a lot harder to find that research material online.

'When you have these tech companies that scrub their servers of all of this content, it actually becomes kind of hard,' Foley said. 'So much of the content that's been up has been taken down.' In addition to percolating through social media, conspiracy narratives can be spread by political and cultural elites who amplify that message with their platform. For example, a conspiracy theory about the death of Democratic National Committee staffer Seth Rich stayed in the news cycle for weeks when political commentator Sean Hannity continued to talk about it on his Fox News show. Often, these individuals or media organizations have economic and political incentives for spreading these narratives. 'There is a class of people that does have incentives to insinuate or even outright make these claims,' he said. 'That group, we have to think about differently than the everyday person who may just believe these things.'

Foley noted that narratives about conspiracies often have certain characters that make them more credible and more likely to gain additional media coverage. There's the hero scientist who makes an amazing discovery but is persecuted for it; their scientific background lends them academic credibility. Then, there are real people who are affected by the issues and are pulled into the narrative. In general, these individuals are more likely to seek out information via media, Foley said. Take for example the families of 9/11 victims 'They're the person who is the material embodiment of the negative effects of this broad conspiracy that's happening,' Foley said.

Further studying how conspiracy narratives travel across media and society helped reposition the question about people who believe in them away from only asking why someone believes in a conspiracy. Rather, the question becomes how is that theory talked about, and how does it make its way around the political and media system. Foley is interested in continuing to research the interaction between journalism and politics beyond his dissertation project. He said SJMC does a wonderful job of starting students with important foundational theories, which helped him get started as a researcher. 'This project crystallized probably two years into the program, and it was very much a result of the seminars I was taking, the professors I was working with and the research groups I was part of, and then bringing in the rhetoric side of things,' he said.

5G

In the 1970s, the bogeyman was power lines. Low-frequency electromagnetic fields were emanating from them all the time, and a shocking 1979 study suggested that children who developed cancer lived near power lines "unduly often." Around the same time, because of Cold War panic about radiation in general, televisions and microwave ovens also became a possible human health catastrophe. Later, concern bubbled up around a slew of other household appliances, including hair dryers and electric blankets.

Now the advance of cellphones and, more recently, the new high-speed networks built to serve them have given rise to a paranoid coalition who believe to varying degrees in a massive cover-up of deleterious harm. The devices are different, but the fears are the same: The radiation from the things we use every single day is destroying us; our modern world is a colossal mistake. The stakes are about as high as they could possibly be: If it were true that our cellphones were causing brain tumors, that our wireless devices were damaging our DNA, and that radiation emanating from cell towers was sickening us in any untold number of ways, this would be the greatest human health disaster the world has ever known. As well as, perhaps, its greatest capitalist conspiracy.

It's too big to be true. The science is confusing, but the World Health Organization, noting decades of research, has found no significant health risks from low-level electromagnetic fields. Yet amid a broader tech backlash—against screens, against social media, against power consolidating in a handful of companies, against a technology industry that rolls out new products and protocols faster than we can keep up or argue with, against the general fatigue and malaise associated with a life spent typing and scrolling, it's just big enough to seem, to many, like the obvious explanation for so much being wrong.

A wildly disorienting pandemic coming at the same time as the global rollout of 5G, the newest technology standard for wireless networks has only made matters worse. '5G launched in CHINA. Nov 1, 2019. People dropped dead,' the singer Keri Hilson wrote in a now-deleted tweet to her 4.2 million followers in March. As the coronavirus spread throughout Europe, fears about 5G appear to have animated a rash of vandalism and arson of mobile infrastructure, including more than 30 incidents in the U.K. in just the first 10 days of April. In the case of one arson attack in the Netherlands, the words 'Fuck 5G' were reportedly found scrawled at the scene. Mobile- and broadband-infrastructure workers have also reported harassment and threats from deluded citizens: A recent Wired UK report detailed an instance in which a London network engineer was spit on; he later contracted an illness that was suspected to be the coronavirus.

While those theories are flat-Earth-level absurd, legitimate scientists have long been interested in a relationship between wireless technology and cancer, and tens of millions of dollars have been spent investigating it. Activists have lobbied politicians and government agencies, who have been thus compelled to address it. Mothers have always told their children not to stand in front of the microwave. Annals of the New York Academy of Sciences published an overview of electromagnetic-radiation research in 1975, acknowledging the public's concern about how quickly 'Technologic advances' were moving along, resulting in the use of 'Electromagnetic emitting equipment … in medicine, industry, research, military systems, and the home.'

The wildest thing about baseless coronavirus and 5G theories is that they're barely part of the story, they're just the latest headline.

The ranks of the 5G-skeptical include environmental activists, politicians, celebrities, and fringe scientists. In 2015, 190 scientists, doctors, and engineers from about 40 countries sent an appeal to the United Nations, urging the World Health Organization to reconsider the international guidelines for human exposure to the kind of radiation emitted by cellphones and other wireless technologies. In 2017, some of the same group co-signed a letter to the European Union asking that 5G rollout be put on hold pending further investigation. Though this community is far from mainstream, it is large. And it is powerful: In April 2019, Brussels stopped work on its 5G network, with the environmental minister of the region saying that citizens wouldn't be treated as 'Guinea pigs.' A few cities and towns in Northern California have passed ordinances to curb 5G deployment, explicitly because of health concerns, and three members of Congress have written to Federal Communications Commission Chairman Ajit Pai about their constituents' worries over 5G safety.

Last fall, the activist group NYC 5G Wake-Up Call hosts Patti Wood, the executive director of the national nonprofit Grassroots Environmental Education founded by Wood and her husband in 2000 to address issues including pesticides, GMOs, fluoridated water, fracking, and synthetic turf for an event about the ills of wireless technology. The venue is a church in Midtown Manhattan, and the audience is rowdy and simmering with anger at the telecom companies, at the government agencies that are supposed to protect us, at the scientists who ignore the work of other scientists. With white hair and a severe laugh, Wood is a woman you'd gravitate toward in the midst of disaster. 'You have no rights. These are involuntary exposures,' she tells the 30 or so attendees. 'But we need it in order to use our fun little toys,' she shoots at the crowd, many of whom have been on their phone the whole time she's been talking.

The FCC, the FDA, the U.S. Department of Agriculture, and the Environmental Protection Agency are supposed to protect our health, Wood says, but they're failing. People are suffering from electromagnetic hypersensitivity, a condition also known as 'Microwave sickness,' with symptoms including fatigue, dizziness, and nausea, but they're afraid to talk about it. 'These are not 'Wacko' people. These are principals of schools, and doctors who work in emergency rooms, I'm just giving you examples of people, people who work in the IT business,' she says. 'You see a lot of health-care professionals who are dealing with this. And yet, nobody's really talking about it. Nobody's talking about it. It's like nobody talks about vaccinations, you know, because nobody wants them to think that 'I'm a crazy, I'm an anti-vaxxer." (Wood later says she's not an anti-vaxxer. Grassroots Environmental Education says it has never taken a public stance on vaccines.) 'It's all about power,' she says, encouraging activists in the room to band together to exert political influence.

As with any argument about injustice and capitalist conspiracy, it is easy to flirt with believing for moments or hours at a time. Wireless technology could be slowly killing us all, or at least it could be slowly killing some of us (as other profitable things have done from time to time), or at least it could be true that we aren't sure and are moving ahead recklessly. In the 50 or so years since Americans started eyeing our microwaves with suspicion, we've been introduced to a parade of new products so quickly it's hard to feel as if we ever had a choice. In 2020, the average person doesn't get to decide whether she wants a smartphone or an email account or a home computer: They're the default, the instruments we all need to live a functional life. In the case of 5G, the lack of agency is even more obvious. The infrastructure is being built whether we want it or not. So, at some level, the conversation becomes not about the technology itself, but about the fact that ordinary people don't feel as though they had any personal say. And sometimes, in fumbling for lost agency, people grab on to conspiracy theories.

'The fact that the fields produced by electric current … were both invisible and ubiquitous, that exposure was largely beyond one's control, and that the alleged health consequences were depicted as catastrophic helps to account for the intense fear that came to be associated with the question in the public mind,' the cancer epidemiologist Geoffrey Kabat writes in his 2008 book, Hyping Health Risks. He compares looking for evidence of a relationship between various forms of electromagnetic radiation and brain cancer to looking for shapes in the clouds: It's easy to see something if that's what you really want to do.

One of the most careful voices of reason in the debate about electromagnetic fields is the epidemiologist David Savitz. He stresses that 'There's not really been a clear indication that there is a problem' with Wi-Fi but acknowledges the validity of the concern. As far as any individual fear is understandable, fear of cellphones makes sense: They went from basic nonexistence to ubiquity in about a decade. Now nearly every public urban place has Wi-Fi, and we will soon have small cell towers every few blocks. Whether or not you believe this will give you brain cancer, you didn't have a chance to opt out. And if there is anything, even anecdotal evidence to suggest that it might cause cancer that can be uniquely terrifying. 'To be honest, I don't think research can ever put the concern to rest,' Savitz tells me. 'It can bound it. It can raise or lower the level of concern. But … when we do nothing, there are legitimate questions in the order of who knows what it does?'

Activists tend to cite the existence of 'Hundreds' or even 'Thousands' of studies that prove a connection between low-level radiation and various adverse health effects. They aren't wrong about the volume of research. They aren't even wrong that some of the studies find what they're looking for. What is impossible to say in a sentence is that they find any one thing in particular, and no evidence supports the idea that global industry and governments have made a concerted effort to keep shocking findings from the public.

Work that points to dangerous connections between electromagnetic radiation and negative human health outcomes tends to ignore much of what we know about electromagnetic waves and the way they interact with the body. Though the word radiation always conjures up a little something frantic in the gut, there is a diverse spectrum of electromagnetic waves, with big differences among them. Gamma rays and X-ray waves with noticeably short wavelengths and very high photon energies can cause cellular damage because they can knock electrons out of atoms. It is unbelievably bad to be exposed to them for extended periods.

But current wireless technology uses fields in the microwave range, and the FCC sets limits for radiofrequency exposure from cellphones well below the line at which we would expect heating to happen in human tissue. In 1991, the Yale physicist Robert K. Adair wrote in Physical Review that 'There are good reasons to believe' that weak fields 'Can have no significant biological effect at the cell level and no strong reason to believe otherwise.' The best evidence that electromagnetic radiation does not cause brain cancer is simple: We have been placing antennae on our bodies and next to our heads almost 24 hours a day for two decades, and the world has not seen an epidemic of brain cancer. In fact, in the U.S., the rate of new brain-cancer cases was lower in 2017 than in 1992.

For years, scientific attempts to find a meaningful relationship between brain cancer and cellular radiation have failed. For 13 years starting in 1982, scientists followed every adult in Denmark who had a cellphone plan, 420,000 people. In the end, they found no evidence at all of an association between brain tumors and cellphone use. In 2010, the World Health Organization released the results of a decade-long international case-control study. The study's 48 authors took more than four years to decide how to interpret the data, and it's easy to see why: The findings were simultaneously explosive and meaningless. The participants who held their phone to their head most often had a 40 percent increase in risk for developing a glioma, absolutely shocking, and significant. But the group with the second-highest use showed, bafflingly, one of the lowest risks for glioma.

The science remained muddy.

In 2018, the largest-ever study of cellphones and brain cancer, conducted by the U.S.'s National Toxicology Program, tested rats at high-level, full-body exposures far higher than the average cellphone user would experience. It found 'Clear evidence' that cellphone exposure was correlated with malignant heart tumors in male rats (but not females), and 'Some evidence' that exposure was correlated with gliomas and adrenal-gland tumors in male rats (but not females). One of the biggest challenges of studying brain cancer is that it is exceedingly rare. An association between a brain tumor and anything at all would be incredibly difficult to prove, even if the association existed. But there is a reason that the question keeps getting asked and the studies keep getting funded: In addition to being rare, brain cancers are exceptionally deadly. Only one in three people who are diagnosed with brain cancer will be alive five years later.

One afternoon, I attend a NYC 5G Wake-Up Call meeting in a prewar co-op on Manhattan's Museum Mile, overlooking Central Park. When I arrive, five women are sitting in a ring around the edge of a sun-dappled sitting room. They've all brought stacks of paper printouts of studies and reports and pamphlets, along with a couple of sheets that are just lists of video links.

The meeting's host, Stephanie Low, has been an activist for 20 years, working against the Trans-Pacific Partnership, fracking, and now, wireless technology of all sorts. 'I only work on things that are enormous horrors,' she says. She hands me a business card; one of 1,000 she had printed to hand out to parents around the city when she sees them giving their young children a cellphone to play with. The card depicts a cartoon child with a smart meter which emit electromagnetic radiation hovering near their throat and a cellphone near their brain, next to a stop sign and a note: 'Protect Your Kids! Studies show that the developing brains of children from conception to teenage years can be damaged by cell phone use. To be safe, even casual play should be prevented.'

Last June, Low finished treatment for pancreatic cancer. A few months before, she'd become personally involved in the wireless issue because of a friend who is electro-hypersensitive. This friend had lived a normal life in New York City, until her landlord installed 25 smart meters in the building without warning. She didn't sleep for five nights, Low says, and had to come stay with her. Three weeks later, Low's friend was in excruciating pain again whenever she moved. She started living in Low's guest bathroom, the only place that felt slightly less like a frying pan. Eventually, she moved upstate. A week after she left, Low found out that her building had installed smart meters in its basement too, a fact she relays with her eyes burning a hole through the floor at her feet.

The WHO has an exceptionally long informational page about electromagnetic hypersensitivity. It is clearly written to be careful about stories like Low's friend's, describing the suffering as real but the idea that a person with EHS can specifically detect and feel electromagnetic-field exposure as suspect. 'EHS is characterized by a variety of non-specific symptoms that differ from individual to individual. The symptoms certainly are real and can vary widely in their severity,' it reads. Then, 'EHS has no clear diagnostic criteria and there is no scientific basis to link EHS symptoms to EMF exposure. Further, EHS is not a medical diagnosis, nor is it clear that it represents a single medical problem.'

The friend, who asked to remain anonymous for fear of retribution from the telecom industry, calls us from upstate and retells the story, adding, 'We're truth detectives, sorting propaganda from reality.' Of the thousands of isolated bits of pop-culture ephemera floating around TikTok, one of the stickiest is a clip of Khloé Kardashian berating her sister Kourtney in an episode of 'Keeping Up With the Kardashians' that aired in the summer of 2016. 'What the fuck is up with your Wi-Fi?' she demands, walking around her sister's basketball court with a phone outstretched. 'You have this big-ass house, and you can't afford a Wi-Fi box out here?'

'It's not about affording …' Kourtney tells her, looking up from her phone, as if exhausted by the never-ending chore of explaining the world to a slightly younger adult sibling. Then, pinching the air under her chin, emphasizing each syllable as if she's teaching phonetics: 'It's about … radiation.' This does nothing to console Khloé, in fact it seems to offend her on a moral level, and she screams, 'You're going to die anyway; you understand that, right? Die with a good Snapchat going through!'

Though the young people ripping the audio for a 15-second joke probably consider Kourtney the butt of it, a fair number of rich and famous Californians likely side with her. Fran Drescher is best known for her starring role as the titular nanny in The Nanny, but she has spent the past 15 years talking about all sorts of things that could cause cancer, including EMFs. Drescher calls me from her car one Saturday afternoon, using speakerphone but not Bluetooth, Bluetooth turns your car into a microwave, she says. The American people are enabling the 'Greedy sociopaths' of the tech and telecom industries, she argues, and we should be expressing our opinions with our dollars. We can't just sit back and let them use us as guinea pigs. She speaks at the clip of a podcast on 3x playback for most of the conversation, but her voice dips low and a little mournful before we hang up. 'We are part of this planet,' she tells me. 'And we are harmonic with it. We are in disharmony with electromagnetic fields.'

The model Miranda Kerr, who is married to Snap CEO Evan Spiegel, told a beauty-magazine editor that she uses an EMF detector to monitor 'The waves in the air,' and that she installed a kill switch to turn off the Wi-Fi and all the electricity at night (save for the refrigerator and security cameras) in her Malibu house. Jack Dorsey, the CEO of Twitter, said last year that he owns a small sauna with an EMF-shielding tent, to protect him from radiation when he wants to relax. ('It feels a little bit different because you're not getting hit by all the EMF energy,' he explained on a podcast.)

Indeed, as with all fears, you can buy things to ease your mind: Belly Armor, recently featured in People magazine, sells blankets lined with RadiaShield Fabric 'To protect your reproductive organs from exposure to cell phones, laptops and other smart devices while at home or at the office,' as well as radiation-deflecting mouse-shaped baby hats to protect babies' brains once they're outside the womb. Companies like Less EMF sell silver-threaded fabric, polyester window film, and carbon paint, which are often used by people who want to block electromagnetic radiation from their homes.

Heather Askinosic, a co-founder of the California jewelry company Energy Muse, approaches the same problem by selling, among other things, well-designed products made with a mostly carbon mineraloid called shungite. 'Two years ago, we really started selling a lot of shungite to people who were more in tune with EMFs and looking for other modalities of how to harmonize,' she tells me in a phone call. 'More and more people are becoming EMF sensitive. Will shungite protect you from an EMF? I don't have the research to say that it will. But I do think that will harmonize those waves so that you have more of a harmonious energy coming at you.'

The supremacy of wireless technology in American daily life is, really, a capitalist plot—at least as far as the best way to protect yourself from anything is with money. The No. 1 seller in Askinosie's shop is a rectangular shungite sticker ($9.95) that goes on the back of a cellphone case and protects 'Your energy against EMFs.' Second is a shungite phone stand ($34.95), and third is a shungite plate ($14.95), to set any kind of electronic device on. ('By placing your devices on a Shungite Plate, the Shungite stone properties minimize the EMFs emitted by technology.')

The California-based lifestyle brand GIA Wellness offers the typical roster of skin-care products and meal-replacement protein powders alongside a range of Lifestyle Energy Products, including a $64.95 cellphone case that was designed in part 'To help support your body's natural resistance to the stress-related effects of electropollution (EMF) exposure,' a pendant that serves a similar purpose for $312.50 (both use "Energy Resonance Technology," a 'Proprietary process, custom programmed to resonate with, and support your body's energy field'), and a

'Home Harmonizer' that costs $234.50 and has been designed to 'Support an energetically harmonious environment' with up to a 60-foot radius.

'We have really profound results, which is the most exciting thing,' the company co-founder Lynda Cormier-Hanser says. 'When people put a cell guard on their phone, and they no longer have migraine headaches. That's really rewarding when you hear those stories.' When products alone don't seem to have addressed the problem, there are also services on offer. In Santa Fe, New Mexico, the Building Biology Institute offers several types of home-inspector certifications, including one for electromagnetic-radiation specialists (a trademark-pending term). The coursework for that program costs $5,355, and requires a series of online classes, a correspondence course, three one-week sessions in person, plus a final project mentored by a current building biologist.

Inspecting an average 1,800-square-foot home with three to four bedrooms is usually a full day of work, the BBI-certified specialist Stephanie Kerst tells me, including four to six hours on-site and an hour or two of reporting and preparing recommendations for the client. Kerst charges $125 an hour for phone or Zoom consultations, and $150 an hour for in-person inspections. 'I've been doing this about two years now. And I would say, what I have noticed is just a steady increase in the number of clients,' she says in a phone call. 'There's so much work to go around.' To believe that wireless technology is deadly, you can start by believing in a few simple, true things, and then go from there. 'There is so much dishonesty in this field, and people paid by the industry,' one activist tells me coolly, a few moments after we first shake hands. Then she looks at me as if she's about to take notes on the muscles in my face. 'You have to dig for the truth. But are you interested in the truth?'

I am, which is how I end up reading a booklet by Norm Alster titled 'Captured Agency,' subtitled 'How the Federal Communications Commission Is Dominated by the Industries It Presumably Regulates.' It was published in 2015 and is a common reference point for activists. The accusations of corruption it contains are extreme, to say the least. Invoking 'The hardball tactics of the tobacco industry,' Alster accuses the wireless industry of 'Bullying potential threats into submission,' and the FCC of allowing it to happen. The flamboyant prose, and the overreactions throughout the paper over minor connections and shared dinners, makes it rhetorically unpersuasive. But Alster is not wrong that the FCC has been accused, credibly, of blurring the lines between regulation and participation. 'The path from a Commission seat to an aisle seat inside Comcast's private jet and vice versa has been wide open for years,' the Verge editor in chief Nilay Patel wrote in his 2016 interview of the former FCC head Tom Wheeler.

There is an argument to be made that the FCC overreaches, removing community agency and consolidating power. In October, a federal court of appeals upheld the commission's wildly unpopular repeal of net neutrality but shot down its claim that states were not allowed to pass net-neutrality laws of their own. The court also criticized the FCC for a 'Disregard of its duty,' in failing to assess the ways in which eroding an open internet might affect public safety and emergency services. There are also valid criticisms surrounding 5G technology, many of which have been made repeatedly by prominent politicians and mainstream journalists. Even Wheeler, one of 5G's most prominent hype men only a few years ago, has come out against the current FCC administration's handling of 5G cybersecurity. There are scientists involved in this discussion who are genuinely scary, Geoffrey Kabat says. The ones who want to imagine they're saving the world, and call anyone who disagrees with them an industry shill. 'The answers aren't simple, and the science certainly isn't simple, but they want to know who the good guys are and who the bad guys are,' he says. They want to be heroes, and they convince people that they are.

Our 5G lifestyle will be expensive and it will be vulnerable. It will probably enable unprecedented surveillance of public and private space, and it may grossly exacerbate the digital divide, as rural areas get left even further behind. You don't have to think that small cell towers will kill you to think that they will look terrible when dispersed every few blocks; you don't have to believe in any fringe science to be annoyed that 5G may interfere with weather satellites. 5G will definitely generate a lot of economic activity, but it won't change the average person's life. The Internet of Things is an ungraspable future, particularly when the fact of a future for Earth at all sometimes sounds implausible. There is no explanation for disease in the way that a person might want one, especially in the moment that she needs one.

The fear of some generalized capitalist conspiracy comes up, too, in Eula Biss's 2014 book, On Immunity, which discusses the anti-vaccine movement. Biss spent years talking to fellow parents about their suspicions and fears, concluding that while these feelings can be easily justified, what they are most of all is sad: 'That so many of us find it entirely plausible that a vast network of researchers and health officials and doctors worldwide would willfully harm children for money is evidence of what capitalism is really taking from us,' she writes. In the case of anti-wireless activism, the scope of the conspiracy widens to the point where it becomes a worldview: Connectivity for connectivity's sake was a mistake. Why are we carrying it around on our bodies? We could dial back, or we could stop moving so fast, we could stop ruining the night sky with satellites that will do nothing but bring super-fast internet to more people who will soon regret what it does to them.

On an afternoon in December, I have lunch with Ellen Osuna, who attended the NYC 5G Wake-Up Call meeting in Low's apartment, and who I also saw hovering at the back of Patti Wood's speech. She uses a landline phone, has an EMF-shielding headset for her cellphone, and owns a Chromebook that connects to the internet only through an ethernet cable, but we meet at a coffee shop in Manhattan. 'I think there should be hardly any places with Wi-Fi,' she says, when I ask how she feels about the café we're sitting in, the city we live in. 'There should be public access to ethernet.' I meant less specifically. How does she feel about the fact that nobody in here seems to be the slightest bit concerned? 'It's a really heavy thing to carry,' she says. 'It's surreal.'

She bristles when I suggest that some of the evidence is compelling for brain cancer, but none of it is for things like autism and Alzheimer's. But she nods emphatically when I ask if the words some activists use apocalypse, Holocaust, death ray, are frustrating for her to hear. These words don't help; she cringes when they come up. 'Wireless is not like the fossil-fuel industries,' she says. "There is so much more brilliance. Amazing things are being done with technology." But it is like the fossil-fuel industry in that 'We're completely entrenched. We're addicted to it because of what these companies hid.'

Osuna sees herself as just one person doing one person's part, which is talking to as many other people who will listen, doing her best to live a moral life, one that is tinged by grief. In the 1980s, when she was in middle school, a surfeit of scientific evidence proved the reality of climate change, she says, and she remembers her teacher telling her so. 'We could have pulled back then, but we didn't.' The fight against wireless technology is at that point now, she thinks. 'This is the beginning.' She is optimistic, she says. Or more so than she was a few years ago, when it was much harder to find information about the dangers of wireless technology. 'We can't see this with the eye, but we are literally covered in this,' she says. 'We're trying to make the invisible visible.'

She's not exaggerating the challenge of her task. When the WHO declared electromagnetic fields a class 2B carcinogen in 2011, with one doctor stating in a press release that there 'Could be some risk' of cancer from EMF exposure, it was effectively publishing a Rorschach test. Anti-wireless activists are quick to point out that group 2B also includes such poisonous-sounding substances as chloroform and lead. You could just as easily point out that the list also includes aloe vera, pickled vegetables, talc-based body powders, and dry cleaning, things that sound innocuous, but then again, Wi-Fi sounds innocuous too.

The second time I see Stephanie Low, she greets me warmly and presses me to take a photo of her optometrist's business card on my phone—I mention that I'm trying to get glasses; I'm going blind from looking at my computer all day. And this reminds her of a theory she read that our vision is a hologram, as is the entire universe. She recommends a book that changed the way she thinks about everything Michael Talbot's The Holographic Universe and adds that my local library likely has a copy. So, I read it one morning, wondering what comfort there might possibly be in conceiving of the world in a completely unusual way than I have all my life. The book is confusing, and it is beautiful. 'There is evidence to suggest that our world and everything in it—from snowflakes to maple trees to falling stars and spinning electrons are also only ghostly images,' Talbot writes, 'Projections from a level of reality so beyond our own it is literally beyond both space and time.'

The theory that our memories are holographic, and that the world itself is holographic, is, he says, the one that explains such phenomena as near-death experiences, precognition, lucid dreams, the placebo effect, stigmata, miracles, psychics, psychokinetic powers, X-ray vision, and the paranormal. Every unanswered question. It explains the remarkable recovery of a 61-year-old throat-cancer patient, who 'Visualized his cancer cells as weaker as and more confused than his normal cells,' and 'His body's white blood cells, the soldiers of the immune system, coming in, swarming over the dead and dying cancer cells.' Talbot's book is not a work of fiction but extrapolates wildly from the real work of credible scientists. He died of chronic lymphocytic leukemia in 1992.

'In a holographic universe,' Talbot writes, 'A universe in which separateness ceases to exist and the innermost processes of the psyche can spill over and become as much a part of the objective landscape as the flowers and the trees, reality itself becomes little more than a mass shared dream.' The wholeness gets to me, as does the lowering of stakes. I see the appeal of a world that exists only as an illusion yet knits our lives together into one shimmering image of continuity. We could be accountable to one another. We could have unlimited chances to erase pain. The theory comes from science, kind of, if you squint, and shove the puzzle pieces together slightly against their will. Imagine choosing to believe something impossible, over a reality that is also impossible: not hard.

In October, the WHO put out a call for systematic reviews of the relationship between electromagnetic fields and 10 different topics. This is a question that will be asked repeatedly and again. 'By and large, the research is reassuring about there not being, certainly not a major problem, perhaps no problem at all in terms of adverse health effects,' David Savitz tells me. But for a vast number of the people asking, the concern isn't about what holds true 'By and large,' it's about the way they're living, what they're feeling. They feel tired and sick; they sense that it is the result of modern life. All they've been asking for is some solid proof that it isn't.

GLOBAL WARMING

A global warming conspiracy theory invokes claims that the scientific consensus on global warming is based on conspiracies to produce manipulated data or suppress dissent. It is one of a number of tactics used in climate change denial to attempt to manufacture political and public controversy disputing this consensus. Conspiracy theorists typically allege that, through worldwide acts of professional and criminal misconduct, the science behind global warming has been invented or distorted for ideological or financial reasons. Temperature data: Global average temperature datasets from NASA, NOAA, Berkeley Earth, and meteorological offices of the U.K. and Japan, show substantial agreement concerning the progress and extent of global warming: all pairwise correlations exceed 98%.

Causation: The Fourth National Climate Assessment ('NCA4', USGCRP, 2017) includes charts illustrating how human factors, especially accumulation in the atmosphere of greenhouse gases, are the predominant cause of observed global warming. As stated by the Intergovernmental Panel on Climate Change (IPCC), the largest contributor to global warming is the increase in atmospheric carbon dioxide ($CO2$) since 1750, particularly from fossil fuel combustion, cement production, and land use changes such as deforestation. The IPCC's Fifth Assessment Report (AR5) states:

'Human influence has been detected in warming of the atmosphere and the ocean, in changes in the global water cycle, in reductions in snow and ice, in global mean sea level rise, and in changes in some climate extremes. This evidence for human influence has grown since AR4. It is extremely likely (95–100%) that human influence has been the dominant cause of the observed warming since the mid-20th century'

IPCC AR5 WG1 Summary for Policymakers

The evidence for global warming due to human influence has been recognized by the national science academies of all the major industrialized countries. No scientific body of national or international standing maintains a formal opinion dissenting from the summary conclusions of the IPCC. Despite this scientific consensus on climate change, allegations have been made that scientists and institutions involved in global warming research are part of a global scientific conspiracy or engaged in a manipulative hoax. There have been allegations of malpractice, most notably in the Climatic Research Unit email controversy 'ClimateGate.' Eight committees investigated these allegations and published reports, each finding no evidence of fraud or scientific misconduct. The Muir Russell report stated that the scientists' 'Rigor and honesty as scientists are not in doubt,' that the investigators 'Did not find any evidence of behavior that might undermine the conclusions of the IPCC assessments,' but that there had been "a consistent pattern of failing to display the proper degree of openness.' The scientific consensus that global warming is occurring as a result of human activity remained unchanged at the end of the investigations.

Alleged conspiracies by scientists who accept the reality of global warming

Faked scientific data: In 2002, after Clive Hamilton criticized Lavoisier Group, the Cooler Heads Coalition published an article supporting the Lavoisier Group's conspiracy theory that hundreds of climate scientists have twisted their results to support the climate change theory in order to protect their research funding. In 2007, John Coleman wrote a blog post claiming that global warming is the greatest scam in history. He wrote 'Our universities have become somewhat isolated from the rest of us. There is a culture and attitudes and values and pressures on campus that are quite different.... They all look askance at the rest of us, certain of their superiority.... These scientists know that if they do research and results are in no way alarming, their research will gather dust on the shelf and their research careers will languish. But if they do research that sounds alarms, they will become well known and respected and receive scholarly awards and, very importantly, more research dollars will come flooding their way. So, when these researchers did climate change studies in the late 90's they were eager to produce findings that would be important and be widely noticed and trigger more research funding. It was easy for them to manipulate the data to come up with the results they wanted to make headlines and at the same time drive their environmental agendas. Then their likeminded PHD colleagues reviewed their work and hastened to endorse it without question.'

The climate deniers involved in Climategate in 2009 claimed that researchers faked the data in their research publications and suppressed their critics in order to receive more funding (i.e., taxpayer money). Some climate change deniers claim that there is no scientific consensus on climate change, and they sometimes claim that any evidence that shows there is scientific consensus is faked. Some of them even claim that governments have used the research grant money to pervert the science. Corrupted peer-review process: It is claimed that the peer-review process for papers in climate science has become corrupted by scientists seeking to suppress dissent. Frederick Seitz drafted an article in Wall Street Journal in 1996 criticizing IPCC Second Assessment Report. He suspected corruption in the peer-review process, writing that 'A comparison between the report approved by the contributing scientists and the published version reveals that key changes were made after the scientists had met and accepted what they thought was the final peer-reviewed version. The scientists were assuming that the IPCC would obey the IPCC Rules--a body of regulations that is supposed to govern the panel's actions. Nothing in the

IPCC Rules permits anyone to change a scientific report after it has been accepted by the panel of scientific contributors and the full IPCC.'

Alleged political conspiracies

Aiming at global governance: In a speech given to the US Senate Committee on the Environment and Public Works on July 28, 2003, entitled 'The Science of Climate Change', Senator James Inhofe (Republican, for Oklahoma) concluded by asking the following question: 'With all of the hysteria, all of the fear, all of the phony science, could it be that man-made global warming is the greatest hoax ever perpetrated on the American people?' He further stated, 'Some parts of the IPCC process resembled a Soviet-style trial, in which the facts are predetermined, and ideological purity trumps technical and scientific rigor.' Inhofe has suggested that supporters of the Kyoto Protocol such as Jacques Chirac are aiming at global governance. William M. Gray said in 2006 that global warming became a political cause because of the lack of any other enemy following the end of the Cold War. He went on to say that its purpose was to exercise political influence, to try to introduce world government, and to control people, adding, 'I have a demonic view on this.' The TV documentary The Great Global Warming Swindle was made by Martin Durkin, who called global warming 'A multi-billion-dollar worldwide industry, created by fanatically anti-industrial environmentalists.' In the Washington Times in 2007 he said that his film would change history and predicted that 'In five years the idea that the greenhouse effect is the main reason behind global warming will be seen as total bunk.'

Liberal extremists: There are theories claiming that 'Climate change is a hoax perpetrated by leftist radicals to undermine local sovereignty,' or 'Climate science is less about science and more about socialist ideology.' In 2017, James Inhofe told the 12th International Conference on Climate Change 'The liberal extremists are not going to give up. Obama has built a culture of radical alarmists, and they'll be back. You and I and the American people have won a great victory, but the war goes on. Stay vigilant.' Green scam: 'Another conspiracy theory argues that because many people have invested in renewable-energy companies, they stand to lose a lot of money if global warming is shown to be a myth. According to this theory, environmental groups therefore bribe climate scientists to doctor their data so that they are able to secure their financial investment in green energy.'

China is behind it: In 2010, Donald Trump claimed that 'With the coldest winter ever recorded, with snow setting record levels up and down the coast, the Nobel committee should take the Nobel Prize back from Al Gore....Gore wants us to clean up our factories and plants in order to protect us from global warming, when China and other countries couldn't care less. It would make us totally noncompetitive in the manufacturing world, and China, Japan and India are laughing at America's stupidity.' Then in 2012, he tweeted that 'The concept of global warming was created by and for the Chinese in order to make U.S. manufacturing non-competitive.' Later in 2016 during his presidential campaign he suggested that his 2012 tweet was a joke saying that 'Obviously, I joke. But this is done for the benefit of China because China does not do anything to help climate change. They burn everything you could burn; they couldn't care less. They have very, you know, their standards are nothing. But they in the meantime, they can undercut us on price. So, it's ridiculously hard on our business.' To promote nuclear power: One of the claims made in The Great Global Warming Swindle is that the 'Threat of global warming is an attempt to promote nuclear power.'

Negative effects

Climate change conspiracy theories have resulted in poor action or no action at all to effectively mitigate the damage done by global warming. In some countries like the United States of America, 40% of Americans believe that climate change is a hoax in spite of the fact that there is a 100% consensus among climate scientists that it is not according to a report in 2019. President Donald Trump previously even pulled the United States out of the Paris Agreement, which was set up in the hopes of reducing global warming. There may be an ideology of climate change denial in some regions of the world, which would lead to disagreements over how to handle climate change and what should be done in the face of it.

Condemnation

Steve Connor links the terms 'Hoax' and 'Conspiracy,' saying, 'Reading through the technical summary of this draft (IPCC) report, it is clear that no one could go away with the impression that climate change is some conspiratorial hoax by the science establishment, as some would have us believe.'

The documentary The Great Global Warming Swindle received criticism from several experts. George Monbiot described it as 'The same old conspiracy theory that we've been hearing from the denial industry for the past ten years.' Similarly, in response to James Delingpole, Monbiot stated that his Spectator article was 'The usual conspiracy theories... working to suppress the truth, which presumably now includes virtually the entire scientific community and everyone from Shell to Greenpeace and 'The Sun to Science." Some Australian meteorologists also weighed in, saying that the film made no attempt to offer a 'Critical deconstruction of climate science orthodoxies,' but instead used various other means to suggest that climate scientists are guilty of lying or are seriously misguided. Although the film's publicist's asserted that 'Global warming is 'the biggest scam of modern times", these meteorologists concluded that the film was 'Not scientifically sound and presents a flawed and very misleading interpretation of the science.'

Former UK Secretary of State for Environment, Food and Rural Affairs David Miliband presented a rebuttal of the main points of the film and stated, 'There will always be people with conspiracy theories trying to do down the scientific consensus, and that is part of scientific and democratic debate, but the science of climate change looks like fact to me.' National Geographic fact-checked 6 persistent scientific conspiracy theories. Regarding the persistent belief in a global warming hoax, they note that the Earth is continuing to warm, and the rate of warming is increasing as documented in numerous scientific studies. The rise in global temperature and its rate of increase coincides with the rise of greenhouse gases in the atmosphere due to human activity. Moreover, global warming is causing Arctic sea ice to thaw at historic rates, many species of plants are blooming earlier than expected, and the migration routes of many birds, fish, mammals, and insects are changing.

Funding

There is evidence that some of those alleging such conspiracies are part of well-funded misinformation campaigns designed to manufacture controversy, undermine the scientific consensus on climate change and downplay the projected effects of global warming. Individuals and organizations kept the global warming debate alive long after most scientists had reached their conclusions. These doubts have influenced policymakers in both Canada and the US and have helped to form government policies.

Since the late 1980s, this well-coordinated, well-funded campaign by contrarian scientists, free-market think tanks and industry has created a paralyzing fog of doubt around climate change. Through advertisements, op-eds, lobbying and media attention, greenhouse doubters (they hate being called deniers) argued first that the world is not warming; measurements indicating otherwise are flawed, they said. Then they claimed that any warming is natural, not caused by human activities. Now they contend that the looming warming will be minuscule and harmless. 'They patterned what they did after the tobacco industry,' says former senator Tim Wirth, who spearheaded environmental issues as an undersecretary of State in the Clinton administration. 'Both figured, sow enough doubt, call the science uncertain and in dispute. That's had a massive impact on both the public and Congress.'

The truth about denial, S. Begley, Newsweek

Greenpeace presented evidence of the energy industry funding climate change denial in their 'Exxon Secrets' project. An analysis conducted by The Carbon Brief in 2011 found that 9 out of 10 of the most prolific authors who cast doubt on climate change or speak against it had ties to ExxonMobil. Greenpeace have said that Koch industries invested more than US$50 million in the past 50 years on spreading doubts about climate change. ExxonMobil announced in 2008 that it would cut its funding to many of the groups that 'Divert attention' from the need to find new sources of clean energy, although in 2008 still funded over 'Two dozen other organizations who question the science of global warming or attack policies to solve the crisis.' A survey carried out by the UK Royal Society found that in 2005 ExxonMobil distributed US$2.9 million to 39 groups that 'Misrepresented the science of climate change by outright denial of the evidence'.

Books written by 'Conspiracy Theorists'

1. Inhofe, James. The Greatest Hoax, How the global warming conspiracy threatens your future.
2. Bell, Larry. Climate of Corruption, Politics, and power behind the global warming hoax.
3. Andrew Montford. The Hockey Stick Illusion, Climate, and the corruption of science.
4. Solomon, Lawrence. The Deniers, The world-renowned scientists who stood up against global warming, political persecution, and fraud.
5. Michaels, Pat and Balling, Robert. Climate of Extremes, Global warming science they don't want you to know.
6. Sussman, Brian. Climategate, A veteran meteorologist exposes the global warming scam.
7. Isaac, Rael Jean. Roosters of the Apocalypse, How the junk science of global warming nearly bankrupted the Western world.

Fictional representations

The novel State of Fear by Michael Crichton, published in December 2004, describes a conspiracy by scientists and others to create public panic about global warming. The novel includes 20 pages of footnotes, described by Crichton as providing a factual basis for the non-plotline elements of the story. In a Senate speech on 4 January 2005, Inhofe mistakenly described Crichton as a 'Scientist', and said the book's fictional depiction of environmental organizations primarily 'Focused on raising money, principally by scaring potential contributors with bogus scientific claims and predictions of a global apocalypse' was an example of 'Art imitating life.' In a piece headed Crichton's conspiracy theory, Harold Evans described Crichton's theory as being 'In the paranoid political style identified by the renowned historian Richard Hofstadter,' and went on to suggest that "'If you happen to be in the market for a conspiracy theory today, there's a rather more credible one documented by the pressure group Greenpeace,' namely the funding by ExxonMobil of groups opposed to the theory of global warming.

On the Dark and Dangerous Underbelly of Climate 'Conspiracy Theories'

In July, as temperatures across the United States started to soar in the triple digits, Mike Adams was, for a rare moment, in a celebratory mood. 'The climate change hoax,' he exulted on Natural News, the website he founded, 'Has collapsed.' New research, Adams claimed, had shown that human activity has 'Virtually no measurable impact on the temperature of the planet.' The 'Extreme alarmism of climate change lunatics' could be safely ignored, he assured his audience, as it had been vigorously proven that it was 'All based on nothing but fearmongering media propaganda and faked science.'

Adams has dubbed himself 'The Health Ranger,' and Natural News is his long-running and exceedingly strange pet project, which blends dubious health tips and thinly sourced blogs about dodgy alternative treatments with floridly fake news about geopolitics from a far-right perspective. According to reporting from the Daily Beast, before Facebook banned the site for promoting spam, it had more followers than InfoWars, a much better-known conspiracy engine. (Adams, who's not a very measured guy, responded to the latest ban by urging Donald Trump to break up big tech companies using military force.)

Adams was responding to the news of a new, exceedingly fringe study from Finnish scientists claiming that cloud coverage is responsible for global temperature changes; the study, which was also hyped on Fox News, was not peer-reviewed and other scientists have identified substantial flaws in its methodology. All that besides, there was hardly a more inopportune moment for Adams to make such a sweepingly wrong statement. July saw some of the hottest temperatures on Earth since record-keeping began in 1880, including brutal heat waves across Western Europe, Japan and the United States, and an abnormal number of deaths in the Netherlands, which the country's national statistics agency attributed to the heat. More recently, a United Nations report warned that climate change is threatening the world food supply.

By any measure whatsoever, our climate crisis is a dire and increasingly unfixable emergency. But climate conspiracy theorists tell a very different story: that climate change is either an entirely manufactured hoax engineered by world governments, or else that it's a natural event, the earth heating and cooling again on a predictable cycle, being played up by ambitious scientists and government agencies for their own, greedy ends. 'Nobody denies the climate is constantly in flux,' fossilized conservative talk radio host Rush Limbaugh declared recently. 'And nobody should deny there's nothing we can do about it.'

So, what drives climate conspiracy theories today? A broad skepticism of government institutions and scientific experts is common, as is a more specific suspicion that dire climate warnings are a pretext for seizing more control over the lives of citizens. (At the most extreme end, climate change is described as a myth propped up by the United Nations as part of their desire to institute a tyrannical one-world government.) Together, climate denialism is rapidly coalescing into a truly toxic stew, one ladled out by far-right politicians, conservative media personalities and conspiracy peddlers alike. And there's compelling evidence that the narrative they're pushing has potentially disastrous consequences.

In a twist that 'Conspiracy Theorists' might love, there's some evidence that climate denialism is, itself, a conspiracy.

And there are bigger, more concerning actors at work here than Mike Adams and his florid blogs, of course. In 2012, the current president of the United States referred to climate change as 'A hoax' perpetrated by the Chinese to make US manufacturing less competitive (he's also displayed a baffling hostility to wind turbines). Brazil's authoritarian president Jair Bolsonaro, in the midst of a push to roll back environmental protections, appointed a Minister of Foreign Affairs, Ernesto Araújo, who's expressed skepticism on numerous occasions that climate change is happening. 'I don't believe in global warming,' he commented during a cabinet meeting, according to the magazine Época. 'See, I went to Rome in May and there was a huge cold wave. This shows how global warming theories are wrong.' (Other countries simply largely ignore the problem where it's inconvenient; Poland, for instance, which is, not coincidentally, the largest coal producer in the European Union has exceptionally low rates of media coverage on climate change and climate policy, one study found.)

Among ordinary citizens, the United States is among the countries with the most serious climate denialism problems, according to a large global survey conducted by YouGov and the Cambridge Globalism Project, The Guardian reported. Denial that human beings are responsible for climate change is a more widely-held belief here, per the survey, than almost anywhere else in the world that they studied, with only Indonesia and Saudi Arabia showing higher percentages. A full 17 percent of people in the US agreed with the statement that 'The idea of manmade global warming is a hoax that was invented to deceive people.'

But in a twist that conspiracy theorists might love, there's some evidence that climate denialism is, itself, a conspiracy. The author and associate professor Martin Hultman, who writes frequently about environmental issues, told the German news outlet Deutsche Welle in December 2018, 'Until the mid-1980s, there was a really strong consensus between politicians and scientists that climate change is really acute and that we have to do something about it.' But then, he says, something changed: the oil and coal industries started to produce their own research to 'Prove' that climate change wasn't real, or wasn't as serious as was previously shown, and to work with think tanks who backed that point of view, like the libertarian, 'Free market'-oriented Heartland Institute, which holds regular conventions dedicated to showcasing the few "scientists" who reject the broad consensus on climate change. Multiple interested parties were attacking credible science from all sides: Greenpeace has reported that the Koch brothers spent roughly $127 million between 1997 and 2017 to fund a broad spectrum of climate change denialist groups, at the same time that Exxon Mobil was publicly downplaying climate change reporting that its own internal research knew to be true.

As with most conspiracy theories, though, climate change denialists can point to events and data points they say justify their skepticism. A major one came to be dubbed 'Climategate,' when, in 2009, a server at the Climate Research Unit at the University of East Anglia in the United Kingdom was hacked, just before a major global summit on global warming in Copenhagen. Thousands of emails were stolen and then uploaded to a server in Russia, soon spreading across the web. Denialists, the Heartland Institute chief among them claimed that the emails showed climate scientists were conspiring to manipulate data and cover up weak evidence for global warming, as well as suppress dissent. The people involved in the leaked emails said they'd been taken seriously out of context and badly misinterpreted by a non-scientist audience. But the damage was already done: the idea that climate science is a global conspiracy still comes up regularly and is routinely utilized by the organizations pushing the idea.

'Conspiracy Theories' about environmental science aren't limited to the climate, either

There's tangible evidence that exposure to climate conspiracy theories lead to a particularly worrisome form of apathy and inaction among the public, encouraging passivity at a time when we can least afford it. A 2013 study from Daniel Jolley and Karen Douglas, two researchers at the University of Kent, shows that exposure to climate conspiracy theories reduced their commitment to cutting down their carbon footprints. More interestingly, they found that exposure to those conspiracy theories also lessened people's intentions to 'Engage in politics' altogether. It's not unlike 'Conspiracy Theories' that mass shootings are staged by government-backed 'Crisis actors' to promote a gun control agenda: the intent in both cases is to encourage passivity, telling people to ignore the fire alarm even as smoke fills the room.

'Conspiracy Theories' about environmental science aren't limited to the climate, either. One longstanding conspiracy theory holds that the High Frequency Active Auroral Research Program, a research project in Alaska that's partly funded by the federal government is a secret weather-controlling device or worse. Former Venezuelan president Hugo Chávez said it was used to create a 2010 earthquake in Haiti, according to the Associated Press. Former Minnesota Governor Jesse Ventura appeared in a 2009 TV series with a famous HAARP 'Conspiracy Theorist' named Nick Begich, the son of a late congressperson, to claim that the research project was capable of mind control.

Elsewhere, a growing number of conspiracy theorists on social media have fixed their suspicions on earthquake science, accusing the United States Geological Survey of hiding the real causes of earthquakes or claiming quakes had a lower magnitude than the one in the official record. The effects of this kind of storytelling are, again, evident: at their core, they can push people to disregard scientific consensus, or, worse, view scientists themselves as part of a sinister conspiracy. Mika McKinnon is a geophysicist and disaster researcher who also works as a science communicator, and she's well-aware of the risks of climate and environmental 'Conspiracy Theories.' She's skilled at talking about scientific concepts to a general, and sometimes skeptical, audience, and has developed some rules about how, and when, to debunk a false idea.

'I don't try to argue with a 'Conspiracy Theorist," she told Lit Hub. 'But I also won't let bad information stand. I'll make a correction and I'll move on.' She's very aware, she says, that she's not going to change the mind of the person making the false or conspiratorial argument. 'Instead, I'm really speaking to everybody who's listening, everybody on the Twitter thread or everyone else in the room.' One of the key things she's pushing back against, McKinnon says, is the climate denialist idea that nothing can be done about our global environmental emergency. 'Nihilism is appealing,' she says. 'It's easy. I hate that we've changed the conversation from, 'Climate change isn't happening' to 'It's too late, who cares, why bother?' We have to do something."

LOSS OF CIVIL RIGHTS

Important human rights failings of the United States were laid bare in 2020. The grossly disproportionate impact of Covid-19 on Black, brown, and Native people, connected to longstanding disparities in health, education, and economic status, revealed the enduring effects of past overtly racist laws and policies and continuing impediments to equality. The police killing of George Floyd in May, and a series of other police killings of Black people, sparked massive and largely peaceful protests, which in many instances were met with brutality by local and federal law enforcement agents.

The administration of President Donald Trump continued to dismantle the United States asylum system, limit access to women's health care, undermine consumer protections against predatory lenders and abusive debt collectors, and weaken regulations that reduce pollution and address climate change. After election officials across the US tallied the votes for the presidential election, determining that Joe Biden was the president-elect, Trump made baseless allegations of voter fraud.

In its foreign policy, the United States worked on several fronts to undermine multilateral institutions, including through the use of sanctions to attack the International Criminal Court. It flouted international human rights law as it partnered with abusive governments, though it did sanction a number of individuals and governments for committing human rights abuses.

Racial Justice

The Covid-19 pandemic has had a disproportionate impact on racial and ethnic minorities, primarily Black, Latinx, and Native communities, which faced increased risk for infection, serious illness, and death from the disease, as well as severe economic impacts. These disparities are linked to longstanding inequities in health outcomes and access to care, education, employment, and economic status.

Some localities and the state of California recognized that these disparities are connected to the legacy of slavery and considered various forms of reparations to address them. At the federal level, HR 40, a bill in Congress proposing the establishment of a commission to investigate slavery's legacy and create reparations proposals, gained unprecedented momentum, with 170 co-sponsors in the House of Representatives and 20 co-sponsors in the Senate as of November.

In May, Human Rights Watch urged state and local authorities in Tulsa, Oklahoma, to provide reparations to descendants and the remaining survivors of the 1921 Tulsa Race Massacre, in which a white mob killed several hundred Black people and destroyed an affluent Black neighborhood. Thousands of people of Asian descent reported incidents of attacks and racial discrimination after the outbreak of the Covid-19 pandemic. President Donald Trump repeatedly described the virus using racist language.

Poverty and Inequality

The Covid-19 pandemic exacerbated poverty and inequality in the United States, and disproportionately affected Black, Latinx, and Native communities. The pandemic and public health measures necessary to slow its spread resulted in lost wages or jobs, reduced health coverage, and reduced access to other essential goods and services. People of color, particularly women and immigrants continued to be over-represented in low-wage service jobs, putting them at greater risk. Many, particularly in agriculture and food production, faced unsafe working conditions leading to outbreaks.

Increased unemployment protection and direct payments in relief packages that Congress passed significantly stemmed poverty rate growth. However, many protections expired in July and August. The relief bills lacked protections for those unable to pay bills or medical care costs, and excluded certain workers, including immigrants. The administration continued to undermine consumer protections against predatory lenders and abusive debt collectors. The Consumer Financial Protection Bureau gutted a rule seeking to prevent small lenders, including so-called payday lenders from charging exorbitant interest rates.

California voters passed a ballot initiative sponsored by app-based companies stripping app-based rideshare and delivery drivers of the minimum wage, paid sick leave, and other critical labor protections provided by a state law passed in 2019, setting a dangerous precedent for workers' rights in the US and globally.

Criminal Legal System

Police killings of George Floyd and Breonna Taylor and the shooting of Jacob Blake provoked massive protests calling for police accountability, reduction in the scope and power of police, elimination of extortionate court fines and fees, and investment in Black communities. Rather than address problems of poverty or health that contribute to crime, many US jurisdictions focus on aggressive policing in poor and minority communities, fueling a vicious cycle of incarceration and police violence.

While no governmental agency tracks police killings, the Washington Post database has documented about 1,000 killings by shootings each of the past five years, revealing significant racial disparities. Black people report being subjected to many forms of police abuse, including non-lethal force, arbitrary arrests and detentions, and harassment, at higher levels than white people. Police subjected Native American people to similar abuse and killed them at even higher rates than they killed Black people.

The US continues to lead the world in reported incarceration rates. Approximately 2.3 million people were locked up on any given day in 2020. There are about 10 million admissions into jails each year. Based on 2017-18 data, about 4.4 percent of the US adult population were on probation or parole. In August, Human Rights Watch reported that violations of probation and parole are adding to jail and prison populations. Many people in the criminal legal system continue to face extortionate fines and fees, as well as bars to accessing public assistance, public housing, and the right to vote.

While their relative incarceration rates have declined steadily over the past decade, Black people, and to a lesser extent Latinx people, are still more likely to be imprisoned than white people. Some of the nation's worst outbreaks of Covid-19 occurred in jails and prisons, with over 169,286 people in prison testing positive and at least 1,363 deaths by November. Some prisons lacked adequate safety and health measures. Some jurisdictions took steps to release people or to limit the influx of new people, but few institutions made reductions sufficient to limit the spread of Covid-19.

Five US states had executed a total of seven men in 2020 at time of writing; the federal government had executed an additional eight by November, the first death sentences carried out by the federal government since 2003. Colorado joined 21 other states in abolishing the death penalty. Three other states have imposed moratoriums in recent years.

The US Congress has not passed further reform legislation since the 2018 First Step Act. Its implementation has had mixed results. While several thousand people's sentences were reduced, the government frequently opposed reductions for crack cocaine sentences. Advocates criticized programs for earning credits toward release as inadequate. A risk assessment tool used for release eligibility may create racial disparities and can be manipulated to prevent initial release.

Nearly half-a-million people are held in local jails pretrial in the United States on any given day. Pretrial incarceration pressures many people to plead guilty regardless of actual guilt or to take on debt to pay money bail. Many jurisdictions have replaced or supplemented money bail with algorithm-based risk assessment tools, which do not necessarily reduce incarceration rates and entrench racial bias. California voters rejected a law that abolished money bail but required courts to use risk assessment tools in pretrial incarceration decisions. New York implemented pretrial reform without these tools, resulting in substantial reductions in pretrial jail populations.

Children in the Criminal and Juvenile Justice Systems

Arrests of children under 18 for violent crimes have dropped by more than 50 percent over the last 20 years, and the number of incarcerated children has dropped by 60 percent since 2000. However, stark racial and ethnic disparities continue. Youth of color make up approximately one-third of teenagers under 18 but two-thirds of incarcerated youth in the United States. A movement to utilize alternatives to incarceration for youth who commit certain offenses is reducing incarceration in California, Hawaii, Kentucky, Georgia, Florida, Mississippi, and Texas.

Vermont, Michigan, and New York also increased the age at which people can be tried in juvenile court. Even so, all US states have laws that permit or require children accused of serious offenses to be prosecuted as adults. Since 2009, 22 states have narrowed their adult transfer provisions. Over 200,000 people were on sex offender registries for offenses committed when they were children, a Juvenile Law Center report found. Many were required to register, sometimes for life, for acts such as streaking, sexting, or consensual sexual activity between teenagers.

Drug Policy

Voters approved the country's first ballot initiative to expand access to evidence-based drug treatment and support and decriminalize the possession of all drugs for personal use in Oregon. Ballot initiatives legalizing marijuana for adult or medical use passed in Arizona, Mississippi, Montana, New Jersey, and South Dakota, bringing the total states legalizing adult-use marijuana to 15 and medical marijuana to 36. The US House of Representatives passed the Marijuana Opportunity Reinvestment and Expungement Act, a bill that, if enacted into law, would end federal marijuana prohibition.

However, drug possession for personal use remains by far the single most arrested offense in the United States. Arrests are marked by stark racial disparities, even though people report similar rates of use across racial groups; according to a 2020 report by the American Civil Liberties Union, in 2018, Black people were 3.64 times more likely to be arrested for marijuana possession than white people. In the months following the declaration of a national public health emergency in response to Covid-19, the US experienced a surge in already high drug overdoses, roughly 17 percent higher than in 2019, according to one study. Access to the overdose-reversal drug naloxone has increased in recent years, but drug laws are an obstacle to life-saving harm reduction services in many states, and evidence-based treatment for substance use disorder is not available to many people who need it.

Rights of Non-Citizens

The administration continued to attack the rights of migrants and asylum seekers. Returns of non-Mexican asylum seekers to Mexico to wait for US asylum adjudications under the "Migrant Protection Protocols" continued with a substantial decrease from April to July, exposing tens of thousands, including many children, to precarious, dangerous conditions and denying fair hearings.

Human Rights Watch identified 138 cases of Salvadorans who were killed after being deported to El Salvador from the United States since 2013, illustrating the toll of inadequate US protection processes. The Trump administration expanded fast-track deportation procedures for families at the border and sent Honduran and Salvadoran asylum seekers to Guatemala under the problematic Asylum Cooperation Agreement. Human Rights Watch reported on how US restrictions on access to asylum harms LGBT people fleeing persecution, including sexual violence, in El Salvador, Guatemala, and Honduras.

As Covid-19 cases increased in March, the Centers for Disease Control and Prevention (CDC) issued an order closing the land borders, over-ruling career-CDC public health officials' opinions it was not warranted. This led to the expulsion of more than 330,000 people 0,000 people along the US-Mexico border, including children, without screening for eligibility for asylum or other protections. Throughout the year, the administration proposed a series of regulations to severely restrict eligibility for asylum and other forms of protection. US officials suspended some forms of immigration enforcement during the pandemic, but continued deportations of migrants detained in the United States, risking spreading the virus globally.

Deaths in US immigration detention spiked to a 15-year high with at least eight fatalities related to Covid-19. In April, Human Rights Watch reported on the detention system's expansion since 2017 in privately run facilities where noncitizens are subjected to threats and use of force, due process violations, and unsanitary and crowded conditions. Though some were released in response to the pandemic, by November, more than 7,000 people had contracted Covid-19 while in detention.

A federal judge ruled in June that the US government was not in compliance with a settlement agreement limiting the detention of children in prison-like conditions to 20 days. In September, a whistleblower brought allegations of medical neglect and abuse by a doctor working with an immigration detention facility in the state of Georgia; subsequent reporting uncovered accounts of hysterectomies and other gynecological procedures performed without informed consent. Lawmakers called for a full investigation.

Health and Human Rights

At time of writing, the United States led the world in coronavirus cases and deaths. Trump and other government officials spread disinformation about the coronavirus. The US has made coronavirus testing largely free, but states have struggled to increase testing capacity. Millions of people are uninsured and unable to access affordable health care. Costs of treatment may have forced many to forgo care or face financial ruin. Rates of people without health insurance in the US were rising before the pandemic, including nearly 10 million women without coverage. Pandemic-related job loss likely increased this number dramatically, with a disproportionate impact on women. Healthcare workers faced serious shortages of protective equipment.

Voting Rights

Election officials' responses to the Covid-19 pandemic seriously impaired some people's access to voting in primary elections, but access improved by the general election in November. A federal appeals court ruled people with criminal convictions in Florida had to pay fines imposed before being able to vote. As media organizations projected Biden had won the presidential election, President Trump made baseless allegations of voter fraud and filed lawsuits challenging certain states' electoral processes.

Right to Education

Schools were closed at some point in all 50 states in response to the pandemic. While closed, many schools switched to online learning, but one in five school-aged US children do not have access to a computer or high-speed internet at home. Numerous studies warned school closures would widen racial and economic inequalities in education, with a particularly significant impact on children with disabilities.

Environment and Human Rights

The Trump administration weakened car emission and air quality standards and suspended many requirements for environmental monitoring. United States farms continue to use more than 70 pesticides that are banned or in the process of complete phase out in the European Union, Brazil, or China, putting the health of farmworkers and nearby communities at risk. Air pollution from industry, transportation, and wildfires, which are increasing due to climate change, continued to impact people in the US, particularly communities of color. A Harvard University study suggested people with Covid-19 are more likely to die if they are exposed to high levels of air pollution.

Some communities, especially Native Americans living on reservations, faced the Covid-19 pandemic without adequate access to water. Detroit failed to reconnect households, mostly minority, whose water had been shut off before the pandemic. We the People of Detroit, an organization committed to community research, found in July that zip codes with more water shutoffs correlated with more Covid-19 cases. The United States is the world's second largest emitter of greenhouse gases. Trump withdrew the US from the Paris Agreement, which took effect on November 4. Biden vowed to rejoin the agreement on his first day in office.

Extreme weather events increased in frequency and intensity in part due to climate change and had a disproportionate impact on already marginalized communities. The summer of 2020 was one of the warmest documented? Some local governments warned about heat-related illness and mortality, but most plans excluded pregnant people, who are more vulnerable to heat stress. Premature birth is also linked with heat. Black women, who already suffer higher rates of giving birth prematurely, are especially vulnerable.

Women's and Girls' Rights

Lack of access to health care contributes to higher rates of maternal and cervical cancer deaths than in comparable countries. Human Rights Watch documented in 2020 how Alabama is failing to provide young people with necessary information on sexual and reproductive health and failing to persuade the public to take the human papillomavirus (HPV) vaccine, which prevents several types of cancer, including cervical cancer. Vaccination rates throughout Alabama remain low in a state with one of the highest rates of preventable cervical cancer deaths in the country, with Black women more likely to die.

The Trump administration continued to limit access to women's health care. Since the "gag" rule went into effect in 2019, barring doctors receiving federal family planning (Title X) funds from giving women information on the full range of pregnancy options available to them, the patient capacity of the Title X network has been reduced by half. In July, the Supreme Court upheld rules permitting employers to opt out of contraceptive coverage in employee health insurance plans by claiming religious or moral objections. Some states, like Ohio and Texas, used the pandemic as an excuse to further restrict access to abortion. In July, a law took effect in Florida requiring anyone under 18 to obtain consent from a parent or legal guardian before an abortion.

Older People's Rights

More than 40 percent of state-reported Covid-19 deaths in the US, but just 8 percent of total cases, were among people living in long-term care institutions. Nursing home operators pushed state and federal governments to give them broad legal immunity. Nursing facilities' longstanding infection control problems and reduced public oversight of nursing homes during the Covid-19 crisis put already vulnerable older residents at greater risk. The Centers for Medicare and Medicaid Services (CMS) announced a 'No visitors' policy for all nursing facilities in response to the pandemic, with limited exceptions for end-of-life visits, cutting off over 1.5 million older residents from families and friends. Such visitors supplement care by staff, advocate on residents' behalf, and provide essential emotional support. CMS updated guidance in September to allow for visitation in some circumstances, though protocols varied widely across states.

Sexual Orientation and Gender Identity

In June, the Supreme Court ruled a federal law prohibiting sex discrimination in employment prohibits discrimination based on sexual orientation and gender identity. Despite the ruling, the Trump administration attempted to roll back health and housing protections for transgender people. More than a dozen states also considered bills restricting gender-affirming care for children, putting their health and rights at risk. At least 28 transgender people were killed in the United States in 2020. Congress failed to reauthorize the Violence Against Women Act, which includes provisions for LGBT survivors of violence, or pass the Equality Act, which would prohibit discrimination based on sexual orientation and gender identity.

Freedom of Expression and Assembly

President Trump continued to attack news outlets that questioned his administration's policies. After Twitter placed a fact-check label on Trump's tweets, the president issued an executive order that attempts to remove legal protections for social media platforms, an attack against online freedom of expression globally. Local law enforcement agencies in several jurisdictions reacted with excessive force toward people protesting police violence. President Trump took aggressive action against protesters demanding racial justice. He had federal police remove peaceful protesters from a park next to the White House to facilitate his appearance for photographs at a nearby church. Against the wishes of local officials, his administration sent federal officers to Portland, despite questions about their authority to take enforcement actions. Reports of excessive force and other misconduct followed.

National Security

In October, state and federal authorities charged 14 men linked to extreme-right movements with plotting to kidnap the governor of Michigan and overthrow the state government because of Covid-19 related restrictions. The men discussed "taking" the governor of Virginia for the same reason, the FBI said. That same month, the Department of Homeland Security identified white supremacists, along with cyber and other forms of election interference by China, Iran, and Russia, among top threats facing the US.

Also in October, a federal court charged two Islamic State (ISIS) suspects with involvement in the torture and killings of US journalists and aid workers. The UK shared key intelligence on the pair after the US agreed not to seek the death penalty. The US reported completing repatriations of all citizens held as ISIS suspects and family members in Syria and Iraq, placing the total at 27.

In January, psychologists James Mitchell and John Bruce Jessen, architects of the Central Intelligence Agency's post-September 11, 2001 "enhanced interrogation" techniques, defended their use of torture on dozens of detainees in their first public testimony on the illegal program. The pair testified at the Guantanamo Bay Naval Base pre-trial military commission hearings for five men charged as co-conspirators in the September 11 attacks. Further proceedings were postponed to at least 2021 due to Covid-19 and the consecutive resignations of two presiding judges. Concerns persist regarding prison conditions and access to counsel for the 40 detainees still held at Guantanamo, most without charge.

Foreign Policy

The United States continued to disengage from multilateral institutions. The administration took unprecedented action in June in issuing an executive order authorizing asset freezes and family entry bans against International Criminal Court (ICC) officials and others assisting them; in September it designated two ICC officials for sanctions. In July, the US took steps to withdraw from the World Health Organization.

This followed its previous withdrawal from the UN Human Rights Council and decision to end US funding for the UN Population Fund (UNFPA) and Palestinian refugee agency, United Nations Relief and Works Agency for Palestine Refugees in the Near East (UNRWA). The US Department of State's Commission on Unalienable Rights, a body established in 2019 to "reexamine" US commitments to international human rights, released a report in August advocating a hierarchical approach to human rights and relegating abortion and marriage equality to 'Divisive social and political controversies.'

In January, the Trump administration cancelled a policy to eliminate all antipersonnel landmines. The administration continued to entrench and expand implementation of its dangerous iteration of the 'Global Gag Rule,' and omitted gender identity and sexual orientation from a draft policy on gender by the US Agency for International Development. The United States admitted 11,814 refugees in fiscal year 2020, an 85 percent decrease from the 85,000 admitted in 2016. In October, the Trump administration set the lowest US refugee resettlement cap on record, 15,000 for fiscal year 2021.

President Trump continued to praise authoritarian leaders, and his administration continued to provide military assistance and approve arms sales to states with poor human rights records. The administration also continued to support the Saudi-led coalition's war in Yemen despite numerous laws-of-war violations and pursued a $478 million arms sale to Saudi Arabia despite two bipartisan votes in Congress to restrict weapons sales. The United States imposed sanctions on perpetrators of grave human rights violations and corruption, including officials in Equatorial Guinea, Uganda, and South Sudan; Chinese and Hong Kong government officials, state agencies, and companies; and 39 Syrians, including Bashar Al-Assad.

Congress passed legislation highlighting human rights concerns in China and Hong Kong, yet some administration responses—including restricting visas for Chinese journalists, increasing scrutiny of students from China, and efforts to ban applications by Chinese tech companies—raised human rights concerns. The US signed an agreement with the Taliban on terms for a US troop withdrawal from Afghanistan. The agreement did not address human rights concerns, but the US did press for greater inclusion of women and civil society in the Afghan government's delegation for negotiations with the Taliban that began in September. The US did not publicly press the Afghan government on its abuses.

In Latin America, the administration focused on serious human rights abuses in Venezuela, Cuba, and Nicaragua but failed to scrutinize abuses in allied countries, such as Brazil, Colombia, El Salvador, and Mexico. In the Middle East, the administration presented in January a plan to formalize Israeli annexation of large parts of the occupied West Bank and helped broker agreements to normalize Israel's relations with the United Arab Emirates and Bahrain in September. Meanwhile, the US took an increasingly hostile approach to Iran. In January, the US killed Qassem Soleimani, commander of Iran's Islamic Revolutionary Guard Corps Quds Force in a drone strike in Iraq; afterwards, President Trump tweeted that retaliation from Iran would be met by targeting Iranian cultural sites, which would constitute a war crime.

In September, following the UN Security Council's refusal to renew an arms embargo that expired in October as part of the Joint Comprehensive Plan of Action (JCPOA), the US argued it could reimpose UN sanctions. Other permanent members of the council and parties to the JCPOA, as well as the UN secretary-general, refused to accept the US position, since the US had withdrawn from the agreement.

In Africa, the US focused on normalizing relations with Sudan's transitional government and removed Sudan from the State Sponsors of Terrorism list; Sudan began a process of normalizing relations with Israel, reportedly in exchange. The US continued its military activity in Somalia, conducting dozens of airstrikes, some of which resulted in apparent civilian casualties that were not adequately investigated or acknowledged.

In May, the Department of Defense released its third annual report on civilian casualties, documenting civilian harm from certain US military activity and estimating 132 civilian deaths or injuries in 2019, a significantly lower estimate than those by nongovernmental organizations.

The report also listed the number of allegations of civilian harm that had been received, concluding that only a fraction of the allegations were 'Credible.'

Big Pharma

The so-called Big Pharma conspiracy theory shares a number of features with all other 'Conspiracy theories.' First, it shares the same basic plot: a relatively small number of people are working in secret against the public good. Second is a belief that most people are ignorant of the truth and that only a small number of people with secret or suppressed knowledge (the conspiracy theorists) know the real score. Third is the conspiracy theorists' backward approach to evidence: lack of evidence for the conspiracy is evidence for the conspiracy, as is any dis confirming evidence. Lastly, the way supposedly confirmatory evidence is handled capitalizes on common mental shortcuts, misperceptions, and non-rational cues, which make the conspiracy theories all the more memorable, compelling, and contagious. This maddening mixture of mistakes makes conspiracy theories very difficult to combat. Big Pharma conspiracy theories, however, in all their variety, constitute their own genre within the larger category of conspiratorial narratives. In much the same way that the gothic novel has its own conventions (for example, a heroine imprisoned, set in a dark old spooky house riddled with hidden passages, and hints of the paranormal), the Big Pharma conspiracy theory has a number of conventions that set it apart from other conspiracy theories. In this case, the villain is the Pharmaceutical Industry. It's not the actual pharmaceutical industry; rather it is the pharmaceutical industry as they imagine it. In these stories, 'Big Pharma' is shorthand for an abstract entity comprised of corporations, regulators,

NGOs, politicians, and often physicians, all with a finger in the trillion-dollar prescription pharmaceutical pie. Eliding all of these separate entities into a monolithic agent of evil allows the conspiracy theorist to mistakenly ignore the complex and conflicting interests that they represent. This agent is, as are all antagonists in conspiratorial narratives, improbably powerful, competent, and craven, and it allows the conspiracy theorist to cast himself in the role of crusader and defender of a way of life, a Manichean dichotomy that was identified in Richard Hofstadter's classic treatise on America's recurring Conspiracism, 'The Paranoid Style in American Politics.'

Like many conspiracy theories, there may be real tangible facts that undergird the elaborate 'Conspiracy Theory.' For instance, pharmaceuticals have side effects, many of which are unpleasant, some of which can be fatal. This basic fact of pharmacology, however, has become the basis of blanket claims about the universal dangerousness of pharmaceutical products. Additionally, not all medical interventions are successful, and in our litigious culture people often seem to not understand that sometimes adverse outcomes occur when everything is done correctly. Nowhere are these ideas more prevalent than in conspiracy theories involving cancer treatments. Cancer treatments are often invasive and dangerous, and while the best practices, in the aggregate, improve outcomes for patients, they can still be unpleasant, even traumatic. They may fail certain patients entirely, so that a patient may experience all of the side effects of a treatment and none of the hoped-for benefits. To the conspiracist, ubiquitous advertisements by pharmaceutical companies become 'mind control' or 'brainwashing,' while industry lobbying becomes 'corruption.' Conspiracy theories may be a way to reassure oneself that there is an order to our lives, that calamity and disaster are not meaningless or random. This in turn enables people to identify an enemy to fight.

When patients (and their loved ones) are forced to accept a serious disease, they often experience powerlessness, especially when no cure is available. This may itself trigger a search for a culprit to blame for their suffering. Big Pharma is a convenient target and is often imagined as with holding a cure. Indeed, a major premise of the Big Pharma 'Conspiracy Theory' is the 'cui bono' fallacy: he who benefits from misfortune must be the cause of that misfortune. Such logic has been used in other, non-medical conspiracy theories: Franklin D Roosevelt got the war he wanted, therefore, he was behind the Japanese attack on Pearl Harbor; George W Bush and his handlers wanted to go to war in the Middle East, so they brought down the World Trade Centre as a pretense to invade Iraq; European Jews were de-ghettoized as Napoleon swept across the continent–they must have been behind the revolution that led to his ascent to power.

In the case of the Big Pharma conspiracy theory, cui bono reasoning appears in a pair of often-levelled charges. The more common charge is that a cure is being withheld to keep people on more expensive, less effective medical regimes. In the case of cancer, the cheap, easy, and 'natural' suppressed cures range from baking soda, to marijuana, to vita mins, to apricot kernels (which are banned because the amygdalin they contain breaks down into hydrogen cyanide). The more extreme charge is that diseases are deliberately manufactured molecule-by-molecule or weaponized in labs and released onto the populace in order to give companies an excuse to sell medications. One such high profile accusation of this, I think, was during the 2009 H1N1 swine flu outbreak. Mike Adams, an inexplicably popular online health guru (he calls himself the 'Health Ranger') who advocates nearly every conspiracy theory, made this charge in 2009 in a bizarre little rap called 'Don't Inject Me (The Swine Flu Vaccine Song)': Don't you know the swine flu was made by man Pharmaceutical scam…

All you parents grab your kids and shoot 'em up just like guinea pigs, Inject your teens and your babies in the crib; And when they get paralyzed, that's when you realize there's no way to undo what you did. The big drug companies are makin' a killing Collectin' the billions and gettin' away like a James Bond villain because they're willin' to do almost anything. Just to make money with the flu vaccine. Adams actually embraces both cui bono claims, that all you need is vitamin D to ward off the swine flu (but that drug companies can't charge as much for it) and that the flu was manufactured in order to sell the vaccine. He also manages to invoke a global depopulation conspiracy alongside creating a market for vaccines: two agendas that are hard to reconcile, as one involves killing people and the other saving as many people as possible by selling them vaccines. This is a typical feature of conspiracist thought, a 2012 study by Wood, Douglas, and Sutton found that the 'Endorsement of mutually incompatible conspiracy theories are positively correlated'.

Anti-vaccine conspiracy theories play on many of the same fears that run-of-the-mill Big Pharma 'Conspiracy Theories' do include fears over side effects, 'unnatural' substances in them and a general suspicion of the profit motive in health care – but these theories are often supercharged by the fears of parents. Parents who believe that their children are 'vaccine-damaged' and who are struggling to understand and assign blame for an intractable, life-changing disease with no cure, have created one of the most stubborn and dangerous conspiracy theories. Following the widespread attention received by Andrew Wakefield's entirely fraudulent 1998 Lancet article linking the MMR vaccine to autism (withdrawn by the journal in 2011), childhood vaccination rates plummeted below levels needed to support community immunity in many areas, and children started to contract diseases that many younger physicians had never seen. The resilience of the conspiracy theory targeting vaccine manufacturers and researchers can be seen in the fact that it persists despite over a dozen studies demonstrating otherwise, including one Cochrane review that had a sample size of about 14.7 million children. The theory is as popular as ever and is still pushed by the likes of Jenny.

McCarthy, Generation Rescue, and innumerable alternative medicine practitioners. Fear, it seems, is more contagious than reason. So, what can be done to combat the Big Pharma conspiracy theory? Sadly, the theory will always be around because peddlers of alternative medicine find Big Pharma to be a useful adversary in their quest to sell their questionable remedies and because of the role that belief plays in people's lives. Furthermore, once the theory has taken root in someone's mind, Blaskiewicz – The Big Pharma conspiracy theory 260 Medical Writing 2013 VOL. 22 NO. 4 it's often impossible to dislodge it, as the conspiracy theory turns those who argue against it into 'Paid shills' or 'Sheeple'. It is best to catch people before they fall into conspiratorial beliefs. Secrecy and ignorance beget conspiracy theories; they are best combated by education and transparency.

MIND CONTROL

Project MKUltra (or MK-Ultra) was the code name of an illegal human experimentation program designed and undertaken by the U.S. Central Intelligence Agency (CIA). The experiments were intended to develop procedures and identify drugs such as LSD that could be used in interrogations to weaken individuals and force confessions through brainwashing and psychological torture. MKUltra used numerous methods to manipulate its subjects' mental states and brain functions, such as the covert administration of high doses of psychoactive drugs (especially LSD) and other chemicals, electroshocks, hypnosis, sensory deprivation, isolation, and verbal and sexual abuse, in addition to other forms of torture.

MKUltra was preceded by two drug-related experiments, Project Bluebird, and Project Artichoke. It began in 1953, was reduced in scope in 1964 and 1967, and was halted in 1973. It was organized through the CIA's Office of Scientific Intelligence and coordinated with the United States Army Biological Warfare Laboratories. The program engaged in illegal activities, including the use of U.S. and Canadian citizens as unwitting test subjects. MKUltra's scope was broad, with activities carried out under the guise of research at more than 80 institutions, including colleges and universities, hospitals, prisons, and pharmaceutical companies. The CIA operated using front organizations, although some top officials at these institutions were aware of the CIA's involvement.

MKUltra was first brought to public attention in 1975 by the Church Committee of the United States Congress and Gerald Ford's United States President's Commission on CIA activities within the United States (also known as the Rockefeller Commission). Investigative efforts were hampered by CIA Director Richard Helms's order that all MKUltra files be destroyed in 1973; the Church Committee and Rockefeller Commission investigations relied on the sworn testimony of direct participants and on the small number of documents that survived Helms's order. In 1977, a Freedom of Information Act request uncovered a cache of 20,000 documents relating to MKUltra, which led to Senate hearings. Some surviving information about MKUltra was declassified in July 2001. In December 2018, declassified documents revealed that the CIA made six dogs run, turn, and stop via remote control and brain implants as part of MKUltra.

Background

Sidney Gottlieb approved of an MKUltra sub-project on LSD in this June 9, 1953, letter. The project's CIA cryptonym is a combination of the digraph MK, indicating the sponsorship of the Technical Services Staff (TSS), and the word Ultra which formerly designated the most secret classification of World War II intelligence. Other related cryptonyms include Project MKNAOMI and Project MKDELTA.

Origin of project

According to author Stephen Kinzer, the CIA project 'Was a continuation of the work begun in WWII-era Japanese facilities and Nazi concentration camps on subduing and controlling human minds.' Kinzer wrote that MKUltra's use of mescaline on unwitting subjects was a practice that Nazi doctors had begun in the Dachau concentration camp. Kinzer proposes evidence of the continuation of a Nazi agenda, citing the CIA's secret recruitment of Nazi torturers and vivisectionists to continue the experimentation on thousands of subjects, and Nazis brought to Fort Detrick, Maryland, to instruct CIA officers on the lethal uses of sarin gas.

Aims and leadership

Sidney Gottlieb, Sept. 21, 1977. The project was headed by Sidney Gottlieb but began on the order of CIA director Allen Dulles on April 13, 1953. Its aim was to develop mind-controlling drugs for use against the Soviet bloc in response to alleged Soviet, Chinese, and North Korean use of mind control techniques on U.S. prisoners of war during the Korean War. The CIA wanted to use similar methods on their own captives and was interested in manipulating foreign leaders with such techniques, devising several schemes to drug Fidel Castro. It often conducted experiments without the subjects' knowledge or consent. In some cases, academic researchers were funded through grants from CIA front organizations but were unaware that the CIA was using their work for these purposes.

The project attempted to produce a perfect truth drug for interrogating suspected Soviet spies during the Cold War, and to explore other possibilities of mind control. Subproject 54 was the Navy's top-secret 'Perfect Concussion' program, which was supposed to use sub-aural frequency blasts to erase memory; the program was never carried out. Most MKUltra records were destroyed in 1973 by order of CIA director Richard Helms, so it has been difficult for investigators to gain a complete understanding of the more than 150 funded research subprojects sponsored by MKUltra and related CIA programs.

The project began during a period of what English journalist Rupert Cornwell described as 'Paranoia' at the CIA, when the U.S. had lost its nuclear monopoly and fear of communism was at its height. CIA counter-intelligence Chief James Jesus Angleton believed that a mole had penetrated the organization at the highest levels. The agency poured millions of dollars into studies examining ways to influence and control the mind and to enhance its ability to extract information from resistant subjects during interrogation. Some historians assert that one goal of MKUltra and related CIA projects was to create a 'Manchurian Candidate'-style subject. American historian Alfred W. McCoy has claimed that the CIA attempted to focus media attention on these sorts of 'Ridiculous' programs so that the public would not look at the research's primary goal, which was effective methods of interrogation.

Scale of project

One 1955 MKUltra document gives an indication of the size and range of the effort. It refers to the study of an assortment of mind-altering substances described as follows:

1. Substances which will promote illogical thinking and impulsiveness to the point where the recipient would be discredited in public.
2. Substances which increase the efficiency of mentation and perception.
3. Materials which will prevent or counteract the intoxicating effect of alcohol.
4. Materials which will promote the intoxicating effect of alcohol.
5. Materials which will produce the signs and symptoms of recognized diseases in a reversible way so they may be used for malingering, etc.
6. Materials which will render the induction of hypnosis easier or otherwise enhance its usefulness.
7. Substances which will enhance the ability of individuals to withstand privation, torture, and coercion during interrogation and so-called "brain-washing".
8. Materials and physical methods which will produce amnesia for events preceding and during their use.
9. Physical methods of producing shock and confusion over extended periods of time and capable of surreptitious use.
10. Substances which produce physical disablement such as paralysis of the legs, acute anemia, etc.
11. Substances which will produce "pure" euphoria with no subsequent let-down.
12. Substances which alter personality structure in such a way the tendency of the recipient to become dependent upon another person is enhanced.
13. A material which will cause mental confusion of such a type of the individual under its influence will find it difficult to maintain a fabrication under questioning.

14. Substances which will lower the ambition and general working efficiency of men when administered in undetectable amounts.

15. Substances which promote weakness or distortion of the eyesight or hearing faculties, preferably without permanent effects.

16. A knockout pill which can be surreptitiously administered in drinks, food, cigarettes, as an aerosol, etc., which will be safe to use, provide a maximum of amnesia, and be suitable for use by agent types on an ad hoc basis.

17. A material which can be surreptitiously administered by the above routes and which in very small amounts will make it impossible for a person to perform physical activity.

Applications

The 1976 Church Committee report found that, in the MKDELTA program, 'Drugs were used primarily as an aid to interrogations, but MKULTRA/MKDELTA materials were also used for harassment, discrediting, or disabling purposes.

Other related projects

In 1964, MKSEARCH was the name given to the continuation of the MKULTRA program. The MKSEARCH program was divided into two projects dubbed MKOFTEN and MKCHICKWIT. Funding for MKSEARCH commenced in 1965 and ended in 1971. The project was a joint project between the U.S. Army Chemical Corps and the CIA's Office of Research and Development to find new offensive-use agents, with a focus on incapacitating agents. Its purpose was to develop, test, and evaluate capabilities in the covert use of biological, chemical, and radioactive material systems and techniques of producing predictable human behavioral and/or physiological changes in support of highly sensitive operational requirements.

By March 1971 over 26,000 potential agents had been acquired for future screening. The CIA was interested in bird migration patterns for chemical and biological warfare (CBW) research; subproject 139 designated 'Bird Disease Studies' at Penn State. MKOFTEN was to deal with testing and toxicological transmissivity and behavioral effects of drugs in animals and, ultimately, humans. MKCHICKWIT was concerned with acquiring information on new drug developments in Europe and Asia, and with acquiring samples.

Experiments on Americans

CIA documents suggest that they investigated 'Chemical, biological, and radiological' methods of mind control as part of MKUltra. They spent an estimated $10 million or more, roughly $87.5 million adjusted for inflation. Early CIA efforts focused on LSD-25, which later came to dominate many of MKUltra's programs. The CIA wanted to know if they could make Soviet spies defect against their will and whether the Soviets could do the same to the CIA's own operatives. Once Project MKUltra got underway in April 1953, experiments included administering LSD to mental patients, prisoners, drug addicts, and prostitutes, 'People who could not fight back,' as one agency officer put it. In one case, they administered LSD to a mental patient in Kentucky for 174 days. They also administered LSD to CIA employees, military personnel, doctors, other government agents, and members of the general public to study their reactions. LSD and other drugs were often administered without the subject's knowledge or informed consent, a violation of the Nuremberg Code the U.S. had agreed to follow after World War II. The aim of this was to find drugs which would bring out deep confessions or wipe a subject's mind clean and program them as 'A robot agent.'

In Operation Midnight Climax, the CIA set up several brothels within agency safe houses in San Francisco to obtain a selection of men who would be too embarrassed to talk about the events. The men were dosed with LSD, the brothels were equipped with one-way mirrors, and the sessions were filmed for later viewing and study. In other experiments where people were given LSD without their knowledge, they were interrogated under bright lights with doctors in the background taking notes. They told subjects they would extend their 'Trips' if they refused to reveal their secrets. The people under this interrogation were CIA employees, U.S. military personnel, and agents suspected of working for the other side in the Cold War. Long-term debilitation and several deaths resulted from this. Heroin addicts were bribed into taking LSD with offers of more heroin. At the invitation of Stanford psychology graduate student Vik Lovell, an acquaintance of Richard Alpert and Allen Ginsberg, Ken Kesey volunteered to take part in what turned out to be a CIA-financed study under the aegis of

MKUltra, at the Menlo Park Veterans' Hospital where he worked as a night aide. The project studied the effects of psychoactive drugs, particularly LSD, psilocybin, mescaline, cocaine, AMT and DMT on people.

The Office of Security used LSD in interrogations, but Dr. Sidney Gottlieb, the chemist who directed MKUltra, had other ideas: he thought it could be used in covert operations. Since its effects were temporary, he believed it could be given to high-ranking officials and in this way affect the course of important meetings, speeches, etc. Since he realized there was a difference in testing the drug in a laboratory and using it in clandestine operations, he initiated a series of experiments where LSD was given to people in "normal" settings without warning. At first, everyone in Technical Services tried it; a typical experiment involved two people in a room where they observed each other for hours and took notes. As the experimentation progressed, a point arrived where outsiders were drugged with no explanation whatsoever and surprise acid trips became something of an occupational hazard among CIA operatives. Adverse reactions often occurred, such as an operative who received the drug in his morning coffee, became psychotic and ran across Washington, seeing a monster in every car passing him. The experiments continued even after Frank Olson, an army chemist who had never taken LSD, was covertly dosed by his CIA supervisor, and nine days later plunged to his death from the window of a 13th-story New York City hotel room, supposedly as a result of deep depression induced by the drug. According to Stephen Kinzer, Olson had approached his superiors some time earlier, doubting the morality of the project, and asked to resign from the CIA.

Some subjects' participation was consensual, and in these cases they appeared to be singled out for even more extreme experiments. In one case, seven volunteers in Kentucky were given LSD for seventy-seven consecutive days. MKUltra's researchers later dismissed LSD as too unpredictable in its results. They gave up on the notion that LSD was 'The secret that was going to unlock the universe,' but it still had a place in the cloak-and-dagger arsenal. However, by 1962 the CIA and the army developed a series of super-hallucinogens such as the highly touted BZ, which was thought to hold greater promise as a mind control weapon. This resulted in the withdrawal of support by many academics and private researchers, and LSD research became less of a priority altogether.

Other drugs

Another technique investigated was the intravenous administration of a barbiturate into one arm and an amphetamine into the other. The barbiturates were released into the person first, and as soon as the person began to fall asleep, the amphetamines were released. Other experiments involved Heroin, Morphine, Temazepam (used under code name MKSEARCH), mescaline, psilocybin, scopolamine, alcohol, and sodium pentothal.

Hypnosis

Declassified MKUltra documents indicate they studied hypnosis in the early 1950s. Experimental goals included creating 'Hypnotically induced anxieties', 'Hypnotically increasing ability to learn and recall complex written matter', studying hypnosis and polygraph examinations, 'Hypnotically increasing ability to observe and recall complex arrangements of physical objects', and studying 'Relationship of personality to susceptibility to hypnosis' They conducted experiments with drug-induced hypnosis and with anterograde and retrograde amnesia while under the influence of such drugs.

Experiments on Canadians

Donald Ewen Cameron c. 1967. The CIA exported experiments to Canada when they recruited British psychiatrist Donald Ewen Cameron, creator of the "psychic driving" concept, which the CIA found interesting. Cameron had been hoping to correct schizophrenia by erasing existing memories and reprogramming the psyche. He commuted from Albany, New York to Montreal every week to work at the Allan Memorial Institute of McGill University and was paid $69,000 from 1957 to 1964 (US$579,480 in 2021, adjusted for inflation) to carry out MKUltra experiments there, the Montreal experiments. These research funds were sent to Cameron by a CIA front organization, the Society for the Investigation of Human Ecology, and as shown in internal CIA documents, Cameron did not know the money came from the CIA.

In addition to LSD, Cameron also experimented with various paralytic drugs as well as electroconvulsive therapy at thirty to forty times the normal power. His 'Driving' experiments consisted of putting subjects into drug-induced comas for weeks at a time (up to three months in one case) while playing tape loops of noise or simple repetitive statements. His experiments were often carried out on patients who entered the institute for common problems such as anxiety disorders and postpartum depression, many of whom suffered permanent effects from his actions. His treatments resulted in victims' urinary incontinence, amnesia, forgetting how to talk, forgetting their parents, and thinking their interrogators were their parents. During this era, Cameron became known worldwide as the first chairman of the World Psychiatric Association as well as president of both the American Psychiatric Association and the Canadian Psychiatric Association. Cameron was also a member of the Nuremberg medical tribunal in 1946–1947.

Motivation and assessments

His work was inspired and paralleled by the British psychiatrist William Sargant at St Thomas' Hospital, London, and Belmont Hospital, Sutton, who was also involved in the Secret Intelligence Service and who experimented on his patients without their consent, causing similar long-term damage. In the 1980s, several of Cameron's former patients sued the CIA for damages, which the Canadian news program The Fifth Estate documented. Their experiences and lawsuit was made into a 1998 television miniseries called The Sleep Room. Naomi Klein argues in her book The Shock Doctrine that Cameron's research and his contribution to the MKUltra project was not about mind control and brainwashing, but about designing 'A scientifically based system for extracting information from 'resistant sources'. In other words, torture.' Alfred W. McCoy writes, 'Stripped of its bizarre excesses, Dr. Cameron's experiments, building upon Donald O. Hebb's earlier breakthrough, laid the scientific foundation for the CIA's two-stage psychological torture method,' referring to first creating a state of disorientation in the subject, and then creating a situation of 'Self-inflicted' discomfort in which the disoriented subject can alleviate pain by capitulating.

Secret detention camps

In areas under American control in the early 1950s in Europe and East Asia, mostly Japan, Germany and the Philippines, the CIA created secret detention centers so that the U.S. could avoid criminal prosecution. The CIA captured people suspected of being enemy agents and other people it deemed "expendable" to undertake diverse types of torture and human experimentation on them. The prisoners were interrogated while being administered psychoactive drugs, electroshocked, and subjected to extremes of temperature, sensory isolation, and the like to develop a better understanding of how to destroy and to control human minds.

Revelation

Frank Church headed the Church Committee, an investigation into the practices of the U.S. intelligence agencies. In 1973, amid a government-wide panic caused by Watergate, CIA Director Richard Helms ordered all MKUltra files destroyed. Pursuant to this order, most CIA documents regarding the project were destroyed, making a full investigation of MKUltra impossible. A cache of some 20,000 documents survived Helms's purge, as they had been incorrectly stored in a financial records building and were discovered following a FOIA request in 1977. These documents were fully investigated during the Senate Hearings of 1977. In December 1974, The New York Times alleged that the CIA had conducted illegal domestic activities, including experiments on U.S. citizens, during the 1960s. That report prompted investigations by the United States Congress, in the form of the Church Committee, and by a commission known as the Rockefeller Commission that looked into the illegal domestic activities of the CIA, the FBI and intelligence-related agencies of the military.

In the summer of 1975, congressional Church Committee reports, and the presidential Rockefeller Commission report revealed to the public for the first time that the CIA and the Department of Defense had conducted experiments on both unwitting and cognizant human subjects as part of an extensive program to find out how to influence and control human behavior through the use of psychoactive drugs such as LSD and mescaline and other chemical, biological, and psychological means. They also revealed that at least one subject, Frank Olson, had died after administration of LSD. Much of what the Church Committee and the Rockefeller Commission learned about MKUltra was contained in a report, prepared by the Inspector General's office in 1963, that had survived the destruction of records ordered in 1973. However, it contained little detail. Sidney Gottlieb, who had retired from the CIA two years previously and had headed MKUltra, was interviewed by the committee but claimed to have very little recollection of the activities of MKUltra.

The congressional committee investigating the CIA research, chaired by Senator Frank Church, concluded that 'Prior consent was obviously not obtained from any of the subjects.' The committee noted that the 'Experiments sponsored by these researchers ... call into question the decision by the agencies not to fix guidelines for experiments.' Following the recommendations of the Church Committee, President Gerald Ford in 1976 issued the first Executive Order on Intelligence Activities which, among other things, prohibited 'Experimentation with drugs on human subjects, except with the informed consent, in writing and witnessed by a disinterested party, of each such human subject' and in accordance with the guidelines issued by the National Commission. Subsequent orders by Presidents Carter and Reagan expanded the directive to apply to any human experimentation.

1977 United States Senate report on MKUltra

In 1977, during a hearing held by the Senate Select Committee on Intelligence, to look further into MKUltra, Admiral Stansfield Turner, then Director of Central Intelligence, revealed that the CIA had found a set of records, consisting of about 20,000 pages, which had survived the 1973 destruction orders because they had been incorrectly stored at a records center not usually used for such documents. These files dealt with the financing of MKUltra projects and contained few project details, but much more was learned from them than from the Inspector General's 1963 report.

On the Senate floor in 1977, Senator Ted Kennedy said: 'The Deputy Director of the CIA revealed that over thirty universities and institutions were involved in an 'Extensive testing and experimentation' program which included covert drug tests on unwitting citizens 'At all social levels, high and low, native Americans and foreign.' Several of these tests involved the administration of LSD to 'Unwitting subjects in social situations." At least one death, the result of the alleged defenestration of Dr. Frank Olson, was attributed to Olson's being subjected, without his knowledge, to such experimentation nine days before his death. [citation needed] The CIA itself subsequently acknowledged that these tests had little scientific rationale. The officers conducting the monitoring were not qualified scientific observers.

In Canada, the issue took much longer to surface, becoming widely known in 1984 on a CBC news show, The Fifth Estate. It was learned that not only had the CIA funded Dr. Cameron's efforts, but also that the Canadian government was fully aware of this and had later provided another $500,000 in funding to continue the experiments. This revelation largely derailed efforts by the victims to sue the CIA as their U.S. counterparts had, and the Canadian government eventually settled out of court for $100,000 to each of the 127 victims. Dr. Cameron died on September 8, 1967, after suffering a heart attack while he and his son were mountain climbing. None of Cameron's personal records of his involvement with MKUltra survived because his family destroyed them after his death.

1994 U.S. General Accounting Office report

The U.S. General Accounting Office issued a report on September 28, 1994, which stated that between 1940 and 1974, DOD and other national security agencies studied thousands of human subjects in tests and experiments involving hazardous substances. The quote from the study: 'Working with the CIA, the Department of Defense gave hallucinogenic drugs to thousands of "volunteer" soldiers in the 1950s and 1960s. In addition to LSD, the Army also tested quinuclidinyl benzilate, a hallucinogen code-named BZ. (Note 37) Many of these tests were conducted under the so-called MKULTRA program, established to counter perceived Soviet and Chinese advances in brainwashing techniques. Between 1953 and 1964, the program consisted of 149 projects involving drug testing and other studies on unwitting human subjects'.

Deaths

Given the CIA's purposeful destruction of most records, its failure to follow informed consent protocols with thousands of participants, the uncontrolled nature of the experiments, and the lack of follow-up data, the full impact of MKUltra experiments, including deaths, may never be known. Several known deaths have been associated with Project MKUltra, most notably that of Frank Olson. Olson, a United States Army biochemist, and biological weapons researcher was given LSD without his knowledge or consent in November 1953, as part of a CIA experiment, and died by suicide by jumping out of a 13th-story window a week later. A CIA doctor assigned to monitor Olson claimed to have been asleep in another bed in a New York

City hotel room when Olson fell to his death. In 1953, Olson's death was described as a suicide that had occurred during a severe psychotic episode. The CIA's own internal investigation concluded that the head of MKUltra, CIA chemist Sidney Gottlieb, had conducted the LSD experiment with Olson's prior knowledge, although neither Olson nor the other men taking part in the experiment were informed as to the exact nature of the drug until some 20 minutes after its ingestion. The report further suggested that Gottlieb was nonetheless due a reprimand, as he had failed to take into account Olson's already-diagnosed suicidal tendencies, which might have been exacerbated by the LSD.

The Olson family disputes the official version of events. They maintain that Frank Olson was murdered because, especially in the aftermath of his LSD experience, he had become a security risk who might divulge state secrets associated with highly classified CIA programs, about many of which he had direct personal knowledge. A few days before his death, Frank Olson quit his position as acting chief of the Special Operations Division at Detrick, Maryland (later Fort Detrick) because of a severe moral crisis concerning the nature of his biological weapons research. Among Olson's concerns were the development of assassination materials used by the CIA, the CIA's use of biological warfare materials in covert operations, experimentation with biological weapons in populated areas, collaboration with former Nazi scientists under Operation Paperclip, LSD mind-control research, and the use of psychoactive drugs during 'Terminal' interrogations under a program code-named Project 'Artichoke.' Later forensic evidence conflicted with the official version of events; when Olson's body was exhumed in 1994, cranial injuries indicated that Olson had been knocked unconscious before he exited the window.

The medical examiner termed Olson's death a 'Homicide.' In 1975, Olson's family received a $750,000 settlement from the U.S. government and formal apologies from President Gerald Ford and CIA Director William Colby, though their apologies were limited to informed consent issues concerning Olson's ingestion of LSD. On 28 November 2012, the Olson family filed suit against the U.S. federal government for the wrongful death of Frank Olson. The case was dismissed in July 2013, due in part to the 1976 settlement between the family and government. In the decision dismissing the suit, U.S. District Judge James Boasberg wrote, 'While the court must limit its analysis to the four corners of the complaint, the skeptical reader may wish to know that the public record supports many of the allegations in the family's suit, farfetched as they may sound.' A 2010 book by H. P. Albarelli Jr. alleged that the 1951 Pont-Saint-Esprit mass poisoning was part of MKDELTA, that Olson was involved in that event, and that he was eventually murdered by the CIA. However, academic sources attribute the incident to ergot poisoning through a local bakery.

Legal issues involving informed consent

The revelations about the CIA and the army prompted a number of subjects or their survivors to file lawsuits against the federal government for conducting experiments without informed consent. Although the government aggressively, and sometimes successfully, sought to avoid legal liability, several plaintiffs did receive compensation through court order, out-of-court settlement, or acts of Congress. Frank Olson's family received $750,000 by a special act of Congress, and both President Ford and CIA director William Colby met with Olson's family to apologize publicly. Previously, the CIA and the army had actively and successfully sought to withhold incriminating information, even as they secretly provided compensation to the families. One subject of army drug experimentation, James Stanley, an army sergeant, brought an important, albeit unsuccessful, suit. The government argued that Stanley was barred from suing under the Feres doctrine.

In 1987, the Supreme Court affirmed this defense in a 5–4 decision that dismissed Stanley's case: United States v. Stanley. The majority argued that 'A test for liability that depends on the extent to which particular suits would call into question military discipline and decision making would itself require judicial inquiry into, and hence intrusion upon, military matters.' In dissent, Justice William Brennan argued that the need to preserve military discipline should not protect the government from liability and punishment for serious violations of constitutional rights. The medical trials at Nuremberg in 1947 deeply impressed upon the world that experimentation with unknowing human subjects is morally and legally unacceptable. The United States Military Tribunal established the Nuremberg Code as a standard against which to judge German scientists who experimented with human subjects.... In defiance of this principle, military intelligence officials ... began surreptitiously testing chemical and biological materials, including LSD.

Justice Sandra Day O'Connor, writing a separate dissent, stated. No judicially crafted rule should insulate from liability the involuntary and unknowing human experimentation alleged to have occurred in this case. Indeed, as Justice Brennan observes, the United States played an instrumental role in the criminal prosecution of Nazi officials who experimented with human subjects during the Second World War, and the standards that the Nuremberg Military Tribunals developed to judge the behavior of the defendants stated that the 'voluntary consent of the human subject is absolutely essential ... to satisfy moral, ethical, and legal concepts.' If this principle is violated, the very least that society can do is to see that the victims are compensated, as best they can be, by the perpetrators.

In another lawsuit, Wayne Ritchie, a former United States Marshal, after hearing about the project's existence in 1990, alleged the CIA laced his food or drink with LSD at a 1957 Christmas party which resulted in his attempting to commit a robbery at a bar and his subsequent arrest. While the government admitted it was, at that time, drugging people without their consent, U.S. District Judge Marilyn Hall Patel found Ritchie could not prove he was one of the victims of MKUltra or that LSD caused his robbery attempt and dismissed the case in 2005.

Notable people: Experimenters

1. Harold Alexander Abramson
2. Donald Ewen Cameron
3. Sidney Gottlieb
4. Harris Isbell
5. Martin Theodore Orne
6. Louis Jolyon West

Documented subjects

American poet Allen Ginsberg first took LSD in an experiment on Stanford University's campus where he could listen to records of his choice (he chose a Gertrude Stein reading, a

Tibetan mandala, and Richard Wagner). He said the experience resulted in 'A slight paranoia that hung on all my acid experiences through the mid-1960s until I learned from meditation how to disperse that.' He became an outspoken advocate for psychedelics in the 1960s and, after hearing suspicions that the experiment was CIA-funded, wrote, 'Am I, Allen Ginsberg, the product of one of the CIA's lamentable, ill-advised, or triumphantly successful experiments in mind control?'

Ken Kesey, author of 'One Flew over the Cuckoo's Nest,' is said to have volunteered for MKUltra experiments involving LSD and other psychedelic drugs at the Veterans Administration Hospital in Menlo Park while he was a student at nearby Stanford University. Kesey's experiences while under the influence of LSD inspired him to promote the drug outside the context of the MKUltra experiments, which influenced the early development of hippie culture. Robert Hunter was an American lyricist, singer-songwriter, translator, and poet, best known for his association with Jerry Garcia and the Grateful Dead. Along with Ken Kesey, Hunter was said to be an early volunteer MKUltra test subject at Stanford University. Stanford test subjects were paid to take LSD, psilocybin, and mescaline, then report on their experiences. These experiences were creatively formative for Hunter:

Sit back picture yourself swooping up a shell of purple with foam crests of crystal drops soft nigh they fall unto the sea of morning creep-very-softly mist ... and then sort of cascade tinkley-bell-like (must I take you by the hand, ever so slowly type) and then conglomerate suddenly into a peal of silver vibrant uncomprehendingly, blood singingly, joyously resounding bells ... By my faith if this be insanity, then for the love of God permit me to remain insane. Boston mobster James 'Whitey' Bulger alleged he had been subjected to weekly injections of LSD and subsequent testing while in prison in Atlanta in 1957.

Alleged subjects

Ted Kaczynski, an American domestic terrorist known as the Unabomber, was said to be a subject of a voluntary psychological study alleged by some sources to have been a part of MKUltra. As a sophomore at Harvard, Kaczynski participated in a study described by author Alston Chase as a 'Purposely brutalizing psychological experiment,' led by Harvard psychologist Henry Murray. In total, Kaczynski spent 200 hours as part of the study. Lawrence Teeter was the attorney for Sirhan Sirhan, who was convicted of murdering Robert F. Kennedy, and he believed that Sirhan was 'Operating under MK-ULTRA mind control techniques.' After retiring in 1972, Gottlieb dismissed his entire effort for the CIA's MKUltra program as useless. The CIA insists that MKUltra-type experiments have been abandoned

OUTCOME BASED EDUCATION

Outcome-based education or outcomes-based education (OBE) is an educational theory that bases each part of an educational system around goals (outcomes). By the end of the educational experience, each student should have achieved the goal. There is no single specified style of teaching or assessment in OBE; instead, classes, opportunities, and assessments should all help students achieve the specified outcomes. The role of the faculty adapts into instructor, trainer, facilitator, and/or mentor based on the outcomes targeted.

Outcome-based methods have been adopted in education systems around the world, at multiple levels. Australia and South Africa adopted OBE policies from the 1990s to the mid-2000s but were abandoned in the face of substantial community opposition. The United States has had an OBE program in place since 1994 that has been adapted over the years. In 2005, Hong Kong adopted an outcome-based approach for its universities. Malaysia implemented OBE in all of their public schools systems in 2008. The European Union has proposed an education shift to focus on outcomes, across the EU. In an international effort to accept OBE, The Washington Accord was created in 1989; it is an agreement to accept undergraduate engineering degrees that were obtained using OBE methods. As of 2017, the full signatories are Australia, Canada, Taiwan, Hong Kong, India, Ireland, Japan, Korea, Malaysia, New Zealand, Russia, Singapore, South Africa, Sri Lanka, Turkey, the United Kingdom, Pakistan, China, and the United States.

OBE can primarily be distinguished from traditional education method by the way it incorporates three elements: theory of education, a systematic structure for education, and a specific approach to instructional practice. It organizes the entire educational system towards what are considered essential for the learners to successfully do at the end of their learning experiences. In this model, the term 'Outcome' is the core concept and sometimes used interchangeably with the terms 'Competency,' 'Standards,' 'Benchmarks,' and 'Attainment targets.' OBE also uses the same methodology formally and informally adopted in actual workplace to achieve outcomes. It focuses on the following skills when developing curricula and outcomes:

1. Life skills;
2. Basic skills;
3. Professional and vocational skills;
4. Intellectual skills;
5. Interpersonal and personal skills.

In a regional/local/foundational/electrical education system, students are given grades and rankings compared to each other. Content and performance expectations are based primarily on what was taught in the past to students of a given age of 12-18. The goal of this education was to present the knowledge and skills of an older generation to the new generation of students, and to provide students with an environment in which to learn. The process paid little attention (beyond the classroom teacher) to whether or not students learn any of the material.

Benefits of OBE

Clarity: The focus on outcomes creates a clear expectation of what needs to be accomplished by the end of the course. Students will understand what is expected of them and teachers will know what they need to teach during the course. Clarity is important over years of schooling and when team teaching is involved. Each team member, or year in school, will have a clear understanding of what needs to be accomplished in each class, or at each level, allowing students to progress. Those designing and planning the curriculum are expected to work backwards once an outcome has been decided upon; they must determine what knowledge and skills will be required to reach the outcome.

Flexibility

With a clear sense of what needs to be accomplished, instructors will be able to structure their lessons around the student's needs. OBE does not specify a specific method of instruction, leaving instructors free to tutor their students using any method. Instructors will also be able to recognize diversity among students by using various teaching and assessment techniques during their class.] OBE is meant to be a student-centered learning model. Teachers are meant to guide and help the students understand the material in any way necessary, study guides, and group work are some of the methods instructors can use to facilitate students learning.

Comparison

OBE can be compared across different institutions. On an individual level, institutions can look at what outcomes a student has achieved to decide what level the student would be at within a new institution. On an institutional level, institutions can compare themselves, by checking to see what outcomes they have in common, and find places where they may need improvement, based on the achievement of outcomes at other institutions. The ability to compare easily across institutions allows students to move between institutions with relative ease. The institutions can compare outcomes to determine what credits to award the student. The clearly articulated outcomes should allow institutions to assess the student's achievements rapidly, leading to increased movement of students. These outcomes also work for school to work transitions. A potential employer can look at records of the potential employee to determine what outcomes they have achieved. They can then determine if the potential employee has the skills necessary for the job.

Involvement

Student involvement in the classroom is a key part of OBE. Students are expected to do their own learning, so that they gain a full understanding of the material. Increased student involvement allows students to feel responsible for their own learning, and they should learn more through this individual learning. Other aspects of involvement are parental and community, through developing curriculum, or making changes to it. OBE outcomes are meant to be decided upon within a school system, or at a local level. Parents and community members are asked to give input in order to uphold the standards of education within a community and to ensure that students will be prepared for life after school.

Drawbacks of OBE

Definition: The definitions of the outcomes decided upon are subject to interpretation by those implementing them. Across different programs or even different instructors outcomes could be interpreted differently, leading to a difference in education, even though the same outcomes were said to be achieved. By outlining specific outcomes, a holistic approach to learning is lost. Learning can find itself reduced to something that is specific, measurable, and observable. As a result, outcomes are not yet widely recognized as a valid way of conceptualizing what learning is about.

Assessment problems

When determining if an outcome has been achieved, assessments may become too mechanical, looking only to see if the student has acquired the knowledge. The ability to use and apply the knowledge in unusual ways may not be the focus of the assessment. The focus on determining if the outcome has been achieved leads to a loss of understanding and learning for students, who may never be shown how to use the knowledge they have gained. Instructors are faced with a challenge: they must learn to manage an environment that can become fundamentally different from what they are accustomed to. In regards to giving assessments, they must be willing to put in the time required to create a valid, reliable assessment that ideally would allow students to demonstrate their understanding of the information, while remaining objective.

Generality

Education outcomes can lead to a constrained nature of teaching and assessment. Assessing liberal outcomes such as creativity, respect for self and others, responsibility, and self-sufficiency, can become problematic. There is not a measurable, observable, or specific way to determine if a student has achieved these outcomes. Due to the nature of specific outcomes,

OBE may actually work against its ideals of serving and creating individuals that have achieved many outcomes.

Involvement

Parental involvement, as discussed in the benefits section can also be a drawback, if parents and community members are not willing to express their opinions on the quality of the education system, the system may not see a need for improvement, and not change to meet student's needs. Parents may also become too involved, requesting too many changes, so that important improvements get lost with other changes that are being suggested. Instructors will also find that their work is increased; they must work to first understand the outcome, then build a curriculum around each outcome they are required to meet. Instructors have found that implementing multiple outcomes is difficult to do equally, especially in primary school. Instructors will also find their work load increased if they chose to use an assessment method that evaluates students holistically.

Adoption and removal

Australia: In the early 1990s, all states and territories in Australia developed intended curriculum documents largely based on OBE for their primary and secondary schools. Criticism arose shortly after implementation. Critics argued that no evidence existed that OBE could be implemented successfully on a large scale, in either the United States or Australia. An evaluation of Australian schools found that implementing OBE was difficult. Teachers felt overwhelmed by the amount of expected achievement outcomes. Educators believed that the curriculum outcomes did not attend to the needs of the students or teachers. Critics felt that too many expected outcomes left students with shallow understanding of the material. Many of Australia's current education policies have moved away from OBE and towards a focus on fully understanding the essential content, rather than learning more content with less understanding.

Western Australia

Officially, an agenda to implement Outcomes Based Education took place between 1992 and 2008 in Western Australia. Dissatisfaction with OBE escalated from 2004 when the government proposed the implementation of an alternative assessment system using OBE 'levels' for years 11 and 12. With government school teachers not permitted to publicly express dissatisfaction with the new system, a community lobby group called PLATO as formed in June 2004 by high school science teacher Marko Vojkavi. Teachers anonymously expressed their views through the website and online forums, with the website quickly became one of the most widely read educational websites in Australia with more 180,000 hits per month and contained an archive of more than 10,000 articles on the subject of OBE implementation. In 2008 it was officially abandoned by the state government with Minister for Education Mark McGowan remarking that the 1990s fad 'To dispense with syllabus' was over.

European Union

In December 2012, the European Commission presented a new strategy to decrease youth unemployment rate, which at the time was close to 23% across the European Union. The European Qualifications Framework calls for a shift towards learning outcomes in primary and secondary schools throughout the EU. Students are expected to learn skills that they will need when they complete their education. It also calls for lessons to have a stronger link to employment through work-based learning (WBL). Work-based learning for students should also lead to recognition of vocational training for these students. The program also sets goals for learning foreign languages, and for teachers continued education. It also highlights the importance of using technology, especially the internet, in learning to make it relevant to students.

Hong Kong

Hong Kong's University Grants Committee adopted an outcomes-based approach to teaching and learning in 2005. No specific approach was created leaving universities to design the approach themselves. Universities were also left with a goal of ensuring an education for their students that will contribute to social and economic development, as defined by the community in which the university resides. With little to no direction or feedback from the outside universities will have to determine if their approach is achieving its goals on their own.

Malaysia

OBE has been practiced in Malaysia since the 1950s; however, as of 2008, OBE is being implemented at all levels of education, especially tertiary education. This change is a result of the belief that the education system used prior to OBE inadequately prepared graduates for life outside of school. The Ministry of Higher Education has pushed for this change because of the number of unemployed graduates. Findings in 2006 state that nearly 70% of graduates from public universities were considered unemployed. A further study of those graduates found that they felt they lacked, job experience, communication skills, and qualifications relevant to the current job market. The Malaysian Qualifications Agency (MQA) was created to oversee quality of education and to ensure outcomes were being reached. The MQA created a framework that includes eight levels of qualification within higher education, covering three sectors; skills, vocational and technical, and academic. Along with meeting the standards set by the MQA, universities set and monitor their own outcome expectations for students

South Africa

OBE was introduced to South Africa in the late 1990s by the post-apartheid government as part of its Curriculum 2005 program. Initial support for the program derived from anti-apartheid education policies. The policy also gained support from the labor movements that borrowed ideas about competency-based education, and Vocational education from New Zealand and Australia, as well as the labor movement that critiqued the apartheid education system. With no strong alternative proposals, the idea of outcome-based education, and a national qualification framework, became the policy of the African National Congress government. This policy was believed to be a democratization of education, people would have a say in what they wanted the outcomes of education to be. It was also believed to be a way to increase education standards and increase the availability of education. The National Qualifications Framework (NQF) went into effect in 1997. In 2001 people realized that the intended effects were not being seen. By 2006 no proposals to change the system had been accepted by the government, causing a hiatus of the program. The program came to be viewed as a failure and a new curriculum improvement process was announced in 2010, slated to be implemented between 2012 and 2014.

United States

In 1983, a report from the National Commission on Excellence in Education declared that American education standards were eroding, that young people in the United States were not learning enough. In 1989, President Bush and the nation's governors set national goals to be achieved by the year 2000. GOALS 2000: Educate America Act was signed in March 1994. The goal of this new reform was to show that results were being achieved in schools. In 2001, the 'No Child Left behind Act' took the place of Goals 2000. It mandated certain measurements as a condition of receiving federal education funds. States are free to set their own standards, but the federal law mandates public reporting of math and reading test scores for disadvantaged demographic subgroups, including racial minorities, low-income students, and special education students. Various consequences for schools that do not make "adequate yearly progress" are included in the law. In 2010, President Obama proposed improvements for the program. In 2012, the U.S. Department of Education invited states to request flexibility waivers in exchange for rigorous plans designed to improve students' education in the state.

India

India has become the permanent signatory member of the Washington Accord on 13 June 2014. India has started implementing OBE in higher technical education like diploma and undergraduate programs. The National Board of Accreditation, a body for promoting international quality standards for technical education in India has started accrediting only the programs running with OBE from 2013.

The National Board of Accreditation mandates establishing a culture of outcomes-based education in institutions that offer Engineering, Pharmacy, Management programs. Outcomes analysis and using the analytical reports to find gaps and carry out continuous improvement is essential cultural shift from how the above programs are run when OBE culture is not embraced.

Outcomes analysis requires huge amount of data to be churned and made available at anytime, anywhere. Such an access to scalable, accurate, automated, and real-time data analysis is possible only if the institute adopts either excelsheet based measurement system or some kind of home-grown or commercial software system. It is observed that excelsheet based measurement and analysis system doesn't scale when the stakeholders want to analyze longitudinal data.

SMART METERS

A smart meter is an electronic device that records information such as consumption of electric energy, voltage levels, current, and power factor. Smart meters communicate the information to the consumer for greater clarity of consumption behavior, and electricity suppliers for system monitoring and customer billing. Smart meters typically record energy near real-time, and report regularly, short intervals throughout the day. Smart meters enable two-way communication between the meter and the central system. Such an advanced metering infrastructure (AMI) differs from automatic meter reading (AMR) in that it enables two-way communication between the meter and the supplier. Communications from the meter to the network may be wireless, or via fixed wired connections such as power line carrier (PLC). Wireless communication options in common use include cellular communications, Wi-Fi (readily available), wireless ad hoc networks over Wi-Fi, wireless mesh networks, low power long-range wireless (LoRa), Wize (high radio penetration rate, open, using the frequency 169 MHz) ZigBee (low power, low data rate wireless), and Wi-SUN (Smart Utility Networks).

The term Smart Meter often refers to an electricity meter, but it also may mean a device measuring natural gas, water, or district heating consumption. Similar meters, usually referred to as interval or time-of-use meters, have existed for years, but 'Smart Meters' usually involve real-time or near real-time sensors, power outage notification, and power quality monitoring. These additional features are more than simple automated meter reading (AMR). They are similar in many respects to Advanced Metering Infrastructure (AMI) meters. Interval and time-of-use meters historically have been installed to measure commercial and industrial customers but may not have automatic reading. Research by the UK consumer group, showed that as many as one in three confuse smart meters with energy monitors, also known as in-home display monitors.

The installed base of smart meters in Europe at the end of 2008 was about 39 million units, according to analyst firm Berg Insight.

Globally, Pike Research found that smart meter shipments were 17.4 million units for the first quarter of 2011. Visiongain determined that the value of the global smart meter market would reach US$7 billion in 2012. As of January 2018, over 99 million electricity meters were deployed across the European Union, with an estimated 24 million more to be installed by the end of 2020. The European Commission DG Energy estimates the 2020 installed base to have required €18.8 billion in investment, growing to €40.7 billion by 2030, with a total deployment of 266 million smart meters. By the end of 2018, the U.S. had over 86 million smart meters installed. In 2017, there were 665 million smart meters installed globally. Revenue generation is expected to grow from $12.8 billion in 2017 to $20 billion by 2022.

Smart meters may be part of a smart grid, but do not themselves constitute a smart grid.

In 1972, Theodore Paraskevakos, while working with Boeing in Huntsville, Alabama, developed a sensor monitoring system that used digital transmission for security, fire, and medical alarm systems as well as meter reading capabilities. This technology was a spin-off from the automatic telephone line identification system, now known as Caller ID. In 1974, Paraskevakos was awarded a U.S. patent for this technology. In 1977, he launched Metretek, Inc., which developed and produced the first smart meters. Since this system was developed pre-Internet, Metretek utilized the IBM series 1 mini-computer. For this approach, Paraskevakos and Metretek were awarded multiple patents.

Purpose

Since the inception of electricity deregulation and market-driven pricing throughout the world, utilities have been looking for a means to match consumption with generation. Non-smart electrical and gas meters only measure total consumption, providing no information of when the energy was consumed. Smart meters provide a way of measuring electricity consumption in near real-time. This allows utility companies to charge different prices for consumption according to the time of day and the season. It also facilitates more accurate cash-flow models for utilities. Since smart meters can be read remotely, labor costs are reduced for utilities.

Smart metering offers potential benefits to customers. These include, a) an end to estimated bills, which are a major source of complaints about many customers b) a tool to help consumers better manage their energy purchases, smart meters with a display outside their homes could provide up-to-date information on gas and electricity consumption and in doing so help people to manage their energy use and reduce their energy bills. With regards to consumption reduction, this is critical for understanding the benefits of smart meters because the relatively small percentage benefits in terms of savings are multiplied by millions of users. Smart meters for water consumption can also provide detailed and timely information about customer water use and early notification of possible water leaks in their premises. Electricity pricing usually peaks at certain predictable times of the day and the season. In particular, if generation is constrained, prices can rise if power from other jurisdictions or more costly generation is brought online. Proponents assert that billing customers at a higher rate for peak times encourages consumers to adjust their consumption habits to be more responsive to market prices and assert further, that regulatory and market design agencies hope these "price signals" could delay the construction of additional generation or at least the purchase of energy from higher-priced sources, thereby controlling the steady and rapid increase of electricity prices.

An academic study based on existing trials showed that homeowners' electricity consumption on average is reduced by approximately 3-5% when provided with real-time feedback. Another advantage of smart meters that benefits both customers and the utility is the monitoring capability they provide for the whole electrical system. As part of an AMI, utilities can use the real-time data from smart meters measurements related to current, voltage, and power factor to detect system disruptions more quickly, allowing immediate corrective action to minimize customer impact such as blackouts. Smart meters also help utilities understand the power grid needs with more granularity than legacy meters. This greater understanding facilitates system planning to meet customer energy needs while reducing the likelihood of additional infrastructure investments, which eliminates unnecessary spending or energy cost increases. Though the task of meeting national electricity demand with accurate supply is becoming ever more challenging as intermittent renewable generation sources make up a greater proportion of the energy mix, the real-time data provided by smart meters allow grid operators to integrate renewable energy onto the grid in order to balance the networks. As a result, smart meters are considered an essential technology to the decarbonisation of the energy system.

Criticism of Smart Meter Roll-out in the UK

Citizens Advice said in August 2018 that 80% of people with smart meters were happy with them. Still, it had 3,000 calls in 2017 about problems. These related to first-generation smart meters losing their functionality, aggressive sales practices, and still having to send smart meter readings.

Ross Anderson of the Foundation for Information Policy Research has criticized the UK's program on the grounds that it is unlikely to lower energy consumption, is rushed and expensive, and does not promote metering competition. Anderson writes, 'The proposed architecture ensures continued dominance of metering by energy industry incumbents whose commercial interests are in selling more energy rather than less,' and urged ministers 'To kill the project and instead promote competition in domestic energy metering, as the Germans do and as the UK already has in industrial metering. Every consumer should have the right to appoint the meter operator of their choice.' In a 2011 submission to the Public Accounts Committee, Anderson wrote that Ofgem was 'Making all the classic mistakes which have been known for years to lead to public-sector IT project failures' and that the 'Most critical part of the project—how smart meters will talk to domestic appliances to facilitate demand response—is essentially ignored.'

The high number of SMETS1 meters installed has been criticized by Peter Earl, head of energy at the price comparison website comparethemarket.com. He said, 'The Government expected there would only be a small number of the first-generation of smart meters before Smets II came in, but the reality is there are now at least five million and perhaps as many as 10 million Smets I meters.' UK smart meters in southern England and the Midlands use the mobile phone network to communicate, so they do not work correctly when phone coverage is weak. A solution has been proposed but was not operational as of March 2017.

In March 2018, the National Audit Office (NAO), which watches over public spending, opened an investigation into the smart meter program, which had cost £11bn by then, paid for by electricity users through higher bills. The National Audit Office published the findings of its investigation in a report titled "Rolling out smart meters" published in November 2018. The report, amongst other findings, indicated that the number of smart meters installed in the UK would fall materially short of the Department for Business, Energy & Industrial Strategy (BEIS) original ambitions of all UK consumers having a smart meter installed by 2020. In September 2019, smart meter rollout in the UK was delayed for four years.

Ross Anderson and Alex Henney wrote that 'Ed Miliband cooked the books' to make a case for smart meters appear economically viable. They say that the first three cost-benefit analyses of residential smart meters found that it would cost more than it would save, but 'Ministers kept on trying until they got a positive result... To achieve 'profitability' the previous government stretched the assumptions shamelessly.' An economist at Ofgem with oversight of the roll-out of the smart meter program who raised concerns with his manager was threatened with imprisonment under a law intended to protect national security. The Employment Appeal Tribunal found that the law was in contravention of the European Convention on Human Rights.

Technology

Communication is a critical technological requirement for smart meters. Each meter must be able to reliably and securely communicate the information collected to a central location. Considering the varying environments and places where meters are found that problem can be daunting. Among the solutions proposed are the use of cell and pager networks, satellite, licensed radio, combination licensed and unlicensed radio, and power line communication. Not only the medium used for communication purposes, but also the type of network used, is critical. As such, one would find fixed wireless, wireless mesh network and wireless ad hoc networks, or a combination of the two. There are several other potential network configurations possible, including the use of Wi-Fi and other internet related networks. To date no one solution seems to be optimal for all applications. Rural utilities have vastly different communication problems from urban utilities or utilities located in difficult locations such as mountainous regions or areas ill-served by wireless and internet companies. In addition to communication with the head-end network, smart meters may need to be part of a home area network, which can include an in-premises display and a hub to interface one or more meters with the head end. Technologies for this network vary from country to country, but include power line communication, wireless ad hoc network, and ZigBee.

Protocols

ANSI C12.18 is an ANSI Standard that describes a protocol used for two-way communications with a meter, mostly used in North American markets. The C12.18 Standard is written specifically for meter communications via an ANSI Type 2 Optical Port and specifies lower-level protocol details. ANSI C12.19 specifies the data tables that are used. ANSI C12.21 is an extension of C12.18 written for modem instead of optical communications, so it is better suited to automatic meter reading. ANSI C12.22 is the communication protocol for remote communications.

IEC 61107 is a communication protocol for smart meters published by the IEC that is widely used for utility meters in the European Union. It is superseded by IEC 62056 but remains in wide use because it is simple and well-accepted. It sends ASCII data using a serial port. The physical media are either modulated light, sent with an LED and received with a photodiode, or a pair of wires, usually modulated by EIA-485. The protocol is half-duplex. IEC 61107 is related to, and sometimes wrongly confused with, the FLAG protocol. Ferranti and Landis+Gyr were early proponents of an interface standard that eventually became a sub-set of IEC1107.

The Open Smart Grid Protocol (OSGP) is a family of specifications published by the European Telecommunications Standards Institute (ETSI) used in conjunction with the ISO/IEC 14908 control networking standard for smart metering and smart grid applications. Millions of smart meters based on OSGP are deployed worldwide. On July 15, 2015, the OSGP Alliance announced the release of a new security protocol (OSGP-AES-128-PSK) and its availability from OSGP vendors. This deprecated the original OSGP-RC4-PSK security protocol which had been identified to be vulnerable.

There is a growing trend toward the use of TCP/IP technology as a common communication platform for Smart Meter applications, so that utilities can deploy multiple communication systems, while using IP technology as a common management platform. A universal metering interface would allow for development and mass production of smart meters and smart grid devices prior to the communication standards being set, and then for the relevant communication modules to be easily added or switched when they are. This would lower the risk of investing in the wrong standard as well as permit a solitary product to be used globally even if regional communication standards vary. Some smart meters may use a test IR LED to transmit non-encrypted usage data that bypasses meter security by transmitting lower level data in real-time.

Smart Meter Equipment Technical Specifications (SMETS)

In the UK, smart meters variants are classified as Smart Meter Equipment Technical Specifications (SMETS), with first generation smart meters commonly known as SMETS1 and second generation smart meters known as SMETS2. In August 2020, smart meter installer SMS plc was the first company to fit the new three-phase SMETS2 meter – developed by Aclara Technologies – on behalf of UK energy supplier, Good Energy.

Data Management

The other critical technology for smart meter systems is the information technology at the utility that integrates the Smart Meter networks with utility applications, such as billing and CIS. This includes the Meter Data Management system. It also is essential for smart grid implementations that power line communication (PLC) technologies used within the home over a Home Area Network (HAN), are standardized and compatible. The HAN allows HVAC systems and other household appliances to communicate with the smart meter, and from there to the utility. Currently there are several broadband or narrowband standards in place, or being developed, that are not yet compatible. To address this issue, the National Institute for Standards and Technology (NIST) established the PAP15 group, which studies and recommends coexistence mechanisms with a focus on the harmonization of PLC Standards for the HAN. The objective of the group is to ensure that all PLC technologies selected for the HAN coexist as a minimum. The two leading broadband PLC technologies selected are the HomePlug AV / IEEE 1901 and ITU-T G.hn technologies.

Technical working groups within these organizations are working to develop appropriate coexistence mechanisms. The HomePlug Powerline Alliance has developed a new standard for smart grid HAN communications called the HomePlug Green PHY specification. It is interoperable and coexistent with the widely deployed HomePlug AV technology and with the latest IEEE 1901 global Standard and is based on Broadband OFDM technology. ITU-T commissioned in 2010 a new project called G. hnem, to address the home networking aspects of energy management, built upon existing Low Frequency Narrowband OFDM technologies. The Google.org's PowerMeter, until its demise in 2011, was able to use a smart meter for tracking electricity usage, as can eMeter' Energy Engage as in, for example, the PowerCentsDC (TM) demand response program.

Advanced Metering Infrastructure

Advanced metering infrastructure (AMI) refers to systems that measure, collect, and analyze energy usage, and communicate with metering devices such as electricity meters, gas meters, heat meters, and water meters, either on request or on a schedule. These systems include hardware, software, communications, consumer energy displays and controllers, customer associated systems, meter data management software, and supplier business systems. Government agencies and utilities are turning toward advanced metering infrastructure (AMI) systems as part of larger 'Smart grid' initiatives. AMI extends automatic meter reading (AMR) technology by providing two-way meter communications, allowing commands to be sent toward the home for multiple purposes, including time-based pricing information, demand-response actions, or remote service disconnects.

Wireless technologies are critical elements of the neighborhood network, aggregating a mesh configuration of up to thousands of meters for back haul to the utility's IT headquarters. The network between the measurement devices and business systems allows the collection and distribution of information to customers, suppliers, utility companies, and service providers. This enables these businesses to participate in demand response services. Consumers can use the information provided by the system to change their normal consumption patterns to take advantage of lower prices. Pricing can be used to curb the growth of peak demand consumption. AMI differs from traditional automatic meter reading (AMR) in that it enables two-way communications with the meter. Systems only capable of meter readings do not qualify as AMI systems.

Opposition and Concerns

Some groups have expressed concerns regarding the cost, health, fire risk, security, and privacy effects of smart meters and the remote controllable "kill switch" that is included with most of them. Many of these concerns regard wireless-only smart meters with no home energy monitoring or control or safety features. Metering-only solutions, while popular with utilities because they fit existing business models and have cheap up-front capital costs, often result in such "backlash". Often the entire smart grid and smart building concept is discredited in part by confusion about the difference between home control and home area network technology and AMI. The (now former) attorney general of Connecticut has stated that he does not believe smart meters provide any financial benefit to consumers, however, the cost of the installation of the new system is absorbed by those customers.

Security

Smart meters expose the power grid to cyberattacks that could lead to power outages, both by cutting off people's electricity and by overloading the grid. However, many cyber security experts state that smart meters of UK and Germany have a relatively high cybersecurity and that any such attack there would thus require extraordinarily high efforts or financial resources. The EU Cyber security Act took effect in June 2019, which includes Directive on Security Network and Information Systems establishing notification and security requirements for operators of essential services. Through the Smartgrid Cybersecurity Committee, the U.S. Department of Energy published cybersecurity guidelines for grid operators in 2010 and updated them in 2014. The guidelines '…present an analytical framework that organizations can use to develop effective cybersecurity strategies…'

Implementing security protocols that protect these devices from malicious attacks has been problematic, due to their limited computational resources and long operational life. The current version of IEC 62056 includes the possibility to encrypt, authenticate, or sign the meter data. One proposed smart meter data verification method involves analyzing the network traffic in real-time to detect anomalies using an Intrusion Detection System (IDS) By identifying exploits as they are being leveraged by attackers, an IDS mitigates the suppliers' risks of energy theft by consumers and denial-of-service attacks by hackers. Energy utilities must choose between a centralized IDS, embedded IDS, or dedicated IDS depending on the individual needs of the utility. Researchers have found that for a typical advanced metering infrastructure, the centralized IDS architecture is superior in terms of cost efficiency and security gains.

In the United Kingdom, the Data Communication Company, which transports the commands from the supplier to the smart meter, performs an additional anomaly check on commands issued (and signed) by the energy supplier. As Smart Meter devices are Intelligent Measurement Devices which periodically record the measured values and send the data encrypted to the Service Provider, therefore in Switzerland these devices need to be evaluated by an evaluation Laboratory and need to be certified by METAS from 01.01.2020 according to Prüfmethodologie (Test Methodology for Execution of Data Security Evaluation of Swiss Smart Metering Components). According to a report published by Brian Krebs, in 2009 a Puerto Rico electricity supplier asked the FBI to investigate large-scale thefts of electricity related to its smart meters. The FBI found that former employees of the power company and the company that made the meters were being paid by consumers to reprogram the devices to show incorrect results, as well as teaching people how to do it themselves.

Health and Safety

Most health concerns about the meters arise from the pulsed radiofrequency (RF) radiation emitted by wireless smart meters. Members of the California State Assembly asked the California Council on Science and Technology (CCST) to study the issue of potential health impacts from smart meters, in particular whether current FCC standards are protective of public health. The CCST report in April 2011 found no health impacts, based both on lack of scientific evidence of harmful effects from radio frequency (RF) waves and that the RF exposure of people in their homes to smart meters is likely to be minuscule compared to RF exposure to cell phones and microwave ovens. Daniel Hirsch, retired director of the Program on Environmental and Nuclear Policy at UC Santa Cruz, criticized the CCST report on the grounds that it did not consider studies that suggest the potential for non-thermal health effects such as latent cancers from RF exposure. Hirsch also stated that the CCST report failed to correct errors in its comparison to cell phones and microwave ovens and that, when these errors are corrected, smart meters 'May produce cumulative whole-body exposures far higher than that of cell phones or microwave ovens.'

The Federal Communications Commission (FCC) has adopted recommended Permissible Exposure Limit (PEL) for all RF transmitters (including smart meters) operating at frequencies of 300 kHz to 100 GHz. These limits, based on field strength and power density, are below the levels of RF radiation that are hazardous to human health. Other studies substantiate the finding of the California Council on Science and Technology (CCST). In 2011, the Electric Power Research Institute performed a study to gauge human exposure to smart meters as compared to the FCC PEL. The report found that most smart meters only transmit RF signals 1% of the time or less. At this rate, and at a distance of 1 foot from the meter, RF exposure would be at a rate of 0.14% of the FCC PEL.

Issues surrounding smart meters causing fires have also been reported, particularly involving the manufacturer's Sensus. In 2012. PECO Energy Company replaced the Sensus meters it had deployed in the Philadelphia region after reports that a number of the units had overheated and caused fires. In July 2014, SaskPower, the province-run utility company of the Canadian province of Saskatchewan, halted its roll-out of Sensus meters after similar, isolated incidents were discovered. Shortly afterward, Portland General Electric announced that it would replace 70,000 smart meters that had been deployed in the state of Oregon after similar reports. The company noted that it had been aware of the issues since at least 2013, and they were limited to specific models it had installed between 2010 and 2012. On July 30, 2014, after a total of eight recent fire incidents involving the meters, SaskPower was ordered by the Government of Saskatchewan to immediately end its smart meter program and remove the 105,000 smart meters it had installed.

Privacy Concerns

One technical reason for privacy concerns is that these meters send detailed information about how much electricity is being used each time. More frequent reports provide more detailed information. Infrequent reports may be of little benefit for the provider, as it doesn't allow as good demand management in the response of changing needs for electricity. On the other hand, widespread reports would allow the utility company to infer behavioral patterns for the occupants of a house, such as when the members of the household are probably asleep or absent. Furthermore, the fine-grained information collected by smart meters raises growing concerns of privacy invasion due to personal behavior exposure (private activity, daily routine, etc.). Current trends are to increase the frequency of reports. A solution that benefits both provider and user privacy would be to adapt the interval dynamically. Another solution involves energy storage installed at the household used to reshape the energy consumption profile. In British Columbia, the electric utility is government-owned and as such must comply with privacy laws that prevent the sale of data collected by smart meters; many parts of the world are serviced by private companies that are able to sell their data.

In Australia debt collectors can make use of the data to know when people are at home. Used as evidence in a court case in Austin, Texas, police agencies secretly collected smart meter power usage data from thousands of residences to determine which used more power than 'Typical' to identify marijuana growing operations.

Smart meter power data usage patterns can reveal much more than how much power is being used. Research has demonstrated that smart meters sampling power levels at two-second intervals can reliably identify when different electrical devices are in use. Ross Anderson has written about privacy concerns. He writes 'It is not necessary for my meter to tell the power company, let alone the government, how much I used in every half-hour period last month;' that meters can provide 'Targeting information for burglars;' that detailed energy usage history can help energy companies to sell users exploitative contracts; and that there may be 'A temptation for policymakers to use smart metering data to target any needed power cuts.'

Opt-out Options

Reviews of smart meter programs, moratoriums, delays, and 'Opt-out' programs are some responses to the concerns of customers and government officials. In response to residents who did not want a smart meter, in June 2012 a utility in Hawaii changed its smart meter program to 'Opt out'. The utility said that once the smart grid installation project is nearing completion, KIUC may convert the deferral policy to an opt-out policy or program and may charge a fee to those members to cover the costs of servicing the traditional meters. Any fee would require approval from the Hawaii Public Utilities Commission.

After receiving numerous complaints about health, hacking, and privacy concerns with the wireless digital devices, the Public Utility Commission of the US state of Maine voted to allow customers to opt-out of the meter change at the cost of $12 a month. In Connecticut, another US state to consider smart metering, regulators declined a request by the state's largest utility, Connecticut Light & Power, to install 1.2 million of the devices, arguing that the potential savings in electric bills do not justify the cost. CL&P already offers its customers time-based rates. The state's Attorney General George Jepsen was quoted as saying the proposal would cause customers to spend upwards of $500 million on meters and get few benefits in return, a claim that Connecticut Light & Power disputed.

Lack of Savings in Results

There are questions about whether electricity is or should be primarily a 'When you need it' service where the inconvenience/cost-benefit ratio of time-shifting of loads is poor. In the Chicago area, Commonwealth Edison ran a test installing smart meters on 8,000 randomly selected households together with variable rates and rebates to encourage cutting back during peak usage. In Crain's Chicago Business article 'Smart grid test underwhelms. In the pilot, few power down to save money.' it was reported that fewer than 9% exhibited any amount of peak usage reduction and that the overall amount of reduction was 'Statistically insignificant'. This was from a report by the Electric Power Research Institute, a utility industry think tank who conducted the study and prepared the report. Susan Satter, senior assistant Illinois attorney general for public utilities said, 'It's devastating to their plan......The report shows zero statistically different result compared to business as usual.'

By 2016, the 7 million smart meters in Texas had not persuaded many people to check their energy data as the process was too complicated. A report from a parliamentary group in the UK suggests people who have smart meters installed are expected to save an average of £11 annually on their energy bills, much less than originally hoped. The 2016 cost-benefit analysis was updated in 2019 and estimated a similar average saving. The Australian Victorian Auditor-General found in 2015 that 'Victoria's electricity consumers will have paid an estimated $2.239 billion for metering services, including the rollout and connection of smart meters. In contrast, while a few benefits have accrued to consumers, benefits realization is behind schedule and most benefits are yet to be realized'

Erratic Demand

Smart meters can allow real-time pricing, and in theory this could help smooth power consumption as consumers adjust their demand in response to price changes. However, modelling by researchers at the University of Bremen suggests that in certain circumstances, 'Power demand fluctuations are not dampened but amplified instead.'

In the Media

In 2013, Take Back Your Power, an independent Canadian documentary directed by Josh del Sol was released describing "dirty electricity" and the aforementioned issues with smart meters. The film explores the various contexts of the health, legal, and economic concerns. It features narration from the mayor of Peterborough, Ontario, Daryl Bennett, as well as American researcher De-Kun Li, journalist Blake Levitt, and Dr. Sam Milham. It won a Leo Award for best feature-length documentary and the Annual Humanitarian Award from Indie Fest the following year.

Echo and Alexa Spying on you

Amazon Echo and the Alexa voice assistant have had widely publicized issues with privacy. Whether it is the amount of data they collect or the fact that they reportedly pay employees and, at times, external contractors from all over the world to listen to recordings to improve accuracy, the potential is there for sensitive personal information to be leaked through these devices. But the risks extend not just to our relationship with Amazon. Major privacy concerns are starting to emerge in the way Alexa devices interact with other services – risking a dystopian spiral of increasing surveillance and control. The setup of the Echo turns Amazon into an extra gateway that every online interaction has to pass through, collecting data on each one.

Alexa knows what you are searching for, listening to, or sending in your messages. Some smartphones do this already, particularly those made by Google and Apple who control the hardware, software, and cloud services. But the difference with an Echo is that it brings together the worst aspects of smartphones and smart homes. It is not a personal device but integrated into the home environment, always waiting to listen in. Alexa even features an art project (not created by Amazon) that tries to make light of this with the creepy "Ask the Listeners" function that makes comments about just how much the device is spying on you. Some Echo devices already have cameras, and if facial recognition capabilities were added we could enter a world of pervasive monitoring in our most private spaces, even tracked as we move between locations.

Do experts have something to add to public debate?

This technology gives Amazon a huge amount of control over your data, which has long been the aim of most of the tech giants. While Apple and Google – who face their own privacy issues – have similar voice assistants, they have at least made progress running the software directly on their devices, so they won't need to transfer recordings of your voice commands to their servers. Amazon doesn't appear to be trying to do the same. This is, in part, because of the firm's aggressive business model. Amazon's systems appear not just designed to collect as much data as they can but also to create ways of sharing it. So, the potential issues run much deeper than Alexa listening in on private moments.

Sharing with law enforcement

One area of concern is the potential for putting the ears of law enforcement in our homes, schools, and workplaces. Apple has a history of resisting FBI requests for user data, and Twitter is relatively transparent about reporting on how it responds to requests from governments. But Ring, the internet-connected home-security camera company owned by Amazon, has a high-profile relationship with police that involves handing over user data. Even the way citizens and police communicate is increasingly monitored and controlled by Amazon.

This risks embedding a culture of state surveillance in Amazon's operations, which could have worrying consequences. We've seen numerous examples of law enforcement and other government bodies in democratic countries using personal data to spy on people, both in breach of the law and within it but for reasons that go far beyond the prevention of terrorism. This kind of mass surveillance also creates severe potential for discrimination, as it has been shown repeatedly to have a worse impact on women and minority groups.

If Amazon isn't willing to push back, it's not hard to imagine Alexa recordings being handed over to the requests of government employees and law enforcement officers who might be willing to violate the spirit or letter of the law. And given international intelligence-sharing agreements, even if you trust your own government, do you trust others? In response to this issue, an Amazon spokesperson said: 'Amazon does not disclose customer information in response to government demands unless we're required to do so to comply with a legally valid and blinding order. Amazon objects to overbroad or otherwise inappropriate demands as a matter of course.'

'Ring customers decide whether to share footage in response to asks from local police investigating cases. Local police are not able to see any information related to which Ring users received a request and whether they declined to share or opt out of future requests.' They added that although local police can access Ring's Neighbors app for reporting criminal and suspicious activity, they cannot see or access user account information.

Tracking health issues

Health is another area where Amazon appears to be attempting a takeover. The UK's National Health Service (NHS) has signed a deal for medical advice to be provided via the Echo. At face value, this simply extends ways of accessing publicly available information like the NHS website or phone line 111 – no official patient data is being shared. But it creates the possibility that Amazon could start tracking what health information we ask for through Alexa, effectively building profiles of users' medical histories. This could be linked to online shopping suggestions, third-party ads for costly therapies, or even ads that are potentially traumatic (think women who've suffered miscarriages being shown baby products).

An Amazon spokesperson said: 'Amazon does not build customer health profiles based on interactions with nhs.uk content or use such requests for marketing purposes. Alexa does not have access to any personal or confidential information from the NHS.' The crudeness and glitches of algorithmic advertising would violate the professional and moral standards that health services strive to maintain. Plus, it would be highly invasive to treat the data in the same way many Echo recordings are. Would you want a random external contractor to know you were asking for sexual health advice?

Transparency

Underlying these issues is a lack of real transparency. Amazon is disturbingly quiet, evasive, and reluctant to act when it comes to tackling the privacy implications of their practices, many of which are buried deep within their terms and conditions or hard-to-find settings. Even tech-savvy users don't necessarily know the full extent of the privacy risks, and when privacy features are added, they often only make users aware after researchers or the press raise the issue. It is entirely unfair to place such a burden on users to find out and mitigate what these risks are. So, if you have an Echo in your home, what should you do? There are many tips available on how to make the device more private, such as setting voice recordings to automatically delete or limiting what data is shared with third parties. But smart tech is almost always surveillance tech, and the best piece of advice is not to bring one into your home.

I hope you enjoyed this as much as I did researching it…

~Fin~

Printed in Great Britain
by Amazon

82922521R00371